COLONIAL BRITISH AMERICA

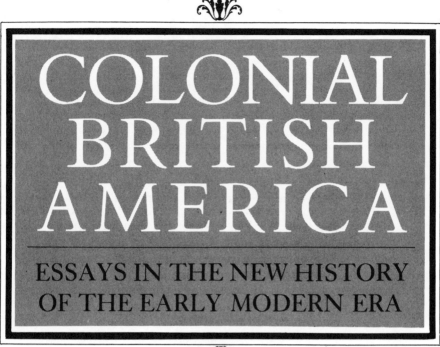

COLONIAL BRITISH AMERICA

ESSAYS IN THE NEW HISTORY OF THE EARLY MODERN ERA

EDITED BY

JACK P. GREENE

AND

J. R. POLE

THE JOHNS HOPKINS UNIVERSITY PRESS

BALTIMORE AND LONDON

The Johns Hopkins University Press
2715 North Charles Street
Baltimore, Maryland 21218-4319
The Johns Hopkins Press Ltd., London

Library of Congress Cataloging in Publication Data

Main entry under title:
Colonial British America
Based on papers presented at a conference held at
St. Catherine's College, Oxford, Aug. 1–7, 1981.
Includes bibliographical references and index.
1. United States—History—Colonial period, ca. 1600–
1775—Historiography—Congresses.   I. Greene, Jack P.
II. Pole, J. R. (Jack Richon)
E188.C72 1983   973.2´0722   83–48060
ISBN 0-8018-3055-9 (pbk.)

A catalog record for this book is available from the British Library.

CONTENTS

TABLES

PREFACE

his volume developed out of a series of discussions between the editors over a period of several years. For reasons elaborated in the introduction, we conceived the plan of bringing together a group of scholars in mid-career to reconsider the state of British-American colonial history between 1607 and 1763. This plan resulted in a small invitational conference sponsored jointly by The Johns Hopkins University and St. Catherine's College, Oxford, and held at St. Catherine's College August 1–7, 1981. During the past year, fourteen of the fifteen papers presented at that conference have been thoroughly reconsidered and revised by their authors. Along with the editors' introductory essay, they are published here.

The conference and the book have been made possible by grants from the National Endowment for the Humanities, the British Academy, the Commonwealth Fund of New York, and Barclay's Bank International Ltd. The editors wish to thank Mrs. Dorothy Brothers of the Center for Advanced Study in the Behavioral Sciences at Stanford, Mrs. Elizabeth Paynter of The Johns Hopkins University, and Ms. Helen Farr of St. Catherine's College, who provided necessary secretarial and administrative help in organizing the conference; Jacqueline Megan Greene and Granville Greene, who reproduced the papers for the conference; and Joyce L. Chaplin of The Johns Hopkins University, who assisted with the final editing. Mrs. Paynter also played a major role in getting the papers ready for publication and Jacqueline Megan Greene prepared the index. Jack P. Greene also wishes to thank the Center for Advanced Study in the Behavioral Sciences at Stanford, where he was a fellow during the year in which the conference was initially planned and organized. Support for his fellowship was provided through the center by the National Endowment for the Humanities.

The editors apologize in advance to the readers for the inconvenience caused by the placement of the notes at the end of the essays rather than at the foot of the page, a step that was dictated by financial considerations.

COLONIAL BRITISH AMERICA

1

RECONSTRUCTING BRITISH-AMERICAN COLONIAL HISTORY: AN INTRODUCTION

JACK P. GREENE AND J. R. POLE

I f history is impossible to predict, so are the changing interests of historians. In March 1947 ten prominent early American historians assembled at Princeton to consider the state of their field. The following December in Cleveland, Carl Bridenbaugh, director of the recently created Institute of Early American History and Culture in Williamsburg, reported on their deliberations to the annual meeting of the American Historical Association. If Bridenbaugh's report accurately reflected their mood, they must have felt like an endangered species. By every measure Bridenbaugh could devise—the amount of time devoted to the period in survey courses, the numbers of specialized courses on the period offered in colleges and universities, the quantity of publications and new dissertations in the field, the numbers of scholars and graduate students engaged in active research—interest in colonial and Revolutionary America, eras that had absorbed a large proportion of the attention of the first two generations of professional historians between 1875 and 1925, seemed to have declined dramatically during the previous quarter-century. Indeed, several leading graduate training centers—Princeton, Pennsylvania, Johns Hopkins, Chicago, and Berkeley—no longer had any historian actively working in the field; at still others, including Columbia, Northwestern, and Duke, teaching responsibilities for early American history fell entirely upon people whose primary field of interest was the early national period. Probably correctly, Bridenbaugh attributed this decline largely to the widespread impression within the profession that "colonial history" had "all been written." Decrying the notion that America's colonial and Revolutionary pasts had been "mined out," Bridenbaugh called attention to how little was known about the social and cultural history of colonial America, especially during the years from about 1680 to 1750, and exhorted his listeners to join in "a concerted effort to re-establish the field as a prominent [area of] study."[1]

But Bridenbaugh's jeremiad did not immediately lead to a palpable revival of interest in American colonial history. Notwithstanding the gradual emergence of the *William and Mary Quarterly* as the liveliest and most interesting medium of historical discourse in the United States and the appearance of important and sophisticated new works—by, among others, Wesley Frank Craven on the early southern colonies; Perry Miller on the New England mind; Louis B. Wright, Bridenbaugh, Max Savelle, and Frederick B. Tolles on aspects of the sociocultural life of the colonies; and Merrill Jensen, John R. Alden, John C. Miller, and Edmund S. Morgan on the American Revolution—it would have been impossible as late as the mid-1950s to predict the remarkable renaissance in early American studies that would occur over the following quarter-century, much less to anticipate the course that renaissance would take.

Indeed, the landscape of colonial American history had changed very little over the previous generation. The major problems had been identified mainly during the three decades between 1890 and 1920, and the main interest had long been, and continued to be, in making slight additions to existing information or modest shifts in points of view. In both a formal and a substantive sense, colonial history before 1763 was dominated by its characterization as "the colonial period." Despite the insistence of Charles M. Andrews, Lawrence Henry Gipson, and other historians of the Imperial school that the proper frame of reference for British-American colonial history included all the British colonies in America and not just the thirteen that revolted in 1776, the prevailing conception of colonial history, even for Andrews and Gipson, was strongly conditioned by the knowledge that the colonial period had been followed by the American Revolution and the foundation of the American nation. Such questions as arose from the operation of the navigation laws, the character of British imperial policy, the quality of British colonial administration, and the development of provincial and local political institutions in the colonies all tended to be colored by an implicit consensus that the underlying questions to be addressed were how such matters affected the movement for independence, how far and in what ways they were "responsible" for the Revolution, and how far back such responsibility might be traced. Even a local uprising in Virginia in 1676, a full hundred years before the Declaration of Independence, could be interpreted and was thought to be best understood as a "forerunner" of the eventual revolt against Britain. These observations do not hold for the careful contextual work of Craven or the profound scholarship of Miller, who analyzed the New England mind in terms that took their bearings from the contemporary interplay between theological aspirations and secular conditions. But the power and implications of Miller's work were slow to intrude upon the existing conception of the subject, a testimony to the force that conception continued to exert over the contracting world of early American studies.

Nor was that force much shaken by contemporary trends in the interpretation of later periods of American history. For at least fifteen years after World War II the prevailing conception of the American past continued to be that formulated during the first three decades of the twentieth century by Charles Beard, Vernon L. Parrington, and others and now known as the "Progressive" point of view. As John Murrin points out in his essay in this volume, these "Progressive historians" were not much interested in, wrote very little about, and hence had relatively little impact upon the ways historians looked at the colonial period per se. Equally important, the Progressive interest in history primarily as the analysis of *political* conflict meant that their salutary concern with getting at underlying social and economic development was limited largely to an interest in how those developments affected political life. Thus, to the small degree that the Progressive point of view influenced the ways colonial historians thought about their area of study, it tended to encourage a search for the socioeconomic roots of political behavior, especially as they were manifested during the Revolutionary era. It thereby served to strengthen the traditional view of the colonial period as interesting chiefly as a prelude to the Revolution. Moreover, because it kept the focus of attention so directly upon politics, the Progressive point of view failed to engender a new comprehension of the significance of socioeconomic history as a subject worthy of study in its own right and probably even helped to inhibit the immediate development of a full appreciation of the important implications of the new work in sociocultural history for understanding the colonial past.

Much the same can be said about the initial effects of the growing interest in American studies between 1945 and 1960. Throughout these years, the American studies movement was guided by two basic assumptions. First was the definition of American studies as the analysis of only those areas that were or would become part of the United States. Thus, no less than the Progressive conception, the American studies approach was at bottom a variation on the Whig interpretation of history. Important in the colonial period were those aspects that seemed to explain the Revolution and the subsequent development of U.S. history. As a consequence, at the same time that it stimulated a renewed interest in many aspects of colonial culture, the American studies movement tended to channel that interest into an anachronistic search for the colonial roots of later American culture and to analyze colonial developments largely in terms of the extent to which they exhibited a process of Americanization. A second pervasive assumption underlying this approach was that America, at least in its continental British-American variant, was and had always been fundamentally different from Europe and that any variations among localities and regions within America were far less important than the similarities that made American culture, defined as the culture of the United States, different from that of Europe. This emphasis upon *American exceptionalism*, reinforced by the new postwar notion of "consensus," tended to homogenize differences in time as well as in space in the American past and thereby further contributed to blur the boundaries between the colonial and national periods and to inhibit the emergence of a conception of the colonial period as having an integrity of its own.

Precisely why and how the colonial period came during the next quarter-century to acquire such an integrity and to become one of the most exciting and attractive areas of American historical study is complex and probably not yet very well understood. A subject of such considerable significance for an appreciation of the transformation of historical knowledge during the last half of the twentieth century demands far more serious and extended analysis than can be attempted here. But any such analysis will have to give primary attention to three interrelated developments *within* the field of early American history itself. First, during the 1950s the works of Perry Miller finally began to exert an influence commensurate with their subtlety and brilliance. A growing recognition that Miller was not only the most original and profound historian in the entire history of American history but perhaps the only American historian whose work was qualitatively comparable to that of the great European historians of his and the previous generation inevitably stimulated interest in early America and set a high standard of historical discourse that in itself attracted prospective young historians into the field. Second, primarily through the *William and Mary Quarterly* and an increasingly distinguished book publication program, the Institute of Early American History and Culture was both providing an outlet for a steadily expanding volume of high-quality research in the field and serving as a forum for the exchange of new ideas and points of view. Third, a well-situated group of unusually effective graduate teachers in several of the major graduate training centers—Edmund S. Morgan at Brown and Yale, Oscar Handlin and Bernard Bailyn at Harvard, Richard B. Morris at Columbia, Wesley Frank Craven at Princeton, and Merrill Jensen at Wisconsin, to name only the most prolific teachers—attracted into early American history a growing proportion of the enlarging pool of graduate students who began, especially after 1955, to seek a career in professional historical studies. Within a decade, students of these and other teachers were assuming posts at major universities and beginning to train students of their own. To cater to the new interest, universities and colleges that prior to World War II had abandoned work in early American history revived the subject, and some universities doubled—a few eventually tripled—the number of historians teaching in the field.

Whatever the explanations for the proliferation of interest in early American history during these years, by the late 1950s, a mere decade after Bridenbaugh's 1947 lament, it was no longer possible to speak of early American history as "a neglected subject."[2] While the number of people teaching in the "first half" of American history was still equal to only a fraction of those covering the nineteenth and twentieth centuries, the proportions had shifted dramatically within a relatively short period. By the last half of the 1960s the number of Ph.D.'s in early American history produced in any given year considerably exceeded those for entire decades between 1920 and 1950, and the same could be said for the quantity of publications. Nor was interest in early America confined to historians and students of early American literature and art. Young scholars in the social sciences—sociology, historical geography, econometric history, anthropology, even psychology and psychiatry and political science—began to find attractive research opportunities in the early American period.

Of course, by no means all of this new interest was directed at the colonial era. Indeed, until the late 1960s a large proportion centered on the Revolution and the deepening of the analysis of such traditional questions as why the Revolution occurred, what kind of phenomenon it was, and how it related to the new Constitution of 1787–88, itself a focus of major investigation. Even among those scholars who did choose to concentrate upon the earlier period, attention was initially rather strongly directed towards conventional institutional and political subjects within established frameworks of interpretation. With the dramatic proliferation of scholars working in early American history through the 1960s, however, more and more of them began to investigate an ever-widening range of topics relating to the one hundred fifty years before the Revolutionary disturbances. Increasingly, they directed their questioning less towards existing answers than towards the questions themselves. Inspired by Miller's work on Puritanism as a moral and explanatory system that changed with social and economic circumstances, they turned first to intellectual history, working out and modifying Miller's own portrait of Puritan religious and intellectual development, analyzing the history of political and social thought, showing how inherited notions about themselves and other peoples conditioned European attitudes towards the non-Europeans they encountered in America.

This revived respect for ideas and values as important components of historical situations, a respect that was very greatly enhanced by intensive studies by Bailyn, Gordon S. Wood, and others on the political ideology of the late colonial and Revolutionary years, was soon accompanied by a new interest in the economic, demographic, and social history of the colonies, areas that had previously been only vaguely charted. To some small extent, this development seems to have been a function of ever larger numbers looking for new research topics in unexplored areas and of an internal, almost self-generating logic that operated to push the boundaries of inquiry from one new area outward into another. For example, when publications on suffrage and representation revealed that ownership of property had been more widespread and the suffrage itself more widely distributed than earlier historians had supposed, others were led to look more closely at probate records as sources of information about social structure, standards of living, and economic expectations.

Probably much more important, however, were powerful stimuli deriving from two external sources. Perhaps the most significant of these came from related social science disciplines, which in the decades immediately after World War II acquired, especially in the United States, a new respectability and a new sophistication. Social science influences intruded upon colonial history in two ways. First, a few social scientists—primarily econometric historians, historical geographers, historical sociologists, and cultural anthropologists—made important contributions to the field. But the impact of the social sciences upon British-American colonial historical studies was far too pervasive to be explained solely by the examples of so few people. As the influence of the social sciences penetrated into the undergraduate curriculi of most universities and colleges, at least in the United States, and reached even into popular social literature, historians themselves increasingly began to take over and to employ, if usually only implicitly, the language, concepts, methods, and concerns of the social sciences, especially sociology, psychology, economics, and anthropology. In time, this development encouraged a demonstrable interest, unusual in historians of earlier generations, in the explicit use of theory and methods, including statistics and quantification, drawn very largely from the social sciences. To the extent that the impact of the social sciences was both earlier and greater among colonial historians than among students of later periods of American history, it was probably because the traditional conception of history as the history of politics was far less strongly entrenched in an area in which so little political history was shared.

But the new interest among colonial historians in social, economic, demographic, and other areas of history was also powerfully reinforced by the example of new schools of methodology and historical inquiry on the other side of the Atlantic. The French *Annales* school had for a generation been striving for an *histoire totale* that would subordinate the history of public life to a more expanded concern for the recovery of all aspects of a population's experience, from the environmental and material to the social and intellectual, from the macro-level to the micro-level, and from the most prominent inhabitants to the most marginal. By the early 1960s the orientation of this group had been taken up by those involved in the study of early modern England, where a powerful intensification of interest in Tudor and Stuart history was already in progress. Scholars concerned with the social sources of the English Revolution of the mid–seventeenth century; with the relationship between social structure, culture, and belief systems; and, especially as it was manifested by the recently formed Cambridge Group for the History of Population and Social Structure, with the interaction between population history and economic, social, and political change, provided students of colonial British-America with attractive new models of how the new interest in the concerns of social science could translate into an illumination of a particular era of the past.

At the same time, the findings of these historians provided colonial historians with an expanded context for their work and served to draw them more fully than ever before into the historian's world of the past, a world in which subjects were judged to be significant less for what they might reveal about subsequent events than for what they told about the specific world of which they were a part. If the social sciences turned the attention of colonial historians in the direction of socioeconomic and cultural history, the work of early modern historians in France and Britain taught them the virtues of endeavoring to recreate past societies in their own integrity, within their own terms of reference, and, insofar as possible, without the distortions of teleology. An important concomitant of this development was a renewed respect for and interest in various levels of local history.[3]

Whatever the influences that aroused so much new interest in British-American colonial history and turned that interest so strongly in the direction of an expanded conception of the subject in the 1960s and 1970s, the result was a veritable explosion of monographs and articles and a profusion of information about many aspects of the field. But not all of the results of this new prosperity have been entirely salutary. For some time now, it has been clear that the wealth of new information generated annually by students of colonial history has given rise to a severe case of intellectual indigestion. As knowledge has become more abundant and detailed, scholars have become more and more specialized, and the field of colonial British-America has fragmented into a series of subspecialties—regional, temporal, thematic, and methodological. To a deplorable extent, one special expertise has excluded others until specialists in one area disclaim any more knowledge about other areas of colonial British-America than they have about, for instance, nineteenth- or twentieth-century history in general. At the same time, while many of the old general contours and themes around which the field had traditionally been organized have been destroyed or rendered obsolete, there has been a notable lack of systematic attention to the problem of replacing them with new ones. As scholars have concentrated more and more upon smaller and smaller units in their laudable efforts to recover the context and texture of colonial life in as much detail as the sources and scholarly ingenuity will permit, there has been surprisingly little effort to relate their findings to the larger picture of British-American development over the whole period from the beginning of the seventeenth century through the middle decades of the eighteenth. One paradoxical result of the reinvigoration of British-American colonial history has thus been a signal loss of overall coherence until we are now less clear than ever before about precisely what the central themes and the larger questions are in the field as a whole.

A second problem is that the profusion of scholarship about colonial

America inevitably has been uneven. We know vastly more, for instance, about New England and the Chesapeake than we do about other areas, about rural life than about urban, about religion than about secular culture, about external trade than about internal, about political ideology than about political process, about static wealth structures than about the dynamics of social development, about adult, white, independent males than about other elements in the population. Yet, although everyone is aware that we know more about some areas and questions than about others, no one has sought in a systematic and comprehensive way to assess what we do know and what we do not or to identify those areas and problems—and they are many—to which scholars in the field might now profitably turn their attention.

In a conscious effort to address these problems, we organized a conference to consider a series of papers by mature scholars who had both lived through and themselves made significant contributions to the first impressive stages of the current transformation of colonial British-American history. The goal was to recruit scholars primarily from among members of the generation who, having received their doctorates in the 1950s or early 1960s and having now held professorial posts for between one and two decades, were already in mid-career and who, because of their past, present, or prospective roles in training doctoral students, seemed to be strategically well placed to be able both to define developments to date and to suggest guidelines for those of the future.

Our intention was for the conference to be as intellectually comprehensive as possible. This objective might have been achieved through either a spatial or a temporal approach. But considerations of economy as well as our feeling that the current preoccupation with distinctions observable over space and time had been a powerful contributing force in undermining a holistic conception of the subject decided us to adopt a structural approach, and we divided the subject into fourteen topics, each of which was to be covered by a scholar with a demonstrated interest in it: Jacob M. Price and Richard B. Sheridan on economic development; James T. Lemon on spatial organization and settlement patterns; Jim Potter on population trends; Richard S. Dunn on labor systems; T. H. Breen and Gary B. Nash on cultural interaction and social relations; James A. Henretta on social structure; Joyce Appleby, David D. Hall, and Richard L. Bushman on value systems and aspects of religious and social behavior; and W. A. Speck, John M. Murrin, and Stanley N. Katz on political, constitutional, and legal development. The particular subject division we adopted reflects contemporary notions about the sociology of knowledge as it has been defined over the past generation by the social sciences and, more specifically in historical studies, by the *Annales* school. Its heavy emphasis upon the economic, demographic, spatial, social, and cultural dimensions of the colonial past also mirrors the contemporary distribution of interest and activity within the field itself.

In setting out guidelines for the authors, we asked each of them to treat his or her topic in its broadest possible dimensions, to cover both the seventeenth and the eighteenth centuries, both the island colonies and those on the continent, and all segments of society. Insofar as relevant, they were to consider regional variations, changes over time, external and internal (metropolitan and colonial) dimensions, and the role of women and minorities as well as the dominant male members of society. Specifically, we asked them to focus upon (1) where we are now and how we got here; (2) what problems require more attention; (3) what, in view of existing sources and ways of manipulating them, the best strategies for attacking these problems are; (4) how problems and findings in the topic area relate to those in the other areas; and (5) what *general* themes that seem to be emerging from research already published or under way might help to structure studies not just of the subject area of the paper itself but in the field of British-American colonial history as a whole. Finally, we requested the authors to try to detach themselves from the teleology imposed by the American Revolution and the establishment of a separate American nation and to consider colonial British-America between 1607 and 1763 as a broad socioeconomic, cultural, and political unit only some portions of which seceded between 1776 and 1783.

Predictably and probably desirably, the final essays as published in this volume, all of which have been revised in the light of the discussions at the conference at which they were initially presented in August 1981, do not conform in all cases to these prescriptions. Some authors, specifically Henretta and Katz, felt that they could best elucidate their topics by looking at them from the vantage point of later, specifically American developments, while a majority, including Appleby, Lemon, Potter, Nash, Henretta, Hall, Bushman, and Katz, either ignored the Caribbean colonies completely or gave them only cursory mention. No one treats in a systematic or sustained way the less populous island colonies of Bermuda, the Bahamas, and Newfoundland or the most northern continental colony, Nova Scotia. Similarly, although they have by no means been ignored, the roles of women and children certainly and those of Indians and lower-class whites probably have not been accorded the prominence their numbers, contemporary socioeconomic and cultural importance, and recent scholarly attention demand and will, we hope, receive over the next few decades. To a considerable degree, these underemphases, like the relative inattention to the colonies of the Lower South, arise out of the absence of extensive research on which the contributors might have drawn. To that extent, they provide powerful testimony to the continuing failure of a significant proportion of the colonial American historical community to adopt a larger conception of their subject or, perhaps, fully to accept the desirability of a nonteleological *histoire totale*.

To the degree that our original objective of comprehensiveness has not been completely fulfilled, it cannot be attributed only to the orientations of individual authors. Several important topics, including the development of language, communications networks, occupational structures, the professions, and secular social institutions above the level of the family simply fell through the interstices of our topical division of the subject, and we must take full responsibility for these and similar omissions. Yet, even by virtue of its failure to achieve a comprehensive treatment of the subject, the volume implicitly fulfills one of its major objectives: the denotation of important areas demanding additional research.

Nor do these omissions represent the only failure of objectives that can be attributed to the organization of the volume. As critics of the *Annales* school have frequently pointed out, one of the most obvious weaknesses of a sectoral approach to historical and social analysis is the difficulty of tying various sectors together and showing how through a series of complex interactions they operate to shape the historical and/or social process, and this weakness is doubtless enhanced when each sector is treated by a different author. Thus, it is scarcely surprising that few of the authors displayed much concern with trying to articulate systematically *"general* themes that . . . might help to structure studies . . . in the field of British-American colonial history as a whole."

This is not to suggest, however, that they have been inattentive to the utility of explanatory frameworks and models in the organization of historical analysis. Indeed, several authors affirm the continuing usefulness of existing models for explaining developments within the particular sectors for which they had responsibility, albeit they often recommend changes in those models to make them fit the complex situations they purport to help analyze. Thus, Price and Sheridan both seem to agree that a combination of the staple and population-market models still provides the most productive approach to colonial economic development, Lemon finds no better substitute for a modified central-place theory for explaining colonial settlement patterns, Breen advocates the use of a revised interactionist model in looking at relations among cultures, Bushman proposes what is essentially a diffusion framework for the interpretation of colonial cultural development, and Appleby points out many positive benefits to be derived from a critical employment of the value-and-society approach to the study of colonial belief systems.

On a more general level, however, the authors seem to be almost unanimous in their conviction that no existing model is very satisfactory, and this negative judgment seems to apply equally to both older and more recent frameworks of explanation. The early twentieth-century interpretive systems associated with Frederick Jackson Turner, the Imperial historians, or the Progressives all now seem to be far too one-dimensional to be of more than limited use, and none of the authors shows any disposition to try to revive them. Similarly, except for Hall, none of them has a good word to say for the concept of American exceptionalism, which provided the intellectual underpinning for both Turnerian analysis and much of the work deriving out of the post–World War II American studies movement and the so-called Consensus school of American history.

Nor are they any happier with the gemeinschaft-gesellschaft model, with its view of Western historical development as a process of "declension" from an organic, communal subsistence, religious, and personal society to a more individualistic, market-oriented, secular, and impersonal one. Perhaps because it seemed to fit rather well the New England experience as it was limned by Miller and several younger historians of the New England community, over the past quarter-century this model has been used more widely by colonial historians than any other. But over the past decade it has become powerfully obvious that it fundamentally distorts the experiences of all of the colonies outside New England and, perhaps more serious, that it gives excessive emphasis to the power of tradition and the resistance to change at the same time that it underestimates the adaptive capacities of societies and the individuals who compose them. Much the same can be said about the more recent variant of this conception that looks at change in the early modern era in terms of a movement from traditional to modern. Both the gemeinschaft-gesellschaft and the traditional-modern frameworks are teleological and almost invariably laden with distorting value judgments. While the former proceeds from a lament for the passage of older, presumably warmer forms of social interaction, the latter is rooted in a celebration of the rush into an enlightened present. Finally, insofar as the authors show any explicit concern for the problem, none of them demonstrates much optimism that the social sciences may yield new general models that will either prove more suitable for analyzing colonial development as a whole or not be freighted with theory that, in Appleby's words, overdetermines the interpretive outcomes.

If, however, existing general frameworks are all unsatisfactory and none of the authors of the papers in this volume has proposed an alternative, those papers do, we would suggest, provide a foundation for the development of a new, more inclusive framework for the reconstruction of colonial history. Although this is not the place to attempt to elaborate it in detail, we can suggest, in a preliminary way at least, what its most essential features may be.

What seems to be indisputably clear from this collection of papers is that any workable general framework will have to be based upon recognition that colonial British-America comprised several distinctive socioeconomic regions that transcended political boundaries. Colonial historians have of course traditionally distinguished between the island and the continental colonies and between the southern and the northern colonies on the continent. More recently, a few scholars have also divided the colonies into two broad categories: *colonies of exploitation* and *colonies of settlement*, the former term referring to those colonies that employed large numbers of slaves to produce staples on plantations in the Caribbean and southern North America and the latter to those colonies that did not.[4] Originally developed by students of nineteenth-century imperialism to distinguish between colonies in which a small population of Europeans conquered and exploited the labor and resources of a large indigenous population and colonies in which large numbers of European immigrants and their increase occupied previously only thinly settled lands as permanent settlers, this particular typology is fundamentally misleading when applied to the early modern British-American colonies, every one of which was a colony of settlement in the sense that it involved the expropriation and settlement of land with new immigrants, whether voluntary, as in the case of most Europeans, or forced, as in the case of virtually all Africans, and the subsequent organization of settler societies. Strictly speaking, not even the small British trading factories on the African coast or in India during this period were colonies of exploitation in the original sense of that term.[5]

An earlier typology developed before the advent of the new imperialism and the establishment of large numbers of colonies of exploitation of the classic type during the later nineteenth century would seem to be more useful. In his *Lectures on Colonization and Colonies*, a collection of lectures delivered at Oxford between 1839 and 1841, Herman Merivale also separated colonies into two types. But his distinction was between those that had *"no peculiar advantages for the production, by agricultural or mining labour, of articles of value in the foreign market"* and those that did, the former being characterized by mixed farming, free labor, less involvement in international markets, and a less stratified social structure and the latter by staple agriculture, bound labor, deep involvement in international markets, and greater extremes of wealth.[6] Of course, this distinction between *farm colonies* and *plantation colonies* cannot be too rigidly applied. No early modern British-American colony was entirely without large landholdings worked by bound labor, and none, not even the Leeward Islands, were purely plantation colonies without small agricultural landholders. But it nevertheless can serve as a useful classificatory device for distinguishing between the two broad categories of colonies of settlement within the early modern British-American world.

As scholars have moved strongly away from political history to social and economic history during the 1960s and 1970s, however, they have recognized the crudeness of these older categorizations and have gradually developed a more refined system of *regional* classification based largely upon differences in methods of land use, settlement patterns, socioeconomic organization, and cultural orientation. As will be apparent from the papers published in this volume, there is by no means yet complete agreement as to precisely how many regions there were or how and where the boundaries among them should be drawn. But a strong preference seems to be emerging for a five-part division. By order of settlement, these parts are the *Chesapeake*, comprising Virginia, Maryland, northern North Carolina, and perhaps southern Delaware; *New England*, composed of Massachusetts and its offshoot colonies Connecticut, Rhode Island, New Hampshire, and Nova Scotia; the *Caribbean*, including until 1763 Barbados, the Leeward Island colonies of Antigua, Montserrat, Nevis, and St. Christopher, and Jamaica; the *Middle Colonies*, comprising New York, New Jersey, Pennsylvania, and northern Delaware; and the *Lower South*, containing South Carolina, southern North Carolina, and Georgia. To these five groups some scholars would add two others, neither of which receives much mention in this volume: first, a group of non-staple-producing small island colonies made up of Bermuda and the Bahamas, and second, the New West, which beginning in the 1730s formed in the back countries of Pennsylvania, Maryland, Virginia, and the Carolinas.[7] It is interesting that in this more refined system of regional classification, before 1763 only three regions—New England, the Small Island colonies, and the New West—can be defined as almost wholly farm colonies, and only two—the Caribbean and the Lower South—as predominantly plantation colonies. Both the Chesapeake and the Middle Colonies fall somewhere in between these two types. No doubt, this seven-part division will be refined still further as scholars develop an even more acute appreciation of important differences between areas within these larger regional categories. Already, in fact, it is obvious that before 1763 there were at least three important sub-regions within both New England and the Caribbean and two within the Chesapeake and the Middle Colonies.

If, however, we are ever going to develop a satisfactory comprehensive general framework for interpreting the whole of the early modern British-American experience, we will have to move beyond an appreciation of regional differences to an emphasis upon important similarities that in themselves served as important underlying unities that make it possible, indeed necessary, to conceive of these separate regions as parts of a larger British-American world.

Five major similarities now appear to have been of special importance. First, each region was initially a *new* society whose members were faced with the problems of organizing an unfamiliar landscape, finding ways to exploit that landscape so as to satisfy their basic material needs, and creating a social and political system that would enable them to live together in an orderly manner. Second, each region was tied into the emerging transatlantic trading network, itself, like the colonies themselves, a result of the vigorous commercial (and military) expansion of Europe outwards during the early modern period. Third, unlike people in the European societies from which the dominant white settlers emanated, the settlers all lived, as both Breen and Nash emphasize in their chapters in this volume, in multiracial and, within each racial category, multiethnic societies whose plural character was sooner or later reflected in considerable heterogeneity in both religious and secular life. Fourth, no less than the societies from which they came, these new societies were all fundamentally exploitative in character, not just of their new environments but of any of the people living in those environments who were susceptible to exploitation. Indeed, in colonies as well as in the metropolitan societies of Europe, people's status was in great measure determined by the extent to which they could or could not exploit other people. Fifth, it cannot be emphasized too strongly that all these new American societies were also *colonial* societies. Most obviously, their status as colonies meant that they were subjected to a common imperial policy and operated within a roughly similar political framework. It also meant that they were not only frequently engaged in hostilities with neighboring Indians and colonists of rival European nations but also drawn into imperial wars between Britain and its French, Spanish, and Dutch enemies for at least half of the long period between 1607 and 1763. Finally, their status as colonies also meant that they were economic and social extensions of Britain and that their existence, material well-being, and, until very late in the colonial period, actual safety were in important degrees intimately dependent upon Britain. Even more important, however, their colonial status meant that no matter how distant they might be from Britain or how much latitude they may have had in their internal development (and notwithstanding their different countries of origin), they were all cultural provinces of Britain whose legal and social systems, perceptual frameworks, and social and cultural imperatives were inevitably in large measure British in origin and whose inhabitants thereby shared a common identity as British peoples living in America.

Arguably the most important similarity among the several regions of colonial British-America, this common identity imposed upon British-Americans in all regions a common set of expectations for their new societies, which they looked upon not merely as vehicles for their own sustenance and enrichment but also as places that would eventually be recognizable approximations of Albion itself. They thus came to the New World expecting, not to create something wholly new, but, insofar as possible, to recreate what they had left behind, albeit without some of its less desirable aspects. Their expectation, their hope, was that the simple societies with which they began would in time develop into complex, improved, and civilized societies as those terms were defined by their metropolitan inheritance.

These contemporary expectations provide a basis for the further elaboration of a general *developmental framework* of the colonial process that can encompass the experiences of all regions of colonial British-America before 1763. Like the emerging system of regional classification, this conception is doubtless in need of much further refinement, but it encourages and permits us to conceive of the development of the several colonial regions as part of a long-range social process that can be divided into three sequential phases. The first phase involved the *social simplification* of inherited forms that so many scholars have noted for the first generations in every new colony. With very few exceptions, this early phase was characterized by much unsettlement and disorientation, as people sought to find ways to manipulate their new environments for their own sustenance and advantage while endeavoring, with limited success, to impose upon that environment social arrangements that, except possibly in the orthodox colonies of Puritan New England, bore little more than a crude resemblance to those they had left behind. As social arrangements gradually became more settled, population grew more dense (and usually more heavily creole), and the inhabitants acquired greater economic wherewithal, the simple social conditions that had characterized the first phase of settlement gave way to more elaborate ones. This second phase, one of *social elaboration*, thus involved the articulation of socioeconomic, political, and cultural institutions, structures, and values that, although they were usually highly creolized variants of those found in the more developed areas of Britain, were sufficiently functional to enable local populations to assimilate to them with relatively little difficulty. If this second phase was marked by a growing acculturation of the inhabitants to their social environment, that acculturation was not so complete as to inhibit demands, emanating largely from emerging elites, for a restructuring of their societies along lines that would make them more demonstrably British. Through the last decades of the period, colonial societies became more populous, offered prospects for greater comfort and affluence, grew more settled (if not in all cases much more orderly), and became internally more complex. In the common language of the times, these developments were subsumed under the term "improvement." With these and other "improvements," colonial societies approximated more closely to the established societies of the Old World and entered into still a third phase of development, a phase of *social replication*. In this phase members of the strategically placed elites, who by the late colonial period almost everywhere dominated and gave tone and definition to their societies, displayed a keen desire to recreate British society in America and took pride in the extent to which their societies were becoming increasingly Anglicized. By no means all members of the less affluent ranks of society shared this desire so fully, however, and some of the signs of sharp conflict in the colonies over religion, economics, and politics during the three or four decades before the Revolution can be attributed to opposing notions about precisely what directions the process of social development should take. For this reason, this third phase cannot by any means be seen as one of harmonious solidification under an image of Anglicized replication.

The timing of this process and the duration of each phase varied from region to region, and it led to widely varying results. The rate and character of population growth (including the changing ratios among the sexes, racial groups, and immigrants and Creoles), economic growth, territorial expansion, and date of settlement would seem to have been the central variables in determining differences in timing. Variations in results, on the other hand, were obviously a function of a much more numerous group of variables, including the nature of economic organization and the labor system, levels of socioeconomic differentiation, the depth and character of the religious orientation and goals of the populace, the healthfulness of the situation, the authority and responsiveness of colonial political leaders and institutions, and the degree of direct involvement with metropolitan Britain.

At every stage in this process of social development, it is important to keep in mind, these variables operated within a general framework of persisting tension between what we might, for convenience, refer to as experience and inheritance. By *experience* we mean to connote the complex of demands made upon the inhabitants by the necessity for their societies to function effectively within their several specific physical and social environments. By *inheritance* we mean to signify those traditions, cultural imperatives, and conceptions of the proper social order that the colonists derived initially from the metropolis—traditions, imperatives, and conceptions that they or their ancestors had brought with them from the Old World and that subsequently had been reinforced or modified through a process of continuous interaction with that world. The balance of force between experience and inheritance shifted from one phase of social development to the next according to local circumstances and the imperial and international context. But the general direction of movement before 1763 seems to have been towards the growing importance, though not necessarily in all cases the predominance, of inheritance.

If our aims in putting forth this conception seem ambitious, the spirit in which we do so is both tentative and inquiring. We offer it as no more than a preliminary effort to call attention to the need for and to articulate a general framework that will help historians of colonial British-America to process the enormous amount of data they are assembling without losing sight of the underlying coherence of the field as a whole or doing violence to the period, places, and structures they study. As R. G. Collingwood observed, all history is an interim report on work in progress. The fourteen substantive essays that follow, like the general model they helped to inspire, are tendered to the reader as precisely that, as a series of provisional reflections upon what has been achieved and what areas require additional research. In this spirit, we commend the essays to our own and succeeding generations of historians of colonial British-America.

NOTES

1. Carl Bridenbaugh, "The Neglected First Half of American History," *American Historical Review* 53 (April 1948): 506–17.

2. Lester J. Cappon, "'The Historian's Day'—From Archives to History," in *The Reinterpretation of Early American History: Essays in Honor of John Edwin Pomfret*, ed., Ray Allen Billington, (San Marino, Calif., 1966), 234–38.

3. In stressing these particular influences from within the disciplines of historical studies, we do not wish to minimize general social developments, such as the disillusionment with the American dream which, beginning in the mid-1960s, sent many people off on what now appears in retrospect to have been a nostalgic search for a more attractive, communal past, one that some of them found in the relatively egalitarian and communally oriented family farming communities of preindustrial New England.

4. See, for instance, Franklin W. Knight, *The Caribbean: The Genesis of a Fragmented Nationalism* (New York, 1978), 50–60. A highly sophisticated elaboration of a similar typology can be found in Philip Mason, *Patterns of Dominance* (London, 1971), 66–136.

5. To argue that all the British-American colonies were settler societies does not imply either that some of them (notably those in the Caribbean) did not subsequently become colonies of

exploitation (in the Leeward Islands this may have already happened by the middle of the eighteenth century) or that they were not basically exploitative in character. Indeed, in addition to being settler societies, all of the colonies were fundamentally exploitative of both the environments in which they lived and of any subordinate groups of people within them whose labor and persons could be exploited by those with greater power and resources. For an illuminating discussion of the problem of developing a workable typology of colonies see M. I. Finley, "Colonies—An Attempt at a Typology," *Transactions of the Royal Historical Society*, 5th ser., 26 (1976): 167–88.

6. Herman Merivale, *Lectures on Colonization and Colonies* (New York, 1967), 260–61.

7. In this connection, see the suggestive essay by Robert D. Mitchell, "The Formation of Early American Cultural Regions: An Interpretation," in *European Settlement and Development in North America: Essays on Geographical Change in Honour and Memory of Andrew Hill Clark*, ed., James R. Gibson, (Toronto, 1978), 66–90.

2

THE TRANSATLANTIC ECONOMY

JACOB M. PRICE

INTRODUCTION

he external economy of British North America in the seventeenth and eighteenth centuries is a subject that has attracted a great deal of scholarly attention in the past century and might well merit a serious bibliographic review here. However, such a review would now be supererogatory, for exactly such a survey—and a superb one at that—has recently been conducted by two able scholars. In October 1980 a conference was held at Williamsburg, Virginia, on the economy of British America from 1607 to 1790. To that conference John J. McCusker and Russell R. Menard presented a 350-page report surveying current knowledge in the field with very comprehensive bibliographical apparatus. This report will soon be published in the Needs and Opportunities series of the Institute of Early American History and Culture. There is therefore no need for me to duplicate what they have done. Instead I propose to present some of my own ideas on the critical and interpretative problems that arise when one tries to look at the colonial economy from the outside, and suggest some areas where useful work remains to be done.

When confronted with the topic of external aspects of early American economic history, the average listener or reader will most likely be reminded of the modern concern with the relationship of foreign trade to economic growth. Ordinary historians, of course, have not usually been very rigorous in their use of the term "growth." Sometimes they are simply indulging in a common organic metaphor comparing a given polity to a plant or animal that "grows"; more often they mean little more than "increase," or the process that results in greater aggregates of whatever is being discussed. By contrast, when economists in recent decades have used the term "economic growth," they have meant something much more precise: usually the process of economic change resulting in higher income per head within a given polity or geographic unit. For all its clarity, this restrictive definition of economic growth can pose problems for the working historian. One can have the greatest admiration for the econometricians who prepare current national income estimates and for the scholars who carry these calculations back in time and yet be wary of a concentration of interest that may confine future historical research within the cul-de-sac of inadequate data. For when the best trained quantitative explorer reaches the eighteenth century, he begins to enter a wilderness so ill provided with his sort of data that he cannot proceed except with the most extraordinary caution.

Almost the only data available for income estimates are hard external trade figures and estimates of population. Most conceivable methods of estimating income therefore are likely to make the internal production of goods and services vary with the population and to leave external trade as the only independent variable (besides population), hence the one that has to bear the full burden of accounting for any changes in per capita income. This becomes less and less satisfactory as the growing complexity of the colonial economy over time leaves the external sector a progressively smaller part of the whole.

One could of course do a better job if one had better estimates of the value of the manufacturing and service sectors in the colonial period. I do not intend to discuss industrial production, which lies within Richard Sheridan's zone of responsibility. I am, however, optimistic enough to imagine the not too distant day when through careful censuses of colonial iron furnaces and forges, fulling mills, breweries, distilleries, and the like, as well as the output of shipyards, we shall be able to suggest rough estimates of colonial industrial production. These and rougher but improved estimates of the value of services should enable a future generation of talented quantifiers to construct significantly better estimates of gross national product, or "national income," for the colonial period. When that day comes, we may usefully begin to pose many questions of economic change in terms of economic growth strictly defined. We cannot do that yet, and therefore I must deny myself the pleasure of talking about "economic growth" and instead confine my remarks to the simple-minded aggregation of traditional historians.

SOURCES

Traditional historians have done a lot with simple aggregation of late, and they can do much more. The external sector of the colonial economy is particularly rich in its available quantitative and quantifiable materials. The various offices of inspectors general of exports and imports have left behind in the Public Record Office the series Customs 2 and 3 on English foreign trade, including that with the colonies; Customs 14, on Scottish trade from 1755, and Customs 16/1, on colonial trade from 1768 to 1772. In addition, there survive in the Colonial Office and Treasury records at the Public Record Office hundreds of quarterly reports from "naval officers" or inspectors of navigation in the North American and West Indian colonies from the late seventeenth century. British historians seemed almost totally oblivious to the value of this material even after the publication of Sir George Clark's handbook in the 1930s;[1] and it was not until the 1950s and 1960s, with the publication of Elizabeth Schumpeter's tables and two important articles by the late Ralph Davis,[2] that the possible value of these materials began to be dimly perceived by British economic historians. Significant breakthroughs came with the publication of B. R. Mitchell and Phyllis Deane's *British Historical Statistics* and Henry Hamilton's *Economic History of Scotland*.[3] American economic historians had been no more forward in using these resources, even though for two generations they had had Charles M. Andrews's *Guide*, pointing out exactly where the materials were to be found.[4]

When I first started working with such materials around 1950, I was unaware of any American economic historian—except my fellow student Richard Sheridan[5]—who had used or was using such data. My own work soon convinced me at least of the great utility of using both the English and the Scottish customs returns together, while the later work of James Shepherd and Gary Walton made very clear the value of the American series (Customs 16/1) and intelligent sampling of naval officers' reports.[6] Their work was based in part on the very ambitious collection of inspector general and naval officer accounts that Lawrence A. Harper had begun collecting in the 1930s and 1940s, a collection made possible by the introduction of microfilm in the late 1930s. Harper was also the chief mover behind the addition of chapter Z on colonial data to the 1960 edition of the *Historical Statistics of the United States*.[7] That was probably the most important single step in publicizing many of the materials available for the quantitative study of the early American economy—particularly its external aspects—and making such data available to students everywhere.

In the 1960s Harper started transferring his holdings into machine-readable, or computer, form.[8] This made it possible to ask new questions of the data. I understand that William Davisson, of Notre Dame University, has also put large amounts of naval officer material into machine-readable form. I should, however, like to question whether such private machine archives best serve the interests of the economic history profession. I am informed that Harper has been forced to remove part of his collections from his office to his home, and I hope that there is no danger that his valuable archive will be dispersed. I should like to suggest that there is a need for a strong machine archive on early American external trade and shipping based in an institution that will give it continuing support and open it to all interested users for a reasonable fee. Such an archive should not be confined to material already in summary forms (such as the reports in Customs 2, 3, 14, and 16) but should include the relatively undigested material both in the American naval officers' reports and in the English and Scottish port books. The English port books for the seventeenth century can help fill part of the great lacunae in American data. A patient individual can process a lot of such data with little more than a pencil and a desk calculator. But there are better ways.

The naval officers in the American ports sent their reports in quarterly. In even the best series there are no reports for some quarters. Where reports for only one quarter in a given year are missing in any series it should be possible to interpolate an estimated figure for that quarter based on other evidence available for that and the immediately preceding and following years. Where a colony—such as New York—has only a single port, such interpolations will be relatively risky; where a colony—such as Virginia—contains a good number of busy ports, the risk may be considerably reduced. With totals of each commodity and each port available in machine-readable form, it should be possible, with the advice of professional statisticians, to work out a system of limited interpolation that would minimize the risks of serious error. Ultimately I think that a single if substantial volume could be published containing all the most important data from the naval officers' reports and the port books. Time series of trade data could be arranged by commodity, port of shipment, port of destination, and, in some cases for the eighteenth century, merchant firms. Comparable series could be printed for shipping activity. Interpolated data could be indicated by italics. This presupposes a collective effort and financial support that may be difficult to obtain in the short run. However, much of the necessary work may already have been done by the teams of Harper, Davisson, and others, so that the costs may not be as great as imagined. Such a volume would be the greatest boon to the study of colonial trade since the publication of chapter Z in 1960.

Besides physical quantities, the most important data needed by early American economic historians are prices. An International Scientific Committee on Price History was set up in the 1920s. Under its auspices, many volumes were published giving price data for many parts of Europe and North America. The volumes of Arthur Cole and Anne Bezanson are well known.[9] Early American economic historians have also made some use of the volumes edited by Sir William Beveridge and N. W. Posthumus.[10] Not very much, however, has been done in the field of price publication in the past thirty years. This is rather unfortunate for students of early American economic history whose needs go far beyond Bezanson's Philadelphia series.

Ideally the best series are those based on printed price currents prepared by publicly recognized brokers. Unfortunately, none was printed in America in the colonial period, and those printed in London have not survived in usable numbers for the years 1715–75.[11] The situation is much better at Hamburg and Amsterdam, where additional price currents have come to light since Posthumus was published. Nor is it generally appreciated that Posthumus did not publish everything available of American interest; for example, he published only the price series for Virginia tobacco, although the Amsterdam price currents also contain a series for Maryland tobacco. It probably would be useful to publish a volume supplementary to Posthumus reporting more fully Amsterdam prices for commodities of American interest. Such a volume might also cover Hamburg.

On this side of the Atlantic, the absence of good printed price currents has forced economic historians to be much more ingenious in their development of price series. Bezanson and colleagues used both prices published in newspapers and prices obtained from merchants' accounts. Since their publications appeared, some interesting new price series have been developed from estate inventories.[12] Those who have made the greatest use of this source have checked it against other sources and report their confidence in the inventory prices. My own feeling is that such confidence may be justified in particular cases but that the validity of inventory prices needs constant checking against other sources, particularly merchants' accounts. Merchants' accounts from the seventeenth century are very few and far between, so that inventory data are likely to remain our chief source for price history. Merchants' accounts from the eighteenth century, however, are somewhat more plentiful, particularly in large commercial centers such as Philadelphia, New York, and Boston. For the Chesapeake and more southerly colonies they are fewer and more scattered, but they can make a valuable supplement to and check on the inventory data. Systematic work in price history would be considerably helped if one institution in each of the thirteen original states made itself responsible for preparing lists and collecting microfilm of seventeenth- and eighteenth-century merchants' accounts and other materials (originating in its state) rich in price data. These might eventually be the raw materials for the publication of series to supplement those in Cole and Bezanson.

INTERPRETATIONS AND FOCI

If the study of the internal American economy in the seventeenth and eighteenth centuries suffers from an absolute lack of data on many key points of production and distribution, the study of the external economy has been held back not so much by the absence of data (particularly in the eighteenth century) as by the bulk and intractability of much of the available material. If a beneficent foundation announced tomorrow that it was going to pay for the compilation and publication of all available quantitative data on colonial trade, shipping, and prices, the problems of bulk and intractability would be much closer to solution, but we would still have the problem of approach and interpretation.

There have been four dominant foci of attention for the study of colonial economic history: the empire, the colony, the community, and the commodity. The first and the last are essentially outward-looking, the second and the third more inward-looking. At the beginning of this century the imperial approach seemed very rewarding. The colonial economies were built, it seemed, if not precisely according to an imperial legislative blueprint, then at least within the protecting and restricting confines of an imperial trading "system." The weakness of the "imperial system" at the time and of the imperial approach in modern historiography is that both have tended to underrate the full influence of the market or of what Harold Innis called "the penetrative powers of the price system" both on the supply side (as in the West Indies sugar and molasses trades) and on the demand side (as in the tobacco, wheat, and slave trades). A relatively small number of scholars are still cultivating the imperial garden, but except for a few articles on the costs of the navigation acts,[13] the impact of the imperial approach on the writing of early American economic history of late has not been impressive.

Antedating the imperial school, running parallel to it, and continuing strongly to the present has been the tradition of using the individual colony as the unit of scholarly focus in early American economic history as well as in political, institutional, and religious history. This approach makes perfect sense when one considers the logistics of research. Both manuscript sources and printed sources tend to be arranged by colonies. A project that is confined to one colony is logistically an efficient project. The colony is also a logical conceptual unit for framing problems in political, institutional, and religious history and for those aspects of economic history that are concerned with public policy. Even trade data are arranged by colonies, though the English inspectors general lumped together New England, the Chesapeake, and the Carolinas and ignored New Jersey and Delaware. However, the colony is probably a very unsatisfactory unit for the study of the external aspects of the economy. Most serious students of the sugar economy of the West Indies have preferred treating the British West Indies collectively as the appropriate unit of study, and John McCusker, like Richard Pares before him, considers the whole Antilles as the proper unit of investigation.[14]

For similar reasons, students of the external economy of the continental colonies may well find the individual province too confining a unit and prefer to think in the mode of a Harold Innis of a fur zone (from Hudson Bay to the Mississippi Valley), a fish zone (from Newfoundland to Massachusetts), a cereal zone (from New York or Connecticut to northwestern Virginia), a tobacco zone (from tidewater Maryland to north-central North Carolina), and a rice and indigo zone (extending from the lower Cape Fear River to Georgia). Other transcolonial divisions could be suggested.

Of late, however, much attention has turned from the colony to the community. Perhaps the most striking innovation of the last twenty years has been the success of a number of scholars in using the community (the town, parish, and county in particular) as the working unit for serious social and economic investigation. At this level of magnification, the study of the family and household becomes practical, and European techniques of family reconstitution can be fruitfully employed. For all their great successes, however, the community studies, even more than the provincial, have been inward-looking and have tended to isolate the community studied from the broader imperatives of the market. There have, of course, been effective exceptions—notably the work of Paul Clemens, Russell Menard, and Gloria Main on Maryland[15]—in which the greater outside world is ever-present through the penetrative powers of the price system.

Finally, there remains the commodity. There is nothing new about this approach, at least since Innis's day.[16] Freshmen and sophomores know all about staples, but serious scholars have done relatively little with them. If there have been popular or semipopular studies of the early modern trades in sugar, tea, coffee, and other exotic commodities,[17] "serious scholars" in English-speaking countries have been slow to follow the example of a Louis Dermigny or a Kristof Glamann and to organize their work on the acceptance of the integrity and utility of an internationally traded commodity as an effective unit for study.[18] We still await comprehensive international studies of most American commodities, particularly wheat, rice, and dyestuffs. Even the relatively well-studied iron and fish trades have yet to be put in their fullest international context. (Noel Deerr attempted this for sugar, but his important effort is only a beginning.)[19]

Part of the problem is that the commodity approach is too difficult. For example, a comprehensive study of the North Atlantic wheat trade in the second half of the eighteenth century must include, in addition to American production, exports, and prices, a discussion of European population trends, the subsistence policies of the principal western European states, and some appreciation of the significance of the Russian conquest of the southern Ukraine and the opening of the Black Sea to international trade. At the other extreme, it is all too easy to throw in a few sentences about "staples" or staple models and think that one has really placed an export trade in its international context.

Nevertheless, it seems likely that the most profitable coming work on the external economy of British North America will be based on either commodity/staple models or population models exploiting the skills of the community historians, but paying more attention to the weight of the market. Let us look at each in turn.

STAPLE AND/OR POPULATION MODELS

When the market price of any commodity rises relative to that of other commodities, there should be a tendency for some of the factors of production—land, labor, capital, and entrepreneurship—to be reallocated away from other uses towards the production of the now more attractive commodity. The staple thesis as usually understood describes the effect of such reallocation upon a country producing a raw material for export. In such a situation, the reallocation of resources may, if permitted, be international in scope and directed not only directly towards increased production of the commodity in question but also towards the provision of support facilities. (Today we think of pipelines and tankers; in the eighteenth century these support facilities may only have been dirt roads, wooden bridges, wagons, flats, coopers' shops, and vessels of two hundred tons or less.) The reallocation should stimulate other aspects of the affected economy; it should result in the more efficient use of resources, and if it is substantial enough, it may result in true economic growth, that is, higher income per head in the territory affected. Whether this true growth is achieved will depend upon the relative importance of the commodity in question in the economy of that territory and upon its population trends.

When we try to carry the "staple model" back to the seventeenth and eighteenth centuries, we run into certain immediate difficulties with numbers. The staple model seems to work best in the very earliest years of settlement, when there was very little in the way of income or production (the base for subsequent calculations) and all resources except unimproved land were sadly lacking. In that dawn, any new resources could seemingly be productively and profitably employed, and slight increases might appear significant in percentage terms. In the era of large-scale indentured-servant trade, the reallocation of resources is not just a vague abstraction. However, when we come to the eighteenth century, we run into some problems in the application of full-blown staple theory. Tobacco, the most important export from North America then, provides an illuminating example. Between 1697–1702 and 1771–75, tobacco exports increased roughly threefold, while population in the tobacco colonies increased about 7.4-fold. Since there is no evidence of a decline in income per head, it is fairly obvious that a lot was going on in the Chesapeake besides growing tobacco. Eighteenth-century Virginia and Maryland in fact also exported many other commodities, including wheat, flour, provisions, naval stores, pig iron, and ships. The staple effect was still working—that is, external demand was encouraging the direction of further resources towards tobacco production—but the monocausal, single-commodity staple thesis is no longer very helpful.

With the conventional staple thesis, or model, more helpful for the seventeenth century than for the eighteenth, scholars working on the early American economy should consider models that better explain or help explain the evolution of the colonial economy. One of these may be a population, or mixed population-market, model. The staple thesis as already noted works best in the early days of settlement, when both labor and capital have to be attracted to the new colony by more or less rational market considerations.[20] However, at a certain stage—fairly early (the first generation) in New England, later in the Chesapeake—normal family life was established, and the primary determinant of the size of the labor force became not immigration but the natural growth of the population, both free and slave. With this more or less independent growth in population and the labor force went a growth in the productive capacity of the colony, although there may have been a transitional decline in income per head as a colony changed from a primarily adult community to a society supporting an exceptionally large number of children.

Less obvious is the proposition that this growing population could create its own capital almost automatically. The most obvious elements in the wealth of the colonies were land and slaves. The slave population tended to increase *pari passu* with the free population, considerably enhancing the wealth and productive resources of slaveholders. Land, too, tended to increase in value *pari passu* with the increase in population. If land beyond the frontier was almost worthless, land in settled areas varied in value with fertility, degree of improvement, and relative access to markets. The growth of population moved the frontier outwards and gave value to hitherto valueless land; the growth of population also created the labor force, both free and slave, to improve and render more valuable hitherto unimproved land. (In an economy where land is abundant and cheap, labor should be more productive than in an economy where land is scarce; thus a smaller proportion of the total labor force should be needed to provide for subsistence, leaving a larger proportion available for other employments, including land improvement and the creation of fixed and movable capital.) The increase in the value of his land or slaves increased the land- or slaveholder's ability to borrow (both from local and British sources), whether on mortgage or on his personal credit. This increased credit-worthiness may have been squandered on more luxurious consumption; it may have been used to buy more land and more slaves and to make agricultural improvements; or it may have been invested in industry (such as an ironworks) or trade. Some of the greatest fortunes in the plantation colonies were in fact made by those who combined landowning and trade. (Undeveloped land held for appreciation might still be valuable enough to support some credit and thus indirectly be productive.)

If then the primary motive power in the expansion of the productive capacity of the colonial economies was the independent natural increase in population with the concomitant increase in aggregate wealth, the question still remains, How were these constantly increasing quanta of labor and capital to be employed? In the agricultural sector this was for most landowners and even tenants a rational, market-oriented decision reflecting the quality and price of land available, transport costs to market, and the current market price of possible alternative productions. Limited migration was a real option, but only in exceptional periods such as that of the Seven Years' War was distant migration within the colonies anything but rare. For those determined to stay where they were, both soil quality and transport costs could be taken as fixed. (Soil exhaustion was compensated for by moving the area of cultivation within the plantation.) The only great variable in the short or medium term was the market.

Thus we return to where we started. Whether one thinks that the economic evolution of the colonies can best be explained by the elegantly simple staple model or by the somewhat sloppier mixed population-market model, one is forced to start with the market to explain much if not all of the short- and medium-term behavior of the colonial economy. A market is made by supply and demand. The writing of most early American economic history has concentrated upon supply. For many branches of the economy the great unexplored frontier may well be demand.

THE DEMAND SIDE OF COLONIAL ECONOMIC HISTORY

The principal commodities exported from British North America in the colonial period are relatively well known. In table 2.1 they are listed, in order of importance as of 1770, along with the proportions of each going to the principal destinations: Great Britain and Ireland; southern Europe; the West Indies and Africa. Some, the so-called enumerated commodities of the acts of trade and navigation, went almost exclusively to Great Britain: tobacco, rice, masts and yards, furs and skins, indigo, whale products, iron, potash and

Table 2.1

PRINCIPAL EXPORTS FROM THE BRITISH CONTINENTAL COLONIES
(INCLUDING NEWFOUNDLAND, THE BAHAMAS, AND BERMUDA), 1770,
AT OFFICIAL VALUES

Export Commodity	Value (£ sterling)	Destination		
		Great Britain and Ireland (%)	Southern Europe (%)	West Indies and Africa (%)
Tobacco[a]	£906,638	99.80%	0 %	0.20%
Bread and flour	504,553	8.37	40.34	51.28
Fish	397,945	3.24	61.73	35.03
Rice[b]	340,693	48.92	23.97	27.12
Wheat, oats, maize	176,086	11.95	56.64	31.41
Timber and wood products	171,737	—	—	—
Masts, yards, etc.[a]	*16,630*	99.90	0	0.01
Pine, oak, and cedar boards	*58,618*	14.84	1.14	84.03
Staves and heading	*61,619*	37.72	8.18	54.10
Furs and skins[a]	149,326	100.00	0	0
Indigo[a]	131,552	99.99	0	0.01
Whale oil and fins[a]	104,134	92.25	3.06	4.69
Horses and livestock	80,212	0	0	100.00
Iron[a]	70,250	96.55	0.12	3.33
Beef and pork	66,035	0	1.36	98.46
Potash and pearl ash[a]	64,661	100.00	0	0
Flaxseed	35,169	99.76	0.24	0.00
Tar, turpentine, etc.[a]	35,076	94.35	0	5.65
Other native produce[c]	122,094			
Total native produce	£3,356,160			
Re-exports	81,555			
Total exports	£3,437,715			

Source: U.S. Bureau of the Census, *Historical Statistics of the United States, Colonial Times to 1970,* 2 vols. (Washington, D.C., 1975), 2:1183–84.

Note: Italicized items represent subdivisions of the "timber and wood products" category.

[a]Enumerated commodities

[b]Enumerated, except for southern Europe

[c]New England rum, peas and beans, butter, cheese, copper and lead ores, among others.

pearl ash, tar and turpentine. Other products not needed in Great Britain and therefore not enumerated went both to the West Indies and to southern Europe: bread and flour, fish, cereals. Still other products went primarily to the West Indies: boards, horses and livestock, beef and pork. Only rice went in significant quantities to all three major market areas. The results of these diffuse trading patterns are summarized in table 2.2, covering the years 1768–72. In those five years some 52.7 percent of North American exports went to Great Britain; 25.7 percent went to the West Indies; and 17.9 percent went to southern Europe and the Wine Islands.

Britain of course, imported "colonial" goods not only from North America but from the West Indies as well. The value of English imports from both the American areas has been summarized for selected years over the eighteenth century in a well-known article by Ralph Davis (see table 2.3). Davis's data, of course, refer only to England. The omission of Scotland is more distorting for some trades than for others. Scotland's sugar imports add only 3.9 percent to England's (by value) in 1772–74, and her cotton imports add only 6.4 percent; but her tobacco imports add 87.9 percent to the value of South Britain's.[21] Even so, the preeminent place of sugar as the leading colonial import is unassailable. Strongly in second place (after Scotland is added in) was tobacco, followed after a significant gap by West Indian coffee and Carolina rice. Much further behind—in the £80,000–160,000 range—came West Indian spirits, dyestuffs, and cotton and North American timber products (masts, etc.), skins and hides, and whale products. Cereal imports from North America were important only in isolated years of bad harvests at home.

All in all, therefore, in 1772–74, on the eve of the American Revolution, Great Britain imported over £5.4 million worth of produce (almost all raw

Table 2.2
ESTIMATED VALUE OF TOTAL COMMODITY EXPORTS FROM BRITISH NORTH AMERICAN COLONIES BY DESTINATION, 1768–72 (IN THOUSANDS OF POUNDS STERLING)

Destination	1768	1769	1770	1771	1772	Annual Average
Great Britain	1,360	1,540	1,449	1,761	1,828	1,588 (52.7%)
Ireland	69	80	133	105	74	92 (3.1%)
Southern Europe and Wine Islands	378	604	565	557	592	539 (17.9%)
West Indies	583	699	815	813	964	775 (25.7%)
Africa	13	24	21	16	29	21 (0.7%)
Total	2,403	2,947	2,983	3,252	3,487	3,014

Source: James F. Shepherd and Gary M. Walton, *Shipping, Maritime Trade, and the Economic Development of Colonial North America* (Cambridge, 1972), 94–95.

Table 2.3
PRINCIPAL ENGLISH IMPORTS FROM NORTH AMERICA AND THE WEST
INDIES, 1699–1774 (IN THOUSANDS OF POUNDS STERLING)

Import Commodity	1699–1701	1722–24	1752–54	1772–74
Sugar	630	928	1,302	2,360
Spirits (rum)	0	6	70	163
Tobacco	249	263	560	518
Coffee	0	0	3	414
Rice	0	52	167	340
Dyestuffs	85	152	97	167
Timber	14	13	90	114
Skins and hides	23	34	46	111
Oil (whale, etc.)	19	26	43	93
Cotton	23	45	56	88
Drugs	6	22	55	55
Cereals	0	0	0	51
Iron and steel	0	0	5	10
Total	1,107	1,679	2,684	4,769

Source: Ralph Davis, "English Foreign Trade, 1700–1774," *Economic History Review*, 2d ser., 15 (1962): 300–301.

materials or semiprocessed goods) from her colonies in North America and the West Indies. (Of this, £4.77 million came to England and £662,884 to Scotland.)[22] A century and a half before, almost nothing had come from the same area. Whence rose the demand in George III's subjects for so much that their ancestors could do without? The simplest explanation would be the old, dependable doctrine of comparative advantage taken by itself. That is, when Englishmen, Irishmen, and Scotsmen settled in the American colonies, they found that they could produce more economically in the colonies than at home certain familiar products for which there was a known demand in Europe. Therefore they set to work making these familiar products, and their relatives at home, finding that these products could be more economically obtained from the colonies, reduced production at home and turned their attention to items in the production of which they had a comparative advantage. At both ends of the imperial system, people specialized in what they could do best, to their mutual advantage and with higher ultimate income for all. Or so we should expect.

In fact, this rationalization happened only to a very limited extent. From the beginning, emigrants to America brought with them the tools, skills, breeding stock, and seed of north European agriculture, and from the beginning they used these to produce the arable and animal products they needed for their own subsistence. In time, they found vents for their surplus production of these items (along with fish and forest products) in the West Indies and southern Europe—but not in Britain itself. When they threatened to send home products that would compete with the output of domestic agriculture, the home government sometimes prohibited the importation of such commodities—as did the British government in the case of colonial wheat and flour, and the French government in the case of colonial rum. For permanent and attractive markets at home the colonists had to turn to tropical products, which could not be produced at home, to forest products (masts, pitch, tar, and the like), in short supply at home, and to new products, such as tobacco, hitherto unknown at home. When it was discovered that tobacco could in fact be grown in northern Europe, its production was prohibited in both England and France, not so much to help colonial trade as to protect the king's revenue. This meant that Britain's (and France's) import trade from the East Indies and from the Americas in the seventeenth and eighteenth centuries developed around a congeries of new products (coffee, tea, chocolate, tobacco, tropical dyestuffs) or products hitherto imported indirectly and in very small quantities (sugar, pepper, silk, cotton).[23] In both cases substantial changes in consumption patterns were needed to create the effective demand that would support the volume of colonial and Asian trade achieved by the third quarter of the eighteenth century.

We are not talking about trifling quantities. Very often taxes had to be paid on the various colonial products imported, and the products underwent processing that added to their final cost to the consumer. The petty retail price was likely to be at least two or three times the wholesale value at importation. This wholesale value for all retained imports in 1765–74 was close to £12 million sterling,[24] of which perhaps a third was accounted for by products from America and the West Indies. If this American produce only doubled in value by the time it reached the consumer, then about £8 million per annum was spent by English consumers on transatlantic products, or something over £1 per head. If the American produce trebled in price by the time it reached retail sale, then the consumer expenditure on American produce would have been about £12 million, or near £1 13s. per head. A very optimistic estimate places per capita income at this time at about £18 per head;[25] even if it were only two-thirds as much, there was ample capacity to support this level of consumption. However, either way, there had been a significant reorientation of consumer demand towards colonial produce. How were consumers able to bear this?

There are two fairly obvious models that might explain this shift in consumer demand. One assumes that there was a more or less steady increase in income per head during the seventeenth and eighteenth centuries; the other starts from the premise that there was not. If there was an increase in income per head, then a very plausible explanation of the new consumption patterns is at hand: the English and later British consumer used part of the increase in his real income for colonial and other exotic products: tobacco, sugar, tea, coffee, rice, cottons, and all sorts of textiles dyed with the superior tropical or semitropical dyes. This explanation of the changed consumption patterns may be simplistic and one-dimensional, but it is at least consistent. But where did the increased real income that in this model accounts for the changed consumption patterns come from? Part may have come from a slowing in the rate of population growth after 1660. Part may have come from increased productivity in the domestic economy, including agriculture. Part may have come from increased foreign demand for British manufactures—including colonial demand. Such increased demand would have permitted a more productive allocation of labor and other resources, particularly if one assumes a situation at the beginning of the seventeenth century characterized by substantial unemployment and underemployment of labor. However, there is no evidence that export markets for any major branch of British manufactures except woolens ever exceeded 20 percent of output before 1776. (In the small cotton industry it may have been as high as 25 percent.) Colonial markets only became an important part of export markets in the generation or two preceding 1776, and in the case of woolens the increase in the colonial market only compensated for decline in the European market.[26] It is of course possible to imagine a model in which higher income per head at home created an enhanced demand for colonial produce which in turn created increased colonial demand for British manufactures, engendering further increases in income per head at home; however, the small share of output taken by colonial markets, particularly during the first century of colonization, makes it improbable that colonial demand could have been the principal cause for any increase in real income per head that took place.

Pessimists may of course deny that there was any increase in real income per head for substantial stretches of the seventeenth or eighteenth centuries. Some would even argue that there was a decline in income per head during the decades 1600–1660 caused by rising population and prices and secular difficulties in traditional export industries. If such were the case, how could there have been a change in consumption patterns towards newer exotic and nonessential commodities? It can be argued that the new consumption was classbound. Even while the generality of the population was suffering a decline in real income per head, landlords and their hangers-on, office-holders, merchants, and some manufacturers of luxury products were gaining ground; they thus can be seen as the market for these new exotic imports.

Were, however, the new consumption patterns confined only to limited circles of the population? It is not unreasonable to suggest that even in a world of constant real incomes, significant shifts in consumption could take place. Do tea or coffee drinkers drink as much beer as those who drink only beer? Do those who take treacle with their bread need as much bread? Even in the seventeenth century men were aware that tobacco dulled the appetite and thus might substitute for some food or drink in the budgets of the poor. Thus, it is not inconceivable that, even with constant or declining incomes, the poorer sections of the population may have supported the newly acquired habits of tobacco, tea, sugar, and the like by consuming less beer, bread, or meat. (Increased cereal exports after 1690 and stagnant beer consumption give some credibility to this hypothesis.)[27] It was also alleged by late seventeenth-century and early eighteenth-century "moralists" that many obtained the wherewithal to purchase Indian calicoes by buying fewer woolen garments.[28]

It is not necessary to accept one explanation *in toto* and reject all others. Historians have always been good at syncretism. A pessimistic model may appear more useful for the early seventeenth century, while a more optimistic model may seem more applicable to the century after 1660. The historian of the colonial economy working on any one commodity is unlikely to get very far in his project if he insists on starting by first solving the problem of whether income per head in Britain was increasing or decreasing in each decade of the colonial period, any more than if he insists on starting by solving the same riddle for the colonies. He must, however, recognize that his story starts with the changing pattern of consumer preference in Europe or the changing demographic situation in Europe that creates the demand for the particular American product he is studying.

Tobacco was probably the most exotic new product introduced into Europe from America. Its strangeness accounts for the extreme slowness of its adoption. On the eve of the American Revolution, some two hundred years after its introduction into England, consumption was barely two pounds per head per annum. By contrast, annual consumption in many countries in the twentieth century is above five pounds per head of population. In most continental countries where there were monopolies, consumption was probably lower than in Britain. If the British consumer after 1685 paid an average price for small retail purchases of as much as 2s.6d. per pound, retail expenditure was at most 5s. per head of population per year; and in France it was unlikely to have been much more than 2s. per head. The student must always remember that the cultural penetration of tobacco, which probably reached its peak after the Second World War, had only gone a small part of the way by 1775. The incomplete cultural victory of tobacco combined with high taxation created a marked inelasticity of demand. Despite attendant low prices, the gluts created by periodic overproduction in the century before 1776 did not evoke compensating upsurges in demand and could only be worked off very slowly. Conversely, when supplies were sharply reduced, the same inelasticity could lead to very marked rises in wholesale prices: tenfold in the extreme case of the American Revolution.

Sugar was known in Europe long before tobacco, and its use was widespread, at least geographically. However, consumption per head remained very low until the seventeenth and eighteenth centuries. When cheaper, slave-grown sugar facilitated an increase in consumption in the seventeenth century, not all parts of Europe developed a sweet tooth at the same rate. English consumption of unrefined imports rose from 5.3 lb. per head per annum in 1699–1703 to 24 lb. per head in 1771–75 (at least 30 percent should be deducted to arrive at refined equivalents). By contrast, modern consumption is over 100 lb. per head. We need to know more about comparable consumption patterns in other European countries, particularly France, which appears to have reexported a higher percentage of its imports than did Britain, so that its consumption in 1783 was reportedly only 2 lb. per head.[29] Future work on sugar must start with all the new forms of demand, including the soft-drink revolution, which linked the fates of sugar, tea, chocolate, and coffee. Carolina rice is supposed to be particularly well suited and traditionally used for rice pudding. If all the Carolina rice retained in England around 1770 had been made into rice pudding, how many tons of sugar would have been used therein?

Given the extraordinary importance of the textile industries in Britain, I am surprised that more attention has not been given to the demand for American dyestuffs. Colonial historians are of course aware of the importance of indigo to South Carolina, but a wider perspective would find room for logwood, Brazil wood, cochineal, and others. How important were qualitative differences between different competing dyes? When we recall that the dying stage could sometimes double the value of a piece of cloth, we can perhaps appreciate the strategic importance of the dyestuffs trade for the hundreds of thousands of persons employed in the textile industries in Britain alone. Since such a study should ideally embrace the French, Spanish, and Portuguese colonies as well as the English, it is not recommended for anyone in a hurry.

LEGAL AND FISCAL BARRIERS

After the future economic historian of colonial trade has chosen his commodity and clearly established the character of the demand for it, he will have to ask what real market choices were open to merchants trying to meet that demand. This will of course bring him to "the old colonial system" so beloved of the imperial school of historians. After Beer and Andrews and Lawrence Harper, one would expect that little more can be said about the acts of trade and navigation and the directing role of the state. Yet I suspect that there are three aspects of the regulative apparatus that have not yet received all the attention that is their due: (1) the political, (2) the administrative/strategic, and (3) the fiscal.

First, English and British legislation rather obviously arose out of a process of competition and compromise between separate and sometimes conflicting interests. A slow but steady trickle of new works reminds us that we do not know all there is to know about the inner political history of most of the important legislative measures touching colonial trade. This trickle of new interpretation will undoubtedly continue.

Second, not all the interests involved were private. Some were state interests of great weight. One such was the need of the Royal Navy and the British merchant marine for a safe, dependable source of masts, ship timbers, naval stores, and flax and hemp for sails, cables, and cordage. To avoid a dangerous dependence on Russia and the Scandinavian countries, the British government in the eighteenth century encouraged by subsidies the importation of most of the key naval raw materials from North America. We know a good bit about this policy as far as it affected the New England mast and timber trade,[30] but much less about the Carolinas and the naval stores trade generally and the unsuccessful efforts to encourage the production of hemp and flax in America. A quite different state interest was the security of the food supply. If the British government in the eighteenth century normally left this to private enterprise, continental governments did not. We know next to nothing about the attitudes and activities of continental governments, including the French, towards the burgeoning North American wheat trade to southern Europe during the last decades preceding the Revolution.

And third, the most important thing about the fiscal interest of the state is that it almost always conflicted with the maximum development of colonial trade. But since governments need taxes, fiscal considerations often won out over other interests of state, including colonial. The extreme case was, of course, tobacco, which paid duties of several hundred percent in most European countries. The fiscal interest of the French state and the private interest of the French tobacco monopoly united to make France almost totally dependent on the British colonies for its tobacco between 1723 and 1775, even though it would have been possible—at a price—for the French colonies or France itself to supply all the tobacco France needed.[31] Other state monopolies, including the Spanish, also bought British tobacco. No other trade was as completely dominated by fiscal considerations, but other colonial products, including sugar and coffee, were taxed, though their fiscal history remains largely untouched.

Taxation inevitably requires regulation. To protect its revenues, the British government—like the French government—prescribed the ship and the package in which the tobacco could be imported. These regulations and the purely financial requirements of bonding and paying the duties are generally thought to have squeezed smaller firms out of the trade and to have encouraged its concentration in fewer hands. Since this same concentration can be detected in most colonial trades, it might be useful to investigate the restrictive and anticompetitive implications of both taxation and regulation in most such trades.

THE IMPORT TRADES

The bulk of this paper, like the bulk of the literature, has been devoted to staple exports and their problems. By contrast, the colonial import trades are much less studied than the export trades; hence, more attention to them may prove profitable. We know too little about the quantities or qualities involved. A mere perusal of merchants' invoices or the ledgers of the inspector general of exports and imports suggests much about the quality of life in early America, and students of consumption could perhaps make fuller use of such sources.

Many but not all of British North America's imports were tropical, Asiatic, or luxury products that did not compete with goods manufactured or grown within the thirteen colonies. Included in this category would be unrefined sugar, molasses, coffee, tea, silks, fancier millinery and haberdashery, most books, and so on. There was, however, a large range of goods (woolens, linens, cottons, shoes and other leather goods, ironmongery) which competed with some colonial manufactures by 1775—although not in all qualities. If we had detailed breakdowns of imports by precise categories and by colonies, we could make some crude but interesting guesses about the relative progress of different manufactures in different colonies over time. Such material may be particularly suggestive if used in conjunction with censuses of colonial ironworks, fulling mills, distilleries, breweries, and the like.

I have the impression that colonial demand for imported manufactures was particularly pressing at the top and the bottom of the price range—at the top for quality goods not made in America; at the bottom for goods like inexpensive German linens, cheaper than anything obtainable in the colonies.[32] In the middle was a price range where some colonial products could compete. Only a very tedious analysis of the inspector general's ledgers—which contain price data—will indicate whether this is anything more than the optical illusion of tired eyes.

AN INTERDEPENDENT SYSTEM

The import trades of course included the trades in slaves and indentured servants, hardly neglected topics, least of all today, when we have a new journal devoted entirely to the history of slavery and emancipation. These will be even less neglected when we have digested David Galenson's new book[33] and have an opportunity to read Bernard Bailyn's promised major book on the peopling of America. However, for all the attention it has received, the slave trade still poses some big problems. I suspect that it was the single most important factor encouraging the descendants of eighteenth-century merchants to destroy their ancestors' papers or at least not to make them available to researchers. Some have suggested that there may still be large bodies of such papers in private possession.[34] Perhaps the attractive prices recently attained at manuscript auctions (by the Codrington Papers in particular) will draw some of these out of hiding. If so, we may be able to answer with a bit more assuredness than now some important questions about the profitability of the slave trade.[35]

One does not have to accept the full argument that the profits of the slave

trade financed the industrial revolution[36] to see that in the final analysis we
are not dealing only with a series of distinct economies producing commodities to be exported to Europe in bilateral exchange for European and
Asian goods. Such a picture may in large part fit the tobacco, rice, indigo,
masts, and naval stores trades but not others. Fish, flour, and wheat were
exported to southern Europe, and the proceeds of sales were remitted to
England to pay for goods to be sent thence to the northern fish- and wheat-
producing colonies. Fish, flour, provisions, livestock, and forest products
were exported to the West Indies, and the proceeds were either returned to
North America in sugar, molasses, and other West Indian produce or remitted to Britain to pay for supplies needed thence.

If there had been no West Indies, how much trade would New England
and the Middle Colonies have had? How many people then would have been
content to emigrate to or reside in those areas? If there had been no slavery,
would there have been any West Indies trade? What about Virginia and
Maryland and the Carolinas? I detect a certain impatience with counterfactual propositions in much recent critical literature. These nevertheless are
not unreasonable questions, even though we may never obtain answers to
them that will give general satisfaction. I personally think that the Chesapeake and much of North Carolina would have developed almost but not
quite the same productive capacity without slavery. Slavery was never necessary for the production of tobacco, even if it was necessary for the optimal
exploitation of large landholdings. I am not so sure about coastal South
Carolina and Georgia. There and in the West Indies, were nonslave economies conceivable? How high would the price of sugar have had to be to
attract free labor to the West Indian cane fields? Under the medical conditions of the seventeenth and eighteenth centuries, could such a population
have survived long enough to reproduce itself? These are some of the questions we must at least consider before we attempt to pass on the absolute
indispensability of slavery. However, since such questions are uncongenial
to most professional historians, most analysis will prefer to start with slavery
and the slave trade as givens.

To speak of an interdependent multilateral trading system is to speak of a
trading system requiring a complex multilateral payments mechanism. It had
to be possible to realize anywhere in the system credits earned or held
elsewhere in the system. In fact, such transfers could be made anywhere in
the Atlantic world and most parts of Europe (and even India) through the
general use by businessmen of the bill of exchange. Joseph Ernst has reminded us of the great importance of exchange rates,[37] and John McCusker's
excellent handbook makes available for the first time the basic exchange data
for the whole North Atlantic world.[38] We still need, however, to know more
precisely how the system worked, particularly in the West Indies and between points in the thirteen colonies.

The international-payments mechanism provided by the bill of exchange supported armies abroad and could have handled such capital movements as took place. We know, though, very little about capital movements. Most of the debts owed by colonists to persons in Britain on the eve of the Revolution appear to have risen from normal commercial transactions and thus were simply unpaid balances on trading accounts rather than evidence of cash loans. Even sums owed on bonds and mortgages appear very often to have their origin in commercial transactions, though more work is needed on this topic. However, there was some direct British investment in America. Persons in Britain owned land in America—in a few cases plantations, in other cases unimproved land held speculatively. British firms not only owned stores in America but also held shares in nominally American firms. They had to invest as well in warehouses, wharves, and small craft in connection with their trading activities; some also invested in distilleries and ironworks. In addition to the post-1790 claims concerning unpaid prewar debts, there are also in the Public Record Office detailed records of the compensation paid by the British government around 1783–89 to persons who lost real estate in America as a result of the Revolution. Many of the claimants were loyalist émigrés, but there was a significant element of British investors claiming compensation for lost ironworks and the like. By separating out the records (claims and compensation) of this class, one could obtain a rough idea of direct British investment in American real estate and plant before the war. One would, however, have to allow something for underreporting, for when ironworks and the like were owned jointly by British and American residents, the Americans, if they accepted the Revolutionary government, were probably able to conceal the shares of their British partners. However, even a rough estimate would be helpful here.

I hope that my recent work on capital and credit in the Chesapeake trade will encourage those working in other trades to try to reconstruct more systematically what we can know of the origins and volume of the capital and credit employed in transatlantic trade.[39] How frequently did American merchants have British partners? Was the Chesapeake's "cargo trade," with its long credits, not characteristic of all branches of British-American commerce? Was most of the capital employed in the American trades accumulated out of the profits of the same trades, as Richard Pares suggested?[40] Were silent partners unknown outside of Glasgow? What about all those widows and orphans who lent money on bond to merchants trading to America, or to the wholesalers who supplied them? The study of the capital market in Britain has only just begun.

A SENSE OF SCALE

It is a truism in the social sciences that at some point in every process of growth quantitative change evokes qualitative change. A city is more than a large village; a factory is more than a large workshop. Students working on the early American economy are very much aware of certain changes in scale—population, volume of exports, and so on—that may affect the structure as well as the aggregates of the colonial economies. Other changes in scale have gone relatively unobserved. One of these is the revolutionary change in scale of British firms trading to America and of indigenous American firms. To give a few examples from my own work, the two largest importers of tobacco in London in 1775 imported as much tobacco as the entire trade of more than a hundred firms in the 1660s.[41] At Glasgow, the largest single firm in 1775 imported more tobacco than the entire trade (ninety-one firms) in 1728–31.[42] Thus the world of the firm in 1775 is radically different from that of 50 or 100 years before. Though I do not have equivalent data, it is my impression that a comparable, if not as extreme, change of scale took place in the African, West Indian, and other North American trades.[43]

   This change of scale and associated concentration was not the result of any conscious government policy and must reflect the survival of the fittest in a competitive market in which entry was easy but large firms had certain strategic advantages over smaller firms. These advantages probably included easier access to capital (both partners' "stock" and long-term loans on bond) and credit from banks and suppliers. The reputations of larger firms were more clearly established, so that their bills of exchange and acceptances also passed more readily from hand to hand and were easily discounted. The larger purchases of export goods by the greater firms must have attracted the most favorable terms either in price or in length of credit—even though smaller firms may have been able to select their export goods more carefully. In many trades these larger firms should also have been in a stronger negotiating position when selling to monopsonistic buyers like the French tobacco monopoly or oligopsonistic buyers like the relatively few sugar refineries in each outport. Finally, the larger firms had opportunities for the more economic utilization of shipping denied to smaller firms. A firm importing a quarter-shipload of sugar or tobacco had little room for maneuver and usually had to accept the added costs of long delays. The firm importing five or more shiploads of sugar or tobacco per year should have been and was able to utilize shipping more efficiently and to reduce freight charges in the final accounting.

   Shepherd and Walton, among others, have already explained to us that the improved efficiency in the use of shipping is almost the only significant productivity improvement that we can definitely detect in the colonial period.[44] This improved efficiency was closely associated with the changing scale of the firm and with the increased availability of marine insurance. In the seventeenth century ships going out to the Americas characteristically carried "adventures" for a large number of relatively small firms. The individual firm, by dividing its ventures among many vessels, could in a sense insure itself when external insurance was not available. However, such complex chartering commitments undoubtedly slowed down the loading of the ship, particularly at the American end, and contributed to the long "stays in the country" characteristic of the seventeenth century. The increased availability of insurance from the late seventeenth century reduced the risk of buying or chartering whole vessels and thus enabled the larger firms to obtain some economies of scale.

Even with the valued contribution of Shepherd and Walton and Ralph Davis, there is opportunity for further useful investigation of the economics of shipping in the colonial period. Equally necessary is serious attention to marine insurance on both sides of the Atlantic. Available scraps of evidence would suggest that lower insurance rates were one of the great advantages that the British had over the French in the eighteenth century—particularly in wartime. We need investigations that will go beyond the anecdotal histories of Lloyds of London and attempt the serious study of marine insurance and insurance rates. Outside of London, almost everything remains to be done on insurance in the English outports, Scotland, and the major North American ports.

Investigators must constantly be alert for signs that changes in scale opened the doors for other changes—that is, that the larger firm size was necessary before new institutional forms or new trades could be attempted. For example, the Glasgow store system in the Chesapeake would appear to have required larger capitalization both per firm and per unit of export or import than did the simpler consignment or earlier peddling trades. Similarly, the development of the wheat export trade to southern Europe very likely required the existence in Philadelphia and other wheat-exporting ports of firms larger than those common in the West Indian provision trade. Much work and much thought is needed on the ramifications of the relationship of scale to the institutional history of the various trades.

CONCLUSION

This paper reflects more the current state of my thinking about the early American external economy than it does the results of any systematic effort to catalog and evaluate all possible "significant" topics deserving attention. I have had to neglect some important subjects, including fishing and fish exports, shipbuilding,[45] and shipping earnings—though these have not been totally neglected in the existing literature. Much more could also be said on the internal organization of the firm.

In general in this paper I have been concerned as much with pointing out problems that need serious reflection as with marking topics that will make prize-winning dissertations. I hope that my weakness for intractable problems will not create the impression that early American economic history is just one dark dead end after another. If no one is likely to produce very soon a generally acceptable time series of per capita colonial income from 1607 to 1775, there are still numerous problems whose systematic investigation will produce interesting and illuminating results. The great success as always will go to those who combine disciplined imagination in defining problems with shrewdness in the choice of methodology and fearlessness in attacking the most forbidding sources. We are only now learning what secrets lay hidden so long in parish registers and inventories post-mortem. Who knows what treasures still lie buried in Admiralty, Chancery, or Exchequer? The best is yet to come.

NOTES

1. G. N. Clark, *Guide to English Commercial Statistics, 1696–1782,* Royal Historical Society Guides and Handbooks, No. 1 (London, 1938).

2. Elizabeth Boody Schumpeter, *English Overseas Trade Statistics, 1697–1808* (Oxford, 1960); Ralph Davis, "English Foreign Trade, 1660–1700," *Economic History Review,* 2d ser., 7 (1954–55): 150–66; idem, "English Foreign Trade, 1700–1774," ibid. 15 (1962): 285–303. Equally noteworthy is Davis's *The Industrial Revolution and British Overseas Trade* (Leicester, 1979).

3. B. R. Mitchell and Phyllis Deane, *Abstract of British Historical Statistics* (Cambridge, 1962); Henry Hamilton, *An Economic History of Scotland in the Eighteenth Century* (Oxford, 1963).

4. Charles McLean Andrews, *Guide to the Materials for American History to 1783 in the Public Record Office of Great Britain,* 2 vols. (Washington, D.C., 1912–14).

5. See Richard B. Sheridan, *Sugar and Slavery: An Economic History of the British West Indies, 1623–1775* (Baltimore, 1974), appendix.

6. See James F. Shepherd and Gary M. Walton, *Shipping, Maritime Trade, and the Economic Development of Colonial North America* (Cambridge, 1972).

7. Lawrence A. Harper, in U.S. Bureau of the Census, *Historical Statistics of the United States, Colonial Times to 1957* (Washington, D.C., 1960); the chapter was expanded in the 1976 edition.

8. See Lawrence A. Harper, "United We Stand; Divided We Fall: A Plea and a Plan for the Use of Modern Technology in Cooperative Research," in *Of Mother Country and Plantations: Proceedings of the Twenty-Seventh Conference in Early American History,* ed. Virginia Bever Platt and David Curtiss Skaggs (Bowling Green, Ohio, 1971), 71–127.

9. Arthur H. Cole, *Wholesale Commodity Prices in the United States, 1700–1861* (Cambridge, Mass., 1938); Anne Bezanson, Robert D. Gray, and Miriam Hussey, *Prices in Colonial Pennsylvania* (Philadelphia, 1935); idem, *Wholesale Prices in Philadelphia, 1784–1861,* 2 vols. (Philadelphia, 1936–37); Anne Bezanson, *Prices and Inflation during the American Revolution: Pennsylvania, 1770–1790* (Philadelphia, 1951).

10. William Henry Beveridge, *Prices and Wages in England from the 12th to the 19th Century* (London, 1939); Nicolaas Wilhelmus Posthumus, *Inquiry into the History of Prices in Holland,* 2 vols. (Leiden, 1946–64).

11. See Jacob M. Price, "Notes on Some London Price Currents," *Economic History Review,* 2d ser., 7 (1954–55): 240–50. John McCusker, of the University of Maryland, is now compiling a bibliography of all price currents and analogous materials published in Europe and America in the seventeenth and eighteenth centuries.

12. See, for example, Russell R. Menard, "Farm Prices of Maryland Tobacco, 1659–1710," *Maryland Historical Magazine* 68 (1973): 80–85; and idem, "A Note on Chesapeake Tobacco Prices, 1618–1660," *Virginia Magazine of History and Biography* 84 (1976): 401–10.

13. For example, Gary M. Walton, "The New Economic History and the Burdens of the

Navigation Acts," *Economic History Review*, 2d ser., 24 (1971): 533–42, which reviews earlier work by Peter D. McClelland, Robert P. Thomas, and Lawrence A. Harper. For further contributions by F.J.A. Broeze, McClelland, D. J. Loschky, and Walton see ibid. 26 (1973): 668–91.

14. For example, Sheridan, *Sugar and Slavery*; and Richard S. Dunn, *Sugar and Slaves: The Rise of the Planter Class in the English West Indies, 1624–1713* (Chapel Hill, 1972). See also Richard Pares, *War and Trade in the West Indies, 1739–1763* (Oxford, 1936).

15. See Paul G. E. Clemens, *The Atlantic Economy and Colonial Maryland's Eastern Shore: From Tobacco to Grain* (Ithaca, N.Y., 1980); Russell R. Menard, "Secular Trends in the Chesapeake Tobacco Industry, 1617–1710," *Working Papers from the Regional Economic History Research Center* 1 (1978): 1–34; idem, "The Tobacco Industry in the Chesapeake Colonies, 1617–1730: An Interpretation," *Research in Economic History* 5 (1980): 109–77; and Gloria L. Main, *Tobacco Colony: Life in Early Maryland, 1650–1720* (Princeton, 1983).

16. See Harold A. Innis, *The Fur Trade in Canada* (1930; reprint, New Haven, 1970); and idem, *The Cod Fisheries* (New Haven, 1940). See also E. E. Rich, "Russia and the Colonial Fur Trade," *Economic History Review*, 2d ser., 7 (1954–55): 307–28.

17. The vast literature on the new beverages is surveyed in A. W. Noling, *Beverage Literature: A Bibliography* (Metuchen, N.J., 1971).

18. See Louis Dermigny, *La Chine et l'occident: le commerce à Canton au XVIIIᵉ siècle, 1719–1833*, 4 vols. (Paris, 1964); and Kristof Glamann, *Dutch-Asiatic Trade, 1620–1740* (Copenhagen, 1958).

19. Noel Deerr, *The History of Sugar*, 2 vols. (London, 1949–50).

20. On the "rationality" of the indentured-servant trade see David W. Galenson, *White Servitude in Colonial America: An Economic Analysis* (Cambridge, 1981), esp. pts. 3 and 4.

21. For Scottish data see Hamilton, *Economic History of Scotland*, 412–13, 416, 419.

22. English totals are from table 2.3, Scottish totals are from the National Library of Scotland, Edinburgh, MS. 60.

23. Only for forest products and iron was import substitution important, imports from North America in the eighteenth century making it less necessary to depend on the northern countries.

24. Phyllis Deane and W. A. Cole, *British Economic Growth, 1688–1959* (Cambridge, 1962), 48.

25. Ibid., 156.

26. See Jacob M. Price, "Colonial Trade and British Economic Development," in *La Revolution américaine et l'Europe*, Colloques internationaux du Centre Nationale de la Recherche Scientifique, no. 577 (Paris, 1979), 221–42; an earlier version is in *Lex et scientia* 14 (1978): 106–26.

27. Peter Mathias, *The Brewing Industry in England, 1700–1830* (Cambridge, 1959), 542–43. Total output of taxed beer was no higher in 1771–73 than it had been in 1701–3, though population had increased in the interim.

28. Alfred P. Wadsworth and Julia de Lacy Mann, *The Cotton Trade and Industrial Lancashire, 1600–1780* (Manchester, 1931), 117, 132–34.

29. John Ramsay McCulloch, *A dictionary, practical, theoretical, and historical, of commerce and commercial navigation: illustrated with maps and plans*, 2d ed., 2 vols. (London, 1834), 2:1088.

30. See, for example, Joseph J. Malone, *Pine Trees and Politics: The Naval Stores and Forest Policy in Colonial New England, 1691–1775* (London, 1964).

31. See Jacob M. Price, *France and the Chesapeake: A History of the French Tobacco Monopoly, 1674–1791, and of Its Relationship to the British and American Tobacco Trades*, 2 vols. (Ann Arbor, 1973); and idem, "The Tobacco Trade and the Treasury: British Mercantilism in Its Fiscal Aspects" (Ph.D. diss., Harvard University, 1954).

32. "The Slaves are cloath'd with Cottons, Kerseys, Flannel & Coarse Linnen, all imported" (Board of Trade report on the colonies, Sept. 8, 1721, Cholmondeley Papers, Cambridge University Library).

33. See n. 20 above.

34. See F. E. Sanderson, "Liverpool and the Slave Trade: Guide to Sources," *Transactions of the Historic Society of Lancashire and Cheshire* 124 (1972): 154–76.

35. Much of the relevant literature is cited in J. E. Inikori, "Market Structure and the Profits of the British African Trade in the Late Eighteenth Century," *Journal of Economic History* 41 (1981): 745–76.

36. See Eric Williams, *Capitalism and Slavery* (New York, 1966).

37. Joseph Albert Ernst, *Money and Politics in America, 1755–1775: A Study in the Currency Act of 1764 and the Political Economy of Revolution* (Chapel Hill, 1973).

38. John J. McCusker, *Money and Exchange in Europe and America, 1600–1775: A Handbook* (Chapel Hill, 1978).

39. Jacob M. Price, *Capital and Credit in British Overseas Trade: The View from the Chesapeake, 1700–1776* (Cambridge, Mass., 1980).

40. Richard Pares, *Merchants and Planters*, Economic History Review supp. 4 (Cambridge, 1960).

41. *Joshua Johnson's Letterbook, 1771–1774*, ed. Jacob M. Price, London Record Society 15 (London, 1979), 158–59.

42. Northampton Record Office, Fitzwilliam-Burke MSS., A.xxv.74 (for 1775); PRO T.36/13 (for 1728–31).

43. On concentration in the British African slave trade see Inikori, "Market Structure," 748–53.

44. Shepherd and Walton, *Shipping, Maritime Trade and Economic Development*, chap. 5.

45. See Joseph A. Goldenberg, *Shipbuilding in Colonial America* (Charlottesville, 1976); and Jacob M. Price, "A Note on the Value of Colonial Exports of Shipping," *Journal of Economic History* 36 (1976): 704–24. No one has ever checked to see how complete is the coverage of *Lloyd's Register*. If it is incomplete to a significant degree, then colonial shipbuilding may have been larger than suggested in these works.

3

THE DOMESTIC ECONOMY

RICHARD B. SHERIDAN

I

The internal, or domestic, sector of the economy of British America performed a variety of functions. It provided subsistence goods that could not be obtained on the market, supplied goods to domestic and overseas markets, and distributed imported goods. Foreign trade, however important it was as an energizing force, constituted only around 9–12 percent of colonial gross output. On the other hand, the agricultural sector engaged 80–90 percent of the work force. As Edwin Perkins observes, "The real strength of the colonial economy was its prodigious agricultural production for local consumption and urban centers." The production of foodstuffs for personal consumption was the chief source of real income for southern as well as northern farmers. Perkins contends that even without the stimulus of foreign markets, the living standards of colonial Americans "would have still ranked among the highest in the world, primarily because of the availability of so much fertile and productive land for the existing population."[1]

Notwithstanding the obvious importance of the domestic sector, economic historians of British America today are concerned primarily with external relations extending throughout the Atlantic community of maritime nations, colonies, trading stations, and fisheries. They focus attention on growth and development, the commercial sector, overseas trade and capital flows, the export industries, the great planters in the South, and the wealthy urban merchants in the North. They have adopted the staple approach to the study of economic history, whereby staple exports are considered the leading sector, setting the pace for economic growth and shaping the process of colonial development. They argue that because domestic markets were limited or nonexistent, European colonists took advantage of an abundance of land relative to labor and capital to develop resource-intensive exports, or staples. They contend that economic development is a process of diversification around the export base, that increased activity in the export sector tended to induce investment in the domestic market by means of various "linkage" effects.[2] Moreover, they argue that the size and structure of the domestic sector in an export-led economy is shaped by the particular characteristics of the dominant staple. For example, the "spread effects" of the fur trade were limited by comparison with those of wheat growing and flour milling for export markets.[3]

In their recent historiographical and analytical study of the economy of the British colonies, John J. McCusker and Russell R. Menard give the staple thesis a reasonably sound bill of health. They find it useful for identifying pressing research needs and for showing how "a focus on exports can illuminate the process of colonization, the growth of colonial economies, and the emergence of regional differences within British America." In defending the utility of the staple approach to the economic history of British America, McCusker and Menard observe that

> resource-intensive exports—furs, fish, forest products, wheat and corn, tobacco, rice, indigo, and sugar—were important to the growth process and left distinctive imprints on colonies which specialized in one or another of them. Further, reflection on regional differences in British America argues for the power of the plantation-farm dichotomy as organizational categories. Roughly, and with some obvious exceptions, the colonies describe a spectrum ranging from north to south, from New England to the West Indies, marking out a fairly steady progression from farm colony to plantation colony. And it is a simple task to construct a list of linkages, instances in which the requirements of a staple export led directly to domestic production of a good or service.[4]

McCusker and Menard contend that the principal concern of the staple theory is the relationship between exports and domestic developments. But the fact is, as these authors point out, that few studies have thus far been undertaken that seek to test the propositions of the staple theory against quantitative and qualitative evidence. Whatever the promise of the staple thesis, moreover, it has so far, as various critics have pointed out, tended to direct attention away from internal or domestic processes.[5]

What we know about the domestic economy of colonial America derives primarily from local and regional studies, many of which have appeared over the past decade. The following sections of this paper will consider this literature in terms of what it tells us about each of five main regions—the Chesapeake, the Caribbean, New England, the Middle Colonies, and the Lower South. This regional discussion will be followed by an analysis of the present state of knowledge of some of the more important problems that require further illumination.

II

Britain's oldest American colonial region, comprising the Chesapeake colonies of Virginia and Maryland, has been the subject of an outpouring of first-rate scholarship over the past fifteen years. Employing the voluminous probate records and tax lists of counties and parishes, Aubrey Land was the first scholar to attempt the systematic analysis of the economic base and the social structure of these colonies with his carefully constructed profiles of eighteenth-century Maryland planters. Wesley Frank Craven, Edmund S. Morgan, Lois Green Carr, Russell Menard, and Alan Kulikoff, among others, have explored similar records in even more depth over the past decade, and they and their colleagues have produced a series of studies ranging over the whole socioeconomic history of the region. They have analyzed such topics as immigration and migration patterns, growth of settled land and expansion into virgin lands, subsistence and commercial agriculture, regional shifts in the production of tobacco and wheat, fluctuations in staple prices and production, the shift from white servants to black slaves, work patterns, demographic patterns and trends, settlement patterns, social mobility, the role of women in the economy and society, and wealth distribution. Using the staple theory, they have given major attention to the impact of changing demand for tobacco, the chief staple of the region, upon social structure, wealth, economic opportunity, the labor system, agricultural diversification, and demography.[6]

The younger group of Chesapeake scholars has divided the colonial history of the region into four distinct periods between 1607 and 1765.[7] Despite the tobacco boom, white immigrants before 1650 met with great hardships. By the late 1640s, however, the chaos of earlier decades had diminished, and from 1650 to 1680 the Chesapeake experienced rapid growth in population and tobacco production in the "age of the small planter." On the other hand, the decades from 1680 to 1720 witnessed deep recession in the tobacco industry, leading marginal growers to substitute grain for tobacco. At the same time, white immigration declined and planters replaced servants with African slaves. The decades after 1720 saw a return to economic expansion involving the extension of tobacco culture and growing attention to wheat production and demographic change characterized by natural increase of both the white and black populations.[8]

The traditional question of why Chesapeake planters shifted to African slave labor between 1680 and 1720 has been a special subject of concern for these scholars. Thus, Menard contends that Chesapeake planters turned to slaves when the supply of servants was inadequate to meet their needs and that they eventually came to regard slavery as a highly profitable labor system. Although the initial investment was high, credit was easy to obtain and slaves received only the necessities—often only the barest of necessities—from their owners, grew the greater part of the food they ate, and were capable of learning skills and performing a wide variety of tasks. Eventually, they even more than reproduced themselves by natural means.[9]

Traditionally, scholars of the Chesapeake have concentrated upon the wealthy gentlemen, who sometimes owned several plantations and vast numbers of slaves.[10] The new school of Chesapeake historians has been somewhat neglectful of this group. In her general study of wealth distribution in the late colonial period, however, Alice Hanson Jones has shown that the slave-powered staple economy of the southern colonies had indeed been generous to many of its free inhabitants. Although Jones does not distinguish between the Chesapeake and the colonies of the Lower South, she finds that the southern colonies as a whole were richer in aggregate physical wealth than the colonies to the north, whether or not slaves and servants are included. On the eve of the American Revolution, the southern colonies contained almost half of the total population and nearly 90 percent of the more than 480,000 slaves in the continental colonies. Dividing the nonhuman wealth of the thirteen colonies among the total population (black and white, free and unfree, men, women, and children), Jones finds that per capita wealth was £36.4 sterling for the South, the same for New England, and £40.2 for the Middle Colonies. However, when she added the value of holdings in slaves and servants to the physical wealth of the South, the per capita wealth was £60.2 sterling for all free persons and £252.0 for those free people who actually were wealthholders.[11]

But this aggregate picture and the prominence of wealthy landed gentlemen distorts actual socioeconomic conditions in the Chesapeake. More concerned with the pattern of land usage of the many than with the great estates of the few, several recent scholars have looked at the middle and lower end of the free social order and have found that small farms and farmers predominated in the Chesapeake and South Atlantic colonies, as they did in those to the north; that agriculture became more diversified, especially with the expansion of wheat and corn growing in the eighteenth century; that tenancy and poverty became chronic among the inhabitants of certain tidewater areas at the same time that population pressure was not relieved by migration to frontier regions; but that crop yields were sustained despite the growing "Malthusian" situation in long-settled parts of the Chesapeake region.

That crop diversification and self-sufficiency were long-term trends as well as responses to short-term fluctuations in staple prices is the contention of Carville V. Earle and Paul G. E. Clemens. In his study of All Hallow's Parish, Maryland, Earle found that planters and their slaves had the equipment and skills to fashion wood, textiles, leather, shoes, and in some cases metal. The typical plantation contained a variety of crafts, crops, and livestock. Planters diversified their food supply by the addition of livestock, wheat and other small grains, beehives, and fishing gear. In his study of Maryland's Eastern Shore, Clemens found that although few inhabitants abandoned tobacco completely or ended their reliance on the export trade, planters managed to diversify agricultural production, and the transition from tobacco to grain modified the colonial staple economy.[12]

Gregory A. Stiverson, in his *Poverty in a Land of Plenty*, has joined Earle and Clemens in casting doubt on the older consensus that there were relatively few tenants in the Chesapeake colonies and that tenancy was only a temporary status for persons who soon moved into the landowning class. By the end of the colonial period, Stiverson found "nonlandowners comprised at least half of the heads of households in the older settled counties of Maryland," while "a large proportion of the householders were tenants in all sections of the province." Tenants devoted the greater part of their land to growing foodstuffs for family consumption, leaving little land for cash crops to meet annual rent charges and pay for essential goods and services. The upshot was a level of poverty among the tenant farmers of Maryland that prevented them from climbing to higher rungs on the agricultural ladder.[13] Nor did most Maryland tenants find it possible to change to nonagricultural occupations or to resettle on distant frontiers. Factors limiting migration to the frontier were the reluctance to sever long-established family connections, frontier dangers and hardships, the high cost of moving long distances, and the engrossing of large tracts of frontier land by speculators.[14]

Contrasted with the tidewater settlements were those of the back country, where agriculture was more primitive and self-sufficient, freehold tenure was more common, dependent laborers were less prevalent, livestock raising was often a major industry, and hunting and gathering were supplementary activities. Thus, in his study of Lunenburg County, Virginia, Richard R. Beeman found that while the local gentry moved from pioneer farming to the intensive cultivation of tobacco with slave labor, the overwhelming majority of the citizens remained at a more primitive level of economic and social development.[15]

Despite the impressive body of new Chesapeake literature, questions remain to be explored. According to McCusker and Menard, "The growth of self-sufficient activities and production for local markets in the Chesapeake colonies are neglected topics in the economic history of the region: scholarship has focused on exports." They attribute the neglect in part to the difficulties of evidence and in part to the false assumption that self-sufficient activities were relatively static and unimportant to dynamic processes in Chesapeake society. Instead of becoming more specialized, they contend, plantations came to supply a wider range of goods and services internally, without resort to the market, at the same time that they continued to produce tobacco and foodstuffs.[16]

III

The Caribbean colonies constitute a second group of colonies to which the staple thesis seems especially applicable; like the Chesapeake colonies, those in the Caribbean—Barbados, the Leeward Islands, and Jamaica—have been the subject of growing historical interest. This development has been stimulated in part by an increased historical consciousness in the islands, a consciousness that is closely related to the growing sense of nationalism that emerged

in the region from the 1940s and led to political independence in the major
territories in the 1960s. To a large extent this increased activity was initiated
by one man, who was both historian and politician. The late Eric Williams
not only wrote *Capitalism and Slavery* (1944), which inaugurated the modern
period of West Indian historiography, but he also edited *The Caribbean Historical Review*, the first professional journal to provide "a medium for historical
writing of and within the area." Moreover, after its inception in 1948, the
University of the West Indies, with branches in Jamaica, Barbados, and
Trinidad, developed a strong tradition of historical studies. As chairman of
the history department at Mona, Jamaica, Douglas Hall made notable contributions. He encouraged *The Jamaican Historical Review* to include articles of
general Caribbean interest and later was instrumental in founding *The Journal
of Caribbean History*. Also, Hall was the prime mover in the publication of
chapters for a projected three-volume *History of the West Indies* and in the
establishment of the Caribbean Universities Press.[17]

But the new concern with the colonial Caribbean is also a by-product of
the rising interest in the history of early Anglo-American colonization in
general. Whatever the explanation, nearly a half-century of neglect that saw
the publication of only a few studies of the economic development of these
colonies and virtually nothing at all on their social history was followed
beginning in the late 1960s by what Jack P. Greene referred to in 1974 as a
"sudden efflorescence of scholarship." That efflorescence, Greene contended, brought us to "the verge of achieving a more systematic and thorough
understanding of the economic and social development of the Caribbean
colonies than we have for any other segment of the early modern British
overseas empire."[18]

The bountiful harvest referred to by Greene included a series of important
journal articles and eleven separate monographs concerned with the British
West Indies in the period prior to slave emancipation in 1834. These works,
written by West Indians, North Americans, Britons, and Australians, by
historians and anthropologists with expertise in sociology, archaeology, demography, geography, politics, and economics, were informed by a new
perspective. This perspective, most fully developed in the "new school" of
historians at the University of the West Indies, insists that the history of the
West Indies is worthy of study for its own sake and not simply as an appendage of European and North American history. This perspective also insists
that West Indian history be a history of *all* the West Indian peoples—those of
Amerindian, African, and Asian as well as of European origin—and that it be
a history of all classes and conditions of men and women—slaves, peasants,
cane cutters and domestic servants, as well as planters, merchants, lawyers,
and politicians.

Not surprisingly, king sugar and his slaves have attracted the attention of
numerous historians. Carl and Roberta Bridenbaugh and Richard S. Dunn
are concerned in their monographs to show how the sugar revolution trans-

formed the agricultural economy and effected a thoroughgoing social revolution in the English West Indies, chiefly in the seventeenth century. Both are primarily social histories, containing trade and census figures, economic analysis, and fascinating narratives of the daily life of all the people. Dunn, however, breaks more new ground in his analysis of demographic data, disease environments, and the role of family life. He asserts that the Barbados sugar planters were the wealthiest men in English America in 1680, showing a striking correlation between wealth, privilege, and power.[19] In my study of the slave-plantation economy in both its internal and external dimensions, I argue that however inhumane, the sugar industry made a notable contribution to the wealth and maritime supremacy of Great Britain. I discuss such internal developments as the settlement of the sugar colonies, geographic and economic influences, development of individual colonies, careers of leading planters, the art of plantership, plantation slavery, and the profitability of sugar and slavery.[20] Drawing on an extensive body of private records, Michael Craton and James Walvin trace the fortunes of one Jamaican sugar plantation over the course of three centuries, with special emphasis on the pioneering period and the golden age of sugar in the eighteenth century. They claim to have written the history of Jamaica and the British West Indies "from the inside out."[21] In their study of slave life in Barbados to 1838, Jerome S. Handler, Frederick W. Lange, and Robert B. Riordan have used archaeological, ethnographic, and historical methods to achieve specific results not shown by older methods.[22]

Arthur Young, the agricultural writer, calculated that in 1770 "the sugar colonies added three million a year to the wealth of Britain; the rice colonies near a million, and the tobacco ones almost as much." Recent wealth estimates support Young's contention that the sugar colonies far outdistanced the rice and tobacco colonies. They show that wealth per free white person in the period 1770–75 amounted to £1,196 sterling in Jamaica, £131.90 in the South, £51.30 in the Middle Colonies, and £32.70 in New England. "Our tobacco colonies," wrote Adam Smith, "send us home no such wealthy planters as we see frequently arrive from our sugar islands." Absentee proprietorship so drained the islands of their sugar wealth that it gives pause to any attempt to apply the staple thesis to the Caribbean colonies. Indeed, economist George L. Beckford argues that since very little income was available to residents from plantation production, the plantation did not provide the impetus for development.[23]

Although many of the most impressive of these studies deal with the period beyond the time limits of this book,[24] several deal directly with the development of the Caribbean colonies down to 1763 and present a rather clear picture of the development of their internal economy.

As with the economies of the Chesapeake and the Lower South, the West Indies began as colonies of settlement, or farm colonies, and were later transformed into colonies of exploitation, or plantation colonies. As on the mainland, early English settlers in the islands sought to replicate the institutions of their homeland and to create a quality of life and an environment superior to that left behind. They hunted, fished, cleared forests, and planted subsistence crops and staple exports in what was a relatively self-sufficient economy. In time, however, a combination of factors enabled sizable numbers to amass sufficient land, labor, capital, and technology to produce what was to become the preeminent staple, muscovado sugar, and its by-products molasses and rum. With the assistance of masses of African slaves, they turned to raising staple articles of produce for the European market and importing luxuries for the planter elite and foodstuffs, clothing, plantation tools, and equipment for the white indentured servants and black slaves. In other words, the islands reputedly conformed to the ideal model of mercantile theorists, producing what they did not consume and consuming what they did not produce.[25]

It is perhaps correct to say that the staple theory has done more to disguise domestic economic developments in the Caribbean region prior to 1763 than to illuminate them. But all is not lost, since a number of monographs and articles have sought to integrate the external and internal segments of the economy and to show that "to a certain extent every settler society had its exploitation component and every exploitation society its settler dimension."[26]

Dunn has noted the common elements in the early settlement of the English colonies from Maryland south to the Caribbean islands. "They employed similar colonizing techniques and shared similar colonizing experiences," he writes. "Tobacco was initially the staple crop in Barbados and the Leeward Islands as in Virginia and Maryland."[27] The islanders were similar to the mainlanders in their dependence on Amerindians, who supplied seeds and planting material and taught the Europeans to grow a variety of food crops and staples. Other similarities were dependence on wild game and fish for sustenance, as well as the need to clear the dense forests, which in the islands were often impenetrable jungles that required back-breaking toil. The islanders grew a wider range of crops than the mainlanders, including cassava, plantains, yams, pineapples, citrus, millet (or "Guinea corn"), arrowroot, cacao, cotton, ginger, pimento, indigo, and sugar cane. The pre-sugar era varied in duration from island to island, occupying some fifteen to twenty years in Barbados, three to four decades in the Leeward Islands, and as many as forty to fifty years in Jamaica. On his Worthy Park plantation in Jamaica, Francis Price is thought to have grown little more than provision crops and pasture grass to feed livestock prior to 1689.[28]

It is true that in the course of several decades the West Indies experienced a marked decline in the number of yeomen farmers, small planters, and white servants at the same time that there emerged numerous sugar plantations, each of substantial acreage, capital, and slave labor force. Food crops and livestock tended to be sacrificed to cane, thus leading the sugar planters to import many of their food, livestock, and wood products from England, Ireland, and New England.[29]

But that the big planters bought up all the land in the sugar colonies is a myth. The census of 1680 shows that in Barbados, where the sugar revolution began early and succeeded rapidly, the great majority of the property holders were small farmers who grew cotton, ginger, and provision crops and bred livestock. Carl and Roberta Bridenbaugh, while they show how the sugar revolution was both cause and effect of the growing international division of labor, caution that the primacy of sugar must not be permitted to conceal the importance of other Caribbean staples such as cotton, ginger, indigo, cacao, pimento, and dyewoods.[30]

The internal economy of the sugar islands was more substantial than is generally indicated by studies that concentrate on the staple industries. Products of the forests, savannas, fields, rivers, and coastal waters were exploited not only for export markets but also for local fabrication and consumption. Locally bred horses, oxen, and mules powered sugar mills and drew cane carts, but they also supplied a variety of domestic needs, as did such small stock as goats, pigs, and poultry. Forests supplied timbers and boards for buildings and boats, thatch for roofs, firewood, rare woods for furniture, dyewoods, and medicinal plants. Deposits of clay were mined and fashioned into pottery. Diets were enhanced by fresh- and salt-water fish, crabs, and turtles. Above all, a variety of seed crops, root crops, and tree crops were grown for local food consumption.

Although the islands depended in varying degrees on imported foodstuffs and other products, they were not entirely committed to a one-crop economy. John H. Parry contends that the islands' economic history should be the story of yams, cassava, and salt fish no less than of sugar and tobacco. "Of the larger islands," he writes, "Jamaica was probably the most successful in evolving a workable balance between crops for export and crops for local consumption, and in avoiding the worst dangers of monoculture." He observes that while the story of crops grown in the West Indies for export to Europe and North America has been told many times, the story of crops grown to feed West Indians has still to be written. Sidney W. Mintz and Douglas Hall have investigated the origins of the Jamaican internal marketing system. Slaves were encouraged to feed themselves by being granted marginal lands and time away from plantation labor to grow foodstuffs and raise small livestock and poultry. Surplus produce from the slaves' provision grounds were taken to local markets and exchanged for other commodities or sold for cash. Mintz has also investigated the problem of retaining coins of small denomination in Jamaica, the greater part of which currency facilitated the island's small-scale trade, which was said to be entirely in the hands of the slaves.[31]

Other recent studies, including those by Bridenbaugh and Bridenbaugh, Craton and Walvin, Dunn, Handler and Lange, Orlando Patterson, and

myself, are in general agreement with Mintz and Hall that the peasant economy and its marketing pattern originated within the slave plantation. Patterson contends that Jamaica was the first island to utilize the provision-ground
system as the main source of food supply for the slaves and that "by about
the middle of the eighteenth century the entire population of free people
became dependent on the slaves not only to provide the labour that was the
life-blood of the economic system, but almost all their vegetable and cash
crop." Patterson notes, however, that loopholes in the provision-ground system led many slaves to beg and steal for their daily sustenance.[32] More
recently, I have questioned certain features of the provision-ground system
and local markets that impinged on the welfare of the slaves. Questions need
to be raised and answered concerning the performance of this system. Were
the slaves given ample time away from plantation labor to cultivate their
grounds? Did they have the will and energy to grow food for themselves?
How great a distance separated the slave huts from the provision grounds,
and how much time was needed to walk to and from these grounds and the
markets where their surplus produce was sold? Were the slaves allotted large
enough plots of land of suitable quality to grow sufficient foodstuffs? Did
they diversify crop production sufficiently to compensate for adverse weather and seasonal variation in growing conditions? Were adequate reserves set
aside for a rainy day? Were adequate measures taken to prevent theft and
pilfering and the trespass of livestock and predators? Was the provision-
ground system adapted to the needs of aged, infirm, and young slaves?
Future historians will need to address these and other questions by drawing
on more authentic sources than the thinly disguised propaganda of the plan-
ter-historians of the eighteenth century.[33]

The domestic economy of the sugar colonies calls for further clarification
of concepts and a resolution of issues and debates. First on the agenda is the
need to delineate the component parts of the domestic economy, to quantify
this sector, and to show how it interacted with the external economy. For
example, we need to know more about the role played by planters, farmers,
smallholders, ranchers, merchants, artisans, and others, differentiating
among whites, free coloreds and blacks, black slaves, and maroons. More
could be done to trace and account for the rise and decline of individual
planter families and the planter class, island by island and collectively. We
know that some families had extensive property interests that were built up
over several generations and held for a century or more.[34] On the other hand,
there is the view of the islands as plunder preserves or lotteries where lucky
individuals made great fortunes that were soon dissipated. Although absentee proprietorship is generally viewed as an unmitigated evil, this view has
been questioned by Douglas Hall, who says that absenteeism varied so much
in extent and nature that broad generalizations about its consequences are
likely to be indefensible.[35] Whether slaves were treated harshly or mildly is
the subject of a complex and lively debate that deals with such things as diet,

housing, clothing, work loads, punishment, passive and active resistance, provision of medical services, and treatment of pregnant women and nursing mothers. Opportunities for further research on these and other topics is abundant, especially in the period prior to 1763.

IV

Textbooks typically contend that the economies of the three colonies of the Lower South—North Carolina, South Carolina, and Georgia—thrived on the production and export of rice, indigo, and naval stores and that a slave-plantation society developed that was markedly similar to the societies of the Chesapeake and Caribbean regions. That these staple industries were slow to develop and that a complex pattern of development characterized these colonies is the burden of several recent studies. In his *Economic Beginnings in South Carolina, 1670–1730*, Converse D. Clowse emphasizes the problems of achieving self-sufficiency in food and the difficulty of finding a suitable agricultural commodity to exchange for European manufactured goods. Lacking an agricultural staple, Carolinians resorted to trading with the Indians for deerskins and furs, selling Indian slaves, and raising livestock and exporting meat and provisions to the West Indies. Deerskins were the most important export commodity until they were overtaken by rice in the early decades of the eighteenth century, while naval stores yielded substantial export earnings. Indian wars, piracy, political and financial troubles, and depression characterized the years from 1715 to 1730 and led to serious disruption of the staple trades of South Carolina.[36]

The role of Caribbean planters and African slaves in the development of rice and indigo as staple crops has been emphasized by Peter H. Wood and Daniel C. Littlefield in their monographic studies. Barbados provided seasoned settlers and their slaves, capital, and knowledge of tropical agriculture, according to Wood. Slaves who came from rice-growing areas of West Africa contributed technical knowledge about rice cultivation, as well as menial labor, to the colony's first agricultural staple. Relative immunity to malaria and yellow fever gave the slaves certain physical advantages over the whites and helps to explain the eventual success of wet rice cultivation in colonial South Carolina.

Littlefield, in his recent study of rice and slaves in colonial South Carolina, is concerned with the major cultural regions from which slaves were recruited, their physical and cultural characteristics, and their contribution to the rice-growing industry of South Carolina. He contends "that blacks were active rather than passive (if often unwilling) participants in the founding of American civilization, that they were sometimes both physically and culturally better suited than their masters to the tasks of survival and construction in a new environment, and that Europeans were occasionally both perceptive and acquisitive of African capabilities." In particular, Littlefield relates African ethnicity, cultural survivals, and technical expertise to African contributions to American civilization, contending that the economic and social structures of American slave societies were a mutual accomplishment.[37]

Whites and blacks from the West Indies also played an important part in the introduction of indigo, the dye that became the staple second in importance only to rice in South Carolina and Georgia. The story of Eliza Lucas Pinckney and her experiments with the seeds she received from her father in Antigua is an old one. Recent scholars, however, have emphasized that her achievement in growing indigo commercially was shared with her father, husband, and others, that there had been an earlier local indigo culture, and that the success of the industry owed much to bounties offered by the colonial and metropolitan governments.[38]

Slave-produced rice and indigo brought great wealth to South Carolina. Indeed, Alice Hanson Jones found that the "extreme" wealth of the planters and merchants of Charleston was not found in samples anywhere else in the continental colonies. Moreover, the number of slaves per individual owner in the Charleston District was larger than elsewhere in the mainland colonies.[39]

On either side of South Carolina, Georgia and North Carolina were gradually incorporated into this staple economy. Georgia began in 1732 as a colony with philanthropic, imperialistic, and mercantilist goals, according to which the indigent city poor of Westminster and London were brought over to grow mulberry trees, silkworms, and olive trees and to live on small parcels of land without the benefit of slave labor. But the colony's failure to fulfill most of these ends left it open for colonization by settlers from South Carolina. Joining forces with some of the original settlers, these new immigrants agitated against the ban on slavery and succeeded in getting it abolished by London authorities. As experienced planters, they took the lead in establishing rice and indigo as the dominant staples of Georgia's economy and thereby made Georgia to a large extent simply an economic extension of South Carolina.[40] As Harry Roy Merrens's study of the historical geography of colonial North Carolina reveals, the southeastern section of North Carolina had a similar experience. Yet, as he points out, "the distinctiveness of North Carolina was evident in the concentration upon the production of naval stores and wood products, the comparatively low proportion of nonwhite inhabitants, the very small number of wealthy and extensive plantation units, and the nonreciprocal dependence of North Carolinians upon Virginia and South Carolina trade outlets."[41]

Further work is needed to fill in gaps and augment our understanding of the domestic economy of the Lower South. The task is complicated by the unique characteristics of the region. From the standpoint of its early settlement and development by West Indians, its plantation staples of rice and indigo, and its dependence on Africa for slaves, the Lower South was more completely a part of the South Atlantic system than any other portion of eighteenth-century North America. Two recent monographic studies add much to our understanding of the rice industry in its internal and external aspects.[42] On the other hand, apart from several articles and printed documents, indigo has received little attention, despite its substantial contribution to the prosperity of the region during the third quarter of the eighteenth century.

Besides its South Atlantic orientation, the Lower South was as unique as the Middle Colonies in the great diversity of its population groups and economic activities; it drew heavily on immigrants not only from the West Indies but also from colonies to the north, and, like the Chesapeake region, it was never a cohesive section in the same way that New England was. "Its society is less well organized," writes Clarence L. Ver Steeg, "its communication system less sophisticated, and its consciousness of status, at least until the 1680s, less well developed."[43] For these and other reasons, Mc-Cusker and Menard assert: "We simply know less about the economy of the Lower South than of any other region of British America."

Within the region, less is known of the interior than of the seaboard, riverine, and staple-producing areas. The southern colonial frontier, which more than half a century ago was the subject of Verner W. Crane's study from 1670 to 1732, recently has been extended in time and scope by W. Stitt Robinson in a study that adds significantly to our understanding of such topics as the movement of peoples and their institutions, the contributions they made to economic development, Indian-white relations, and the occupation of the back country by numerous groups that remained divided by cultural attitudes, social heritage, language, and religion.[44]

Apart from the production and marketing of major staples, agriculture in the Lower South has been much neglected in recent years. Lewis Cecil Gray's monumental two-volume *History of Agriculture in the Southern United States to 1860* remains, nearly half a century after its publication, the basic work in the field. Gray probed deeply into virtually every aspect of southern agriculture, relied heavily on quantitative data and economic analysis, and devoted much space to the colonial period. The book not only stands on its own merit but is also valuable for its heuristic potentiality. Gray moves across the landscape from tidewater planter to back-country farmer. Much remains to be learned also about why the interior and port towns and cities were so limited in number and how those that did emerge fitted into the regional economy.[45]

V

Perhaps at least in part because they produced so few staples, the New England colonies, more than any colonial region of British America, have suffered from a neglect of their internal economic development in favor of their extensive involvement in Atlantic commercial enterprise. The only comprehensive economic and social history of New England was published in 1890, and it is largely of antiquarian interest today. The most frequently cited history of agriculture in the northern colonies was published in 1925. Other major works from the early decades of the present century are those concerned with colonywide household manufactures and forest industries.[46] Recent decades have witnessed the production of a growing and vibrant literature on colonial New England's intellectual, social, political, ethnographic, and economic history. As a result, an extensive secondary literature describes and analyzes commerce, shipping, wealth distribution, various crafts and industries, agriculture, and transportation, but the primary emphasis continues to be on the external economy. Although few subjects have escaped monographic attention, it is surprising, as one economic historian has recently noted, that "no one has attempted a systematic analysis that would provide an overview of the economic development of the region or of any one colony in it."[47]

Export-oriented historians of the New England economy have tended to emphasize the development of extractive industries related to the sea, forests, and commercial agriculture. They have noted, for example, that Puritan farmers produced a surplus to supply immigrant colonists. The outbreak of the English Civil War brought a halt to the immigrant-based prosperity. But New Englanders responded by developing import-substitution industries, supplying markets in the Atlantic islands and West Indies with fish, corn and other products, and creating a commercial economy based on the carrying trade. Divided roughly into thirds, the cargoes consisted of foodstuffs, fish, and wood products. These historians have also argued that commercial agriculture grew both absolutely and relatively down to the American Revolution, despite such limitations as the cold climate, rocky soil, low yields, and primitive transportation. As the decades passed, it became more and more the goal of rural New Englanders to grow for the market at least some farm products beyond their family's requirements. That they succeeded is the contention of Howard S. Russell, who writes that pork, cattle, horses, onions, boards, staves, pitch, and other farm and forest produce were sent seaborne to the West Indies and southern markets, serving as a basis for economic health at home. Once the French and Indian War had ended, emigrants, who represented the overspill from increasing population in the older towns, headed south, west, and north to carve new farms from the wilderness.[48]

Casting doubt on the view that external market forces played a major role in shaping New England's internal economy are the findings of the "new" social historians. In an attempt to synthesize the contributions of these historians, Kenneth A. Lockridge investigated early New England at large and in particular the agricultural towns of eastern Massachusetts in the years 1630–1790. He found that landholdings per head of household shrank to less than one-third those held in the first generation; that a population increase of from 1 to 5 percent a year was a normal condition of life; that land values easily doubled and often tripled over the century; that migration was limited, mostly by patterns of inheritance; and that the rich were becoming more numerous and relatively more rich, while "the poor were becoming more numerous and relatively poorer." The upshot was a Malthusian situation of population pressure on a finite supply of land which was not relieved until after 1790, when the opening of western lands began to serve as a "safety valve."[49]

Lockridge admitted that his findings rested on a limited geographical and data base and challenged historians to engage in further research. From the long list of specific questions he thought should be answered were the following of an economic nature. "Was the decline in landholdings general? Was there an improvement in agricultural techniques and in the man-land ratio? Was there an improvement in access to markets? Did non-farm occupations offer alternative sources of income? Was the distribution of wealth changing with time? Was forty acres enough to support a large family?"[50]

Darrett B. Rutman responded to Lockridge's challenge. He pointed out that in all of New England in the late eighteenth century there were a thousand-odd towns and that only about a dozen had been analyzed by the "new" social historians. Rutman gathered a variety of data for the 198 inhabited towns in New Hampshire in the period 1767–90. He found that, contrary to Lockridge's findings, the inhabitants had ample economic opportunities other than agriculture and that the "Turnerian safety valve" opened early enough in the eighteenth century to prevent the emergence of overpopulation and the appearance of an agricultural proletariat.[51]

Support for Rutman's findings can be found in Bruce C. Daniels's recent article on economic development in colonial and revolutionary Connecticut. Farming, which had been "extensive and wasteful rather than intensive and careful" in seventeenth-century Connecticut, became more specialized and commercialized in the eighteenth century. Farming patterns changed—from grain to meat and dairy production—as settlements spread to upland areas suited to grazing. The colony responded to the demands of commercial agriculture on the primitive transportation network with "an outburst of intertown road construction in the 1750s." As a result of transportation and other improvements, "towns became more differentiated in size and function as some emerged as major mercantile centers and others as secondary centers of collection and distribution. Large-scale merchants appeared and developed contacts with much of the Atlantic world. A larger proportion of the population engaged in manufacturing; in particular, a sizable business developed in processing foodstuffs for market." Finally, Daniels contends that those who failed to share in these and other opportunities found a safety valve after 1760 in the unsettled lands in northern New York and in New Hampshire and Vermont.[52]

But still other studies concerned with wealth and income estimates cast doubt on the extent of internal economic growth in the New England colonies. Working with probate and other records, Terry L. Anderson argues that after rising in the seventeenth century, New England's real wealth per capita tended to slow or stagnate from 1700–1709 to 1770–79. He describes the first eighty years of the eighteenth century as "the one bleak period" in New England's growth history. Even more bleak was the trend in agricultural productivity, which was clearly downward during the same period. In her monumental *Wealth of a Nation to Be*, Alice Hanson Jones finds that in 1774 private physical wealth per capita in New England was £36.6 sterling. This compares with £41.9 for the Middle Colonies, £54.7 for the South, and £46.5 for the thirteen colonies combined. Moreover, New England had the greatest extremes in net worth, and the Middle Colonies the least. In 1774 the richest 10 percent of people who left probate records held 57 percent of the net worth in New England, compared with 49 percent in the South and 42 percent in the Middle Colonies. (The degree of inequality represented by these percentages is overstated because no allowance is made for age-wealth differences.) Jones believes that the relatively greater inequality in New England may be explained by the harshness of the climate, poor soil, and other difficulties encountered by small farmers on the one hand and by the opportunities for wealth accumulation in trade, shipping, shipbuilding, distilling, and other export-oriented activities on the other hand.[53]

What is perplexing about the economic and social history of colonial New England is the differences between the economic and social historians in their approaches, methods, findings, and interpretations. Economic historians have tended to focus on the external economy and see the domestic economy as the producer and processor of export commodities and as a market for imported goods. Emphasis has been placed on the production and exportation of fish, timber and timber products, farm and craft products; the importation of European goods and tropical products; shipbuilding; and the carrying trades, certain import-substitution industries, domestic processing and manufacture, as well as industries such as rum distilling and sugar refining which contributed to the reexport trade. It has been argued, for example, that the growth of external markets had the effect of transforming subsistence and semisubsistence farmers into producers who were more specialized by town and region, that commercial farming advanced, and that these developments were both cause and effect of the development of roads; bridges; ferries; grist, flour, and saw mills; tanneries; and ironworks. New England thus followed the path of material progress.

Contrasted with the externally oriented economic historians are the social historians, who are committed to rewriting American colonial history from the bottom up. They have explored the structure and character of society in studies that examine the experience of individuals, families, and groups in particular communities over long periods of time. Communities that were relatively stable and self-contained in the seventeenth century are said to have exhibited such characteristics by the middle decades of the eighteenth century as increasing population density, pressure on the land supply, economic hardship, increased social inequality, commercial dependency, migration, and absentee proprietorship—all of which changes, it is argued, occurred in the absence of a substantial rise in per capita income.

How to reconcile these differences is no easy matter. As a first approximation, staple historians could benefit perhaps from studies of individual towns, localities, and industries; the cycles of growth, stability, flux, and decline; and the extent to which localities, regions, or colonies were economically isolated or interconnected.[54] On the other hand, social historians are aware that their generalizations have been constructed on too thin a base; they have made repeated appeals for more local, demographic, and economic studies. While many more New England towns need to be studied, at the same time these towns need to be seen in their individual regional settings. It has been recommended that a colonial data bank be established. Such a project would provide an opportunity to tackle such problems as underregistration and bias in probate records and thus contribute to the formulation of more standardized methodologies. Traditional narrative history might well be combined with structural presentations derived from systematic analysis of long-term social, economic, and demographic change, drawing on not only quantitative data but also letters, sermons, journals, and the like.[55]

VI

Frederick Jackson Turner called attention to the role played in American history by the Middle Colonies of New York, New Jersey, Pennsylvania, and Delaware. This was a region that "mediated between New England and the South, and the East and West." "It had a wide mixture of nationalities, a varied society, the mixed town and county system of local government, a varied economic life, many religious sects." Though it became the "typical American region," the Middle Colonies have been traditionally neglected by historians. Among the reasons for this neglect is the difficulty of isolating unifying themes and historical patterns. As Douglas Greenberg has observed, the Middle Colonies were "populated by an extraordinarily large number of ethnic and religious groups, economically diversified, politically fragmented, and socially heterogenous." Despite their bewildering complexity, however, the Middle Colonies, as Greenberg notes, have become a focus of intense interest in the past decade.[56]

The middle region was entered by the Hudson and Delaware rivers. Coming first to the region were the Dutch, whose prime interest was profits from trade, not colonization. They established scattered trading posts on the Hudson, the Delaware, and Connecticut rivers. Recent studies add to our knowledge of New York's economic development under both Dutch and English rule. They have been concentrated on the role played by Dutch and English merchants and magnates in the fur trade centered around Albany, the gradual supplanting of furs by grain as the colony's leading export during the early eighteenth century, and the rise, structure, and functioning of the four largest manors in the Hudson River Valley, as well as New York agrarian society as a whole where tenancy prevailed.[57] Yet the only comprehensive treatment of New York's colonial economic history presently available consists of a single chapter in Michael Kammen's history of the colony. According to Kammen, the colony's first major period of concentrated commercial growth did not come until after the cessation of war in 1713. The decades that followed witnessed not only the expansion of external trade but also the expansion and diversification of the internal economy to include not just furs but naval stores, lumber, wheat and flour, and livestock. Among the rising entrepreneurs, Caleb Heathcote "engaged in trade as a merchant and contractor, built gristmills, a leatherworking shop, a fulling mill, a linseed oil mill, and a sawmill; raised flax and hemp; speculated in real estate; and became the collector of Westchester County taxes, a lucrative post." But New Yorkers were unable to sustain the momentum, and the colony's growth was inhibited by land grabbing, political and economic domination by the landed class, and a landlord-tenant system in which tenants suffered from many kinds of discrimination. The upshot was that New York lagged behind the other colonies in population growth. "By 1756 it had some 97,000 persons, as compared with 220,000 in Pennsylvania, which had been initially colonized two generations after its northern neighbor."[58]

Pennsylvania outgrew New York because it had better-quality and more abundant farm lands, its land disposal policies were more egalitarian, immigrants of diverse national origin and religion were encouraged, the much heralded "Puritan ethic" of the inhabitants stimulated capital accumulation, and Philadelphia emerged as the largest city in the colonies by serving the foodstuffs-producing areas of southeastern New Jersey and Pennsylvania and linking the colony to external markets. Pennsylvania was the foremost "bread colony," producing substantial quantities of corn, wheat, rye, oats, and barley and, like New York, exporting large quantities of flour. It led the colonies in iron production and shipbuilding and had extensive raw-material–processing industries, workshop crafts, and household manufacturing industries.

Unfortunately, no comprehensive economic history of colonial Pennsylvania has been written. On the contrary, more attention has been given to urban and rural studies of particular localities, communities, and industries than to synthetic or broadly unifying themes.

A Pennsylvanian observed in 1773 that "many thousands, rather than go farther back into the country where lands are cheap or undertake the arduous task of clearing new lands, turn to manufacturing, and live upon a small farm, as in many parts of England."[59] This observation is supported by historical studies: Victor Clark tells of numerous artisans who plied their crafts in the towns of Lancaster, Germantown, Trenton, and Wilmington and of workers in the mill industries in the surrounding countryside.[60] But the picture we have of these activities is fragmented, largely perhaps because social and economic historians have been attracted by the prosperous farmers of southeastern Pennsylvania, particularly by those of Chester County. This is a level and rolling country of productive soils, a long growing season, and easy access to navigable waterways, markets, and transshipment points. It was populated chiefly by members of the Society of Friends, or Quakers, who carved farms out of the wilderness and developed a pattern of mixed farming with wheat and flour as the chief export commodities. Chester County is also remarkable for possessing one of the richest collections of data for studying, on a microscopic level, the social and economic characteristics of the "bread" colonies.

From the ample records of Chester County have issued a remarkable number of dissertations, articles, and monographs that investigate almost every facet of colonial life and seek to relate local patterns and trends to those of broader scope in time and place. Unfortunately, the picture that emerges is to a considerable extent blurred, inconsistent, and often confusing. Some of the studies point to an egalitarian society and economy of hard-working and thrifty farmers, expanding in population and per capita wealth, becoming more diversified as an increasing number of Chester County men and their families found nonfarming livelihoods or migrated to areas of greater opportunity, and without any strong evidence of "over-crowding" or other social dislocations implied by the term "Europeanization."[61]

Other historians find reasons to question the extent to which Chester County conformed to the image of a democratic society of prosperous yeomen farmers. Careful studies of tax lists and inventories point to a gradual concentration of wealth and a relative widening of the gap between rich and poor. By the decade before the Revolution not quite half of the men living in the county were landless, while tenant farmers had increased in numbers and as a percentage of all taxpayers, indicating lessened opportunity to rise from the bottom of the economic ladder. Moreover, a slow rate of increase in agricultural productivity is difficult to square with the general impression of substantial affluence in the pre-Revolution era. If the prosperity of the middle-wealth farmers of Chester County held inequality there to a low measure, the same was not so apparent elsewhere. There was widespread discontent in many of the long-settled agricultural regions, as is evidenced by the uprising of small tenant farmers against the landlords and speculators in New Jersey. While it is true that migration alleviated the problem to some extent, it is also true that western regions were plagued with battles over disputed land claims and troubles with the Indians.[62]

Despite the above-mentioned new literature, the domestic economy of the

Middle Colonies affords ample opportunities for further study. The fur trade of New York, while it has been brilliantly analyzed in several monographs, has yet to be treated comprehensively from its Dutch beginnings to the end of British colonization. There are several unpublished dissertations that would help to complete the study. Albany under both Dutch and British rule attracted land speculators and traders in furs, lumber, and grain, and their activities have been carefully documented during the past two decades.[63] Land distribution, an issue of heated controversy among colonial New Yorkers, continues to agitate historians and calls for further research. In dispute is the question whether New York's landed estates formed an insurmountable obstacle to the aspirations of many colonists. Moreover, more could be known about the ethnic groups other than the Dutch and the English who settled in New York, as well as why the population of the colony grew slowly by comparison with that of neighboring Pennsylvania. Then there are opportunities for studies in such fields of New York's economic history as agriculture, household industries, mill and furnace industries, internal trade and transportation, and public credit and paper money.[64]

Douglas Greenberg says that the three most sophisticated examples of community studies in the recent historiography of the Middle Colonies are James T. Lemon's *The Best Poor Man's Country: A Geographical Study of Early Southeastern Pennsylvania*, Stephanie Grauman Wolf's *Urban Village: Population, Community, and Family Structure in Germantown, Pennsylvania, 1683–1800*, and Thomas J. Archdeacon's *New York City, 1664–1710: Conquest and Change*.[65] Although Lemon's study has generated an impressive number of dissertations and articles concerned with Chester County, historians of this county differ as to just how representative it was of the mainland colonies as a whole or even of the rural Middle Atlantic Colonies. There is no denying the advantages that the county enjoyed in terms of soil quality, length of growing season, access to water transportation and markets, and quality of early settlers. In their study of agricultural productivity, Ball and Walton admit that "the limited geographical coverage of this analysis and the incomplete and crude nature of the data cry out for more research."[66] Historical records permitting, it remains for historians of the Middle Colonies to study what Jackson Turner Main calls "frontier societies" and "subsistence farming societies" as thoroughly as those who have investigated the predominantly "commercial farming" communities of Chester County.[67] One area that calls for comprehensive economic and social study is the Pennsylvania back country.[68] Other questions include the impact made on the economy and society by settlers whose national and religious backgrounds were different, and why the farmers of Pennsylvania apparently had more opportunities for seasonal labor in rural handicrafts and mill and furnace industries than their counterparts in other northern colonies. Furthermore, we need a thorough study of large commercial flour mills in the mid-Atlantic region and of sawmills in the principal lumbering regions.[69]

VII

The role of women in the domestic economy of British America varied according to such criteria as race, class, age, education, skill, marital status, and residence. In this section I will survey the literature on women's work, region by region, in search of unifying themes and areas of strength and weakness.

Women in the staple colonies of the Chesapeake, the Caribbean, and the Lower South were active in various lines of work. Before Africans were imported in numbers sufficient to supplant white labor in plantation production, white female indentured servants sometimes worked in the fields with their male counterparts. Moreover, as Lois Green Carr and Lorena S. Walsh point out, wives in households too poor to afford bound labor might well tend tobacco plants, as well as perform customary household tasks. After slavery became entrenched, black women and black men often worked together in the fields. Slave women on both the Washington and Jefferson plantations were engaged in plowing, hoeing and grubbing the land, spreading manure, sowing, harrowing, and harvesting. On the other hand, female slaves were frequently trained by planters' wives as cooks, seamstresses, housekeepers, dairy maids, gardeners, and "chicken merchants." Female field labor in the colonies is a much neglected topic. We need to know more about its incidence among blacks and whites, northerners and southerners, British and non-British ethnic groups, and those living in seaboard and back-country areas.[70]

Southern white women had a wider range of lifestyles than their sisters in the North. Women in the back settlements had to depend on their own labor and ingenuity, providing their families with a wide range of goods and services, as well as assisting their husbands in field labor. The wives of farmers in settled areas often had several indentured servants and slaves to train and supervise, besides the household tasks they undertook themselves. Plantation mistresses, on the other hand, had the supervision of the largest households in North America. They were almost always directors rather than performers, overseeing large numbers of household workers in such tasks as procuring supplies, preparing food, making cloth and slave clothing, nursing the sick, and caring for the children and the aged. A number of women supervised all the plantation business as well as their household affairs. This was the case during the absence or at the death of their husbands. Eliza Lucas Pinckney was the exceptional female planter who managed three plantations after her father was recalled to his regiment in Antigua. With the encouragement and assistance of her father and husband, she experimented with ginger, cotton, lucerne, cassava, indigo, and other plants. She was the outstanding woman planter in the colonies who "reintroduced indigo seed into South Carolina, persevered in her experiments with it, and produced dye and, more important, seed for broader trials."[71]

The role of women in Jamaica during the slavery era was researched by Lucille Mathurin Mair. She shows how the life patterns of white, brown, and black women were shaped by the environment of racism, colonialism, and sexism. White women ranged widely in status from indentured servants to the wives of planters and top government officials. To a considerable extent, both the servant girls and mistresses of the great house declined in relation to the total white population, the one being replaced by female slaves and free women of color, the other frequently becoming absentees living in Europe. For those who stayed, the planter household was the dominant domestic norm. Here the white women were carefully sheltered from the life of industry and commerce. The rapidly growing mulatto class sprang from the deeply entrenched concubinage of brown and black females and white males. Because of the conspicuous absenteeism of the white elitist women, mulatto women tended to adopt the role of surrogate whites.

Mair found that the conditions for Jamaican slave women were less tolerable in the eighteenth century than in the seventeenth. This was owing in part, to the replacement of white servants by black women in field labor and in part to black women's replacing black men withdrawn from field labor to be trained as artisans and subordinate supervisors. The crunch came when planters turned to pronatalist policies after abolition of the slave trade in 1807 at the same time that their female slaves were expected to continue strenuous field labor. Indeed, sustained manual labor proved to be "inconsistent with the physical demands made on women by menstruation, pregnancy, lactation, infant and child care," to the extent that Jamaica continued to experience a net annual decrease in its slave population.[72]

Despite the cultural, legal, and economic restrictions imposed upon their activities, women played a major role in the internal economy of the farm colonies from New England south to Pennsylvania. From servant and slave girl to the large landholder's wife, from the pioneer woman of the back country to the wife of the affluent merchant in the city, women in colonial America participated actively in production, distribution, and marketing. Whether rural or urban, the household was the domain of colonial women. In the main they were involved in the primary processes of making apparel, food, drink, and other goods for household consumption. Besides supplying household needs, women commonly produced a variety of products for the market. As Mary Beth Norton observes, "A majority of the employed women worked at jobs that were extensions of the feminine sphere—sewing, housekeeping, teaching small children, nursing, and selling food or clothing." In addition, they ran dry goods, millinery, or grocery shops, inns and taverns, together with a variety of businesses first established by their now-deceased husbands, outside or attached to the home.[73]

The work activities of colonial women have been investigated by several recent historians. In her study of northern New England between 1650 and 1750, Laurel Thatcher Ulrich found "that the economic lives of women and men were clearly differentiated, that self-sufficient households were atypical, and that relationships between women were far more crucial than most scholars have supposed." Regardless of social position, women were responsible for cooking, washing, plain sewing, milking, tending a garden, and feeding swine. Some of them added the female specialities of cheesemaking, spinning, knitting, poultry raising, or cultivation of flax. Ulrich singles out woolen and linen clothmaking to demonstrate that self-sufficient households were atypical. Very few families commanded the tools, skills, and labor to perform all the steps in making cloth at home. On the other hand, there is evidence that women shared not only commodities but also the work that produced them. This "friendly neighborliness" went far to establish a condition of local or community self-sufficiency.[74]

Carole Shammas lends support to the Ulrich thesis that self-sufficient households were atypical. She found that rural households in New England performed one or two steps in the production process and then relied on craftspeople for the rest of the processing. "In addition," she writes, "they supplemented home grown products with textiles, flour, butter, and meat bought from tradesmen, peddlers, and neighboring producers." Shammas emphasizes the part played by goods imported from outside the mainland colonies in supplying the consumer demands of colonial households.[75]

Other studies of women's work in the farm colonies are focused on the second half of the eighteenth century. Nancy F. Cott notes that subsistence farming and household production for family use prevailed in the towns of New England. This activity was supplemented by individual craftspeople and by small industrial establishments. Mothers and daughters shared the labor of food preparation and preservation, dairying, gardening, cleaning, laundering, soapmaking, candlemaking, knitting, and textile and clothing manufacture. During the 1760s the first "manufactories" were established in major cities to collect yarn spun and cloth woven in farm homes by traditional hand methods. Norton, in her study of women in the Revolutionary War period, calls attention to the seasonal nature of much of farm women's labor. While the farmer's basic cycle was yearly, that of his wife was daily and weekly, with additional obligations superimposed seasonally. Men were able to break their routine by making frequent trips to town or going hunting or fishing, "whereas their wives, especially if they had small children, were tied to the home." However, not all wives were tied to the home. Bidwell and Falconer observe that in Pennsylvania "the marketing was largely done by farm women, who carried their produce, butter, poultry, fresh meat, etc., in large wallets or panniers slung across horses. Two-horse carts came into general use about the middle of the century."[76]

VIII

From the above-mentioned regional and topical studies certain large themes relating to the domestic economy of early America emerge very clearly. Reliance on staple exports and their impact on the domestic economy is one such theme. Such reliance varied widely among the five groups of colonies. Per capita commodity exports in pounds sterling for the years 1768–72 amounted to £4.75 for the British West Indies, £1.82 for the Chesapeake region, £1.78 for the Lower South, £1.03 for the Middle Colonies, and £0.84 for New England. Per capita exports from the British West Indies were 2.6 times those of the Chesapeake and 3.5 times the average of the British North American colonies.[77]

How the reliance on staple exports influenced the development of the internal economy is a question that is only imperfectly understood. For purposes of clarification, it seems advisable to distinguish two types of staples. Primary staples were produced in tropical and semitropical regions, on plantations worked by white indentured servants and/or African slaves. They were generally classified as "enumerated" commodities, giving rise to a shuttle-type trade between the colony and the metropolis. Secondary staples, on the other hand, were produced in temperate-zone regions, on farms worked by family members, white servants, and wage laborers. One school of thought argues that they were produced primarily for subsistence and only secondarily for sale in local, regional, or overseas markets. Since they were "unenumerated," they could be sold to foreigners as well as to inhabitants of Great Britain and her colonies. They were secondary chiefly in the sense that they supplied the plantation colonies and other external markets with intermediate products and common items of consumption.

As viewed by British mercantilists, the West Indies were "ideal" colonies. They supplied the mother country with commodities hitherto obtained from rival nations. Their primary staples could be processed and reexported to provide credits on the balance-of-payments statement, and they yielded tax revenues, provided the means to pay for British exports, and gave employment and gain to British ships and seamen as well as merchants, commission agents, insurance underwriters, warehousemen, bankers, and others. Except for a group of planters and merchants, primary-staple colonies yielded limited benefits to local factors of production. Profits of staple production and trade tended to be siphoned off by interested parties in the metropolis; few linkages, or "spread effects," developed in the colonies where sugar monoculture prevailed; wealth and income were grossly maldistributed, as between lordly planters and impoverished slaves; and wealthy planters often chose to become absentees.

Whereas the inhabitants of "ideal" plantation colonies produced what they did not consume and consumed what they did not produce, those in farm colonies consumed most of what they produced and produced most of what they consumed. The latter colonies had a more equal distribution of wealth and income; the higher demand for goods and services led to the growth of local and regional markets. Backward and forward linkages developed to add value to products of the land and sea. Urban centers developed to provide mercantile and other services that linked internal to external markets.

Compared with the West Indies, the plantation colonies in the Chesapeake region and the Lower South were less than ideal. Outside the rice belt and the Tobacco Coast, mixed production of primary and secondary staples coexisted with subsistence agriculture. Diversified farming, which was commonplace in many parts of the mid-Atlantic and New England colonies, spread to the Upper and Lower South in the thirty years or more before the American Revolution. Farmers in the tobacco colonies responded to the expansion of the Atlantic grain market by diversifying their production. As Paul G. E. Clemens points out, "They found they could grow more wheat and corn without reducing the amount of land and labor they devoted to tobacco." In time, however, population growth reduced the land-labor ratio, inducing many small planters and farmers on Maryland's Eastern Shore to shift to wheat because it brought better returns than tobacco. According to David Klingaman, "The grain sector not only was vital as a basis for feeding a rapidly growing population but also served at the margin as an increasingly important source of export earnings." Nothwithstanding the growth of the grain sector, tobacco continued to dominate the Chesapeake throughout the colonial period, accounting for three-quarters of all exports on the eve of independence.[78]

Advocates of the staple thesis maintain that although commercial agriculture was limited by geographical, technological, and economic factors, most farmers, attuned to the potentials of the market, were motivated by liberal, entrepreneurial, individualistic, or capitalist values, seeking to maximize income and profits and willing to take risks and accept innovations. Staple adherents argue that as population expanded, many people were able to move to frontier areas and relieve the pressure on the resources of long-settled areas. In his study of the early agricultural society of southeastern Pennsylvania, James T. Lemon found that a century of development brought prosperity to many residents of the area. "Although the people followed fairly well-established European ways of organizing their lives and using the land," he writes, "their individualistic drives and the richness of the land contributed greatly to their success." Those who were not so fortunate looked to the West as "a place to try again, a place to conquer. Resources were there in abundance, or so they thought."[79]

In recent years, however, this line of argument has been challenged by a group of historians who have raised a second major criticism of the staple approach. These scholars, the "Malthusians," emphasize the limits placed upon the liberal and acquisitive market mentality by continued population pressure on resources, low productivity, and subsistence and semisubsistence production stemming from constraints of a geographical, technological, and economic nature, as well as from social relationships and cultural expectations. They underscore the centrality of farms and plantations in colonial America, stress the fact that up to 85 percent of the population depended upon agriculture for their livelihood, and emphasize the extent to which, despite regional variations in soil and climate, farmers and planters endeavored to supply their own requirements for foodstuffs. Thus, in his studies of early American agriculture Stiverson found that although farmers were concerned to grow commodities for sale, inadequate transportation and marketing facilities and the rudimentary nature of existing technology forced them to focus their planting priorities on feeding themselves and their dependents. To make sure that they had a safeguard against crop failure, farmers typically overplanted food crops, thus providing a "subsistence-surplus," from which came the greater part of the crops put on the market.[80]

Others have supported Stiverson in this "Malthusian" interpretation. Daniel Scott Smith and James A. Henretta may be singled out for special mention. Smith has tried to shift the focus from a market-oriented, export-led approach to an essentially demographic interpretation of colonial economic development. He argues that birth rates outdistanced death rates in older communities, leading to limited resources, higher rents, smaller yields, increased inequality, and a subsistence pattern of production. Although some rural dwellers managed to migrate to the frontier, they were too few in number to prevent the "Europeanization" of American society. Although Smith finds it difficult to refute the rough conclusion that economic progress more or less kept pace with the rapid march of population growth in the Malthusian era, he insists that "urbanization, the extension of the frontier, and the growth in the number of political offices had difficulty matching the pace of demographic expansion" and that even though they dominated the market sector, staples were not an engine of widespread economic transformation in the Malthusian era.[81]

Unlike Stiverson and Smith, who focus attention on economic and demographic factors, Henretta argues the case for a system of subsistence and semisubsistence production based primarily on social and cultural factors. He contends that the family persisted as the basic unit of agricultural production, capital formation, and property transmission and that the economic behavior of most northern farm families was determined fundamentally by ethnic, linguistic, and religious ties and only secondarily by market forces and values. He suggests that in this relatively static society, at least prior to about 1750, "elaborate networks of family and kin, of European inheritance patterns, and of traditional social values" played a far greater role in determining economic behavior than did the market-stimulated desire for wealth emphasized by "liberal" historians such as Lemon. More research is obviously needed to examine the evidence and assess the validity of the arguments advanced by proponents of the liberal and Malthusian interpretations.[82]

IX

Other important areas have been neglected by the literature on the regions and/or treated by the general literature. These areas include manufacturing, the role of government in economic life, the money supply, the service sector, internal trading patterns, and the role of the Indians. Like Adam Smith, modern economic historians point on the one hand to the comparative advantage of agricultural pursuits and on the other to the formidable obstacles to manufacturing in the colonies. These obstacles included low population density, few urban markets, poor inland transportation, low freight charges on manufactures carried on "back-haul" voyages on ships built to carry bulky staples to Europe, scarce capital and labor, and mercantile restrictions on certain branches of colonial manufacturing. According to a contemporary writer, the colonists found "it more their interest to cultivate their lands and attend the fisheries than to manufacture."[83]

Colonial manufacturing, though of small importance in an imperial context, was vital to inhabitants of interior settlements and is a topic that merits further research. To manufacture, according to a seventeenth-century definition, was to make articles or material by physical labor or mechanical power. Denominated "household manufactures," countless articles were made by the physical labor of colonial men and women, assisted by simple hand tools. In urban areas and commercial farming regions manufactured goods were produced for a wide market by persons who depended entirely upon the income derived from such activity for their support. Market-oriented production covered a wide spectrum, ranging from commercial processors of agricultural commodities to "mill and furnace industries."[84] In his study of the markets for northern farm products from 1750 to 1775, Max George Schumacher finds that despite the high degree of self-sufficiency, there was a good demand for the leading export products—wheat, horses, beef, pork, and flaxseed. At strategic points in the interior and in coastal towns there grew up commercial meatpackers, water-driven bolting mills, tanneries, and sawmills. Among the middlemen were country dealers, many of whom were themselves farmers or graziers, who were active in buying up cattle in outlying areas.[85]

Mill and furnace industries included flour and gristmills, sawmills, ironworks, glassworks, paper mills, breweries and distilleries, fulling and powder mills, and shipyards. Compared with other branches of manufacturing, mill and furnace industries were more closely geared to overseas markets, employed a larger labor force, required heavier investment in plant and equipment, and depended in large measure on water power and at times wind power.

Shipbuilding and iron-making are among the leading mill and furnace industries researched for doctoral dissertations. In his study of the shipbuilding industry in the Delaware Valley of eastern Pennsylvania and West Jersey from 1684 to 1775, Simeon John Crowther details the construction of ocean vessels in terms of numbers, tonnage, average size, and vessel type. Paul F. Paskoff has examined the formation and growth of large colonial-owned iron firms in Pennsylvania and Maryland during the period 1725–75. Merchants who had accumulated capital reserves in commerce saw investment in iron production as a desirable alternative to more extensive involvement in trade. Although the technology of iron production remained virtually unchanged in the half-century before the Revolution, labor productivity increased by such means as improved organization and the substitution of capital for labor. Limits of space preclude comment on other well-researched and perceptive studies of colonial manufacturing. Unfortunately, little effort has been made to integrate these fragmentary studies and give them broader unity and coherence.[86]

One stereotypical view of early American history is that the colonists revolted against political and economic tyranny imposed by the British government with the goals of establishing a small property-owning democracy and a system of competitive enterprise free from intervention by government. Countering this laissez-faire myth is the view that within their restricted sphere of influence, colonial governments sought to control, regulate, restrain, and stimulate activity and thus to guide economic and social development. Colonial governments responded to popular demand by establishing public markets and regulating the price of country produce entering towns and cities. They enacted laws to fix wages in certain occupations; to license such quasi-public functionaries as porters, draymen, millers, smiths, and gravediggers; to fix wharfage and storage rates and fares on ferries; to set prices on bread and other basic commodities. Besides wage and price controls, colonial authorities laid down standards of quality and measure for commodities and certain manufactured goods. Moreover, able-bodied males were required to work a certain number of days in the year on such public-works projects as roads, bridges, fortifications, meeting houses, and prisons. By means of compulsory or statute labor and tax revenues, Indian trails and bridle paths were upgraded to wagon roads that served as arteries of migration and trade, linking interior farms and villages to navigable waterways and seaport cities. In sum, political establishments sought to foster development through building roads and bridges, establishing ferries and ports, organizing postal services, building lighthouses and canals, and upgrading exports by establishing inspection standards.[87]

The literature on the role of government in the economy can be divided into two parts. In the first place, we have seen that governments fixed wages and prices, established and regulated town markets, fixed various rates and fares, issued licenses, extracted compulsory labor, and established inspection standards. In his monumental *Government and Labor in Early America*, Richard B. Morris analyzed government in its fundamental role as a regulator of economic and class interests. He examined wage- and price-fixing; restrictions on admission to crafts and trades; compulsory labor on public-works projects; licenses, fees, and fares; and quality controls. He noted that colonial wage and price controls were most widespread in Massachusetts Bay, "the happy hunting ground for paternalistic controls over religion, morals and business." Gary Nash, in his monograph on social and political change in major urban areas, added to our understanding of regulated public markets for foodstuffs, price controls, corporately owned and licensed businesses, and workhouses, where the able-bodied poor were segregated, relieved, and rehabilitated. Mary McKinney Schweitzer analyzed the causes and consequences of the Maryland Tobacco Inspection Act of 1747 in a recent article. Regulating the quality of tobacco exports had several significant effects on the Maryland economy. Tobacco prices and revenues were increased, the economy became more diversified, transaction costs were reduced, wealth was redistributed, and the money supply was affected by the circulation of inspection notes. Schweitzer laments the fact that while much has been written about England's attempts to control the economies of the American colonies, relatively little has been written about the colonial governments' efforts to influence their own economic activities.[88]

Closely linked with the regulation of economic and class interests was the role played by government in developing systems of transportation and communication. We have seen that these systems included navigable waterways, roads, bridges, ferries, wharfs, lighthouses, and postal services. As population grew by natural increase and immigration, settlers occupied areas inaccessible to navigable waterways. Road building became of vital importance, linking farms to nearby villages and towns and interior regions of settlement to waterways and seaboard cities. What we know of inland transportation development in British America is very limited except for certain colonies and areas or regions. Studies show that from about 1700 to 1760 Connecticut developed a system of primary and secondary roads which, though expensive and difficult to maintain, went far to link interior towns to markets in Providence, Hartford, and Boston.[89] Maryland is another colony whose transportation developments are quite well documented. Carville V. Earle shows how settlement dispersal in the tidewater Chesapeake region encouraged sweeping changes in transport arrangements. Water transport lost its sole cost advantage, and increased reliance was placed on "the horse, the road, and the ferry as the modes and media of transport."[90] Considerable attention has also been given to transport developments in the Philadelphia trading area[91] and to the southern piedmont or back country, with special reference to the Shenandoah Valley. Robert D. Mitchell is concerned in his monograph with the direct and indirect effects of government policies on the settlement and development of the early Shenandoah Valley. He traces the development of the Great Wagon Road, which ran west and south from Philadelphia to form the backbone of the highway system of the southern interior. Located along this road were the region's major towns, which provisioned and lodged wagoners and animals, repaired vehicles, and shod horses. From a local standpoint, county courthouses served as focal points for roads, while secondary focuses were mills, meeting houses, churches, and ferries.[92]

The impressive body of research on the money supply of the colonies of British America published in recent decades has challenged older viewpoints, raised new issues, utilized new data sources, and sought to achieve a broader synthesis. Though not focused directly on the money supply of the colonies, two recent studies add much to our understanding of capital, credit, money, and exchange in the context of the Atlantic economy. In his handbook of money and exchange in Europe and America, John McCusker has published some sixty-five tables of exchange rates compiled from newspapers and unpublished business records. Moreover, the tables in this most valuable handbook are introduced by useful essays on the colonial money systems of the mainland and West India colonies. In his latest study of Anglo-Chesapeake trade and finance, Jacob M. Price investigates the origin and development of money markets in London and the outports and the role played by capital and credit in the trade between Britain and the colonies of Virginia and Maryland. Of particular interest is his contention that the immense debts of tobacco growers contributed to psychological unease and a revolutionary ethos.[93]

The traditional view that emissions of colonial paper currency tended to be inflationary and enabled debtors to defraud creditors has been refuted by several historians. In his well-received doctoral dissertation, Leslie V. Brock claims that "the distinctive contribution of the American colonies to financial and monetary practice was the paper currency issued under government auspices." These issues served as necessary instruments of government finance, provided long-term credit, and served as a medium of exchange. Brock's views are supported by E. James Ferguson, who contends that on balance colonial paper-money practices proved successful. Joseph Albert Ernst casts his net widely in his *Money and Politics in America, 1755–1775*. He examines British monetary policy and its impact on colonial politics, money, and economic life. Ernst finds numerous reasons to question the methodology and findings of historians who have used the quantity theory of money to show how monetary policy influenced overall price levels and exchange rates. Similarly, Robert Craig West presents strong evidence that any generalization about the inflationary effects of paper-money issues will probably be incorrect. Without these new types of means of settlement, he contends, internal economic growth during the colonial period might have been severely retarded.[94]

Besides paper money, the money supply of the colonies included wampum, various forms of commodity money, and specie. In Virginia and Maryland tobacco was made legal tender in payment of debts and the settlement of contracts. Tobacco was used to pay taxes, duties, court fees, and the salaries of clergymen. A refinement of this system was the establishment of official storehouses and the quality inspection of tobacco; depositors received warehouse receipts or tobacco notes, which circulated as currency. Although not accorded legal-tender status, such widely demanded commodities as molasses and rum tended to take on the character of commodity money in the colonies. Whether there was a chronic drain of specie to settle colonial trade balances with the mother country is a question of dispute. West observes that there was both an inflow and an outflow of specie, and at times of crisis the outflow certainly exceeded the inflow. However, doubt on the "chronic drain" thesis has been strengthened by research on the balance of payments and the discovery in probate records of gold and silver in the wealth holdings of individuals.[95]

One controversy of some importance is whether to include book credit in the colonial money supply. In order to overcome the lack of specie, merchants commonly sold imported and other goods on credit, and payment was made later in commodities of local origin, with the transaction being recorded in the money of account. W. T. Baxter calls this "bookkeeping barter," or barter of a "refined and subtle" form which frequently involved third parties in balancing accounts. Stuart Bruchey contends that book credit in the colonial period no more belongs to the money supply than credit cards do today, and that while bookkeeping barter did facilitate commodity exchanges, it was still barter, and one function of money is to make barter unnecessary. Ernst, on the other hand, contends that merchants early developed an extensive and efficient system of book credit and barter to make up for the deficiency of coin and that it is an error to focus on the visible money supply (paper currency, coin, commodity notes) and ignore the bulk of the money supply in the form of book credit. Similarly, West maintains that book credit made up a substantial portion of the transactions and that it worked for the American colonists much as demand deposits work in modern economies. Believing that book credit had important implications regarding the structure of the colonial economy and its susceptibility to financial and commercial crises, West calls for closer scrutiny of merchants' records to discover clues concerning the velocity at which book credit was used.[96]

Improvements in the money system no doubt helped to shift the colonial economy from a subsistence to a commercial basis, which in turn gave rise to the need for commercial and other services. The service sector included the rural artisans, mills, and stores, as well as seaport merchants and other middlemen. Where markets were lacking, each family or village unit had to produce for its own consumption. As a New England clergyman observed, "The house was a factory on the farm, the farm a grower and producer for the house."[97] Besides preserving and processing the food they ate, isolated farm families made homespun cloth, candles, soap, and other products and entered into sharing arrangements with local sawmills, gristmills, and tanneries. In his economic history of the inland farming communities of early New England, Percy Wells Bidwell found that the towns were small and the purchasing power of the farmers set within very narrow limits. In these circumstances a community could not furnish sufficient demand for the products and services of specialized nonagricultural workers and professional men. There was no market for agricultural produce because of the union of all trades, businesses, and professions with agriculture. In other words, there were carpenter-farmers, miller-farmers, storekeeper-farmers, lawyer-farmers, and clergymen-farmers but no nonagricultural specialists who resided in the isolated inland towns.[98]

Contrasted with the isolated inland towns were coastal towns, where the people got their living from both the sea and the land. Here was found a strictly nonagricultural population that derived its income from such activities as fishing, trade, handicraft production, milling, shipbuilding, and maritime activities. Town markets opened up opportunities for commercial agriculture and an urban-rural exchange of goods and services. Market penetration was facilitated by new settlements accessible to navigable waterways and the construction of farm-to-market roads. Some rural areas developed cottage industries organized under a putting-out system, whereby farmers and their wives and children were employed part time as nailmakers, shoemakers, and textile workers.[99]

Colonial historians' neglect of the organization and patterns of internal trade is by no means a recent phenomenon. However, the neglect may have been greater in recent years because of the bias imparted by the staple approach. The trading class in the colonies included individuals who ranged from poor frontier storekeepers to wealthy seaport merchants and shipowners. Generally speaking, seaport merchants established networks to gather commercial intelligence, coordinated the production and consumption of goods and services, dealt in a wide range of goods, engaged in both wholesale and retail trade, and performed many functions that were later assumed by commercial banks. Seaboard merchants and factors not only saw ships and cargoes depart and enter Atlantic ports but also looked inwards to oversee the assembling of commodities for export and the distribution of imported goods. They frequently directed a commercial network that extended from the major cities to towns, villages, hamlets, and frontier trading posts. Agents of seaport merchants frequently settled in back-country towns, where they acted as buyers, wholesalers, retailers, moneylenders, and organizers of transport services. A variation of this pattern consisted of chains of stores established by Glasgow tobacco merchants in the Chesapeake region. Needless to say, more research is needed on the role played by seaport merchants in internal trade and economic development.[100]

Compared with what is known about the seaport merchants and factors, little is known about the organization and patterns of internal trade except in certain well-researched geographical areas. As key units in the network of trade, country stores and storekeepers should be studied more systematically, using probate and other records and the techniques of historical geographers. The stock in trade of country stores included such European goods as textiles, crockery, glassware, and metal goods and such West Indian goods as salt, molasses, rum, and sugar. These and other imported goods were bartered for tobacco, flaxseed, deerskins, furs, and other produce of the surrounding countryside. According to Schumacher, country stores were the most widely distributed agency for collecting produce. The wagons and boats that carried local produce to city markets returned with imported goods purchased from wholesale merchants. In a financial capacity, country store-keepers sold goods on credit and made loans to local farmers and craftsmen. Stuart Bruchey has asked the following important questions about country stores: "How far west were these stores to be found? What were their precise locations in relation to settlements and to roads and rivers connecting with the coast? In what numbers did they exist, and what was their scale of operations?" "If we had answers to these questions," he writes, "we would be able to draw more meaningful conclusions concerning the commercial impact of rural markets on upcountry agriculture."[101]

Finally, by its assumption that America was a continent of "empty" lands, the staple approach has neglected the vital role played by Amerindians in supplying food and otherwise enabling early settlers to survive and cope with the environment. This criticism arises directly out of recent work by eth-nohistorians, who by uniting archaeology, ethnology, history, and linguis-tics, have contributed substantially to broadening understanding of the range and depth of culture contacts along the colonial-Indian frontier. Recent stud-ies have increased tenfold or more the estimated number of Indians who occupied the Americas in 1492 and have discovered that few Indians lived exclusively by the hunt; that Indians along the Atlantic seaboard had cleared substantial areas to provide village sites and fields for their crops; that, lack-ing immunity to smallpox and other communicable diseases brought in by Europeans, the Indian population had fallen off dramatically by the time of the first English settlements. Perhaps even more than the fur trade, agricul-ture pervaded the history of Indian-white contacts. As Thomas R. Wessel observes, "Indian agriculture fed the first colonists at Jamestown and Plym-outh and largely accounted for their survival. . . . The coastal tribes' ability to feed themselves and the white settlements belied the popular conception of Indian agriculture in that region as bare subsistence."[102]

Moreover, Indians guided explorers and traders and established trails through the wilderness. They exchanged furs and hides for blankets, rum, firearms, and other goods, thus providing a stimulus for European and colo-nial industry and trade. The fur trade revolutionized the Indian's way of life. He ceased to be self-sufficient: he neglected his crops and became the sup-plier of a single export, which made him dependent on the white trader and his trade goods. As the Indians receded further into the interior in search of peltries, the lands they had formerly occupied were taken over by white settlers and speculators.[103]

X

No little progress has been made in understanding the nature, dimensions, and performance of the internal economy of British America during recent decades. We have seen that much greater attention has been given to all

aspects of West Indian economic history and to the role of indentured servants and the rise of slavery in the Chesapeake and the West Indies. For all of
the colonies there is a greater understanding of demographic patterns, the
process and dimensions of economic growth, and the distribution of wealth.
Intensive parish and county studies have been undertaken, particularly in
New England, Chester County, Pennsylvania, and the counties of Maryland. These studies, which draw heavily on probate documents and tax lists,
reveal such things as family and social structure; demographic, wealth, and
productivity changes; and trade patterns.

From the above survey of the literature on the economic history of British
America it is evident that as scholars have become more and more specialized, they have tended to narrow their focus and excessively fragment
their studies into a series of subspecialties in terms of regions, periods,
themes, and methodologies. To the extent that broader conceptual schemes
and analytical frameworks have been employed, they have tended to focus on
economic growth and development, the economic analysis of quantitative
phenomena, the thrust of the commercial sector with special emphasis on
external economic relations, and the key roles played by planters in the
South and seaport merchants in the North. The Malthusian school, on the
other hand, has focused on the internal economy and society of British
America. Members of this school find that population increased in relation to
the supply of good land, that the size of farms declined to the point where
they did not provide a full living for their owners, that farm tenancy became
entrenched in certain areas, and that the gap between rich and poor grew
wider. What we need now is some conceptual scheme that avoids the extremes of cosmopolitanism on the one hand and parochialism on the other.
What we mainly need is a lot of empirical research about the domestic
economy.

Specifically, we need to fit the internal economies of British America into
the broader setting of the Atlantic economy and to compare their patterns of
economic development. Compared with what we know about trade and
shipping, however, we know relatively little about how internal development
was influenced by disease environments, crop introductions, demographic
patterns, and immigration. In these and other respects intercolonial comparisons are only beginning to be undertaken by economic historians. Stanley L.
Engerman has compared the economic and demographic experience of the
slaves in the southern mainland states with those in the West Indies, while
Robert W. Fogel in the forthcoming book analyzes the slave economies and
demographics of these two regions. Richard S. Dunn and Peter H. Wood,
among others, have shown how the sugar revolution in Barbados influenced
the development of South Carolina, while Dunn has compared a sugar plantation in Jamaica with a tobacco plantation in Virginia. David W. Galenson
has analyzed indentured servitude in all its aspects and the change from
primary reliance on bound white labor to the use of slaves in the islands and

on the mainland. Intercolonial economic and social comparison can be a fruitful field of research.[104]

From the side of the international economy, we need to know more about how outside events and developments affected the internal economy. The economic impact of imperial wars and restrictions on manufacturing and trade are little-touched research topics. The military impact was both positive and negative. At the same time that wars wreaked destruction on certain frontier settlements, other communities benefited from contracts that the British government awarded to local traders and merchants for provisions, fodder, wagon freighting, and various services. The Seven Years' War was particularly traumatic because it was followed by the British government's effort to reorganize the old colonial system. Colonials resisted, in part, by becoming more economically self-sufficient. Colonial textile production increased rapidly after 1760 both in the countryside and in the towns. The domestic economy became more important in the decade before the Revolution.[105]

Turning from the exterior to the interior, frontier studies of the mainland colonies tend to be regional in their focus and concern economic and social life more from a descriptive standpoint than from an analytical one. In order to weigh the merits and demerits of the Malthusian thesis, we need both micro and macro studies of the amount, quality, price, and availability of western lands, the distance and accessibility to markets, and the feasibility of self-sufficient existence. To what extent did the depletion of soil through wasteful unscientific methods of farming serve, along with population growth and land scarcity, as a stimulus to the westward movement?

Variations in economic behavior by ethnic groups is another subject in need of further study. German farmers are reputed to have cleared their crop land of trees and stumps, plowed deeply, and farmed intensively with family labor. Rather than permit their livestock to range widely for forage, they grew hay and grain and built large barns to shelter their animals in winter, thus concentrating manure to fertilize their crops. On the other hand, the Germans, like other settlers, are said to have been tempted by the cheapness of the land to exploit it for immediate profit. Can these contradictory positions be reconciled?[106]

We need to know to what extent the production in various regions was intended for and entered into the market sector; the nature and magnitude of localized, intraregional trade in each area; the relative importance of push-pull factors in internal migration; the relationships between wealth distribution and demographic variables. To what extent did capital markets emerge that were independent of external sources of capital? We could better understand the factors influencing differential fertility and mortality, as between the slaves in the West Indies and those in the southern mainland colonies. There is a need to undertake more regional analysis, as opposed to that of towns and counties; to determine whether cycles of prosperity and depres-

sion were synchronous, as among the various colonies and regions, or disparate. More research is needed on the internal economy of the Lower South
and the British West Indies. More serious attempts should be made to assess
the influence of cultural forces—Puritanism, Enlightenment ideas, the Protestant work ethic, mercantilism, and so on—on economic activity, and vice
versa.

Any discussion of the strategies to be employed in the writing of colonial
economic history must necessarily involve the controversial question of
methodology. F. J. Fisher said in his inaugural lecture at the London School
of Economics and Political Science in 1956 that the previous generation of
economic historians had had as their main requirement the ability to read,
since most of their sources were literary. However, by the mid-1950s the
first requirement of economic historians was the ability to count, since their
materials were largely statistical. The learned monograph of the "reader" was
said to consist of a "thin rivulet of text meandering through wide and lush
meadows of footnotes," while the learned monograph of the "counter" consisted of a stream of text that "tumbles from table to table and swirls round
graph after graph."[107] We should keep in mind that economic history is the
product of the marriage of two separate disciplines, that its survival depends
on maintaining a balance between the historian's interest in the process of
change and the study of personal and cultural elements on the one hand and
the economist's interest in theory and quantitative evidence to verify hypotheses on the other. We should keep in mind that many, if not most, of the
important questions in economic history do not lend themselves to quantitative treatment, that quantitative methods are only a tool, and that explanation requires both quantitative and qualitative evidence.[108]

These cautionary remarks notwithstanding, there is a promising future for
a "balanced" economic history of British America, a history which would
combine the best of traditional and contemporary methodologies and draw
on the humanities and social sciences to enrich our understanding of the
processes of the past.

On a more mundane level, we should search for more farm account books
to supply data on production and sales, make use of birth and death registers
in family histories, and make greater use of plantation letter books and account books, of which a substantial number pertaining to the West Indies
have come into the public domain in recent years. Jacob Price reminds us
that despite their limitations, probate records are the most valuable single
source we have for the economic and social history of extended communities.
There are valuable repositories of probate and other records in Jamaica,
Barbados, and other Caribbean islands which should be used more widely by
historians of British America. A worthy project would be to arrange exchanges of archival personnel and historians between the mainland and the
islands.[109]

Three orientations are suggested by the contents of this paper. The first is the part played by colonial Americans in establishing the foundations of the national economy. The second is the important interrelationships between North and South, farms and plantations, Yankees and Creoles. A point of special emphasis is the role played by black slaves in creating wealth and income throughout the Atlantic economy. The third orientation is that between Europe and America, particularly the British Isles and the colonies from Maine to Tobago. J. R. Pole underscores the truth when he writes that ever since the sixteenth century the people of Europe and America have been locked into a growing complex of economic, demographic, and political systems from which none of them could ever escape. He urges us to grasp the totality of Anglo-American history.[110]

NOTES

For helpful suggestions in preparing this paper I am indebted to Stanley L. Engerman, David W. Galenson, Alice Hanson Jones, John J. McCusker, Russell R. Menard, Edmund S. Morgan, and Jacob M. Price.

1. Edwin J. Perkins, *The Economy of Colonial America* (New York, 1980), 31–35.

2. Melville H. Watkins, "A Staple Theory of Economic Growth," *Canadian Journal of Economics and Political Science* 29 (1963): 141–58; David W. Galenson and Russell R. Menard, "Approaches to the Analysis of Economic Growth in Colonial British America," *Historical Methods* 13 (1980): 3–18.

3. John J. McCusker and Russell R. Menard, "The Economy of British America, 1607–1790: Needs and Opportunities for Study" (Draft for discussion, Conference on the Economy of British America, Williamsburg, Va., October 1980, mimeographed), 9–25.

4. Ibid., 10, 22.

5. The staple theory is limited in other ways. It is difficult to separate the impact of a particular staple from that of a slave labor system; its assumption of "empty" lands or regions neglects the vital role played by Amerindians in supplying food and otherwise enabling early settlers to survive; and by concentrating on successful cases of export-led growth and development, it neglects those colonial and neocolonial regions that have been caught in a "staple trap" of underdevelopment (see ibid., 18–25 and n. 16; Watkins, "Staple Theory," 149–51; Robert E. Baldwin, "Patterns of Development in Newly Settled Regions," *Manchester School of Economics and Social Studies* 24 [1956]: 161–79; and Andre Gunder Frank, *Dependent Accumulation and Underdevelopment* [New York, 1979], 112–28).

6. Thad W. Tate, "The Seventeenth-Century Chesapeake and Its Modern Historians," in *The Chesapeake in the Seventeenth Century: Essays on Anglo-American Society*, ed. Thad W. Tate and David L. Ammerman (Chapel Hill, 1979), 32–49.

7. Allan Kulikoff, "The Colonial Chesapeake: Seedbed of Antebellum Southern Culture?" *Journal of Southern History* 45 (1979): 513–40.

8. Recent dissertations, articles, essays, and monographs concerned with the economic and social history of the Chesapeake region have been authored by Richard R. Beeman, Lois G. Carr, Paul G. E. Clemens, Carville V. Earle, David W. Galenson, Peter M. G. Harris, Ronald Hoffman, Rhys Isaac, David S. Klingaman, Allan Kulikoff, Gloria L. Main, Russell R. Menard, Gerald W. Mullin, Edward C. Papenfuse, Jr., Jacob M. Price, Gregory A. Stiverson, Thad W. Tate, and Lorena S. Walsh.

9. Russell R. Menard, "From Servants to Slaves: The Transformation of the Chesapeake Labor System," *Southern Studies* 16 (1977): 355–90; Edmund S. Morgan, *American Slavery— American Freedom: The Ordeal of Colonial Virginia* (New York, 1975), 5, 344–45, 369.

10. *The Diary of Colonel Landon Carter of Sabine Hall, 1752–1778*, ed. Jack P. Greene, 2 vols. (Charlottesville, 1965); Jack P. Greene, *Landon Carter: An Inquiry into the Personal Values and Social Imperatives of the Eighteenth-Century Virginia Gentry* (Charlottesville, 1965); Louis Morton, *Robert Carter of Nomini Hall: A Virginia Tobacco Planter of the Eighteenth Century* (Williamsburg, 1941); Louis B. Wright, *Letters of Robert Carter, 1720–1727: The Commercial Interests of a Virginia Gentleman* (San Marino, Calif., 1940).

11. Alice Hanson Jones, *Wealth of a Nation to Be: The American Colonies on the Eve of the Revolution* (New York, 1980), 54–59, 301–3.

12. Carville V. Earle, *The Evolution of a Tidewater Settlement System: All Hallow's Parish, Maryland, 1650–1783* (Chicago, 1975), 131–32; Paul G. E. Clemens, *The Atlantic Economy and Colonial Maryland's Eastern Shore: From Tobacco to Grain* (Ithaca, N.Y., 1980).

13. Gregory A. Stiverson, *Poverty in a Land of Plenty: Tenancy in Eighteenth-Century Maryland* (Baltimore, 1977), ix, 102–3, 137–39.

14. Ibid., 139–42. Tenant farming problems are also discussed in Earle, *Tidewater Settlement System*, 12–13, 225–26; and Edward C. Papenfuse, Jr., "Planter Behavior and Economic Opportunity in a Staple Economy," *Agricultural History* 46 (1972): 297–311.

15. Richard R. Beeman, "Social Change and Cultural Conflict in Virginia: Lunenburg County, 1746 to 1774," *William and Mary Quarterly*, 3d ser., 35 (1978): 455–76.

16. McCusker and Menard, "Economy of British America," 77–79.

17. Woodville K. Marshall, "Review of Historical Writing on the Commonwealth Caribbean since c. 1940," *Social and Economic Studies* 24 (1975): 271–307.

18. Jack P. Greene, "Society and Economy in the British Caribbean during the Seventeenth and Eighteenth Centuries," *American Historical Review* 79 (1974): 1499–1517; see also William A. Green, "Caribbean Historiography, 1600–1900: The Recent Tide," *Journal of Interdisciplinary History* 7 (1977): 509–30.

19. Carl Bridenbaugh and Roberta Bridenbaugh, *No Peace beyond the Line: The English in the Caribbean, 1624–1690* (New York, 1972); Richard S. Dunn, *Sugar and Slaves: The Rise of the Planter Class in the English West Indies, 1624–1713* (Chapel Hill, 1972).

20. Richard B. Sheridan, *Sugar and Slavery: An Economic History of the British West Indies, 1623–1775* (Baltimore, 1974).

21. Michael Craton and James Walvin, *A Jamican Plantation: The History of Worthy Park, 1670–1970* (Toronto, 1970).

22. Jerome S. Handler, Frederick W. Lange, and Robert B. Riordan, *Plantation Slavery in Barbados: An Archaeological and Historical Investigation* (Cambridge, Mass., 1978).

23. Arthur Young, *Annals of Agriculture*, vol. 1 (London, 1784), 13; McCusker and Menard, "Economy of British America," table 4.2 (p. 41); Adam Smith, *An Inquiry into the Nature and Causes of the Wealth of Nations* (New York, 1937), 158; George L. Beckford, *Persistent Poverty: Underdevelopment in Plantation Economies of the Third World* (New York, 1972).

24. Elsa V. Goveia, *Slave Society in the British Leeward Islands at the End of the Eighteenth Century* (New Haven, 1965); Edward Brathwaite, *The Development of Creole Society in Jamaica, 1770–1820* (Oxford, 1971); Barry W. Higman, *Slave Population and Economy in Jamaica, 1807–1834* (Cambridge, 1976); William A. Green, *British Slave Emancipation: The Sugar Colonies and the Great Experiment, 1830–1865* (Oxford, 1976); Seymour Drescher, *Econocide: British Slavery in the Era of Abolition* (Pittsburgh, 1977); Michael Craton, *Searching for the Invisible Man: Slaves and Plantation Life in Jamaica* (Cambridge, Mass., 1978).

25. Franklin W. Knight, *The Caribbean: The Genesis of a Fragmented Nationalism* (New York, 1978), 51–65.

26. Ibid., 56–57.

27. Dunn, *Sugar and Slaves*, xiii.

28. Bridenbaugh and Bridenbaugh, *No Peace beyond the Line*, 41–45, 98, 271–76; Craton and

Walvin, *A Jamaican Plantation*, 37–41; F. C. Innes, "The Pre-Sugar Era of European Settlement in Barbados," *Journal of Caribbean History* 1 (November 1970): 1–22.

29. Sheridan, *Sugar and Slavery*, 119–21, 128; Dunn, *Sugar and Slaves*, 19–20, 46–47, 59, 67, 272; Bridenbaugh and Bridenbaugh, *No Peace beyond the Line*, 280.

30. Dunn, *Sugar and Slaves*, 67–97; Bridenbaugh and Bridenbaugh, *No Peace beyond the Line*, 94, 99, 267.

31. John H. Parry, "Plantation and Provision Ground: An Historical Sketch of the Introduction of Food Crops into Jamaica," *Revista de historia de America* (Mexico) 39 (1955): 1–20; Sidney W. Mintz and Douglas Hall, "The Origins of the Jamaican Internal Marketing System," *Yale University Publications in Anthropology*, no. 57 (1960): 1–26; Sidney W. Mintz, "Currency Problems in Eighteenth Century Jamaica and Gresham's Law," in *Process and Pattern in Culture*, ed. Robert A. Manners (Chicago, 1964), 248–65. For currency problems in the West Indies see also John J. McCusker, *Money and Exchange in Europe and America, 1600–1775: A Handbook* (Chapel Hill, 1978), 234–74; and idem, "The Rum Trade and the Balance of Payments of the Thirteen Continental Colonies, 1650–1775" (Ph.D. diss., University of Pittsburgh, 1970).

32. Orlando Patterson, *The Sociology of Slavery: An Analysis of the Origins, Development and Structure of Negro Slave Society in Jamaica* (London, 1967), 216–30.

33. Richard B. Sheridan, "Labor, Diet and Punishment," in *Doctors and Slaves: A Medical and Demographic History of Slavery in the British West Indies, 1680–1834* (forthcoming); see also Roderick A. McDonald, " 'Goods and Chattels': The Economy of Slaves on Sugar Plantations in Jamaica and Louisiana" (Ph.D. diss., University of Kansas, 1981), 47–110.

34. Jerome S. Handler, *The Unappropriated People: Freedmen in the Slave Society of Barbados* (Baltimore, 1974); Richard B. Sheridan, "The Rise of a Colonial Gentry: A Case Study of Antigua, 1730–1775," *Economic History Review*, 2d ser., 13 (April 1961): 342–57.

35. Douglas Hall, "Absentee-Proprietorship in the British West Indies, to about 1850," *Jamaican Historical Review* 4 (1964): 15–35.

36. Converse D. Clowse, *Economic Beginnings in Colonial South Carolina, 1670–1730* (Columbia, S.C., 1971).

37. Peter H. Wood, *Black Majority: Negroes in Colonial South Carolina from 1670 through the Stono Rebellion* (New York, 1974); Daniel C. Littlefield, *Rice and Slaves: Ethnicity and the Slave Trade in Colonial South Carolina* (Baton Rouge, 1981), xi, 176–77.

38. David L. Coon, "Eliza Lucas Pinckney and the Reintroduction of Indigo Culture in South Carolina," *Journal of Southern History* 42 (1976): 61–76; C. Robert Haywood, "Mercantilism and South Carolina Agriculture, 1700–1763," *South Carolina Historical Magazine* 60 (1959): 15–27.

39. Jones, *Wealth of a Nation to Be*, 118–20, 356, 358, 420. In her inventories for the Charleston District, Jones shows that 32 planters owned in the aggregate 1,590 slaves. Holdings ranged from 5 to 245 slaves. The mean is 48, and the median 21 (idem, *American Colonial Wealth: Documents and Methods*, 3 vols. [New York, 1977], 3: 1473–1619).

40. Milton LaVerne Ready, "An Economic History of Colonial Georgia, 1732–1754" (Ph.D. diss., University of Georgia, 1970); Betty Christina Wood, " 'The One Thing Needful': The Slavery Debate in Georgia, 1732–1750" (Ph.D. diss., University of Pennsylvania, 1975); David Rogers Chestnutt, "South Carolina's Expansion into Colonial Georgia, 1720–1765" (Ph.D. diss., University of Georgia, 1973).

41. Harry Roy Merrens, *Colonial North Carolina in the Eighteenth Century: A Study in Historical Geography* (Chapel Hill, 1964), 179.

42. Littlefield, *Rice and Slaves*, 1–2; McCusker and Menard, "Economy of British America," 110–18 and n. 30.

43. Clarence L. Ver Steeg, "Historians of the Southern Colonies," in *The Reinterpretation of Early American History: Essays in Honor of John Edwin Pomfret*, ed. Ray Allen Billington (San Marino, Calif., 1966), 81–84.

44. Verner W. Crane, *The Southern Frontier, 1670–1732* (Durham, N.C., 1929); W. Stitt Robinson, *The Southern Colonial Frontier, 1607–1763* (Albuquerque, 1979).

45. Lewis Cecil Gray, *History of Agriculture in the Southern United States to 1860*, 2 vols. (Wash-

ington, D.C., 1933), 1: 438–43; Carville V. Earle and Ronald Hoffman, "The Urban South: The First Two Centuries," in *The City in Southern History: The Growth of Urban Civilization in the South,* ed. Blaine A. Brownell and David R. Goldfield (Port Washington, N.Y., 1977), 23–51; idem, "Urban Development in the Eighteenth-Century South," *Perspectives in American History* 10 (1976): 7–78.

46. William B. Weeden, *Economic and Social History of New England, 1620–1789,* 2 vols. (Boston, 1890); Percy Wells Bidwell and John I. Falconer, *History of Agriculture in the Northern United States, 1620–1860* (Washington, D.C., 1925); Rollo M. Tryon, *Household Manufactures in the United States, 1640–1860* (Chicago, 1917); Robert G. Albion, *Forests and Sea Power: The Timber Problem of the Royal Navy* (Cambridge, Mass., 1926); Joseph J. Malone, *Pine Trees and Politics: The Naval Stores and Forest Policy in Colonial New England, 1691–1775* (London, 1964).

47. Bruce C. Daniels, "Economic Development in Colonial and Revolutionary Connecticut: An Overview," *William and Mary Quarterly,* 3d ser., 37 (1980): 429–50; James F. Shepherd and Gary M. Walton, *Shipping, Maritime Trade, and the Economic Development of Colonial North America* (Cambridge, 1972); idem, *The Economic Rise of Early America* (Cambridge, 1979).

48. Darrett B. Rutman, "Governor Winthrop's Garden Crop: The Significance of Agriculture in the Early Commerce of Massachusetts Bay," *William and Mary Quarterly,* 3d ser., 20 (1963): 396–415; Bernard Bailyn, *The New England Merchants in the Seventeenth Century* (New York, 1955), 82–111; Howard S. Russell, *A Long, Deep Furrow: Three Centuries of Farming in New England* (Hanover, N.H., 1976), 112–75, 206–7.

49. Kenneth A. Lockridge, "Land, Population and the Evolution of New England Society, 1630–1790: And an Afterthought," in *Colonial America: Essays in Politics and Social Development,* ed. Stanley N. Katz (Boston, 1971), 466–91.

50. Ibid., 482–83.

51. Darrett B. Rutman, "People in Process: The New Hampshire Towns of the Eighteenth Century," *Journal of Urban History* 1 (1975): 268–91.

52. Daniels, "Economic Development in Colonial and Revolutionary Connecticut," 429–50.

53. Terry L. Anderson, "Economic Growth in Colonial New England: 'Statistical Renaissance,' " *Journal of Economic History* 39 (1979): 243–57; Jones, *Wealth of a Nation to Be,* 54, 129, 161–69, 183.

54. McCusker and Menard, "Economy of British America," 62–63.

55. These two approaches have been combined in an excellent manner by Robert A. Gross in *The Minutemen and Their World* (New York, 1976).

56. Frederick Jackson Turner, *The Significance of the Frontier in American History,* edited, with an introduction, by Harold P. Simonson (New York, 1976), 44, 48–49; Douglas Greenberg, "The Middle Colonies in Recent American Historiography," *William and Mary Quarterly,* 3d ser., 36 (1979): 396–98.

57. Thomas Elliot Norton, *The Fur Trade in Colonial New York, 1686–1776* (Madison, Wis., 1974); Sung Bok Kim, *Landlord and Tenant in Colonial New York: Manorial Society, 1664–1775* (Chapel Hill, 1978). See also Douglas Edward Leach, *The Northern Colonial Frontier, 1607–1763* (New York, 1966).

58. Michael Kammen, *Colonial New York: A History* (New York, 1975), 161–90.

59. William Pollard to Benjamin and John Bower, April 6, 1773, *Pollard Letterbook,* Historical Society of Pennsylvania, quoted in Marc Egnal, "The Economic Development of the Thirteen Continental Colonies, 1720 to 1775," *William and Mary Quarterly,* 3d ser., 32 (1975): 219.

60. Victor S. Clark, *History of Manufactures in the United States: Volume I, 1607–1860* (Washington, D.C., 1929), 185–86.

61. James T. Lemon and Gary B. Nash, "The Distribution of Wealth in Eighteenth-Century America: A Century of Change in Chester County, Pennsylvania, 1693–1802," *Journal of Social History* 2 (1968): 1–24; James T. Lemon, *The Best Poor Man's Country: A Geographical Study of Early Southeastern Pennsylvania* (Baltimore, 1972), 8–13; Duane E. Ball, "Dynamics of Population and Wealth in Eighteenth-Century Chester County, Pennsylvania," *Journal of Interdisciplinary History*

6 (1976): 621–44; Jackson Turner Main, *The Social Structure of Revolutionary America* (Princeton, 1965), 180–83; Jones, *Wealth of a Nation to Be*, 185, 217, 272.

62. Lemon and Nash, "Distribution of Wealth," 10–15; Main, *Social Structure of Revolutionary America*, 180–83; Duane E. Ball and Gary M. Walton, "Agricultural Productivity Change in Eighteenth-Century Pennsylvania," *Journal of Economic History* 36 (1976): 102–17; James A. Henretta, *The Evolution of American Society, 1700–1815: An Interdisciplinary Analysis* (Lexington, Mass., 1973), 72–74, 103–5, 120–21; Ramon S. Powers, "Wealth and Poverty: Economic Base, Social Structure, and Attitudes in Prerevolutionary Pennsylvania, New Jersey and Delaware" (Ph.D. diss., University of Kansas, 1971), 165–70.

63. Norton, *Fur Trade in Colonial New York*; Greenberg, "Middle Colonies," 404; Stephen Earl Sale, "Colonial Albany: Outpost of Empire" (Ph.D. diss., University of Southern California, 1973); Oliver Albert Rink, "Merchants and Magnates: Dutch New York, 1609–1664" (Ph.D. diss., University of Southern California, 1976); David Arthur Armour, "The Merchants of Albany, New York: 1686–1760" (Ph.D. diss., Northwestern University, 1965); Stephen Hosmer Cutcliffe, "Indians, Furs, and Empires: The Changing Policies of New York and Pennsylvania, 1674–1768" (Ph.D. diss., Lehigh University, 1976).

64. See Thomas J. Archdeacon, review of *Landlord and Tenant in Colonial New York*, by Sung Bok Kim, *William and Mary Quarterly*, 3d ser., 36 (1979): 622–24; and Greenberg, "Middle Colonies," 404–5.

65. Greenberg, "Middle Colonies," 407; Lemon, *Best Poor Man's Country*; Stephanie Grauman Wolf, *Urban Village: Population, Community, and Family Structure in Germantown, Pennsylvania, 1683–1800* (Princeton, 1976); Thomas J. Archdeacon, *New York City, 1664–1710: Conquest and Change* (Ithaca, N.Y., 1976).

66. Ball and Walton, "Agricultural Productivity Change," 116–17.

67. Main, *Social Structure of Revolutionary America*, 7–43.

68. Jack M. Sosin, *The Revolutionary Frontier, 1763–1783* (New York, 1967); George William Franz, "Paxton: A Study of Community Structure and Mobility in the Colonial Pennsylvania Backcountry" (Ph.D. diss., Rutgers University, 1974); Russell Sage Nelson, Jr., "Backcountry Pennsylvania (1709 to 1774): The Ideals of William Penn in Practice" (Ph.D. diss., University of Wisconsin, 1968).

69. Joseph E. Walker, *Hopewell Village: A Social and Economic History of an Iron-Making Community* (Philadelphia, 1966); James M. Ranson, *Vanishing Ironworks on the Ramapos: The Story of the Forges, Furnaces, and Mines of the New Jersey–New York Border Area* (New Brunswick, N.J., 1966).

70. Lois Green Carr and Lorena S. Walsh, "The Planter's Wife: The Experience of White Women in Seventeenth-Century Maryland," *William and Mary Quarterly*, 3d ser., 34 (1977): 542–71.

71. Coon, "Eliza Lucas Pinckney," 65–68; Julia Cherry Spruill, *Women's Life and Work in the Southern Colonies* (New York, 1938), 74–84, 305–11; Alan D. Watson, "Women in Colonial North Carolina: Overlooked and Underestimated," *North Carolina Historical Review* 58 (1981): 1–23; *The Letterbook of Eliza Lucas Pinckney*, ed. Elise Pinckney (Chapel Hill, 1972).

72. Lucille Mathurin Mair, "A Historical Study of Women in Jamaica from 1655 to 1844" (Ph.D. diss., University of the West Indies, 1974), 1–5, 21, 53–57, 100–103, 127–37, 225–57, 287–311.

73. Mary Beth Norton, *Liberty's Daughters: The Revolutionary Experience of American Women, 1750–1800* (Boston, 1980), 138; Carol Ruth Berkin and Mary Beth Norton, eds., *Women of America: A History* (Boston, 1979), 37–138.

74. Laurel Thatcher Ulrich, "'A Friendly Neighbor': Social Dimensions of Daily Work in Northern Colonial New England," *Feminist Studies* 6 (1980): 392–405.

75. Carole Shammas, "The Myth of Early American Self-Sufficiency" (Paper, Department of History, University of Wisconsin–Milwaukee, Milwaukee, Wis.). I am indebted to Dr. Shammas for sending me a copy of her paper.

76. Nancy F. Cott, *The Bonds of Womanhood: "Woman's Sphere" in New England, 1780–1835*

(New Haven, 1977), 24–36; Norton, *Liberty's Daughters*, 10–12; Bidwell and Falconer, *History of Northern Agriculture*, 138.

77. Shepherd and Walton, *Shipping, Maritime Trade, and Economic Development*, 47. The estimate for the British West Indies is my own.

78. Clemens, *From Tobacco to Grain*, 168–205; David C. Klingaman, "The Significance of Grain in the Development of the Tobacco Colonies," *Journal of Economic History* 29 (1969): 268–78; McCusker and Menard, "Economy of British America," 82; Ronald Hoffman, *A Spirit of Dissension: Economics, Politics, and the Revolution in Maryland* (Baltimore, 1973), 69–91; Stiverson, *Poverty in a Land of Plenty*, 85–103.

79. Lemon, *Best Poor Man's Country*, 218–28.

80. Gregory A. Stiverson, "Early American Farming: A Comment," *Agricultural History* 50 (1976): 37–44.

81. Daniel Scott Smith, "A Malthusian-Frontier Interpretation of United States Demographic History before 1815," in *Urbanization in the Americas: The Background in Comparative Perspective*, ed. Woodrow Borah, Jorge Hardoy, and Gilbert H. Stelter (Ottawa, 1980). I am indebted to Dr. Smith for sending me a typescript copy of his paper.

82. James A. Henretta, "Families and Farms: *Mentalité* in Pre-Industrial America," *William and Mary Quarterly*, 3d ser., 35 (1978): 3–32; and James T. Lemon, "Comment on James A. Henretta's 'Families and Farms: *Mentalité* in Pre-Industrial America,'" with a reply by Henretta, ibid. 37 (1980): 688–700. See also Perkins, *Economy of Colonial America*, 41–66.

83. Smith, *Wealth of Nations*, 575. Quoted in Clark, *History of Manufactures, Volume I*.

84. Clark, *History of Manufactures, Volume I*, 100, 164.

85. Max George Schumacher, *The Northern Farmer and His Markets during the Colonial Period* (New York, 1975), 73–75, 78, 145–47.

86. Simeon John Crowther, "The Shipbuilding Industry and the Economic Development of the Delaware Valley, 1681–1776" (Ph.D. diss., University of Pennsylvania, 1970); Paul F. Paskoff, "Colonial Merchant-Manufacturers and Iron: A Study in Capital Transformation, 1725–1775," *Journal of Economic History* 37 (1977): 261–63.

87. Curtis P. Nettels, "British Mercantilism and the Economic Development of the Thirteen Colonies," *Journal of Economic History* 12 (1952): 105–14; McCusker and Menard, "Economy of British America," 211–17.

88. Richard B. Morris, *Government and Labor in Early America* (New York, 1946), vii–viii, 6–10, 20–21, 55, 84–91; Gary B. Nash, *The Urban Crucible: Social Change, Political Consciousness, and the Origins of the American Revolution* (Cambridge, Mass., 1979), 32, 129–36, 188; Mary McKinney Schweitzer, "Economic Regulation and the Colonial Economy: The Maryland Tobacco Inspection Act of 1747," *Journal of Economic History* 40 (1980): 551–69.

89. Daniels, "Economic Development in Colonial and Revolutionary Connecticut," 443–44; Richard L. Bushman, *From Puritan to Yankee: Character and the Social Order in Connecticut, 1690–1765* (Cambridge, Mass., 1967), 61–64, 114; Isabel S. Mitchell, *Roads and Road-Making in Colonial Connecticut* (New Haven, 1933), 1–32.

90. Earle, *Tidewater Settlement System*, 142–57; Clarence P. Gould, *Money and Transportation in Maryland, 1720–1765* (Baltimore, 1915), 122–70.

91. Carl Bridenbaugh, *Cities in the Wilderness: The First Century of Urban Life in America, 1625–1742* (New York, 1938), 334–35, 349–50, 356; Lemon, *Best Poor Man's Country*, 114–15; John Flexer Walzer, "Transportation in the Philadelphia Trading Area, 1740–1775" (Ph.D. diss., University of Wisconsin, 1968).

92. Robert D. Mitchell, *Commercialism and Frontier: Perspectives on the Early Shenandoah Valley* (Charlottesville, 1977), xi, 149–90; Merrens, *Colonial North Carolina*, 143–45, 162–76; Carville V. Earle and Ronald Hoffman, "Staple Crops and Urban Development in the Eighteenth-Century South," *Perspectives in American History* 10 (1976): 51, 56–57, 65–66; Edward G. Roberts, "The Roads of Virginia, 1607–1840" (Ph.D. diss., University of Virginia, 1950).

93. McCusker, *Money and Exchange;* Jacob M. Price, *Capital and Credit in British Overseas Trade: The View from the Chesapeake, 1700–1776* (Cambridge, Mass., 1980).

94. Leslie V. Brock's published 1941 dissertation, *The Currency of the American Colonies, 1700–1764* (New York, 1975), 17; E. James Ferguson, "Currency Finance: An Interpretation of the Colonial Monetary Practices," *William and Mary Quarterly,* 3d ser., 10 (1953): 153–80; Joseph Albert Ernst, *Money and Politics in America, 1755–1775: A Study in the Currency Act of 1764 and the Political Economy of Revolution* (Chapel Hill, 1973), 6–10, 16–17; Robert Craig West, "Money in the Colonial American Economy," *Economic Inquiry* 16 (1978): 5.

95. Ernst, *Money and Politics,* 6–8; Perkins, *Economy of Colonial America,* 101–22; West, "Money in the Colonial American Economy," 12–14.

96. W. T. Baxter, *The House of Hancock: Business in Boston, 1724–1775* (Cambridge, Mass., 1945), 17–26; Stuart Bruchey, review of *Money and Politics,* by Ernst, *William and Mary Quarterly,* 3d ser., 31 (1974): 673–75; Ernst, *Money and Politics,* viii, 20–21; West, "Money in the Colonial American Economy," 7–8, 10–14.

97. Horace Bushnell, "The Age of Homespun," in *Work and Play: or Literary Varieties* (New York, 1864), 392.

98. Percy Wells Bidwell, "Rural Economy in New England at the Beginning of the Nineteenth Century," *Transactions of the Connecticut Academy of Arts and Sciences* 20 (1916): 267–68, 352–54.

99. Egnal, "Economic Development of the Thirteen Continental Colonies," 219–22.

100. Lemon, *Best Poor Man's Country,* 114–15, 125–26, 134–39; Jacob M. Price, "The Rise of Glasgow in the Chesapeake Tobacco Trade, 1707–1775," *William and Mary Quarterly,* 3d ser., 11 (1954): 179–99; Perkins, *Economy of Colonial America,* 85.

101. Schumacher, *Northern Farmer and His Markets,* 146–47; Stuart Bruchey, *The Roots of American Economic Growth, 1607–1861: An Essay in Social Causation* (New York, 1965), 27–28.

102. Thomas R. Wessel, "Agriculture, Indians, and American History," *Agricultural History* 50 (1976): 9–19; Francis Jennings, *The Invasion of America: Indians, Colonialism, and the Cant of Conquest* (Chapel Hill, 1975).

103. Wilbur R. Jacobs, "The Indian and the Frontier in American History—A Need for Revision," *Western Historical Quarterly* 4 (1973): 43–56.

104. Stanley L. Engerman, "Some Economic and Demographic Comparisons of Slavery in the United States and the British West Indies," *Economic History Review,* 2d ser., 29 (1976): 258–75; Robert W. Fogel, *Without Consent or Contract: The Rise and Fall of American Slavery* (forthcoming); Dunn, *Sugar and Slaves,* 46–116; idem, "The English Sugar Islands and the Founding of South Carolina," *South Carolina Historical Magazine* 72 (1971): 81–93; Wood, *Black Majority,* 3–34; Dunn, "A Tale of Two Plantations: Slave Life at Mesopotamia in Jamaica and Mount Airy in Virginia, 1799 to 1828," *William and Mary Quarterly,* 3d ser., 34 (1977): 32–65; David W. Galenson, *White Servitude in Colonial America: An Economic Analysis* (Cambridge, 1981); idem, "White Servitude and the Growth of Black Slavery in Colonial America," *Journal of Economic History* 41 (1981): 39–47.

105. Egnal, "Economic Development of the Thirteen Continental Colonies," 219–21.

106. Richard H. Shryock, "British versus German Traditions in Colonial Agriculture," *Mississippi Valley Historical Review* 26 (1939): 39–54; John G. Gagliardo, "Germans and Agriculture in Colonial Pennsylvania," *Pennsylvania Magazine of History and Biography* 83 (1959): 192–218.

107. F. J. Fisher, "The Sixteenth and Seventeenth Centuries: The Dark Ages in English Economic History?" *Economica,* n.s., 24 (1957): 2–18.

108. David Landes, "On Avoiding Babel," *Journal of Economic History* 38 (1978): 3–12.

109. Jacob M. Price, "Quantifying Colonial America: A Comment on Nash and Warden," *Journal of Interdisciplinary History* 6 (1976): 701–9. See also Gloria L. Main, "Probate Records as a Source for Early American History," *William and Mary Quarterly,* 3d ser., 32 (1975): 89–99.

110. J. R. Pole, *Paths to the American Past* (New York, 1979), xvii, xxi.

4

SPATIAL ORDER: HOUSEHOLDS IN LOCAL COMMUNITIES AND REGIONS

JAMES T. LEMON

EARLY AMERICAN REGIONS

y the mid-eighteenth century America's rural population had spread over an area far greater than that of England. Over much of the seaboard the original, discrete settlements had expanded to merge with one another, while new ventures presaged post-Revolution occupation of Indian lands beyond the Appalachians. The American landscape carried the marks of the dispersed society, one that was organized extensively more than intensively.

But America was still a part of England and of Europe; in fact, from one perspective it was England and Europe on the move. Americans of European origin and descent organized themselves into households, local communities, and regional structures. At the household level, most lived much of their lives within nuclear families on dispersed farms largely held in freehold tenure. These farms were contained within open-country localities organized into parishes, townships, or towns that in turn were enclosed within counties and then connected through courts, religious organizations, and trade to broad regional hinterlands that often crossed provincial boundaries. Ultimately, farmers were linked through political, religious, and economic institutions and social and cultural ties to England and to the larger Atlantic world. Some were participants in alternative world images shaped by the Bible, religious tradition, and deep cultural folkways. Notwithstanding their extensive scattering over the American landscape, colonial peoples could locate themselves within this complex set of institutional and cultural relationships. Then as now, all experience was mediated by forms and rules—

hidden and explicit. Extensive colonial American society was rooted in and continued to be bound to a more intensive England. Even as patterns of action diverged, variations were defined in English terms.

Interpretations of local communities and regions in early America must, then, take into account both New World conditions and Old World antecedents. Turnerian terms like "frontier," "free land," and "rural" have acquired emotive connotations that have come to imply an environmental determinism: American character and institutions developed out of the settlers' encounters with the open American landscape. Turner's egalitarian frontier was at most a fleeting condition, however: communities rapidly showed signs of becoming more "European" as they developed significant contrasts of wealth and power, dense settlement, intensive economic and social activity, and urbanization.[1] To achieve a more balanced interpretation requires recognition of the continuing force of the conditions the settlers left behind as well as of those they encountered. America was new. Yet it was also Europe, particularly England, expanding.

Of central importance in approaching early America, and not least from a spatial perspective, is the issue of property relations. Land was not literally free. While cheaper than in England, it was first of all collectively owned by the Indians. Then, vast chunks were appropriated by companies, proprietors, and speculators, who organized the land. Into this template of property divided into fee-simple plots of varying sizes came the settlers. Variations on the theme of fee simple were minor and temporary. As developed in England over centuries prior to 1600, fee-simple ownership of real property denoted the nearly absolute right of the owner to, and the exclusion of all others from, the use of that piece of property, as defined by deed and physically marked by blazes, walls, or fences. The almost universal adoption of fee simple in America paralleled and grew out of the drive towards enclosure in England. What was a long-term process in England, however, was in America an almost instantaneous and repeatable event as the settlers occupied the land. Englishmen were well prepared to carve up communally held Indians lands. Indeed, the passion for fee-simple ownership proved a powerful stimulus to expansion.

Equally fundamental was the Englishman's need for reciprocal relationships within the locality, among neighbors, and at the "higher" scales of the county and region. Households rubbed up against one another. They shared boundary lines and often built mutual fences. Even their disputes over property lines tied them to one another. More positively, they all joined to contribute taxes and manpower to build and maintain the roads, bridges, churches, and courthouses that linked them to each other and to the larger world. Similarly, reciprocal neighboring at such social gatherings as bees, dances, and games pulled people together, while those affluent people with strong outside connections were linked to people of lesser means through trading and credit relations. Finally, congregations meeting in a sacred place "elevated" people above their worldly struggles while reminding them of their moral duties.

In the frontier model, community formation in America has been seen largely as a result of a voluntary coming together of free individuals on free land, in contrast with that in Europe, where it was marked by deeply entrenched customary obligations. Certainly, it is necessary to recognize this element of voluntarism and cooperation. Yet the problem of status, and the obligations it imposed, did not disappear in the Atlantic crossing or in the setting up of new places inland. Indeed, status could be more difficult to identify for people in the more apparently open, individualistic social climate of America than where distinctions between plebians and patricians were more conspicuous and more settled. Paradoxically, as Alexis de Tocqueville later noted, status in America quickly came to depend upon everyone's conforming, particularly pursuing the ownership of land in fee simple. To ensure that one's children retained their status, parents sought to accumulate more and more land. This pressure on the land meant that within any given area space soon became rather more finite than free. In all localities, independent households soon became locked into community structures reflecting this social pressure.

Even though local communities up and down the seaboard tended to share these characteristics, variations occurred from region to region and within regions. In this discussion many of these differences will be noted. But we will also deal with regional and the intermediate county-level organization, remembering that political, economic, and social connections and their areal patterns did not always coincide. Still, these "higher"-order activities did tend to come together in urban places. We can, therefore, use the notion of the urban system as a key to unlock the organization of regions. As in the case of local communities, interpretations of the urban system remain problematic in some areas.

In developing an areal framework for discussing local and regional organization, it is first necessary to point out briefly the difficulties in marking out various regions. Unlike the Caribbean with its discrete islands, the mainland was continuous. As a result, the creation of colonies resulted in controversial overlaps and border disputes. This fact complicates attempts at definition. Nevertheless, regions can be defined according to differing scales. First and foremost, there was the large-scale distinction noted by Andrew Burnaby and many others between North and South, a distinction based on climate and especially slavery.[2] This distinction, especially as it related to slavery, would become even more obvious during the nineteenth century.

A second common way to break up the seaboard is to divide the South into Upper and Lower, and the North into Middle and New England colonies. This finer-grained view has the advantage of distinguishing the tobacco colonies of the Chesapeake, often considered by geographers as a "hearth" for subsequent development, from the newer rice/indigo-growing area extending out from Charleston in South Carolina (and indirectly from its source island, Barbados). In the North, the mixed farming and seafaring colonies of New England, also notable as a hearth, are distinguished from the newer grain-exporting or Middle Colonies to the south.[3]

Of course, these distinctions are not without problems. If tidewater South Carolina was the focus of the Lower South, Georgia (despite the original intentions of the founders) became an appendage, as did the adjacent parts of southeastern North Carolina. But other parts of North Carolina were pulled economically towards other regions, the northeast towards the Chesapeake and the Piedmont, like the Shenandoah Valley of Virginia, in part towards the Middle Colonies. By moving to wheat, even the tidewater Chesapeake itself was shifting to the "middle" by the 1740s and 1750s.

In the North similar problems arise. Far from being a single homogeneous region, the Middle Colonies seem to fall into two still largely discrete regions, one focusing upon Philadelphia, the other upon New York, with western New Jersey looking towards the former and eastern New Jersey towards the latter. Though economic and social patterns were similar, the lower-middle region, surrounding Philadelphia, was much more quickly and densely settled than the upper-middle, stretching out from New York, at least some of which (on Long Island and in eastern New Jersey) was settled from New England. Within New England itself, there were marked intraregional variations, the coastal settlements showing a strong orientation to the sea, and western Connecticut and Massachusetts being increasingly pulled into the economic orbit of New York port.

It should be obvious from this discussion that economic, social, and, even more comprehensively, cultural regions did not coincide with political boundaries. Indeed, that sociocultural regions extend across political lines has long been recognized; for centuries, Englishmen have been aware of the Midlands, the Home Counties, lowland Scotland, and so on. Not surprisingly, in a generalized sense, colonists also were aware of similarities stretching beyond their own provinces, though perhaps somewhat less than modern-day scholars, who follow customary distinctions but also search for commonalities that transcend political designations.

In any overview from a geographical vantage point, political, economic, social, and cultural dimensions must be considered. But in a short essay it is impossible to be comprehensive. As already noted, the central spatial issue is the extensive dispersion of rural populations on both the local and regional levels. The internal workings of families, households, and farms and patterns within urban places will be largely ignored. In social terms, at the local level issues of property and status loom large, while at the regional level the urban system, with its political and economic vectors, will be the chief focus of attention. Throughout, there will be an attempt at an interpretative balancing of culture and environment, of inherited antecedents and the new land, of rural and urban.

SETTLEMENT IN LOCAL COMMUNITIES

The standard pattern of settlement throughout the Anglo-American colonies in the seventeenth and eighteenth centuries was the rural farmstead, occupied by a single household composed of parents, children, and servants and/or slaves. There were some notable exceptions to this pattern.

In the Caribbean, the Chesapeake, and the Lower South, high death rates and an unbalanced sex ratio inhibited the formation of standard nuclear-family households. Throughout much of the seventeenth century high profits from staple agriculture encouraged the formation of what would become, first in the Caribbean in the 1650s and 1660s, then more gradually in the Chesapeake between 1680 and 1720, and finally in the Lower South during the early decades of the eighteenth century, the large-scale, slave-powered plantation settlements, whose internal social structures closely resembled the family-dominated factories of the early industrial revolution. Even in the plantation colonies, however, initial settlements had all followed the standard pattern, and except perhaps in a few of the smaller Caribbean islands, a majority of settlements continued to be small, individual farmsteads, even after the emergence of the plantation system.

But the predominant pattern was one of individual farmsteads, often initially much dispersed but gradually coalescing into apparently loose rural communities and neighborhoods. In most places these individual farmsteads were separated from one another by contiguous fields and were not clustered on small home lots in agricultural villages, surrounded by open fields and common meadows and pastures. This nearly universal pattern presented a sharp contrast with the spatial organization of much of western Europe in early modern times, although the settlement of Anglo-America occurred while England itself was undergoing through the enclosure movement the protracted transformation of its lowland plains from open-field agriculture to the open-country pattern. Today, only one agricultural village survives in England, subsidized to remain so by the central government.[4]

While defense needs, which in many colonies were a sporadic if serious consideration, might have encouraged concentration, four factors seem to have operated in favor of dispersion and enclosure: efficiency, productivity, control, and ownership.[5] The problem of efficiency turned on distance to fields. With strips in open fields a central location for farmsteads made sense. Yet, divisions into strips also meant more aggregate travel than if holdings were consolidated and farmsteads located on them. Because it is possible to recognize efficiency in sharing lots and collective sowing of grain, however, we must look further to explain dispersion and enclosure. Productivity per unit of land is difficult to separate from other factors because it depends on willingness to cooperate. With maximum cooperation, communal organization of production could theoretically yield more than individually worked lands (as, say, in China). The key lies primarily in control over production.

In early modern England the enclosure movement clearly shifted the way farms were run; increasingly, decisions concerning higher productivity and greater efficiency were no longer collective, but individual, at least from the perspective of the household. The most successful seventeenth-century farmers in England were tenants on long leases who had more complete control over decisions on what and how to produce than did large estate holders, and small owner-operators actually declined in numbers and status. In America ownership more clearly coincided with control from the beginning, and experience replicated the tighter household control over production that was only just being achieved by the enclosure movement in England. Yet, although tenancy was not absent in the American experience, ownership was much more common. Perhaps it would not be going too far to say that American settlers were in fact reacting to tenancy (successful in England only for relatively few) and to the long-run deterioration of owner occupancy. The desire for independence from landlord influence and from local constraints appears to have been an important consideration. Put positively, people wanted a strong degree of autonomy over production and of privacy.[6]

The process of enclosure and dispersion did not, however, put an end to community life, though it has often been argued that community bonds were weakened by the erosion of customary rights and the loosening of community structures. Yet, as in all times, people reformulated their community experience and institutions to fit the new conditions. Quite possibly, attachment to locality was even stronger in England on the eve of settlement than it had been earlier, albeit within a more unified nation.[7]

In America settlers organized local communities that persisted. Propinquity always encourages some interaction in rural as well as urban areas, and new localities rapidly were overlain by networks of interaction both within and outside of their own bounds, networks that knit them together and tied them to the outside world. Within communities, local government and church congregations, as well as less formal voluntary organizations and informal neighboring, provided institutional cement. In open-country landscapes these social patterns were often only vaguely defined because church buildings, mills, taverns, and stores were not usually clustered. Nor were community boundaries usually visually marked, though residents knew in which parish or township they lived and paid taxes, were aware of congregational territories, however ill-defined, and were conscious of the accessible points of economic activities.

Pennsylvania was a prototype of such settlement patterns. Tightly organized Quakers, Mennonites, and Amish lived in this open-country pattern, often sharing the community landscape with other religious groups. Networks of relations were combined with and grew out of propinquity. Few communitarian alternative settlements broke this pattern—William Penn's attempts to promote agricultural villages were most remarkable for their almost total failure. Nevertheless, though community may possibly have been formally weaker in these open-country settlements than it would have been in agricultural villages, it was not absent. No society has ever existed without local community action and structures.

If Pennsylvania adheres closely to a standard found in most other Anglo-American communities, seventeenth-century New England (notably Plymouth, Massachusetts, and Connecticut) has often been put forth as the single major exception to this pattern. The argument in this essay is that not even the earliest New England settlements were so sharply different as has been depicted, that the presumed tendency to slip into an open-country landscape during the eighteenth century was present from the beginning. Bruce Daniels's *The Connecticut Town* serves as a springboard for exploring this issue. Although subtly and with qualifications, Daniels, following a long tradition in New England studies, argues that a marked communal impulse in the early settlements had eroded by 1675 into an evident individualism that was reflected in local government, churches, and economic institutions and accelerated still more after 1750. The basic and relevant issue raised by Daniels is "why Connecticut Puritans were so willing to jettison the agricultural village" and disperse.[8]

An even more fundamental question, however, is whether the process of settlement was in fact one of jettisoning the agricultural village. In another recent study, Joseph Wood, a geographer, has found that most initial settlements were dispersed and that there were only about twenty-eight agricultural villages formed in the early decades of New England. Even most of these were "not closely gathered about a meeting house, but stretched out along a broad street." About half of the total were located in the Connecticut River Valley. Wethersfield, the most famous example, and others were laid out in the "French" mode, that is, in long lots like those along the St. Lawrence and the Detroit rivers, with the result that householders lived in close proximity. Elsewhere, there were a few nucleated settlements in southwestern Connecticut, Newtown being the last formed, in 1708. But the remainder of Connecticut settlements were of the dispersed type from the beginning. In Plymouth and Rhode Island dispersal was the norm from the start. In eastern Massachusetts Bay several places were nucleated, some even briefly with open fields, and there was one nucleated settlement in New Hampshire. Analyzing early local records and nineteenth-century histories, Wood further argues that nucleation was the result of late eighteenth- and especially early nineteenth-century urbanization, the "traditional" village greens being converted meetinghouse lots, not erstwhile commons.[9]

Whether a town began as a dispersed settlement such as Watertown, rapidly dispersed such as Cambridge, or more slowly dispersed such as Sudbury, Dedham, and Andover, the process seems to have begun during the first two generations, and not during the eighteenth century, as the conventional view—a twentieth-century invention, Wood argues—has seen it. To clear the way to understanding dispersion in New England, we must first ask briefly why there was variety at the outset. The only clear answer is that of prior practice and experience. Sumner C. Powell and David Grayson Allen have argued forcefully for direct transference from England: Rowley to Rowley represented a conservative agricultural village pattern; Essex and Suffolk to Watertown, a dispersed-enclosed pattern reflecting even capitalist practices; and Sudbury, whose settlers came from diverse regions, had to undergo a fierce political struggle before implementing an initially conservative pattern. Its second-generation offshoot, Marlborough, dispersed.[10] Within a half-century virtually all communities had dispersed.

Many scholars of New England have associated settlement patterns with defense and land quality, but defense was not a problem in early years. Had Indians been more belligerent, perhaps more concentration would have been in evidence. Yet, even in the more exposed Connecticut Valley it was not. Indeed, Windsor inhabitants ignored an early decision to establish a concentrated defensive center. Older generations of scholars of European settlement assigned plains to arable open-field/village agriculture (that is, champion country), and uplands to dispersed pastoralism. But recent studies hardly support this distinction.[11] In the American case, it might be argued that areas like eastern Massachusetts, which had only pockets of arable land separated by rocky hills and meadows, were not conducive to nucleated settlement. Yet, dispersion occurred even on the best level land.

For dispersion, as Daniels points out, distance to fields was a crucial variable; farmers simply did not want to undergo long journeys to scattered plots in open fields. Yet, it is possible to view distance to fields as an instrumental variable that was a direct result neither of tradition nor of land quality but of social and political conditions. The cogency of this view is clearly evident in the process of land distribution. Take conservative Andover, where four distributions of land were required to increase the size of holdings. Original home lots had ranged in size from four to twenty acres, the largest of which was scarcely conducive to day-to-day interaction. By 1662 the smallest holdings comprised about 122 acres and the largest 610 acres. Even though much of this land was being reserved for division among children or for sale and therefore was not cultivated, farmers had probably cleared the best soils, and because the best soils were not concentrated immediately around the village center, farmers found it impossible to live in a village context.[12]

Even the provincial government of Massachusetts had to admit its incapacity to prevent dispersion. In 1635 the General Court tried to impose a residential limit of one-half mile from the meetinghouse, and the ambiguity of this act concerning the number of towns covered forced the magistrates explicitly to extend it to all places in 1637. But in 1639 the General Court exempted five persons, and the next year it had to repeal the whole. The original law obviously had not worked. Similarly, the symmetrical community scheme set forth in an "essay on the ordering of Towns" (ca. 1635)

advocating settlement within a radius of one and one-half or two miles apparently carried no more weight than did William Penn's similar proposal for
Pennsylvania later in the century.[13]

Everyone strove to get out on the land—his own land. Even in New
England the drive for independent ownership, control, and autonomy thus
underlay the organization of space in the Anglo-American spatial process,
though the power of the market should not be underemphasized. Independence, of course, has a fine Crèvcoeurian ring: to be free from constraints, to
provide for one's family, to raise one's status. But these settlers came out of
an English context where population was for the time dense, where landlords, in some areas at least, demanded high rents, where Charles I was
trying to centralize control, where the danger of being proletarianized was
apparent—with the poor a constant reminder of the perils of being reduced to
wage-labor status. Following a dangerous sea crossing and confrontations
with disease, Indians, and the intractable wilderness in the New World,
immigrants sought land—and land over which they had maximum control.
Indeed, in New England the often noted Puritan passion for control probably in many ways enhanced the drive for independence and autonomy that
was so evident throughout Anglo-America.[14]

The market was a second, related early force towards dispersion. As Allen
shows, East Anglians and Hampshiremen, if not east Yorkshiremen, had
already been strongly enmeshed in market relations dealing with land and
commodities before they left Britain. The settlers of the remote Connecticut
Valley above Middletown sought high-quality land for subsistence, as well as
accessibility to the sea—and to markets—via the river. The most prominent
valley settlers, William and John Pynchon, brought in tenants and actively
involved themselves in trade in furs and agricultural goods. Even earlier,
landowners had put tenants on large farms in Rhode Island and encouraged
trade. By 1647 they were breeding horses especially for export. Similarly,
Boston merchants, Ipswich sheepherders, and Marblehead fishermen were
active in provisioning new settlers and finding overseas markets. Even earlier, about 1630, Plymouth farmers had dispersed from the village of Plymouth in search of better lands to raise provisions to feed their new Puritan
neighbors. Cooperative farming had not been efficient enough in Plymouth;
independent household organization would be. Later Puritan settlements
learned the same lesson quickly. John Winthrop and other leaders led the
way into trade and independent action, and the capable followed.[15]

Initially, market opportunities in New England were, however, quite limited. As provision requirements slowed following the decline of immigration
after 1640 a depression underlined the limits of the market. There were just
too many people and not enough opportunities for the market to remain a
constant dominant force in the lives of any but the most vigorous entrepreneurs, even in settlements endowed with good soils and easy access to the
sea. Nevertheless, the process of dispersion did not stop.

Independent action and market involvement did not mean that community structures lost their force. On the contrary, local institutions initially and subsequently sustained and limited households. But they do not appear to have been so thoroughly restrictive as the conventional view of closed settlement patterns would suggest. The increasingly open-country landscape points to something more akin to Pennsylvania. Yet, for most of the seventeenth century and even beyond, local structures seem to have been stronger in New England than in Pennsylvania. In contrast to the situation in Pennsylvania, first of all, towns, not speculators with monopoly rights nor a central land office, distributed lands, and this mode of distribution by proprietors persisted in new towns established in New England throughout the colonial period, even though speculation was by no means absent, as was apparent very early in eastern Connecticut.[16] In all of the colonies to the south orderly settlement became even less common as individuals and groups of settlers went off on their own, even without survey warrants, when land offices did not function well. In the end, of course, fee-simple tenure and trade in land prevailed in both areas.

Second, the spatial and constitutional congruence between town and congregation was more apparent in early New England than anywhere else, with the possible exception of Anglican Virginia, where congregations were slower to take shape. Although New England towns had separate covenants for the secular municipality and the sacred congregation, and membership in the two did not altogether coincide, these two formal institutions fitted more closely. William Penn might have preferred a similar fit, but he failed to persuade his coreligionists, and by inviting people other than Quakers and English, he himself undercut this goal. On the other hand, while the Puritan insistence upon congruity between church and state gave rise to religious and civil schisms and physical secessions, fewer separations occurred in Pennsylvania and other non-Puritan colonies, despite frequent political conflict and squabbles within congregations.[17]

Third, New England communities were more intentionally of the alternative utopian type than were communities even in Pennsylvania, although Quakers, Mennonites, and a few others were moved by some degree of millennialism. Unlike a gemeinschaft-like community into which one is born, the first settlements in Massachusetts were the work of people who were very deliberately promoting a gemeinschaft ideal. Yet, the subsequent colonywide adoption of the halfway covenant points to a decline in the force of this ideal as a corporate goal. Fourth, counties were slower to emerge as powerful intermediate units of government, especially in Connecticut. Finally, common grazing lands may have persisted longer in New England, though no data has been assembled to enable us to know for sure.

Some of the differences between New England and the other colonies may be explained by the time of settlement and are therefore related to conditions in England and America. New England had the first substantial settlements organized by radical Protestants and composed to a large degree of families, with the flow slowing drastically after 1640. Earlier colonies—Roanoke, Jamestown, New France, and Plymouth—had demonstrated the need for careful planning and tight organization. Thirty to forty families composed a rational grouping for town building—small enough for acquaintance, large enough not to be totally embraced in intimacy. But this planning was rooted in local experience in England. The migration itself and the strength of New England localism were in part a rebellion against the centralizing push of Charles I. In Massachusetts itself Puritan settlers resisted central authority, and in the long run the New England colonies probably retained somewhat more residual local secular power in their orderly if not always peaceable little kingdoms than did other Anglo-American colonies, though perhaps not more than did England.[18]

In the limits of local autonomy—from above in regulating public order and from below in dealing with the economy and property—the New England colonies were not very different from the others. From above, the central government restricted local control. In fact, according to David Konig, the General Court did not define town functions until 1636, at the very same meeting at which it first set out the powers of counties, with county courts clearly designed to "supervise local affairs." Towns were thus never "self-contained." By 1643 local quarterly courts had revealed such "inherent town weaknesses" that the General Court sought a remedy in the creation of the Essex county court.[19] As in England, higher-level authority was needed to channel disputes and litigation. Eventually, the center gained greater power, partially through the agency of the county governments. A great exception proved the rule. Failure of central secular and church authorities to halt quickly the Salem witch trials of 1692 underlined the importance of society's control over community.

From below, not only were central powers resisted but the authority of towns were circumscribed by the desires and actions of the inhabitants. At the material level, the town exercised some control. It divided up the land, assigned and policed grazing rights on town commons, chose people to view fences and build and maintain roads, regulated weights and measures, and, briefly during the early years, tried to establish wage and price controls. But it had no explicit control over the major area of material life: it did not specify what and how much individual families should produce or by what methods. The absence of an obvious staple meant, however, that most farmers diversified. "From time out of mind," Englishmen had produced small grains, vegetables, and fruits and had raised cattle, sheep, pigs, chickens, and horses; New Englanders simply followed established English practices in these activities. In this repetition of culture no explicit rules were necessary on what to grow or raise. Individual households regulated production according to their own needs and opportunities. Rationally adding in maize and cucurbits and game fowl and animals, most farmers achieved a good mixture and a dietary balance. Similarly, tools were very largely those used "over home"—sickles, scythes, threshing flails, and so on—while modes of maintaining the quality of seed and livestock breeding were probably customary. In none of those areas was there much need for the community to control individual households.[20]

From the perspective of the market rather than of custom, some towns actually attempted to encourage specialization before 1660, hence local trade and higher productivity. In the industrial sector, they granted incentives in the form of tax abatements, land, and start-up costs to artisans and craftsmen, including brickmakers, blacksmiths, and corn mill operators. What happened in the nineteenth century was already foreshadowed: local municipalities sought to gain essential services for their inhabitants by priming the pump through handouts to private business. In at least one instance the provincial government also stepped in to ensure productivity, enjoining local constables to "require artificers or handicrafts men to labour or work by the day for their neighbours, needing them in mowing, reaping and inning." This law strongly suggests that voluntary cooperation among residents did not always happen automatically. But interaction was achieved as many farmers took up crafts to supplement or even exceed returns from the land. Records of trading were kept in money terms.[21]

Long before Grant's entrepreneurs settled in Kent, Connecticut, in the mid-eighteenth century, New Englanders with a similar bent had sought to increase productivity and profits, especially in places where trading possibilities presented themselves: Springfield, Ipswich, Rhode Island, Plymouth, Wethersfield. Towns did not control individual production. They did not inhibit those able to get into the market. The stress on localism did not mean control over production and trade. Indeed, asked William Pynchon, one of the Bay colony's leaders: "If the magistrates in N.E. should *ex officio* practice such a power over men's properties, how long would Tyranny be kept out of our habitations?" Pynchon was asserting that not only Charles I but the provincial government of Massachusetts should not stand in the way of individual economic action. The economy largely lay beyond government scrutiny, permissively separated from the political and social sphere. Economic democracy as described by Grant meant freedom to produce, to trade, and to accumulate, according to individual family abilities and inclinations.[22]

But the economy could not, of course, be separated from the social sphere. To link the economic and the social dimensions, let us consider the problem of property in land, particularly the size of holdings, including speculative holdings. Holdings were not equal; equality was not a primary consideration in distributing land. New Haven and Portsmouth / Newport, with initial acreage ratios of 100/1 (nearly 1000 acres to 10) and 182/1 (730 to 4), may have been extreme. Yet, in all the early towns a hierarchy based on wealth from England was evident. In New Haven, according to Daniels, most settlers were near the average, and "only nine men received more than 300 acres.". But to turn this observation around, why did nine men receive 300 acres? The answer of course is that the nine brought with them higher status, and this practice of granting more land to the rich than to the poor seems to have rested on an implicit compact, a consensus. The middling and lesser sorts accepted the differences as part of the customary social design. Yet, as in England, those few with the greater determination, skill, and luck could actually emulate their betters and find ways to get rich too. In England, the Reverend Ralph Josselin of Essex provides an interesting example of how one person (with Puritan leanings) could amass land even in a thickly settled area.[23]

Those proprietors at the top clearly held an advantage; they were the great speculators, who must hold our attention. By what *moral* right did Pynchon, William Coddington of Rhode Island, or indeed James Fitch and John Winthrop, Jr., engross great amounts of land? This is not the morality of the Indians, who held land collectively, nor of those few other societies where public constraints impose some degree of equality of possessions. For ordinary people, even in conservative Dedham and other towns where the distribution of wealth was not particularly marked, accumulation through the spatial expansion of the society was seen as a right. If initially in New England settlement had been largely by groups to achieve success in that "howling wilderness," New Englanders were early participants in a grand American custom: individual proprietors created, as it were, rural "land" from the natives, not unlike urban developers in the twentieth century producing urban "land" from the rural so that the middle class can own houses and factories and offices can be built. Use value cannot be separated from exchange value or, even more fundamentally, from social or status value. The consensus that individuals should be as independent as possible in determining how they should settle and what and how much they should produce was accompanied by a further consensus that accumulation would necessarily be differential. The "social" level represented by this twin consensus was and is more fundamental than the strictly economic level. Town structures thus set the framework for economic activities but emphatically did not make any effort to promote what is now called equality of condition. Nor did religion hinder the drive towards individual accumulation of wealth; in fact it may well have morally sustained independent action and market participation among individuals and differential status within society.[24]

But at the same time, the moral basis of the material lives of Puritans was complicated by the difficulty of resolving contradictions of exclusiveness and inclusiveness within their communities. As in English parishes, authorities warned off the poor, the marginal. Beyond that, they faced the sectarian problem of defining the elect. If everyone could confess and be saved, then election would lose its aura. So a quarter of the population was excluded from membership. Besides, material prosperity or the lack of it did not guarantee sainthood, so that objective behavioral measures were not certain.

And, as is often the case in sects, an enthusiastic first generation gave way to a more flaccid second generation: the children of saints did not have to prove that they were also of the elect.[25]

Beyond this, in New England there was a further difficulty. In contrast with other social environments with sectarian groups, Puritan society was nearly monolithic, so that the contradiction between exclusiveness and inclusiveness had to be faced not only in the religious sphere but in the civil sphere as well, not merely in an alternative landscape of a "new heaven and a new earth" but in practical terms, in the actual spatial dimensions of society. Inhabitants of outlying areas, practically excluded by their place of residence, sought separation to form their own inclusive towns and congregations, but they were prevented for long periods by the older communities' reluctance to abandon the goal of inclusiveness for the whole town.[26]

The Salem witchcraft crisis of 1692 represented a particularly dramatic exposure of the tensions these contradictions produced. As a poorer and outlying (but not inaccessible) precinct of the municipality of Salem Town, Salem Village (not an agricultural village) sought separation from the more powerful urban place after having earlier succeeded in creating its own congregation. Frustrated by the town's intransigence, envious of the town's commercial success, and uncertain of who was of the elect, the community turned in destructively on itself. The daughters acted out for the community and for all places in orthodox New England a chilling definition of exclusion within a community. The hysterical displacement of problems onto quintessential outsiders—witches—brought into sharp relief previously latent structural tension in all spheres—economic, political, religious. In the process, this episode also exposed formerly hidden networks within the community and showed that New England communities were complex and irreducible to a one-dimensional "circle of loved, familiar faces, known and fondled objects." The Puritan goals of order and communal affection could not be sustained in the face of such tensions, which would probably have been even more intense had the settlers all lived in tight agricultural villages.[27]

To recapitulate the general argument, dispersal onto contiguous holdings separating households from daily contact involved a rejection neither of aspirations for community nor of formal, local structures. If in 1635 the General Court in Massachusetts was sufficiently alarmed to attempt stricter control of settlement, it had to give up the attempt fairly quickly, even to the point of explicit repeal. With people scattered over large holdings that were later split up into smaller units among sons, New England settlements became like those in the earlier Chesapeake colonies and in later Pennsylvania and Carolina. Thus, New England, like those colonies, was also an extension of English developments such as the enclosure movement. Yet, the situation there was more complicated, in terms of timing and of the tighter mechanisms of control that once established were not so easily modified.

This position is at variance with other perspectives on early New England, perspectives that take as their main themes declension, the importance of visions of alternative community, the dichotomy between traditional and modern, and a populist yet structuralist Marxism. The "declension" view of New England argues that it was composed of a series of mini-Puritan commonwealths, closed and corporate in character and representing an intense localism, whose communal and religious impulses were slowly eroded by increasing population growth, which brought about unanticipated and unfortunate results, including mobility of sons and daughters to new areas or occupations other than farming and poverty. These major changes, this declension, had occurred by 1662 in Andover, by 1686 in Dedham, and by the eighteenth century everywhere, as Puritans became Yankees. After the transformation life was more easygoing; religion, except for periodic renewals, was looser, if not always quieter; town meetings were much less frequent (at least in Connecticut); and people were turning away from spiritual life in quest of individual social and economic objectives.

In contrast to this view, I would argue that the initial founding of towns took a great deal of energy and organizational ingenuity. If there was declension, it occurred soon after the initial outburst of making convenants, dividing lands, building roads, and otherwise establishing order, a process that was more or less repeated with each new town. More basically, however, my contention is that however strong their religious and communal impulses, Puritan settlers were by no means exempt from developments in contemporary England towards a quickening of economic life through increased commercial and industrial activity in many parts of the countryside as well as in towns. England was clearly becoming more intensively commercialized, even entering the early phases of industrialization. To a large extent, it was already capitalist in its orientation. I cannot enter the debate on the transition from feudalism. But despite the strong criticism accorded it, Alan Macfarlane's view that individualism and trade in land and commodities not only were hardly new but may even have been dominant cannot be lightly dismissed. Hence, while Puritans may have been reacting to conditions in England, their reaction did not involve a retreat into feudalism or corporatism, but a protest against what they perceived as mounting social disorder and a rebellion against central control, which seemed likely to inhibit their ability to control their own destinies.[28]

But to explain the movement across the Atlantic exclusively in such reactionary terms is inadequate. Puritan religious zeal may have been reactionary, but many of the leading Puritans were adventurers who shared the accumulative acquisitive instinct abroad in England at the time. If resistance to central authority, the maintenance of localism, and the emphasis upon order and deference were characteristic of Puritan New England, so also was this acquisitive instinct, continually reinforced in New England by spatial expansion, by capital growth, and eventually by technological developments. Like the migration to the other American colonies, the Puritan migration thus represented a point in the long development of a capitalism that is still evolving. Put another way, it is too simple to say that people were forced out of Sudbury or Dedham by population pressure. Those who felt pushed, the marginal ones (at times many people), were the victims of the successful aggrandizement of property by their more fortunate coresidents. The Malthusian interpretation cannot stand on its own. From the beginning, inside the Puritan was the Yankee.[29]

If the declension view of New England needs to be qualified, interpretations that treat the Puritan settlements largely as alternative communities also have serious problems. Thomas Bender's *Community and Social Change in America* is one of the most succinct statements of this position. It describes early New England as a series of tight, exclusive little alternative communities hermetically sealed from the outside world and characterized by face-to-face intimacy. All was comfortable consensus, the local economy was managed, everyone was undifferentiated. That people lived with kin and friends all over the early modern Anglophone world can be seen in the networks of Ralph Josselin and John Cleveland. But these networks extended beyond the bounds of immediate community. Also, there were some at the bottom who were kinless and friendless. Bender cannot easily fit into his scheme the tensions reflected and created by the Salem witch trials and Indian wars, the activities of Boston and Salem merchants, and the adversity suffered by the poor. At most, the New England town was only a halfway alternative community.

Bender does admit a slight modification in the eighteenth century: as the population of towns grew, the circle of nonintimates increased. Yet, according to Bender, it was not until 1870 that all this wonderful quietude of gemeinschaft based on locality was "shattered" by the market, by gesellschaft based on networks. But like the family, community (including networks) and society have always been with us, even if their shapes have changed. Gemeinschaft and gesellschaft are nothing more than ideal analytical constructs that bear little resemblance to historical reality.[30]

Similarly, as E. P. Thompson has contended, the modern/traditional dichotomy must be rejected. As another critic has argued, this paradigm has neither delivered much nor stimulated comparative studies. What is not modern is traditional. A recent attempt to discuss post-Revolution Massachusetts farmers as traditional fails. David Szatmary's benighted rebelling farmers were not traditional, as he argues, but marginal. They wanted paper money, not a "return" to Eden. The "two worlds" of New England accorded more closely with those of the affluent and the poor than with traditional and modern. Like "gemeinschaft" and "gesellschaft," "traditional" and "modern" are much too general to be of use. What is more important, even if only employed as "ideal" types, they seem so easily to become historical and literal, transformed to reified "stages" and thereby tending to serve as obstacles to understanding what persists and what changes.[31]

Finally, the view that a distinctive "independent mode of production" preceded a "capitalist mode of production" encounters similar difficulties. Aware that no feudal peasantry existed in New England, writers who take this view nevertheless are bent upon distinguishing between early subsistence farming, on the one hand, and a situation characterized by the factory, free wage labor, market commodity exchange, and the treatment of land as a commodity, on the other. According to this view, subsistence farmers were drawn into the market only reluctantly. Capitalism was therefore purely an exogenous force, presumably insinuating itself like a hidden hand from England. New cultural heroes, independent farmers thus held back capitalism by fighting a desperate rear-guard action as long as they could.[32]

In fact, opportunities in agriculture and land speculation probably did slow down industrialization. With only 20 percent of the American population free wage laborers in 1775, compared with 50 percent in Britain (or over one-third landless, including slaves), it is clear that America possessed a weaker base for factory organization than Britain, where rural manufacturing was growing ever more evident. But independent farmers did not prevent the emergence of factories in America. Indeed, to turn the matter around, it can be asked why, given the much lower percentage of wage laborers in America, factories appeared as early as they did. Far from being opposed to the market, "independent" farmers eagerly sought English manufactured goods and in other ways acted as agents of capitalism: individualism, accumulation and property, and commercial-exchange value were intimately intertwined and cannot be so casually separated. Land carried use, exchange, and especially status value—in New England as well as in all the other colonies.[33]

To this point, primarily New England has been considered, largely because it is the most problematic region. By comparison, debates on Pennsylvania and other northern colonies seem bland. Differing interpretations over New England rest in part on some of the peculiar conditions found there, where internal trade was less obvious, the standard of living probably lower, the soil less bounteous, and awareness of local communities more explicit. But current disagreements over New England are also partially a result of scholars' preoccupation with religion and their relative lack of interest in internal economy, labor, and county political structures. On the other hand, in places like Pennsylvania and New York local controls (if not so formal) were undoubtedly stronger than scholars have traditionally emphasized. The power of the county courts, litigation, and internal trade all tied people together. A "liberal" society is not without community ties.[34]

With regard to settlements in the South, our understanding is less problematic. What is hidden in New England and elsewhere in the North is more clearly observable in the Chesapeake, where much fruitful work has been done recently. Plantations large and small were dispersed, and settlement was carried out by individuals and informal groups rather than by formally covenated communities or corporate groups of proprietors, as in New England. This is not to say that the process was haphazard. According to Kevin P. Kelly, in Surry County, Virginia, settlers choosing land rationally sought water for access and consumption. As elsewhere, later arrivals had to take up land on less accessible and then unnavigable streams and on interfluves. A similar pattern was followed in All Hallow's Parish in Maryland. Nowhere in the Chesapeake was the survey pattern neat. As in Pennsylvania, individuals had wide scope in deciding where to settle, and the result was irregular patterns of holdings, as settlers consistently tried to search out the best lands.[35]

Size of individual holdings was also larger than in the North. In Surry County in the seventeenth century holdings averaged 433 acres. Even eighteenth-century tenant holdings on Maryland proprietary manors averaged between 150 and 200 acres. The inability of many freed servants to exercise their headrights of fifty acres and the trade in these headrights operated to keep sizes up. Those servants who survived the high death toll and were able to find wives in a region that in 1700 still saw a white sexual imbalance of three to two sometimes found that speculative holdings blocked them in accessible regions, while from time to time Indian threats held back frontier expansion. Yet, sooner or later poor ex-servants began to brave the frontiers and to search out places, even if they were on poorer, less accessible but cheaper lands. Dispersion onto large holdings, only later subdivided among offspring or tenants, may have limited contacts among households, while urban places were slow to take hold. Courthouses, churches, schools, mills, artisan shops, stores, and tobacco inspection warehouses were scattered about the countryside. In All Hallow's, London Town rose and then fell after 1740 as secondary and tertiary functions increasingly were performed on the larger plantations.[36]

Again, however, community structures and controls lay behind the dispersal pattern. Even more explicitly, power relationships in the Chesapeake were apparent. Theoretically inclusive local parishes exercised some powers, as colony legislatures in an attempt to curtail the volume of litigation over land in county courts assigned parish vestries authority to define property boundaries by annual "land processioning." "Safeguarding its possession" was "of paramount importance." Vestries were also responsible for the very poor squatters, who were excluded by the beating of the bounds of properties. Unlike England, where the poor retained customary rights to nooks and crannies, Virginia eventually made sure that squatting was prohibited, thus forcing the poor to move on or to fall into dependency on the larger planters.[37]

The larger planters increasingly dominated the local social environment. They controlled the vestries and the county courts. Even as early as the mid-seventeenth century in Lancaster County, Virginia, county justices drawn from the elite held "at least twice as much land as the average householder, controlled nearly half the labor force in the county, and were major creditors." As a consequence, by 1700 in older, settled places like All Hallow's one-third of householders were tenants or laborers; as on nearby proprietary manors, over time these tended to become permanently fixed poor who were derided as "ignorant and abject." The eighteenth century saw even more consolidation of power in the hands of large planters. Tobacco inspection acts helped large planters because small planters with insufficient labor or capital more often produced inferior crops. In an environment of unequal power, regulation created even more inequality. Business cycles also helped the large planter. During economic downturns the least wealthy became even more enmeshed in debt to the more affluent, who dominated retailing and credit. In Maryland at least, the large plantation came more and more to be almost a company town. Although some tenants were able partially to escape their obligations by removing to the frontier safety valve, others were stuck in debt under a local government system biased in favor of their creditors.[38]

Yet, the gradual replacement of white servants by black slaves between 1680 and 1720 helped, as Edmund Morgan has argued, to produce a marked solidarity among all whites, as big, middling, and poor white planters, Anglican and sectarian, combined to control the slaves. The full weight of official terror meted out through the courts on the poor of England was inflicted on the slaves. When the court granted Robert "King" Carter the right "to dismember runaways" early in the eighteenth century, it recognized that local social control had to be based on not only deference but intimidation and fear. Local government was certainly conducted in "a personal, face-to-face manner." Far more important, it also operated through both well-defined and subtle institutions representing unequal rights. Standing before the magistrate, the runaway slave or even the indebted tenant, like the accused witch in Salem or the vagabond in Shropshire, must have taken cold comfort in knowing that relations were "face to face" as they were being used as examples for defining and maintaining the local order. As everywhere, personal relations were mediated through institutions. American freedom was and is grounded in the institution of property in fee simple and built on the unequal structure of economic life and the unequal power relationships represented in the courts.[39]

REGIONAL ORGANIZATION AND THE PROBLEM OF URBANIZATION

Households and local communities, whether organized as towns, parishes, or counties, combined into larger regional organizations. When we speak of regional organization, we have in mind the transport of goods and services, the movement of ideas and information, and the flow of authority—political, economical, and social—between places. By general agreement some places are considered to be more important than others; indeed, we all hold to some sense of dominance and control. By the early seventeenth century London already dominated England and in many respects early America. At a lower level, Philadelphia and New York dominated their respective hinterlands rather more than, say, Leacock Township, in Lancaster County, Pennsylvania, or Kent, in Litchfield County, Connecticut. Of course, to their inhabitants, these last places were in one sense the "center of the world," the focus of their radiating and overlapping networks. Yet, the biggest urban places loomed large, with the county seats of Lancaster and Litchfield eventually mediating in large measure between major centers and small rural communities. All places, even the most rural of areas, were connected to cities. Within an imperfect hierarchy of traders, coastal cities, and county seats, regional actions during the first century and a half of Anglo-American colonization occurred in an extensively organized fashion, that is, among only poorly articulated or unevenly spread urban centers. Regional variations were notable, yet all regions were tied to London.[40]

Three models can be invoked for dealing with regional organization and the problem of urbanization. The most important derives from central-place theory and was developed with retailing as the prime focus, though it has subsequently been modified by other considerations. According to this theory, whether a good is traded depends on a threshold population, and the volume of trade for the item in turn depends on its range. With regard to all goods, a hierarchy of towns develops, theoretically in layered hexagonal regions of differing sizes. The sorting out depends on other processes, including specialization, agglomeration through people clustering together and thereby cutting the costs imposed by distance, and the emergence of economies of scale within particular activities. Higher-order places deal in higher-order goods and services, which are scarcer and more expensive, and not only lower-order goods, as is exclusviely the case with small places. Hierarchies of places from metropolis, cities, towns, farm-service urban villages, and hamlets can be worked out with one at the top and many at the bottom. The larger the population, the greater the number of activities and of established needs per activity and the more definite the clustering spatially. Form, function, and population are mutually supportive.[41]

Despite its elegance, this model is not easily applied in early America. Retailing hardly encompasses all economic activity. Transport, wholesaling, manufacturing, and finance complicate the picture. Further, political and social connections are as crucial in defining regional flows as the strictly economic. Public administration of order through courts, legislatures, governors, and church structures did not totally correspond in flow with economic activity. County seats may have mediated questions of order between top and bottom, but by no means did they mediate all those concerning economic matters. Before 1775 the central-place hierarchy made most sense towards the top (London and coastal cities) but less so "below."[42]

James Vance has developed an alternative model of regional organization, the mercantile, based on wholesaling of imports and of staple exports. The key to this model is the establishment of points of attachment from the outside, that is, entrepôts. Whereas the central-place model is endogenic, the mercantile is exogenic. Obviously the entrepôts fit more easily with early America, where the seaboard cities were connected with the metropolis. Only gradually did a central-place system emerge, based on internal economic development.[43]

Carville Earle has put forward an important modification of the mercantile model based on monopoly power. While the mercantile model stresses the merchants' role, Earle emphasizes the importance of monopoly control granted by government to companies, at least in the first phases of settlement. The English preferred one city per colony, where possible, located at midpoints on colonial shorelines. The staple trade in the first instance was not their exclusive concern. Rather, imperial expansion demanded strong defensive and organizing points for settlements that were expected to be largely self-sufficient and to serve as means to keeping settlers orderly and civilized: "Monopolists channeled capital and colonists into a single, centrally located port town, thereby avoiding the redundancy and resource inefficiencies of multiple ports." This development, according to Earle, was the genius of British settlement policy, which was in contrast with that of the Dutch. If the mercantile model based on free trade calls for several potential urban sites that would later be sorted out by the market, this monopoly model limits the number severely. The subsequent establishment of county seats by central authorities can be seen through this monopoly lens. Over the long run, with the relative weakening of ties with Britain, internal growth encouraged the development of central places, as well as manufacturing towns that did not fit a neat central-place pattern. Throughout the colonial period, however, very imperfect intensification occurred.[44]

Using the central-place and mercantile models with the political dimension added by Earle, we can consider regional organization and urban systems of New England, the Chesapeake, and Pennsylvania. This approach permits greater complexity in systematic analyses. Regional organization in colonial New England was never very clear-cut, in part because there were so many small colonies and in part because the emphasis on fishing led to the establishment of a large number of ports. Moreover, at least by 1700 western Connecticut and Massachusetts were being pulled economically more and more towards New York. Use of the word *town* to denote a political unit that was not necessarily an urban place itself is misleading in terms of any analysis of the problem of urbanization and complicates discussion of regional patterns.

Although the issue remains problematic, it is nevertheless safe to conclude that all studies suggest an extensive society. With the onset of occupation, planned urban settlements developed: Boston, Newport, New London, Norwich, New Haven, Hartford, and Springfield, the latter two on the Connecticut River, navigable at least to Hartford. All of these persisted as urban places, although Boston clearly gained a substantial degree of hegemony over much of eastern New England, while Newport, for a time its chief rival, subsequently lost strength to Providence, and both to Boston. The Connecticut case involved several settlements and, for a time, two colonies, Connecticut and New Haven, none of which was able to rise clearly above the others according to the central-place model; they were eventually absorbed into New York's and Boston's higher-order regions.[45] Few other urban places emerged. Indeed, several Bay Colony towns, although the General Court granted them periodic market days and thus designated them urban sites along English lines, were unable to fulfill their aspirations to become market towns.[46] Only when county seats become firmly established with mutually supportive judicial, administrative, and commercial functions does the next rank of urban place become apparent. The General Courts established county courts in Massachusetts in 1636 and in Connecticut in 1664 but did not initially fix them in place.

Four recent studies using central-place notions help us to understand regional structure and urban patterns in eighteenth-century New England.[47] Edward M. Cook and Bruce Daniels provide new perspectives on regional organization primarily in terms of its social and political aspects, though neither has adequately connected these aspects to the economy. Taking a sample of seventy-four eighteenth-century towns, Cook develops a five-level "typology" of towns: frontier, egalitarian, secondary rural centers/suburbs of cities, major county towns, and cities. These are based on a combination of 5 indices: percentage of population serving in town leadership, average number of terms served by influential leaders, percentage of all terms served by influential leaders, percentage of taxes paid by the wealthier, and percentage of prominent individuals. Cook quite explicitly lays out experimental methodologies through various steps in reaching this final typology. He also provides a commercial index for all towns in New England (1765–74) by dividing "each town's share of the colony's taxes by the total area of the town, and thereby computing an index of the hypothetical average of the property in the town." Cook concludes that a central-place pattern is more appropriate to describe the region than Jackson Turner Main's four regional bands of urban, commercial farming, subsistence (plus) farming, and frontier. At the very least, the pattern was certainly lumpier than Main allows.[48]

Less statistical and somewhat less systematically analytical is Daniels's study of eighteenth-century Connecticut towns.[49] He develops a three-level hierarchy: urban centers (5); secondary centers, some directly in the export business and some inland market centers (27); and country towns (43). Although Daniels provides nine useful maps, including four on periods of town incorporations, three on population, and one on "overall land quality," unfortunately he does not show cartographically the results of his categorizing of towns. Like Cook, Daniels provides considerable material, much of it quantitative, on political aspects of towns; some statistical calculations on religious societies; tables on incorporation, including numbers of families involved and size of town; and an important table correlating the number of artisans with population. Let us consider some of his substantive points briefly.

Municipalities called towns were at first large in acreage and small in population. Daniels shows that in the period 1635–75 at the date of town incorporation the average number of families was 31 and the average town size was 106.3 square miles. Between 1686 and 1734 groups averaged 20.4 families within much smaller areas, the mean being 64.9 square miles. The tendency in the next period, 1737–66, was for the number of families to rise but the size of towns to fall to 45.9, towards the magical figure of 36 square miles, which presumably was one basis for the development of the Jeffersonian "template" for midwestern rural settlement. Overlaying the town pattern was the county system, though Daniels does not systematically analyze this system including the county towns. Religious societies did not totally correspond to towns; indeed, Daniels states that in 1790 in Connecticut there were 101 towns and 307 ecclesiastical societies, making the parish areas of religious bodies considerably smaller than those of the towns. Yet, in spite of these changes, even as late as the 1770s artisans were nearly proportionate to population in all towns, which suggests little regional or subregional concentration of manufacturing. Why were sizes reduced as the population grew? The data suggest an intensification of society, defined by population density. But do they specify specialization and concentration of activities?[50]

Illuminating as these studies are, they raise problems. First is the problem of comparability. Why Daniels did not at least discuss the possibility of following Cook's typology, since he used similar criteria, including officeholding, as the basis for his hierarchy, is puzzling. Instead, he chose to start de novo. In the third study, Daniel Scott Smith has in fact reworked Cook's data using a statistical technique, discriminant analysis, which sorts out place by various indices. His fit is quite close to Cook's, though county-level towns did not correspond quite so well as did those in Cook's other four categories. Some achieved higher-level city status, while others lagged. One might expect this development to be the result of the level of economic development in various counties, a consequence of timing of settlement or of land quality (given equal technologies). This suggestion is confirmed by comparing Cook's commercial index for all Connecticut towns in 1774 with Daniels's categorization of land quality for each town. More recently settled areas lagged behind their potential, while some earlier settled but theoretically less productive towns ran ahead.[51]

A more serious question has to do with what is meant by the terms "urban" or "central places." Cook, Daniels, and even Smith fail to differentiate rural from urban. A town in New England was not necessarily what English historians and geographers have usually meant by "town." The New England definition referred to political units, municipalities, and communities, whether rural ("township" elsewhere) or urban, whereas in normal scholarly usage "urban" refers to places with secondary and tertiary activities (or primary if mining) and not agricultural. One can grant that there is often no clear line between urban and rural; modern U.S. censuses define non-agricultural places of less than twenty-five hundred as rural. But these studies do not clearly confront the problem. Their central-place schemes appear to include large farming populations. Conceivably, a totally rural town, one with farms, could be classified as higher than one that was urban—affluent Wethersfield may be a case in point. This weakness derives partly from the total shift of the terms of defining "central place" away from economic towards political and social aspects. All places had officeholders, and all had land to tax, but these do not necessarily make them "urban," with clustered shops, taverns, warehouses, public places, and the like.

Perhaps these studies were assuming that all towns had urban clusters or that all towns had urban functions. Again, following the recent study by Joseph Wood, it would be dangerous to claim, however, that all or even many towns possessed a neat cluster of urban dwellers centrally located around village greens, at least before the late eighteenth century. Although these studies try to establish clear categories, a town below the county-seat level should not be considered a central place as defined by nucleation. Density of population, degree of wealth, and the status of politicians do not clarify the issue of urban clustering, because economic issues and the role of urban subdividers are not considered. In short, Cook, Daniels, and Scott develop typologies of municipalities called towns, not central-place systems.[52]

In a fourth study of the central-place issue and of urbanization a geographer, Bonnie Barton, does consider economic functions. Taking eight places representing "the full spectrum of colonial settlements, ranging from the most to the least important places," she attempts to correlate place-specific economic activities with population growth. The data assembled suggest that mills and taverns were the earliest nonfarming activities, with others developing as population grew. Yet, Barton argues that populations levels and the emergence of central activities do not correspond well across all places. Indeed, from a systems perspective, she concludes that New England in 1790 was a "two-layered landscape consisting of a set of agricultural towns whose centrality status is unstable and a system of central places powered by the entrepreneur." They are interconnected, however; Boston and other cities depended on their hinterland, and vice versa. But like the others, she does not focus on nucleation within towns. Because population growth and functions did not fit together, perhaps neither did clustering.[53]

The obvious difficulty of melding together these various approaches leads us to one inescapable conclusion: the urban-system question for New England remains problematic. Yet, together these studies tell us enough to make us conclude that the region was an extensively organized one in which a clear urban articulation had to await the later intensification of commerce and industrialization. But do the extensive spatial pattern and the decline of

urban population relative to rural point to a "ruralization or decommercialization," as Smith concludes? Boston's population actually stagnated and
even declined, but Philadelphia continued to grow, although it accounted for
less and less of Pennsylvania's total population, the result, as Smith himself
points out, of the extension of the rural population over more and more
space. This was certainly ruralization, but was it decommercialization? One
could argue, harking back to Earle, that even while becoming numerically
less important, cities continued to fulfill their commercial and administrative
roles very well. And the alleged eighteenth-century agricultural crisis, if it
forced people deeper into subsistence, might be taken to suggest decommercialization. But Robert Gross has suggested that in Concord, Massachusetts,
this was not clearly the case. In fact, by the 1760s improved agriculture was
apparent. Winifred Rothenberg, too, argues for the presence "early on" of
markets not tied to central marketplaces but fitting an inland free-trade system, and such a system seems to have persisted. Imports from Britain increased. What we may be observing is a situation of very little overall development with no long-run rise in the standard of living which resulted in a
New England that was poorer than other regions. But this does not mean
that commerce was not present from the beginning. Without an omnipresent
commerce, no matter how weak, it is difficult to explain either the emergence
of Yankee ingenuity and zeal or the periodic demand for paper money.[54]

But what did commerce signify in that era? It involved not only trade but
money in some form. Certainly, when compared with present-day corporate
farms that employ wage labor and operate within the fully capitalized and
specialized paraphernalia of credit and interest, early farms were indeed
primitive. But despite the glacial velocities of money, shortages of cash, and
quantitatively greater proportions of products produced by subsistence techniques, one wonders whether it is possible to draw a sharp line or locate a
critical transition period between that era and our own when it comes to
capitalism.

Merchants' records are instructive. A mid-seventeenth-century Salem
dealer, for example, bought farm produce not only from nearby towns but
from as far away as Andover and Lynn for provisioning of ships and for sale
in Boston.[55] He imported goods from England and dealt with Boston's merchants. Goods carried a monetary value, and he obviously profited. As elsewhere, this merchant was indebted on long terms to London, and hinterland
farmers were indebted to him. All were enmeshed in the credit nexus,
whether through bills of exchange or by bookkeeping. Face-to-face transactions between merchants and farmers settled accounts, or partially so, from
time to time, and then the cycle renewed. Interestingly, farmers' debts did
not bear interest to the shopkeeper as similar transactions today would.
Perhaps because of this fact as well as because of the obvious shortage of
cash, those arguing that colonial New England was precapitalist would seem
to have a point.

But do they? Let me draw on my own experience. I grew up in a small town in Ontario where my grandfather and father ran a general retail store. They bought goods from wholesalers at thirty or sixty days' "nett" and in turn sold these "imports" to farmers and townspeople. Prior to 1945 they more often than not recorded sales in accounts and, especially during the depth of the Depression, took goods in return, including chickens, geese, and butter (which often went rancid in the cellar). As in the seventeenth-century, these accounts were settled when crops and livestock were sold, and debts did not bear interest, no matter how long they ran or how high they were. No shopkeeper dared charge interest. Banks, a specialized instrument themselves, made profits through interest on loans, as had some, though not all, merchants and rich farmers in earlier times. But all these conditions, which were characteristic of economic relations in rural areas prior to the corporatization of agriculture after 1945, could be described, misleadingly of course, as "precapitalist."

Consider also the problem of cash itself. It was scarce in colonial New England, which is why farmers periodically demanded paper money to help pay off debts. Over the long run, after 1700, scarce specie was gradually replaced by paper currency. Today cash is still scarce relative to the total money supply, notably, as then, for people at the bottom of society, for precisely those who do not have access to other instruments of exchange. Cash has always been nearly irrelevant for those with abundant capital. Those who stress the importance of cash, therefore, believe the monetarist fallacy that government-issued money is the only money. Monetarist strategies then and now fall most heavily on the poor. What marks us off from the past is a far larger volume of money moving far more rapidly through more specialized instruments. Capitalism developed because people were willing to use these means more and more in an open society. As we saw in the last section, property relations were a fundamental basis for this development.

If, as Fernand Braudel has pointed out, money is a sign of urban life, urban and rural in colonial America merged.[56] Of course it is clear that money was not the only measure of things in rural and even urban life; indeed, not until recently could we say that agriculture was nearly totally commercialized. Then, most produced was consumed at home. Yet, local "money," whether in the form of barter, bookkeeping credit/debt, or cash, was a part of everyday life, and it must be seen as part of the credit system focused on London via Boston and New York and to a lesser degree the other smaller cities. Commercial production in New England may have been at a low level, but it existed and increased, not just in favored spots like Wethersfield, with its onions, or Narragansett Bay or places like Dedham, supplying lumber and other produce to Boston. Even marginal places were to some degree tied in to the credit nexus. Thus, I would contend, no clear temporal line can be drawn between noncapitalist and capitalist relations among farmers. Gradually, if haltingly, because of business cycles, they were drawn into—and most allowed themselves to be—ever-deepening capital relations. Over the long run fewer and fewer family farms became more and more capitalized, eventually corporatized. The roots of this process lay in England before America was founded.

What I have concluded for New England comes very close to the position of Joseph Ernst and Roy Merrens on urbanization in the South. Urban functions there were often carried on in small places or indeed even in rural settings. Scottish stores, Scottish factors, and pedlars performed urban functions in the countryside. In the Chesapeake, in All Hallow's Parish, and in South Carolina large planters were retailers and bankers, just as were hustlers in Charles Grant's Kent. In North Carolina trade was decentralized and county seats were often tiny. By the late eighteenth century urban places, strictly defined, were far more numerous but still mostly small and not evenly distributed.[57]

But the South did differ somewhat from New England in its regional organization and urban systems. First, the firm coastal anchor points desired by the English did not arise except in the special case of Charleston, which for many decades had a relatively small agricultural hinterland. Nowhere in the Chesapeake did a large port emerge early. Jamestown and St. Mary's failed, and the settlers complained of the lack of what they understood as towns. Williamsburg and Annapolis, too, were more seasonal places of courts and politics than of trade. North Carolina ports never became very large.[58]

The obvious explanation for this slow urban development lies largely in the tobacco trade. Paradoxically, the most commercialized region was the least urban, containing no large or even substantial seaport as did New England and the Middle Colonies. Even more than New England, the top central place of London (along with Glasgow) loomed so large that no important intermediaries were needed in organizing trade. Linkages were so forward that strong urban initiatives in the Chesapeake were unnecessary. The estuarine coastline providing convenience for shipping from plantation wharves was a secondary consideration.[59]

This picture runs contrary to colonial Third World urbanization, where primate cities of large size such as Rangoon dominate the regional scene;[60] in such places the surplus was drawn from an almost totally subject population. In the Chesapeake only half of the people were fully a subject population by the mid-eighteenth century. The other half shared with London the economic surplus. If it is true that within this white half a few large planters took the largest portion, the central-place system was preempted by a system of large planters controlling the economic levers, as well as, if to a lesser extent, the political and religious lives of ordinary farmers.

After 1750 this pattern changed. Not only did the Shenandoah Valley follow the Pennsylvania pattern of strong county market towns but the rise of wheat induced the same in the northern Chesapeake and on the Piedmont, and a rapidly rising Baltimore pulled back the linkage controls to America. Yet, interestingly, unlike Philadelphia, Baltimore was not a capital. The time had come when granting a monopoly to a seaport was unnecessary for success. Indeed, Baltimore's rise signaled a break between the political and the economic and hence to a degree pointed to the weakening strength of London's political economy.[61]

In Pennsylvania the emergence of new counties and new county towns moved that province over a short period of time towards intensification and hence toward a central-place system. No less than the first coastal cities, mid-century towns were the responsibility of monopolies, several owned by the Penn family itself. In Pennsylvania's political economy sheer survival was scarcely a consideration in the drive to establish towns. More important were the desires to secure public order through establishing county courts, to expedite trade, and not least, to increase incomes from urban subdivisions. The Penns did in fact earn incomes from these urban lands.[62]

Below the county-town level the pattern was hardly complete before 1776 and should not quite be graced with the term "system." At mid-century many individuals strove to gain the unearned increment by laying out urban places, but few of these places gained much population, and many of their residents were poor. Spatially, the pattern was patchy, as if urban subdivision activity was a fad of speculative gentlemen with spare capital. Yet a few places did grow, and during the post-Revolution division of old counties and the laying out of new ones a few of the most accessible succeeded through lobbying efforts on the part of their proprietors in becoming county seats. Harrisburg even became the capital. Eventually, over the next century, a more definite central-place hierarchy did emerge, the neat theoretical spatial clarity distorted by the rise of manufacturing towns at water-power sites.

In the meantime, in Pennsylvania as elsewhere much "urban" activity, that is, actively involving money, occurred in the countryside, some at crossroads hamlets not centrally located in townships and the rest on farms among farmers. Even with high incomes per capita, this region, too, was organized extensively, with affluent farmers loaning money to less affluent farmers and decentralized millers controlling the milling of flour and presumably the selling of fresh seed. Although intensification of the urban system occurred in the mid-eighteenth century, sustained growth appeared only in the 1790s.[63]

Much existing literature presents a rural society sharply distinguished from an urban society. Christopher Jedrey's recent characterization of Chebacco, Massachusetts, is one example among many. Chebacco, according to Jedrey, was connected to "relatively few extra-communal sources of information [and] a proportionately larger part of one's world view" was "simply passed from the previous generation." But it is highly doubtful that Chebacco, orginally part of Ipswich, near Salem, was so isolated as to prevent information from flowing freely from a variety of sources. That place could hardly have been different from Myddle, a far more remote community, in Shropshire, which was "not as cut off from the mainstream of national life as might be supposed." Moreover, that parents in Chebacco were, as in most societies, the main source of information for their children does not necessarily mean that information from outside was not available, absorbed, and acted upon. Not all cosmopolitans lived in cities, nor for that matter did all locals live in the country, and differences between urban and rural were indistinct. Even without newspapers or with only a few, information got around through a variety of connections, leading to, among other things, the emergence of the *regional* material culture described by Richard Bushman in this volume.[64]

Of course within the social hierarchies that existed in rural places, some persons could and needed to tap the flow of information more fully than others. Knowledge of prices in Salem, Boston, and London was crucial to a few and, at least in an immediate sense, incidental to the rest. The same was true in the political, religious, and cultural spheres. Undoubtedly, the most powerful, the leaders of places, were the most conscious of the need for access to information in all areas. Indeed, it is not going too far to suggest that social status depended in large measure on "controlling" information in much the same way as it does in today's society, notwithstanding differences in technical means and the greater intensification. The composition of social hierarchies may have changed, but their existence has persisted. In Western society at least, some people seem always to have been more equal than others.

PERSPECTIVE

In *The Country and the City* Raymond Williams provides a valuable spatial and temporal perspective for consideration.[65] While obviously different, rural and urban are difficult to separate even in the relatively undifferentiated world of early modern colonial Anglo-America. In our highly urbanized society it is easy to forget the earlier realities of the country and the tensions that many have felt between urban and rural. Drawing on literary works, Williams shows that images have been contradictory: pastoral innocence versus urban corruption, yet country bumpkins as opposed to the civilizing city. But the country and the city have also been complementary. The real or imagined quiet country scene is set off against the bright lights and bustle of the city. Even in the colonial era the two coexisted: indeed, the biblically derived message fixing human origins in Eden and futures in the New Jerusalem accentuated this tendency to juxtapose opposites.

Williams also casts some light on the problem of change. Focusing on the issue of community stability, he shows that the theme of the decline and imminent collapse of the organic rural life, even of rural society itself, has been a persistent one among English writers at least as far back as *Piers Plowman*. Here we confront an instance of infinite regress: obviously, all did not collapse, and the English have somehow continued to muddle through. Indeed, recent protesters against urban freeways and the destruction of Covent Garden Market invoked the same arguments for customary rights of the commons as did opponents of enclosure. In short, on one level we can speak of the timeless dialectic between city and country. Similarly, individual, household, community, and society have always been intertwined. No society could hold together without some definition of individual integrity and institutional frameworks to mediate communication, trade, and power.

Property is a critical institution bearing on human interaction. In this essay I have stressed individual (male head of household) rights to property notably in land but also in slaves and the importance of money as persistent qualities of early Anglo-American life. In contrast to the Indians' communal ownership, among English-speaking peoples and other Western Europeans, in varying degrees for many centuries individual property rights have been given great stress. By 1600 practices had weakened community controls to such an extent that fee simple, the least restrictive form of tenure, had become the norm in England. Such was clearly also the case throughout America and has continued to be so. Despite legal hedges, the property of General Motors is generally seen more in terms of individual right than in terms of collective rights. We cannot work backward in America to find a time when fee simple was not the norm.

It is within this context, then, that changes must be seen. Fundamentally, property was not evenly held. Nor was power, because unequal property enabled some people to acquire unequal power over others and, just as important, unequal status, by which people identified one another. In early America the most important spatial and social change was the extension of freehold property, or put another way, the expansion into and accumulation of Indian lands by fee-simple colonies. (Henry Nash Smith's "empire" was not apparent, however, until the nineteenth century.) In every wave of movement onto new lands early appearances of equality were rapidly supplanted by inequality: seemingly small initial differences in status and material condition magnified even to the point of landlessness for some as each new area reached the limits of its growth, since those limits were established by the amount of available property to be held in fee simple and by the economic opportunities possible within the structures of the time.

As each area reached these limits, it became either a seedbed for new areas of settlements or a foundation for intensification of population, of secondary and tertiary economic activities, of court cases, of capital. Such changes varied regionally and temporally and occurred in waves of longer and shorter duration, but over the long run they were incremental and led to a higher degree of commercialization, even industrialization at some points. Even before 1776 there were, for example, eight mills on the Brandywine just above Wilmington.[66] In every place some individuals with more property, or with aspirations to acquire more, led the way towards intensification, and others followed. Those who could not follow were marginalized; some were even pauperized. Neither the extension of settlement nor the intensification of economic and social structures could have happened without prior intensification in England and in colonial cities. Eventually the intensification within the colonies and their unification into a nation allowed the vast spatial expansion and periodic explosions of technologies during the nineteenth century. Within the slow, perhaps even almost no-growth colonial era lay the basis for later rapid development, with all of its social costs.

It is within this context that politics, court actions over property, sectional differences, urban and rural political controversies, and the striving for status and salvation occurred. Even a few religious communitarian groups arose to throw into sharp relief how property-minded the society was and how limited they were in achieving their goals, including commercial ownership. The extension of America and its subsequent intensification would not have happened without all the decisions and actions of individuals, households, and other small groups. Structures do not just happen; people make them. The formal politics of government at various levels was and is the final arena in which people expect to—and do—get things done for themselves and others. All individual and collective actions and choices, all face-to-face relations, all experiences were mediated through institutions defined by language. The landscape of early America was not only the stage on which these messages were articulated but a vehicle for them as the inhabitants developed a spatial order.

NOTES

For comments I am grateful to Bruce Daniels, Carville Earle, Joseph Ernst, Harriet Friedmann, Carolyn Lemon, David Levine, Ian Parker, Paul Romney, Daniel Vickers, and Joseph Wood, to the editors of this volume, and to those who participated in a seminar at the University of Toronto. I am also grateful to those whose works are cited in my "Early Americans and Their Social Environment," *Journal of Historical Geography*, 6 (1980): 115–31.

1. Henry Nash Smith, *Virgin Land: The American West as Symbol and Myth* (New York, 1950), esp. chaps. 12 and 18.

2. Andrew Burnaby, *Travels through the Middle Settlements in North America in the Years 1759–1760*, 2d ed. (1775; reprint, Ithaca, N.Y., 1960), 110–11.

3. Wilbur Zelinsky, *The Cultural Geography of the United States* (Englewood Cliffs, N.J., 1973); Robert D. Mitchell, "The Formation of Early American Cultural Regions: An Interpretation," in *European Settlement and Development in North America: Essays on Geographical Change in Honour and Memory of Andrew Hill Clark*, ed. James R. Gibson (Toronto, 1978); Douglas Greenberg, "The Middle Colonies in Recent American Historiography," *William and Mary Quarterly*, 3d ser., 36 (1979): 396–427.

4. Laxton, in northern Nottinghamshire. In the village are the church, the pub, and farm-steads. In July 1981 the wheat was maturing nicely in the open fields.

5. Michael Chisholm, *Rural Settlement and Land Use: An Essay on Location* (London, 1962), is a standard work.

6. Lawrence Stone, *The Causes of the English Revolution, 1529–1642* (London, 1972), 67–76. On conditions in western England see James Horn, "Servant Emigration to the Chesapeake in the Seventeenth Century," in *The Chesapeake in the Seventeenth Century: Essays on Anglo-American Society*, ed. Thad W. Tate and David L. Ammerman (Chapel Hill, 1979), 51–95. See also David H. Flaherty, *Privacy in Colonial New England* (Charlottesville, 1972).

7. E. P. Thompson, "The Grid of Inheritance: A Comment," in *Family and Inheritance: Rural Society in Western Europe, 1200–1800*, ed. Jack Goody, Joan Thirsk, and E. P. Thompson (Cambridge, 1976), 331; T. H. Breen, *Puritans and Adventurers: Change and Persistence in Early America* (New York, 1980); Clive Holmes, "The County Community in Stuart Historiography," *Journal of British Studies* 52 (1980): 54–73.

8. Bruce C. Daniels, *The Connecticut Town* (Middletown, Conn., 1979), 143. Among general works drawing sharp differences are Thomas Bender, *Community and Social Change in America* (New Brunswick, N.J., 1978), esp. chap. 3; Ruth Sutter, *The Next Place You Come To* (Englewood Cliffs, N.J., 1973), 84–85; Conrad Arensberg, "American Communities," *American Anthropologist* 17 (1955): 1143–62; Glenn T. Trewartha, "Types of Rural Settlement in Colonial America," *Geographical Review* 36 (1946): 568–96; and Edna Scofield, "The Origin of Settlement Patterns in Rural New England," ibid. 27 (1938): 652–63.

9. Joseph Wood, "The Origin of the New England Village" (Ph.D. diss., Pennsylvania State University, 1978), esp. map 149; and idem, "Village and Community in Early Colonial New England," *Journal of Historical Geography* 8 (1982): 333–46. Wood has suggested that there may have been four more nucleated, but this hardly alters the issue (personal communication, 1981). See also Flaherty, *Privacy*, chap. 1; Darrett B. Rutman, *The Husbandmen of Plymouth: Farms and Villages in the Old Colony, 1620–1692* (Boston, 1967), 14, 23; John Demos, *A Little Commonwealth: Family Life in Plymouth Colony* (New York, 1970), 9–12; and Kenneth A. Lockridge, *A New England Town: The First Hundred Years, Dedham, Massachusetts, 1636–1736* (New York, 1970), 79, 82.

10. Sumner C. Powell, *Puritan Village: The Formation of a New England Town* (Middletown, Conn., 1963); David Grayson Allen, *In English Ways: The Movement of Societies and the Transferal of English Local Law and Custom to Massachusetts Bay in the Seventeenth Century* (Chapel Hill, 1981). On p. 232, however, Allen cites without criticism advocates of the convention: Edna Scofield and Glenn Trewartha, both pre-1950 geographers, noted above.

11. Joseph Wood, "Origin of the New England Village," 104; James T. Lemon, *The Best Poor Man's Country: A Geographical Study of Early Southeastern Pennsylvania* (Baltimore, 1972), 106–7.

12. Daniels, *Connecticut Town*, 144; Philip J. Greven, Jr., *Four Generations: Population, Land, and Family in Colonial Andover, Massachusetts* (Ithaca, N.Y., 1970), 58–59.

13. Nathaniel B. Shurtleff, ed., *Records of the Governor and Company of the Massachusetts Bay in New England*, 5 vols. in 6 (Boston, 1853–54), vol. 1, *1628–1641*, 157, 181, 257, 291; also noted in Flaherty, *Privacy*, 26. Greven, *Four Generations*, 55–56, discusses futile gestures by the town meeting to control dispersion. See also Massachusetts Historical Society, *Winthrop Papers*, 5 vols. (Boston, 1929–47), vol. 3, 181–84.

14. David Levine has been working on the expansion of the English proletariat from 1540 to 1850, suggesting a rise from 25 percent of the population to 75 percent (personal communication, 1981). See also Horn, "Servant Emigration"; and Michael Walzer, *The Revolution of the Saints: A Study in the Origins of Radical Politics* (Cambridge, Mass., 1965).

15. Allen, *In English Ways*; Douglas R. McManis, *Colonial New England: Historical Geography* (New York, 1975), 45, 92; Stephen Innes, "Land Tenancy and Social Order in Springfield, Massachusetts, 1652–1702," *William and Mary Quarterly*, 3d ser., 35 (1978): 33–56; Howard S. Russell, *A Long, Deep Furrow: Three Centuries of Farming in New England* (Hanover, N.H., 1976),

42, 60, 62, 68, 119, 133, 142; Sydney V. James, *Colonial Rhode Island: A History* (New York, 1975), esp. 50; Carl Bridenbaugh, *Fat Mutton and Liberty of Conscience: Society in Rhode Island, 1636–1690* (Providence, 1974), esp. 58; Darrett B. Rutman, *Winthrop's Boston: Portrait of a Puritan Town, 1630–1649* (Chapel Hill, 1965); idem, *Husbandsmen*, 23.

16. Daniels, *Connecticut Town*, 20–22.

17. Lockridge, *New England Town;* Jerome H. Wood, Jr., *Conestoga Crossroads: Lancaster, Pennsylvania, 1730–1790* (Harrisburg, Pa., 1979), chap. 9; Laura L. Becker, "Diversity and Its Significance in an Eighteenth-Century Pennsylvania Town," in *Friends and Neighbours: Group Life in America's First Plural Society*, ed. Michael Zuckerman (Philadelphia, 1982), 200.

18. Carville V. Earle, "The First English Towns of North America," *Geographical Review* 67 (1977): 45, notes that family migrations occurred during depressions. See *Winthrop Papers*, vol. 1, passim, for evidence on tight organization and the great array of commodities carried over. See also Stephen Foster, *Their Solitary Way: The Puritan Social Ethic in the First Century of Settlement in New England* (New Haven, 1971), xvi; and Breen, *Puritans and Adventurers*, chap. 1.

19. David T. Konig, "English Legal Change and the Origins of Local Government in Northern Massachusetts," in *Town and County: Essays on the Structure of Local Government in the American Colonies*, ed. Bruce C. Daniels (Middletown, Conn., 1978), 12–43. On the subsequent and specialized development of the courts and on increasing litigation see Peter E. Russell, "The Massachusetts Superior Court and the American Revolution: The Professionalization of a Judicial Elite, 1740–1775," in *Man and Nature: Proceedings of the Canadian Society for Eighteenth-Century Studies* 1, ed. Roger L. Emerson et al. (London, Ont., 1982), 109–18.

20. Robert A. Gross, *The Minutemen and Their World* (New York, 1976), 84; idem, "The Problem of the Agricultural Crisis in Eighteenth-Century New England: Concord, Massachusetts, as a Test Case" (Paper presented at a meeting of the American Historical Association, Atlanta, Ga., 1975), 8; Shurtleff, *Records of Massachusetts Bay*, 3: 102, 1: 72; Daniels, *Connecticut Town*, 69–70.

21. Eric Nellis, "Labor and Community in Massachusetts Bay: 1630–1660," *Labour History* 18 (1977): 538, 542; Russell, *A Long, Deep Furrow*, 76; Shurtleff, *Records of Massachusetts Bay*, 3: 102; Nellis, "Work and Social Stability in Pre-Revolutionary Massachusetts," Canadian Historical Association, *Historical Papers/Communications Historiques Presented at the Annual Meeting 1981*, 81–100.

22. Quoted in Breen, *Puritans and Adventurers*, 23. See also Charles S. Grant, *Democracy in the Connecticut Frontier Town of Kent* (New York, 1961), 167; and Rutman, *Winthrop's Boston*, 203.

23. Daniels, *Connecticut Town*, 120; Robert E. Wall, Jr., *Massachusetts Bay: The Crucial Decade, 1640–1650* (New Haven, 1972); Alan Macfarlane, *The Family Life of Ralph Josselin: A Seventeenth-Century Clergyman* (New York, 1977).

24. Innes, "Land Tenancy"; Bridenbaugh, *Fat Mutton*, 133–34; Daniels, *Connecticut Town*, 20–22; Lockridge, *New England Town*, chap. 1 and 2. On religion and the everyday life see Christopher Jedrey, *The World of John Cleaveland: Family and Community in Eighteenth-Century New England* (New York, 1979), esp. 104–19; and more generally, Gregory Baum, *Religion and Alienation: A Theological Reading of Sociology* (New York, 1975).

25. Douglas L. Jones, "The Strolling Poor: Transiency in Eighteenth-Century Massachusetts," *Journal of Social History* 8 (1975): 28–49; Kenneth A. Lockridge, *Settlement and Unsettlement in Early America: The Crisis of Political Legitimacy before the Revolution* (Cambridge, Mass., 1981), 24.

26. Gross, *Minutemen*, 102; Joan Hoff Wilson, "The Illusion of Change: Women and the American Revolution," in *The American Revolution: Explorations in the History of American Radicalism*, ed. Alfred E. Young (De Kalb, Ill., 1976), 383–445; Daniels, *Connecticut Town*, 81, 95, 100, 171; Lockridge, *New England Town*, 31.

27. Paul Boyer and Stephen Nissenbaum, *Salem Possessed: The Social Origins of Witchcraft* (Cambridge, Mass., 1974); Wood, "Village and Community," fig. 1, which notes that the term "village" was most widely used in Essex County; Bender, *Community and Social Change*, 60, quoting Peter Laslett.

28. Joan Thirsk, *Economic Policy and Projects: The Development of a Consumer Society in Early Modern England* (Oxford, 1978); Alan Macfarlane, *The Origins of English Individualism: The Family, Property and Social Transition* (New York, 1979); Rosamond Faith, review of Macfarlane, *Origins*, in *Journal of Peasant Studies* 7 (1980): 384–89; Breen, *Puritans and Adventurers*, chap. 1.

29. Daniel Scott Smith, "A Malthusian-Frontier Interpretation of United States Demographic History before c. 1815," in *Urbanization in the Americas: The Background in Comparative Perspective*, ed. Woodrow Borah, Jorge Hardoy, and Gilbert Stelter (Ottawa, 1980), 16–17.

30. Darrett B. Rutman, "The Social Web: A Prospectus for the Study of the Early American Community," in *Insights and Parallels: Problems and Issues of American Social History*, ed. William L. O'Neill (Minneapolis, 1973), 57–89; Macfarlane, *Ralph Josselin*; Jedrey, *The World of John Cleaveland*. On the German terms see the critical analysis in Baum, *Religion and Alienation*, 45–46.

31. E. P. Thompson, "Eighteenth-Century English Society: Class Struggle Without Class?" *Social History* 3 (1978): 133; Dean C. Tipps, "Modernization Theory and the Comparative Study of Societies: A Critical Perspective," *Comparative Studies in Society and History* 15 (1973): 199–226; David Szatmary, *Shays' Rebellion: The Making of an Agrarian Insurrection* (Amherst, 1980). Cf. Robert Zemsky, *Merchants, Farmers, and River Gods: An Essay on Eighteenth-Century American Politics* (Boston, 1971); Micael Zuckerman, "Introduction: Puritans, Cavaliers, and the Motley Middle," in Zuckerman, *Friends and Neighbours*, esp. 20, an unhelpful polarization using these categories.

32. Kevin D. Kelly, "The Independent Mode of Production," *Radical Review of Political Economics* 11, no. 1 (1979): 38–48; Michael Merrill, "Cash Is Good to Eat: Self-Sufficiency and Exchange in the Rural Economy of the United States," *Radical History Review* 4 (1977): 42–71; Christopher Clark, "Household Economy, Market Exchange and the Rise of Capitalism in the Connecticut Valley, 1800–1860," *Journal of Social History* 13 (1979): 169–89; Robert Brenner, "The Origins of Capitalist Development: A Critique of Neo-Smithian Marxism," *New Left Review*, no. 104 (1977): esp. 88–90; James A. Henretta, "Families and Farms: *Mentalité* in Pre-Industrial America," *William and Mary Quarterly*, 3d ser., 35 (1978): 3–32 (see also reply by James T. Lemon and comment by Henretta, ibid. 37 [1980]: 688–700).

33. Jackson Turner Main, *The Social Structure of Revolutionary America* (Princeton, 1965), 66, 221–23; David Levine, personal communication, on estimates of English numbers; Robert Sherry, "Comments on O'Connor's Review of the Twisted Dream: Independent Commodity Production versus Petty Bourgeois Production," *Monthly Review: An Independent Socialist Magazine* 28 (May 1976): 52–63; J. P. Cooper, "In Search of Agrarian Capitalism," *Past and Present*, no. 80 (1978), 20–65; Carole Shammas, "Consumer Behavior in Colonial America," *Social Science History* 6 (1982): 67–86.

34. See James T. Lemon, "The Weakness of Place and Community in Early Pennsylvania," in Gibson, *European Settlement and Development in North America*, 190–207, in which the local government is the focus.

35. Kevin P. Kelly, "'In Dispers'd Plantations': Settlement Patterns in Seventeenth-Century Surry County, Virginia," in Tate and Ammerman, *The Chesapeake in the Seventeenth Century*, 183–205; Carville V. Earle, *The Evolution of a Tidewater Settlement System: All Hallow's Parish, Maryland, 1650–1783* (Chicago, 1975), chaps. 1, 5, 7, maps on 21, 190.

36. Kelly, "'In Dispers'd Plantations,'" 190, 198, 202, 186–89; Gregory A. Stiverson, *Poverty in a Land of Plenty: Tenancy in Eighteenth-Century Maryland* (Baltimore, 1977), 8; Edmund S. Morgan, *American Slavery—American Freedom: The Ordeal of Colonial Virginia* (New York, 1975), 219–26, 420. The ratio is from Lockridge, *Settlement and Unsettlement*, 67. See also Earle, *Tidewater Settlement System*, 96–97, 81; and Harry Roy Merrens, *Colonial North Carolina in the Eighteenth Century: A Study in Historical Geography* (Chapel Hill, 1964), 121–22.

37. William H. Seiler, "The Anglican Church: A Basic Institution of Local Government," and Lois Green Carr, "The Foundations of Social Order: Local Government in Colonial Maryland," both in Daniels, *Town and County*, 134–59, 72–110, 151; Thompson, "The Grid of Inheritance."

38. Seiler, "Anglican Church," 139; Robert Wheeler, "The County Court in Virginia," in

Daniels, *Town and County*, 114; Earle, *Tidewater Settlement System*, 207, 169–81; Stiverson, *Poverty in a Land of Plenty*, 84, 100.

39. Morgan, *American Slavery—American Freedom*, 344; Douglas Hay, "Property, Authority and the Criminal Law," in *Albion's Fatal Tree: Crime and Society in Eighteenth-Century England*, ed. Douglas Hay et al. (New York, 1975), 17–64; Wheeler, "The County Court," 127, 129.

40. E. A. Wrigley, "A Simple Model of London's Importance in Changing English Society and Economy, 1650–1750," *Past and Present*, no. 37 (1967): 44–70.

41. The classic work is Walter Christaller, *Central Places in Southern Germany*, trans. C. W. Baskin (Englewood Cliffs, N.J., 1966). See also Bonnie Barton, "The Creation of Centrality," *Annals, Association of American Geographers* 68 (1978): 34–44; and James W. Simmons, "The Organization of the Urban System," in *Systems of Cities*, ed. Larry S. Bourne and James W. Simmons (New York, 1978), 61–69. The issue of centrality is by no means settled. But even though the pure model is not applicable, there is no reason to reject key ideas, as John McCusker and Russell R. Menard seemingly do while overstressing staples in "The Economy of British America 1607–1790: Needs and Opportunities for Study" (Draft for discussion, Conference on the Economy of British America, Williamsburg, Va., October 1980, mimeographed), chap. 13.

42. Michael Conzen, "The American Urban System in the Nineteenth Century," in *Geography and the Urban Environment: Progress in Research and Applications, Volume IV*, ed. D. T. Herbert and R. J. Johnston (Chichester, Eng., 1981); Diane Lindstrom, *Economic Development in the Philadelphia Region, 1810–1850* (New York, 1978).

43. James Vance, *The Merchant's World: The Geography of Wholesaling* (Englewood Cliffs, N.J., 1970).

44. Earle, "The First English Towns of North America," 33–50, 42. See also Sylvia D. Fries, *The Urban Idea in Colonial America* (Philadelphia, 1977).

45. McManis, *Colonial New England*, chap. 3; Carl Bridenbaugh, *Cities in the Wilderness: The First Century of Urban Life in America, 1625–1742*, 2d ed. (New York, 1955).

46. Russell, *A Long, Deep Furrow*, 80; Winifred B. Rothenberg, "The Market and Massachusetts Farmers, 1750–1855," *Journal of Economic History* 61 (1981): 312. But see Gross, *Minutemen*, 91.

47. Konig, "English Legal Change"; Bruce C. Daniels, "The Political Structure of Local Government in Colonial Connecticut," in Daniels, *Town and County*, 44–71.

48. Edward M. Cook, *The Fathers of the Towns: Leadership and Community Structure in Eighteenth-Century New England* (Baltimore, 1976), esp. chap. 7; p. 79.

49. Daniels, *Connecticut Town*, esp. chap. 7.

50. Ibid., 14, 183–84, 171, 100, 194–95.

51. Smith, "Malthusian-Frontier Interpretation," 18–19. A map of residuals for Connecticut correlating Daniels's land quality with Cook's commercial index of 1774 shows some interesting results. I divided Cook's list exactly as had Daniels, in levels from 8 down to 1, with two towns at level 8, and so on. Sixty-nine of seventy-four towns could be analyzed. Nineteen places showed no residual, twenty-four plus or minus 1. For example, New Haven was in rank 5 in both scales. More interesting were residuals of plus or minus 2 (15), 3 (7), 4 (4). Negative residuals are strongly clustered in the northwest and to a lesser extent in the far east. But the positive residuals are at the mouth and upstream to Middletown on the Connecticut River and by a lesser degree up the Thames. What does this mean? The northwest at least was settled late; hence even by 1774 it may not have reached the "potential" provided by land quality. On the other hand, it would appear that Durham, Killingworth, Colchester, East Haddam, and Hebron (all plus 4 or 3 and not particularly urban it seems) were ahead of their potential. This is suggestive not only of timing, because New London and New Haven were early, but of a stronger degree of commercialization than other data, including Daniels's hierarchy, showed. With the exception of Norwich, this area is not singled out in Lester Cappon, with Barbara Bartz Petchenik and John Hamilton Long, eds., *Atlas of Early American History: The Revolutionary Era, 1760–1790* (Princeton, 1976), 31, by 1775 for significant industrialization. Of course, Jared Eliot of Killingworth may have persuaded all farmers in this not particularly auspicious area to

commercialize intensively! Two other points: early settled and commercialized Wethersfield stands at the top. But why Colchester was second and New Haven only fifteenth on Cook's index should be looked into. This exercise (available on request) shows one possible way of correlating data without a computer and the like: it is useful as a diagnostic tool in teasing out issues for analysis from what tax collectors, town clerks, and others kept for us. A recent study by Thomas Reed Lewis, Jr., "From Suffield to Saybrook: An Historical Geography of Connecticut River Valley in Connecticut before 1800" (Ph.D. diss., Rutgers University, 1978), esp. 217, raises questions from a population perspective, notably on East Haddam. See also 1790 town densities in Barton, "Centrality," 43.

52. Wood, "Origin of the New England Village," and idem, "Village and Community." Both contain mapped examples of settlement patterns.

53. Barton, "Centrality"; using local histories and other scattered data, Barton generated graphs correlating population and activities. See Van Beck Hall, *Politics Without Parties: Massachusetts, 1780–1791* (Pittsburgh, 1972), for a categorization of towns.

54. Smith, "Malthusian-Frontier Interpretation," 19; Gross, "The Problem of the Agricultural Crisis"; Rothenberg, "The Market and Massachusetts Farmers"; U.S. Bureau of the Census, *Historical Statistics of the United States, Colonial Times to 1957* (Washington, D.C., 1960), 757; Carville V. Earle, "A Geographer's Observations on an Economist's Pursuit of 'Exact History,'" review essay of *Wealth of a Nation to Be: The American Colonies on the Eve of the Revolution*, by Alice Hanson Jones, *Annals of Scholarship* 1 (1980): 107–16. Earle presents recalculations showing that per capita wealth in New England was lower than Jones's result. Overall he reduces her wealth growth rate from 0.35 percent per year to 0.27 percent and so suggests no decline after 1774. See also James A. Henretta, "Wealth and Social Structure," in this volume.

55. George Corwin Papers, notably Account Book 1653–1654, Essex Institute, Salem (reported to me by Daniel Vickers); Nellis, "Work and Social Stability," 99–100. On the nature of money see Joseph Albert Ernst, *Money and Politics in America, 1755–1775: A Study in the Currency Act of 1764 and the Political Economy of Revolution* (Chapel Hill, 1973), viii.

56. Fernand Braudel, *Capitalism and Material Life, 1400–1800*, trans. Miriam Kochan (New York, 1973), 400.

57. Joseph Albert Ernst and Harry Roy Merrens, "Camden's Turrets Pierce the Skies! The Urban Process in the Southern Colonies during the Eighteenth Century," *William and Mary Quarterly*, 3d ser., 30 (1973): 549–74, esp. 555. Hermann Wellenreuther, "Urbanization in the Colonial South: A Critique," ibid. 31 (1974): 653–68, presents an articulate response with some good points, as does a letter by Fred Siegel. See also James O'Mara, "Urbanization in Tidewater Virginia during the Eighteenth Century: A Study in Historical Geography" (Ph.D. diss., York University, 1979); Earle, *Tidewater Settlement System;* Michael Mullin, ed., *American Negro Slavery: A Documentary History* (Columbia, S.C., 1976), introduction; Merrens, *Colonial North Carolina*, chap. 7; Carville V. Earle and Ronald Hoffman, "Staple Crops and Urban Development in the Eighteenth-Century South," *Perspectives in American History* 10 (1976): 7–78.

58. On Williamsburg see Fries, *Urban Idea in Colonial America*, chap. 4.

59. Jacob M. Price, "Economic Function and the Growth of American Port Towns in the Eighteenth Century," *Perspectives in American History* 8 (1974): 123–86; Morton Rothstein, "Antebellum Wheat and Cotton Exports: A Contrast in Marketing Organization and Economic Development," *Agricultural History* 41 (1967): 91–100; Lemon, *Best Poor Man's Country*, 127; Harry Roy Merrens, "The Physical Environment of Early America: Images and Image-Makers in Colonial South Carolina," *Geographical Review* 59 (1969): 530–56.

60. Brian J. L. Berry, "City Size Distributions and Economic Development," *Economic Development and Cultural Change* 9 (1961): 573–87.

61. Robert D. Mitchell, *Commercialism and Frontier, Perspectives on the Early Shenandoah Valley* (Charlottesville, 1977), esp. 191; Paul G. E. Clemens, *The Atlantic Economy and Colonial Maryland's Eastern Shore: From Tobacco to Grain* (Ithaca, N.Y., 1980), esp. 198–204.

62. Lemon, *Best Poor Man's Country*, chap. 5; Wood, *Conestoga Crossroads;* Stephanie Grauman

Wolf, *Urban Village: Population, Community and Family Structure in Germantown, Pennsylvania, 1683–1800* (Princeton, 1976); Becker, "Diversity and Its Significance."

63. Lemon, *Best Poor Man's Country*, 132–37; Lindstrom, *Economic Development in the Philadelphia Region.*

64. Compared with what was described in, for example, John M. Bumsted and James T. Lemon, "New Approaches in Early American Studies: The Local Community in New England," *Histoire Sociale/Social History: A Canadian Review* 2 (November 1968): 98–112. See Jedrey, *The World of John Cleaveland*, xiii; Flaherty, *Privacy*, 106–10; Richard Gough, *The History of Myddle*, ed. David Hey (Harmondsworth, 1981), 18; and Richard L. Bushman, "American High-Style and Vernacular Cultures," in this volume.

65. Raymond Williams, *The Country and the City* (New York, 1973), esp. chaps. 2 and 25.

66. Anna T. Lincoln, *Wilmington, Delaware: Three Centuries under Four Flags, 1607–1937* (Rutland, Vt., 1937), map endpapers.

5

DEMOGRAPHIC DEVELOPMENT
AND FAMILY STRUCTURE

JIM POTTER

INTRODUCTION

etween the middle 1930s, when three major works appeared,[1] and the publication in 1962 of Y. Yasuba's pioneering study of the American birth rate in the nineteenth century,[2] American demographic history was a neglected subject. With the exception of incidental references, not always (as has subsequently emerged) accurate or adequately documented, colonial demography continued to attract little attention for several more years. Then in the second half of the 1960s the writings began to appear of a number of researchers who, unknown to each other at the time, had been independently pursuing their own separate lines of enquiry.

Since 1965 a rapidly growing volume of work on American population history has been published, enabling one of its major contributors, Maris Vinovskis, to write in 1979 that "most of the work in this field has been done during the past fifteen years."[3] But, as Vinovskis went on to state, this work was "still unfamiliar to large segments of the scholarly world." Shortly before the appearance of the Vinovskis's compilation, another American commentator had complained in 1977: "Indeed, foreigners—a Japanese, a Briton and two Australians—are responsible for several of the most important research contributions in the last two decades."[4]

To be sure, a great deal of this recent work in American demographic history has been concerned with the national period, but even so, there has been a very significant increase in both general and monographic studies of different aspects of colonial population history. (The notes to this chapter consist mainly of writings since 1965.)

Of course an important element in this upsurge of interest in historical

123

demography in America was the gradually increasing awareness of the European work in the field, which had been going on for some time, work above all associated with the *Annales* school in France and the Cambridge Group for the History of Population and Social Structure in England.[5] But this extraneous circumstance is not enough to explain the development of an interest in population studies for the first time in the whole of the long historiography of America. The first cause was indubitably an illustration of Dr. Johnson's famous dictum, "Depend upon it, Sir, when a man knows he is to be hanged in a fortnight, it concentrates his mind wonderfully." The late 1960s saw a new growth industry in American publishing. They were "days of wrath and doom impending": books with such inflammatory titles as *The Population Bomb, Famine 1975*, or simply *Too Many Americans* all declared, with neo-Malthusian foreboding, that population growth and its supposedly resultant or associated problems had reached crisis proportions.[6] Demography, if those popular works deserved to be described as such, became suddenly fashionable, although the appeal turned out to be ephemeral.[7] The doomsters were less interested in the historical record (and occasionally displayed appalling ignorance and misinformation about it) than they were in making dire predictions, but their view that the whole world, with America showing the way, was facing a demographic calamity of enormous magnitude did concentrate a lot of minds on demographic questions, and a few more people began to recognize the importance of examining America's demographic experience. Interest was awakened, for instance, in the writings of the Reverend T. R. Malthus and in the relevance of his theories for America and the world today (but not enough interest in what Malthus actually wrote about the American colonies).

Other trends and changes within American academe also gave a timely impetus to the study of the national demographic history. First, the development for very different reasons of black studies inevitably drew attention to the black demographic experience both during and after slavery. This development was of particular relevance for colonial studies, and an important part of recent work has been concerned with demographic aspects of slavery and the slave trade in the seventeenth and eighteenth centuries.

The subsequent development of other ethnic studies came to include the American Indian, obviously of special significance in the colonial period, as well as every identifiable immigrant group, from the earliest Portuguese and Spanish travelers and settlers through the Scotch-Irish and English, the Palatine Germans and Salzburgers, to the recent enormous Hispanic invasion. Many contemporary American problems of the 1970s added to the momentum towards the study of ethnicity and thus, inevitably, population history.

Together, black and other ethnic studies brought increasing realization that even in the colonial period not all regions and subregions had homogeneous populations and cultures. At different points in time the different colonies offered contrasting mixes of Indian, black, and European peoples; and within the European population the composition varied significantly, by country and region of origin, religion, age and sex structure, marital behavior, and cultural heritage.

Second, the Women's Movement, by whatever description it is known, created its own brand of history, women's history, and for a time in the 1970s scholarly historical meetings almost came to be dominated by that theme. To the extent that women's studies also drew attention to the family as a social institution, as well as to woman's role in society, age of marriage, sex relations, childbearing, and lactation practices, their relevance to population history is obvious. Indeed the development of family history as yet another separate discipline has made vital contributions to population history more generally.[8]

An associated permissive factor assisting the development of demographic history—the word *permissive* is used quite deliberately here—has been the removal of barriers in the United States, indeed in most parts of the Western world, to the serious academic study and discussion of sexual relations (without which there could be no demography). Yet as recently as 1965, when the Library of the Kinsey Institute, in Bloomington, Indiana, offered one of the few collections of appropriate materials, many still considered the subject to be not quite suitable for a serious historian.[9] It may be added that where these various areas of interest have coincided, especially but not exclusively those of black studies and the family, the results have been particularly valuable to the demographic historian.[10]

The final factor conducive to the growth of demographic history will no doubt prove in the long run to have been the most important. If the circumstances so far mentioned helped determine the themes, the last element—the computer—has been decisive in determining the methodology. The development of cliometrics, that is, the increased use of statistical data and the ability to handle a quantity of data many times greater than before, together with much greater sophistication in the manipulation of those data, has influenced most areas of historical enquiry. In the last decade and a half many branches of American historiography have become increasingly mathematical, or at least numerical. The "new" highly quantitative economic history (or econometric history) of the late sixties and early seventies has been succeeded by the "new" highly quantitative social history of the late seventies and early eighties. Given the obvious fact that many, even most, aspects of demographic history are quantitative in their very nature, using as their raw materials the regular censuses of the national period and the irregular "counts" of the colonial period, the cliometricians themselves have finally discovered demography and recognized what a fertile field for further quantification is offered there; currently we are perhaps in the midst of something of a takeover bid for control of the subject by the cliometricians.

Traditional literary historians may be justified in regarding this development with some alarm and trepidation. The invasion of different fields of study by cliometricians has often been professionally divisive. The mathematically trained practitioners, with one or two notable exceptions, are more skilled at computerization than at verbalization and have usually failed lamentably to explain themselves to the uninitiated; they have shown a low tolerance for the nonmathematically inclined, who find the mathematical techniques difficult or impossible to understand. An American colonial historian accustomed perhaps to reading seventeenth-century sermons or eighteenth-century lawsuits may be excused for adverse reaction when on opening a history book he is confronted by pages of seemingly incomprehensible algebra.[11]

This sets a real problem for the integration of some of the recent developments in demographic history with the mainstream literary writings. One of the leading interpreters of the specialist writers to the layman, Daniel Scott Smith, has stated the problem clearly.[12] Starting from the sweeping but justifiable claim that "historical demography is perhaps the most multidisciplinary area of historical research," he states his qualifications for the aspiring historical demographer: "(1) a knowledge of the methods of demography and the comparative findings of historical demography; (2) a concern for the accuracy of facts deriving from, among other sources, the scientific historiography of the period under examination; and (3) an interpretive framework based on informed historical speculation or an explicit social science model applied to a topic of substantive significance."[13]

To take but the first of these criteria: even without the more extreme manifestation of algebraic formulations, demography is itself a highly technical subject into which the general historian strays at his peril. Smith himself proceeds in the article cited to take to task several of his fellow practitioners for their technical "errors," "demographic slips," or "fallacies"; many of his examples are from the recent writings on colonial demography, including numerous works mentioned in the notes to this chapter.

At one extreme, the claim has been made that the demographic historical writings of the past decade and a half have approached closer to the ideal of "total history" than any other branch of the discipline; at the same time, technical problems remain. The historian and the demographer have gradually been learning to fuse their disciplines; historians have begun to master demography, demographers to be less technical. The historian above all has been learning the limits of possibility and when he ought to be surprised by his findings.[14]

By now the point has surely been adequately made that numerous features of the intellectual climate in the United States since 1965 have greatly encouraged a heightened interest in American demographic history, not least in the colonial period. The past decade and a half has indeed witnessed a considerable output of demographic studies; and the rest of this chapter will attempt to summarize the present state of knowledge about colonial population and colonial family life.[15] Daniel Scott Smith's cautionary words must, however, be kept constantly in mind. Compared with the state of the subject in many other countries, demographic history in the United States is still in its infancy. Since a number of significant points of agreement are emerging, despite Smith's strictures on his colleagues, it would be too strong to say, as Gary Nash does in his chapter on social development, that demographic history is "in glorious disarray." But although enormous progress has been made, the work has only just begun; what has been accomplished is small in comparison with what is still uncertain or still awaits investigation.

Above all it is to be regretted that the impact of these studies of population history on "mainstream" American historiography is still rather limited. To quote Richard Easterlin again, speaking of the area with which he is particularly acquainted: "American economic historians have virtually ignored exciting new works on colonial demography by their colleagues in social history."[16] There is as yet quite inadequate investigation of the broader implications for political, economic, social, and cultural history of such demographic variables as population growth rates, in total and for specific groups, as well as sex ratios, age structure, age of marriage, incidence of childbearing, mortality, household and family size and composition, ethnic mix, and mobility and the differences over time and between regions in all these variables.

THE QUESTIONS

The demographic history of colonial America, possibly more than any other branch of its history, must be studied in constant awareness both of the length of the period and of the total size, as well as of the geographical and climatic diversity, of the colonies. The most important single result of the recent research described above has been to emphasize the danger of generalization. This is equally true whether one is considering the dynamics of population growth either in total or for separate regions and colonies or attempting cross-sectional comparisons of the demographic situation in different places at particular times. The early studies of the 1960s were inclined to generalize and indeed were to some extent characterized by a deliberate search for generalization. The later studies of the 1970s and beyond, sometimes using more sophisticated techniques of analysis, have insisted on the need to particularize.

In many, or even most, significant respects, the seventeenth-century picture is very different from that of the eighteenth century (and the same applies to separate decades within each); in the broadest terms, the New England studies produced different findings from those of the later Chesapeake studies. The most usual division into three regions—New England, the Middle Colonies, and the South—itself appears inadequate: intraregional differences may be as significant as interregional differences; the "South" is too large and diverse to be a useful category for demographic purposes and needs to be subdivided into Upper and Lower. Within every separate colony the newly settled territories, the "frontier," had a different profile from those settled earlier: some areas offered much more benign ecological conditions than others; emergent small towns showed markedly different patterns from the prevailing rural patterns. One could extend much further the areas of enquiry where other comparisons might be found: by ethnicity (native Indian; black, slave or free, rural or urban; white, first, second, third, and subsequent generations; white considered by European origin; or white considered by social class or economic status); by marital behavior (age of marriage, frequency of marriage, illegitimacy, bridal pregnancies); by demographic structure (age structure and in particular the producer-dependent ratio, sex ratios, the relative contribution to population growth of in-migration and natural growth, respectively); by mortality (life expectancy, infant and child mortality, incidence of widowhood and orphanhood). These different factors all interacted with each other, often in complicated ways: the continuance of indentured servitude in the Chesapeake and elsewhere created a male surplus and, because of the period of indenture, postponed the marriage of females, the former lowering the potential birth rate, the latter the fertility rate; male life expectancy affected the age at which a man's sons inherited property and thus, arguably, their own age of marriage; the very fact of rapid population growth, where it occurred, created an age structure with a particularly large proportion of the population under fifteen, or even under ten, years of age.

Even if generalizations have come to appear increasingly dubious, the important task still remains of attempting to assess in what ways American demographic experiences in the colonial period had unique features and to what extent these experiences diverged from those in other parts of the world at a comparable stage of development. International comparisons may be useful to provide yardsticks against which the American rate can be measured. How different was the fate of the aboriginal American population, the Indians, from that of aboriginals elsewhere, such as the Maoris of New Zealand or, for that matter, the Indians in other parts of the Americas? How did slave demography in the mainland American colonies differ from that in the West Indies? Did it take more or less time for new white settlements, for example, in Australia or Canada, to establish themselves as self-sufficient in food supplies? How did the rate of growth of the free white population, once the initial seasoning period (however long that may have been in different regions) was over, compare with growth rates in contemporary Europe? In most socioeconomic questions, international comparisons are notoriously hazardous, but it is at least arguable that demographic data, dealing with such universals as births and deaths, offer rather greater safety in numbers.

Although the answers are liable to be (but will not necessarily be) different for every region and subregion, every generation, and every ethnic (or otherwise culturally differentiated) group, it is still possible to ask the same questions. A very suitable framework of reference is provided by the assertions of the late-eighteenth-century writers, above all Benjamin Franklin, Ezra Stiles, and Edward Wigglesworth the Younger in America and Richard Price and above all T. R. Malthus in Britain.[17] We may turn into questions the statements made by these contemporaries about American population and ask them not about an unrealistic aggregate called "the American colonies" but about every region and every ethnic group in every time period, adding a further set of supplementary questions and observations.[18]

How far, then, does recent research support the contemporary assertions that in colonial America:

1. "throughout all the northern colonies, the population was found to double itself in twenty-five years . . . a rapidity of increase probably without parallel in history" (Malthus);

2. "in the back settlements [that is, in newly settled frontier lands] . . . they were found to double their own number in fifteen years" (Malthus);

3. "this rapid population of the Americas arises, partly from the great accession of foreigners, but principally from the natural increase of the inhabitants" (Wigglesworth);

4. "marriages in America are more general, and more generally early, than in Europe" (Franklin) and "Americans are induced to marry earlier in life, and consequently their families of children are more numerous" (Wigglesworth);

5. "if in Europe they have but four births to a marriage (many of their marriages being late), we may reckon eight; of which if one half grow up . . . our people must at least be doubled every twenty [sic] years" (Franklin);

6. "the ease of procuring subsistence for a family is occasioned by the boundless tracts of uncultivated forests, bordering on their plantations. For every new-married couple can, at small expense, purchase a freehold; which by their industry, will afford them and their children a comfortable support" (Wigglesworth); and "in the inland parts of North America, in the back settlements, where almost everyone occupies land for himself, there is an increase so rapid as to have hardly any parallel" (Price);[19]

7. "political institutions . . . were favourable to the alienation and division of property [significance of inheritance]" (Malthus); and

8. "where there are few people, and a great quantity of fertile land, the power of the earth to afford a yearly increase of food may be compared to a great reservoir of water, supplied by a moderate stream. The faster

population increases, the more help will be got to draw off the water, and consequently an increasing quantity will be taken every year" (Malthus)?

The supplementary questions to be attached to these contemporary statements are as follows:

1. Does the twenty-five-year period of doubling apply to all the colonies throughout the colonial period? Each new community underwent an initial period of settlement, in which population growth depended on in-migration. The first objectives of these first colonizers were survival, then self-sufficiency, and then growth. The loss of life in the first phase, the "seasoning period," was often very high. One estimate indicates, for example, that in the early years of Virginian settlement at least fifteen thousand migrants were required over a forty-year period to produce a population of about half that total; for a considerable time Virginia was simply "a death trap for most of those who went there."[20]

The questions that follow are central to the demographic experience of every settlement and every region. How long was the "seasoning period" before the population could become both self-supporting economically and self-generating demographically? Was it longer in the seventeenth century than in the eighteenth century? Did it vary greatly from region to region? The evidence strongly suggests that the "seasoning period" was much shorter in New England than further south. The recent Chesapeake studies depict conditions that indicate that it was not until well into the eighteenth century that, after quite catastrophic losses of life, the population can be said to have become self-reproducing.

In the next stage, after the achievement of self-sufficiency, what growth rates were achieved and by what date? The Franklin-Malthus formula of a doubling in a generation (whether twenty or twenty-five years) does not represent the experience of every colony (some were faster, some were slower) in this eventual phase of self-sustained growth.

2. Is the supposition that population growth was more rapid at the frontier than in the older settlements supported by evidence? The founding of a new "colony" to the west (or north, or south, or wherever the new lands were being brought into cultivation) replicated the process of original colonization: first a phase of struggle for survival, then the gradual achievement of self-sufficiency, and then the eventual growth. Such new settlements may be regarded as a process of investment: present satisfactions were sacrificed in the anticipation of future benefits. How great were the necessary sacrifices (perhaps in terms of lives lost or living standards forgone), and for how long did they continue? How great were the ultimate rewards, and how did they vary from

place to place according to ecological circumstances? How long was it before the very rapid growth rate indicated by a doubling every fifteen years was achieved?

3. What were the contributions to growth made by natural increase and migration, respectively, in both the seasoning and subsequent periods? Franklin attributed more weight to "the accession of foreigners" (no doubt reflecting his vantage point in Philadelphia) than did Malthus, who almost totally ignored migration.

The very concept of "migrant contribution" requires clarification.[21] Are we concerned with the total number of emigrants leaving Europe, the number actually arriving in the colonies, or the number surviving as permanent settlers. What has been termed "gate mortality" refers to deaths both on the journey and during the first difficult months of acclimatization.

It is now clear that the migrant contribution varied greatly from decade to decade, perhaps reflecting conditions of war or peace, and between regions. As already observed, it affected the age and sex structure of the colonies. The conditions of the migration—slave, indentured, or free—obviously affected subsequent events in many different ways, for example, illegitimate births and age of eventual marriage. Further, what "cultural baggage" did migrants carry with them to influence their subsequent social behavior, and for how long was it influential?

4. The age and incidence of marriage are now, following the findings of the Cambridge Group for the History of Population and Social Structure, coming to be accepted as the most important single determinant of population growth. If it was true that marriages occurred earlier in America than in Europe, by how many years were they earlier, and how did this vary in different parts of the colonies? Did the age of marriage change over time during the colonial period?

5. What was the size of families in colonial America? Franklin's statement is remarkably pessimistic, assuming as it does that only half of all children born reached adulthood. If age of marriage is the most important single variable in determining family size, other factors that nevertheless have to be considered are the spacing of children and infant mortality. Recent research on other parts of the Western world give some guidance as to what may be considered usual. Even in areas of very high population growth (the Hutterites usually being considered the group against which others can be measured), an interval between births of about two years has been found to have been normal (owing primarily to the prolongation of lactation but possibly also to other methods of family limitation). Similarly, figures for infant mortality from late-seventeenth-century England of about 180 per 1,000 live births (but varying between extremes of 100 and 300) set bench marks

against which to compare any figures found for the American colonies.[22]

Family structure is also affected by the age of death of parents and grandparents. In this context, it is appropriate to mention the significance of diet. The eventual (this word begging the question of when that was) high productivity and the variety of colonial agriculture, with meat-producing wild and domesticated animals, high-yield grains, edible vegetables, with a remarkable regularity of harvests and absence of failures, supplemented by fish from the sea, rivers, and lakes, led not merely to survival and self-sufficiency but to a standard of diet that permitted sturdy health. This was not merely important demographically for pregnant and nursing women. The protein and calories provided by the food supplies were transformed into human energy, without which land abundance would have been meaningless. Certainly, studies of colonial nutrition are lacking, but what evidence there is suggests that once the growth period had been reached, malnutrition was minimal and food consumption was at a level permitting long, hard, and heavy labor. In this respect it is worth noting a recent finding that has indicated that human stature in America reached a peak around the end of the colonial period and then remained more or less constant until the middle of the twentieth century.[23]

6. These assertions that frontier conditions were superior to those in settled areas raise the question of the impact on population data, birth rates, and above all death rate of the growth of small towns in the older areas. Much recent evidence indicates a deterioration of conditions as urbanization progressed. As in England, infant mortality does appear to have been closely related to population density; that of the colonial towns may have been as high as that in contemporary English towns of comparable size.

7. The importance of the size of landholdings is worth consideration. A general land abundance was translated into individual farms considerably in excess of those in the Old World. To the family, land abundance meant not only access to new territories but also a farm acreage more than adequate to ensure eventual self-sufficiency. The ancient virgate of medieval Europe (differing greatly, but perhaps generally about thirty acres) was considered the size of landholding which would allow self-sufficiency. In the American colonies the size of farms was often one hundred acres or above (not all cultivable of course until the labor-intensive task of forest clearing had been accomplished).

8. In the final question, Malthus is suggesting that so long as frontier conditions continue to exist, the combination of land and labor will sustain the growth of population.[24] Here, as mentioned earlier, the question of age structure and producer-dependent ratio has to be examined.

THE EVIDENCE

THE INDIAN POPULATION

Although it is not central to the theme of this chapter, it is nevertheless important to recognize the presence of an aboriginal population in the Americas in the seventeenth and eighteenth centuries. Its population history, one of catastrophic decline, not of growth, is very different from that of the white settlers or even of the black slaves.

Until recently, the commonly repeated figure for the Indian population was that there were just over 1,000,000 Indians north of Mexico (846,000 in the eventual central territory of the United States, 220,800 in Canada, and 72,000 in Alaska). This estimate, probably originating just before 1910,[25] was accepted more or less without challenge for many decades. The last few years have seen a major revision of that figure. Recent work, principally at the Newberry Library Center for the History of the American Indians, has cast serious doubts on the accepted figures and indeed has suggested a figure some ten times as great: "The Americas were densely populated at the time Europeans found their way to this New World. Recent estimates place the hemispheric population at 100,000,000 in about 1490. Perhaps two-fifths of that total [i.e., 40,000,000] inhabited North America including the civilized state in Mexico (which contained some 30,000,000 people)."[26]

The implication here that the Indians had a total population not of one million but of ten million obviously necessitates an enormous reappraisal of the history of the Tribes over the subsequent centuries. If their original population was ten times greater than has generally been supposed, then so also (or approximately) must have been the calamitous decline in their numbers, through disease and warfare, during the next three hundred years.[27]

The inquiries of the British government during the colonial period showed little concern about the number of Indians (who were sometimes reported in the returns for "Blacks") except in order to assess their military danger. On the other hand, it is noteworthy that some interbreeding did occur and that some individual governors actively encouraged marriages between settlers and Indians, with the ostensible motive of reducing the need for emigration from England.

THE PROBLEM OF COLONIAL NUMBERS

A number of recent studies have been concerned primarily with colonial population statistics. In 1969 James Cassedy confirmed the notion that Americans have always had a high propensity to count.[28] He suggested two main reasons why more statistical information is in fact available for colonial America than for most parts of Western Europe; first religion, second the very fact of colonial status. More recently still, Robert Wells has compiled and analyzed a list of 124 censuses, or counts, held in twenty-nine American colonies between 1623 and 1775, all in response to requests for information about colonial population (usually for military reasons) from the British government.[29] Wells's book has the advantage of including *all* the American colonies, not merely those eventually incorporated in the United States, and thus provides information about Canada, Newfoundland, Nova Scotia, Bermuda, and the West Indies. Wells shows clearly that, unfortunately, the incidence of the materials bears no relationship to the size or importance of the colony: the best information is available for the Leeward Islands, with nine enumerations between 1678 and 1756; at the other extreme, the scantiest data are those for the two most important colonies: Virginia, with no censuses between 1634 and 1699 (of which little remains) and after counts in 1701 and 1703 no other before the Revolution; and Pennsylvania, with no counts at all.

The available materials therefore vary greatly from colony to colony. At best, they are detailed and probably reliable. At worst, there are few statistical landmarks. Nevertheless, American population problems are of measurable dimensions in that there is a known starting point of zero population and a point of time, 1790, for which the first national census provides a reasonably complete statistical picture, as we will see below.

The differing growth rates of the colonial white population resulted in a wholesale redistribution of the population over the course of the colonial period. Whereas in 1650, 85 percent of the total population was in four colonies (Virginia, 37 percent; Massachusetts, 31 percent; Maryland, 9 percent; and Connecticut, 8 percent), by 1700 the leading four colonies accounted for only two-thirds of the total (Massachusetts, 25 percent; Virginia, 19 percent; Maryland, 12 percent; and Connecticut, 11 percent), by 1750 only 57 percent of the total (Massachusetts, 20 percent; Virginia, 14 percent, Pennsylvania, 12 percent; and Connecticut, 11 percent), and by 1780 less than half the total (Pennsylvania, 14 percent; Virginia, 14 percent; Massachusetts, 12 percent; and Connecticut, 9 percent).

In order to explain these shifts and these varying rates of population growth, we must analyze natural growth (depending on age and sex structure, fertility, and mortality), the contribution to growth from foreign migrants (whether voluntary or involuntary), and internal migration. Of these three variables, least is known about the last, internal migration. However, merely to recognize that there was significant internal migration—not merely to new, "frontier" settlements but also between the older settlements, not merely short-distance, intracolonial movements to the embryonic towns or to new areas but also longer-distance, intercolonial movements—is itself an important step towards a clearer picture of colonial society.

A number of recent studies have indicated that early settlers continued to move after their arrival in America and that both early New Englanders and Virginians were mobile.[30] Population mobility seems to have increased with the passage of time, being much more intense in the eighteenth century than in the seventeenth century. At first, movement was predominantly of single males, but increasingly the most common type of movement came to be of family groups. Increasingly also, perhaps, the movement became longer-distance. Of the movement of Virginian Quakers in the eighteenth century, over fifty percent was by family groups and about 80 percent consisted of movements of over one hundred miles. Differential economic opportunities seem almost universally to have been the main motivation for migration, although religion, war, and social disqualifications also played their part.

This mobility, although not quantifiable in aggregate terms, seems to have been at a level that can only be described as rapid and high. Its social and religious implications were as far-reaching as those for demographic analysis. The trends of migration contributed to the redistribution of population that occurred during the colonial period and to the different growth rates demonstrated by the different colonies. Two generalizations appear to be safe: first, colonial urban populations were as volatile as urban populations have been shown to be in the nineteenth century;[31] second, by the end of the colonial period all the regions of early settlement, but especially the southern part of New England, had become areas of emigration (with the corollary that, as in the nineteenth century, there was a corresponding transmission of the ways of life, attitudes, and religion of the older settlements).

Recent evidence makes it possible to estimate better the contributions made by foreign migrants to colonial population growth. For the seventeenth century, Henry A. Gemery has derived figures that lead him to conclude that just over 150,000 migrants entered the mainland colonies (116,000 to the South, 39,000 to the North) between 1630 and 1700.[32] More than half of the total migration (including that to the Caribbean) occurred between 1630 and 1660; during those three decades *total* population increase in all the colonies was slightly less than half the total migration. It would be dangerous to deduce from that figure a proportionate estimate for the mainland colonies, but it would seem unlikely that migrants contributed more than 100,000 at the very maximum to population growth in the seventeenth century. If Gemery's allocation between northern and southern colonies is reasonably accurate, however, one important conclusion does follow. The aggregate increase in the northern colonies over this time period exceeded that in the southern colonies by some 50,000, yet according to Gemery's figures, migration into the southern colonies exceeded that into the northern colonies by some 70,000. This disparity must result from one or both of two causes: either the loss of migrant population during the seasoning period was very much greater in the southern colonies than in the northern colonies or the natural growth rate in the northern colonies was very much greater than in the southern colonies. These are conditions that confirm the findings of the research (using quite different sources) in the Chesapeake region.

The second contribution comes from David W. Galenson, who presents estimates of decennial net migration to the British mainland colonies between

1650 and 1780.[33] His figures add up to 90,000 white persons for the period 1650–1700 and just under 370,000 for the period 1700–1780. The first total is readily compatible with Gemery's seventeenth-century data, although the distribution among the colonies is somewhat different. The second figure is very close to an earlier estimate of 350,000 for the eighteenth century.[34]

Whatever the precise figures for the number of in-migrants, it is clear that white population growth in all the continental colonies stemmed largely from natural increase. Indeed, recent evidence has not fundamentally disturbed confidence in the basic Malthusian assertion that the population of the American colonies doubled itself by natural increase every twenty-five years. After allowance has been made for the contribution of growth made by migration, the natural-growth-rate figure falls slightly, but not significantly, below that required to satisfy the Malthusian formula.

No attempt will be made at this stage to make generalizations about the cause of this rapid rate of growth beyond the observation that, as in England, the age of marriage, accompanied as it was by low infant mortality, appears to have been the critical determinant. This basically confirms the insight of Benjamin Franklin in his own attempt to explain the faster growth rate of the American population. Marriages were more numerous, occurred at a lower age, and were therefore more fertile in England (because of the age of marriage, not because of higher fertility within marriage). More children were born in each family, and consequently more survived, with the result that, on the average, two parents produced four surviving children (thus the normal total family size was six); as these children repeated in their own lives a similar pattern of marriage and fertility, the population doubled itself with each successive generation.[35]

THE BLACK POPULATION

The comments so far have concerned the white population exclusively; before we look at the regions separately, it is necessary to intrude a brief section on the black population.[36] The same analytical questions apply to the black population as to the white: what population growth resulted from migration (that is, slave importation) and what from natural growth? The most important conclusion to emerge from the available information is that for most of the colonial period the black population grew more rapidly than the white, resulting in a rising percentage of blacks in the total population. Indeed, the black percentage reached its highest point in the second half of the eighteenth century, when between 20 percent and 21 percent of the total population was black.[37]

The first national census, in 1790, showed a black population of three-quarters of a million. If the figure of total slave importation before that date of about 300,000 is accepted, then natural growth clearly played an important part in the growth of the black population, although obviously much less of a part than it played in the growth of the white population.

Table 5.1
DECENNIAL RATES OF POPULATION GROWTH 1630–1790, WHITE AND
BLACK COMPARED

	Percentage Increase		Black as % of of Total Population at End		Percentage Increase		Black as % of Total Population at End of
	White	Black	Decade		White	Black	Decade
1630–40	450%	900%	2%	1710–20	38%	53%	15%
1640–50	87	168	3	1720–30	36	32	14
1650–60	48	82	4	1730–40	41	65	17
1660–70	49	55	4	1740–50	24	57	20
1670–80	35	54	5	1750–60	36	38	20
1680–90	34	40	8	1760–70	33	41	21
1690–1700	15	66	11	1770–80	31	25	21
1700–1710	29	61	14	1780–90	44	32	19

Source: Data calculated from U.S. Bureau of the Census, *Historical Statistics of the United States, Colonial Times to 1970,* 2 vols. (Washington, D.C., 1975), table 21–19, 2:1168.

At what date the slave population began to generate some of its own increase, and how that date and the contribution made by natural growth differed from colony to colony, cannot be stated with certainty. Already in the first decade of the eighteenth century, however, the total increase in the number of slaves of about 17,000 was almost double the likely slave importation in that decade. By the 1730s, when the figures are perhaps safer, the difference is even clearer: an increase of some 60,000 in the total slave population, compared with an importation of 23,000; in the 1760s, when the number of slaves increased by 144,000, the largest increase in any decade, imports accounted for just under one-half.

The fact that the slave population of the American colonies was not entirely reliant on the slave trade for its increase, but was already increasing naturally, is of immense historical significance. It is in sharp contrast with the experience of slave societies in most other parts of the world, but in particular with the West Indies during this same period. The mainland experience was very different from that of the Caribbean, particularly perhaps in Jamaica, where the population history of the black population was nothing short of disastrous.

The final observation to be made about the black population is that it was, of course, very unevenly distributed. After 1690 over 80 percent of all black people in American were to be found in the southern colonies, where they were heavily concentrated in Virginia and the Carolinas. Similarly, the Negro proportion in the population of the South was far higher than that of other regions, as can be seen in Table 5.2.

By 1700 one-quarter of the Virginia population was black, and it rose to

Table 5.2
BLACKS AS A PERCENTAGE OF TOTAL POPULATION, 1640–1790, BY REGION

	1640	1670	1700	1730	1760	1770	1780	1790
Massachusetts	2%	1%	2%	2%	2%	2%	2%	1%
Rhode Island	—	5	5	10	8	6	5	6
Total New England	1	1	2	3	3	3	2	1.7
New York	12	12	12	14	14	12	10	8
New Jersey	—	6	6	8	7	7	7	8
Pennsylvania	—	—	2	2	2	2	2	2
Total Middle Atlantic	12	11	7	8	7	6	6	6.2
Maryland	3	9	11	19	30	31	33	35
Virginia	1	6	28	26	41	42	41	41
North Carolina	—	4	4	20	30	35	34	27
South Carolina	—	15	43	66	61	61	54	44
Total South Atlantic	2	6	21	27	38	40	38	36.4
Kentucky						16	16	17
Tennessee						20	15	11
Total America	2	4	11	14	20	21	21	19.3

Source: See table 5.1.

over 40 percent after 1750 (in 1860 the percentage was 34); after 1750 Virginia also had 40 percent of all Negroes in the mainland colonies. Maryland reached 20 percent by 1710 and 30 percent by 1750, and stayed above that level to the end of the colonial period (25 percent in 1860). The North Carolina proportion remained below 10 percent until after 1710, reaching 20 percent two decades later and 30 percent by 1760 (36 percent in 1869). South Carolina, with its much smaller white population, quickly came to surpass North Carolina, and later even Maryland, in its number of slaves; in 1720 the number of Negroes amounted to as much as 70 percent of the colony's population, declining slowly thereafter to two-thirds and eventually to one-half (59 percent in 1860). It is of considerable importance that the highest-percentage slave component at any period occurred in South Carolina in 1720, just on the eve of the founding of Georgia. In the South as a whole, the Negro proportion was always over 20 percent after 1700 and always over 30 percent after 1740.

The most rapid absolute increase in the slave population was in the Chesapeake Bay area. During the colonial period some hundred thousand slaves were imported into Virginia alone, and the 1790 census showed 300,000 slaves in that state.

REGIONAL DEMOGRAPHIC AND SOCIAL CONTRASTS

As suggested earlier, different colonies experienced very different growth rates at different periods. Despite the much smaller numbers of arriving migrants, the New England colonies grew apace in the seventeenth century at a rate that probably exceeded that of any other contemporary society. While percentages calculated from a low base figure are misleading, the New England growth rate, if calculated from 1640, when the white population had reached 13,700, grew at an average rate of just over 45 percent per decade for the next fifty years, reaching 87,000 by 1690. The contrast with the slower growth rate in the Chesapeake is sharpest if Massachusetts is compared with Virginia; their respective populations were, in 1700, 56,000 and 42,000, again, it must be repeated, despite the much heavier contribution made from the outside world in Virginia.

In the eighteenth century the story changed: growth in New England showed retardation, in the southern colonies acceleration. The average decennial growth rate in New England between 1700 and 1780 was 27 percent; in the southern colonies it was 33 percent: Massachusetts averaged 22 percent, compared with Virginia's 30 percent. The most significant demographic change in the eighteenth century, however, was the expansion of the Middle Colonies, whose white population grew from 48,000 in 1700 to 638,000 in 1780, with Pennsylvania (at 320,000) outstripping both Massachusetts and Virginia (at 264,000 and 317,000, respectively) by 1780. The decennial growth rate of the Middle Colonies between 1700 and 1780 averaged 38 percent, 44 percent for Pennsylvania alone.

Among the various areas of research of the past fifteen years, studies of the family and of mortality have been the most innovative. The works fall broadly into two main groups: the first, those which appeared in the decade after 1965, mainly concerned with New England; the second, those since the early 1970s, concerned with the Chesapeake region.

It is common to both groups that all writers emphasize the primacy of the family among colonial institutions. It is true that the nature of the family varied, but everywhere it was the central human institution. The case is stated particularly aptly by P. D. Hall:

> It is hardly an exaggeration to say that until the late eighteenth century, the major social and economic organization in Massachusetts was the family. . . .
> Lacking a state bureaucracy, standing army and police force, implementation of state policy depended on the family. The church was . . . dependent on the family for daily supervision of morality and behaviour, for it was nonhierarchi-

cal and lacked any direct means of enforcing its mandates. . . . The family was also the center of economic activity, for there were no banks, insurance companies, corporations or other formal economic organizations. Thus whatever capital a merchant might require for his entrepreneurial activities was personal capital. [38]

The regular household consisted of husband, wife, and their own children; rarely was the home shared with an older generation or with married or single siblings. In the New England studies, Demos found marriage contracts providing a house for the betrothed couple; Greven's study of the colonial family strongly stresses its nuclear structure.

The evidence for New England largely confirms the older view of the significance of the nuclear-family unit. [39] Marriage was a contract resulting from a decision to marry, not from falling in love. The establishment of a separate household was an integral part of the institution of marriage, and the woman's place was indubitably in the home. Another point of confirmation is that the basic family pattern was generally maintained after the death of a spouse by the rapid remarriage of the survivor, often within one year, sometimes within six months. The good Puritans of New England controlled their affections, and immoderate mourning after the death of a partner was a sign of excessive self-indulgence.

The new data appear to confirm the earlier impression of a high incidence of marriage. Demos's sample of seven hundred persons who lived to age fifty showed that 60 percent of men and 75 percent of women married once and smaller percentages contracted second and third marriages (unfortunately, he does not give a figure for the never-marrieds). The later Governor's Report for Connecticut showed almost 75 percent of persons between the ages of twenty and seventy to be married in the year of the count (1774); in Litchfield County, with its male surplus, over 80 percent of all women were married.

The findings concerning the age of marriage are particularly important. Contrary to the earlier view, teenage marriage was rare. Demos found that in Plymouth Colony in the seventeenth century the average age of marriage for men was 27, and for women "over" 20, in the early period of settlement; the gap narrowed in the later years, with an average age of 25 for men and 22 for women. Lockridge found that in Dedham, Massachusetts, around the turn of the century the average age for men was 25.5, and for women 22.5. In Andover, Massachusetts, according to Greven, 5 percent of men married before the age of 21, 35 percent between 21 and 24, and 38 percent between 25 and 29; thus the average age of marriage for men was 26.6 years. Just over one-third of females married before the age of 21 and 40 percent between 21 and 24 (that is, 75 percent below the age of 24, compared with 40 percent for men); thus the average age of marriage for women was 22.3. Daniel Scott Smith's calculation of mean age of marriage in Watertown, Massachusetts, produced the figures of 22.4 years between 1641 and 1720 and 22.0 years between 1721 and 1800. Later in the eighteenth century the Governor's Report for Connecticut contained statistics that showed that under 2 percent of men between the ages of 15 and 19 years were married, and under 6 percent of the women. The highest proportion of women married in this age group was in the newer county of Litchfield.

All the evidence thus converges upon an average marriage age for men of twenty-four or twenty-five, and for women of twenty-one or twenty-two. While it does not confirm the picture of teenage marriage, this finding does confirm the assumption that marriage in New England usually occurred at an earlier age than in contemporary Europe.

Childbearing was spread throughout a woman's married life, until menopause. Children within a family might range from infants to grownups of twenty years; the older children, especially girls, were expected to help bring up the younger children. The first child was usually born within nine to fifteen months of marriage, and the subsequent children were often spaced at two-year intervals. This pattern might result from the death of an intervening child or from the practice of some form of deliberate family limitation, through either abstinence from sexual intercourse or prolongation of lactation, since babies were usually breast-fed; there is little or no evidence of artificial contraception during the colonial period (though a different story would have to be told of urban America from the early nineteenth century on). Families thus grew slowly, and family size was directly related to age of parents.

Finally, on the subject of maternal mortality, we may observe that Demos found deaths of women in childbirth to have occurred in about one birth in thirty. If women on the average had six children, then as many as one in five may have died in childbirth.

Infant mortality, according to all the new evidence, was far lower in New England than had been suggested by the earlier writings. The highest was in the study of Demos, who found a death rate of one-quarter of all live-born children before the age of twenty-one years; in other words, three-quarters survived to adulthood. Greven found a higher rate of survival: of 247 live births, 39 died before the age of 21; thus the survival rate was 85 percent. Scott Smith estimated an infant mortality rate of 5–10 percent. From figures in the Governors' Reports for New Jersey a rate of survival to adulthood of about 80 percent may be deduced.

There is a possible objection to all these estimates. It is very likely that no record was kept of stillbirths or births of infants who died in the first days, or even weeks, of life. Scott Smith observed, for example, that few infants appear to have died in their first month. These were probably events best forgotten. It must be assumed that an unknown number of children were born, and died, leaving no trace in the records. The fact that recorded births of survivors are often spaced at two-year intervals greatly increases the uncertainty. It is theoretically possible that there were twice as many actual births as reported births but that death followed quickly enough for the event to pass unrecorded.

To summarize the above findings, one may suggest that the rapidity of natural growth in early New England was due to a combination of factors: marriages between the ages of twenty and twenty-five; births spaced at two-year intervals for the next fifteen to twenty years, producing a total of, say, eight children; and the survival to adulthood of at least three-quarters, and probably more, of the infants whose births were recorded.

The other region to which the greatest attention has been paid in recent research is the early Chesapeake.[40] The picture that has emerged is in sharp contrast to that painted in the earlier writings about New England. The seasoning period was much more protracted in the Chesapeake than in New England. The diseases associated with its subtropical climate took an appalling toll in deaths, similar to that reported for the Caribbean colonies. Mortality continued to be very high, and life expectancy was correspondingly low. Consequently, throughout the seventeenth century the growth of population was very much more dependent on a constant replenishment from the outside; and it was not until well into the eighteenth century that this region became self-reproducing.[41] During the eighteenth century the gap between mortality rates in the Chesapeake and New England seems to have diminished quite sharply, with death rates declining in the former and possibly even rising (in association with urbanization) in the latter.

The continuing arrival of indentured servants produced a sexual imbalance that affected the whole social structure of the region; the male preponderance was at times and in places as high as three to one. While theoretically this imbalance might have been expected to lower the age and increase the incidence of female marriage, it was offset by the fact that so many marriageable girls were indentured servants whose age on arrival was between eighteen and twenty-two, causing a postponement of their marriage until the end of their servitude at least four years later. Consequently, the average age of female marriage appears to have been some three or four years higher than in New England. If the assertion made earlier in this chapter that the lower age of marriage was the most important single reason for the larger size of families was valid, then this postponement of marriage was a further reason why it took longer for the Chesapeake region to reach the stage of rapid, self-generated population growth. Although the late seventeenth century saw a particularly large number of prosecutions of servant girls for illegitimacy, and this development was an obvious source of extramarital births, one punishment for the "crime" of bearing an illegitimate child was the extension of the term of servitude by an appropriate period, thus postponing the age of eventual marriage correspondingly.

While marital fertility itself does not appear to have been significantly different from that found in New England, resultant family size was reduced by a higher infant mortality and also by earlier parental death. Family structure itself was affected by the large number of orphans and in particular by the number of women left at the head of families. One study finds that in about four hundred marriages examined in seventeenth-century Maryland, the wife outlived the husband in about twice as many cases as those in which the husband outlived the wife. These various features all contributed to a degree of instability in the Chesapeake region that contrasted with the stability of the institution of marriage and family in New England.

Before we turn our attention to the region of the Mainland colonies, where population growth was the most rapid, a brief word must be said about the colonies where the other extreme was to be found, namely, the Caribbean colonies.[42] All the evidence points to an extremely high mortality for both the white and the black populations that persisted at least until the end of the eighteenth century in most islands. Population was maintained only through a continuing flow of arrivals from the outside, particularly white servants and black slaves, without which population would have declined. The white population of Jamaica, for example, appears to have reached a peak in 1670, continuing at that level until about 1750 only because of a regular reinforcement by imported servants. By the end of the century the average household size in Jamaica may have doubled, but this may reflect a change in household structure rather than in family size.

It is of course true that conditions varied sharply between the islands, between large and small plantations, between rural and urban (if that description can be used at all), and according to such occupational variables as seagoing activities which took the menfolk away from the islands. But a high mortality rate was everywhere the predominant feature, varying only in its intensity. Family size was small, often extremely small: indeed, one author comments how few "normal" families (that is, consisting of two parents with several children) there were in Barbados. There was a large male surplus in many areas, a low incidence of marriage even among females, and a very low ratio of children to adults. What was usual was that deaths regularly exceeded births. In Jamaica, for example, of the 12,000 inhabitants who had arrived there since 1656 only 3,874 remained in 1661; and between 1670 and 1750, according to one estimate, the white population would have declined by as much as 2 percent per year but for immigration. If that is the story for the white population, the story for the black population was very much grimmer still.

The other region of which a brief word must be said is that where population growth was the greatest, that is, the Middle Colonies in the eighteenth century. The rapid economic development of this region in the eighteenth century had an exact parallel in the growth of its population. The middle regions followed a demographic pattern strikingly different from that of either New England or the southern colonies. This was the region with the most rapid growth of all, far outstripping the national rate of increase.

Before 1700 the Middle Colonies had under one in ten of the white population (and a similar proportion of total population). These were nearly all in New York. By the second half of the eighteenth century the population of this region had grown to one in four of total population and three in ten of the white population. New York's population had increased steadily. New Jersey had 6 percent of the American white population by 1700 and remained fairly constant at that level. But the outstanding feature was the rise of Pennsylvania from virtually zero population before William Penn's advent in 1680 to America's second most populous colony by 1770 and the colony with the largest number of white people in 1780. It was in the Middle Colonies that the combination of high natural growth with a high level of in-migration is best demonstrated.

Finally, it should be noted briefly that recent studies have indicated the impact of urbanization on population.[43] Although most colonial towns were still in their infancy and very small, these urban places suffered a mortality rate very similar to that of towns of comparable size in England.

EVIDENCE FROM THE FIRST TWO CENSUSES

In the final section of this chapter I will review the evidence from the national censuses concerning demographic conditions in the closing decades of the colonial period. The fact that this evidence in many respects confirms the conclusions drawn from the colonial counts and literary evidence will give greater confidence to these findings. In addition, the censuses make possible a number of fresh assertions.

The first observation to be made from the 1790 census is that the nation as a whole had a male surplus (50.9 percent) but certain clearly defined states had a low sex ratio, that is, a surplus of females. New England as a whole had a female surplus (the male ratio was 49.8 percent), and, apart from Maine and Vermont, all New England states had a sex ratio below the national average. At the other end of the scale the two trans-Appalachian regions, Kentucky and Tennessee, both had a high sex ratio.

The natural growth of the American population was probably most rapid in the closing decades of the eighteenth century. The most important result was confirmation of the youthful age structure revealed, for example, in the New York and New Jersey colonial counts. The 1790 census showed the median age of whites to be about sixteen; that is to say, almost half the entire white population at that date comprised children and youths born after the Declaration of Independence. Again in 1800 half the white population was under the age of fifteen years, that is, born considerably after the end of the war with Britain; the more detailed age breakdown of the second census also enables one to say that under one-third of the population was over twenty-five, that is, survivors from the colonial period, born before the Declaration.

A similar age structure probably existed, at least in the areas of old settlement, for most of the eighteenth century. It implied a high proportion of dependents and a low proportion of active producers. Less than 40 percent of the population was between sixteen and forty-five years of age; about half of these were males. If it is assumed that these made up the main producing group, even though their efforts were supplemented by female and child labor, then one economically active person was required to produce for himself *plus* perhaps three, certainly over two, other members of the population. The assumption of an American labor "shortage" usually has not taken into account this age structure, which must be regarded as "unfavorable" from the point of view of production. Moreover, injections of immigrant labor, with a very differently biased age structure, take on an added significance. The social implications are just as important. With one in three in the population under ten years of age and one in two under fifteen, the need to devote a large amount of men's and, even more women's energies into the nurturing and upbringing of children was far greater than in modern or contemporary European societies. An inevitable conflict must have arisen between the desirability of achieving an early entry of children into the work force and the desirability of, and demands for, education.

Looking at the detailed information available in 1800, one finds confirmation of the variance of age structure from region to region, of which glimpses are given in the colonial counts. The lowest percentage of children and the highest percentage of adults over age forty-five are found in the early settled areas and those from which there is evidence of emigration (above all the eastern and southern parts of Connecticut and Massachusetts). Conversely, the newly settled immigration areas (such as Kentucky, Tennessee, and Ohio) in 1800 had the greatest proportion of children and the smallest number of adults over forty-five years old. The picture is simplest in the areas from which people were moving: thus the older New England states group together at both ends of the age scale, with the fewest children and the most old people. They are also areas with a female surplus, as noted above. If it is true that in migrant societies those who leave are the malcontents, the dissatisfied, the ambitious, and the dynamic, while those who stay are the contented, the satisfied, sometimes the shiftless, certainly the static, then both age structure and temperament may combine to give such areas of emigration an inclination to be socially and politically conservative.

The pattern in the receiving areas is not so simple. The first intrusion into a new region of settlement was of people with an age structure more like that of the later European immigrants into America: they were predominantly adult, and generally there was a slight, and sometimes a pronounced, male surplus. In 1800 Washington, D.C., and Indiana had the greatest proportion of "producers." Not only was 45 percent of Indiana's still small population (of five thousand) between the ages of sixteen and forty-five (compared with the national 38 percent) but 24 percent were males between those ages (compared with the national 19 percent). At first the new areas had few old people and few children; families were nonexistent or small.

A decade or more later the second stage arrived. The initial age and sex structure, with a large percentage in the fertile age group and a male surplus, plus the tendency to higher fertility at the frontier, soon transformed the situation. Large numbers of children were born and families grew quickly (family size characteristically exceeding that of the older areas). One result of this second phase of frontier settlement was the reversal of the initial productively favorable age structure and the development of one with a particularly high number of dependents. By 1800 the states with the greatest percentage of children were those whose main settlement had been under way during the two preceding decades, especially in the mid-1780s: Tennessee, Kentucky, Ohio, the Mississippi Territory. The first two of these illustrate the argument in an extreme manner: they led all other states in the proportion of children under age nine but were at the bottom of the list in the proportion of persons between sixteen and forty-five years (though they still had a greater than average male surplus between those ages).

Although such detailed materials are not available for the colonial period, the sporadic data do appear to indicate a similar pattern of behavior. The argument of this survey must be that both the national averages and the regional differences in age (and also sex) structure throughout the eighteenth century deserve far greater attention in considering virtually every aspect of American life.

A related topic is, of course, that of family size, and with it the troublesome question of defining to what extent "family" and "household" may be considered identical. Without taking up the latter question at this stage, we can apply simple arithmetic to the 1790 census to find around 540,000 white families with an average size of 5.7 persons per family.

To obtain a rather more detailed picture, a sample of 3,600 family entries in the return of the 1790 census was examined. They revealed that for America as a whole a family size of four persons was the one most commonly recurring—there were 554 such four-person families out of the total of 3,600. This family size of four persons was the mode in eight of the twelve states. Two states had a mode of three persons, two others a mode of six persons. Exactly 40 percent of all families (1,440) consisted of three, four, or five persons; more than half the families (1,905, or 53 percent) consisted of between three and six persons.

The incidence of the smallest households—the single-person or two-person households—was greatest in two types of area. It occurred most regularly, as one would expect from the above remarks about age structure, in counties of very recent settlement, where a disproportionately large number of single men or couples who had not yet had children was to be found. There was a relatively large number of such families in the four southern states for which data are available, single-person households showing up strikingly in Virginia, Maryland, North Carolina, and South Carolina. These single-person households in the South, however, generally consisted of one white person, the "head of family" (sometimes a woman), and a number of black slaves.

Another intrastate distinction is that the urban family size was below that of the average for the state: Baltimore, 4.1 (Maryland 5.2); Philadelphia, 4.4 (Pennsylvania 5.5); New York City, 5.6 (New York State 5.8); Boston, 4.9 (Massachusetts 5.7); Providence, 4.5 (Rhode Island 5.9); Norfolk, 4.6 (Virginia 5.8); Charleston, 4.1 (South Carolina 5.5). The conclusion in the sample of figures for these towns reduces somewhat the average for the states in which they are situated. New York City conforms to the general pattern, but only just. As may be seen from similar data from the subsequent censuses, New York City had its own special characteristics which made it an exception to most rules. The urban figures, however, may be more susceptible to inaccuracies arising from the sampling method used. The pattern of one street might be very different from that of another, because of its location, social structure, type of house, economic activities, and so forth.

Finally, however, it is important to note that counting by households in this way may lead to a misleading conclusion. The statistical fallacy is analogous to that involved in analyses of the size of firms: although there may well be more small firms than large, more workers are employed by large firms than by small. To discover the modal family experience of individuals, we have to move higher up the statistical scale. It is in families of six or of seven persons that we find the greatest number of individuals (2,790 in families of six, 2,786 in families of seven, out of the total of 19,194 individuals caught up in the sample). In fact, about two-thirds of the sample (12,560 individuals) are recorded in families of between five and nine persons, there being almost as many individuals in the nine-person families (2,160) as in the four-person families (2,214).

Should one conclude from all this that the size of American families in 1790 was "large," "medium," or "small"? This is a subjective judgment and depends largely on the preconceptions with which one approaches the matter. Not surprisingly, the evidence confirms the view that the average family size in America of between 5.5 and 6 persons was greater than that in contemporary England, where the average was about 4.5 persons. On the other hand, the difference does not appear to be so great as might have been expected by those contemporary writers who described the "large" numbers of children (that is, ten or more) supposedly so common in the late colonial period. The data in the sample examined revealed over three hundred families (9 percent of the sample) of ten persons or more, and no doubt encounters with several such examples would remain as a vivid memory with foreign visitors. But statistically the evidence that families of four or five persons predominated appears overwhelming. In other words, the structure was that of the nuclear family. Individuals married and produced offspring when they had the means to set up a separate household. The Jeffersonian ideal of the responsible, self-sufficient family does not appear to have been very far away from the truth.

Conclusions and Summary

From the foregoing survey a number of features emerge that may be considered characteristic of the demographic experience of colonial America. In some respects, these features were normal for the seventeenth and eighteenth centuries and for the general human experience of fresh colonial settlement; in a number of important respects, however, the American experience may be regarded as unusual, if not unique.

1. As with most contemporary experience, "gate mortality" was very high, though decreasing with the passage of time. In some regions improvement in this respect may not have occurred until the very end of the period.

2. The impact of fresh settlement on the aboriginal inhabitants was, as in many other known instances, devastating. The gradual and not so gradual attrition of the Indian population through warfare and through the newly introduced diseases appears, in the light of recent research, to have been far more serious than was assumed in earlier writings.

3. The loss of life among the European settlers during the "seasoning period" was always high in the early phase of first settlement. It varied greatly between colonies. The loss of life was doubtless greatest among the slave population of the West Indies. At the other extreme, seventeenth-century New England appears to have overcome the initial difficulties of settlement relatively quickly and with less severe consequences than elsewhere, achieving first self-sufficiency and then very rapid growth by the middle of the century. The natural growth rate of Massachusetts and Connecticut in particular in the second half of the seventeenth century was extremely unusual, if not unique, in human history. The "seasoning period" elsewhere, particularly in the South for both white and slave populations, was prolonged and the death rate high. The weakening effect of malaria rendered human beings highly susceptible to other ailments. Although there is less direct evidence, it appears likely that the experience of the Middle Colonies approximates that of New England, while the experience of the southernmost colonies was similar to that of the colonies of the Chesapeake region.

4. Once the "seasoning period," of varying lengths, was over, colonial populations grew essentially from natural increase rather than from the "accession of strangers." Eventually, most colonies came close to the Malthusian thesis of a doubling every twenty-five years. Regions

that did not achieve that growth rate were characterized by one or more of the following features: a continuing high death rate, out-migration, urbanization. Regions that exceeded that growth rate were those to which in-migration, either from Europe or from other colonies, augmented the natural growth or were characteristically new frontier areas once their own problems of first settlement had been overcome.

5. The most important determinant of the rapid growth rate of the population appears to have been the age of marriage, especially of women. This was generally some four or five years younger than in contemporary Europe, though in areas where indentured servitude was common the terms of indenture may have postponed marriage by two or three years and thus slowed down the growth rate. Teenage marriage appears to have been unusual in all colonies.

6. Population structure in many colonies was unlike that of contemporary Europe in that it generally showed a male surplus. This was very marked in certain areas, especially where in-migration made a particularly large contribution to population growth. On the other hand, the male surplus was usually conducive to a high incidence of female marriage and thus to a high fertility rate.

7. There is no evidence that either illegitimacy or fertility within marriage was significantly, if at all, greater than in contemporary England. The spacing of births at two-year intervals from an early age of marriage created a higher lifetime fertility rate. Once the growth phase had been reached, an infant mortality rate that was marginally but not greatly lower than in contemporary England produced a significantly larger family size and thus a significantly higher growth rate.

8. Rapid growth entailed an age structure both for the population in aggregate and for separate families that was "youthful." While in the long run large families contributed to solving the problem of labor shortage, in the short run they increased the burden on producers by increasing the dependent-producer ratio. All members of the family were therefore involved in the productive activities of the family as soon as and whenever possible.

9. In the early phases of settlement a great deal of labor-intensive work was often involved in land preparation before the natural advantages of climate and the soil could yield results. In this phase the problem of the low producer-dependent ratio was particularly acute; the use of indentured servants to augment family labor affected population structure in a number of ways, increasing the male preponderance but also changing the age structure more favorably from the point of view of production. Where a plantation economy developed on the basis of slave labor, the ethnic pattern of the population structure was

changed. The ratio of slaves to free population varied greatly from colony to colony, even within the South, and in different time periods.

10. The number of foreign-born, whether black or white, in a colony's population thus affected many aspects of its demographic experience: growth rate; age and sex structure; religious foundations for family life.

11. Life expectancy also varied greatly among the different colonies, being lowest in the regions where uncontrollable diseases continued to take their toll throughout the period. The age of death of family members affected intergenerational attitudes, the incidence of orphanage, inheritance customs and laws, widowhood and remarriage and influenced patterns of behavior in terms of an individual's expected life span. The relatively low infant mortality was aided by both religious attitudes and practical considerations that led to children being regarded as a blessing, not a curse.

12. In the final analysis, the basic Malthusian proposition that population survival and growth are dependent on food supplies remains unassailable. The eventual rapid growth of the population of the American colonies was made possible by the eventual high productivity of American agriculture, which resulted from land abundance, the ability of the labor force (because of its adequate diet) to work the land, and the ecological conditions which permitted high-yield crops in wide variety to prosper and offered a wide variety of both wild and domesticated animals for both work and meat. The resultant diet was not merely adequate but, as it was appropriately described, one of "rude plenty." Where these conditions were maximized, as in the Middle Colonies in the eighteenth century, both population growth and economic growth surpassed not merely those of other American colonies but also those of contemporary Europe.

NOTES

I wish to acknowledge my great debt to Professor E. A. Wrigley, my colleague at the London School of Economics, for all the ways in which he contributed to the final version of this chapter.

1. E. B. Greene and V. D. Harrington, *American Population before the Federal Census of 1790* (New York, 1932); W. S. Thompson and P. K. Whelpton, *Population Trends in the United States* (New York, 1933); Stella H. Sutherland, *Population Distribution in Colonial America* (New York, 1936).

2. Y. Yasuba, *Birth Rates of the White Population in the United States, 1800–1860: An Economic Study* (Baltimore, 1962).

3. Maris A. Vinovskis, ed., *Studies in American Historical Demography* (New York, 1979), 20. This compilation by Vinovskis supplies the best published list—well over one hundred items—of the studies that had appeared since 1965.

4. R. A. Easterlin, "Population Issues in American Economic History: A Survey and Critique," in *Research in Economic History. Supplement 1. Recent Developments in the Study of Business and Economic History: Essays in Memory of Herman E. Krooss*, ed. R. E. Gallman (Greenwich, Conn., 1977). The writings to which Easterlin here refers are: Yasuba, *Birth Rates;* Jim Potter, "The Growth of Population in America, 1780–1860," in *Population in History*, ed. D. V. Glass and D. E. C. Eversley (London, 1965); and C. Forster and G. S. L. Tucker, *Economic Opportunity and White American Fertility Ratios, 1800–1860* (New Haven, 1972).

5. The many early publications of the Cambridge Group culminated in 1981 in the definitive summary of their work in E. A. Wrigley and R. S. Schofield, *The Population History of England, 1541–1871: A Reconstruction* (London, 1981). That work is mentioned in this context because of its examination of emigration from England, which has obvious relevance for migration to the North American colonies.

6. L. H. Day and A. T. Day, *Too Many Americans* (New York, 1964); Paul H. Ehrlich, *The Population Bomb* (New York, 1968); W. Paddock and P. Paddock, *Famine—1975! America's Decision: Who Will Survive?* (Boston, 1967).

7. In lectures under the title "Malthus and America" on the American West Coast in 1970 I spoke to overflow (and sometimes hostile, but always concerned) audiences. Using precisely the same title in 1974, I was politely heard by a small handful of listeners.

8. An informative analytical survey of this development is to be found in Louisa A. Tilly and Miriam Cohen, "Does the Family Have a History? A Review of Theory and Practice in Family History," *Social Science History* 6, no. 2 (1982): 131–79. The many relevant works in women's history and family history include: Edmund S. Morgan, *The Puritan Family*, rev. ed. (New York, 1966); Peter Laslett, ed., *Household and Family in Past Time* (Cambridge, 1972); Roger Thompson, *Women in Stuart England and America* (London, 1974); Stephanie Grauman Wolf, *Urban Village: Population, Community, and Family Structure in Germantown, Pennsylvania, 1683–1800* (Princeton, 1976); Nancy F. Cott, *The Bonds of Womanhood: "Woman's Sphere" in New England, 1780–1835* (New Haven, 1977); Tamara K. Hareven, ed., *Family and Kin in Urban Communities, 1700–1930* (New York, 1977); John Demos and Sarene S. Boocock, eds., *Turning Points: Historical and Sociological Essays on the Family*, supp. to *American Journal of Sociology* 84 (1978); Nancy F. Cott and Elizabeth Pleck, eds., *A Heritage of Her Own: Toward a New Social History of American Women* (New York, 1980); Philip J. Greven, Jr., "Family Structure in Seventeenth-Century Andover, Massachusetts," *William and Mary Quarterly*, 3d ser., 23 (1966): 234–56 (reprinted in Vinovskis, *Studies*); idem, "The Average Size of Families and Households in the Province of Massachusetts in 1764 and the United States in 1790: An Overview," in Laslett, *Household and Family;* John Demos, "Families in Colonial Bristol, Rhode Island: An Exercise in Historical Demography," *William and Mary Quarterly*, 3d ser., 25 (1968): 40 ff.; idem, "Demography and Psychology: The Historical Study of Family Life: A Personal Report," in Laslett, *Household and Family;* A. J. Coale, "Age Patterns of Marriage," *Population Studies* 25, no. 2 (1971): 193–216; Robert V. Wells, "Demographic Change and the Life Cycle of American Families," *Journal of Interdisciplinary History* 11 (1971): 273–82 (reprinted in Vinovskis, *Studies*); idem, "Family Life and Fertility Control in Eighteenth-Century America: A Study of Quaker Families," *Population Studies* 25, no. 1 (1971): 73–82; idem, "Quaker Marriage Patterns in a Colonial Perspective," *William and Mary Quarterly*, 3d ser., 29 (1972): 428–80; Glen H. Elder, Jr., "Approaches to Social Change and the Family: A Sociological Perspective," in Demos and Boocock, *Turning Points*, 1–38; Susan L. Norton, "Marital Migration in Essex County, Massachusetts, in the Colonial and Early Federal Periods," *Journal of Marriage and the Family* 35, no. 3 (1973): 419–28 (reprinted in Vinovskis, *Studies*); R. Frisch, "Demographic Implications of the Biological Determinants of Female Fecundity," *Social Biology* 22 (Spring 1975); Nancy Osterud and John Fulton, "Family Limitation and Age of Marriage: Fertility Decline in Sturbridge, Massachusetts, 1730–1850," *Population Studies* 30, no. 3 (1976): 481–93 (reprinted in Vinovskis, *Studies*); Lois Green Carr and Lorena S. Walsh, "The Planter's Wife: The Experience of White Women in Seventeenth-Century Maryland," *William and Mary Quarterly*, 3d ser., 34 (1977): 542–71; Carole Shannon, "The Domestic Environment in Early Modern England and

America," *Journal of Social History* 14 (1980): 3–24; Nancy F. Cott, "Eighteenth-Century Family and Social Life Revealed in Massachusetts Divorce Records," in Cott and Pleck, *Heritage*.

9. Of the numerous recent historical works that have subsequently appeared in which sexual behavior is discussed and described in detail one might simply note: R. Wheaton and Tamara K. Hareven, *Family and Sexuality in French History* (Philadelphia, 1976); Lawrence Stone, *The Family, Sex and Marriage in England, 1500–1800* (London, 1977); M. Gordon, ed., *The American Family in Social Historical Perspective* (New York, 1978); E. Le Roy Ladurie, *Montaillou: The Promised Land of Error* (New York, 1978); and Carl Degler, *At Odds: Women and the Family in America, 1776 to the Present* (New York, 1980). An older study is Edmund S. Morgan, "The Puritans and Sex," *New England Quarterly* 15 (1942): 591–607.

10. Especially Herbert G. Gutman, *The Black Family in Slavery and Freedom, 1750–1925* (New York, 1976).

11. An extreme example would be found on pages 90–95 of Peter H. Lindert, *Fertility and Scarcity in America* (Princeton, 1978).

12. Daniel Scott Smith, "The Estimates of Early American Historical Demographies: Two Steps Forward, One Step Back, What Steps in the Future?" *Historical Methods* 12, no. 1 (1979): 24–38.

13. Ibid., 24.

14. These problems are well examined in Allan N. Sharlin, "Historical Demography as History and Demography," *American Behavioral Scientist* 21, no. 2 (1978): 245–62. Other discussions of the relationship between the two disciplines include: Louis Henry, "Historical Demography," *Daedalus*, Spring 1968; idem, "The Verification of Data in Historical Demography," *Population Studies* 22, no. 1 (1968): 61–82; and Maris A. Vinovskis, "Recent Trends in American Historical Demography: Some Methodological and Conceptual Considerations," *Annual Reviews in Sociology* 4 (1978): 603–27 (reprinted in Vinovskis, *Studies*). I make no pretense that this chapter, written by a historian dabbling in demography, will be any less prone to error than other essays in the field.

15. The summary will not attempt to identify in notes the source of information in every particular.

16. Easterlin, "Population Issues in American Economic History."

17. Benjamin Franklin, *Observations Concerning the Increase of Mankind and the Peopling of Countries* (1751); Ezra Stiles, *Discourse on the Christian Union* (1761); Edward Wigglesworth the Younger, *Calculations on American Population* (1775); Richard Price, *Concerning Observations on the Expectation of Lives, the Increase of Mankind* (1769); T. R. Malthus, *An Essay on the Principle of Population* (1798), esp. chap. 6. These were not the only contemporary writers on population of course, but they were doubtless the most influential. There is considerable interaction between them and similarity in phraseology in their writings; yet although they use almost identical words at some points, there is no evidence that Malthus was aware of the writing of Edward Wigglesworth the Younger, the second Hollis Professor of Divinity at Harvard University. The views are summarized, and interconnections discussed, in Potter, "The Growth of Population in America"; and idem, "American Population," *Population and Economics*, ed. Paul Deprez (Winnipeg, 1968).

18. This is of course a counsel of perfection that will not be fulfilled in this chapter but may be regarded as providing an agenda for future work.

19. A copy of Price's *Observations* in Malthus's library was heavily scored in the margin at this point, and an inserted calculation about the doubling process suggests that it is the original source of Malthus's population theory.

20. Edmund S. Morgan, *American Slavery—American Freedom: The Ordeal of Colonial Virginia* (New York, 1975), 158–59. It is also relevant to growth rates to observe that so long as the main source of growth was migration, the resultant large surplus of young males was not conducive to rapid growth (although it may have been conducive to high fertility of the proportionately small number of females). On the other hand this circumstance—an unusually large number of males in their early twenties and relatively few dependent children—created a producer-dependent ratio favorable to production.

21. The word *immigrant* is being deliberately avoided because it did not come into use until the beginning of the national period.

22. The figures here cited have been supplied by E. A. Wrigley. Much more detail will be found in Wrigley and Schofield, *Population History of England.*

23. *Social Science History* 6, no. 4 (1982) is a special issue entitled *Trends in Nutrition, Labor Welfare and Labor Productivity,* edited by Robert W. Fogel and Stanley L. Engerman. The following contributions are of particular relevance to this discussion: Robert W. Fogel, Stanley L. Engerman, and J. Trussell, "Exploring the Uses of Data on Height," 401–21; K. L. Sokoloff and Georgia Villaflor, "The Early Achievement of Modern Stature in America," 453–81; and R. A. Margo and R. H. Steckel, "The Heights of American Slaves: New Evidence on Slave Nutrition and Health," 516–38.

24. It is generally agreed that Malthus greatly underestimated the eventual improvements to the human condition brought about by medical science. The evidence suggests, however, that medicine, and still less surgery, contributed little to solving the demographic problem in colonial America. The medical contribution to population growth is discussed in: J. Duffy, *Epidemics in Colonial America* (1953; reprint, Baton Rouge, 1971); J. B. Blake, *Public Health in the Town of Boston, 1630–1822* (Cambridge, Mass., 1959); Richard M. Shryock, *Medicine and Society in America, 1660–1860* (New York, 1960); idem, *Medicine in America: Historical Essays* (Baltimore, 1966); Herbert Thoms, *The Doctors of Yale College, 1702–1815* (New Haven, 1960); George E. Winslow, *A Destroying Angel: The Conquest of Smallpox in Colonial Boston* (Boston, 1974); Otto Beall and Richard M. Shryock, "Cotton Mather: First Significant Figure in American Medicine," *Proceedings of the American Antiquarian Society* 63 (1963): 37–274; Philip D. Curtin, "Epidemiology and the Slave Trade," *Political Science Quarterly* 83 (1968): 190–216.

25. James Mooney, "Population," in *Handbook of the American Indians North of Mexico,* ed. F. W. Hodge, Smithsonian Institution Bureau of American Ethnology Bulletin 30, 2 vols. (Washington, D.C., 1910).

26. Henry T. Dobyns, *Native American Historical Demography* (Bloomington, Ind., 1976).

27. It is in no way to minimize the catastrophe to the Indian tribes to point out that such a decline has been the common experience of aboriginal populations when confronted by the invasion of new settlements; the Maoris of New Zealand (whose numbers declined through disease alone rather than extermination in war) showed an even more catastrophic decline than did the American Indians.

28. James H. Cassedy, *Demography in Early America: Beginnings of the Statistical Mind* (Cambridge, Mass., 1969).

29. Robert V. Wells, *The Population of the British Colonies in America before 1776* (Princeton, 1975).

30. Darrett B. Rutman, *Winthrop's Boston: Portrait of a Puritan Town, 1630–1649* (Chapel Hill, 1965); John Demos, *A Little Commonwealth: Family Life in Plymouth Colony* (New York, 1970); T. H. Breen and Stephen Foster, "Moving to the New World: The Character of Early Massachusetts Immigration," *William and Mary Quarterly,* 3d ser., 30 (1973): 189–222; Linda A. Bissell, "From One Generation to Another: Mobility in Seventeenth-Century Windsor, Connecticut," ibid. 31 (1974): 79–110; Morgan, *American Slavery—American Freedom;* Douglas L. Jones, "The Strolling Poor: Transiency in Eighteenth-Century Massachusetts," *Journal of Social History* 8 (Spring 1975): 28–54; L. D. Gragg, *Immigration in Early America: The Virginia Quaker Experience* (Ann Arbor, 1980).

31. See, for example, Peter R. Knights, *The Plain People of Boston, 1830–1860* (New York, 1971); and Howard P. Chudacoff, *Mobile Americans* (New York, 1972).

32. Henry A. Gemery, "Emigration from the British Isles to the New World, 1630–1700: Inferences from Colonial Population," *Research in Economic History* 5 (1980): 179–232.

33. David W. Galenson, *White Servitude in Colonial America: An Economic Analysis* (Cambridge, 1981). Other works by Galenson in this field are "Immigration and the Colonial Labor System: An Analysis of the Length of Indenture," *Explorations in Economic History* 14, no. 4 (1977): 360–77; "British Servants and the Colonial Indenture System in the Eighteenth Century," *Journal of Southern History* 41, no. 1 (1978): 44–66; " 'Middling People' or 'Common Sort'? The

Social Origins of Some Early Americans Re-examined," *William and Mary Quarterly*, 3d ser., 35 (1978): 499–524; "Literacy and the Social Origins of Some Early Americans," *Historical Journal* 22, no. 1 (1979): 75–91; "The Social Origins of Some Early Americans: Rejoinder," *William and Mary Quarterly*, 3d ser., 36 (1979): 264–77 (rejoinder to Mildred Campbell, "Response," ibid. 35 [1978]: 525–40); "Demographic Aspects of White Servitude in Colonial British America," *Annales de démographie historique*, 1980, 239–52; "White Servitude and the Growth of Black Slavery in Colonial America," *Journal of Economic History* 41 (1981): 39–49; and "The Market Evaluation of Human Capital: The Case of Indentured Servitude," *Journal of Political Economy* 89 (1981): 446–67.

34. Potter, "The Growth of Population in America."

35. It was Wigglesworth and Malthus who decided on a twenty-five-year span. Franklin spoke almost interchangeably about twenty years and twenty-five years, indicating that his time unit was really generational. It might be worth observing that Wigglesworth was a good example of one who broke his own rule. His own family consisted of only three generations, covering almost the entire colonial period. His grandfather, Michael Wigglesworth (1631–1705), arrived in Massachusetts Bay as a child in 1638. His first wife died childless; in 1679 he married his second wife (his serving maid, Martha Mudge, aged 20—earning him the rebuke of Increase Mather and a warning that such a marriage would shorten his life), who bore him six children before her death (*pace* Increase Mather) in 1690; his third wife, a widow, bore him one child, Edward Wigglesworth the Elder (1693–1765), who became the first Hollis Professor of Divinity at Harvard. Edward the Elder married twice, his second wife bearing him four children, including Edward the Younger (1732–94), who succeeded him as second Hollis Professor of Divinity at Harvard. Thus when Edward Wigglesworth the Younger died in 1794, only three lives—from his grandfather Michael to himself—spanned a century and a half of Massachusetts history, from early colonial days to full statehood. Wigglesworth Hall at Harvard University commemorates the name of this family.

36. Recent publications which discuss slavery and the black population in colonial America include: Philip D. Curtin, *The Atlantic Slave Trade: A Census* (Madison, Wis., 1969); Wesley Frank Craven, *White, Red and Black: The Seventeenth-Century Virginian* (Charlottesville, 1971); Peter H. Wood, *Black Majority: Negroes in Colonial South Carolina from 1670 through the Stone Rebellion* (New York, 1974); Henry A. Gemery and Jan S. Hogendorn, "The Atlantic Slave Trade: A Tentative Economic Model," *Journal of African History* 15, no. 2 (1974): 223–46; idem, eds., *The Uncommon Market: Essays in the Economic History of the Atlantic Slave Trade* (New York, 1979); Richard R. Beeman, "Labor Forces and Race Relations: A Comparative View of the Colonization of Brazil and Virginia," *Political Science Quarterly* 86 (1971): 609–36; Gary B. Nash, "Slaves and Slaveowners in Colonial Philadelphia," *William and Mary Quarterly*, 3d ser., 30 (1973): 223–56; Allan Kulikoff, "A 'Prolifick People': Black Population Growth in the Chesapeake Colonies, 1700–1790," *Southern Studies* 16 (1977): 391–428; Cheryll Ann Cody, "A Note on Changing Patterns of Slave Fertility in the South Carolina Rice Dsitrict, 1735–1865," ibid., 457–63; Sarah S. Hughes, "Slaves for Hire: The Allocation of Black Labor in Elizabeth County, Virginia, 1782–1810," *William and Mary Quarterly*, 3d ser., 35 (1978): 260–86; Herbert S. Klein and Stanley L. Engerman, "Fertility Differences between Slaves in the United States and the British West Indies: A Note on Lactation Practices and Their Possible Implications," ibid., 357–74; Stanley L. Engerman, "Studying the Black Family," *Journal of Family History* 3, no. 1 (1978): 78–101; and David W. Galenson, "White Servitude and the Growth of Black Slavery in Colonial America," *Journal of Economic History* 41 (1981): 39–47.

37. The percentage declined steadily throughout the nineteenth century and into the twentieth, reaching its lowest point (the lowest, it might be noted, since 1690) in 1930, with 9 percent. Since 1930 the black percentage has slowly increased.

38. P. D. Hall, "Farming Structure and Economic Organization: Massachusetts Merchants, 1700–1850," in *Family and Kin in Urban Communities, 1700–1930*, ed. Tamara K. Hareven (New York, 1977). Hall goes on to consider the importance of inheritance laws and customs in the

process of capital accumulation.

39. See John Demos, *A Little Commonwealth*; Philip J. Greven, Jr., *Four Generations: Population, Land, and Family in Colonial Andover, Massachusetts* (Ithaca, N.Y., 1970); idem, *The Protestant Temperament* (New York, 1977); Kenneth A. Lockridge, *A New England Town: The First Hundred Years, Dedham, Massachusetts, 1636–1736* (New York, 1970); idem, "Land, Population and the Evolution of New England Society, 1630–1790," *Past and Present*, no. 39 (April 1968) (reprinted in *Colonial America: Essays in Politics and Social Development*, ed. Stanley N. Katz [New York 1977]); Gordon E. Geddes, *Welcome Joy: Death in Puritan New England* (Ann Arbor, 1981); David E. Stannard, *The Puritan Way of Death: A Study in Religion, Culture, and Social Change* (New York, 1977); R. Higgs and H. L. Stettler, "Colonial New England Demography: A Sampling Approach," *William and Mary Quarterly*, 3d ser., 27 (1970): 291 ff.; Susan L. Norton, "Population Growth in Colonial America: A Study of Ipswich, Massachusetts," *Population Studies* 25, no. 2 (November 1971): 433–52; Daniel Scott Smith, "The Demographic History of Colonial New England," *Journal of Economic History* 32 (1972): 165–68 (reprinted in Vinovskis, *Studies*); idem, "Parental Power and Marriage Patterns: An Analysis of Historical Trends in Hingham, Massachusetts," *Journal of Marriage and the Family* 35, no. 3 (1973): 406–18; idem, "Old Age and 'The Great Transformation': A New England Case Study," in *Aging and the Elderly: Humanistic Perspectives in Gerontology*, ed. Stuart Spicker, Kathleen Woodward, and David Van Tassel (Atlantic Highlands, N.J., 1978); idem, "The Estimates of Early American Historical Demographers: Two Steps Forward, One Step Back, What Steps in the Future?" *Historical Methods* 12 (1979): 24–38; idem, "A Malthusian-Frontier Interpretation of U.S. Demographic History before 1815," in *Urbanization in the Americas: The Background in Comparative Perspective*, ed. Woodrow Borah, Jorge Hardoy, and Gilbert A. Stelter (Ottawa, 1980); Daniel Scott Smith and Michael S. Hindus, "Premarital Pregnancy in America, 1640–1971: An Overview and Interpretation," *Journal of Interdisciplinary History* 5 (1975): 537–70 (reprinted in Vinovskis, *Studies*); Terry L. Anderson and Robert Paul Thomas, "White Population, Labor Force and Extensive Growth in the New England Economy in the Seventeenth Century," *Journal of Economic History* 33 (1973); and David E. Stannard, "Death and Dying in Puritan New England," *American Historical Review* 78 (December 1973): 1305–30.

40. The ensuing brief summary is based mainly on the following recent works: Thad W. Tate and David L. Ammerman, eds., *The Chesapeake in the Seventeenth Century: Essays on Anglo-American Society* (Chapel Hill, 1979), esp. articles by Carr and Menard, Horn; Vinovskis, *Studies*, articles by Vinovskis, Dethlefsen, Hecht, Rutman and Rutman, Menard; Duffy, *Epidemics in Colonial America*; Allan Kulikoff, "The Colonial Chesapeake: Seedbed of Antebellum Southern Culture?" *Journal of Southern History* 45 (1979): 513–40; Lorena S. Walsh and Russell R. Menard, "Death in the Chesapeake: Two Life Tables for Men in Early Colonial Maryland," *Maryland Historical Magazine* 69 (1974): 211–74; Russell R. Menard, "From Servants to Slaves: The Transformation of the Chesapeake Labor System," *Southern Studies* 16 (1977): 355–90; David Souden, "'Rogues, Whores and Vagabonds'? Indentured Servant Emigrants to North America," *Social History* 3 (1978): 23–41.

41. Although not strictly within the subject matter of this book, another region of North America worthy of note (whose experience shows marked similarities to the Chesapeake experience) is the quite separate Spanish colonial development in the Mississippi Valley before the Louisiana Purchase. In his work *La Población de Luisiana Española, 1763–1803* (Madrid, 1979), Antonio Acosta-Rodriguez examined the size, composition, and family structure of these primarily, but not exclusively (and their composition is an interesting revelation), Spanish settlements; the age of marriage was generally lower than in New England, with a resultant higher fertility rate. But the large male surplus and high mortality rate (especially the infant-mortality rate) in the eighteenth century resemble the Chesapeake data. By the late eighteenth century these Spanish settlements had reached the stage of self-generated growth, albeit very slow growth.

42. On the Caribbean see in particular Elsa V. Goeia, *Slave Society in the British Leeward Islands at*

the End of the Eighteenth Century (New Haven, 1965); Barry W. Higman, *Slave Population and Economy in Jamaica, 1807–1834* (Cambridge, 1976); Michael Craton, *Searching for the Invisible Man: Slaves and Plantation Life in Jamaica* (Cambridge, Mass., 1978); Wells, *Population of the British Colonies;* Richard S. Dunn, "The Barbados Census of 1680: Profile of the Richest Colony in English America," *William and Mary Quarterly,* 3d ser., 28 (1971): 287–300; Hans Christian Johansen, "Slave Demography of the Danish West Indian Islands," *Scandinavian Economic History Review* 29, no. 1 (1981): 1–20.

43. See Blake, *Public Health;* Rutman, *Winthrop's Boston;* Michael Zuckerman, *Peaceable Kingdoms: New England Towns in the Eighteenth Century* (New York, 1970); Woodrow Borah, Jorge Hardoy, and Gilbert A. Stelter, eds., *Urbanization in the Americas: The Background in Comparative Perspective* (Ottawa, 1980); R. Holmes, *Communities in Transition: Bedford and Lincoln, Massachusetts, 1729–1858* (Ann Arbor, 1980); K. J. Friedman, "Victualling Colonial Boston," *Agricultural History* 47 (1973): 189–205; James A. Henretta, "Economic and Social Studies in Colonial Boston," *William and Mary Quarterly,* 3d ser., 22 (1965): James T. Lemon, "Urbanization and the Development of Eighteenth-Century Pennsylvania and Adjacent Delaware," ibid. 24 (1967): 504–10; Billy G. Smith, "Death and Life in a Colonial Immigrant City: A Demographic Analysis of Philadelphia," *Journal of Economic History* 37 (1977): 863–89.

6

SERVANTS AND SLAVES: THE RECRUITMENT AND EMPLOYMENT OF LABOR

RICHARD S. DUNN

he history of labor in colonial America is a large subject because it embraces more than half the colonial population during a 170-year span, as well as labor practices in seventeenth- and eighteenth-century England, West Africa, Ireland, Wales, Scotland, and Germany, the chief catchment areas for immigrant colonial laborers. It is a complex subject because each region of British America evolved a distinctive labor system: in the Caribbean sugar colonies, a quick dependence on African slave labor; in the southern mainland colonies, a slow conversion from white servants to black slaves, with heavy use also of white family labor; in the mid-Atlantic colonies, a mix of family and wage labor with immigrant servants and slaves; and in New England, a prime reliance upon native-born family and wage labor. Finally, it is a difficult subject because it treats the history of the inarticulate—laboring men and women who left few records or artifacts and who must be studied chiefly through the observations of their employers. It is much harder to reconstruct the bygone experiences and work habits of obscure servants and slaves than those of prominent planters and merchants, yet the effort must be made if we are to comprehend the labor systems of colonial America.

Before World War II, colonial historians took little interest in the topic. Marcus Jernegan, author of the only general work, devoted scant space to labor practices and conditions and wrote instead about "upper class" assistance to the "lower classes."[1] Immediately after the war, Richard B. Morris and Abbot Emerson Smith opened the subject to fruitful inquiry for the first time. Morris's *Government and Labor in Early America* (1946) was the first serious attempt to describe colonial employment practices; surveying twenty thousand court cases, Morris established the numerous friction points between colonial laborers and their employers. Smith's *Colonists in Bondage: White Servitude and Convict Labor in Colonial America, 1607–1776* (1947) was the first serious attempt to describe colonial labor recruitment; surveying the transatlantic servant and convict trades, Smith demonstrated the harsh features of the system of immigrant bound labor. In the thirty-five years since World War II much more excellent work has been done, particularly on colonial slave labor, not dealt with by Morris or Smith. Yet in some respects the history of American colonial labor is almost untouched. We know next to nothing about the female half of the colonial work force, and will likely remain ignorant, since female laborers are even harder to trace through the surviving records than male laborers. We know far too little about major categories of workmen who *can* be investigated, such as merchant seamen, fishermen, lumbermen, shipbuilders, road builders, fort builders, and rank-and-file soldiers. Even worse, we remain generally ignorant about labor practices on small family farms. And as yet we are in no position to assess the *quality* of the labor performed in colonial America, to determine, for example, whether unskilled and semiskilled laborers worked any differently— harder, more purposefully, or more efficiently—than their counterparts in the Old World.

My purpose in this essay is not so much to call attention to neglected topics as to survey work already done and to consider some of the chief issues currently under debate. To make this survey manageable, I will define a colonial laborer as any person who performed manual labor, with or without wages, for a head of household: a slave, a servant, an apprentice, a wage laborer, or a dependent family worker. This definition *excludes* a great many colonial manual workers: self-employed small farmers and craftsmen, because they were independent producers; tenant farmers, because they were semi-independent producers; and members of the armed forces, because they were employed by the state rather than by individual entrepreneurs. All of these people, especially the tenants and the soldiers, deserve much fuller attention. And yet the laborers I *do* attempt to discuss in this essay constituted a majority of the American colonial population. Following the lead of Abbot Emerson Smith, I will consider the recruitment of servants and slaves from England, Ireland, Germany, and Africa. What sort of workers went where, and when? How and why did the recruitment process change during the seventeenth and eighteenth centuries? Then, following the lead of Richard B. Morris, I will survey labor practices in four regions of British America—the Caribbean, the southern mainland, the mid-Atlantic, and New England. How and why did each region develop its own distinctive labor system? What were the most significant social and economic features of each system?

The recruitment of labor for the American colonies was a vital issue from the 1580s to the American Revolution. From the outset, the promoters of

colonization, particularly in the Chesapeake and the Caribbean, had no intention of performing the necessary manual work themselves, and hence they
needed servile laborers. Initially, following the Spanish precedent, they
hoped to mold the native Indians into an acceptable work force, but when
this strategy quickly collapsed, they imported workers, voluntary and involuntary, from Europe and Africa—either white servants indentured temporarily or black slaves captured permanently.

White servants were initially preferred to black slaves. By the close of the
seventeenth century servants were largely replaced by slaves in the Caribbean and the southern mainland, but they were still in heavy demand in the
northern colonies; and in the eighteenth century many servants continued to
migrate to America, particularly to Pennsylvania and Maryland. Precise
figures are impossible to obtain, since the surviving evidence is so faulty.
One must extrapolate from scattered servant registration lists in England and
America; from defective shipping lists, which rarely distinguish between
servants and free passengers; from servant headright claims in the southern
land records; and from a few colonial census tabulations that enumerate
servants (although they do not distinguish between immigrant and native
servants). Systematic analysis of servant data in the court records and military records for several colonies is now under way, which should improve
our understanding of the changing size and character of the white immigrant
labor force. Drawing as best I can upon the evidence currently available, I
offer the following exceedingly rough estimate of servant importation into
British America:

80,000 servants from England, Ireland, and Scotland, 1580–1650
90,000 servants from England, Ireland, and Scotland, 1651–1700
25,000 servants from England, 1701–75
70,000 servants from Ireland and Scotland, 1701–75
35,000 servants from Germany, 1701–75
50,000 convicts, vagabonds, and political prisoners transported from
　　　　England, Ireland, and Scotland, 1607–1775

350,000 white laborers imported, 1580–1775

This estimate suggests that about half of the whites who came to the colonies
from Britain and continental Europe during the colonial period arrived as
servants.

In the seventeenth century most servants came from England. They were
bound for terms of varying length, commonly from four to seven years. The
first Roanoke colonists were Sir Walter Raleigh's servants. The first Jamestown colonists were Virginia Company servants, and when the Virginia
Company could no longer afford to buy laborers, it devised the headright
system to encourage private investors to ship their own servants. By 1625,
when a census was taken, over 40 percent of the Virginia colonists were listed

as servants.[2] (This very high ratio seems to have continued through the next generation in many parts of the Chesapeake.) In the West Indies, the first Barbados colonists, in 1627, were Sir William Courteen's servants. Here as in Virginia, private investors quickly began to stake out plantations and equip them with their own servants; by 1638 well over half of the Barbados colonists were servants.[3] In New England, settled primarily by family groups, servants were much less numerous, but they were far from negligible. Twenty of the 104 Pilgrims who sailed to Plymouth on the *Mayflower* (some died en route) were servants;[4] the Massachusetts Bay Company sent 180 servants to Salem in 1628; Governor Winthrop brought eight servants with him on the *Arbella* in 1630;[5] and about 15 percent of the passengers on ships bound for New England during the great Puritan migration of the 1630s can be identified as servants.[6] Thus even in New England, servants constituted about a third of the initial work force.

The flow of English servants into America probably peaked in the 1650s and 1660s and then declined. The best surviving English evidence—a Bristol servant registry for 1654–86—shows a precipitous drop in the 1670s and 1680s.[7] This pattern can be explained in part by alterations in the American labor market. After 1640 New England imported few servants, depending instead upon local labor. After 1660 Barbados imported few servants, depending instead upon African slave labor. A decade or two later the other Caribbean colonies followed suit. In the older established tidewater districts of the Chesapeake the ratio of servants and the career opportunities for servants also declined during the late seventeenth century.[8] On the other hand, settlers pushing into the frontier districts of the Chesapeake created a fresh demand for servant labor. And the newly founded Restoration colonies provided another strong new market for servant labor. In early Pennsylvania, for example, about a third of the first arrivals in the 1680s appear to have been servants.[9] Thus, despite the Caribbean conversion to slave labor and the beginnings of a parallel conversion to slavery in the southern mainland colonies, the overall American demand for indentured servants may not have contracted greatly in the late seventeenth century. But the supply pattern did shift: after 1680 the servants came chiefly from Ireland and Germany, not from England.

This pattern of rise and decline in the English indentured servant trade raises several obvious questions: Who were these English emigrant servants? why did they come to America in the seventeenth century? and why did they stop coming in the eighteenth century?

In early modern England unskilled and semiskilled agricultural and textile workers normally did not bind themselves to long-term contracts. They were wage laborers, and much of the work available to them was casual, paid by the day, the job, or the season. Nearly all of it was drudge work, requiring little skill or training. Whereas yeomen and artisans, several notches higher in the social scale, entered apprenticeships in order to become skilled craftsmen or farmers or household managers, the cottagers and laborers were offered minimal incentives and responsibilities. Their employers had no interest in labor-saving devices nor in reducing monotony.[10] Cheap labor was far more important than quality labor: "the surest wealth consists in a Multitude of laborious poor."[11] Most recent analysts agree that the English laboring poor experienced deteriorating conditions between 1550 and 1650. Rapid population expansion created a labor surplus among agricultural and textile wage workers and domestic servants. The price revolution pushed real wages down by 50 percent. Unemployment, long-range migration within England in search of work, and prosecutions for vagrancy, begging, and theft all seem to have increased notably. Some laborers attempted to stage a moral rebellion in the 1640s and 1650s by joining such groups as the Fifth Monarchy Men, the Levellers, the Diggers, the Seekers, the Ranters, or the Quakers.[12] Others contracted for indentured servitude in America. Contract labor was of course no novelty in England: youths from the middling classes normally received craft training through long-term apprenticeship. In America, however, the need was for cheap unskilled farm labor, not for craft apprenticeship. The solution was to transport laborers to the colonies, at a cost of about six pounds per head, and to present them with incentives and restrictions not usually given to unskilled wage workers in England. The chief incentive was that they could eventually acquire farms or businesses of their own, unobtainable at home. The chief restriction was that they had to work without wages for terms of four to seven years.

When Abbot Emerson Smith surveyed the English servant trade, he concluded that only rogues, whores, vagabonds, paupers, and other unwanted rabble could be recruited into American contract labor. But Mildred Campbell proposed in 1959 that the English servants "were drawn from the middling classes: farmers and skilled workers, the productive groups in England's working population."[13] Campbell based her appealing argument upon analysis of lists of servants emigrating from Bristol and London. However, recent reexamination of these same lists by David Galenson, James Horn, and David Souden has modified her conclusions considerably. Horn characterizes the seventeenth-century emigrating servants as "a representative cross section of the ordinary working men and women of England."[14] In these lists, a few servants described themselves as from the gentry or trained in a profession; many of them [Campbell's people] described themselves as yeomen, husbandmen, or artisans; a small number described themselves as laborers; about half had no stated occupation. The current view is that these anonymous servants were younger and less skilled than the others. Furthermore, an additional cadre of emigrant laborers did not appear on English servant lists because they came over without signing indentures in England. These unindentured emigrants can only be traced through the labor contracts they made in the local colonial courts. Lorena Walsh's analysis of unindentured servants in seventeenth-century Maryland indicates that they "were younger, served longer terms, and possessed fewer skills than those with indentures."[15] Thus a majority of the English emigrant laborers appear to have had low status and little training.

More important than the social origins of these servants were their economic circumstances: many of them were desperate for work. The three decades from 1630 to 1660, when especially large numbers of servants migrated to America, were years of extreme hardship for laborers in England. There was always a great deal of internal labor migration within England, mostly short-range, from the countryside to nearby village and towns, but in times of subsistence crisis young adults traveled long distances in search of food and work.[16] There appears to be a direct connection between these subsistence migrants and servant emigrants. David Souden has recently compared lists of emigrating servants with lists of apprentices in the city of Bristol in the 1650s; he finds that more apprentices than servants identified themselves as residents of Bristol and that those servants who had traveled to Bristol in search of work came from a much wider geographical area than the apprentices.[17] They were young people, less well-connected than the apprentices, who had been wandering along the main roads until they reached the city; if they found no work in Bristol, they sailed on to the colonies.

If this argument is correct, it suggests that seventeenth-century English servant laborers emigrated to America not because they wanted to but because they had to. Push was more important than pull. The combination of hard times at home and labor demand in the colonies, facilitated by a well-organized servant trade in the chief English port towns, drew thousands of people who knew little or nothing of the Chesapeake or the Caribbean into emigration abroad. Only such a pattern can explain why English laborers flocked in great numbers to Virginia and Barbados at a time when disease, mortality rates, and agricultural working conditions were so disadvantageous to newcomers.

In a recent book David Galenson presents a quantitative analysis of 20,657 English servants who contracted for labor in America between 1654 and 1775.[18] Galenson's data base has some obvious defects: the servant lists he analyzes provide no information on the crucial initial labor migration of 1607–53; his sample is skewed towards the eighteenth century, when the English trade became much smaller; his sample contains too many servants from Bristol and not enough from London or the other outports; and his registration lists are of greatly varying quality. Nonetheless, he deals with a large cohort from three cities, and his statistical findings are instructive. His servants were single individuals, mostly young and mostly male: 82 percent of them were men and boys, which confirms information from many other sources that the sex ratio among white servants in the colonies was exceedingly unbalanced, especially in the seventeenth century. In consequence, the male laborers were sex-starved, and men who remained in the colonies after their indentures expired had trouble finding wives. In colonies largely populated by servants and ex-servants family formation was hindered and the birth rate was handicapped for many years. In Maryland, for example, females did not balance males in the white adult population until the early eighteenth century.[19] Among the servants in Galenson's sample who stated their ages, 68 percent of the males and 81 percent of the females were in the 15–24 age bracket and therefore of much the same age as apprentices and domestic servant girls in England. But whereas in English towns apprentices could be disciplined and controlled by the masters and clergy and town elders, and in the English countryside unsatisfactory farm and household workers could be readily dismissed, in such colonies as Virginia and Barbados there were few familial or institutional mechanisms whereby the swarms of incoming young laborers could be socialized into docility. Very quickly the colonial contract laborers became more unruly than their counterparts at home.

Not surprisingly, the older servants in Galenson's sample, and the more highly skilled, were able to negotiate shorter terms of indenture. In the mid-seventeenth century there was little correlation between the servant's level of skill or occupation in England and his destination in America; much the same proportion of yeomen or carpenters or weavers went to Jamaica as to Maryland. By the eighteenth century servants bound for the Caribbean were older and more skilled than those bound for the mainland, perhaps because by this time white servants in the islands were no longer manual laborers, and many of their jobs (such as bookkeeping on the sugar estates) required literacy. There was also a marked seasonal pattern in the shipment of servants to particular American destinations. Caribbean servants were sent in the winter and spring, between October and May, while Chesapeake servants were sent in the late summer and fall, between July and October; thus servant ships could return with sugar from the West Indian spring harvest and tobacco from the Chesapeake fall harvest. If, as has been argued above, many servants signed up because they had no alternative employment, they were given little choice about which colony to go to, but migrated to one part of America or another depending upon the season of the year.

Why did this English servant supply decline in the 1670s and 1680s and remain relatively low until just before the America Revolution? Gregory King's famous survey of 1688, in which he reckoned that only half of the people in England were earning enough to share in the country's surplus wealth, while the other half were "decreasing the wealth of the kingdom" by living below the poverty line, surely indicates that the English still had a huge pool of depressed "laborious poor."[20] Nevertheless, it appears that the young people who had been migrating to America by the thousands every year in search of employment stayed at home in the 1680s and 1690s because they were finding jobs. In the first systematic effort at reconstituting England's population history, E. A. Wrigley and R. S. Schofield argue that the population of England stopped growing and may even have declined between

1640 and 1710 and that during this period real wages were rising percepti-
bly.[21] Thus it was easier than before for marginal workers to make ends
meet. Furthermore, a long series of good harvests helped to ameliorate English living conditions. Peter Clark's study of labor migration patterns within
England from 1660 through 1730 suggests that people were still making
short-range searches for work, as in the early seventeenth century, but not
the long-distance migrations previously associated with subsistence crises.
Vagrants who attempted long-distance travel were now harassed more systematically than earlier by local officials, who wanted to keep strange
paupers out of their villages and towns.[22] The English government continued to use America as a dumping ground for outcasts and undesirables,
sending debtors to Georgia and convicted felons to Maryland. But among
voluntary migrants we find a paradoxical pattern. English laborers poured
over in the early and mid-seventeenth century, when American conditions
were at their least favorable for struggling newcomers, and they came in
much smaller numbers during the eighteenth century, when opportunities
for the little man were much improved in most of the colonies.

During the 1640s and 1650s in the Caribbean and during the 1680s and
1690s in the Chesapeake, black slaves from West Africa began to replace
English servants as the mainstay of the labor force. Until recently very little
was known about the Atlantic slave trade. Thirty years ago, when Noel
Deerr attempted to estimate the overall proportions of the trade, he exaggerated the number of Africans shipped to British North America from 1607
through 1780 by about 550 percent because he reckoned by analogy from the
numbers shipped to the British West Indian colonies.[23] Now, thanks to the
new interest in Afro-American history and the cliometricians' discovery of
slave-trade statistics, the overall pattern of this vast forced labor migration is
far better understood. Slave-trade statistics for the seventeenth and eighteenth centuries, while extremely faulty, are markedly more satisfactory than
servant-trade statistics. In commercial records, slave ships are more readily
identifiable than servant ships because they sailed to or from Africa. No
shipping records from the servant trade can begin to match the records of the
Royal African Company in the Public Record Office, which incorporate a
wide range of information about some 150,000 slaves shipped to America
over a forty-year span.[24] Colony governments frequently taxed incoming
slave cargoes, and so they kept better importation records for slaves than for
servants. Slaves were usually separately enumerated in population counts,
tax lists, and probate records. Time series of slave prices can be generated.
Often, the regional African tribal origins of the slaves can be detected. Thus
it is possible to piece together a reasonably clear picture of slave recruitment
for the English colonies from 1607 to the American Revolution.

Philip Curtin's *The Atlantic Slave Trade* places the English trade within its
wider international context. He reckons that about 1,480,000 slaves were

imported from Africa to the British colonies between 1600 and 1780—or more than four times my estimate for the number of bound white servants imported to the British colonies during this span. Curtin's figures are very crude, and they are probably too low.[25] Several cliometricians have attempted to improve upon them, for example, by using the Jamaican slave-importation time series as a model for recalculating the Barbados and Leeward Islands imports or by using model life tables derived from modern nonenslaved populations to calculate the proportion of African-born and creole-born slaves in the various colonies.[26] In my view, such counterfactual hypotheses are not particularly helpful because they substitute a new, fictive certitude for old, sloppy ignorance. At any rate, Curtin's estimates, such as they are, indicate the slave recruitment pattern presented in table 6.1.

Obviously the slave trade was a far larger business in the eighteenth century than in the seventeenth century, and a far larger business in the Caribbean than in North America. Only about 17 percent were sent to the mainland colonies. Comparison between the import totals and the population totals as of 1780 also points up the stark contrast between slave demography in the islands and on the mainland. Those Africans who were shipped to the sugar colonies experienced long-term natural decrease, while those shipped

Table 6.1
ENGLISH SLAVE IMPORTS TO AMERICA, 1600–1780 (IN THOUSANDS)

Years	West Indies	Southern Mainland	Mid-Atlantic	New England	Total
1601–25	—	—	—	—	—
1626–50	21	—	—	—	21
1651–75	69	—	—	—	69
1676–1700	174	10	—	—	184
1701–20	160	28	2	—	190
1721–40	199	64	4	2	269
1741–60	267	63	1	1	332
1761–80	335	80	2	—	417
Total	1,225	245	9	3	1,482
Black population in 1780	346	519	42	14	921

Sources: The slave import figures are taken from Philip D. Curtin, *The Atlantic Slave Trade: A Census* (Madison, Wis., 1969), 119, 140, and have been modified by my own effort to distribute Curtin's North American totals between the South, the mid-Atlantic region, and New England. The figures for the West Indian black population in 1780 come from Frank Wesley Pitman, *The Development of the British West Indies, 1700–1763* (New Haven, 1917), 373–83; the mainland population figures come from U.S. Bureau of the Census, *Historical Statistics of the United States, Colonial Times to 1957* (Washington, D.C., 1960), series Z 1–19.

to the tobacco colonies soon experienced natural increase. Possible explanations for this demographic contrast will be considered later in this essay when we compare the character of the labor system in the two regions.

First, however, it is necessary to consider why the colonists turned from white contract labor to black slave labor, and why the Barbados planters adopted this new labor system half a century before the Chesapeake planters. Economic and social historians offer differing explanations. For the economic analysts, the chief factors are cost, profit, and productivity. When the price of a lifetime slave became competitive with the price of a short-term servant, the planters bought slaves because they were the cheapest form of labor. Barbados sugar planters, with their lucrative new crop, could afford to assemble large gangs of slaves in the 1640s and 1650s. At this date Virginia planters had less money to spend on labor, and they reckoned that servants were cheaper, because the high mortality rate in the Chesapeake made it extremely risky to pay extra money for lifetime workers who might die within a few years. By the 1680s and 1690s, however, life expectancy had improved significantly in the Chesapeake, and the tobacco planter could now calculate that an African slave was the better investment.[27] For social historians, the trouble with this cost-efficient line of argument is that it omits the human element. Seventeenth-century Englishmen were a narrowly ethnocentric people prejudiced against foreigners of any sort, even Scots, Irish, and Dutchmen, not to mention Jews, Indians, and Africans. Winthrop Jordan has assembled much evidence to demonstrate that they considered Africans to be ugly, barbaric, apelike, and devilish.[28] Colonists who wanted to make their homes in the New World must have preferred to keep America a white man's country. Hence the prospective slaveholder had to be persuaded that an African bondsman possessed other attractions beyond cheapness.

In making a choice between white servants and black slaves, the Caribbean and Chesapeake planters seem to have taken both economic and social factors into account. In Barbados, white servants in the 1620s and 1630s adjusted poorly to tropical conditions: they resented cultivating tobacco and cotton in the hot sun and either idled or tried to escape. When the Barbados planters introduced sugar production in the 1640s and 1650s, the new crop required strenuous, continuous, regimented labor that was vastly more taxing and less seasonal than any form of English agriculture. Sugar is a labor-intensive crop, and the Barbados planters needed to enlarge their labor force for sugar-making purposes just at the time of the English Civil War, when English shipping to the island, and the English servant trade, was disrupted. At this juncture Dutch traders showed the colonists how to make sugar and sold them African laborers on easy terms. The Barbados planters quickly discovered that they could compel the Africans to perform the heavy, unskilled gang labor required on the sugar plantations. The slaves were deeply rebellious and unwilling, to be sure, but they were also more patient, tractable, disciplined, and rugged than English servants. Of course the planters never described their African slaves in such positive terms; rather, they stereotyped them as black, uncivilized heathen who ranked several notches lower in the social order than the unprivileged laboring poor at home and so were especially suitable for drudge work in the cane fields. In this fashion, racism conveniently justified and bolstered the use of forced black labor.[29]

In Virginia at mid-century the situation was quite different. The planters continued to grow tobacco, and while the white servants grumbled, their labor was less strenuous and regimented than in sugar production. Like the Barbadians, the Virginians faced a cutback in their servant supply during the English Civil War, but as yet they had no prospect of slave labor. In the 1640s and 1650s the Atlantic slave trade was directed mainly towards Brazil; Barbados was the northernmost slave market in America, and the Chesapeake was too remote for Dutch slavers to bother with when they could sell their cargoes to customers who lived much closer to Africa. Even in the 1670s and 1680s, when the Royal African Company undertook to deliver slaves to the English colonies on a large scale, it concentrated almost exclusively on the West Indies market and sent very few shipments on the longer journey to the Chesapeake. But if the Virginia planters had no real labor choice, by the 1670s both masters and servants were becoming dissatisfied with the status quo. Edmund Morgan has traced in rich detail the labor tensions in Virginia that climaxed when the "terrible young men"—servants and ex-servants— who felt trapped, cheated, and impoverished, turned to open war against the Indians and rebellion against Governor Berkeley in 1676.[30] "How miserable that man is," Berkeley protested on the eve of Bacon's Rebellion, "that Governes a People wher six parts of seaven at least are Poore Endebted Discontented and Armed."[31] It was to resolve this dilemma, according to Morgan, that the Virginians turned from servant to slave labor in the years after the rebellion was suppressed. They could do so only because a supply of African laborers was at last becoming available. After the Glorious Revolution, the Royal African Company lost its monopoly of the English slave trade, private slavers rushed into business, and the Atlantic trade zoomed fantastically. For the first time, sizable shipments reached the Chesapeake.

It is difficult to compare the slave trade with the servant trade because historians have approached the two subjects rather differently. Historians of slavery tend to concentrate upon those quantifiable aspects of the trade for which comparable servant data is lacking—size of ships and crews, value of trade goods, prices, length of voyage, mortality in transit, and profits to the English traders. On the other hand, historians of slavery have little information as yet about slave hunting and gathering within Africa, nor do they know why slave traders kept shifting from region to region along the West African coast. In general we are even more ignorant about slave recruitment in Africa than about servant recruitment in Britain.[32]

From 1640 to the abolition of the English trade in 1807, the volume of English slave shipments from Africa increased almost continuously, rising from about ten thousand slaves loaded per year in the 1690s to about forty thousand slaves loaded per year in the 1790s. To some extent the slaving business became more cost-efficient over time, for the ships used in the trade in the late eighteenth century were larger than earlier and carried more slaves per vessel. English slavers learned to assemble their cargoes more quickly, although in the 1790s they still spent about four months on average cruising along the African coast or negotiating with local dealers.[33] Slave gathering was always a slow business because each ship captain wanted to mix captives from various tribes so as to hinder them from combining in shipboard plots and rebellions.[34] As the trade kept expanding, the English traders shifted their operations east and south along the African coast. In the 1690s they drew about two-thirds of their cargoes from Senegambia, Sierra Leone, and the Windward and Gold coasts. By the 1790s they drew about 70 percent of their cargoes from the Bight of Biafra and the Congo basin. Though English colonial customers much preferred Guinea slaves to Angolan slaves, over time this consideration was clearly outweighed by African coastal trading conditions. The voyage from Liverpool to Angola, and from Angola to Jamaica, was considerably longer than the voyage to and from Guinea, but the Liverpool slaver more than made up this difference by reducing by about two months the time he spent on the African coast.[35]

Better information is needed on the age and sex ratios of African slaves shipped to the American colonies. In the late seventeenth century, according to Kenneth G. Davies, some 86 percent of the slaves transported by the Royal African Company were adults, and 60 percent were males. One hundred years later, according to Herbert S. Klein, 93 percent of the slaves arriving in Jamaica were adults, and 62 percent were males.[36] There are indications that the male ratio was sometimes as high as among English servants in the seventeenth century. The demographic effects of this skewed sex ratio were certainly important in the West Indian colonies, where the African-born proportion of the slave population was so large, but the sex ratio among imported slaves was soon modified by another factor: once slaves were put to work, especially on the Caribbean sugar estates, the men died faster than the women. Caribbean census returns and probate records from the late seventeenth century show a female slave majority among the slaves. Slave inventories from eighteenth-century sugar estates, during the peak period of African importation, generally show a male majority. But by the 1820s, shortly after the slave trade had closed, slave registration figures in Jamaica once again show more females than males.[37]

Mortality rates on the Middle Passage declined very markedly over time. In the 1680s, when a Royal African Company trader could buy a slave in Africa for about one-fifth of his selling price in America, 23 percent of these slaves died during the Atlantic crossing. By the 1790s a slave in Africa cost close to half of his sale price in America. High mortality would now erase all profit, and accordingly the death rate on the passage to Jamaica fell to below 6 percent.[38] Like English servant ships, African slave ships arrived in the several regions of English America at differing seasons of the year. Slave ships bound for the West Indies arrived principally between November and March—a pattern quite similar to that of the servant shipments. But slave ships bound for the Chesapeake usually arrived in the summer months, whereas servant ships arrived in the fall. No African ships arrived in Virginia in the coldest winter months, when the local demand for labor was at its lowest ebb and when the new slaves would have experienced the most difficult climatic adjustment.[39] Little comparative work has been done on the mechanics of slave sales in the various American ports. Chesapeake-bound slave ships carried smaller cargoes than Caribbean-bound ships, yet the selling procedure in the Chesapeake was generally more protracted, involving many more shoppers and buyers. For example, a Bristol ship carrying 150 slaves to Virginia in 1717 sold these slaves to 65 different buyers, after weeks of haggling.[40] In the sugar islands, sales were generally quick because individual planters bought new slaves in large groups, ten or twenty at a time. The African entering Jamaica was certainly treated no better than the African entering Virginia, but he encountered a more impersonal, faster, production-line system of purchase by his new American master.

Though African slaves formed by far the largest body of laborers imported into English America after 1680, three other groups of workers arrived in very sizeable numbers during the course of the eighteenth century: Irish indentured servants, English convicts, and German redemptioners.

Many more indentured servants came to America from Ireland in the eighteenth century than from England. Some were Catholics, but the majority were Scotch-Irish from Ulster. No surviving Irish emigration lists have been found, so we cannot tell how many came, which were Catholics and which Protestants, nor which were paying passengers and which servants. However, through newspaper advertisements we can trace a very large number of servant ships sailing to America from the Irish ports. R. J. Dickson has studied the Scotch-Irish emigration from Ulster between 1718 and 1775. While he undoubtedly exaggerates the number of Ulstermen who emigrated as servants rather than as paying passengers, he demonstrates that most of the Ulster emigrants were hard-pressed tenant farmers forced out by food shortages and rack-renting in northern Ireland. They were also vigorously solicited by recruiting agents. By ingenious use of newspaper advertisements, Dickson is able to follow the activities of agents who toured the Ulster towns and villages on market days to recruit servant emigrants, and he also traces the embarkation from Ulster ports of 442 vessels carrying servants to America between 1750 and 1775. Audrey Lockhart has similarly traced the embarkation from southern Irish ports of 252 additional servant ships between 1750 and 1775.[41]

As table 6.2 shows, these Irish ships sailed to different parts of America than did the London servant ships in these same years. Whereas 77 percent of

Table 6.2
AMERICAN DESTINATIONS OF SERVANTS, 1750–75

Destination	London Servants ($N = 3,958$)	Ulster Ships ($N = 442$)	Southern Irish Ships ($N = 252$)
Canada	0%	3%	5%
New England	0	1	4
New York	1	19	13
Pennsylvania	17	55	38
Maryland	58	5	15
Virginia	19	1	12
Carolina and Georgia	1	16	9
West Indies	3	0	3
Other, unknown	1	0	1
Total	100%	100%	100%

Sources: David W. Galenson, *White Servitude in Colonial America: An Economic Analysis* (Cambridge, 1981), app. I; R. J. Dickson, *Ulster Emigration to Colonial America, 1718–1775* (London, 1966), app. E; and Audrey Lockhart, *Some Aspects of Emigration from Ireland to the North American Colonies between 1660 and 1775* (New York, 1976), app. C.

the London servants in 1750–75 were bound for Maryland and Virginia, and 17 percent for Pennsylvania, Dickson shows that 74 percent of the Ulster servant ships sailed to the mid-Atlantic colonies, with Carolina next, and only 6 percent sailed to Maryland and Virginia. The southern Irish ships traced by Lockhart pursued still another pattern, sending passengers to every part of America, with prime focus on those colonies known for their religious and ethnic diversity—where Catholics would be least unwelcome. Earlier in the eighteenth century nearly half of the London servants had gone to Jamaica, but by 1750–75 very few London servants or Irish ships sailed to any of the West Indian islands.

The English convict trade also was very sizable in the eighteenth century; it deserves more study, if not by genealogists then by social and economic historians. Beginning in 1718 English felons convicted of minor crimes could be transported to the colonies as laborers on seven-year terms, while felons convicted of major crimes were to serve fourteen years. Registers in the Public Record Office list the names of 17,740 felons from jails in and near London, together with the 190 ships that transported them to the colonies between 1719 and 1772. Records in Maryland show that 9,360 convicts arrived in that colony between 1746 and 1775; 58 percent were shipped from London, and 35 percent from Bristol. Abbot Emerson Smith reckons that about 30,000 convicts were transported overseas from British jails from 1718 through 1775 and that about 20,000 of them reached Maryland or Virginia.[42] His figures, taken in conjunction with Galenson's and Lockhart's, demonstrate that the Chesapeake planters, despite their large slave holdings, were especially eager for white bound labor in the eighteenth century.

Kenneth Morgan has found evidence suggesting that most Maryland buyers of convict laborers purchased them one at a time; 739 incoming convicts in the years 1767–75 were distributed among 405 different buyers. Convicts were relatively cheap; they fetched less than one-third of the price of African slaves, and female felons were special bargains, selling for only two-thirds of the price of males.[43] At least one of the leading Chesapeake planters was engaged in the convict trade: John Tayloe II, the master of some 300 slaves, imported two shiploads of London convicts in 1773–74. Tayloe must have sold most of them to other planters, but he used convict labor on his own estate. Between 1757 and 1776 he offered rewards in the *Virginia Gazette* for six convict servants who had run away. Three of them were ironworkers at his furnace, and three were sailors on his river schooners. One of the sailors bore "the mark of the Irons he wore in Goal on one of his Ancles," the second had stolen clothing from his fellow crew members before absconding, and the third, a man of "bold countenance," had been the skipper of the schooner *Occaquan* before he took off. These men must have been pleasant company for the slave sailors who also worked on Tayloe's river fleet.[44]

All of the immigrant laborers considered so far—whether English servants, African slaves, Ulster servants, or English convicts—arrived in America as single individuals. Our final category of immigrant workers, the German redemptioners, came in family groups and sometimes in larger neighborhood or community groups. Systematic study of the eighteenth-century exodus from southwestern Germany and Switzerland is only just now beginning, but present evidence indicates that these German peasants left the Rhineland and the Palatinate more because they were attracted by the advertising campaigns of recruiting agents than because they were forced out by famine or rack-renting. They traveled to America in large numbers—about 70,000 arrived in Philadelphia on 348 ships between 1727 and 1776—but America was only one of their choices. Groups of Germans moved in large, sudden waves: 13,000 to England in 1709; 37,000 to Philadelphia in 1749–54; 13,000 to Russia in the 1760s. The Germans who migrated to America appear to have been in better shape than most of the other immigrant laborers. Marianne Wokeck, who is currently studying the German migration to Pennsylvania, estimates that about two-thirds of the people who landed in Philadelphia paid their own way or were able to finance the cost of the trip through sale of goods in Pennsylvania or through loans. The remaining third were the redemptioners, or contract workers, who sold their own or their children's labor in order to cover the cost of the Atlantic passage. Up to the mid-1750s it was common for an arriving German family to bind one or several children—boys until the age of twenty-one, girls until eighteen—

while the other family members worked for their own profit. But in the 1760s and 1770s this family-immigration pattern declined, and the arriving Germans, like other contract laborers, were mostly young, single males.[45]

In sum, the chief common feature among the nearly two million bound workers recruited from Europe and Africa in the seventeenth and eighteenth centuries is that they came to America under duress. Unlike their successors from Europe and Asia in the nineteenth and twentieth centuries, almost all of them came over as singles, not as families. But like their successors, they were rejects from the Old World. Most of them—the Africans, the Irish Catholics, and the convicts in particular—encountered deep prejudice and open contempt in the colonies, but they were readily admitted, purchased, and put to work because cheap unskilled labor was scarce in colonial America.

By the mid-eighteenth century the American colonists had developed four strikingly different labor systems in the Caribbean, the southern mainland, the mid-Atlantic colonies, and New England. Let us briefly consider the functional aspects of each system and compare some of their social and economic characteristics.

In the Caribbean, ever since the days of Hawkins and Drake the English had pursued economic exploitation more than full-scale settlement. The sugar boom of the 1640s legitimated this tendency. Not only did the sugar planters convert from white to black workers but they became totally dependent upon massive slave imports. Between 1640 and 1780 the islanders bought about 1,225,000 Africans to stock their slave gangs, keeping just enough white overseers, doctors, and clerical workers on hand to maintain control. This social mode, a small cadre of white masters driving an army of black slaves, was totally without precedent in English experience. Already by 1680 in Barbados the gulf between the privileged gentry and the un-privileged laborers was much greater than at home.[46] At this date the Barbados slaves outnumbered their masters by only two to one. By 1750 the Barbados ratio had climbed to four to one. In the Leeward Islands the ratio was seven to one: in the parish of St. Mary, in Antigua, as of 1767 only 65 whites paid taxes, and they held an average of 86 slaves apiece.[47] Jamaica was the chief English sugar island by 1750, and it had a slave ratio of ten to one. A few hundred big entrepreneurs owned all of the best acreage and farmed on a very large scale. They raised cattle, cut timber, and cultivated indigo, cocoa, pimento, ginger, coffee, and cotton, but sugar was by far the most important crop. Surveys of the island taken in 1739, 1768, and 1832 disclose that half or more of the Jamaican slaves were attached to sugar estates, living and working in village-sized compounds.[48] By 1814 in Westmoreland Parish, Jamaica, half of the slaves lived in gangs of 200 or more, and only 10 percent were placed in gangs of less than 30.[49] While the black laborers were thus congregated into factorylike units, many of their employers had retired to England as absentees, leaving their estates in the hands of attorneys and overseers.

In recent years a number of Caribbean historians have inspected this slave labor system by studying the business records of individual sugar estates, paticularly those records preserved by absentee proprietors in England. Thus J. Harry Bennett and I have reconstructed the operations of Bybrook plantation in Jamaica, 1669–1713, Richard Pares has studied the Pinney plantations in Nevis, 1685–1809, J. Harry Bennett has examined the Codrington plantations in Barbados, 1710–1808, Jerome S. Handler, Frederick W. Lange, and Robert B. Riordan have analyzed the Newton estate in Barbados, 1670–1834, Michael Craton and James Walvin have described the estate management and the labor force on Worthy Park in Jamaica from the 1720s into the twentieth century, and Barry Higman has explored conditions on a sample of early nineteenth-century Jamaican estates.[50] Such microcosmic studies have obvious shortcomings: the slave laborers themselves are silent, and observations about labor conditions have to be filtered through the writings of white owners, attorneys, and overseers. The estates studied so far may not be very representative, yet their records generate specific information about employment patterns, labor routines, purchase and sale of slaves, health care, and sex roles, which adds a much needed human dimension to the macrocosmic analysis of slave productivity and profitability generated by the cliometricians.

To illustrate what can be learned by close study of Caribbean plantation records, let us consider the slave labor system in the Westmoreland sugar district of western Jamaica, as documented by the estate records of Mesopotamia plantation and by the diary of a Westmoreland estate manager, Thomas Thistlewood. The Mesopotamia records provide the fullest documentation yet found for any Caribbean slave community; they include eighty-five inventories of the slave force taken between 1736 and 1832.[51] By correlating these inventories, we can reconstruct the careers of eleven hundred individual slaves, often from birth (or purchase) to death. Thistlewood's diary is the most minutely detailed day-by-day record yet discovered for the activities of any colonial planter. He kept this diary for thirty-six years, from his arrival in Jamaica in 1750 to his final illness in 1786, and he discloses almost more than the reader can bear about the underside of slave management.[52]

Reading through Thistlewood's diary, one wonders how the slaves he dealt with could possibly endure such a regime and why they did not rebel far more frequently and violently. Thistlewood's first job in Jamaica was to manage a cattle pen in a remote mountain district. During the twelve months he held this job, in 1750–51, Thistlewood lived alone with forty-two slaves most of whom were African-born. In the first few days Thistlewood was there, the owner of the pen inspected the place and showed him how to manage the slaves: he ordered that the head slave, driver Mulatto Dick, be tied to an orange tree in the garden and given nearly three hundred lashes "for his many crimes and negligencies." It was nine days before Dick emerged from his cabin to go back to work. Thistlewood got the message: in the next twelve months he had 35 slaves whipped a total of 52 times. The punishment ranged from 50 to 150 lashes per whipping. In his diary Thistlewood recorded that he kept a slave mistress, with whom he had intercourse almost nightly. He also had sex with nine of the other fifteen females who lived at the pen. Thistlewood frequently reported that the slaves were shirking their work. Nine of them ran away at least once, and two of them disappeared repeatedly. All of them complained of hunger and kept stealing food. Several became violent: one man hacked a woman with a machete, and two men pulled knives when they were cornered. Yet Thistlewood was never personally threatened. He quit the job because he quarreled with the owner, not the slaves. Indeed, he went on lengthy hunting and fishing trips with some of the men whom he had flogged and whose wives he had raped, and he distributed rum, food, and other presents all round on leaving.[53]

Turning to the Mesopotamia records, one begins to understand why these Jamaican slaves were not more rebellious: they were trapped into a labor routine that kept them exhausted, enervated, sickly, and dull. Mesopotamia was a fairly typical Jamaican sugar production unit, staffed by a labor gang that fluctuated in size between 250 and 350 during the last century of Jamaican slavery. Between 1762 and 1832, when the Mesopotamia records are most complete, nearly twice as many slaves died as were born on this estate, and the work force was sustained by introducing 147 new Africans—mostly male teenagers—and 278 "seasoned" slaves, bought from neighboring estates. During this seventy-year span only 4 slaves were sold, 12 were manumitted, and 9 escaped.[54] Slaves born at Mesopotamia had a definite occupational advantage over slaves purchased from the slave ships or from other estates: they held the lion's share of the supervisory, craft, and domestic jobs. To some extent craftworkers and domestics secured preferential employment for their children, but the key factor was color. By 1832, 10 percent of the Mesopotamia slaves were mulattoes and quadroons, and these people were always assigned domestic or semiskilled jobs.[55]

The majority of the Mesopotamia laborers were field workers, kept busy six days a week, year round, with twelve hours of monotonous drudge labor: digging cane trenches, weeding and dunging the young cane, tending the cattle, and harvesting the mature cane. The slaves were given simple hand tools and no labor-saving devices. Much of their work would have been performed by draft animals in English or North American agriculture. Sugar was then, as it is now, a seasonal crop, but the overseers stretched out the tasks to keep the slaves fully occupied at all times. The Mesopotamia records show a clear correlation between slave occupation and longevity: field workers broke down in health more quickly, and died younger, than craftworkers. Furthermore, females survived this labor routine better than males. During this seventy-year span 105 more males than females died at Mesopotamia, so that female workers considerably outnumbered male workers on this estate by 1832. A large majority of the field workers were women, even on the First Gang, which performed the heaviest field labor.

The Mesopotamia women who worked so hard produced few living children. Between 1762 and 1832 about half of the female slaves aged eighteen to forty-five were childless, and those who did raise children had small families. The disease environment, dietary deficiencies, and the debilitating labor regimen were probably the most important factors in explaining this infertility. It cannot be a pure coincidence that the Jamaican population began to increase naturally almost immediately after emancipation, when many women withdrew from field labor.[56] According to the Mesopotamia records, about 20 percent of the slave deaths on this estate were attributable to diet and bad hygiene. The absentee owners of Mesopotamia were upset by the high mortality and the low fertility; they attempted to encourage motherhood by excusing from labor women with five or more children. The owners were bothered a good deal more, however, by the fact that so many of their slaves were elderly or invalids. A surprisingly large number of Mesopotamia slaves lived into their sixties and seventies. Although the owners kept adding young male workers, most of the labor was performed by women, and at any one time about 20 percent of the adult slaves were too sick or old for productive labor. Thus at Mesopotamia the Caribbean slave labor system proved to be inefficient as well as inhumane.

Turning to the southern mainland colonies, we find not one labor system but several. At one extreme, the South Carolina low-country rice planters employed slave labor practices reminiscent of those in the West Indies. In a parish like St. James Goose Creek, adjacent to Charleston, blacks outnumbered whites by four to one as early as the 1720s.[57] The slaves were congregated into large work gangs, as in Jamaica, and compelled to plant, hoe, harvest, thresh, and husk the rice by hand. In the 1760s about half of the slaves in the low country were African-born; adult male slaves heavily outnumbered adult female slaves; and 40 percent of the blacks lived and worked in large gangs of at least fifty.[58] At the opposite extreme, in the North Carolina piedmont, an entirely different labor system was in operation. Orange County, one of the few piedmont counties with surviving pre-revolutionary tax records, was a district of corn, wheat, and livestock agriculture. The taxpayers were small farmers of English, Scotch-Irish, or German stock who had migrated south from the Chesapeake or the mid-Atlantic colonies. In 1755 only 10 percent of the Orange County householders owned any slaves, and no planter in the county possessed as many as ten.[59]

A third southern labor pattern, in many respects a median system combining features of the South Carolina low country and the North Carolina piedmont, was to be found in the Chesapeake, especially in the oldest settled tidewater counties of Virginia and Maryland. Here the tobacco planters, while just as interested as their South Carolina or Jamaica counterparts in making money through the exploitation of cheap labor, were also trying to shape a society in which both rich and poor whites had status and could feel comfortably at home. Between the 1680s and the 1750s they created an elaborately tiered social and economic hierarchy with slave laborers at the base, convict and indentured servants ranked next, then tenant farmers, then small landholders, then middling planters, and a handful of large planters— one to five in each county—at the top. By mid-century, slaveholding was very widely distributed throughout Virginia and Maryland. No Chesapeake county was so heavily tilted towards slave labor as the South Carolina rice parishes, but only the remote western frontier counties were without significant slave holdings. In 1755 the population in fourteen of the sixty-three Chesapeake counties was more than half black; all of these counties were in Virginia, served by the James, York, and Rappahannock rivers, where the African slave traders principally brought their cargoes.[60] Maryland had noticeably fewer slaves at this date, which helps to explain why the planters from the upper Chesapeake were especially eager for convict servants.[61] Even in the Virginia counties with the largest black populations slaveholding was far from universal. It is difficult to be precise on this point, since the prerevolutionary Virginia county tax lists have disappeared, but it appears that fewer than half of the small planters and tenant farmers in the Chesapeake were slaveholders in the 1760s and 1770s.

Table 6.3 shows the distribution of slaves within one Virginia tidewater county in 1783, a Barbados parish one hundred years earlier, and a Jamaica parish (the site of Mesopotamia estate) thirty years later. A striking contrast between the Chesapeake and the Caribbean is immediately evident. Richmond County, on the Rappahannock, was 57 percent black in 1783—one of the highest county ratios in Virginia—yet Richmond could still be construed as a white man's society. A third of the white householders in this county stood outside of the slave system. Blacks were held principally by small and middling planters, and they lived and worked in small units. Only two planters in the county, John Tayloe III and Robert Wormeley Carter (son of the diarist Landon Carter), held over one hundred slaves; together, they accounted for 11 percent of the slaves in Richmond. In St. George's Parish, Barbados, and in Westmoreland Parish, Jamaica, the slaves lived and worked in far larger units.

Ideally, our investigation of eighteenth-century Chesapeake slave labor should concentrate upon the small plantations where most slaves lived and worked. But the small slaveholders have left little trace of their doings. Even the business accounts of the great planters are far less informative than in the West Indies. Students of Chesapeake slavery are currently using a diverse

Table 6.3
THE DISTRIBUTION OF SLAVES IN THE CARIBBEAN AND VIRGINIA

	St. George's, Barbados, 1680	Richmond County, Virginia, 1783	Westmoreland, Jamaica, 1814
0	16%	34.0%	11%
1–5	43	54.0	40
16–50	18	10.6	26
51–100	12	1.0	8
More than 100	11	0.4	15
Total	100%	100.0%	100%
Number of slaves per living unit			
1–5	2%	10%	1%
6–15	6	27	4
16–50	17	41	14
51–100	23	11	13
More than 100	52	11	68
Total	100%	100%	100%
Total property holders	120	451	338
Total slaveholders	101	299	302
Total slaves	4,216	3,191	20,596
Average number of slaves per slaveholder	42	11	68

Sources: The Richmond tax list is from U.S. Bureau of the Census, *Heads of Families at the First Census . . . State Enumerations of Virginia; from 1782 to 1785* (Washington, D.C., 1908), 62–63. The St. George's Parish, Barbados, census of 1680 is from John Camden Hotten, ed., *Original Lists of Persons . . . who went from Great Britain to the American Plantations, 1600–1700* (London, 1874), 460–64. The Westmoreland Parish, Jamaica, tax return of 1814 is from Barham Papers, b.34, Bodleian Library.

range of techniques in order to find out how the pre-revolutionary system worked. Michael Mullin has searched newspaper advertisements to find a pattern among slave runaways; Allan Kulikoff has searched the inventories of probated estates to find information about the size and structure of slave working units; and Rhys Isaac has read between the lines in Landon Carter's diary to assess one plantation owner's relations with his black workers.[62] Mullin, Kulikoff, and Isaac all argue for black activism; they show ways in which the Chesapeake slaves were able to challenge or undermine the system. My own reading of the situation is less sanguine. While Chesapeake slavery was certainly not as brutal or repressive as in the Caribbean, the slaveholders seem to me to have stymied black resistance pretty effectively and to have thwarted most forms of black achievement.

In order to set up a meaningful comparison with Jamaican slavery as documented by the Mesopotamia estate records and Thomas Thistlewood's diary, let us consider parallel collections of evidence concerning the slave labor system in the northern neck of tidewater Virginia: the papers of the Tayloe family of Mount Airy, overlooking the Rappahannock, and the diary of Landon Carter, who lived next-door to the Tayloes at Sabine Hall. The Tayloes and the Carters were far from being representative Chesapeake slaveholders. They were among the largest entrepreneurs in the Chesapeake: the slave communities at Mount Airy and at Sabine Hall were equivalent in size to the slave community at Mesopotamia, Jamaica. John Tayloe I held 167 slaves at Mount Airy in 1747; his grandson held 383 slaves at Mount Airy in 1809, as well as hundreds of other slaves elsewhere in the Chesapeake. The Tayloe family papers describe the development of this large work force and include a series of 47 slave inventories, directly comparable to the Mesopotamia inventories, documenting black life at Mount Airy.[63] Just as the Mount Airy records can be set against the Mesopotamia records, so Landon Carter's diary can be set against Thomas Thistlewood's diary. Carter was a considerably less systematic observer than the Jamaican diarist, and a more idiosyncratic one; but he reported on the same scale and with the same attention to detail. How does Virginia slavery, as documented by the Tayloes and Landon Carter, chiefly differ from Jamaican slavery?

In the first place, the Tayloes and Carters saw themselves as patriarchs, in the fullest sense of the term, and this impelled them to manipulate their black workers' private lives and not simply to exploit their labor. In Jamaica, Thomas Thistlewood kept a diary in order to preserve his sanity, but in Virginia, Landon Carter kept a diary in order to nurture his self-image of father/ruler over his white family and black slaves. Through this diary the reader can follow Carter's efforts to supervise the work of his slaves, and manage their lives, for his own profit and their moral betterment. Carter moved constantly among the Sabine Hall field workers as well as the domestics, badgering them to work and doctoring them when sick. He would stay for hours in the threshing house in order to make the threshers work faster and more carefully. He knew his slaves as individuals, identifying some 150 blacks in his diary by name. His comments on slave behavior were almost invariably negative, for despite his wealth and status, Carter suffered acutely from paranoia. His diary in the 1760s and 1770s was a dumping ground, filled with diatribes against the people who betrayed him: his children and grandchildren and his slaves. In Carter's view, the Sabine Hall slaves, through "villanous lazyness," were constantly frustrating his best-laid plans. Thus carpenter Jimmy, who should have been building a corn house, was too lame to work, his legs swollen from wearing tight shoes. Far from feeling sorry for Jimmy, Carter punished this "splay footed rascal" by prohibiting him from going home at night to his wife, who lived on another quarter. Carpenter Tony, who should have been building Carter's garden fence, "goes on pretending with his scheme of old age creeping and whindling about often pretending to be sick." Plowman Manuel also had a scheme: to kill off Carter's oxen and horses by miring them in the mud. Body servant Nassau's strategy was to be constantly drunk.

As Rhys Isaac has pointed out, Carter played his role of patriarch ineptly, and his slaves knew how to outmaneuver and humiliate him. But they did so at great physical and psychic cost. Some of them escaped, at least briefly: Carter reports about forty runaways (mainly short-term) over a twenty-year span. Some of them were flogged: Carter reports twenty whippings in the year 1770 alone. Worse than the whippings must have been the endless intrusion, inspection, and harassment by this crabbed, obnoxious master. The slaves who knew Carter best, such as his body servant Nassau, were the ones most likely to run away. When Lord Dunmore called upon the Virginia slaves to revolt against their masters in 1775, fourteen of Carter's people fled to the British governor. This upset the proud old man very much. He dreamed one night that the runaways, looking "most wretchedly meager and wan," came back and begged for his help.[64] But in truth, Carter's slaves had had quite enough of his help.

Landon Carter can be dismissed, and perhaps he should be, as an aberrant mental case. But the slaves who lived next-door at the Tayloes' Mount Airy plantation were also manipulated and intruded upon to a high degree. Admittedly, they worked less hard and lived much better than the slaves at Mesopotamia, Jamaica. Over a sixty-year span the Mount Airy records show that nearly twice as many slaves were born as died on this plantation. The labor pattern was designed to achieve total self-sufficiency: the field workers raised corn and pork in addition to tobacco, and they tended their gardens in off-hours; slave spinners and weavers made cloth from local cotton and wool; slave shoemakers tanned and dressed local leather; the smiths and joiners made wagons, ploughs, and hoes and shod horses; and the carpenters, masons, and jobbers erected and repaired buildings. Work logs kept by the overseers show a definite seasonal rhythm, with the harvest frenzy in mid-summer and a long slack period in the winter. A third of the Mount Airy black workers were domestics or craftworkers, and women did much less of the heavy field labor than at Mesopotamia.

On the other hand, the lives of the Mount Airy slaves were continually disrupted by the Tayloes' practice of moving workers from one quarter to another or from one plantation to another and by their frequent sale of surplus slaves. There is only fragmentary evidence of this practice in the pre-revolutionary papers but abundant evidence in the post-revolutionary papers. In 1792 John Tayloe III advertised: "For Sale 200 Virginia born, men, women and children, all ages and descriptions."[65] At least 50 Mount Airy slaves were among those sold that year. Between 1809 and 1828 John Tayloe III sold 52 Mount Airy slaves, mainly teenage girls. Between 1828 and 1860 his sons moved 364 Mount Airy slaves to other Tayloe properties, about half of them to distant cotton plantations in Alabama. By this method the Tayloes kept the Mount Airy work force well organized for maximum productivity, with a high percentage of prime-aged male laborers. They clearly played favorites, keeping the domestics and craftworkers they liked best, together with their children, at Mount Airy. But among the field workers, husbands and wives generally lived at separate work quarters, and children were customarily taken from their parents at an early age. Thus the Tayloes' constant shuffling of the slave population, while sensible from a business viewpoint, was destructive of black family life.

To turn from the plantation slavery of tidewater Virginia to the farm, shop, and household environment of the mid-Atlantic colonies is to enter a different world. It was, to be sure, a variegated world, incorporating such laborers as the Yankee tenants, who staffed many of the baronial estates in the Hudson Valley; the Scottish tenants, who preserved their peculiar "farmtoun" style of husbandry in East Jersey; the African slaves, who labored on Quaker farms in West Jersey; the German redemptioners, who worked in rural Pennsylvania; and the Ulster servants, who bound themselves to masters in Philadelphia.[66] But throughout this region the labor pattern differed in three important respects from the labor patterns of the Chesapeake and the Caribbean. First, the mid-Atlantic employers relied overwhelmingly on white labor, not black; and on apprentices, servants, and wage workers, not slaves. Second, they made heavy use of non-English imported white labor, especially Scotch-Irish and German immigrants. Third, the mid-Atlantic employment pattern more closely resembled the pattern in Britain or Europe than that in the plantation colonies. Agricultural laborers raised small grain crops and tended livestock, urban laborers were trained for crafts or tended shops, and female laborers were engaged for domestic service—all much as in the Old World.

Towns were more central work places in the mid-Atlantic economy than in the southern plantation economies; and since we will be focusing upon farm labor when discussing New England, it is appropriate to focus upon urban labor in the mid-Atlantic region. The premier town in this region during the eighteenth century was Philadelphia, which grew from around two thousand inhabitants in 1690 to nine thousand in 1740 and twenty-five thousand in 1776.[67] By the Revolution, Philadelphia was the largest town and employment center in British America. Unhappily, many of the Philadelphia laborers—apprentices, servants, slaves, journeymen, and other wage workers (most particularly the female workers)—are impossible to find in the existing records. Some of them surface in the Philadelphia tax records for 1693, 1709, 1756, 1767, 1769, 1772, 1774, and 1775, in the twenty-four hundred inventories of estates filed between 1682 and 1780, in the newspapers, or in business records kept by merchants, shopkeepers, and artisans.[68] But in many respects the Philadelphia servant or wage laborer remains a more shadowy figure than the Jamaica or Virginia slave.

Our understanding of labor practices in pre-revolutionary Philadelphia has been strongly colored by the example and the writings of Benjamin Franklin. He started out as a bound apprentice, became a wage-earning journeyman, and quickly rose through skill and hard work to be a self-employed printer, bookseller, and newspaper editor. And though he retired from the printing business at age forty-two, he was tremendously proud of his workingman's roots and of his craft as a printer, which enabled him to work with his hands and exercise his brain simultaneously. Franklin's *Autobiography* devotes considerable space to a description of the labor climate in Philadelphia from 1723, when he arrived as a runaway apprentice, to the 1730s, when he established himself as a successful printer. But the *Autobiography* was written for propaganda purposes; it is far more selective and less candid than the private diaries of Thomas Thistlewood and Landon Carter. Looking back as an old man upon his youth, Franklin was more concerned with character building than with the work practices in his printing shop. He encourages the reader to believe that any laborer, through industry, sobriety, and frugality, can rise up in the world. He introduces vignettes of lazy, drunken apprentices and journeymen as exemplars of behavior to avoid. He also contrasts the openness of the Philadelphia labor market with the proletarian restrictiveness of opportunity in London, where he also labored as a journeyman printer. Thanks to Franklin, we have tended to assume that Philadelphia provided an ideal environment for the struggling workingman and that most, if not all, of its inhabitants enjoyed expanding opportunities and a rising standard of living.[69]

Recently this rosy picture has been challenged. A group of historians more influenced by E. P. Thompson's *The Making of the English Working Class* than by Franklin's *Autobiography* has been investigating servitude and slavery in Philadelphia, as well as job opportunities, wages, prices, and the distribution of wealth. Their findings suggest that while laborers in this town enjoyed generally favorable working and living conditions into the 1740s, their circumstances deteriorated badly in the next thirty years. Initially, as elsewhere in seventeenth-century America, the pioneers who founded Philadelphia relied heavily upon bound labor. The early inhabitants brought with them numerous indentured servants, and they purchased a shipload of 150 African slaves in 1684. According to Jean Soderlund, who has made a systematic analysis of all existing city inventories, Philadelphians who died in the 1680s, during the first decade of settlement, held more slaves and servants per capita than at any later date.[70] During the next forty years, from 1690 to 1730, servant imports were low, and slave imports were also fairly low. During this period Philadelphians did not abandon bound labor. Rather, they recruited apprentices and journeymen locally in the urban English fashion or hired migrant laborers from other colonies, such as seventeen-year-old Benjamin Franklin from Boston in 1723. And as the town grew rapidly and the local labor market expanded, Philadelphians bought many of the African slaves and the Irish and German servants who were shipped into the city between 1729 and 1775. These immigrant laborers came in overlapping waves: slave shipments in 1729–41, followed by shipments of German and Irish servants in 1732–56, then slave shipments in 1759–65 (at a time when it was impractical to import servants because the British enrolled large numbers of them into the army during the Seven Years' War), and Irish servants again from 1763 to 1775.

Despite this large-scale infusion of bound labor the proportion of slaves and immigrant servants in the total Philadelphia labor force was probably not rising during the years 1729–62, and it was certainly declining during the years 1763–75. Immigrant servants had to be constantly replaced, since they soon earned their freedom, and slaves had to be replaced also, since they had little chance to develop family life in Philadelphia and were not reproducing themselves. When offered a choice, Philadelphia employers preferred servants to slaves; they bought Africans mainly when immigrant whites were unavailable. And probably Philadelphia employers preferred native-born to immigrant workers. If African slaves and Irish servants had been especially sought-after, one would expect that the rich merchants and professionals, who could pay top prices, would have snapped up most of them. But instead we find that Philadelphia artisans of modest means bought much of the immigrant bound labor. In 1745, two-thirds of the 253 servants imported into the city were bound to artisans, and in 1767 about half of the 905 slaves in Philadelphia were held by artisans.[71]

During and after the Seven Years' War there was a decisive shift away from bound to free wage labor. From 1754 onward the Philadelphia Quakers campaigned actively against slave ownership. Meanwhile, many free white laborers were drawn to the city because the wartime business boom of 1754–63 drove wages up in Philadelphia for mariners, shipwrights, and other semiskilled workers. In the peacetime depression that followed, there was a labor glut, wages fell, and Philadelphia employers discovered that wage labor was cheaper than bound labor. According to Gary Nash, the 1760s and 1770s saw a great constriction in job opportunities for mariners and unskilled laborers and a great increase in the number of underemployed and unemployed workers. According to Billy Smith, the wages of unskilled and semiskilled workers were now no longer adequate to cover the minimum cost of food, rent, fuel, and clothing.[72] The wives and children of the laboring poor had to find marginal employment if families were to survive. The city fathers had to devise new measures of poor relief for the destitute.

Had young Benjamin Franklin wandered into Philadelphia in 1763 instead of 1723, according to this interpretation, he would have had much more difficulty in picking himself up from the bottom. The pre-revolutionary labor surplus in Philadelphia among unskilled and semiskilled workers was a new phenomenon in America, for labor had always been scarce in the colonies. We will encounter a parallel labor surplus—which might be better described as a population surplus—in the farm villages of eastern Massachusetts during the generation before the Revolution. There was also a population surplus in the Chesapeake, but it developed thirty or forty years later, after the Revolution, when tidewater planters sold their superfluous slaves or moved them to new work places in the piedmont or further west and south. But if all the oldest settled parts of America were becoming overstocked with laborers during the late eighteenth century, there was a marked difference between the southern and northern methods of coping with this situation. In Virginia the use of slave labor became more widespread among all white householders, rich and poor; consequently, the institution of slavery became more deeply entrenched in the years between 1750 and 1800.[73] In Philadelphia the opposite occurred: slavery was abolished after the Revolution, indentured servitude sharply declined, and both immigrant and native-born unskilled and semiskilled workers were thrown onto the free wage market.

During the past decade or so, historians of slavery have been stressing the achievements of black laborers in the eighteenth-century South, and not the restrictiveness of the system. Historians of urban labor have been stressing the exploitation of wage workers in Philadelphia and Boston, and not the flexibility of this new wage system. In my opinion, this interpretive tendency somewhat obscures the basic facts of laboring life in eighteenth-century America. The Virginia slaveholders may have been patriarchal and precapitalistic, but as we have seen, the masters of Mount Airy continually sold their slaves or transferred them to new job assignments not of their choice in order to maintain an effective labor force. The businessmen of Philadelphia likewise manipulated their proletarian employees, but the unskilled workers who flocked to this town came out of free choice, and if they were underpaid, they had the further option (which many exercised) of moving on to other places in America where labor was still scarce. I do not wish to minimize the plight of Philadelphia's laboring poor, but they did have an ultimate freedom that was not available to their counterparts in England (where unskilled labor was in permanent surplus) nor to the Afro-American slaves in the Chesapeake and the Caribbean.

In New England, the chief singularity of the labor system was that during the eighteenth century nearly all work was performed by native-born whites. After the great Puritan migration of the 1630s had ended, the New England colonists imported few white servants or black slaves from abroad. Among David Galenson's 20,657 emigrating English servants, only 234 were bound for New England. Among R. J. Dickson's 442 Ulster servant ships, only 5 were bound for Massachusetts.[74] And while slave ships from Newport, Rhode Island, were very active in the African trade, slave imports to New England were significantly lower than those to the mid-Atlantic colonies. The few blacks were employed chiefly in the coastal towns, especially Newport and Boston. In addition to this slave labor, the New Englanders got the local Indians to do some of their dirty work. In 1774 a third of the Indians living in Rhode Island were boarding with white families, employed as servants. On the island of Nantucket the merchants who organized the whaling industry maneuvered the local Indians into manning the whaling boats.[75] But Indians were no longer numerous in New England, having been nearly annihilated in the wars of the seventeenth century. Censuses of the four New England colonies taken during the 1760s and 1770s indicate that the Indians and Negroes together formed a tiny nonwhite minority—only a little over 3 percent of the regional population.[76] The descendants of the Puritans, with their well-established reputation for clannish hostility to strangers and aliens, thus performed most of the labor assigned elsewhere in America to immigrant servants and slaves.

The New Englanders were the only American colonists to develop a homogeneous society, closely resembling in ethnic composition the society their ancestors had known in England. But the New Englanders did not perpetuate the mother country's sharp social division between the propertied, privileged upper and middling orders and the propertyless, unprivileged wage laborers. On the contrary, New England was the most egalitarian sector of colonial America, far less stratified than the Caribbean or Chesapeake colonies and somewhat less stratified than the mid-Atlantic colonies.

To be sure, New England had a growing poverty problem in the mid-eighteenth century. In Boston, more pronouncedly than in Philadelphia, unskilled wage workers began to resemble the permanently depressed laboring poor of England. A very large number of mariners were congregated in the coastal towns. In 1740 it was calculated that 74 percent of the fishing, coasting, and long-distance merchant ships in the American colonies sailed from New England ports.[77] During the war years, wages on naval, privateering, and merchant ships were high; when shipping declined and wages plummeted during peacetime, some seamen quit, but many others became trapped into careers of unattractive, irregular, low-paying wage work. The wages of Boston seamen did not keep pace with commodity prices, and their probated estates declined significantly in value between 1685 and 1775. Sailors ranked below shoemakers and tailors as the most depressed occupational group in Boston.[78] But the plight of the mariners was not indicative of the New England labor system as a whole. Most of the unskilled and semiskilled work in this region was performed on farms and not at sea. To get a sense of farming conditions, we must turn to the country villages, where the majority of New Englanders lived and worked.

Eighteenth-century New England farmers seem to have used formally bound labor—indentured servants or wage workers hired by the year—less than did Pennsylvania or Virginia farmers. For example, in Bristol, Rhode Island, two-thirds of the householders in 1689 had no live-in servants. Every one of these Bristol households included at least one adult woman—a wife, a grown daughter, or a female live-in servant—because men could not or would not do the cooking, needlework, cleaning, and processing of raw farm produce that every household required. Furthermore, nine out of ten Bristol households in 1689 included children, and overall there were 3.2 children per household. While this census does not tell which of these children were old enough to work, a later Bristol census, taken in 1774, divides the population between males and females over sixteen (hence old enough for full-scale work) and boys and girls up to sixteen (too young for work). On average there were three white workers per household. More than a third of these Bristol "adults" were listed as singles: John Demos, who has analyzed this census of 1774, has identified many of them as unmarried sons and daughters.[79] The same pattern reappears in a colonywide census of Massachusetts taken in 1764, which shows 3.4 nonworking children per household and 3.6 "adults." The mean Massachusetts household size of 7.0 white persons in 1764 is very much larger than the mean household size of 4.8 persons found in mid-eighteenth-century England and larger also than the white households of small planters in the Caribbean or the Chesapeake.[80]

Philip Greven's study of family structure in the farming village of Andover demonstrates in concrete terms how these large Massachusetts households generated a great deal of family labor. For example, Deacon John Abbot (1648–1721) started his farm and his family in 1673 and over the next eighteen years sired six sons and two daughters who lived to maturity. The early careers of these eight children may be summarized as follows:

Child	Born	Years Available to Work for Parents	Number of Years of Family Work	Married
John Jr.	1674	c. 1690–1702	c. 12	1703
Joseph	1676	c. 1692–1721	c. 29	1721
Stephen	1678	c. 1694–1707	c. 13	1708
Sarah	1680	c. 1696–1706	c. 10	1707
Ephraim	1682			1715
Joshua	1685			c. 1710
Ebenezer	1689	c. 1705–19	c. 14	1720
Priscilla	1691	c. 1707–21	c. 14	—

When Greven traced twenty-eight Andover families through four generations, he found that fathers delayed their sons' marriages and kept them economically dependent until well into their twenties. Furthermore, "parents often used the labors of adolescent sons for their own interests. Sons were not paid directly; their parents received credit for their wages."[81] In the case of the Abbot children, Joshua moved to Billerica at an early age, and Ephraim was apparently apprenticed to learn a trade. Both Joseph and Priscilla were still unmarried when their father died (though Joseph married immediately afterward), and they presumably lived with their parents. While Greven offers no proof that any of the deacon's children worked on his farm or drew wages for his use by working on neighbors' farms, the presumption is strong, since upon the deacon's death John Jr. and Joseph divided the family homestead and Stephen and Ebenezer also received farmland [from their father] in Andover. Assuming that each child except Ephraim and Joshua was available for work at age sixteen, the deacon had about sixty-eight years of male labor at his disposal, and his wife had twenty-seven years of female labor. For many years of course—from 1673 to about 1690—the children were young and the only family workers were the deacon and his wife. If they needed more labor, they had to hire it. But from about 1694 to 1713 there were always five or six family workers. The Abbots now had a labor surplus, and several of the children could earn money for their father or for themselves by hiring out to neighbors. By 1713 the deacon was sixty-five years old, and the family labor during the last eight years of his life must have been performed mainly by his remaining dependent children: Joseph, Ebenezer, and Priscilla.[82]

This family labor system seems to have functioned to the mutual advantage of Deacon Abbot and his children, except perhaps for "meek and mild" Priscilla, who never married and who spent a long life tending her parents, brothers, nephews, and great-nephews. But this dependence upon the labor of grown sons and daughters became less functional in the next generation of the Abbot family. By the mid-eighteenth century the patriarchal family system was breaking down in Andover because of population pressure and the resultant scarcity of local farmland and jobs. Deacon Abbot's third son, Stephen, and his fourth son, Ephraim, drew much less effectively upon family labor than their father had been able to. Stephen raised only three sons instead of six. Over a twenty-six-year span each of these three sons seems to have worked for Stephen before marrying and setting up on his own. But while this arrangement kept Stephen's farm going, it did not enable him to recompense two of his sons with adequate farmland, so they died poor. Ephraim had six sons, but he was a craftworker who had little employment and no land for his two farmer sons, who moved to New Hampshire and western Massachusetts. The other four sons followed their father into craftwork, but only one of them seems to have worked with Ephraim. Four of Ephraim's six sons found the local job opportunities too discouraging and left Andover.[83]

One may also examine New England farm labor practices through the diary of Ebenezer Parkman, a country parson who served as the minister of Westborough, Massachusetts, from 1724 until his death in 1782. For over sixty years Parkman kept an elaborately detailed diary, comparable in scale and in quality to Thomas Thistlewood's or Landon Carter's (the sections spanning the years 1723–28, 1737–40, and 1743–55 have been published).[84] Parkman was no farmer, but he had to operate a farm in order to make ends meet, since his salary was very small and his family was very large (he had sixteen children). He was always being distracted from his sermon writing and his pastoral duties in order to take care of the seasonal chores or to get someone else to do them. "I was abroad," he noted in March 1726, "about my Spring Business, to hire Labourers, and make Enquiry after a Man to Live with me." Again in April 1738: "I rode abroad for Help in my Farm Business." Unfortunately for Parkman, he did not succeed that year in hiring anyone until May, and so he was forced "to assist at the Team my Self to my great Trouble and affliction." Parkman was a male chauvinist who seldom reported on the female domestic labor in his household, but both his first wife and his second generally had live-in servant girls. In 1728, when Parkman dismissed a hired hand, he pointedly observed: "Now we are intirely alone having no servant nor any one in the House. Our Loneliness give Scope for Thought. God Sanctifie our solitude."[85]

During his early years at Westborough, before he could get his own children to do the brunt of the work, Ebenezer Parkman hired and fired a stream of unsatisfactory laborers. In 1726 he engaged Robert Henry for twenty-three pounds per annum to do the farming, and Silence Bartlett for only eight pounds per annum to do the housework (female domestics were always wretchedly paid). Within three months Parkman had had enough of Robert Henry's blundering incompetence and gave him his liberty. "Perhaps," he reflected, "there may be many more Tedious and Chafing things in Hirelings than ever Mention has been made of."[86] Two years later he bought a Negro slave named Maro for seventy-four pounds, but poor Maro soon died. In 1738 he bought a fifteen-year-old indentured servant, John Kidney, from Waterford in Ireland. This was a disaster: Kidney tried to rape Parkman's thirteen-year-old daughter, whereupon Mrs. Parkman refused to stay "alone with so bruitish a Creature," and the parson quickly sold him to another master.[87] In most years Parkman engaged a hired hand to work for the four summer months. In addition, he drew upon his parishioners for a great deal of free labor. In 1738, for example, he mentions fifty-five different Westborough men and boys who put in a day or two apiece on his place and five women and girls who similarly aided his wife. Many of these helpers can be identified in the Westborough church birth register as teenagers; presumably their parents had sent them over to rescue the minister.

When Parkman's own children were small, they could only pick apples or dig potatoes, but in their early teens the boys began to plough and do the other heavy chores. For seven years, starting when he was eighteen, Ebenezer Jr. managed the farm, and after Ebenezer married, his younger brother Billy took over. But Parkman still engaged a hired hand every summer. In 1748 he encountered a new crisis when the man he had just hired, Joseph Bowker, was impressed into military service at the height of the harvest season. Parkman felt aggrieved because Bowker was the only laborer in Westborough to be called up that summer, and it was the second time that he had lost a hired hand to the army during harvest time. The next Sunday he appealed to his congregation for help, and though he grumbled that they came slowly, during the month of July 1748 twenty-one of his male parishioners did put in a day apiece in his fields. It is hard to believe that all of this irregular "volunteer" labor produced good crops, but Parkman was in no position to complain. "A great Kindness this of my Neibours," he remarked after his hay was finally mowed, raked, and carted from the ministerial meadow. "The Lord reward 'em for it."[88]

Clearly the labor systems in the several regions of colonial America diverged remarkably from each other by 1775. And clearly these divergences held consequences for the future. The New England method, with its prime reliance upon family labor and supplementary help from hired hands and neighbors, was cumbersome and inefficient, but it was a functional method, and one that the New Englanders would carry westward with them after the Revolution as they set up new family farms in Ohio and beyond. The Philadelphia method, with its increasing reliance upon underpaid wage labor supplied by a pool of unskilled and semiskilled casual workers, was exploitive and inhumane, but it too was a functional method that capitalistic entrepreneurs would utilize as they built new western cities and recruited factory workers after the Revolution. The Chesapeake method, with its prime reliance upon unpaid labor by chattel slaves, appears to me to have been rather more exploitive and inhumane than labor practices further north, but here again was a functional method that cotton planters would carry westward after the Revolution as they set up new plantations in Alabama and elsewhere in the Deep South. But the Caribbean method of slave labor, in my view, was becoming truly dysfunctional by 1775. The sugar planters could sustain their work force only through continuous recourse to the African slave trade, and their labor management was so patently inhumane that the abolitionists in England were able to mount an effective parliamentary attack upon them. When Parliament voted to close the slave trade in 1806, the Caribbean labor system was placed in jeopardy, pointing the way towards emancipation of the West Indian blacks and the near paralysis of the West Indian sugar industry. There are of course other reasons for the collapse of the sugar planters. But they were the only colonists in British America whose labor system went bankrupt, in both a moral and a business sense.

NOTES

I wish to thank my colleagues at the Oxford conference and at a subsequent seminar held by the Philadelphia Center for Early American Studies for advice in revising this essay. I am most particularly grateful to Paul G. E. Clemens, Jack P. Greene, P.M.G. Harris, Allan Kulikoff, Marcus Rediker, Jean R. Soderlund, and Marianne Wokeck for their helpful comments.

1. Marcus Wilson Jernegan, *Laboring and Dependent Classes in Colonial America, 1607–1783* (Chicago, 1931). Some passages of Jernegan's book make painful reading today, such as his comparison between "raw" Guinea Negroes and "country-born" American slaves: " 'Country-born' negroes would generally have greater intelligence and a better knowledge of the English language. They would be more docile, more adaptable to their environment, more familiar with the methods of production and, in general, more civilized than freshly imported negroes" (pp. 8–9).

2. Irene W. D. Hecht, "The Virginia Muster of 1624/5 as a Source of Demographic History," *William and Mary Quarterly,* 3d ser., 30 (1973): 75–79.

3. In 1638 there were 764 landholders on Barbados, and 5,705 inhabitants over the age of fourteen (see Richard S. Dunn, *Sugar and Slaves: The Rise of the Planter Class in the English West Indies, 1624–1713* [Chapel Hill, 1972], 51, 55). Since many of the landholders had no wives or children, I reckon that about four thousand of the island inhabitants were servants.

4. William Bradford, *Of Plymouth Plantation,* ed. Samuel Eliot Morison (New York, 1953), 441–43.

5. Edmund S. Morgan, ed., *The Founding of Massachusetts* (Indianapolis, 1964), 161; Richard S. Dunn, "Experiments holy and unholy, 1630–1," in *The Westward Enterprise,* ed. K. R. Andrews et al. (Liverpool, 1978), 274.

6. This calculation is derived from inspection of twenty-one New England passenger lists for the 1630s printed in John Camden Hotten, ed., *Original Lists of Persons . . . who went from Great Britain to the American Plantations, 1600–1700* (London, 1874).

7. Abbot Emerson Smith, *Colonists in Bondage* (Chapel Hill, 1947), 309. The low servant registration figures for Bristol, as well as for London, for the 1680s may be misleading; the English servant trade may have been shifting to more northern ports, such as Liverpool, in the late seventeenth century.

8. Lois Green Carr and Russell R. Menard, "Immigration and Opportunity: The Freedmen in Early Colonial Maryland," in *The Chesapeake in the Seventeenth Century: Essays on Anglo-American Society,* ed. Thad W. Tate and David L. Ammerman (Chapel Hill, 1979), 206–42.

9. Gary B. Nash, *Quakers and Politics: Pennsylvania, 1681–1726* (Princeton, 1968), 50–51.

10. For fuller discussion of these points see Peter Laslett, *The World We Have Lost* (New York, 1965); W. G. Hoskins, *The Midland Peasant* (London, 1957); Alan Everitt, "Farm Labourers," in *The Agrarian History of England and Wales,* vol. 4, *1500–1640,* ed. Joan Thirsk (Cambridge, 1967), 396–465; C. W. Chalkin, *Seventeenth Century Kent* (London, 1965); Keith Thomas, "Work and Leisure in Pre-Industrial Society," *Past and Present,* no. 29 (1964): 50–62; idem, *Religion and the Decline of Magic* (New York, 1971), chap. 1; Margaret Spufford, *Contrasting Communities: English Villagers in the Sixteenth and Seventeenth Centuries* (Cambridge, 1974); Peter Clark and Paul Slack, eds., *Crisis and Order in English Towns, 1500–1700: Essays in Urban History* (London, 1972); A. L. Beier, "Vagrants and the Social Order in Elizabethan England," *Past and Present,* nos. 64 (August 1974) and 71 (May 1976); and John Walter and Keith Wrightson, "Dearth and the Social Order in Early Modern England," ibid., no. 71 (May 1976): 22–42.

11. D. C. Coleman, "Labour in the English Economy of the Seventeenth Century," *Economic History Review,* 2d ser., 8 (1956): 280.

12. Christopher Hill, *The World Turned Upside Down* (New York, 1972).

13. Mildred Campbell, "Social Origins of Some Early Americans," in *Seventeenth-Century America,* ed. James Morton Smith (Chapel Hill, 1959), 76.

14. James Horn, "Servant Emigration to the Chesapeake in the Seventeenth Century," in Tate and Ammerman, *The Chesapeake in the Seventeenth Century,* 94.

15. Lorena S. Walsh, "Servitude and Opportunity in Charles County, Maryland, 1658–1705," in *Law, Society and Politics in Early Maryland,* ed. Aubrey C. Land, Lois Green Carr, and Edward C. Papenfuse (Baltimore, 1977), 112.

16. Peter Bowden, "Agricultural Prices, Farm Profits, and Rents," in Thirsk, *Agrarian History*

of England and Wales, 621; Paul Slack, "Vagrants and Vagrancy in England, 1598–1664," *Economic History Review*, 2d ser., 27 (1947): 364–68.

17. David Souden, " 'Rogues, Whores and Vagabonds?' " *Social History* 3 (1978): 29–33. See also Anthony Salerno, "The Social Background of Seventeenth-Century Emigration to America," *Journal of British Studies* 19 (1979): 31–52.

18. David W. Galenson, *White Servitude in Colonial America: An Economic Analysis* (New York, 1981); see esp. pp. 24–28, 86–93, 103. I am very grateful to Professor Galenson for letting me read his book in manuscript.

19. Robert V. Wells, *The Population of the British Colonies in America before 1776* (Princeton, 1975), 272–74.

20. Gregory King's tabulations are conveniently reproduced in Charles Wilson, *England's Apprenticeship, 1603–1763* (London, 1965), 239.

21. E. A. Wrigley and R. S. Schofield, *The Population History of England, 1541–1871: A Reconstruction* (London, 1981), 161–62, 219, 402, 408.

22. Peter Clark, "Migration in England during the Late Seventeenth and Early Eighteenth Centuries," *Past and Present*, no. 83 (May 1979): 57–90.

23. Noel Deerr, *The History of Sugar*, 2 vols. (London, 1949–50), 2:284.

24. Kenneth G. Davies, *The Royal African Company* (London, 1957).

25. Philip D. Curtin, *The Atlantic Slave Trade: A Census* (Madison, Wis., 1969), pp. 87, 119, 140. Several scholars have found new data on the British trade in the eighteenth century and have revised Curtin's figures upwards; for a survey of this work, see Paul E. Lovejoy, "The Volume of the Atlantic Slave Trade: A Synthesis," *Journal of African History* 23 (1982):483–87. However, none of the revisionists has yet published a breakdown of British slave imports for the years 1600–1780 to replace Curtin's tabulation, cited in table 6.1. Indeed, one of the revisionists, James A. Rawley, in *The Transatlantic Slave Trade* (New York, 1981), p. 167, totals British slave imports for this period at only 1,299,000, which is 12 percent below Curtin's estimate.

26. Richard Nelson Bean, *The British Trans-Atlantic Slave Trade, 1650–1775* (New York, 1975), 223–34; Jack Ericson Eblen, "On the Natural Increase of Slave Populations," in *Race and Slavery in the Western Hemisphere: Quantitative Studies*, ed. Stanley L. Engerman and Eugene D. Genovese (Princeton, 1975), 244–47.

27. Russell R. Menard, "Why African Slavery?" (Paper presented at Rutgers University, May 1980); Richard Nelson Bean and Robert P. Thomas, "The Adoption of Slave Labor in British America," in *The Uncommon Market: Essays in the Economic History of the Atlantic Slave Trade*, ed. Henry A. Gemery and Jan S. Hogendorn (New York, 1979), 377–98.

28. Winthrop D. Jordan, *White over Black: American Attitudes toward the Negro, 1550–1812* (Chapel Hill, 1968), chap. 1.

29. Dunn, *Sugar and Slaves*, chaps. 2, 6, 7; Carl Bridenbaugh and Roberta Bridenbaugh, *No Peace beyond the Line: The English in the Caribbean, 1624–1690* (New York, 1972), chaps. 3–4.

30. Edmund S. Morgan, *American Slavery—American Freedom: The Ordeal of Colonial Virginia* (New York, 1975), chaps. 6, 11.

31. Wilcomb E. Washburn, *The Governor and the Rebel* (Chapel Hill, 1957), 31.

32. For helpful discussion of the African side of the Atlantic slave trade see J. D. Fage, "Slaves and Society in Western Africa, c. 1445–c. 1700," *Journal of African History* 21 (1981): 289–310; Philip D. Curtin, *Economic Change in Precolonial Africa: Senegambia in the Era of the Slave Trade* (Madison, Wis., 1975); Walter Rodney, *History of the Upper Guinea Coast, 1545–1800* (Oxford, 1970); and Mario Johnson, "The Atlantic Slave Trade and the Economy of West Africa," in *Liverpool, the African Slave Trade, and Abolition*, ed. Roger Anstey and P.E.H. Hair ([Liverpool], 1976), 14–38.

33. Curtin, *Atlantic Slave Trade*, p. 150; Roger Anstey, "The Volume and Profitability of the British Slave Trade, 1761–1807," in Engerman and Genovese, *Race and Slavery*, 12; Herbert S. Klein, *The Middle Passage* (Princeton, 1978), 142–44, 157.

34. Rhode Island slavers used much smaller ships and collected smaller cargoes than did English slavers, yet they still spent from three to five months on the African coast. (see Jay Caughtry,

The Notorious Triangle: Rhode Island and the African Slave Trade, 1700–1807 [Philadelphia, 1981], 75, 105).

35. Curtin, *Atlantic Slave Trade*, 129, 150; Engerman and Genovese, *Race and Slavery*, 13, 112; Klein, *The Middle Passage*, 156–57.

36. Davies, *The Royal African Company*, 299; Klein, *The Middle Passage*, 149.

37. Dunn, *Sugar and Slaves*, 316; Barry W. Higman, *Slave Population and Economy in Jamaica, 1807–1834* (Cambridge, 1976), 71–75.

38. Davies, *The Royal African Company*, 292–93; Klein, *The Middle Passage*, 162; Curtin, *Atlantic Slave Trade*, 275–86.

39. Klein, *The Middle Passage*, 126, 143; W. E. Minchinton, "The Slave Trade of Bristol with the British Mainland Colonies in North America, 1699–1770," in Anstey and Hair, *Liverpool, the African Slave Trade, and Abolition*, 40–44.

40. Loyde-Tayloe Account Book, 1708–78, Virginia Historical Society. See also Gerald W. Mullin, *Flight and Rebellion: Slave Resistance in Eighteenth-Century Virginia* (New York, 1972), 14–15; Allan Kulikoff, "The Origins of Afro-American Society in Tidewater Maryland and Virginia, 1700 to 1790," *William and Mary Quarterly*, 3d ser., 35 (1978): 232–35; and Caughtry, *The Notorious Triangle*, 194.

41. R. J. Dickson, *Ulster Emigration to Colonial America, 1718–1775* (London, 1966), esp. chaps. 5 and 7 and appendixes; Audrey Lockhart, *Some Aspects of Emigration from Ireland to the North American Colonies between 1660 and 1775* (New York, 1976), 190–208.

42. Smith, *Colonists in Bondage*, 116–19, 325–29.

43. Kenneth Morgan, "The Organization of the Convict Trade to Maryland, 1718–1776," *William and Mary Quarterly*, forthcoming. I wish to thank Mr. Morgan for letting me read his article.

44. *Virginia Gazette*, Sept. 2, 1757; Dec. 24, 1772; July 8, Oct. 7, 1773; Sept. 22, Nov. 10, 1774.

45. Marianne Wokeck, "The Flow and the Composition of the German Immigration to Philadelphia, 1727–1775," *Pennsylvania Magazine of History and Biography* 105 (1981): 249–78; idem, "A Tide of Alien Tongues: The Flow and Ebb of German Immigration to Pennsylvania, 1683–1775" (Ph.D. diss., Temple University, 1982), chap. 5. I am very grateful to Dr. Wokeck for sharing her findings with me.

46. Richard S. Dunn, "Barbados Census of 1680: Profile of the Richest Colony in English America," *Willam and Mary Quarterly*, 3d ser., 26 (1969): 3–30.

47. Vere Langford Oliver, *The History of the Island of Antigua*, 3 vols. (London, 1894–99), 3:394–97; Richard B. Sheridan, "The Rise of a Colonial Gentry: A Case Study of Antigua, 1730–1775," *Economic History Review*, 2d ser., 13 (April 1961): 342–57.

48. Additional MSS 12,434/1–12, British Library; Richard B. Sheridan, "The Wealth of Jamaica in the Eighteenth Century," *Economic History Review*, 2d ser., 18 (1965): 303; Higman, *Slave Population and Economy*, chap. 2.

49. Clarendon Manuscript Deposit, Barham Papers, b. 34, Bodleian Library; Higman, *Slave Population and Economy*, 70.

50. J. Harry Bennett, "Cary Helyar," *William and Mary Quarterly*, 3d ser., 21 (1964): 53–76; idem, "William Dampier," *History Today* 14 (1964): 469–77; idem, "William Whaley," *Agricultural History* 40 (1966): 113–23; Dunn, *Sugar and Slaves*, 212–23; Richard Pares, *A West India Fortune* (London, 1950); J. Harry Bennett, *Bondsmen and Bishops* (Berkeley, 1958); Jerome S. Handler, Frederick W. Lange, and Robert B. Riordan, *Plantation Slavery in Barbados: An Archaeological and Historical Investigation* (Cambridge, Mass., 1978); Michael Craton and James Walvin, *A Jamaican Plantation: The History of Worthy Park, 1670–1970* (Toronto, 1970); Michael Craton, *Searching for the Invisible Man: Slaves and Plantation Life in Jamaica* (Cambridge, Mass., 1978); Barry W. Higman, "Household Structure and Fertility on Jamaican Slave Plantations," *Population Studies* 27 (1973): 527–50; idem, "A Report on Excavations at Montpelier and Roehampton," *Jamaican Journal* 8 (1974): 40–45; idem, "The Slave Family and Household," *Journal of Interdisciplinary History* 6 (1976): 261–87.

51. The Mesopotamia slave inventories, together with other business records, are filed in the

Clarendon Manuscript Deposit, Barham Papers, Bodleian Library. For a preliminary survey of slave life at Mesopotamia see Richard S. Dunn, "A Tale of Two Plantations: Slave Life at Mesopotamia in Jamaica and Mount Airy in Virginia, 1799 to 1828," *William and Mary Quarterly*, 3d ser., 34 (1977): 32–65.

52. Journals of Thomas Thistlewood, Monson Manuscript Deposit, 31/1–37, Lincolnshire Archives, Lincoln. Thistlewood was born in Lincolnshire in 1721. Apart from his thirty-seven-volume diary, he wrote ten commonplace books and kept thirty-three volumes of Jamaica weather reports, as well as other miscellaneous account books, all now to be found in the Monson collection.

53. Journals of Thomas Thistlewood, Monson 31/1–2. For a more indulgent reading of Thistlewood's diary see J. R. Ward, "A Planter and His Slaves in Eighteenth-Century Jamaica," in *The Search for Wealth and Stability*, ed. T. C. Smout (London, 1979), 1–20.

54. Another eighty-three males and twenty-four females ran away temporarily from Mesopotamia, but they returned. So there was plenty of unrest, as at Thistlewood's cattle pen, but little formal out-migration.

55. This is a high percentage, given the small number of white men who lived at Mesopotamia. I calculate that a white overseer or bookkeeper at Mesopotamia was twice as likely as a black man to sire a slave child. Thomas Thistlewood, so sexually active in 1750–51, continued to molest slave women thereafter. During 1765, for example, when he was managing a sugar estate near Mesopotamia, Thistlewood recorded on one hundred occasions that he had had intercourse with his slave mistress, and he also raped twenty-three other women on fifty-five occasions (Journal of Thomas Thistlewood, Monson 31/16).

56. Craton, *Searching for the Invisible Man*, 287.

57. Peter H. Wood, *Black Majority: Negroes in Colonial South Carolina from 1670 through the Stono Rebellion* (New York, 1974), 147–49.

58. Philip D. Morgan, "Black Society in the Lowcountry South in the Revolutionary Era" (Paper presented at the U.S. Capitol Historical Society Conference, March 1980), tables 2, 5, 6, 7, 8.

59. Harry Roy Merrens, *Colonial North Carolina in the Eighteenth Century: A Study in Historical Geography* (Chapel Hill, 1964), 76–77. The Shenandoah Valley of Virginia and the northern counties of Maryland's Eastern Shore had labor patterns fairly similar to those of Orange County (see Robert D. Mitchell, *Commercialism and Frontier: Perspectives on the Early Shenandoah Valley* [Charlottesville, 1977]; and Paul G. E. Clemens, *The Atlantic Economy and Colonial Maryland's Eastern Shore: From Tobacco to Grain* [Ithaca, N.Y., 1980]).

60. A Virginia list of tithables for 1755 is printed in Robert E. Brown and B. Katherine Brown, *Virginia, 1705–1786: Democracy or Aristocracy?* (East Lansing, 1964), 73 and table 1.

61. A Maryland census of 1755 is summarized in U.S. Bureau of the Census, *A Century of Population Growth, 1790–1900* (Washington, D.C., 1909), 185. See the commentary on this census in Wells, *Population of the British Colonies*, chap. 5. For discussion of the dimensions of the pre-revolutionary Chesapeake slave trade see Klein, *The Middle Passage*, chap. 6 [on Virginia]; and Darold D. Wax, "Black Immigrants: The Slave Trade in Colonial Maryland," *Maryland Historical Magazine* 73 (1978): 30–45.

62. Mullin, *Flight and Rebellion*; Kulikoff, "Origins of Afro-American Society," 226–59; Rhys Isaac, *The Transformation of Virginia, 1740–1790: Community, Religion, and Authority* (Chapel Hill, 1982), 328–46.

63. The Tayloe Papers (Virginia Historical Society, Richmond) are much more detailed for the nineteenth century than for the eighteenth; the Mount Airy slave inventories start in 1808. For fuller discussion of slave life at Mount Airy, and fuller comparison with Mesopotamia, see Dunn, "A Tale of Two Plantations," 32–65.

64. *The Diary of Colonel Landon Carter of Sabine Hall, 1752–1778*, ed. Jack P. Greene, 2 vols. (Charlottesville, 1965), 1:347–48, 363, 373, 396, 554; 2: 1049, 1051, 1064, 1075.

65. *Maryland Gazette*, Oct. 18, 1792. I owe this reference to Michael Mullin.

66. Sung Bok Kim, *Landlord and Tenant in Colonial New York: Manorial Society, 1664–1775* (Chapel

Hill, 1978), esp. 235–50; Ned Landsman, "William Penn's Scottish Counterparts" (Paper presented at the World of William Penn Conference, Philadelphia, March 1981); Jean Soderlund, "Conscience, Interest, and Power: The Development of the Quaker Opposition to Slavery in the Delaware Valley, 1688–1780" (Ph.D. diss., Temple University, 1981), esp. chap. 4.

67. Gary B. Nash, *The Urban Crucible: Social Change, Political Consciousness, and the Origins of the American Revolution* (Cambridge, Mass., 1979), 407–8.

68. See Billy G. Smith, "The Material Lives of Laboring Philadelphians, 1750 to 1800," *William and Mary Quarterly*, 3d ser., 38 (1981): 163–202.

69. This is the view of Carl Bridenbaugh and Jessica Bridenbaugh, *Rebels and Gentlemen: Philadelphia in the Age of Franklin* (New York, 1942); of Jackson Turner Main, *The Social Structure of Revolutionary America* (Princeton, 1965); and of Sam Bass Warner, Jr., *The Private City: Philadelphia in Three Periods of Its Growth* (Philadelphia, 1968).

70. Soderlund, "Conscience, Interest, and Power," chaps. 4, 6. I am very grateful to Dr. Soderlund for discussing her findings with me.

71. For Philadelphia servants see Sharon V. Salinger, "Colonial Labor in Transition: The Decline of Indentured Servitude in Late Eighteenth-Century Philadelphia," *Labor History* 22 (1981): 165–91. I wish to thank Professor Salinger for letting me read two of her essays on servitude. For Philadelphia slaves see Gary B. Nash, "Slaves and Slaveowners in Colonial Philadelphia," *William and Mary Quarterly*, 3d ser., 30 (1973): 249.

72. Gary B. Nash, "Up from the Bottom in Franklin's Philadelphia," *Past and Present*, no. 77 (1977): 57–83; Smith, "Material Lives of Laboring Philadelphians," 163–202.

73. Richard S. Dunn, "Black Society in the Chesapeake, 1776–1810" (Presented at the U.S. Capitol Historical Society Conference, March 1980).

74. A Massachusetts list of arriving immigrants confirms this pattern. According to James A. Henretta, "Fewer than 250 of 2,380 persons entering Boston from 1764 to 1768 were classified as indentured servants" ("Economic Development and Social Structure in Colonial Boston," *William and Mary Quarterly*, 3d ser., 22 [1965]: 83).

75. John A. Sainsbury, "Indian Labor in Early Rhode Island," *New England Quarterly* 48 (1975): 379–80; Danny Vickers, "The Indian Whalemen of Nantucket" (Paper presented at Millersville State College, Millersville, Pa., April 1981).

76. Wells, *Population of the British Colonies*, 71, 81, 90, 100.

77. "A Computation of the Value and Trade of the British Empire of America," Public Record Office, London, CO/323/10. I owe this reference to Marcus Rediker, author of "Society and Culture among Anglo-American Deep Sea Sailors, 1700–1750" (Ph.D. diss., University of Pennsylvania, 1982); I am very grateful to Dr. Rediker for sharing his findings about maritime labor with me. For conditions among English seamen see Ralph Davies, *The Rise of the English Shipping Industry* (Newton Abbot, Devon, 1972), chaps. 6–7.

78. Nash, *Urban Crucible*, app. tables 2, 5, figs. 6, 7, 8. For discussion of rural poverty in New England see Douglas L. Jones, "Poverty and Vagabondage: The Process of Survival in Eighteenth-Century Massachusetts," *New England Historical and Genealogical Register* 133 (1979): 243–54; and idem, "The Strolling Poor: Transiency in Eighteenth-Century Massachusetts," *Journal of Social History* 8 (Spring 1975): 28–54.

79. John Demos, "Families in Colonial Bristol, Rhode Island: An Exercise in Historical Demography," *William and Mary Quarterly*, 3d ser., 25 (1968): 40–57.

80. Peter Laslett, ed., *Household and Family in Past Time* (Cambridge, 1972), chaps. 4, 20.

81. Philip J. Greven, Jr., *Four Generations: Population, Land, and Family in Colonial Andover, Massachusetts* (Ithaca, N.Y. 1970), 69.

82. Ibid., 142–43. Since Greven supplies information only about male members of his Andover families, I have also consulted Abiel Abbot and Ephraim Abbot, *Genealogical Register of the Descendants of George Abbot of Andover* (Boston, 1847).

83. Greven, *Four Generations*, 238–40, 249–50, supplemented by Abbot and Abbot, *Genealogical Register*.

84. *The Diary of Ebenezer Parkman, 1719–1755*, ed. Francis G. Walett (Worcester, Mass., 1974).

85. Ibid., 10, 32–33, 46.
86. Ibid., 10–13.
87. Ibid., 33, 37, 55, 64–65. Many, but by no means all, of Parkman's helpers can be traced in the *Vital Records of Westborough, Massachusetts to the end of the year 1849* (Worcester, Mass., 1903).
88. Ibid., 178–80.

7

CREATIVE ADAPTATIONS: PEOPLES AND CULTURES

T. H. BREEN

he tale of the peopling of the New World is one of human creativity. Colonization of the Caribbean islands and the North American mainland brought thousands of men and women into contact who ordinarily would have had nothing to do with each other. Whether migrants arrived as slaves or freemen, as religious visionaries or crass opportunists, they were forced to adjust not only to unfamiliar environments but also to a host of strangers, persons of different races, cultures, and backgrounds.

These challenges were staggering. Within the constraints of the peculiar circumstances in which they found themselves, blacks and whites learned to live with each other as well as with native Americans. However cruelly some exploited others, however much they resented each other's presence, in their development these three groups became intricately intertwined. How men and women chose to interact, therefore, how much they preserved of their original cultures, how much they borrowed from the strangers are topics of considerable importance, for their decisions made three centuries ago still powerfully affect the character of modern society.

Before the middle of the present century historians seldom described the colonization of North America in terms of cultural interaction. Outstanding scholars of an earlier generation such as Charles M. Andrews focused attention upon the transfer of English culture to the New World—indeed, upon the ideas of a few articulate leaders—and in these older accounts, Indians, blacks, and poorer white settlers rarely played a significant role. Native Americans were either ignored or dismissed as obstacles to progress, while blacks took on interest only insofar as their enslavement facilitated the development of various plantation economies. Indeed, before World War II the most provocative work on the transplantation of Old World cultures was written not by historians but by anthropologists, most notably Melville J. Herskovits.[1]

During the 1960s no topic generated greater excitement or controversy than did the history of race relations in colonial America. The reasons for this explosion of interest were obvious. Blacks and Indians began to achieve civil and political rights so long denied them, and as they did so, they demanded inclusion in our nation's past. A history populated only by white people seemed inadequate, even racist. And in a remarkably short period scholars made great progress in setting the record straight. They provided not only fresh insights into the development of Afro-American and Indian cultures but also searching reexaminations of the processes that allowed white colonists to oppress blacks and dispossess Indians.[2]

To hazard generalizations about the character of this vast revisionist literature may be misleading. The authors addressed diverse topics, and the results of their efforts were extremely uneven. Nevertheless, with the benefit of hindsight, it appears that this work suffered from various conceptual weaknesses. First, studies that purported to be about race relations were often concerned with the experience of a single racial group—whether black, Indian, or white—and paid little attention to relations among colonial peoples of different color. Second, the story of race relations tended to be static, as if early Americans were caught up in unchanging social structures. For instance, little distinction was made between the slavery of the seventeenth century and that of the eighteenth.

Third, perhaps as a result of their concern with the development of discrimination and prejudice, historians sometimes portrayed early American blacks and Indians as victims—as the unfortunate objects of exploitive capitalism or white racism. As Gary Nash has observed, however, to include Africans and Indians "in our history in this way, simply as victims of the more powerful Europeans, is no better than to exclude them altogether. It is to render voiceless, nameless, and faceless people who powerfully affected the course of our historical development."[3] Fourth, studies of race and race relations stressed conflict. While obviously there were instances of tensions flaring into violence, an emphasis on conflict obscures other, more subtle forms of human interaction found in early America. And last, the revisionist literature unwittingly stripped the analysis of race and culture of individuals. Men and women played a part only as stereotypes such as slave or master. They were reduced to abstractions as historians concentrated on questions of status or group identification and neglected to ask how specific individuals shaped their own lives in response to specific, often unique environmental and demographic conditions.

Over the last decade the study of race and culture in early America attained even higher levels of sophistication. Historians—some writing under the banner of "ethnohistory"—brought an extraordinary richness to the analysis of human interaction in the colonial period. These scholars incorporated the insights of other disciplines, especially those of cultural anthropology. Indeed, the writings of Gerald W. Mullin, Peter Wood, Gary Nash, James Axtell, Michael Craton, Cornelius Jaenen, and Bruce Trigger—to name just a few—provided exciting new ways of looking at cultural exchange.[4] They perceived cultural and racial relations as a *process*, as a drawing and redrawing of human boundaries in reaction to changing conditions over which colonial Americans exercised varying degrees of control. The ethnohistorians also insisted that the analysis of the culture of one group was incomplete unless it provided an equally sensitive account of the peoples and cultures with whom that group came into contact. Moreover, no people, no matter how exploited or undermined by disease, passively accepted cultural change. From this perspective, culture was a continuing series of reciprocal relationships, involving borrowing and resistance, conflict and cooperation, modification and invention. A full understanding of the transfer and development of early American cultures, therefore, assumed a thorough knowledge of the specific historical contexts in which interaction occurred.

An obvious objection to this approach to the investigation of past cultures immediately springs to mind. The focus upon specific historical contexts, upon particular incidents of interaction, seems to chop human experience into ever smaller pieces, and one wonders whether such specificity can yield meaningful generalizations about race relations or cultural adaptation. The ethnohistorians appear to have sacrificed the forests for the trees. Or, stating the point in a slightly different way, is there not a danger that emphasis upon microevents occurring in particular regions, communities, and plantations will obscure long-term patterns of discrimination and prejudice?

The answer, I submit, is no. Close analysis of specific historical contexts directs attention precisely where it should be focused, upon particular men and women shaping their lives in response to changing social and environmental conditions. In this sense, culture is a creative process: people construct reality, spin webs of meaning, and make choices about their lives. Whenever colonial historians take a long-term, often presentist, view of cultural and racial relations, they should realize that it was only within specific contexts of interaction that freedom and slavery, dignity and degradation, and a score of other abstractions acquired social meaning. An ethnohistorian, in fact, interprets the cultural "conversations" of the past in terms that the participants themselves would have comprehended.[5] As sociologist Alan Dawe explains, "It is the prime imperative of the sociology of conversations that we ceaselessly listen to and converse with the voices from everyday life . . . listen for detail, for every nuance, every inflection, every change of tone, however slight, in the myriad ways in which people make their lives, in order to recognize and understand and articulate human agency at work."[6]

This creative process generated different results depending upon the social, economic, and environmental situations in which early Americans found themselves. The New World produced a kaleidoscope of human encounters. To suggest that Africans and Indians possessed the same voice in shaping cultural "conversations" as did Europeans would be absurd. Whites clearly enjoyed substantial advantages in such interracial exchanges. But it would be equally mistaken to claim that either blacks or native Americans—or the poorer whites for that matter—were overwhelmed by the dominant white cultures.[7] Within obvious limits, these people also adapted traditional folkways to meet changing conditions, dropping some practices, acquiring new ones, and modifying others. The problem for the historian of colonial cultures, therefore, is to define with precision the constraints upon choice: What actually determined the character of specific conversations?[8]

This essay examines several major constraints upon cultural creativity in early American societies. Examples are drawn from English colonies that developed on the Caribbean islands and on the mainland. Major elements that shaped the way people adapted to each other and to their new homes were (1) the backgrounds of migrants and native Americans before colonization, (2) the perceptions that members of the three racial groups formed not only of themselves but also of representatives of other races, (3) the motives of different white settlers for moving to the New World, (4) the timing of initial contact, (5) the physical environment in which contact occurred, (6) the shifting demographic configurations, (7) the character of local economies, and (8) the force of individual personality. This list is not exhaustive; moreover, it is not intended as a model or prescription for future analyses. This approach merely provides a convenient way of reviewing a vast historical literature while emphasizing at the same time the centrality of the human agent in cultural conversations.

After examining how in particular situations these elements more or less affected the character of interaction between strangers of diverse backgrounds and different races, I maintain that it is still possible to discern certain long-term trends in early American cultural and racial relations. In many English colonies the seventeenth century was a time of openness, of experimentation, of sorting out ideas. Race was important in negotiating social identities, but it was by no means the chief determinant. People formed niches in which they created fluid, often unique patterns of interaction. But during the eighteenth century—and the timing of course varied from community to community—race became more obtrusive in shaping human relations. To understand how this change came about, we must first consider constraints upon adaptation.

CULTURAL CONVERSATIONS: CONSTRAINTS

Background before contact.   Colonization in the New World brought men and women of diverse backgrounds together for the first time. These people did not greet each other as representatives of monolithic racial groups—as blacks, reds, or whites. Ethnic and class divisions, some of them deeply rooted in the history of a particular Old World community, cut across migrant populations. "Those peoples called Indians by Europeans were divided into hundreds of tribes and thousands of societies," observes Robert F. Berkhofer. "Even who was a member of a tribe at any one time and what a tribe was, changed greatly over time."[9] Both immigrants and native Americans were products of dynamic, often locally oriented societies that were changing when the New World was discovered and would have continued to change even if it had remained unknown for centuries. The backgrounds of these peoples before initial contact affected the ways they adapted not only to each other but also to strangers of a different race.

Relatively little is known about the Indians of eastern North America and the Caribbean during the precontact period. Recent archaeological investigations suggest, however, that native American cultures were both dynamic and diverse. Tribal customs changed considerably over time in response not only to other tribes but also to environmental demands. The once accepted notion that the first major alteration in Indian cultures occurred only after the arrival of the white man turns out to have been an error based upon ethnocentrism. The native American population of these regions actually was divided into scores of self-contained tribal groups and bands—best described as ethnic groups—that spoke languages virtually unintelligible to members of other tribes, sometimes even to those living in close proximity. These groups shared no common kinship system. The Hurons of Southern Ontario and the Creeks of the southeast, for example, were agricultural and matrilineal. Most hunting tribes of the Great Lakes area were patrilineal, but significant exceptions can be found to any relation between economy and kinship.[10]

Ethnic differences profoundly affected the way specific tribes reacted to the European challenge. One particularly well-documented example involving the Iroquois and the Hurons reveals why someone interested in cultural interaction must understand Indian heterogeneity. Even before contact, the Iroquois were apparently a bellicose tribe. relying upon warfare to obtain animal skins and hunting territory. The neighboring Hurons gained the same ends largely through trade. "The contrasting responses of the Huron and the Iroquois [to the white man]," explains Bruce Trigger, "reflect not only their different geographical locations, but also *longstanding cultural differences* that had arisen as a result of cultural adaptation to these locations."[11]

The various native Americans with whom the colonist came into contact represented strikingly different levels of technological development. On the eve of the European conquest many tribes living in what became the middle and southeastern mainland colonies experienced a cultural revolution. They adopted the Mississippian cultural complex, the central characteristics of which were "systematic agriculture, hierarchical social and political structures, elaborate exchange networks, and clusters of large, pyramidal mounds."[12] The Mississippian reorganization did not make a substantial impact upon the Algonkian bands that the English and French first encountered in the far Northeast. These less developed peoples were less able to preserve their traditional belief system against the external threat than were the members of southern and inland tribes. "The more advanced Amerindian cultures," Cornelius J. Jaenen reports, "assimilated more rapidly than the less advanced tribes. . . . It was the less advanced, northern and eastern nomadic Algonkian-speaking tribes who were most disorganized in the face of contact."[13]

The cultures of "precontact" Africa were less unified than that of seventeenth-century Europe. Only recently, however, have anthropologists and historians come to appreciate fully the diversity and complexity of West African societies. It is still common to read of a general African heritage, a single background allegedly providing slaves with a set of shared meanings and beliefs once they reached the New World. But as anthropologists Sidney Mintz and Richard Price argue, "Enslaved Africans . . . were drawn from different parts of the African continent, from numerous tribal and linguistic groups, and from different societies in any region."[14] Black men and women were transported to America as members of specific tribes—as Ibos, Yorubas, or Ashantis but not simply as Africans. Indeed, historians accustomed to thinking of European migrants in terms of national origin often overlook African ethnicity, overestimating perhaps the difficulty of obtaining evidence for the heterogeneity of African culture.

African ethnicity is not a modern invention. Colonial planters who purchased slaves recognized distinctions between various West African peoples, and in South Carolina and the Caribbean islands whites sought blacks from specific tribes thought to be particularly docile or strong.[15] Even if the planters had not made such demands, however, the slave population in the English colonies—at least in the earliest years of settlement—would have reflected a wide range of geographic and cultural backgrounds. Different European traders put together human cargoes in areas (usually at the mouths of major rivers) where they had gained commercial rights. Slaves acquired by Dutch merchants, therefore, came from different regions than did those transported by English vessels. Moreover, local political and economic instability sometimes affected the ability of coastal tribes to obtain adequate supplies of slaves, and during the colonial period the locus of the slave trade shifted from one region to another, each change bringing in its wake men and women of different cultural heritages.[16] Such diversity meant that the Africans themselves were often strangers to each other's customs and languages, and if a single African background developed at all, it came into being on board slave ships or plantations, where West Africans were compelled to cooperate in order to survive.

Colonial American historians seldom describe England on the eve of colonization as a "precontact" culture. The reasons for their reluctance are clear.

Elizabethan society seems politically sophisticated, economically expansive, and, by the standards of the seventeenth century, technologically well developed. For the purposes of this essay, however, it is salutary to consider another perspective: to conceive of the earliest migrants as coming not from a well-integrated culture but from localized subcultures scattered throughout the kingdom. English people shared assumptions about the meaning of daily events—just as the eastern woodland Indians or West Africans did—but the lost world of the Anglo-Americans was generally a specific rural area.[17] According to Peter Clark and Paul Slack, the England of 1700 was "still very much a rural nation."[18] Whether a colonist came from Kent or Norfolk, East Anglia or the West Country, therefore, should be a matter of considerable importance for anyone interested in cultural interaction in the New World.

This line of reasoning must not be overstated: even as men and women set out to settle the Caribbean and mainland colonies the localism that had so long characterized the English countryside had begun to dissolve.[19] The process was slow and uneven, affecting regions near London and other urban centers more profoundly than it did outlying areas such as Cornwall and Yorkshire. Moreover, the creation of a national culture involved wealthy county gentry and affluent merchants long before it touched the common folk, many of whom traveled to America as indentured servants. Such social divisions notwithstanding, however, English colonists possessed a greater awareness of a shared culture, especially a common language, than did either the Africans or the Indians. Several historians, including Sumner C. Powell, John J. Waters, and David Grayson Allen, have argued, not that these general centralizing trends should be ignored, but rather that the story of the transfer of English culture to the New World and the attitudes of English colonists towards other Americans is richer once one knows something about the migrants' "local" as well as "national" background.[20]

Perceptions and prejudices. Men and women involved in the colonization of North America generally regarded themselves as superior to the representatives of other groups with whom they came into contact. Such flattering self-perceptions developed long before anyone thought of moving to the New World. When Africans, Europeans, and Indians encountered individuals of unfamiliar races and cultures, they attempted to incorporate them into established intellectual frameworks, and it is not surprising that differences were often interpreted as evidence of inferiority. Early modern English writers left a particularly detailed record of how they viewed blacks and Indians, not to mention the Irish. Historians drawing upon this material concluded that ethnocentric biases pervaded the white colonists' world view. Only recently have scholars become aware that members of other cultures could be just as ethnocentric in their outlook as were the English. To the extent that these ideas and prejudices shaped the ways that persons of different race and culture actually interacted in the New World, they obstructed open, creative adaptation, especially by people of dependent status.

The study of white attitudes about blacks and Indians is flourishing, largely in the area of intellectual history. The writings of David Brion Davis and Winthrop Jordan represent the idealist tradition at its best.[21] Within somewhat different contexts, Jordan and Davis trace European perceptions of black people, and they provide masterful analyses of the ways in which whites subtly and often insidiously developed the justification of slavery. By the time that English colonists set out for America, they had come to equate Africans with evil, paganism, bestiality, and lust—traits that seemed to deny blacks any chance of obtaining freedom and dignity in the New World. Whether these attitudes amounted to full-blown "racism" is a question yet to be resolved. To be sure, blacks became slaves in America in large numbers. There is considerable evidence, however, that the English regarded almost anyone who was not English as inferior and that at least during the early seventeenth century Africans were just one of several groups whom they saw as inferior.[22]

The image of the Indian in the so-called white mind also continues to fascinate early American historians. They have discovered that even as white settlers drove native Americans from the Atlantic coast, exterminating many in the process, they held ambivalent ideas about the Indian, some favorable, some derogatory. How much these complex attitudes affected Indian policy is not entirely clear. Indeed, general intellectual histories may reveal very little about the character of race relations in specific environments. That, however, may not be their goal. According to Roy Harvey Pearce, such accounts tell us a great deal about white fears and obsessions, about self-perceptions threatened by the American "savage." "The Indian became important for the English mind," Pearce explains, "not for what he was in and of himself, but rather what he showed civilized men they were not and must not be."[23]

Whites were not alone in their prejudice. West Africans possessed an image of the white man that was extremely unflattering. Blacks seem to have associated the color white, at least on human beings, with a number of negative attributes, including evil. In one magnificent Danish account compiled in the mid-eighteenth century, it was reported that an African ruler thought "all Europeans looked like ugly sea monsters." He ordered an embarrassed Danish bookkeeper to strip so that he could definitively discover if this was so. After examining the naked Dane, the African exclaimed, "You are really a human being, but as white as the devil."[24] When William Bosman visited Guinea in the late seventeenth century he was surprised to learn from local blacks that while God "created Blacks as well as White Men," the Lord preferred the blacks.[25] How much such ethnocentric attitudes carried over to the New World and affected relations between blacks and whites is not known. There is no reason to believe, however, that Afro-Americans viewed the English any more favorably than the English viewed the blacks.

Reconstruction of native American ideas about Europeans presents a formidable challenge. Our only knowledge of Indian attitudes is derived from white sources, especially those compiled by unsympathetic missionaries and traders. "We are completely ignorant," Trigger admits, "or have only the vaguest ideas about what the majority of Indians thought and felt as individuals and know little about what they did, except in their dealings with Europeans."[26] Despite these obstacles, we have reasons to believe that while Indians were eager to obtain manufactured goods, they maintained a critical, even derogatory, stance towards the whites and their cultures. The northern tribes, for example, regarded Europeans as ugly—too hairy for their tastes. In fact, Jaenen reports that "on a wide range of points of contact . . . the Amerindian evaluation of French culture and civilization was often as unflattering as was the low regard of Frenchmen for Amerindian culture."[27] Indians of tidewater Virginia were as ethnocentric in their outlook as were the first English planters. In fact, there is almost no evidence that native Americans wanted to live in stuffy cabins, attend white schools, give up traditional religious practices, copy English government, adopt European medicines, or, much to the white colonists' amazement, make love to white women.[28]

Once historians have catalogued these ethnocentric biases—white, black, and red—they still do not know much about race relations in specific historical contexts. Recent studies indicate that general attitudes were often modified, muted, or dropped altogether when peoples of different races and cultures came into contact. As James Axtell points out, "Breezy generalizations about 'English' attitudes are much less helpful than distinctions between the attitudes of stay-at-homes and colonists, city folk and frontiersmen, tourists and locals, saints and sinners, and fighers and lovers."[29]

The difficulty of studying race relations from the perspective of intellectual history may be even greater than Axtell admits. Sociologists have found no direct connection between stereotypical notions about other groups and actual discrimination. "It is quite possible," observes George Fredrickson, "for an individual to have a generalized notion about members of another race or nationality that bears almost no relation to how he actually behaves when confronted with them."[30] In other words, if we are to understand the creative choices that people made in the New World, we must pay close attention not only to what they said and wrote but also to what they did. Whatever racial images may have inhabited the "white mind," Englishmen certainly did not treat blacks and Indians the same way throughout the empire.

Ideas that people held concerning members of other groups are best regarded as loose, even inchoate bundles of opinion. These perceptions tended to be ambivalent, and it usually required a major event such as war or rebellion to trigger outbursts of hatred. In themselves, however, popular attitudes about race and culture did not determine the character of human interaction in the English colonies.

Motives for colonization. English men and women moved to the New

World for many different reasons, not the least of which was escape from personal misadventures. However, by concentrating narrowly upon economic and religious incentives for transfer, we can argue plausibly that the further north the colonists settled, the less obsessed they were with immediate material gain. As historians constantly reiterate, Puritans journeyed to New England for more than the reformation of the Church of England, but religious purity was certainly a matter of considerable importance in establishing a "city on a hill." By the same token, some English people undoubtedly thought they were doing the Lord's work in Virginia. The major preoccupation of these settlers, however, was making money—a great deal of it very quickly. As Edmund S. Morgan has pointed out, the Chesapeake colony in the early seventeenth century took on the characteristics of a "boom town," a place where powerful persons were none too particular about the means they used to gain their ends.[31]

These scrambling, greedy tobacco planters look almost saintly when compared with the individuals who crossed the "line" into a Caribbean world of cutthroats and adventurers. "The expectations the English brought with them," writes Richard Dunn, "and the physical conditions they encountered in the islands produced a hectic mode of life that had no counterpart at home or elsewhere in English experience."[32] In these tropical societies organized religion failed to make much impact upon the colonists' avariciousness. Sugar producers could not possibly have comprehended the communal controls over private gain that bound New Englanders together in small covenanted villages.

How much the expectations of early white leaders affected relations between persons of different races and cultures is difficult to ascertain. Unquestionably, for people of dependent status, life in the southern and island colonies was less pleasant than it would have been in Pennsylvania or Massachusetts Bay. Adventurers who demanded quick returns on investment eagerly exploited anyone's labor, whether they were black, white, or Indian. The ambition to become rich in the New World may have transformed planters into cruel and insensitive masters. But however much we recoil at their behavior, we should not confuse exploitation with racism. In early Virginia and Barbados—two well-recorded societies—the Irish, Africans, and native Americans were at equal disadvantage. In these colonies class rather than race may have been the bond that united workers, and the willingness of the poor whites and blacks to cooperate, to run away together, and in some cases to join in rebellion grew out of a shared experience of poverty and oppression.[33]

Timing of transfer. In shaping cultural patterns, the earliest migrants, English and African, enjoyed great advantage over later arrivals. The first colonists established rules for interaction, decided what customs would be carried to the New World, and determined the terms under which newcomers would be incorporated into their societies. According to John Porter, the founders should be regarded as "charter" groups. Porter explains that "the first ethnic group to come into a previously unpopulated territory, as the effective possessor, has the most to say. This group becomes the charter group of the society, and among the many privileges and prerogatives which it retains are decisions about what other groups are to be let in and what they will be permitted to do."[34] A double challenge confronted men and women relocated at a later date. They had not only to adjust to an unfamiliar environment but also to accommodate themselves to the people already living there, to members of their own race as well as to other colonists. Timing of transfer, therefore, functioned as an important constraint upon cultural adaptation.

English "charter" groups exercised considerable influence over subsequent generations. They did so by making decisions about institutional forms, about the treatment of other races, about the allocation of natural resources. And in New England especially these decisions were then published. They became permanent guides to a specific social order. The *Laws and Liberties of Massachusetts* was such a document, as was the *Cambridge Platform*. Even in the southern colonies, where people died like flies and printing presses were scarce, "charter" settlers established customs and traditions, exploitative labor systems, and normative patterns of behavior. The men and women who flooded into Virginia after mid-century, for example, however wealthy and powerful they may have been, were forced to channel their ambitions through existing institutional structures. They were not free to abolish slavery or staple-crop agriculture: these had become expressions of a regional way of life. To be sure, newcomers could tinker with what they found— make modifications, clarify procedures—but the hand of the past restricted the choices available to them. In every English colony white Creoles—persons born and raised in America—came to accept local folkways without question. New immigrants adjusted not to a single English culture transferred to the New World but to a particular creole culture that had developed over time.[35]

Timing was a factor of profound importance in shaping distinct Afro-American cultures. Tensions between black Creoles and newly arrived Africans affected not only the development of specific slave communities but also the ways black people interacted with whites. The fullest evidence comes from the Caribbean islands, especially from Barbados and Jamaica, but similar frictions seem to have occurred in all English possessions south of New England, beginning with the landing of the first African slaves in the early seventeenth century. Frightened and ill, often separated from family and members of their own ethnic groups, these men and women found themselves thrown together with black strangers on ships and later on plantations. Since they spoke different languages, even casual conversation was difficult.

But as Sidney Mintz and Richard Price have argued so provocatively, these early blacks successfully created new cultures that were part African and part American. They transferred some customs familiar to blacks throughout West Africa. The slaves also negotiated compromises, invented new rules and languages, and learned how to deal with whites; in short, they crafted complex social orders in the face of great personal deprivation. The rich oral culture that flourished on plantations transformed these ad hoc measures into viable traditions. Older men and women, particularly obeah men and women, believed to possess special medical or spiritual powers, passed on the decisions of the founders to children born in America. Obviously it took many years and much suffering to establish genuine, stable creole cultures, but they did eventually spring up throughout the Caribbean and southern mainland colonies.[36]

These developments sometimes aggravated hardships experienced by African-born slaves. Creoles established rules for their incorporation into Afro-American plantation communities which often seemed arbitrary to men and women fresh from West Africa. These "outlandish Negroes," "salt-water Negroes," or "Guineybirds"—as they were called by Creole and whites—could barely comprehend the mechanisms that had deprived them of their freedom, much less the customs that governed exchanges between Afro-Americans. Adjustments generated tensions, even hostilities.[37] Consider, for example, the pain of young Olaudah Equiano, who arrived in the Chesapeake region in 1757. This twelve-year-old slave declared, "I was now exceedingly miserable, and thought myself worse off than any . . . of my companions; for they could talk to each other, but I had no person to speak to that I could understand. In this state I was constantly grieving and pining, and wishing for death."[38] In time most Africans in Equiano's position accepted the conventions of Afro-American culture, just as so many European migrants came to terms with Anglo-American culture. Newcomers, whatever their color, did not experience the possibility of creating a new culture. For them, interacting in strange situations required them to break the code—often under great pressure and quite quickly—of creole culture.

Some new African slaves simply could not adjust. Rather than become Afro-Americans, they made a different choice, one that often cost them their lives: they ran off in gangs or violently resisted their white masters. But as Gerald Mullin, Michael Craton, and David Barry Gaspar, among others, have pointed out, whatever the provocation, Creoles and "outlandish" blacks seldom made common cause. In the Antigua slave rebellion of 1736, for example, Creoles who were "assimilated blacks, proficient in English or the local patois, intelligent in bearing, sometimes literate, and usually skilled" planned the enterprise.[39] In contrast, Mullin discovered that in eighteenth-century Virginia "only native Africans who were new arrivals and referred to as 'outlandish,' ran off in groups or attempted to establish villages or runaways on the frontier." Black Virginia Creoles generally slipped away alone and headed for urban areas, where they passed themselves off as free persons.[40]

The timing of contact played a considerably different role in the evolution of native American cultures. The Indians, after all, were already here, and for them, the strains of creolization were not a problem. Nevertheless, the chronology of first interaction with white settlers is a matter of great significance in the native American history. Several tribes that initially encountered Europeans—the Caribs and Arawaks of the Caribbean islands and the Algonkian bands of the Northeast—were ill-equipped to deal with the massive threat presented by the white colonists. Because of their exposed position on the first frontier of settlement, they did not have time to adjust to the external challenge. Disease wiped out many bands; others were quickly dispersed or enslaved. To claim that these men and women had an opportunity to adapt creatively would be disingenuous. In comparison with these unfortunate groups, the inland tribes—many of them more highly developed—were able to adjust to change at a more leisurely pace and thus were able to preserve fundamental elements of their cultures.[41]

Physical environment.   Colonial historians have shown no great interest in systematically investigating the connection between culture and environment. Unlike anthropologists, they seem to take such matters for granted. No one doubts, of course, that cultural relations in the New World were somehow influenced by flora and fauna, by rainfall and temperature, by soil types and natural resources.[42] The question is, How and to what degree did these elements affect the cultural choices made by early Americans?

Certainly such factors operated as constraints upon cultural transfer, for as English colonists discovered, it was far easier to reproduce traditional ways of life in a familiar environment than in one that threatened their very survival. The obvious contrast is between the early settlements of New England and of the Caribbean. The physical environment of Massachusetts Bay was not substantially different from that which East Anglian, West Country, or Kentish migrants had known in the mother country. To be sure, they complained of the harsh American winters, but despite snow and cold, New Englanders quickly reestablished the forms of mixed agriculture that their fathers and grandfathers had practiced before them. These fortuitous similarities meant that Puritans were spared the wrenching adjustments demanded of English people who settled in the tropics. Instead of experimenting with strange staples like rice, sugar, and tobacco, New Englanders immediately turned their attention to recreating as much of English village life in America as they possibly could, and as David Grayson Allen has argued persuasively, they experienced considerable success.[43]

The same claim could not be made for the English people who landed on Barbados or Jamaica. In the hot, damp climate of the Caribbean, colonists stubbornly attempted to recreate English ways of life. As Richard Dunn has explained, their diet and clothes were grossly unsuited for the tropics. Some men and women managed to adjust to this strange environment. Others went home or moved to areas of the New World where they felt more comfortable. But a few unhappy souls were overwhelmed, and according to Michael

Craton, they "sank into a hopeless moral stupor, eating, drinking, and for-
nicating themselves into an early grave."[44] It is not clear exactly how such a
major culture shock—an uprooting from all that was familiar—affected relations in the Caribbean between whites and blacks, or between creole whites
and later arrivals. In what must have seemed alien, exotic surroundings to the
seventeenth-century colonists, the massive exploitation of African peoples
may have appeared more appropriate, even logical, than it did in an environment that looked much like the English countryside.

European colonists insisted, even as they watched African slaves die by the
hundred, that blacks were particularly well-suited to living in a tropical
environment. The West Africans transported to the Caribbean, however,
found the staple-crop, plantation agriculture as alien to their experience as
did the white settlers. As Michael Craton explains, "To Africans accustomed
to subsistence farming, plantation agriculture was dislocatingly strange, if
not unnatural. The planters' profit motive meant nothing to them, and their
spirit probably resisted the forests' despoilation as much as the exploitation of
themselves."[45] These blacks, of course, exercised no choice over where they
would settle and adjusted to unfamiliar surroundings as best they could.

Environmental conditions provided some Afro-Americans with opportunities denied to others. On a few Caribbean islands, but especially on
Jamaica, large maroon communities developed in heavily forested, rugged
regions that the white militia found impossible to patrol. These villages,
populated by ex-slaves and their children, presented an appealing alternative
to bondage. Rebellious men and women knew that they could slip away into
the deep woods; in fact, such people ran away to the maroons so frequently
that in 1740 frustrated Jamaican authorities accepted the independence of
these communities in exchange for peace and assistance in capturing newly
escaped slaves. This form of resistance was not available to Afro-Americans
living on a small, deforested island like Barbados. However much these
slaves resented their treatment, they were constrained by the characteristics
of their environment to channel hostility into other forms of resistance.[46]
Why maroon societies did not flourish in the mainland colonies remains
something of a mystery. Certainly the southern back country afforded many
potential hideaways. One plausible explanation is that these inland areas
were inhabited by powerful Indian tribes who were no more enthusiastic
about the spread of black settlements than they were about those of the
whites.

Native Americans adjusted to ecological niches long before Africans and
Europeans arrived in the New World. To discuss these long-term adaptations is not necessary in an essay of this scope. Of greater significance in
explaining the ways that peoples of different races and cultures interacted is
the simple accident of location. The experience of the Iroquois provides a
good example of the importance of geography. In the early seventeenth
century these Indians found themselves surrounded by Dutch, English, and

French colonists. The Iroquois had obviously not foreseen the commercial advantages of this particular location, but once the Europeans landed, the Indians masterfully played one group off against the others.[47] Had the Iroquois lived in a different area, say, along the Atlantic coast, such complex trade relations with the whites could not possibly have developed.

Demographic configurations. The last two decades have witnessed a revolution in the study of historical demography in this country. We know more about seventeenth-century New Englanders than about almost any other population on earth. More recently, colonial demographers have examined other English settlements, as well as early Afro-American communities. Cultural and social historians have rushed to incorporate this growing literature into their own work, for it seems indisputable that population density, family structure, and mortality rates—just to cite obvious themes—somehow influenced patterns of cultural and racial interaction in the New World.

The relation between culture and population, however, remains fuzzy. Historians sometimes assume a connection merely because it sounds plausible. Take high mortality as an example: How exactly did the terrible death rates experienced by the earliest Chesapeake adventurers affect their attitudes about each other or about dependent peoples? Did the threat of early death make them more hedonistic, more exploitative, or more religious than they might have been in a healthier environment? Currently we do not know. Even if we recognize these interpretative problems, it is clear that historical demography provides marvelous insights into the constraints upon creative adaptation in early America.

Any demographic discussion must begin with New England. New Englanders' remarkable experience, along with other factors we have considered, greatly facilitated the transfer of local English cultures to America. Puritan migrants were unexpectedly blessed with long life. By all rights, persons who moved to the New World in their forties or fifties could not have expected to survive very long. But they did. Many even saw their grandchildren reach maturity, a rare occurrence in contemporary Europe. In fact, once they founded communities, the fathers of New England towns literally became patriarchs, keepers of tradition and symbols of stability. Since these colonists usually migrated in nuclear families, the sex ratio of the population was relatively balanced. Among other things, this demographic structure meant that people immediately had to plan for the well-being of future generations. They established schools and churches, and even in the very earliest settlements young men and women were conscious of being members of extensive kinship networks as well as cohesive farm communities.[48]

Strikingly different demographic configurations developed in the seventeenth-century southern mainland and Caribbean colonies. These settlements drew a disproportionately large number of young males, mostly indentured servants, who generally died within a few years. Warm climates exacerbated the spread of contagious disease, but shallow wells poisoned by salt water and hostile Indians also took a sizable toll.[49]

Continuing high mortality appears to have had a profound impact upon white cultures in these colonies. There was little incentive to plan for the future—at least, a future in the New World. Men wanted to strike it rich and return home as quickly as possible. They paid little attention to the establishment of churches and schools. After all, in societies in which women "were scarcer than corn or liquor," few children were born, and of those, most died in infancy.[50] In the early Chesapeake, Cary Carson finds, "many of the earlier structures were not only *not* built to last, they *were* built in ways that termites could not resist"[51] A similar sense of impermanence pervaded the Caribbean colonies. As Carl and Roberta Bridenbaugh observe, early death combined with the absence of normal family life "made for a slower transit of English civilization to the islands than to New England."[52]

Historical demographers have discovered that mortality in these regions did not significantly improve for generations. In the Chesapeake settlements births did not outnumber deaths among the whites until the end of the seventeenth century.[53] And in Jamaica health conditions remained wretched throughout the entire eighteenth century.[54] What all this means in demographic terms is that these were abnormal societies, comparable to European mercenary armies rather than to English country villages, and those people who managed to survive must have been keenly aware of the tenuousness of life, of the need to grab for as much as one could in the race for wealth. From this evidence alone, one would predict that white males in these colonies would look upon dependent blacks and Indians chiefly as convenient sources of sex and labor.

Besides high mortality, at least two other demographic factors affected the character of early American race relations. Of great importance in the staple colonies was the shifting population ratio of blacks and whites. Recent studies suggest that white attitudes towards blacks were influenced powerfully by the number of Africans with whom the whites *actually* came into contact. In the earliest years of settlement the black populations of Virginia, South Carolina, Barbados, and Jamaica were relatively small, and white planters either treated blacks with indifference—in other words, no worse than they treated everyone else—or allowed some blacks to forge independent niches as farmers or herdsmen. As the black populations increased, however, whites began to draw racial boundaries more rigidly. They also became more vocal in their protestations of black inferiority. In colony after colony demographic change produced racial fears and hostility. Orlando Patterson, in his study of Jamaican society, explains, "In the first few years after the occupation there was a favourable attitude toward Negro freemen. . . . But as more slaves came into the island this policy changed rapidly." White authorities challenged free Jamaican blacks at every turn, and those who could not prove their status were reenslaved.[55]

A second consideration was population dispersion. In Virginia and Maryland slaves generally worked in small groups on tobacco farms scattered across the countryside. In the fields they often toiled alongside their owners. According to Ira Berlin, interaction between members of the two races was "constant and continued," and white planters, even some of the wealthiest, developed a strong paternalistic interest in the affairs of their slaves.[56] In the Carolinas and Georgia and certainly in the Caribbean such intimate relationships over long periods of time were rare. On large rice and sugar plantations blacks were isolated; they might go days without seeing any white person. In the eighteenth century many great planters of Jamaica fled the island altogether, becoming "absentees" living in England. They left behind a skeletal staff of salaried whites to manage several hundred slaves. Since these whites were paid to maintain high production rates and since they were usually frightened out of their wits by the possibility of rebellion, they acted like petty tyrants. Race relations were cruel and arbitrary. Indeed, the whites who remained on Jamaica would probably have regarded the paternalism of a William Byrd II or a Landon Carter as foolish, if not absolutely suicidal.

The formation of distinct Afro-American cultures owes much to demographic forces over which black people exercised little control. Slave traders decided where men and women would be sent and in what numbers. During the seventeenth century, Caribbean planters who negotiated the largest purchases demanded strong, young males. Africans, therefore, faced three particularly severe handicaps in transferring local cultures to the New World: they were unfree; their sex ratios were so badly skewed towards males that normal family life and reproduction was retarded; and they died at appalling rates, either of unfamiliar contagious diseases or of overwork. Only gradually, as life expectancy improved and sex ratios became more balanced, did slaves develop stable kinship networks, as well as sustaining folk traditions. This crucial demographic transition occurred in various colonies at different times. As Allan Kulikoff argues, the slaves of Maryland and Virginia laid the foundations for a secure Afro-American society during the early decades of the eighteenth century. But in the southern, more lethal regions the process may have been slower. "As long as slavery lasted," Michael Craton notes, "West Indian slave society was demographically not self-sufficient, though the gap between deathrate and birthrate gradually narrowed."[57]

A second demographic element in the creation of Afro-American cultures was touched upon in our discussion of the density of various white populations. In areas where the blacks worked in small units, often in close proximity to whites, they found it difficult to maintain independent customs and practices. Their situation compelled them to make subtle adjustments to the demands of a specific work routine. Again, the more southern mainland and Caribbean colonies present a sharp contrast to this experience. In these regions the size of the plantation work force was generally large, sometimes comprising several hundred men and women, and while the tropical environment endangered good health, Caribbean and Carolina slaves lived within communities composed almost entirely of blacks. Several historians suggest that the peculiarities of work culture explain why so many African customs seem to have survived on the sugar and rice plantations. "The West Indian slave," writes Richard Dunn, "barred from the essentials of European civility, was free to retain as much as he wished of his West African cultural heritage. Here he differed from the Negro in Virginia . . . who was not only uprooted from his familiar tropical environment but thrown into close association with white people and their European ways."[58]

For native Americans race relations represented demographic disaster. Smallpox, influenza, and measles swept through Indian peoples, who possessed no natural immunities, and in some areas, particularly in the northeastern and Caribbean colonies, entire tribes were wiped out within a few years of conquest. The impact of lethal epidemics upon Indian cultures varied from region to region and from tribe to tribe. Among some woodland bands of the far North inexplicable suffering called into question the efficacy of traditional religious beliefs. In other places death so eroded their cultures that Indian survivors lost tribal identity and joined remnants of other shattered groups or inland tribes not yet decimated by the contagious killers. The Indian population fell so rapidly that few English colonists seriously regarded native Americans as a potential labor force.[59] As George Fredrickson remarks, "There are several reasons why Indians never became a significant part of the agricultural or industrial labor force in the United States, but the most important is the sheer lack of numbers resulting from the ravages of disease."[60] Removal of native Americans from English work cultures, particularly in the staple economies, meant that Indians developed quite different patterns of relations with the whites than did the plantation blacks.

The story of white-Indian interaction has another, often overlooked demographic dimension. Population density influenced relations between these two races throughout the colonial period. Disease, however devastating its effects, did not hit all tribes with equal intensity. Indians who inhabited the Atlantic coast of New England, for example, suffered major demographic setbacks *before* the Puritans arrived, and as a result of these earlier epidemics, whites outnumbered local native Americans in this region almost from the very beginning of contact.[61] But in central and western New York, in tidewater Virginia, and along the Georgia–South Carolina frontier, Indians presented a formidable challenge to white expansion. To be sure, the colonists eventually dispossessed most of the eastern tribes, but this displacement should not obscure the occasions in which large numbers of reasonably healthy native Americans more than held their own.

Economic constraints. While Europeans largely determined patterns of work and trade in the New World, everyone possessed a voice, however faint, in economic affairs. In fields of sugar, rice, and tobacco or at trading posts where Indians brought food or furs, people carried on subtle forms of cultural bargaining. In these settings they forged mutual dependencies and developed understandings about the limits of cooperation. Not surprisingly, therefore, in early America cultural borrowing and technological exchanges were most frequently associated with work and trade.

The character of the local economies, however, was quite fluid. Colonial agriculturalists switched crops and, depending upon where they lived, substituted staple crops for livestock or livestock for cereals. Moreover, as whites demanded different items from native Americans, the nature of the Indian trade changed. These shifts had a major effect upon the ways that local peoples interacted, for each change affected the exploitativeness of work, the size of the labor force, and, most significantly, the ability of men and women of different races and backgrounds to engage in creative "conversations."

The most dramatic economic transformations—for blacks as well as whites—occurred in the southern mainland and Caribbean colonies during the seventeenth century. Englishmen arrived in the regions filled with ill-conceived notions about how to become rich. They dreamed of finding passages to the Orient, of gold and rubies by the seashore. The harsh realities of the New World dispelled such fantasies, and during the early decades of settlement colonists experimented with different crops. Barbadians did not immediately see the advantages of sugar over cotton and tobacco. Only after years of economic misadventure did tobacco catch on in Virginia, and in South Carolina the planters seem to have stumbled upon rice, and later upon indigo, quite by accident. In each colony, the staple crop radically changed the structure of regional societies. Local gentry demanded, and eventually obtained, large numbers of African slaves, who replaced white servants.[62]

Staples not only created greater reliance upon black laborers but also exacerbated economic inequalities within the English population. As the marquis de Chastellux noted in 1783, "Agriculture which was everywhere the occupation of the first settlers, was not enough to cast them all in one mold, since there are certain types of agriculture [mixed agriculture] which tend to maintain equal wealth among individuals, and other types [staple agriculture] which tend to destroy it."[63] Many poor whites left Barbados, for example, after the switch to sugar, a crop that required a large initial capital investment for machinery.[64] Those who remained were reduced to desperate marginality, the ancestors of modern "redshanks" (the Caribbean equivalent of rednecks in the American South). The effects of staple agriculture on the mainland societies were less striking than the effects on the island societies. Nevertheless, rice and tobacco—and the particular work routines associated with these crops—helped redefine relations between whites, as well as between whites and blacks.[65]

As the world market for American staples expanded, the slave's life became much harder than it had been during the earliest years of settlement. Of course, Africans had always suffered discrimination, but during the first stages of economic development the line between slave and freeman and between black and white seems to have been loosely drawn in some colonies. In South Carolina, for example, slaves worked as "cowboys" along the frontier with only minimal white supervision. In this period even the black's exact legal status remained vague.[66] Once white planters began to realize large profits, however, they pushed their slaves harder, eager to obtain full return on their human investment. Agrarian schedules settled into a dull, mindless routine. As Craton explains of one plantation on Jamaica: "With the clearing of trees and the beginning of sugar planting, the quality of life for those working in Lluidas Vale inevitably deteriorated . . . . a herd of tractable blacks was needed, with no more skills than were called for in the West African agriculture of slashing, burning, and hoeing."[67] Unskilled, often unpleasant work became part of the circular justification for slavery. Slaves performed nasty jobs, and because blacks did them, they obviously made good slaves. Other factors were operating in this process, but it is instructive to compare the experience of Jamaican blacks with the experience of those who worked on small Pennsylvania farms. Jerome Wood reports that the latter were treated relatively well, escaping much of the personal hardship connected with staple agriculture.[68]

Economic change affected white-Indian relations in different ways. At first, English settlers required foodstuffs, and since their needs were obviously desperate, native Americans could drive hard bargains, something Powhatan learned very early in his dealings with the Jamestown adventurers. Both sides profited from these exchanges; both maintained their cultural integrity. But it was not long before the colonists demanded furs and skins. Those tribes that could not generate adequate supplies of pelts were either pushed aside or ignored. Coveted manufactured items went to inland Indians who had access to regions where the animals had not yet been hunted to extinction. Gradually, however, the European market for furs dried up, styles changed, and the Indians, now dependent upon European commerce, had little to offer in exchange for guns and cloth, kettles and knives. Under these conditions, Indians were easily exploited, abused, and cheated out of whatever they still possessed. In a none too subtle fashion, therefore, commercial relations along a moving frontier shaped native American economic behavior.[69] These constraints on interaction did not inevitably produce tragic results. Some Indians developed skills highly marketable in certain white communities. The native Americans on Nantucket and far eastern Long Island, for example, were renowned for their ability to catch whales, and long after many woodland bands had disappeared, these people flourished.[70]

Individual personality. During the colonial period certain persons occasionally broke the rules governing race relations, defied economic trends, and by sheer strength of personality forced other men and women to deal with them on their own terms. Whether these people possessed special genius or courage or luck is impossible to determine. Their existence, however, is not in doubt, and in areas scattered throughout Englis'. America they had a considerable influence upon local cultural conversations. Anthony Johnson was such an individual. He arrived in Virginia a slave, and by hard work and good fortune he purchased his freedom, becoming eventually a successful planter on the Eastern Shore. Johnson's story is clearly exceptional; that is the point: in a small pond he was a very big fish—a shark—and while the Virginia House of Burgesses was busy passing laws restricting black freedoms, he persuaded his white neighbors to treat him and his family with respect.[71] Thomas Mayhew, Jr., a Congregational minister on Martha's Vineyard, helped local Indians preserve many traditional ways of life, and when external authorities threatened his work, he held his ground.[72] Like Johnson, Mayhew set his own standards. Any analysis of creative adaptations that overlooks these special cases will fail to capture the full richness of human relations in early America.

Cultural persistence and white dominance. Before hazarding a general interpretation of cultural and racial relations in colonial America, I should offer two mild caveats. First, for anyone studying cultures over long periods of time, there is an understandable tendency to stress change over persistence. In fact, however, most early Americans were conservative, trying to preserve as best they could familiar customs and traditions, a known way of life. Sometimes what appears to have been a radical cultural reorientation turns out upon closer examination to have been a shrewd compromise, a superficial adjustment masking the survival of a deeper, often symbolic cultural core. The native American experience provides good examples of this process. Under certain conditions, Indians converted to Christianity, a decision that would seem to have threatened the entire fabric of traditional culture. But appearances may have been deceiving. As James Axtell argues, "Even though their conversion entailed wholesale cultural changes, it preserved their ethnic identity as particular Indian groups on familiar pieces of land that carried their inner history." In other words, native Americans used "elements of European religious culture for their own purposes." Historians tracing English and African migrations to the New World report similar creative efforts, often against great odds, to protect at least the main elements of a former cultural system.[73]

Second, while emphasizing human choice in shaping patterns of human interaction, I am fully aware that white people possessed tremendous economic, military, and technological advantages in defining cultural conversations. They often set the terms: they provided foils against which native Americans and Afro-Americans reacted. That much seems self-evident. What colonial historians have generally overlooked is the potential within specific social contexts for creative response.

FROM CHARTER TO CREOLE:
SHIFTING CONTEXTS OF CULTURAL INTERACTION

The movement of so many men and women to America—Africans as well as Europeans—changed Old World cultures in ways that even the participants only vaguely understood. However determined various ethnic groups may have been to recreate familiar patterns of life within the constraints of a new environment, none succeeded in doing so. Traditional values and beliefs were transformed, and out of this process emerged new cultural realities, mosaics in which one could identify certain elements of a former experience but which also contained pieces that were wholly original.

The process began during the earliest period of transfer, and despite local peculiarities, general patterns emerged. Seventeenth-century migrants were involved in two different kinds of cultural interaction. The first brought men and women of the same race together under conditions that most likely would not have occurred in the Old World. East Anglians were forced to deal with West Country and Kentish migrants, Ibos with Akan. Strangers had to sort themselves out, making compromises about institutional structure and rituals connected with the life cycle. These encounters produced *charter* societies, small, often isolated groupings of people scattered over an immense territory from Barbados to Massachusetts Bay. As we have already noted, the members of charter communities set the rules for the incorporation of later arrivals. One either conformed or moved on. In fact, the influence of the initial immigrants—the timing varied from region to region—was disproportionate to their actual numbers. The second form of encounter, the meeting of representatives of different races, took place among various charter settlers and particular native Americans. During the earliest years of colonization, therefore, men and women learned to live with each other in specific local contexts, and it was not until the eighteenth century that new commercial, demographic, and religious factors significantly changed patterns of cultural interaction.

The creation of Anglo-American cultures began the moment men and women departed from mostly rural areas that time out of mind had provided them and their forefathers with a compelling source of personal identity. These people—especially those who journeyed to New England—planned to reproduce the life they had known in Yorkshire or Kent, Suffolk or Sussex. But almost despite themselves, they became social innovators in America. As Michael Zuckerman writes, "Traditional familial ideals and communal norms could be carried intact across the Atlantic and reconstituted in America from the models in the colonists' minds, but such deliberate recourse to tradition was, at bottom, the very antithesis of tradition. The rich particularity of the past could not be remade from models."[74]

To chronicle these local transfers as just so many failures slights the creative qualities that colonization initially inspired. People who had lived in different parts of England established ecclesiastical, military, and legal institutions in America that had no exact precedent in the Old World.[75] In small agricultural communities they effected compromises on sensitive issues, and persons who could not tolerate these arrangements moved on, forming their own charter societies in remote corners of New England.[76] The territory was large enough to accommodate a range of solutions to common social problems. Other founders—William Penn, Lord Baltimore, the earl of Shaftesbury—enjoyed similar charter privileges, and while their economic plans came to nothing, they established legal procedures, institutional forms, and local traditions that in no small way determined how later immigrants would be incorporated into these societies. Virginia was no exception. Even though the founders died by the hundreds, they exercised surprising influence over later generations. After all, the early adventurers made enduring decisions about how to treat Indians and blacks, about the cultivation of staple crops, and about the shape of local government. Strictly speaking, English people who moved to America in the seventeenth century did not become Anglo-Americans. Rather, they joined insulated subcultures, where they were transformed willy-nilly into Anglo–New Englanders, Anglo-Pennsylvanians, Anglo-Barbadians, or Anglo-Virginians. Each was strikingly different from the others. As one historian explains, the Caribbean planters were "as different from their fellows on the mainland as the English were from the Portuguese."[77]

West Africans transported to the New World as slaves also created wholly new cultures. They did so out of fragments—customs taken from one tribe, terms borrowed from another—and within a relatively short time transformed these shards of African experience into scores of separate Afro-American cultures. Slavery placed severe limits on this process. These people were not, however, passive victims. Much like the English migrants who oppressed them, Africans worked with whatever cultural materials they found at hand.

The formation of Afro-American cultures was initially a local process, an interaction among men and women on a single plantation or within a small area. Indeed, some historians argue that the story begins with the mingling of different African ethnic groups aboard slave ships bound for the New World. Whatever the case may have been, once they landed, black migrants attempted to "recreate" familiar customs. During this exciting period of reinvention, probably the most important encounters took place, not between black slaves and white masters, but between Africans of various ethnic backgrounds.

The obstacles to the creation of new cultures were formidable. Individuals spoke different languages; what one person took for granted was often alien to other slaves. Tribal rivalries reappeared in the New World. But by negotiating compromises, by making creative adaptations within hostile physical and social environments, African slaves formed genuine charter societies. In Surinam this cultural sorting out was well advanced within only a few decades. Africans living in the Caribbean quickly developed "the core of a new language and a new religion," and once these highly localized subcultures had taken root, they became vehicles for incorporating newcomers into particular slave communities. According to Mintz and Price, "Subsequent centuries of massive new importations from Africa apparently had little more effect [on the local culture] than to lead to secondary elaborations."[78]

As early migrants went about the business of establishing charter societies—and it is essential to stress that the timing varied from region to region—relations between members of different races remained relatively open. Within specific, semi-isolated localities it was possible for individuals to negotiate social status on the basis of various attributes, only one of which was race. Just as persons had not yet formulated precise rules governing interaction with members of their own race, so too they had not determined a rigid etiquette for interracial encounters. Cultural boundaries were therefore remarkably fluid, and under these conditions borrowing occurred in ways that would become less common, even nonexistent, during the eighteenth century.

In the early stages of colonization flexibility characterized relations between Afro-Americans and Anglo-Americans. Whatever general ideas the whites may have entertained about black inferiority, they seldom treated blacks as mere chattel. To be sure, patterns of race relations differed from colony to colony, but in none, not even in the staple colonies, did white masters draw boundaries solely upon the basis of color.

Explanations for this relative openness are complex. In sparsely populated frontier areas interaction between peoples of different races occurred with some frequency. Blacks and whites were compelled to work together. They fought together. And when white indentured servants and black slaves could no longer tolerate their situation, they conspired to run away. Members of one race may well have regarded people of a different color as inferior, but when confronted with common dangers, men and women often put aside racial prejudice in favor of survival. As Peter H. Wood states in his brilliant study of early South Carolina, "Common hardships and the continuing shortage of hands put the different races, as well as separate sexes, upon a more equal footing than they would see in subsequent generations."[79] White South Carolinians even armed their slaves to fight against the local Indians. And Clarence L. Ver Steeg tells us, "Extant contemporary comments do not suggest that blacks were considered incompetent, inferior, or 'less than men.'"[80] Many examples could be advanced in support of this claim, but perhaps the most poignant is a white settler's report written in 1697 that he had spent many days working "with a Negro man at the Whip saw."[81] Their task forced them to cooperate, and covered with sweat, no doubt complaining of blisters, they discovered each other's humanity while clearing the Carolina frontier. To describe this type of society in stark terms of white over black is a distortion of the past, an exaggeration of the centrality of color in shaping early American social relations.

During the seventeenth century at least, the range of conversations between whites and blacks was immense. The Afro-American's conversion to Christianity, his ability to speak English, and his personal ingenuity figured into local cultural negotiations. The result was that some blacks became slaves, others servants, and a few successful planters who purchased dependent laborers of their own. It should be noted that those seventeenth-century blacks whose lives are well-documented—Anthony Johnson of the Virginian Eastern Shore, for example—were happy to exploit encounters with both blacks and whites to their own advantage, and in spheres of interaction outside the family they revealed no greater obsession with color than did their white neighbors.[82]

Within the constraints of particular local societies, blacks and whites adopted elements of each other's cultures. The question is, How much? Or more precisely, how deeply did this borrowing transform the cultural cores of specific Afro-American or Anglo-American groups? Many slaves professed Christianity, but as historians and anthropologists have demonstrated, one should not be misled by outward forms. Superficial acceptance of white religion allowed enslaved blacks an opportunity to preserve spiritual beliefs and practices that remained distinctly African in character. On their part, Europeans picked up certain African terms, usually ones associated with work. They expressed an uncomprehending admiration for slave music. But despite the fluidity of relations during this formative period, whites seem to have been interested primarily in the Africans' agricultural experience. The classic example is the development of rice culture in South Carolina. As Wood points out, West African slaves had probably grown this difficult crop in the Old World, and they provided instruction to their masters. The irony, of course, was that the introduction of this staple suddenly made slavery more profitable and therefore harsher than it had been.[83] According to Daniel C. Littlefield, "Africans were able to give technical advice and skill which the Europeans not only accepted but actually sought. Even more than is commonly assumed, the economic and social structures of American slave societies were . . . a mutual accomplishment."[84]

Assessment of the full range of early white-Indian relations raises quite different interpretative problems. For one thing, native Americans suffered horribly from disease. As we have already observed, even before the establishment of permanent English colonies explorers introduced devastating illness, and many Indians who had never seen an English settler experienced terrible demographic reverses. This meant that some bands living along the Atlantic coast were at a great disadvantage in dealing with the colonists; for them the threads of traditional culture were coming unraveled. Initial contact, therefore, did not involve a confrontation between two monolithic racial groups. Rather, members of particular tribes, some weakened by sickness, encountered representatives of specific Anglo-American charter societies.

Sustained contact with Europeans challenged native American cultures. Some early English settlers hoped to convert the Indians to Christianity, to persuade them to adopt European habits, and to lure them into an exchange of food and furs for imported goods. Native Americans—those who survived exposure to contagious diseases—reacted to the white man's blandishments in different ways. Indeed, meetings at trading posts and Christian missions should be perceived as creative encounters in which individual Indians accepted some offerings and rejected others. With specific regard to religious conversations, James P. Ronda writes, "Some Indians accepted the new religion and the new life-patterns it commanded. Others incorporated certain Christian elements into their lives while rejecting the essence of the white man's message. Most native Americans reaffirmed their traditional beliefs and strenuously resisted Christianity."[85] No two contexts were identical; each brought members of particular tribes into contact with representatives of distinct English charter societies.

During the seventeenth century—again the precise timing varied from region to region—the range of possible cultural variations was immense. South Carolinians wanted the Indians' bodies for the slave trade. Virginians wanted their lands. New Englanders wanted their souls as well as their lands. New Yorkers wanted their furs. And Marylanders do not appear to have wanted much of anything from their native American neighbors. On the Indians' part, one simply cannot distinguish a "typical" response to the English invaders. The Pequots, Powhatans, and Yamasees—just to cite familiar examples—resisted white advance and were destroyed. The Iroquois balanced competing European interests so successfully that their famed league endured long after other tribes had disappeared. The Piscataway of Maryland accommodated themselves to Lord Baltimore's colonists and thus managed throughout most of the seventeenth century not only to remain alive but also to preserve their cultural integrity.[86]

Borrowing between Indians and whites occurred within highly local contexts. Some whites—usually traders or adopted prisoners of war—found the Indian way of life so alluring that they took up permanent residence in native American villages. Considerably fewer Indians seem to have enthusiastically embraced white culture. For the most part, cultural exchange between members of these two groups involved technical skills that in no obvious way undermined either group's traditional beliefs and customs. Everyone knows the story of how Squanto taught the Pilgrims about the wonders of fish fertilizer. In the earliest days of settlement such incidents were relatively common. Indians taught English colonists how to make snowshoes, how to produce warm garments from pelts, how to find their way in the forest; in other words, they provided them with practical information for living in strange environments three thousand miles from home. Adoption of Indian customs did not threaten English culture. As Axtell explains, "The frontiersmen did not regard themselves as Indians nor did they appreciably alter their basic attitudes toward the native means they employed. If those means were regarded favorably, or at least no longer negatively, it was not because they were Indian but because they *worked* to effect the English conquest of the American environment."[87]

Indians regarded borrowing from the same utilitarian perspective as did white men. They immediately saw the value of metal goods, especially kettles and guns, and they adopted these items into their daily routine without second thought. It was when various Englishmen talked of distant schools and Protestant churches that native Americans became restless. Like Europeans, Indians entered into exchanges with representatives of the other culture chiefly with an eye towards material comfort. This independent turn of mind angered many colonists who assumed that their culture was so superior, so much an expression of God's plan, that any rational being would eagerly adopt it in entirety. When friendly persuasion failed to convert native Americans to this way of thinking, English sometimes employed force, but there is no evidence that coercion greatly increased the Indians' admiration for the nonmaterial aspects of Western culture.[88]

The important point is that in the early stages of colonization borrowing of some sort occurred whenever men and women encountered representatives of other races. So long as cultural boundaries remained relatively open, so long as cultural interaction remained a localized phenomenon, persons of different races displayed receptivity to new ideas, especially those related to material culture.

Creole societies. During the first half of the eighteenth century the peoples of America experienced a cultural transformation as great as that associated with the original transfer. Local "charter" societies began to merge into larger, racially defined "creole" societies. As they did so, patterns of cultural interaction changed profoundly. Many elements contributed to this cultural redefinition, but undoubtedly the most critical was the extraordinary expansion of the Anglo-American and Afro-American populations. Growth heightened cultural density. As these racial groups achieved the ability to maintain and then to expand their numbers through natural reproduction, a process that effected more frequent interaction among native-born adults, racial boundaries became more rigid. Especially in the southern colonies, earlier forms of cultural exchange—open, contingent negotiations based on a range of personal attributes—gave way to an ascriptive system in which people sorted themselves out according to the color of their skins. In fact, one could well argue that white racial prejudice—even racism—owes more to social, economic, and political developments that took place long after initial colonization than it does to general Old World notions about race and color.

During this period, Anglo-Americans increasingly became conscious of a shared cultural identity, a common set of values and beliefs connecting them to English men and women living in other localities. Several historians have drawn attention to this expanding cultural core. John Murrin describes the general standardization of procedures, tastes, and assumptions as the "Anglicanization" of early American society.[89] Anthropologist James Deetz refers to the same phenomenon as "re-Anglicanization."[90] But whatever we call this process, the inclusion first of colonial elites and then of more humble folk into a broad Anglo-American culture had far-reaching effects not only upon white people but also upon their dealings with persons of other races.[91] Curiously, Cornelius J. Jaenen believes a parallel transformation took place in eighteenth-century French Canada. "As the colony grew older and stronger," Jaenen explains, "efforts were made to fashion it more and more in the traditional cadres of the absolute monarchy, the Gallican church, mercantilism, and seigneurialism. . . . As New France became more like Old France it follows that the cultural gap between French and Amerindian widened rather than closed."[92]

The forces bringing about greater homogenization in Anglo-American cultures cannot be treated in detail here. A few, however, should be mentioned. First, English rulers centralized administration and standardized legal procedures. If nothing else, the language of commerce, government, and law became less provincial than it had been during the seventeenth century.[93] Second, the long imperial wars against France provided scattered English colonists with a common enemy, a foil that inevitably reinforced their Englishness even as they remained Virginians, Pennsylvanians, or New Englanders.[94] Third, the religious revivals of mid-century, especially George Whitefield's phenomenally successful American tours, broke down local cultural boundaries. In Pennsylvania, for example, evangelical religion actually strengthened main-line Protestant denominations and thereby incorporated persons dispersed over a large area into larger institutional structures. "As the Reformed and Lutheran churches gained strength," John B. Frantz points out, "the fluidity which had characterized religion among the Germans gave way to solidity based on distinctive doctrines and practices."[95]

Fourth, the eighteeenth century saw a tremendous increase in commerce not only between the various colonies and the mother country but also among the colonies themselves. The magnitude of the rise in intercolonial trade was striking. Marc Egnal estimates that during the middle decades of the century the percentage of tonnage bound for other mainland and Caribbean ports expanded in virtually every major American port. Egnal writes, "New England rum and fish, bread and flour from the middle colonies, corn from the upper South, and Carolina rice found a growing market in other colonies."[96] This developing coastal trade brought Anglo-Americans of quite different backgrounds into communication for the first time. They exchanged views and learned about each other's customs. Without these important commercial links, people living in Rhode Island and New York probably would not have learned in 1765 of Patrick Henry's famous speech protesting the Stamp Act, a momentous event that may have started Americans down the road towards independence.[97]

One final element stimulated the development of an expanded cultural core. White Americans of this period were caught up in a consumer revolution of unprecedented dimensions. English ships flooded colonial markets with manufactured goods of all sorts. The most common item appears to have been Staffordshire ceramics, which found their way into households from Maine to Georgia. Indeed, one might argue without great exaggeration that Staffordshire pottery was the "Coca-Cola" of eighteenth-century British

North America. The desire to purchase imports proved overwhelming. Next to English-made goods, local handicrafts seemed crude and unexciting even to those colonists least able to afford the English goods.[98] In his *Sketches of Eighteenth Century America* Crèvecoeur explained, "Another reason which keeps us in debt is the multiplicity of shops with English goods. These present irresistible temptations. It is so much easier to buy than it is to spin. The allurement of fineries is so powerful with our young girls that they must be philosophers indeed to abstain from them. Thus one fifth of all our labours every year is laid out in English commodities."[99]

None of these five factors had existed in the previous century. At this preliminary stage of our research, it is difficult to discern whether one was more important in effecting cultural transformation than the others. Together, however, they eroded local customs and identities and, in the words of Jack Greene, left "the separate colonies far more alike than they had ever been at any earlier time."[100]

The development of an expanded cultural core meant that white newcomers, migrants from the Old World, were no longer incorporated into distinct subcultures, as they had been in the seventeenth century. Rather, these men and women found themselves confronted with two quite different choices. They could move immediately to the frontier, as did many Ulster Scots, and attempt to create "charter" societies of their own.[101] Such enterprises rarely succeeded for long: with each passing year, it became more difficult to establish separate cultural enclaves, ethnic or religious sanctuaries sealed off from the influence of the Anglo-American world. Bernard Bailyn tells of Scottish migrants who located in Vermont, at that time one of the more isolated areas of colonial America. These people—a not atypical group—rapidly lost their ethnic distinctiveness. "Before the revolutionary war was over," Bailyn claims, "the settlers in that remote spot, once part of a distinctive cultural concentration, had dispersed, lost their identity as Scots, and had become simply a collection of rural New Englanders with families and friends in Scotland."[102]

The new immigrants could also embrace the dominant culture, learning English, changing diet, and altering dress. Certainly, many so-called Pennsylvania Dutch favored assimilation over separation. As Stephanie Wolf explains in her study of Germantown, these people undercommunicated cultural differences that might have frightened or angered their Anglo-American neighbors. In 1702, for example, one German advised his countrymen, "Do not stand upon your head, but take advice from the experience of others. In the mean time one need not act hastily, but await with patience the Divine dispensation, until one learns fully how to establish oneself according to the custom of the country."[103] Jon Butler finds a similar pattern among the Huguenots: within a single generation they had shed all attributes—except perhaps their names—that might have set them apart from the dominant English culture.[104]

The changing contexts of eighteenth-century life affected Afro-Americans both positively and negatively. Without doubt, the expansion of staple agriculture, now firmly tied to a world market, brought great misery to the entire slave population. The mechanisms of labor control on the plantations became crueler as they became more efficient. This was especially true of Jamaica, where absentee owners demanded ever higher returns on investments; since the technology of sugar production did not significantly improve during this period, profits had to be sweated out of black field hands, many of them men and women just imported from Africa. The Caribbean colonies were extreme cases. After all, in Jamaica the ratio of blacks to whites had reached ten to one by 1780.[105] But even in the southern mainland colonies, where the ratios were more balanced, a similar economic reordering took place. The rise of large rice and tobacco plantations, some worked by hundreds of slaves, bound Afro-Americans ever more tightly to the soil and to a monotonous agricultural routine.

But the planters' economic success transformed Afro-American cultures in ways that no one could have foreseen. In the mainland colonies the black population not only increased but also became much healthier. Men and women who would have died in the seventeenth century now lived, bore children, and formed extensive contacts with relatives living on neighboring plantations. Gradually, larger creole cultures began to replace isolated charter societies. The general process was analogous to that which the Anglo-Americans had experienced. Eighteenth-century whites created an expanded cultural core through trade and publication, itinerant ministers and marching armies. By contrast, contacts between Afro-Americans ranged over much smaller territories. The blacks were limited not only by their slavery but also by an oral culture that restricted them to face-to-face exchanges. Nevertheless, by the middle of the eighteenth century we can legitimately speak of regional Afro-American cultures each of which was bound by well-defined rules of kinship, shared rituals and customs, and creole languages. The most striking evidence of this cultural expansion comes from the Chesapeake colonies. As Allan Kulikoff declares, "The Afro-Americans made good use of these opportunities to create their own society. In the years before the Revolution, they developed a sense of community with other slaves both of their own plantation and in the neighborhood."[106] Ira Berlin and Michael Mullin, historians who have considered these developments in detail, analyze eighteenth-century Afro-American societies in terms of four broad regions: the northern colonies, the Chesapeake, the Lower South, and the Caribbean.[107]

The development of larger configurations based primarily upon skin color altered patterns of race relations throughout colonial America. The boundaries between the two groups were more rigidly drawn, in formal legal codes as well as in everyday practice, than they had been in the seventeenth century. With good reason, white colonists worried that black people would rise up and destroy their masters. Whenever rebellions—or threats of rebellion—

occurred, the reaction by the white community was swift and terrible. As Willie Lee Rose observes, the Stono revolt of 1739 provoked the South Carolina legislature to enact "a general 'Negro Act' lumping free blacks and slaves into one category, and prescribing speedy second-class justice for both. . . . South Carolina was on the way to an unenviable reputation as the mainland colony with the harshest slave code."[108] Certainly, English colonists did not attempt to romanticize the slave experience as southern writers did in the early nineteenth century. The great planters of British America generally saw the institution for what it was—nasty, brutal, oppressive, and not a little frightening. Under these conditions, creole blacks (except of course those who worked as domestics) had as little to do with whites as possible. With rare exception, this was obviously not an atmosphere conducive to creative cultural borrowing.

Relations between whites and Indians also changed dramatically during the course of the eighteenth century. As native Americans were either destroyed or driven from traditional lands, they ceased to be important in the lives of most colonial Americans. The early settlers had been forced to deal with local native Americans. Indians appeared frequently in the streets of Boston, New York, and Charles Town. But by the time of the American Revolution, it is doubtful that many farmers living along the Atlantic coast had ever seen an Indian. The decline of the fur trade further reduced the contact between the races. It is perhaps not surprising that the Indian was gradually transformed from a real human being, however alien or threatening he may have appeared, into an abstraction—the "noble savage." "His way of life," writes Ramsay Cook, "was an obstacle to agricultural production organized through private land ownership. His technology and skills, so important in the fur trade, were no longer in demand in the more diversified society. He rarely fitted into the new capitalist economy, even at the lowest level. In North America the proletariat also came from Europe."[109] Pan-Indian movements lay far in the future. For the moment, separate tribes, each hoping to corner the market on manufactured goods, each sustaining ancient rivalries against other native American groups, found themselves confronted with representatives of an expansive, unified Anglo-American culture determined to control the West.

How these transformations affected black-Indian relations is impossible to assess. Scholars have generally ignored this important topic, and there is no way to tell under what conditions members of the two races perceived each other as allies or enemies. Friction between blacks and Indians seems to have been most acute along the frontier. Some native Americans served as "slave catchers"; others owned black slaves.[110] By the same token, blacks assisted their white masters in fighting the bloody Indian wars that took place in South Carolina and Georgia.[111] However, there is another side to black-Indian relations. Indian communities within areas of white control—really reservations—contained a mixture of free blacks, runaway slaves, and surviving native Americans. These isolated, biracial societies developed throughout the mainland colonies and deserve much closer study than they have received so far.[112]

By the middle of the eighteenth century, but probably not before, one could reasonably describe American cultures in terms of color: red, white, and black. The openness of the seventeenth-century colonial frontier had spawned a number of promising experiments in cultural exchange. The charter groups gave way in the eighteenth century to larger, self-contained creole societies that were deeply suspicious of one another. It is tragic that poorer whites did not comprehend that they shared a common oppression with the blacks and Indians. With each passing decade throughout the English empire, their whiteness increasingly blinded them to the most daring, most creative forms of cultural adaptation.

NOTES

I thank James Axtell, Josef Barton, George Fredrickson, Chester Pach, and Ivor Wilks for their helpful suggestions on earlier drafts. I also want to express my gratitude to the Rockefeller Foundation, in whose Villa Serbelloni, at Bellagio, I revised sections of this essay.

1. Especially Melville J. Herskovits, *The Myth of the Negro Past* (Boston, 1941).

2. Two fine reviews of this literature are Peter H. Wood, "'I Did the Best I Could for My Day': The Study of Early Black History during the Second Reconstruction, 1960 to 1976," *William and Mary Quarterly*, 3d ser., 35 (1978): 185–225; and James Axtell, "The Ethnohistory of Early America: A Review Essay," ibid., 110–44.

3. Gary B. Nash, *Red, White, and Black: The Peoples of Early America* (Englewood Cliffs, N.J., 1974), 3.

4. For example, Gerald W. Mullin, *Flight and Rebellion: Slave Resistance in Eighteenth-Century Virginia* (New York, 1972); Peter H. Wood, *Black Majority: Negroes in Colonial South Carolina from 1670 through the Stono Rebellion* (New York, 1974); Nash, *Red, White, and Black*; James Axtell, *The European and the Indian: Essays in the Ethnohistory of Colonial North America* (New York, 1981); Michael Craton, *Searching for the Invisible Man: Slaves and Plantation Life in Jamaica* (Cambridge, Mass., 1978); Cornelius J. Jaenen, *Friend and Foe: Aspects of French-Amerindian Cultural Contact in the Sixteenth and Seventeenth Centuries* (New York, 1976); and Bruce G. Trigger, *The Children of Aataentsic: A History of the Huron People to 1660*, 2 vols. (Montreal, 1976).

5. The term "conversations" was suggested by Richard Rorty in *Philosophy and the Mirror of Nature* (Princeton, 1979). See also Anthony Giddens, *New Rules of Sociological Method: A Positive Critique of Interpretative Sociologies* (New York, 1976).

6. Alan Dawe, "Theories of Social Action," in *A History of Sociological Analysis*, ed. Tom Bottomore and Robert Nisbet (New York, 1978), 414. See also Fredrik Barth, "Introduction," in *Ethnic Groups and Boundaries: The Social Organization of Cultural Difference*, ed. Fredrik Barth (Boston, 1969); and James A. Henretta, "Social History as Lived and Written," *American Historical Review* 84 (1979): 1293–1322.

7. See George M. Fredrickson, *White Supremacy: A Comparative Study in American and South African History* (New York, 1981), chaps. 1–3.

8. A good example of the type of cultural analysis I am advocating is Gerald M. Sider, "The Ties That Bind: Culture and Agriculture, Property and Propriety in the Newfoundland Village Fishery," *Social History* 5 (1980): 1–40.

9. Robert F. Berkhofer, Jr., "The North American Frontier as Process and Context," in *The Frontier in History: North America and South Africa Compared*, ed. Howard Lamar and Leonard Thompson (New Haven, 1981), 45, See also Bruce G. Trigger, "Brecht and Ethnohistory," *Ethnohistory* 22 (1975): 51–56.

10. James Axtell, ed., *The Indian Peoples of Eastern America: A Documentary History of the Sexes* (New York, 1980), xviii; Robert F. Berkhofer, Jr., *The White Man's Indian: In Ages of the American Indian from Columbus to the Present* (New York, 1978), 3–4; Eleanor Burke Leacock and Nancy O. Lurie, eds., "Introduction," *North American Indians in Historical Perspective* (New York, 1971).

11. Trigger, *Children of Aataentsic*, 2:843 (emphasis added).

12. Neal Salisbury, *Manitou and Providence: Indians, Europeans, and the Making of New England, 1500–1643* (New York, 1982), 15.

13. Jaenen, *Friend and Foe*, 196.

14. Sidney W. Mintz and Richard Price, *An Anthropological Approach to the Afro-American Past: A Caribbean Perspective*, ISHI Occasional Papers on Social Change, no. 2 (Philadelphia, 1976), 1, 4–11; J. H. Parry, *The Age of Reconnaissance* (Cleveland, 1963), 277–79; Jerome S. Handler, Frederick W. Lange, and Robert B. Riordan, *Plantation Slavery in Barbados: An Archaeological and Historical Investigation* (Cambridge, Mass., 1978), 20–29.

15. Daniel C. Littlefield, *Rice and Slaves: Ethnicity and the Slave Trade in Colonial South Carolina* (Baton Rouge, 1981). For an interesting colonial account see Richard Ligon, *A True & Exact History of the Island of Barbados* (1657; reprint, London, 1970), 46.

16. Philip D. Curtin, *Economic Change in Precolonial Africa: Senegambia in the Era of the Slave Trade* (Madison, Wis., 1975); Michael Craton, "Jamaican Slavery," in *Race and Slavery in the Western Hemisphere: Quantitative Studies*, ed. Stanley L. Engerman and Eugene D. Genovese (Princeton, 1975), 265; Johannes Postma, "The Origin of African Slaves: The Dutch Activities on the Guinea Coast, 1675–1795," ibid., 33–50; Orlando Patterson, *The Sociology of Slavery: An Analysis of the Origins, Development and Structure of Negro Slave Society in Jamaica* (London, 1967), 113–44.

17. These observations are based upon my reading of *The Agrarian History of England and Wales*, vol. 4, *1500–1640*, ed. Joan Thirsk (Cambridge, 1967); Thomas Garden Barnes, *Somerset, 1625–1640: A County's Government during the "Personal Rule"* (Cambridge, Mass., 1961); Alan Everitt, *Change in the Provinces: The Seventeenth Century*, Department of English Local History Occasional Papers, 2d ser., 1 (Leicester, 1969); Peter Laslett, "The Gentry of Kent in 1640," *Cambridge Historical Journal* 9 (1948): 148–64; Keith Wrightson and David Levine, *Poverty and Piety in an English Village: Terling, 1525–1700* (New York, 1979); Peter Clark, *English Provincial Society from the Reformation to the Revolution: Religion, Politics, and Society in Kent, 1500–1640* (Hassocks, Eng., 1977); Margaret Spufford, *Contrasting Communities: English Villagers in the Sixteenth and Seventeenth Centuries* (Cambridge, 1974); Carl Bridenbaugh, *Vexed and Troubled Englishmen, 1590–1642* (New York, 1968); Mark A. Kislansky, "Community and Continuity: A Review of Selected Work on English Social History," *William and Mary Quarterly*, 3d ser., 37 (1980): 139–46; Peter Clark, "The Alehouse and the Alternative Society," in *Puritans and Revolutionaries: Essays in Seventeenth-Century History Presented to Christopher Hill*, ed. Donald Pennington and Keith Thomas (Oxford, 1979), 68; and John Morrill, "The Diversity of Local History," *Historical Journal* 24 (1981): 717–30.

18. Peter Clark and Paul Slack, *English Towns in Transition, 1500–1700* (Oxford, 1976), 1.

19. Clive Holmes, "The County Community in Stuart Historiography," *Journal of British Studies* 52 (1980): 54–73.

20. Sumner C. Powell, *Puritan Village; The Formation of a New England Town* (Middletown, Conn., 1963); John J. Waters, Jr., "Hingham, Massachusetts, 1631–1661: An East Anglian Oligarchy in the New World," *Journal of Social History* 1 (1967–68): 351–70; David Grayson Allen, *In English Ways: The Movement of Societies and the Transferal of English Local Law and Custom to Massachusetts Bay in the Seventeenth Century* (Chapel Hill, 1981); T. H. Breen, "Persistent Localism: English Social Change and the Shaping of New England Institutions," in *Puritans and Adventurers: Change and Persistence in Early America* (New York, 1980), 3–23. See also Bruce E. Steiner, "Dissension at Quinnipiac: The Authorship and Setting of a *Discourse about Civil*

Government in a New Plantation Whose Design Is Religion," *New England Quarterly* 54 (1981): 14–32; and Edmund S. Morgan, "The Labor Problem at Jamestown, 1607–18," *American Historical Review* 76 (June 1971): 595–611.

21. David B. Davis, *The Problem of Slavery in Western Culture* (Ithaca, N.Y., 1966); Winthrop D. Jordan, *White over Black: American Attitudes toward the Negro, 1550–1812* (Chapel Hill, 1968). See also William McKee Evans, "From the Land of Canaan to the Land of Guinea: The Strange Odyssey of the Sons of Ham," *American Historical Review* 85 (February 1980): 15–43.

22. David Beers Quinn, *The Elizabethans and the Irish* (Ithaca, N.Y., 1966); Nicholas P. Canny, *The Elizabethan Conquest of Ireland: A Pattern Established, 1565–76* (Hassocks, Eng., 1976).

23. Roy Harvey Pearce, *Savagism and Civilization: A Study of the Indian and the American Mind* (1953; reprint, Baltimore, 1971), 5. See also Edmund S. Morgan, *American Slavery—American Freedom: The Ordeal of Colonial Virginia* (New York, 1975), 1–70; Karen Ordahl Kupperman, *Settling with the Indians: The Meeting of English and Indian Cultures in America, 1580–1640* (Totowa, N.J., 1980); H. C. Porter, *The Inconstant Savage: England and the North American Indian, 1500–1660* (London, 1979); and Bernard W. Sheehan, *Savagism and Civility: Indians and Englishmen in Colonial Virginia* (Cambridge, 1980).

24. R. F. Romer, *Tilforledelig Efterretning om Kysten Guinea* (Copenhagen, 1790), 161–63.

25. William Bosman, *A New and Accurate Description of the Coast of Guinea . . .* (1705; reprint, London, 1967), 146. See also David Roediger, "The Meaning of Africa for the American Slave," *Journal of Ethnic Studies* 4 (1977): 1–16.

26. Trigger, *Children of Aataentsic*, 1:22–23.

27. Cornelius J. Jaenen, "Amerindian Views of French Culture in the Seventeenth Century," *Canadian Historical Review* 55 (1974): 261–91.

28. Nancy Oestreich Lurie, "Indian Cultural Adjustment to European Civilization," in *Seventeenth-Century America: Essays in Colonial History,* ed. James Morton Smith (1959; reprint, New York, 1972), 36–58; Axtell, *The European and the Indian,* chaps. 3, 4, 9, 10.

29. James Axtell, "Bronze Men and Golden Ages: The Intellectual History of Indian-White Relations in Colonial America," *Journal of Interdisciplinary History* 12 (1982): 666–67.

30. George M. Fredrickson, "Toward a Social Interpretation of the Development of American Racism," in *Key Issues in the Afro-American Experience,* ed. Nathan I. Huggins, Martin Kilson, and Daniel M. Fox, 2 vols. (New York, 1971), 1:240–54. See also Robert C. Twombly and Robert H. Moore, "Black Puritans: The Negro in Seventeenth-Century Massachusetts," *William and Mary Quarterly,* 3d ser., 24 (1967): 226.

31. Edmund S. Morgan, "The First American Boom: Virginia 1618 to 1630," *William and Mary Quarterly,* 3d ser., 27 (1971): 169–98; Breen, *Puritans and Adventurers,* chaps. 1 and 6.

32. Richard S. Dunn, *Sugar and Slaves: The Rise of the Planter Class in the English West Indies, 1624–1713* (Chapel Hill, 1972), 45. See also Carl Bridenbaugh and Roberta Bridenbaugh, *No Peace beyond the Line: The English in the Caribbean, 1624–1690* (New York, 1972); Craton, "Jamaican Slavery," 249; Patterson, *Sociology of Slavery,* 70.

33. Breen, *Puritans and Adventurers,* 127–47: T. H. Breen and Stephen Innes, *"Myne Owne Ground": Race and Freedom on Virginia's Eastern Shore, 1640–1676* (New York, 1980), 19–35.

34. John Porter, *The Vertical Mosaic: An Anlysis of Social Class and Power in Canada* (Toronto, 1965), 60.

35. See Carole Shammas, "English-Born and Creole Elites in Turn-of-the-Century Virginia," in *The Chesapeake in the Seventeenth Century: Essays on Anglo-American Society,* ed. Thad W. Tate and David L. Ammerman (Chapel Hill, 1979), 274–96; and Brathwaite, *Development of Creole Society,* 296–305. A general analysis of seventeenth-century English immigration patterns is Henry A. Gemery, "Emigration from the British Isles to the New World, 1630–1700: Inferences from Colonial Population," *Research in Economic History: A Research Annual* 5 (1980): 179–232.

36. Mintz and Price, *An Anthropological Approach,* 1–31; Craton, "Jamaican Slavery," 265; Littlefield, *Rice and Slaves;* Patterson, *Sociology of Slavery;* David Barry Gaspar, "The Antigua Slave Conspiracy of 1736: A Case Study of the Origins of Collective Resistance," *William and*

Mary Quarterly, 3d ser., 35 (1978): 308–23; Michael Mullin, "British Caribbean and North American Slaves in an Era of War and Revolution, 1775–1807," in *The Southern Experience in the American Revolution*, ed. Jeffrey J. Crow and Larry E. Tise (Chapel Hill, 1978), 235–67; Ira Berlin, "Time, Space and the Evolution of Afro-American Society in British Mainland North America," *American Historical Review* 85 (February 1980): 44–78; Allan Kulikoff, "The Beginnings of the Afro-American Family in Maryland," in *Law, Society and Politics in Early Maryland*, ed. Aubrey C. Land, Lois Green Carr, and Edward C. Papenfuse (Baltimore, 1977), 171–96; idem, "The Origins of Afro-American Society in Tidewater Maryland and Virginia, 1700 to 1790," *William and Mary Quarterly*, 3d ser., 35 (1978): 226–59. For general trends in the slave trade see Philip D. Curtin, *The Atlantic Slave Trade: A Census* (Madison, Wis., 1969).

37. See Mullin, *Flight and Rebellion;* and Patterson, *Sociology of Slavery*, 146.

38. Cited in Kulikoff, "Origins of Afro-American Society," 246.

39. Gaspar, "Antigua Slave Conspiracy," 319.

40. Mullin, *Flight and Rebellion*, 34–35.

41. See Ramsay Cook, "The Social and Economic Frontier in North America," in Lamar and Thompson, *The Frontier in History*, 175–208; and Allen W. Trelease, *Indian Affairs in Colonial New York: The Seventeenth Century* (Ithaca, N.Y., 1960).

42. An extremely suggestive study of this sort is Julian H. Steward, *The People of Puerto Rico: A Study in Social Anthropology* (Urbana, 1956).

43. Allen, *In English Ways;* Breen, *Puritans and Adventurers*, 68–80.

44. Dunn, *Sugar and Slaves*, 263–99; Michael Craton, *Sinews of Empire: A Short History of British Slavery* (Garden City, N.Y., 1974), 205–6.

45. Craton, *Searching for the Invisible Man*, 55.

46. Dunn, *Sugar and Slaves*, 256–62; Richard Price, ed., *Maroon Societies: Rebel Slave Communities in the Americas* (Garden City, N.Y., 1973).

47. *Handbook of North American Indians*, vol. 15, *Northeast*, ed. Bruce G. Trigger (Washington, D.C., 1978).

48. The literature on this topic is enormous. An excellent, provocative review of the most important work is John M. Murrin, "Review Essay," *History and Theory* 11 (1972): 226–75.

49. Morgan, "First American Boom;" Carville V. Earle, "Environment, Disease, and Mortality in Early Virginia," in Tate and Ammerman, *The Chesapeake in the Seventeenth Century*, 96–126.

50. Morgan, "First American Boom," 179–80; Breen, *Puritans and Adventurers*, 106–26; Irene W. D. Hecht, "The Virginia Muster of 1624/5 as a Source of Demographic History," *William and Mary Quarterly*, 3d ser., 30 (1973): 65–92.

51. Cary Carson, "Doing History with Material Culture," in *Material Culture and the Study of American Life*, ed. Ian M. G. Quimby (New York, 1978), 57.

52. Bridenbaugh and Bridenbaugh, *No Peace beyond the Line*, 101.

53. Lorena S. Walsh and Russell R. Menard, "Death in the Chesapeake: Two Life Tables for Men in Early Colonial Maryland," *Maryland Historical Magazine* 69 (1974): 211–27; Russell R. Menard, "Immigrants and Their Increase: The Process of Population Growth in Early Colonial Maryland," in Land, Carr, and Papenfuse, *Law, Society, and Politics*, 88–110; Lois Green Carr and Lorena S. Walsh, "The Planter's Wife: The Experience of White Women in Seventeenth-Century Maryland," *William and Mary Quarterly*, 3d ser., 34 (1977): 542–71; Daniel Blake Smith, "Mortality and Family in the Colonial Chesapeake," *Journal of Interdisciplinary History* 8 (1977–78): 403–27; Darrett B. Rutman and Anita H. Rutman, "'Now-Wives and Sons-in-Law': Parental Death in a Seventeenth-Century Virginia County," in Tate and Ammerman, *The Chesapeake in the Seventeenth Century*, 153–82.

54. Craton, "Jamaican Slavery," 267–68; Dunn, *Sugar and Slaves*, 313–30.

55. Patterson, *Sociology of Slavery*, 90; Ira Berlin, "The Slave Trade and the Development of Afro-American Society in English Mainland North America, 1619–1775," *Southern Studies* 20 (1981): 122–37: Stanley L. Engerman, "Comments on the Study of Race and Slavery," in Engerman and Genovese, *Race and Slavery*, 504; Wood, *Black Majority*, 95–130; Breen and Innes,

"Myne Owne Ground"; Morgan, *American Slavery—American Freedom*, 293–337; Craton, *Sinews of Empire*, 199–201.

56. Berlin, "The Slave Trade," 136; Mullin, *Flight and Rebellion*, chap. 1.

57. Craton, *Sinews of Empire*, 199. See also Dunn, *Sugar and Slaves*, 224–62; Cheryll Ann Cody, "A Note on Changing Patterns of Slave Fertility in the South Carolina Rice District, 1735–1865," *Southern Studies* 16 (1977): 458; and Kulikoff, "Origins of Afro-American Society."

58. Dunn, *Sugar and Slaves*, 250; Berlin, "Time, Space and the Evolution of Afro-American Society."

59. Calvin Martin, *Keepers of the Game: Indian-Animal Relationships and the Fur Trade* (Berkeley, 1978). A challenge to Martin's thesis is presented in Shepard Krech, ed., *Indians, Animals, and the Fur Trade: A Critique of "Keepers of the Game"* (Athens, Ga., 1981). See also Trelease, *Indian Affairs in Colonial New York*, 179.

60. George M. Fredrickson, "Review Essay," *New York Review of Books*, March 18, 1982, 51.

61. See Breen, *Puritans and Adventurers*, 75–77.

62. Morgan, *American Slavery—American Freedom*, 131–95; Wood, *Black Majority*, 13–66; Dunn, *Sugar and Slaves*, 15–83; Richard B. Sheridan, *Sugar and Slavery: An Economic History of the British West Indies, 1623–1775* (Baltimore, 1973).

63. Marquis de Chastellux, *Travels in North America*, ed. Howard C. Rice, Jr., 2 vols. (Chapel Hill, 1963), 2: 533.

64. Dunn, *Sugar and Slaves*, 110–16.

65. See T. H. Breen, "The Culture of Agriculture: The Symbolic World of the Tidewater Planter, 1760 to 1790," in *Saints and Revolutionaries: Essays in Honor of Edmund S. Morgan*, ed. David D. Hall, John M. Murrin, and Thad W. Tate (New York, 1983). See also Fernando Ortiz-Fernandez, *Cuban Counterpoint: Tobacco and Sugar* (New York, 1947).

66. Wood, *Black Majority*, 30–31, 105–6; Clarence L. Ver Steeg, *Origins of a Southern Mosaic: Studies of Early Carolina and Georgia* (Athens, Ga., 1975), 106–7.

67. Craton, *Searching for the Invisible Man*, 53–54; Eric Williams, "Race Relations in Caribbean Society," in *Caribbean Studies: A Symposium*, ed. Vera Rubin (Seattle, 1960), 54–60; Patterson, *Sociology of Slavery*, 75.

68. Jerome H. Wood, Jr., "The Negro in Early Pennsylvania: The Lancaster Experience, 1730–90," in *Plantation, Town, and Country: Essays on the Local History of American Slave Society*, ed. E. Miller and Eugene D. Genovese (Urbana, 1974), 441–52.

69. Cook, "Social and Economic Frontier," 175–208; David H. Corkran, *The Cherokee Frontier: Conflict and Survival, 1740–62* (Norman, Okla., 1962), 6–14.

70. Trelease, *Indian Affairs, in Colonial New York*, 179; James P. Ronda, "Generations of Faith: The Christian Indians of Martha's Vineyard," *William and Mary Quarterly*, 3d ser., 38 (1981): 369–94.

71. Breen and Innes, *"Myne Owne Ground,"* 7–18.

72. Ronda, "Generations of Faith."

73. James Axtell, "The Invasion Within: The Contest of Cultures in Colonial North America," in Lamar and Thompson, *The Frontier in History*, 268. See also Allen, *In English Ways*; Lurie, "Indian Cultural Adjustment," 58; Mintz and Price, *An Anthropological Approach*, 1–44; and Brathwaite, *Development of Creole Society*, 296, 307.

74. Michael Zuckerman, "The Fabrication of Identity in Early America," *William and Mary Quarterly*, 3d ser., 34 (1977): 194.

75. See G. B. Warden, "Law Reform in England and New England, 1620 to 1660," *William and Mary Quarterly*, 3d ser., 35 (1978): 668, 690; Breen, *Puritans and Adventurers*, 24–49; Stephen Foster, "The Faith of a Separatist Layman: The Authorship, Context, and Significance of *The Cry of a Stone*," *William and Mary Quarterly*, 3d ser., 34 (1977): 375–403; and idem, "New England and the Challenge of Heresy, 1630 to 1660: The Puritan Crisis in Transatlantic Perspective," ibid. 38 (1981): 624–60.

76. Powell, *Puritan Village*; Waters, "Hingham, Massachusetts"; T. H. Breen and Stephen

Foster, "The Puritans' Greatest Achievement: A Study of Social Cohesion in Seventeenth-Century Massachusetts," *Journal of American History* 60 (1973): 5–22.

77. Willie Lee Rose, *Slavery and Freedom* (New York, 1982), 155–56.

78. Mintz and Price, *An Anthropological Approach*, 26; Berlin, "The Slave Trade," 135–36; Craton, "Jamaican Slavery," 265; Jerome S. Handler and Charlotte J. Frisbie, "Aspects of Slave Life in Barbados: Music and Its Cultural Context," *Caribbean Studies* 11 (1972): 5–46.

79. Wood, *Black Majority*, 97; Berlin, "Time, Space and Evolution of Afro-American Society"; Morgan, *American Slavery—American Freedom*; T. H. Breen, "A Changing Labor Force and Race Relations in Virginia," in *Puritans and Adventurers*, 127–47.

80. Ver Steeg, *Origins of A Southern Mosaic*, 106–7.

81. Cited in Wood, *Black Majority*, 97.

82. Breen and Innes, "*Myne Owne Ground*," chaps. 1 and 6.

83. Wood, *Black Majority*, chap. 2.

84. Littlefield, *Rice and Slaves*, 177. See also Craton, *Sinews of Empire*, 210.

85. James P. Ronda, "'We Are Well As We Are': An Indian Critique of Seventeenth-Century Christian Missions," *William and Mary Quarterly*, 3d ser., 34 (1977): 67. See also Edmund S. Morgan, "The American Indian: Incorrigible Individualist," in *The Mirror of the Indian* (Providence, 1958).

86. James H. Merrell, "Cultural Continuity among the Piscataway Indians of Colonial Maryland," *William and Mary Quarterly*, 3d ser., 36 (1979): 548–59. See also Francis Jennings, *The Invasion of America: Indians, Colonialism, and the Cant of Conquest* (Chapel Hill, 1975).

87. Axtell, "The Indian Impact on English Colonial Culture," in his *The European and the Indian*, 272–316. See also Ronda, "Generations of Faith," 369–94; Alden T. Vaughan and Daniel K. Richter, "Crossing the Cultural Divide: Indians and New Englanders 1605–1763," *Proceedings of the American Antiquarian Society* 90 (1980): 23–99; and J. S. Otto and N. E. Anderson, "Slash-and-Burn Cultivation in the Highland South: A Problem in Comparative Agricultural History," *Comparative Studies in Society and History* 24 (1982): 136–38.

88. See Axtell, "The English Colonial Impact on Indian Culture," in his *The European and the Indian*, 245–71; Lurie, "Indian Cultural Adjustment," 36–58; and A. Irving Hallowell, "American Indians, White and Black: The Phenomenon of Transculturation," in his *Contributions to Anthropology* (Chicago, 1976), 498–518.

89. John M. Murrin, "Anglicizing an American Colony: The Transformation of Provincial Massachusetts" (Ph.D. diss., Yale University, 1966).

90. James Deetz, *In Small Things Forgotten: The Archeology of Early American Life* (Garden City, N.Y., 1977).

91. Jack P. Greene, "Search for Identity: An Interpretation of the Meaning of Selected Patterns of Social Response in Eighteenth-Century America," *Journal of Social History* 3 (1970): 216–18.

92. Jaenen, *Friend and Foe*, 197.

93. Allen, *In English Ways*, chap. 12; John M. Murrin, "The Legal Transformation: The Bench and Bar of Eighteenth-Century Massachusetts," in *Colonial America: Essays in Political and Social Development*, ed. Stanley N. Katz (Boston, 1971), 415–49; Stephen Botein, "The Legal Profession in Colonial North America," in *Lawyers in Early Modern Europe and America*, ed. Wilfred Prest (New York, 1981).

94. Douglas Edward Leach, *Arms for Empire: A Military History of the British Colonies in North America, 1607–1763* (New York, 1973), 110; Howard H. Peckham, *The Colonial Wars, 1689–1762* (Chicago, 1964).

95. John B. Frantz, "The Awakening of Religion among the German Settlers in the Middle Colonies," *William and Mary Quarterly*, 3d ser., 33 (1976): 286. See also Martin E. Lodge, "The Crisis of the Churches in the Middle Colonies," *Pennsylvania Magazine of History and Biography* 95 (1971): 195–220.

96. Marc Egnal, "The Economic Development of the Thirteen Continental Colonies, 1720 to

1775," *William and Mary Quarterly*, 3d ser., 32 (1975): 218. See also Gary M. Walton and James F. Shepherd, *The Economic Rise of Early America* (Cambridge, 1979), 87–88; David C. Klingaman, *Colonial Virginia's Coastwise and Grain Trade* (New York, 1975); Bernard Bailyn, "1776: A Year of Challenge—A World Transformed," *Journal of Law and Economics* 19 (1976): 447.

97. The classic account of the role of the newspapers in this event is Edmund S. Morgan and Helen M. Morgan, *The Stamp Act Crisis: Prologue to Revolution* (Chapel Hill, 1953), chap. 7. See also Bernard Bailyn and John B. Hench, eds., *The Press and the American Revolution* (Worcester, Mass., 1980).

98. Deetz, *In Small Things Forgotten*, chap. 3; Joan Thirsk, *Economic Policy and Projects: The Development of a Consumer Society in Early Modern England* (Oxford, 1978); Michael D. Coe, "The Line of Forts: Archeology of the Mid-Eighteenth Century on the Massachusetts Frontier," in *New England Historical Archeology*, ed. Peter Benes (Boston, 1977), 44–45.

99. St. John de Crèvecoeur *Sketches of Eighteenth-Century America*, ed. Henri Bourdin et al. (New Haven, 1925), 94.

100. Greene, "Search for Identity," 216–17.

101. See Carl Bridenbaugh, *Myths and Realities: Societies of the Colonial South* (Baton Rouge, 1952); and James G. Leyburn, *The Scotch-Irish: A Social History* (Chapel Hill, 1962).

102. Bailyn, "1776," 453.

103. Cited in Stephanie Grauman Wolf, *Urban Village: Population, Community, and Family Structure in Germantown, Pennsylvania, 1683–1800* (Princeton, 1976), 131.

104. Jon Butler, "The Ethnic Mirage: Defining and Testing Ethnicity and Religious Loyalty in a Pre-independent America" (Paper presented at the fourth annual meeting of the Social Science History Association, Cambridge, Mass., November 1–4, 1979).

105. Craton, "Jamaican Society," 254.

106. Kulikoff, "Origins of Afro-American Society," 253, 226–59. See also idem, "Beginnings of the Afro-American Family," 171–96.

107. Berlin, "The Slave Trade"; idem, "Time, Space and the Evolution of Afro-American Society"; Mullin, "British Caribbean and North American Slaves."

108. Rose, *Slavery and Freedom*, 161. See also Jordan, *White over Black*, chap. 3.

109. Cook, "Social and Economic Frontier," 181. See also Berkhofer, "North American Frontier," 49–51; Fredrickson, *White Supremacy*, 28, 39; and Corkran, *Cherokee Frontier*, 6–14.

110. R. Halliburton, Jr., "Black Slave Control in the Cherokee Nation," *Journal of Ethnic Studies* 3 (1975): 23–36; Craton, "Jamaican Slavery," 271; Price, *Maroon Societies*, 15–16; Wood, *Black Majority*, 52–53, 260–63.

111. William S. Willis, Jr., "Divide and Rule: Red, White, and Black in the Southeast," *Journal of Negro History* 48 (1963): 157–76.

112. See, for example, Karen I. Blu, *The Lumbee Problem: Making of an American Indian People* (Cambridge, 1980).

8

SOCIAL DEVELOPMENT

GARY B. NASH

he history of social development in colonial America—portrayed in this paper primarily as the history of social relations between groups of people defined by race, gender, and class—is in glorious disarray. Disarray because all of the old paradigms have collapsed under the weight of the last generation of scholarship. Glorious because a spectacular burst of innovative scholarship, the product of those who have crossed disciplinary boundaries, transcended filiopietism, and been inspired in the best sense by the social currents of their own times, has left us with vastly more knowledge of the first century and a half of American history than we ever had before. But the more we have found out about the social development of early America, the less able we are to fit this knowledge into any of the existing frameworks that heretofore have guided us—the Whig framework, the Progressive framework, or the Consensus framework. Hundreds of fresh building blocks have been fashioned, each of them representing a challenge to the structures of earlier architects, but no new master builder has appeared to create an edifice out of these handsome new construction materials.

Colonial social historians of the last generation have done the most exciting, ingenious empirical research that can be found for any period of American history. By severely limiting spatial and chronological sweep, they have illuminated particular aspects of life as it unfolded in dozens of communities along the Atlantic seaboard from the early seventeenth to the late eighteenth century. Scholarly care has been lavished especially on the New England town. One may now read about twenty Puritan community studies published in the last twenty years, and another dozen or more are seeking the light of print. The community-study infection has spread southward to the mid-Atlantic region, where the records of town, church, and family have succumbed to the imaginative gaze and clever computations of another group of social historians. It has moved also to the tobacco colonies of the

Chesapeake, where, substituting the county for the town, social historians have learned all the methodological lessons of their New England predecessors and done them several steps better. Only the rice coast has escaped the community-studies devotees, and surely it too will soon fall before their Gini coefficients, mortality calculations, family reconstitutions, and mobility measurements. But in all of these studies the sociological analysis, as opposed to the social, has been largely wanting. Sociological history—theoretically self-conscious history—"unfolds in a more grandiose fashion, peering down at large segments of the past from the lofty heights of imposing abstractions and generalization."[1] Its contribution is to analyze change broadly, to fathom the causes and nature of social development over extended periods of time.

So much creative work has been done during the last generation that it may seem that the time has arrived to build new models of social development. Yet this still may be premature because in spite of their many virtues, the innovative studies of the past two decades are so male-centered and oblivious to the black and native American peoples of colonial society that any new synthesis would necessarily be constructed with materials that present a skewed and incomplete picture of the social process in the prerevolutionary period.

If social development is defined as changing social relations between different groups in society, then the foundation of any such study must be rigorous analysis of the structural arrangements that did not strictly govern most human interaction but set the boundaries for it in the preindustrial period, as between masters and slaves, men and women, parents and children, employers and employees. Those relationships, moreover, must be examined within the context of a triracial society. This marks a fundamental difference between social development in England and America or in France and America. Of course other differences existed as well, but perhaps none was so great as that produced by the convergence of three broad cultural groups on the North American coastal plain in the seventeenth and eighteenth centuries. Some of the best work in colonial social history has been unmindful of this, drawing conceptually on European historical studies as if the colonies were pure offshoots of English society. While some inspiration can be drawn from the *Annales* school, the English Marxists, and other work accomplished at the macro- and micro-levels, we must regard the social development of colonial America as *sui generis* because of the triracial environment in which most colonists lived their lives. This racial intermingling had profound effects on the social formation of the colonies. Hence, in the years ahead colonial historians will be better advised to perfect their Spanish and Portuguese rather than their French and German. The work of the European historians will remain relevant to American historians, especially those studying the era of industrialization; but for the preindustrial era American historians will need to turn in a direction that has been consistently ignored for decades—the rapidly expanding social history of Spanish and Portuguese America.

Above structure is superstructure. Older arguments that the first determines the second or that base and superstructure are "separable concrete entities" are now passé.[2] Consciousness, cultural institutions, and ideology, it is widely agreed, are indissolubly a part of social development. While studies of social structure involving quantitative measurements stand out as one of the major achievements of the last generation of scholarship, a primary task for the next few decades is to reunite these contributions with studies of social change that deal with the transformations of value and consciousness, often expressed symbolically or ritually, that occurred in the colonial era. The advice of Raymond Williams, who calls for a "theory of social totality," is worth quoting at length. Williams pleads for revaluing "'determination' toward the setting of limits and the exertion of pressure, and away from a predicted, prefigured, and controlled content. We have to revalue 'superstructure' toward a related range of cultural practices, and away from a reflected, reproduced or specifically dependent content. And, crucially, we have to revalue 'the base' away from the notion of a fixed economic or technological abstraction, and toward the specific activities of men [and women], in real social and economic relationships, containing fundamental contradictions and variations and therefore always in a state of dynamic process."[3]

Presuming that it is the interaction of social structure and social consciousness—worked out in the confrontation of three broad cultural groups—that is the bedrock upon which a theory of social development in colonial America must be built, we must be mindful of regional distinctions. It is not to be believed that the social development of a region where male and female colonizers were roughly equivalent in number and where African slaves and Indian inhabitants were relatively few could evolve the same social relationships as a society where male colonizers greatly outnumbered female colonizers for four generations and where the ratio of white to black and white to red was drastically different than in the prior case. The discussion that follows therefore moves regionally from North to South, although for the sake of emphasis I have separated the discussion of Afro-American and native American social development from that of the European colonizers.

NEW ENGLAND

As many historians have noted, the wave of community studies of prerevolutionary New England make the several hundred thousand souls who lived in this region one of the most studied human populations in the annals of history. This is sometimes rationalized with the claim that the New England Puritan town was the prototypical American community. Yet, in terms of its social development, the New England town may be exceptional rather than typical of the early American experience. Especially in its transition to a market economy, a theme that will be resorted to on several occasions in this essay, it may have been the least dynamic region of the British mainland colonies. In its reliance upon free labor, mostly organized in family units, and in the depth of its attachment to communal values it was also atypical of the colonial experience. The point is not apparent in the work of a number of historians who have argued that the intrusion of individualistic, commercialized relations on a corporate, communalized ethos fermented the antinomian controversy in Boston in the 1630s, lay behind the witchcraft trials in Salem in the 1690s, gave meaning to the Great Awakening in many New England towns in the 1740s, partially inspired the American Revolution of the 1770s, and fueled the Second Great Awakening in the early 1800s. Taken together, these accounts make it appear that the transition to mercantile capitalism was occurring—and causing social trauma—at widely spread points in time within a region smaller than the state of North Dakota.[4] But much of the evidence in the New England community studies suggests that social change occurred very slowly. The inhabitants of the early Puritan towns were, in fact, much less peasant in outlook and behavior than Kenneth Lockridge would have us believe, experienced a longer and less divisive transition to a commercialized economy in the late seventeenth century than Paul Boyer and Stephen Nissenbaum portray, and by the end of the colonial era had witnessed less change in social relations than other regional populations in America.[5] In no part of North America, in fact, was rural England more faithfully recreated than in New England.[6]

This is not to argue that no alterations occurred but only that they were slower and more subtle than in other areas, leaving New England's communities unusually stable and relatively static in comparison with communities in other parts of colonial America. In the early years challenges to customary social relations may have been raised with what seemed frightening rapidity to the Puritan leaders by Mortonites, Gortonites, Hutchinsonians, Pequots, and Quakers, each with an alternate vision of how to structure society and mediate between different groups within it. But in each case the "outsiders" were bested and expelled without having affected the deeper-running social processes. Thus, a peculiar Puritan blend of participatory involvement within a hierarchically structured society of lineal families on small community-oriented farms perpetuated itself. The relatively fixed nature of this society owed something to the thin migratory flow into New England by other than English immigrants, the smallest flow in any area of English colonization. It owed much also to the visionary quality of Puritan ideology, the persistence of which was aided by the fact that New England remained a region populated by a culturally homogeneous people. Finally, the economic marginality of the region, which hindered commercial development and obviated the need for bound labor, ensured that New England's social development would change at an unimpressive pace compared with that in other areas.

No historian labors in the eye-straining, frustratingly incomplete, and sometimes nearly intractable sources of local records in order to prove the changelessness of the society he or she is studying. So nearly all of New England's community historians have emphasized change. Change there was, to be sure: demographic shifts at first in fertility, mortality, and marriage age, made possible in the founding generations by the general healthfulness of the climate and the wide availability of land that gave to the extended English family a durability greater than that of its English counterpart; changes in land prices, farm sizes, and patriarchal authority influenced by the new demographic contours; and changes from open-field to independent farming and from partible inheritance to primogeniture as the people-land ratio changed.[7]

In demonstrating these shifts the historians of early New England have made a major contribution, especially in the area of historical demography, where the old model of the extended English family evolving into the nuclear colonial family has been nearly stood on its head. Yet, while we now have a rich demographic history of New England, the economic history of the region is woefully underdeveloped. It is this gap in scholarship that has led to some exaggerated claims for social changes extending beyond the family to society at large. Very slowly, no doubt, the Puritan was becoming a Yankee, to invoke those two overused ideal types. Yet at the end of six generations of settlement social differentiation in the interior New England towns remained considerably less than in most other places in the Europeanized New World; the economy remained relatively underdeveloped; the threshold of expectations remained relatively fixed; and individualistic, opportunistic behavior was not nearly so pronounced as was continued attachment to family and community. New England was not so stable, so undifferentiated, so un-litigious, so religiously harmonious, or so consensual as Michael Zuckerman has argued; but the least favorable physical environment in eastern North America combined with the cultural restraints imposed by Puritanism to retard the advent of behavioral characteristics associated with the spread of the market economy in a way that sets New England off somewhat from the rest of the British mainland colonies.

Because New England's economy was ill-suited to the use of slave labor, except in a few areas such as the Narragansett region of Rhode Island, and because the native population was nearly eliminated by disease and war between 1615 and 1675, by the late seventeenth century the colonizers' society was left to develop relatively unaffected in formal ways by the cultures of non-Europeans.[8] Where New England's history did intersect with the history of "outside" forces was through its peoples' long involvement in a series of exhausting wars against the French in Canada and their Indian allies. These conflicts sapped the productive energies of New England's communities, inflicted casualty rates associated with modern wars, and dislocated the economy, especially in Massachusetts, in ways that produced social strain.[9] Still, so long as New Englanders could comprehend these wars as struggles of the people of light against the people of darkness, social development in the region was not significantly altered.

In summary, New Englanders had come from parts of England undergoing a transformation that involved widespread enclosure of land, unprecedented geographical mobility, widening social differentiation, and a quickening pace of commercial relations. In New England these developments were arrested for much of the seventeenth century as immigrants built a social system where family and community outweighed material acquisition, restless individualism was held in check, and the household mode of production remained the dominant form of economic existence. Over the fifteen decades separating the arrival of the Pilgrims from the beginnings of the American Revolution the morselization of land increased geographical mobility, widened social disparities, and eroded patriarchal authority. But in no place in colonial America did the earliest forms of social development—land use, social differentiation, labor force, mode of production, religious ideology, political institutions, legal codes, and moral discipline—remain so close to the founding patterns as in the *relatively* cohesive, *relatively* insular, and *relatively* homogeneous communities of New England.[10]

THE MID-ATLANTIC

If New England stands as the most homogeneous area in British America in the colonial period, the mid-Atlantic represented the most heterogeneous. This diversity has been noticed most frequently in terms of the ethnic and religious mosaics of New York and Pennsylvania, where religious sects flourished, ethnic enclaves proliferated, and a great commingling of different variants of transplanted European culture occurred. In New York this was so initially because of the cosmopolitan Dutch presence in the area, which was followed by English intrusion, Puritan migration, Huguenot and Jewish arrivals, and German and Scotch-Irish immigration. In Pennsylvania the founding English and Welsh Quakers ensured they they would be engulfed by other religions and ethnic stocks shortly after they grafted themselves onto the scattered Swedish, Finnish, and Dutch settlements by adopting an open-door policy to all newcomers, in vivid contrast to the New Englanders, who used rhetoric, law, and even the hangman's noose to keep outsiders from their doors.

This ethnic and religious heterogeneity in the mid-Atlantic was important to the pluralistic development of the region. But more vital were the forms of social organization imposed upon this temperate grain and cattle area by the founding colonizers of the region and by its basic ecology. If the New England way was to stress individual economic activity within communally oriented towns, the mid-Atlantic contained a variety of economic modes and social formations. In parts of New York and New Jersey some men aggrandized baronial estates and practiced a form of exploitative agrarian capitalism based on leasing land to hundreds of tenant farmers.[11] Though often called manor lords, most of them were more interested in land speculation and maximizing rental income than in exercising the privileges and responsibilities traditionally associated with feudal tenure. While landlordism may not have been as exploitative of tenant farmers as has sometimes been claimed, and while some farmers may have regarded tenantry as a necessary step on the road to a freehold farm, capitalistic manorialism nonetheless stunted the economic development of areas where it prevailed and introduced class disparities that were the most exaggerated for any rural area north of the Chesapeake.[12]

Within the same ecological zone, in other parts of New York and New Jersey and in Pennsylvania and northern Delaware, the social organization evolved very differently: towards a society of freeholders; a competitive market economy; a system of land use and transfer that stressed the commodity value of land; the considerable use of slave, indentured, and wage labor by individual owners of medium-sized farms; and a social ethos notable for the most fully articulated defense of self-interest in colonial America.[13] The prevailing ideal in this region was familial without being communal, so that most farmers were competitively involved in a market economy and many more than in New England utilized credit and purchased the bound labor of indentured servants and slaves.

These commercial farmers of the region watered by the Delaware and Susquehanna rivers engaged in no dramatic antinomian controversies or witchcraft trials, and even the Great Awakening there was mild by comparison with that in New England. Hence, we find little of the social conflict that is said to have been causally joined to the transition to a market economy in New England. Disputes with proprietors and their agents abounded, and Quaker Pennsylvania was wracked by the Keithian controversy in the early years of settlement. But chronic social division was not characteristic of the mid-Atlantic region. What stands out is the rapid settlement of the land by individual farmers, who rarely settled in towns and exhibited several of the key characteristics of a system of commercial agriculture—production of foodstuffs for an export market; purchase rather than home manufacture of cloth; high volume of turnover in land for speculative purposes; and investment in nonfamily labor, whether bound or free. The contrast in growth and development of these two northern regions is notable. Seven decades after it was founded, New England had a population of ninety-three thousand, which drew but little on an external labor supply and imported goods from England at a rate of about one pound per capita annually. Seven decades after its founding, the region embracing Pennsylvania, New Jersey, and Delaware contained about two hundred twenty thousand people who were heavily involved in the slave and indentured servant trade and imported from England nearly twice as much per capita as their New England counterparts. [14]

We will need many more community studies of the mid-Atlantic in the next decade before parity with the state of knowledge for New England is reached; but it is already apparent that real differences existed between the social development of most of New England (excluding parts of the Connecticut River Valley and the Narragansett region) and that of most of the mid-Atlantic region. These differences help reconcile the ongoing argument between James Lemon and James Henretta, two of the principal contributors to recent discussions of social evolution in early America. The argument is largely a false one because Henretta is mainly painting the New England scene, while Lemon is portraying the mid-Atlantic landscape. To be sure, the two regions were not altogether different. The lineal family was important in Pennsylvania, as in New England. Agricultural production for market was not unknown in Massachusetts or Connecticut; "traditional" values were not changeless in one area or entirely swept away in the other. But distinct patterns of social development occurred because the forms of economic existence varied, as did the ideological outlook, partly brought from the homelands of the respective settlers and partly remolded by conditions in the new land. Henretta believes that Lemon assumes "a false homogeneity in colonial society" but himself portrays "the historically distinct social and economic system that developed in America," as if all colonists traveled the same road towards a commercialized economy and at the same pace. [15]

At the heart of the problem, then, lies the dialectic between inherited cultural norms and economic systems brought to the New World and the transforming effects of colonizers' new environment. In the mid-Atlantic, as in New England, traditional values set limitations on how fast and in what ways social relationships changed. But the tempo and character of change depended in turn on the possibilities afforded by particular environments. Following Percy Bidwell, Henretta admits "a direct relationship between the material environment, on the one hand, and the consciousness and activity of the population on the other" and concludes that in America "acquisitive hopes had yielded to geographic realities," thus preserving the precommercial *mentalité*. [16] But geographic realities varied greatly between stony, thinsoiled New England and the rich alluvial soils of Pennsylvania which proved so wonderfully suited to grain production. It was not the "differential access to an urban and international market" that marked the mid-Atlantic off from New England but the productivity of the soils and the greater availability of cleared land in the early period of settlement. The latter fact, not yet fully studied, is likely explained by the pre-Columbian history of the region. Far more agricultural than their Algonkian counterparts of the more northerly latitudes, the native inhabitants of the mid-Atlantic had left far greater amounts of tillable soil to the European immigrants.

Nor did the cultural constraints circumscribing "the extent of involvement in the market economy" apply with equal force in New England and the mid-Atlantic. Puritan communalism kept its grip on New Englanders far longer than did the weaker Quaker communalism of Pennsylvania and New Jersey, partly because the environment itself in New England was less conducive to the breaking out of a bourgeois ethos and partly because New England attracted, or permitted, far fewer non-Puritan immigrants than Pennsylvania attracted, or recruited, non-Quaker newcomers. Even the communally oriented Germans of Pennsylvania make a frail reed upon which to base an argument for resistance to a commercialized, commoditized culture, because the Moravian and Mennonite sectarians represented only a small fraction of the entire pool of newcomers after 1715, which was heavily composed of Scotch-Irish and nonsectarian Germans.

Thus, while Henretta's argument for the persistence of a precommercial ethos has substantial relevance for New England (the maritime towns, the Connecticut River Valley, and the Narragansett country excepted), Lemon's model is more appropriate for the mid-Atlantic. It is likely that additional local studies will show that there the rate of land transfer was higher, social differentiation proceeded faster, per capita accumulation of goods was substantially higher, farmers produced more extensively for external markets, and the bourgeois mentality, less restrained by the community ideal, was developed more fully by the time of the Revolution.

With deeper research the different patterns of social development in New England and the mid-Atlantic may also make better sense of the contrasting resonances of the Great Awakening in the two regions, which in itself offers clues to the course of deeper-running social changes. The much greater intensity of the Awakening in New England can be partly accounted for by the stronger grip that millennialism always had in the region of colonial America that maintained its cultural insularity longest and thus kept alive the sense of providential mission. But the searing force of the Awakening in New England is also attributable to the incipient strain produced by economic marginality (rather than by the transition to capitalism), a disordered monetary system, growing poverty in the port towns, and a series of debilitating wars between 1675 and 1763. The flame-throwing itinerant evangelist James Davenport never preached in Lancaster, Pennsylvania, or Albany, New York; but it seems unlikely that he could have touched off the emotional explosions that occurred when he scorched the townspeople of New London, Connecticut, and Boston, Massachusetts. The Great Awakening in the middle colonies emerged from doctrinal differences within the Presbyterian and Dutch Congregational churches and served primarily to reach a large number of people who were poorly ministered to, if served at all by the established clergy. In New England thousands who had been on the fringes of organized religious activity "flew to Christ"; but a far greater number were swept into the evangelical net because of the precariousness of their position—an insecurity that now could be expressed through the vehicle of religion, which, amidst an ethos of community and cultural homogeneity, was more appropriate than the vehicle of politics. Militant and evangelical Protestantism was best suited to the people in British America who had best maintained their religious and ethnic unity, who were geographically contiguous to the French papist enemy, and who inhabited the least hospitable physical environment along the North American coastal plain.

THE SOUTH

In the Chesapeake and along the rice coast of South Carolina and Georgia local societies developed so differently than in either the mid-Atlantic or New England that they may be designated hinterlands of exploitation rather than of settlement.[17] Three interlocking factors governed the unique development of these areas: first, the peculiarly dismal demographic history of the seventeenth-century South; second, the rapid growth of export-propelled economies; and third, the heavy reliance on bound labor. A spectacular burst of empirical research, almost all of it appearing since 1965, has reshaped our understanding of the colonial South's unique social development and the extent to which it differed from northern social evolution in ways that go far beyond the contrasts implied in the hallowed dichotomy of Cavalier and Yankee.

The last decade of scholarship has nearly reversed the old characterization of the South as precapitalist and neofeudal because it lacked economic diversification and developed a partriarchal planter class whose members supposedly buried capital in the creation of an ostentatious plantation life instead of ploughing it back into productive use. Chesapeake historians, by delving into the economic history of the Chesapeake tobacco coast—in contrast to the New England community historians, who have only scratched the surface of this subject—have pieced together a comprehensive picture of the interaction between cultural traditions and physical environment. These studies portray Chesapeake settlers building a highly exploitative and capitalist economy far more rapidly than did settlers in New England, if we can judge this transition by the rapidity of land exchange, the rise of land speculation, the commoditization of labor, the movement from subsistence to commercial agriculture, and the use of deficit spending to increase production.[18]

The new history of the Chesapeake stresses the development of a staple crop, in wide demand in the metropolitan area, as an engine of growth. Tobacco filled this function for Virginia, Maryland, and southern Delaware in the seventeenth century. Initially, high prices for the leaf spurred investments in the development of the region, which led to large importations of white bound labor and the rapid expansion of output. Over the course of the seventeenth century tobacco prices declined sharply, but for producers this was offset by lower costs in producing, transporting, and marketing the crop. As tobacco prices dropped, the nicotine addiction fell within reach of a broader range of consumers; and even though the limits of the English market had been reached by about 1680, creating a period of stagnation for about three decades, the eighteenth century brought a dizzying new expansion of the market, as France became a major consumer of Chesapeake-produced sotweed.

Subject to booms and depressions far more intense than fluctuations in the northern agricultural sector, Chesapeake tobacco growers became mainland America's foremost users of credit instruments and were the most deeply involved in the international marketplace. With roughly the same population as New England, the Chesapeake colonies exported to and imported from England commodities with aggregate values from six to ten times greater than those imported and exported by their northern counterparts.[19] Even if New England's trade volume is doubled to reflect its extensive participation in the West Indies economy (remembering that the Chesapeake–West Indies commerce, although very considerable, has hardly been studied), the difference in the degree of commercialization in the two regions is marked.

The far more dynamic character of the Chesapeake economy has sometimes been shrouded because so much emphasis has been given to the southern reliance on bound as against free labor, a factor that for some historians disqualifies the region's economy as capitalistic. In fact, it was the ability of southern planters to procure and control a large and unfree labor force— reversing the historical rise of free labor in early modern Europe—that led to a rate of growth, market orientation, and accumulation of wealth that outstripped the performance of New England.[20] The factors that led to changing this labor force from primarily white indentured servants in the seventeenth century to primarily African slaves in the eighteenth has now been pieced together in a skillful examination of both the supply and the demand side of the phenomenon.[21]

One of the major accomplishments of the Chesapeake social historians has been to show how the rapid development of an economy that increased tobacco exports from fifteen million pounds in 1670 to one hundred million pounds in 1770 occurred amidst ghastly demographic conditions that contrast severely with those in other parts of English America. Mortality rates in the seventeenth-century Chesapeake colonies were probably twice as high as New England's in this period. The region also suffered a badly skewed ratio of males to females that left more than half the males womanless for most of the century. These two factors, fearful mortality and a wildly unbalanced sex ratio, produced a dismally low fertility rate, probably not one-fourth of New England's. Yet the population of the Chesapeake grew as rapidly as New England's because of an immigration rate that dwarfed that of the Puritan colonies.[22] New Englanders in the second half of the seventeenth century were mostly the children and grandchildren of healthy, fertile founding immigrants; in the same period Marylanders and Virginians were mostly newly arrived immigrants replacing the sickly and infertile settlers of earlier years.

Social development within a society so demographically sterile and socially mobile but so economically dynamic could not help but differ drastically from northern patterns. First, the labor force was predominatly young, predominantly male, and predominantly unmarried for most of the seventeenth century. Second, by the end of the seventeenth century southern society was relying increasingly on black slave labor. Between 1690 and 1770 the Afro-American population of the South grew from about 13,000 to 410,000. Hence, the advent of a less transitory and more family-centered white society in the South, marked by decreased white immigration, lower mortality rates, more balanced sex ratios, and family formation, occurred simultaneously with the adoption of a labor force that required massive coercion and intimate interracial contacts.[23] Third, because the plantation system was based on dispersed holdings of land, where capital and labor were concentrated as nowhere else on the mainland, the rules governing the supervision of the labor force tended to be set individually by employer-owners rather than by local instruments of government as in New England and the mid-Atlantic. Fourth, the rapidly expanding staple economy produced a much more stratified social system than in the North, with a small number of extremely wealthy planters, who owed their fortunes to land speculation as well as tobacco production; a comparatively shriveled middle class, kept small because of the difficulties for small producers to compete with large planters, the domination of artisan work by black slaves, and the general absence of towns; a sizable white tenant class, which in both absolute and relative terms was growing in the eighteenth century; and a massive number of slaves, who constituted from 40 to 60 percent of the total population in various regions of the South on the eve of the Revolution.

Relying increasingly on chattel slavery in the eighteenth century, this staple-producing society was marked by greater volatility and violence than historians have usually recognized. The substitution of black slave labor for white indentured labor at first seemed to promise differently. The tobacco coast in the 1660s and 1670s seethed with discontent, as servants, who had obligingly died off before serving their term of service during the era when English adventurers launched the tobacco economy, began to live longer and form a class of landless, impoverished, socially blocked, and armed freemen—the stuff of which frontier Indian wars and civil rebellions are made. By relocating their reservoir of servile labor from the impoverished rural villages of England and Ireland to the villages of West Africa while at the same time turning internal class tensions into external violence against native occupiers of fertile land, late-seventeenth-century southern colonizers were able to forge a consensus among upper- and lower-class whites. With new land available through dispossession of Indians, and the pipeline carrying new indentured servants shut down, lower-class southern whites became aspiring landowners, desirious of owning their own black bondsmen and bondswomen, and thus emerged as a stabilizing force in the eighteenth-century plantation society rather than a source of disequilibrium as in the seventeenth. Race became the primary badge of status in a world that heretofore had relied primarily on religious and economic distinctions in creating lines of social stratification.[24]

Despite its promise of allowing for social development free of class tension, racial slavery could only temporarily mend rifts in white society. In fact, the new availability of land following the Chesapeake Anglo-Indian war of 1675–76 and the greater degree of family formation as sex ratios became more balanced in the late seventeenth century were powerful dissolvents of the social acids that ate at the fabric of society in Bacon's and Culpepper's rebellions in the 1670s. Far from narrowing rifts in white society, however, slavery greatly enhanced the class power of the large planters, leading to a concentration of wealth and political leverage and, as it evolved into its patriarchal form in the eighteenth century, allowing the planter to extend his dominance over family, including secondary wives and illicit offspring, poor kin, and neighboring smallholders.[25] But power derived from extensive landholdings and fields full of gang laborers had its limits. Even the creation of a white solidarity myth, which "asserted the unity of the free population, the oneness of those who owned slaves and those who did not" and "assured those whose importance had been reduced, whose labor had been cheapened, that they shared with the slaveholder a fundamental superiority," could not prevent the rise of tensions within white society.[26] By the mid-eighteenth century these tensions were manifesting themselves, and they would continue to rive southern society during the Revolution, when a much larger part of the lower class in the South than in the North turned out under the colors of the loyalists rather than fight alongside a patriot planter class. More delving into this topic is needed, especially for North Carolina and South Carolina, where social historians have only begun to make inroads, but there are signs in recent research that the pressures for racial solidarity among whites were breaking down in the eighteenth century.[27] Comparatively hidden from sight because they frequently took the form of social banditry or localized disruptions rather than being played out on the public stage of provincial politics, the incipient divisions riddling the southern colonies were much greater than in New England or the middle colonies. Social cohesion, attachment to community, the mediating role and moderating effects of local institutions, and a vision of a larger purpose were all attenuated in the staple economies of the South. To no small extent this was related to the peculiar demographic history of the region, where the unbalanced sex ratio, redressed only after four generations, produced a male-centered rather than a family-centered society and an extremely high population turnover, which made attachment to community and social stability elusive. Zuckerman may sometimes have confused the ideal with the real in his study of New England's eighteenth-century communities, but surely the agricultural villages he studied *were* "peaceable kingdoms" compared with either the tidewater or the piedmont counties of Virginia, Maryland, or the Carolinas, all of which lacked most of the centripetal forces operating in the North.

Social volatility and endemic violence in the South also owed much to Indian-white relations. It is customary to think of the South as a much more biracial society than the North, but it was also more triracial. The interaction with small coastal tribes in the early period of settlement was not very different in the two regions. In both cases European diseases did their deadly work, and the remaining strokes were delivered in a series of wars that culminated in both New England and the Chesapeake in 1675. The Euro-Indian confrontation in the Carolinas produced similar results in a different way: the pitting of one local tribe against another for the purposes of primitive accumulation and a disencumbering of the land through an Indian slave trade.[28]

A major North-South difference evolved, however, in relations between the colonizers and the powerful, populous interior tribes. Northern colonists competed little for the land of the Iroquois, since they were valued as trading partners and since it was widely understood that to push them into the arms of the French was suicidal. In the South the Creeks and Cherokees stood in a different relationship to the coastal settlers. Their trade was valued, as was their political neutrality, given Spanish pretensions in this part of the world; but by the eighteenth century the rapid growth of the settler population and the expanding export market for staples such as rice, indigo, and tobacco caused covetous eyes to turn towards native lands. Moreover, holding in bondage a slave population that after 1690 was tripling every twenty-five years in Virginia and Maryland and quadrupling in South Carolina, white colonizers warily regarded the Creeks and Cherokees as providers of refuge for escaping slaves and even as potential coconspirators with blacks against the white population. One solution was to pit the Creeks and Cherokees against each other in a game of double elimination. Another was to render them both dependent on the English through the trade connection. Whatever the strategy, the colonizers of the South were more continuously, intimately, and violently involved in exploiting the Indian societies of their region than were their counterparts in New England or the mid-Atlantic. The mixing of gene pools and cultural traits was also more extensive in the South than elsewhere, affecting social development in ways that historians have only begun to explore.

In sum, environment triumphed over imported cultural traditions more completely than in any other region. The result was a highly developed system of extracting an economic surplus through the coercion of an internal black labor force and the fitfully successful manipulation of an external labor force of indigenous people. This process proceeded all the faster because the

southern colonists lacked widely shared assumptions about a controlling social ideal, such as characterized New England's communities. Nonetheless,
the social development of the South did in time produce ideological constructs peculiar to the region. New expectations and new labor processes
emerged amidst ecological conditions far different than in the North and
eventually gave birth to an ideology that legitimized and gave a veneer of
respectability to the highly exploitative economic system based on the racial
division of labor.

In New England, it may be said, institutions such as religious ideology,
participatory local government, and a town form of settlement greatly restrained economic ambition, which in any case was dampened by the geographical realities of the region. Amid different geographical realities, southern colonizers cast away restraining ideologies and institutions, developed a
labor process unknown in England, and gradually articulated an ideology of
racial paternalism.

THE CITIES

Even though only about 5 percent of the eighteenth-century colonizers
lived in cities (and none of these cities exceeded sixteen thousand in 1750 or
thirty thousand in 1776), the commercial capitals of British North America
were the cutting edge of social change. Almost all the alterations that have
been discussed so far first occurred in the seaports and then radiated outward
to the villages, farms, and plantations of the hinterland.

In the half-century between 1690 and 1740 Boston, New York, and Philadelphia blossomed into commercial centers that rivaled such British provincial ports as Hull, Bristol, and Glasgow. This urban growth reflected the
development of the hinterlands to which they were symbiotically linked.
Gradually these seaports—along with others such as Newport, Providence,
Baltimore, Annapolis, Norfolk, and Charleston—were drawn into the international marketplace, which included not only England, Scotland, and Ireland but also Newfoundland, the West Indies, Africa, and the Iberian penin-
sula. Increasingly a part of an Atlantic world, urban merchants, politicians,
and even artisans made economic decisions in consonance with an emerging
commercial ethic that was eroding traditional restraints on entrepreneurial
activity.[29]

That the cities stood at one end of a continuum of social develoment can be
seen in the rate of geographical mobility, the distribution of wealth, the
rapidity of property transfer, the extent of poverty, the level of investment in
bound and wage labor, and the reliance on modern credit instruments. All of
these phenomena have been examined in some detail in recent years, although the lesser port towns and the inland marketing centers still largely
await study.[30] Persistence rates, for example, which according to Lockridge

were as high as 99 percent in seventeenth-century Dedham, were much
lower in the cities, where as much as 10 percent of the population annually
were in- or out-migrants. The wealth profile in the maritime centers was
much more asymmetrical than in rural areas, with the top 10 percent of the
urban wealthholders typically holding about 70 percent of the wealth,
whereas in northern farming communities at mid-eighteenth century they
usually controlled about 40 percent. Those without property typically constituted about 30 percent of the adult males in farming areas of the North by
the time of the Seven Years' War but nearly double that percentage in the
urban centers. Bound labor—black slaves and white indentured servants—
filled roughly half of the laboring roles of the commercial ports at the end of
the colonial period but less than one-quarter of them in the northern
countryside.[31]

Another mark of urban social development was occupational specialization
and the rise of the professions. In every farming village of the North and on
most large southern plantations a variety of artisans practiced their crafts.
But in the seaboard commercial centers the occupational range increased
enormously, not only because shipbuilding and metalworking flourished but
because crafts such as shoemaking and furniture making were divided into
subspecialities in the eighteenth century. While artisans in twenty-seven
different trades resided in Germantown, Pennsylvania, on the eve of the
American Revolution, for example, more than eighty skills were denoted on
the tax lists of nearby Philadelphia. Likewise, the urban centers became
professional seedbeds because they contained the major institutions of culture and higher learning, which rapidly increased in number during the
prerevolutionary generation; a majority of the colonial lawyers, whose profession grew in tandem with urban commercial development; most of the
government officials, whose ranks swelled with the increase in imperial authority in the eighteenth century; and more than their share of clergymen.[32]
The growing density of social institutions, which was occurring everywhere
in the eighteenth-century colonies but happened most extensively in urban
areas, signaled the maturation of colonial society and played a vital role in the
ability of the colonists to concert themselves politically and militarily when
the imperial crisis erupted following the end of the Seven Years' War.

The spread of the entrepreneurial ethic in the eighteenth century, which
was most noticeable in the commercial centers, where upper artisans as well
as merchants and shopkeepers threw off traditional notions of political economy, was accelerated by the European wars into which the colonies were
drawn. The effect of these international conflicts on colonial social development has gone largely unnoticed and represents one of the important areas of
research ahead. But it is evident, taking King George's War as an example,
that New England was drained of manpower and resources as its inhabitants
engaged in costly attempts to overcome the French enemy to the north.

However, the war also offered opportunities for merchants and others to conduct business on a scale hitherto unknown and to amass profits through lucrative war contracts and privateering. Becoming more stratified by wealth and differentiated by occupation, urban people came to think of themselves as belonging to economic groups that did not always share common goals, began to behave in class-specific ways in response to events that impinged upon their well-being, and manifested ideological points of view and cultural differences peculiar to their rank. This is not to say that all carpenters or all merchants occupied the same position along the spectrum of wealth, or that all ship captains or all ship caulkers thought alike, or that upper-class city dwellers consistently opposed lower-class city dwellers because they occupied different social niches. Evidence is abundant that vertical consciousness was always present in a society where movement up and down the social ladder never stopped and where the natural tendency of economic networks was to create a common interest, as among merchant, shipbuilder, and mariner. Nonetheless, movement between ranks and vertical linkages that were a part of a system of economic clientage could not prevent horizontal bonds from growing stronger. People who had previously thought of themselves as belonging to the lower, middling, or upper ranks but had seen no reason why this should imply incipient social conflict gradually came to associate these rough identifiers of social standing with antagonistic interests and made these differences the basis for political contention.[33]

Much more work needs to be done on the cities before these tendencies can be fully comprehended. Little is yet known about the productive and reproductive lives of urban women. Urban economic networks and economic clientage need further study, as do the phenomena of cultural hegemony wielded from above and deference yielded from below—modes of behavior that may have pertained to the rural populations of the eighteenth century more than the urban.

One aspect of urban development that troubled many contemporaries was the impoverishment of a substantial part of the population of the northern seaports. In part the growth of poverty was a side effect of the mid-century wars that extended over eighteen of the twenty-four years between 1739 and 1763. Casualty rates in these conflicts exceeded those of twentieth-century wars and left in their wake large numbers of disabled men, as well as larger numbers of widows with dependent children, who became the labor force of the first textile factories in America, conceived not out of entrepreneurial inspiration but out of despair at the climbing poor rates and bulging almshouses. Since colonial armies were recruited mainly from the lower classes, and since the cities contained a disproportionate number of propertyless and marginal persons, the urban centers became scenes of considerable suffering at the end of these wars.[34]

The discovery of urban poverty has altered the thinking of some historians about social development in the eighteenth century. For many years it was assumed that progress was almost automatic in the thriving commercial centers of America. We now know differently. In the cities poverty challenged the governing modes of thought, shook confidence in the internal economic system, led to sharp questioning of the imperial relationship, and intensified class feeling. "He that gets all he can honestly, and saves all he gets (necessary Expenses excepted)," Poor Richard counseled, "will certainly become RICH." Such advice, for a growing number of urban dwellers, was only salt on wounds that were not self-inflicted. No amount of exhortation could convince the laboring poor of the relevancy of maxims written in an era of full employment and higher real wages than existed in the period following the end of the Seven Years' War. Out of the grievances of the urban laboring classes came much of the social force that saw in Revolution the possibility of creating a new social order.

Most of the tendencies associated with the development of a bourgeois society are most noticeable in the colonial commercial centers: the transition from an oral to a literate culture, from an organic to an associational patterning of human relationships, from a moral to a market economy, from ethnically and religiously homogeneous to heterogeneous communities, from roles assigned by ascription to roles gained by achievement, and from a communal to an individualistic orientation. In the work that lies ahead, however, it is important that these work pairings not entrap us in the much used model of decline, which, as Thomas Bender points out, traces the movement from gemeinschaft to gesellschaft in terms of decay, declension, dissolution, and disintegration of "community." Enough has been discovered about the dynamics of social development in diverse seventeenth- and eighteenth-century locales to keep historians mindful that communities change at different rates of speed, sometimes in different directions, not always in unilinear fashion, and rarely with all members of the community cleaving to the same values and responding identically to the same stimuli. Bender aptly asks: "Why cannot gemeinschaft and gesellschaft simultaneously shape social life," for both are "forms of human interaction that can act reciprocally on each other"?[35] We may ask also whether homogeneity is the *sine qua non* of community and whether the concept of *pro bono publico* is the only glue of social relations. Even in the seaport towns, where social development carried colonial people closest to the world we call modern, where stratification was most pronounced, population mobility greatest, the market orientation strongest, the concept of self-interest most widely accepted, and the populace the most heterogeneous in terms of ethnicity, occupation, and religion, communities existed and thrived. This is not to say that there was no social conflict. But conflict is not the same as decline or decay. In future work historians may better construct new paradigms of social change by concentrating on social process—the story of people struggling to create, oppose,

defend, and legitimize new circumstances and new structural realities—
rather than by nostalgically documenting the eclipse of community.

NATIVE AMERICANS

Ideally, a discussion of the role of native American societies in the social
development of eastern North America should be regionally organized because there was no unified "Indian" experience and the various tribal histories that ethnohistorians have reconstructed are closely related to the histories
of European colonizers in particular areas.[36] But space limitations permit
only some general remarks about the underdeveloped field of native American history and its connection to the history of the colonizers. It is important
to differentiate between coastal and interior tribes: even though disease and
warfare thoroughly ravaged the numerous seaboard tribes by the third generation of settlement in any colony, these small societies profoundly affected
the shaping of settler communities.

The process of decimation, dispossession, and decline among the Indian
societies of their coastal areas occurred in different ways during the first
century of European colonization. Everywhere that Europeans settled, a
massive depopulation occurred as the invaders' diseases swept through bio-
logically defenseless native societies. Yet this rarely broke the resistance of
the native peoples. In New England that occurred only after the stronger
coastal tribes, such as the Wampanoags and Narragansetts, finally succumbed in a long war of attrition to an enemy who sought no genuine
accommodation. In Virginia and Maryland the tidewater tribes genuinely
strove for accommodation following their unsuccessful resistance movements
of 1622 and 1644. But, as in New England, their inability to function in any
way that served European society finally led to conflict initiated by whites.
Even as a friendly colonized people they were obstacles in the path of an
acquisitive and expanding plantation society. In South Carolina it was not
dead Indians but Indians alive and in chains that benefitted the white settlers. The build-up of the colonizer population was slow enough, and the
desire among the Indians for trade goods intense enough, that the white
Carolinians, most of them transplanted from Barbados, where they had
learned to trade in human flesh, could lure the coastal tribes into obliterating
each other in the wars for slaves.[37]

The result was roughly the same in all the colonies along the seaboard. By
the 1680s in the older colonies and by the 1720s in the new ones the coastal
tribes were shattered. Devastated by disease and warfare, the survivors either incorporated themselves as subjects of stronger inland groups or entered
the white man's world as detribalized servile dependents. Their desire for
European trade goods, which kept them in close contact with European

colonizers, and the persistence of ancient intertribal hostilities, which thwarted pan-tribal resistance, sealed their fate once the growth of the settler population made it apparent that their value as trading partners was incidental in comparison with the value of the land that their destruction would convert to European possession.

Although they were defeated, the coastal cultures served a crucial function for tribes farther inland. Their prolonged resistance gave interior societies time to adapt to the European presence and to devise strategies of survival as the white societies grew in size and strength. "People like the Iroquois," T. J. C. Brasser has pointed out, "owed a great deal to the resistance of the coastal Algonkians, and both peoples were well aware of this."[38] The coastal tribes provided a buffer between the interior Indians and the Europeans, and when the coastal tribes lost their political autonomy, their remnants were often incorporated into the larger inland tribes. This was important in the much stronger opposition that the Iroquois, Cherokees, and Creeks offered to European encroachment—a resistance so effective that for the first century and a half of European settlement the white newcomers were restricted to the coastal plain, unable to penetrate the Appalachians, where the interior tribes, often allied with the French, held sway.

During the first half of the eighteenth century the interior Indian societies demonstrated their capacity for adapting to the presence of Europeans and for turning economic and political interaction with them to their own advantage. Drawing selectively from European culture, they adopted through the medium of the fur, skin, and slave trade European articles of clothing, weapons, metal implements, and a variety of ornamental objects. To some extent this incorporation of material objects robbed the Indians of their native skills. But agriculture, fishing, and hunting, the mainstays of Indian subsistence before the Europeans came, remained so thereafter. European implements such as the hoe only made Indian agriculture more efficient. The knife and fishhook enabled the natives to fish and trap with greater intensity in order to obtain the commodities needed in the barter system. However, pottery making declined, and the hunter became more dependent upon the gun.

Yet, interaction with European societies over many generations sowed seeds of destruction within tribal villages. It is not necessary to turn Indians into acquisitive capitalists to explain their desire for trade goods. They did not seek guns, cloth, kettles, and fishhooks out of a desire to become part of bourgeois culture, accumulating material wealth from the fur trade, but because they recognized the advantages, within the matrix of their own culture, of goods fashioned by societies with a more complex technology. The utility of the Europeans' trade goods, not the opportunities for profit provided by the fur trade, drew native Americans into it, and from the Indian point of view, trade was carried on within the context of political and social alliance.[39]

Nonetheless, the fur trade required native Americans to reallocate their human resources and reorder their internal economies. Subsistence hunting turned into commercial hunting, and consequently males spent more time away from the villages trapping and hunting. Women were also drawn into the new economic organization of villages, for the beaver, marten, or fox had to be skinned and the skins scraped, dressed, trimmed, and sewn into robes. Among some tribes the trapping, preparation, and transporting of skins became so time-consuming that food resources had to be procured in trade from other tribes. Ironically, the reorientation of tribal economies towards the fur trade dispersed villages and weakened the localized basis of clans and lineages. Breaking up in order to be nearer the widely dispersed trapping grounds, Indian villagers moved closer to the nomadic woodland existence that Europeans had charged them with at the beginning of contact.

Involvement in the fur trade also altered the relationship of native Americans to their ecosystem. The tremendous destruction of animal life triggered by the advent of European trade undermined the spiritual framework within which hunting had traditionally been carried out and repudiated the ancient emphasis on living in balance with the natural environment. Trade also broadened vastly the scale of intertribal conflict. With Europeans competing for client tribes who would supply furs to be marketed throughout Europe, Indian societies were sucked into the rivalry of their patrons. As furs became depleted in the hunting grounds of one tribe, they could maintain the European trade connection only by conquering more remote tribes whose hunting grounds had not yet been exhausted or by forcibly intercepting the furs of other tribes as they were transported to trading posts. Thus, the Iroquois decimated the Hurons of the Great Lakes region in the mid-seventeenth century as part of their drive for beaver hegemony.[40]

While the interior tribes were greatly affected by contact with the colonizers, they nonetheless rejected much of what the newcomers presented to them as a superior way of life. Tribes such as the Iroquois, Creeks, and Cherokees were singularly unimpressed with most of the institutions of European life and saw no reason to replace what they valued in their own culture with what they disdained in the culture of others. This applied to the newcomers' political institutions and practices, system of law and justice, religion, education, family organization, and childrearing practices. Many aspects of Indian life were marked by cultural persistency in the long period of interaction with Europeans. Indian societies incorporated what served them well and rejected what made no sense within the framework of their own values and modes of existence.

Despite their maintenance of their traditional culture in many areas of life, the native Americans' involvement in the European trade network hastened the spread of epidemic diseases, raised the level of warfare, depleted ecozones of animal life, and drew Indians into a market economy that over a long period of time constricted their economic freedom. The interior tribes re-organized productive relations within their own communities to serve a trad-ing partner who, through the side effects of trade, became a trading master.

Social development within the British mainland colonies proceeded in some unexpected ways because of the Indian presence. Unable to coordinate themselves militarily and politically in the first 150 years of settlement, English colonizers were unable to conquer or dislodge from their tribal homelands—as did their Spanish counterparts to the south—the powerful interior native American societies. Hence, the settlers' societies, restricted to the coastal plain, developed differently than if they had been free to indulge their appetite for land and their westward yearning. Higher mortality rates associated with the spread of epidemic diseases in more densely settled areas, the rise of tenantry in rural areas, underemployment in the cities at the end of the colonial period, the decline of indentured servitude because of the grow-ing pool of landless free laborers, and the rise of class tensions in older seaboard communities are some of the social phenomena that may be at-tributed in part to the limitations placed upon westward movement by the controlling hand of the major eastern tribes in the trans-Allegheny and even the Piedmont region. The native American was also of primary importance in forging an "American" identity among English, Scotch-Irish, German, and other European immigrants in North America. In their relations with the native people of the land the colonizers in British North America served a long apprenticeship in military affairs. Far more populous than the settlers of New France and therefore much more covetous of Indian land, they engaged in hundreds of military confrontations ranging from localized skirmishes to large-scale regional wars. The allegiance of the diverse immigrants to the land, the annealing of an American as distinct from an English identity, had much to do with the myriad ways in which the colonists interacted with a people who were culturally defined as "the others" but were inextricably a part of the human landscape of North America.[41]

AFRO-AMERICANS

Unless we wish to continue picturing some one million Africans brought to or born in America before the Revolution as mindless and cultureless drones, it will be necessary to push forward recent work on the social devel-opment of black society and then to incorporate this new corpus of scholar-ship into an overall analysis of colonial social development. It bears noting that a large majority of the persons who crossed the Atlantic to take up life in the New World in the three hundred years before the American Revolution were Africans. Their history is still largely untold because so much attention has been paid to the kind of slave systems Europeans fashioned in the New World—the black codes they legislated, their treatment of slaves, the economic development they directed—that the slaves themselves, as active participants in a social process, are often forgotten.

In attempting to remedy this gap, historians have borrowed heavily from the work of anthropologists. The encounter model of Sidney Mintz and Richard Price, developed with reference to the Caribbean world, is especially useful because it explores how Africans who found themselves in the possession of white masters five thousand miles from their homeland created institutions and ways of life that allowed them to live as satisfactorily as possible under the slave regimen imposed upon them by the master class. In their New World encounter with European colonizers the problem was not one of merging a West African culture with a European culture because the human cargoes aboard slave ships were not a single collective African people but rather a culturally heterogeneous people from many tribes and regions. Hence, arriving slaves did not form "communities" of people at the outset but could only become communities through forging a new life out of the fragments of many old cultures combined with elements of the dominant European culture that now bounded their existence. "What the slaves undeniably shared at the outset," according to Mintz and Price, "was their enslavement; all—or nearly all—else had to be created by them."[42]

Recently, major strides have been taken in tracing this process of social adaptation in the Chesapeake region and along the rice coast of South Carolina and Georgia, though much remains to be done.[43] Already, it is apparent that in this process of adaptation there was a premium on cultural innovation and creativity, both because slaves had to adjust rapidly to the power of the master class and because of the initial cultural heterogeneity of the Africans. Unlike the European colonizers, Africans were immediately obliged "to shift their primary cultural and social commitment from the Old World to the New." This required rapid adaptation, learning new ways of doing things that would ensure survival. It is not surprising, therefore, that Africans developed local slave cultures rather than a unified Afro-American culture. In adapting to North American slavery, they adopted "a general openness to ideas and usages from other cultural traditions, a special tolerance (within the West African context) of cultural differences."[44] Of all the people converging in seventeenth- and eighteenth-century North America, the Africans, by the very conditions of their arrival, developed the greatest capacity for cultural change.

The complexity of black culture in America cannot be understood without considering the evolution of distinct, regional black societies as they developed over the long course of slavery.[45] One of the accomplishments of the new social historians of the colonial South is to have broken much new ground on the life cycle, family formation, and cultural characteristics of the black population, which was increasingly creole, or American-born, as the eighteenth century progressed. This new work makes it possible already to go beyond earlier studies of slave life in the colonies, which were based largely on studies of nineteenth-century sources, when discussing the development of Afro-American society in the eighteenth-century colonies.

How much of African culture survived under eighteenth-century slavery is an oft-debated question. There can be little doubt that slave masters were intent on obliterating every Africanism that reduced the effectiveness of slaves as laborers and that they had some success in this. It is also true that slavery eliminated many of the cultural differences among slaves, who came from a wide variety of African cultural groups—Fulanis, Ibos, Yorubas, Malagasies, Ashantis, Mandingos, and others. At the same time, it must be remembered that throughout the eighteenth century, unlike in the nineteenth, large numbers of new Africans arrived each year. Slave importations grew rapidly in the eighteenth century, so that probably never more than half the adult slaves were American-born. This continuous infusion of African culture kept alive many of the elements that would later be transmuted almost beyond recognition. Through fashioning their own distinct culture within the limits established by the rigors of the slave system, blacks were able to forge their own religious forms, their own music and dance, their own family life, and their own beliefs and values. All of these proved indispensable to survival in a system of forced labor. All were part of the social development of black society. And all affected the social development of white society as well.

WOMEN

One final aspect of social development, occasionally alluded to in this essay but indispensable to the work that lies ahead, concerns social relations defined by gender. In the last ten years and especially in the last four or five, a wave of new work has appeared, some of it defined as women's history and some as demographic or family history.[46] This new work shows how rich the possibilities are for those who wish to study the lives of women and female-male relationships. It is crucial to the construction of new paradigms of social development that these studies of women's productive and reproductive lives, which need to be studied with class, racial, and regional differences in mind, be pushed forward at an accelerated pace and then integrated with the studies of the much better understood male half of the population. It is out of the convergence of the already completed demographic and community studies and the studies of women, blacks, and native Americans still remaining to be done that a new understanding of the social development of colonial American will emerge.

NOTES

1. Bryan D. Palmer, *A Culture in Conflict: Skilled Workers and Industrial Capitalism in Hamilton, Ontario, 1860–1914* (Toronto, 1979), xiv.

2. Raymond Williams, *Marxism and Literature* (Oxford, 1977), 81.

3. Raymond Williams, "Base and Superstructure in Marxist Cultural Theory," *New Left Review*, no. 82 (1973): 5–6.

4. Michael Zuckerman, "The Fabrication of Identity in Early America," *William and Mary Quarterly*, 3d ser., 34 (1977): 183–84; Thomas Bender, *Community and Social Change in America* (New Brunswick, N.J., 1978), 47–49.

5. Kenneth A. Lockridge, *A New England Town: The First Hundred Years, Dedham, Massachusetts, 1636–1736* (New York, 1970); Paul Boyer and Stephen Nissenbaum, *Salem Possessed: The Social Origins of Witchcraft* (Cambridge, Mass., 1974).

6. Sumner C. Powell, *Puritan Village: The Formation of a New England Town* (Middletown, Conn., 1963); David Grayson Allen, *In English Ways: The Movement of Societies and the Transferal of English Local Law and Custom to Massachusetts Bay in the Seventeenth Century* (Chapel Hill, 1981).

7. Among the major community studies that wrestle with these changes, utilizing various methodologies, are: Powell, *Puritan Village;* Charles S. Grant, *Democracy in the Connecticut Frontier Town of Kent* (New York, 1961); John Demos, *A Little Commonwealth: Family Life in Plymouth Colony* (New York, 1970); Philip J. Greven, *Four Generations: Population, Land, and Family in Colonial Andover, Massachusetts* (Ithaca, N.Y., 1970); Lockridge, *New England Town;* Darrett B. Rutman, *Winthrop's Boston: Portrait of a Puritan Town, 1630–1649* (Chapel Hill, 1965); Richard L. Bushman, *From Puritan to Yankee: Character and the Social Order in Connecticut, 1690–1765* (Cambridge, Mass., 1967); Robert G. Pope, *The Half-Way Covenant: Church Membership in Puritan New England* (Princeton, 1969); Michael Zuckerman, *Peaceable Kingdoms: New England Towns in the Eighteenth Century* (New York, 1970); Darrett B. Rutman, *The Husbandmen of Plymouth: Farms and Villages in the Old Colony, 1620–1692* (Boston, 1967); Boyer and Nissenbaum, *Salem Possessed;* Paul R. Lucas, *Valley of Discord: Church and Society along the Connecticut River, 1636–1725* (Hanover, N.H., 1976); Richard P. Gildrie, *Salem, 1626–1683: A Covenant Community* (Charlottesville, 1975); Robert A. Gross, *The Minutemen and Their World* (New York, 1976); and Patricia J. Tracy, *Jonathan Edwards, Pastor: Religion and Society in Eighteenth-Century Northampton* (New York, 1979).

8. The Puritan-Algonkian interaction in the first generations of settlement is treated from radically differing perspectives in Alden T. Vaughan, *New England Frontier: Puritans and Indians, 1620–1675* (Boston, 1965); Francis Jennings, *The Invasion of America: Indians, Colonialism, and the Cant of Conquest* (Chapel Hill, 1975); and Neal E. Salisbury, *Manitou and Providence: Indians, Europeans, and the Making of New England, 1500–1643* (New York, 1982).

9. Gary B. Nash, *The Urban Crucible: Social Change, Political Consciousness, and the Origins of the American Revolution* (Cambridge, Mass., 1979), chaps. 3–10.

10. This characterization is most explicitly argued in T. H. Breen and Stephen Foster, "The Puritans' Greatest Achievement: A Study of Social Cohesion in Seventeenth-Century Massachusetts," *Journal of American History* 60 (1973): 5–22; John J. Waters, Jr., "The Traditional World of the New England Peasants: A View from Seventeenth-Century Barnstable," *New England Historical and Genealogical Register* 130 (1976): 3–21; idem, "Patrimony, Succession, and Social Stability: Guilford, Connecticut in the Eighteenth Century," *Perspectives in American History* 10 (1976): 131–60; idem, "Family, Inheritance, and Migration in Colonial New England: The Evidence from Guilford, Connecticut," *William and Mary Quarterly*, 3d ser., 39 (1982): 64–86; and Christopher M. Jedrey, *The World of John Cleaveland: Family and Community in Eighteenth-Century New England* (New York, 1979).

11. Rowland Berthoff and John M. Murrin, "Feudalism, Communalism, and the Yeoman Freeholder: The American Revolution Considered as a Social Accident," in *Essays on the American Revolution*, ed. Stephen G. Kurtz and James H. Hutson (Chapel Hill, 1973), 263–76.

12. Cf. Sung Bok Kim, *Landlord and Tenant in Colonial New York: Manorial Society, 1664–1775* (Chapel Hill, 1978); and Edward Countryman, *A People in Revolution: The American Revolution and Political Society in New York, 1760–1790* (Baltimore, 1981), chaps. 1–3.

13. James T. Lemon, *The Best Poor Man's Country: A Geographical Study of Early Southeastern Pennsylvania* (Baltimore, 1972); Stephanie Grauman Wolf, *Urban Village: Population, Community, and Family Structure in Germantown, Pennsylvania, 1683–1800* (Princeton, 1976); Patricia U. Bonomi, "The Middle Colonies: Embryo of the New Political Order," in *Perspectives on Early*

American History: Essays in Honor of Richard B. Morris, ed. Alden T. Vaughan and George Athan Billias (New York, 1973), 63–92; Jerome H. Wood, Jr., *Conestoga Crossroads: Lancaster, Pennsylvania, 1730–1790* (Harrisburg, Pa., 1979).

14. U.S. Bureau of the Census, *Historical Statistics of the United States: Colonial Times to 1970,* 2 vols. (Washington, D.C., 1975), 2:1168, 1176–77. The mid-Atlantic data are for Pennsylvania.

15. "Mr. Henretta Replies:" *William and Mary Quarterly,* 3d ser., 37 (1980): 696–97.

16. James A. Henretta, "Families and Farms: *Mentalité* in Pre-Industrial America," *William and Mary Quarterly,* 3d ser., 35 (1978): 14; see also James T. Lemon, "Early Americans and Their Social Environment," *Journal of Historical Geography* 6 (1980).

17. The terms are taken from Lloyd Best, "Outlines of a Model of Pure Plantation Economy," *Social and Economic Studies* 17 (1968): 285–87.

18. Jacob M. Price, *France and the Chesapeake: A History of the French Tobacco Monopoly, 1674–1791, and of Its Relationship to the British and American Tobacco Trades,* 2 vols. (Ann Arbor, 1973); Carville V. Earle, *The Evolution of a Tidewater Settlement System: All Hallow's Parish, Maryland, 1650–1783* (Chicago, 1975); Russell R. Menard, "Secular Trends in the Chesapeake Tobacco Industry, 1617–1710," *Working Papers from the Regional Economic History Research Center* 1 (1978); Paul G. E. Clemens, *The Atlantic Economy and Colonial Maryland's Eastern Shore: From Tobacco to Grain* (Ithaca, N.Y., 1980).

19. Bureau of the Census, *Historical Statistics of the United States, Colonial Times to 1970,* 1168, 1176–77.

20. Aubrey C. Land, "Economic Base and Social Structure: The Northern Chesapeake in the Eighteenth Century," *Journal of Economic History* 25 (1965): 639–54; idem, "Economic Behavior in a Planting Society: The Eighteenth-Century Chesapeake," *Journal of Southern History* 33 (1967): 469–85.

21. T. H. Breen, "A Changing Labor Force and Race Relations in Virginia, 1660–1710," *Journal of Social History* 6 (1973): 3–25; Edmund S. Morgan, *American Slavery—American Freedom: The Ordeal of Colonial Virginia* (New York, 1975); Russell R. Menard, "From Servants to Slaves: The Transformation of the Chesapeake Labor System," *Southern Studies* 16 (1977): 355–90; Lois Green Carr and Russell R. Menard, "Immigration and Opportunity: The Freedman in Early Colonial Maryland," in *The Chesapeake in the Seventeenth Century-Essays on Anglo-American Society,* ed. Thad W. Tate and David L. Ammerman (Chapel Hill, 1979), 206–42.

22. Herbert Moller, "Sex Composition and Correlated Cultural Patterns," *William and Mary Quarterly,* 3d ser., 11 (1945): 415–42; Lorena S. Walsh and Russell R. Menard, "Death in the Chesapeake: Two Life Tables for Men in Early Colonial Maryland," *Maryland Historical Magazine* 69 (1974): 211–27; Morgan, *American Slavery—American Freedom;* Darrett B. Rutman and Anita H. Rutman, "Of Agues and Fevers: Malaria in the Early Chesapeake," *William and Mary Quarterly,* 3d ser., 33 (1976): 31–60; Carville V. Earle, "Environment, Disease, and Mortality in Early Virginia," in Tate and Ammerman, *The Chesapeake in the Seventeenth Century,* 96–125.

23. Daniel Blake Smith, "Mortality and Family in the Colonial Chesapeake," *Journal of Interdisciplinary History* 8 (1977–78): 403–27; Lorena S. Walsh, "'Til Death Us Do Part': Marriage and Family in Seventeenth-Century Maryland," in Tate and Ammerman, *The Chesapeake in the Seventeenth Century,* 126–52.

24. William McKee Evans, "Race, Class and Myth in Slaveholding Societies" (Paper presented at a meeting of the Southern Historical Association, Louisville, Ky., 1981).

25. For the rise of patriarchalism see Daniel Blake Smith, *Inside the Great House: Planter Family Life in Eighteenth-Century Chesapeake Society* (Ithaca, N.Y., 1980); Gerald W. Mullin, *Flight and Rebellion: Slave Resistance in Eighteenth-Century Virginia* (New York, 1972), chap. 1; T. H. Breen, "Horses and Gentlemen: The Cultural Significance of Gambling among the Gentry of Virginia," *William and Mary Quarterly,* 3d ser., 34 (1977): 239–57; Jack P. Greene, *Landon Carter: An Inquiry into the Personal Values and Social Imperatives of the Eighteenth-Century Virginia Gentry* (Charlottesville, 1965); and Rhys Isaac, *The Transformation of Virginia, 1740–1790: Community, Religion, and Authority (Chapel Hill, 1982).*

26. Evans, "Race, Class, and Myth."

27. Ronald Hoffman, *A Spirit of Dissension: Economics, Politics, and the Revolution in Maryland* (Baltimore, 1973); David Curtis Skaggs, *Roots of Maryland Democracy, 1753–1776* (Westport, Conn., 1973); Rhys Isaac, "Evangelical Revolt: The Nature of the Baptists' Challenge to the Traditional Order in Virginia, 1765 to 1775," *William and Mary Quarterly*, 3d ser., 31 (1974): 345–68; Gregory A. Stiverson, *Poverty in a Land of Plenty: Tenancy in Eighteenth-Century Maryland* (Baltimore, 1977); Marvin L. Michael Kay, "The North Carolina Regulation, 1766–1776: A Class Conflict," in *The American Revolution: Explorations in the History of American Radicalism*, ed. Alfred F. Young (De Kalb, Ill., 1976), 71–123; Rhys Isaac, "Preachers and Patriots: Popular Culture and the Revolution in Virginia," in ibid., 125–56; Ronald Hoffman, "The 'Disaffected' in the Revolutionary South," in ibid., 273–316; Richard R. Beeman and Rhys Isaac, "Cultural Conflict and Social Change in the Revolutionary South: Lunenburg County, Virginia," *Journal of Southern History* 46 (1980): 525–50; Richard R. Beeman, "Social Change and Cultural Conflict in Virginia: Lunenburg County, 1746 to 1774," *William and Mary Quarterly*, 3d ser., 35 (1978): 455–76.

28. Verner W. Crane, *The Southern Frontier, 1670–1732* (Durham, 1929).

29. Carl Bridenbaugh, *Cities in the Wilderness: The First Century of Urban Life in America, 1625–1742* (New York, 1938); idem, *Cities in Revolt: Urban Life in America, 1743–1776* (New York, 1955); Jacob M. Price, "Economic Function and the Growth of American Port Towns in the Eighteenth Century," *Perspectives in American History* 8 (1974): 123–86; Carville V. Earle and Ronald Hoffman, "Staple Crops and Urban Development in the Eighteenth-Century South," ibid. 10 (1976): 7–78; Carville Earle, "The First English Towns of North America," *Geographical Review* 67 (1977): 34–50; Nash, *Urban Crucible*.

30. See, however, Wolf, *Urban Village*; and Wood, *Conestoga Crossroads*.

31. The many studies on wealth distribution in the colonial period are recapitulated in Alice Hanson Jones, *The Wealth of a Nation to Be: The American Colonies on the Eve of the Revolution* (New York, 1980); and Peter H. Lindert and Jeffrey Williamson, *American Inequality: A Macro-economic History* (New York, 1980), chap. 1. For migration see Douglas L. Jones, *Village and Seaport: Migration and Society in Eighteenth-Century Massachusetts* (Hanover, N.H., 1981). For bound labor in the cities see Gary B. Nash, "Slaves and Slaveowners in Colonial Philadelphia," *William and Mary Quarterly*, 3d ser., 30 (1973): 223–56; and Sharon V. Salinger, "Colonial Labor in Transition: The Decline of Indentured Servitude in Late Eighteenth-Century Philadelphia," *Labor History* 22 (1981): 165–91.

32. On lawyers see John M. Murrin, "The Legal Transformation: The Bench and Bar of Eighteenth-Century Massachusetts," in *Colonial America: Essays in Politics and Social Development*, ed. Stanley N. Katz (Boston, 1971), 415–49; and William E. Nelson, *Americanization of the Common Law: The Impact of Legal Change on Massachusetts Society, 1760–1830* (Cambridge, Mass., 1975). On education see Lawrence A. Cremin, *American Education: The Colonial Experience, 1607–1783* (New York, 1970).

33. Nash, *Urban Crucible*, chaps. 7–13.

34. Douglas L. Jones, "The Strolling Poor: Transiency in Eighteenth-Century Massachusetts," *Journal of Social History* 8 (Spring 1975): 28–54; Billy G. Smith, "The Material Lives of Laboring Philadelphians, 1750 to 1800," *William and Mary Quarterly*, 3d ser., 38 (1981): 163–202; Gary B. Nash, "Poverty and Poor Relief in Pre-Revolutionary Philadelphia," ibid. 33 (1976): 3–30; Raymond A. Mohl, "Poverty in Early America: A Reappraisal: The Case of Eighteenth-Century New York City," *New York History* 50 (1969): 5–27.

35. Bender, *Community and Social Change*, 31, 33.

36. For a review of recent work see James Axtell, "The Ethnohistory of Early America: A Review Essay," *William and Mary Quarterly*, 3d ser., 35 (1978): 110–44.

37. An overview and synthesis of recent work in this area is given in Gary B. Nash, *Red, White, and Black: The Peoples of Early America*, 2d ed. (Englewood Cliffs, N.J., 1982), chaps. 3–6.

38. T.J.C. Brasser, "The Coastal Algonkians: People of the First Frontiers," in *North American Indians in Historical Perspective*, ed. Eleanor Burke Leacock and Nancy O. Lurie (New York, 1971), 73.

39. Calvin Martin, *Keepers of the Game: Indian-Animal Relationships and the Fur Trade* (Berkeley, 1978).

40. Bruce G. Trigger, *The Children of Aataentsic: A History of the Huron People to 1660*, 2 vols. (Montreal, 1976).

41. James Axtell, "The Indian Impact on English Colonial Culture," in *The European and the Indian: Essays in the Ethnohistory of Colonial North America* (New York, 1981), 272–315.

42. Sidney W. Mintz and Richard Price, *An Anthropological Approach to the Afro-American Past: A Caribbean Perspective*, ISHI Occasional Papers on Social Change, no. 2 (Philadelphia, 1976), 4–11; the quote is from p. 10.

43. The most important work includes Mullin, *Flight and Rebellion;* Peter H. Wood, *Black Majority: Negroes in Colonial South Carolina from 1670 through the Stono Rebellion* (New York, 1974); Russell R. Menard, "The Maryland Slave Population, 1658–1730: A Demographic Profile of Blacks in Four Counties," *William and Mary Quarterly*, 3d ser., 32 (1975): 29–54; Allan Kulikoff, "A 'Prolifick People': Black Population Growth in the Chesapeake Colonies, 1700–1790," *Southern Studies* 16 (1977): 391–428; idem, "The Origins of Afro-American Society in Tidewater Maryland and Virginia, 1700 to 1790," *William and Mary Quarterly*, 3d ser., 35 (1978): 226–59; idem, "The Beginnings of the Afro-American Family in Maryland," in *Law, Society, and Politics in Early Maryland*, ed. Aubrey C. Land, Lois Green Carr, and Edward C. Papenfuse (Baltimore, 1977); Daniel C. Littlefield, *Rice and Slaves: Ethnicity and the Slave Trade in Colonial South Carolina* (Baton Rouge, 1981); and Philip D. Morgan, "Black Society in the Lowcountry, 1760–1810," in *Slavery in the Era of the American Revolution*, ed. Ira Berlin and Ronald Hoffman (Charlottesville, 1982). For a comprehensive view of recent work see Peter H. Wood, "'I Did the Best I Could for My Day': The Study of Early Black History during the Second Reconstruction, 1960 to 1976," *William and Mary Quarterly*, 3d ser., 35 (1978): 185–225.

44. Mintz and Price, *An Anthropological Approach*, 26.

45. Ira Berlin, "Time, Space, and the Evolution of Afro-American Society in British Mainland North America," *American Historical Review* 85 (1980): 44–78.

46. For a review of the demographic literature see Daniel Blake Smith, "The Study of the Family in Early America: Trends, Problems, and Prospects," *William and Mary Quarterly*, 3d ser., 39 (1982): 3–28. Among the recent work in women's history see esp. Ben Barker-Benfield, "Anne Hutchinson and the Puritan Attitude toward Women," *Feminist Studies* 1 (1972): 65–96; Alexander Keyssar, "Widowhood in Eighteenth-Century Massachusetts: A Problem in the History of the Family," *Perspectives in American History* 8 (1974): 83–119; D. Kelly Weisberg, "'Under Greet Temptations Heer': Women and Divorce in Puritan Massachusetts," *Feminist Studies* 2 (1975): 183–94; Katherine A. Jacob, "The Woman's Lot in Baltimore Town, 1729–1797," *Maryland Historical Magazine* 71 (1976); Nancy F. Cott, "Divorce and Changing Status of Women in Eighteenth-Century Massachusetts," *William and Mary Quarterly*, 3d ser., 33 (1976): 586–614; John Faragher, "Old Women and Old Men in the Seventeenth-Century Wethersfield, Connecticut," *Women's Studies* 4 (1976): 110–31; Lois Green Carr and Lorena S. Walsh, "The Planter's Wife: The Experience of White Women in Seventeenth-Century Maryland," *William and Mary Quarterly*, 3d ser., 34 (1977): 542–71; Jean P. Jordan, "Women Merchants in Colonial New York," *New York History* 58 (1977): 416–36; Mary Dunn, "Saints and Sisters: Congregational and Quaker Women in the Early Colonial Period," *American Quarterly* 30 (1978): 582–601; Gary B. Nash, "The Failure of Female Factory Labor in Colonial Boston," *Labor History* 20 (1979): 165–88; Marylynn Salmon, "Equality or Submersion? Feme Covert Status in Early Pennsylvania," in *Women of America: A History*, ed. Carol Ruth Berkin and Mary Beth Norton (Boston, 1979), 92–111; Linda K. Kerber, *Women of the Republic: Intellect and Ideology in Revolutionary America* (Chapel Hill, 1980); Mary Beth Norton, *Liberty's Daughters: The Revolutionary Experience of American Women, 1750–1800* (Boston, 1980); Lyle Koehler, *A Search for Power: The 'Weaker Sex' in Seventeenth-Century New England* (Urbana, 1980); Alan D. Watson, "Women in Colonial North Carolina: Overlooked and Underestimated," *North Carolina Historical Review* 58 (1981): 1–22; Laurel Thatcher Ulrich, *Good Wives: Image and Reality in the Lives of*

Women in Northern New England, 1650–1750 (New York, 1982); Joan R. Gundersen and Gwen Victor Gampel, "Married Women's Legal Status in Eighteenth-Century New York and Virginia," *William and Mary Quarterly*, 3d ser., 39 (1982): 114–34; Marylynn Salmon, "Women and Property in South Carolina: The Evidence from Marriage Settlements, 1730 to 1830," *William and Mary Quarterly*, 3d ser., 39 (1982): 655–85.

9

WEALTH AND SOCIAL STRUCTURE

JAMES A. HENRETTA

ealth and social structure is hardly a venerable topic. Indeed, this subject achieved an autonomous status only in 1965. The crucial publication was Jackson Turner Main's *The Social Structure of Revolutionary America*. Before the appearance of Main's volume, scholars had treated colonial wealth and social structure as subsidiary topics. These issues were subordinate to analyses of political events and, to a lesser extent, of the process of social development. This method of treatment constituted the legacy of the great Progressive historians Charles Beard and Frederick Jackson Turner. In his most famous and influential work, *An Economic Interpretation of the Constitution of the United States* (1913), Beard examined the wealth holdings of members of the Constitutional Convention to demonstrate the economic roots of that document and to explain certain of its provisions. He did not attempt a systematic analysis of the social structure. Nor did Frederick Jackson Turner, even though his "frontier thesis" assumed the existence and the evolution of distinct social formations. The concerns of these scholars and of most of their followers rested primarily in the spheres of politics and national character.[1]

Why was this so? Intellectual traditions provide part of the answer. More than most European countries, the United States lacked a radical or socialist tradition of scholarship that fastened attention on social groups and classes. The genteel amateurs and academics who studied the colonial period placed prime emphasis on men and events. A second reason is equally important: before 1950 there was widespread agreement on the character of prerevolutionary American society. Both Progressive historians of the liberal left and Brahmin authors of the conservative right assumed the existence of class divisions in the colonial period, however much they might argue about their political implications. Indeed, the most class-conscious portraits of early

American life were penned by patrician conservatives such as Samuel Eliot Morison and James Truslow Adams. There were "marked social distinctions between the colonists," Adams wrote in *Provincial Society, 1690–1763* (1927), for "economically, societies are always like a pyramid, and the mass of men at the opening of the eighteenth century was composed of those who had made only a moderate success or none at all in the art and practice of living."[2] For these authors the existence of a privileged social and political elite was completely compatible with the relative prosperity of the British mainland colonies in relation to Europe. American "exceptionalism" was a matter of degree, not of kind.

Because of widespread agreement across this narrow ideological spectrum, there were few debates among historians regarding the social structure of early America. Robert E. Brown shattered this complacency in 1955. In his *Middle Class Democracy and the Revolution in Massachusetts, 1691–1780* Brown argued that Massachusetts was a "middle class society in which property was easily acquired"; that the "great majority of men" met the franchise requirements; and that poorer back-country towns were equitably represented in the provincial assembly. Brown's "consensus" interpretation of social stratification and political privilege found few advocates. Indeed, criticism came from three quarters. Neo-Progressive scholars challenged the accuracy of his data on wealth and the franchise, particularly with respect to Boston and other urban areas. Historians with more of a sense of historical complexities accepted his statistics but repudiated his intellectual assumptions. They pointed out that "democracy" was not the operative political theory of the eighteenth century but rather the Whig concept of a "balanced constitution." Because whig principles found institutional expression in a bicameral legislature and a royal executive, the effective power of the demos was strictly limited. These critics insisted, moreover, on the existence of a deferential polity ruled by the wealthy and well-born, whatever the extent of the franchise.[3] Support for this position came from a third quarter. Younger scholars used quantitative methods to demonstrate that those with college educations, judicial appointments, and eastern constituencies dominated the leadership positions in the Massachusetts assembly and in other provincial legislatures.[4]

A quarter of a century later, it is clear that Brown's "thesis" represented a creative failure. Most of its specific propositions have been discredited or modified beyond recognition. And yet Robert E. Brown's work, and that of his wife, B. Katherine Brown, transformed the terms of debate in two major respects. In the first place, *Middle-Class Democracy* (and its less successful sequel, *Virginia, 1705–1786: Aristocracy or Democracy?*) gave importance to the topic of social stratification.[5] Second, their work shifted the attention of social historians to the mass of the adult white male population. Even the best social history written in the 1940s and 1950s had been elitist in orientation and subsidiary to the analyses of political events. The early articles of Jackson Turner Main are a case in point. Through his mentor Merrill Jensen, at the University of Wisconsin, Main inherited the intellectual concerns of the great Progressive historians. Following Beard, he studied the Constitution, but he focused on its Antifederalist opponents. Emulating Turner, he explained its political configurations within the various states. Thus, his early articles on Virginia explored the relationships between wealth, social structure, and voting patterns during the Confederation period.[6] Like Brown's, Main's work was as much traditional as innovative. It utilized new records, such as tax lists, and adumbrated a new methodology, but its emphasis remained political. It sought to explain political formations rather than social processes.

A similar purpose informed Bernard Bailyn's influential essay of 1959, "Politics and Social Structure in Virginia." Bailyn's concern was the vicissitudes of the various political elites who ruled the tobacco colony from its founding until the early eighteenth century. He sought both to explain the breakdown of the hierarchical class structure inherited from England—a classic Turnerian question—and to comprehend the logic of Bacon's Rebellion of 1675–76. These traditional issues were balanced by two innovative features: the application of Namier's prosopographic techniques to early American materials and the causal significance accorded to social and economic factors. For Bailyn, the crucial elements determining the political structure of Virginia were not institutional or ideological. Rather, shifts in political power had social, demographic, and economic roots: cycles of elite immigration, high mortality and low fertility, the boom and bust of the tobacco market. If Brown and Main were innovators in methodology, Bailyn led the way conceptually. His work of the late 1950s demonstrated the evolution of basic social formations—the family, the Virginia aristocracy, the New England merchants—and suggested their autonomous treatment through rigorous historical analysis.[7]

Yet it was Jackson Turner Main who established the independence of wealth and social structure as scholarly topics. His accomplishment was almost accidental. As Main explained in the preface to *The Social Structure of Revolutionary America*, he undertook this study "out of a conviction that an understanding of political history during the revolutionary era depends upon mastery of the underlying social structure." It was only because "the subject proved much too large" and too complex that Main was unable to achieve the desired synthesis: "an essay on the relationship between class and the structure of power." More than chance determined this result. As Main acknowledged, his thinking was deeply influenced by "recent literature on the class structure of contemporary America."[8] In fact, a close analysis of *The Social Structure of Revolutionary America* reveals a significant reorientation of intellectual priorities. Its organization and argument was determined less by the historiographic tradition—or even Main's previous scholarship—than by two theoretical perspectives derived from the social sciences: the analysis of economic development and the study of social mobility.

These intellectual antecedents were of considerable importance, for they shaped the character of Main's interpretation and much of the subsequent scholarship. Beginning in the mid-1950s, American students wrote extensively on the subject of economic development, especially with respect to the superiority of "capitalist" or "communist" models for the Third World. W. W. Rostow composed the most concise and influential argument in 1960 in *The Stages of Economic Growth: A Non-Communist Manifesto*.[9] The ideological bias of these works is less important for our purposes than the analytic assumptions that they fostered. These theories of social development emphasized the primacy of economic forces and market structures in the historical transition to industrial capitalism. In fact, these "economist" assumptions were pervasive in the early 1960s. They suffused the work of many historians, cutting across traditional ideological divisions. They informed my treatment of "Economic Development and Social Structure in Colonial Boston" (1965). In that article I argued that the expansion of mercantile enterprise was the prime cause of the growth of wealth inequality in Boston between 1687 and 1772 and of the appearance of a new social order dominated by "merchant princes" and filled by a large underclass of "proletarians." Main was equally influenced by these theories of economic development. He detected four "subsocieties," or "class structures," in colonial America, each characterized by a specific stage of commercial development and a distinct distribution of wealth. On the undeveloped frontier the richest 10 percent of the property holders owned 33–40 percent of the wealth. In subsistence farming regions the percentage rose to 35–45 percent, while involvement in commercial farming raised the share of the top 10 percent to 45–65 percent. Finally, the port cities stood at the apex of the commercial system. Their merchant elites controlled 55–65 percent of the total taxable wealth.[10] In these schema social structure became a quantified measure of commercial development.

The research of economic historians shaped the substantive as well as the conceptual understanding of the mainland colonies. Inspired by developmental studies of the U.S. economy in the nineteenth century, George Rogers Taylor published an exploratory essay in 1964, "American Economic Growth before 1840." Taylor knew that the gross national product (GNP) per capita had increased 1.6 percent per year between 1840 and 1960. His review of the available literature produced three hypotheses for the preceding two centuries: first, that "until about 1710 growth was slow, irregular, and not properly measured in percentage terms"; second, that from 1710 to 1775 growth rates averaged 1 percent per annum, "relatively rapid for a preindustrial economy"; and finally, that there was little increase in per capita output between 1775 and 1840.[11] Like the Brown "thesis," Taylor's hypotheses generated an intense debate among historians, especially with respect to the alleged stagnation of the early nineteenth century.

However, Taylor's positive evaluation of the eighteenth-century economy provided added support for Main's extremely optimistic interpretation of colonial welfare. If Main turned to economists for causal models of wealth distribution, he sought a sociological explanation of the relationship between wealth and welfare. More precisely, he relied on one particular group of sociologists, American analysts of "social mobility." Once again, the departure from the historiographical tradition was striking. There was no mention of social mobility, not even a separate chapter on social development, in Clarence Ver Steeg's highly regarded survey, *The Formative Years, 1607–1763*, published in 1964. Nor did this concept intrude into the far more innovative study of English preindustrial society by Peter Laslett, *The World We Have Lost* (1965). Yet "social mobility" was very much in the intellectual air in American academic circles in the 1960s. Building on a series of important journal articles and sociological studies, Seymour Martin Lipset and Reinhold Bendix attempted a wide-ranging comparative historical analysis of *Social Mobility in Industrial Society* in 1963. In the following year Stephen Thernstrom published his enormously influential study of the "mobility" of Irish laborers in Newburyport, Massachusetts, while in 1966 Lawrence Stone used the concept to analyze the changing social structure of early modern England.[12]

Main pursued a similar strategy. Indeed, by stressing "mobility," geographic as well as vertical, he restated the classic Turnerian interpretation of American development. There were marked social divisions in colonial society, Main suggested, but they were not fixed. For "westward the land was bright" and "a man's ability to move to a new location . . . gave him a chance to rise." In the end the possibilities of American life impressed Main more than did the "long-term tendency . . . toward greater inequality" revealed by his research. This positive tone suffused not only his chapter "Mobility in Early America" but also "Social Classes in the Revolutionary Era." It closed on a note of romantic optimism: "Since anyone could acquire property, anyone could rise, and the poor man could and occasionally did become a wealthy esquire."[13]

Main's contributions to the social analysis of early America were both substantial and flawed. In retrospect it is clear that *The Social Structure of Revolutionary America* successfully completed the shift in focus begun by Brown; its subject was neither politics nor the wealth of the elite but rather the structure of the entire social order. It demonstrated as well how probate records and tax lists formed the documentary basis for an autonomous social history. Finally, Main's book provided a causative model of commercial development for the "forgotten" period of colonial history—the century separating the end of settlement and the onset of the independence struggle.[14] These accomplishments were undermined, at least in part, by Main's use of two anachronistic models of social change. The theories of economic *development* and social *mobility* imply change, movement, transformation. They were originally devised to explain the nineteenth-century transition from

agricultural to industrial society. Yet no historian maintained that this process of technological change and urban growth had begun in a significant way
in America by 1775. Main's social theories failed to address colonial reality.
They could not comprehend the character and pace of life and the intractability of social arrangements in the predominately agricultural society of
seventeenth- and eighteenth-century America.

Since 1965 historians have attempted, some more consciously than others,
to remedy these interpretive deficiencies. They have proposed various theoretical models to define and elucidate the actual social processes of this
historic epoch. The study of colonial demography and the family produced
the first major conceptual advance. In a series of articles and books published
between 1965 and 1970 the triumivirate of Philip Greven, John Demos, and
Kenneth Lockridge offered a new perspective on the study of social change.
Appropriating methods, insights, and arguments developed by French and
English historians and demographers, these authors demonstrated that men
and women in New England married in their mid- to late twenties; bore
"completed" families of seven to eight (declining over time to five to six)
children; and lived, as did most of their offspring, to an advanced age.[15]
Beyond this, their work suggested that this process of reproduction and
family formation held the key to the distribution of wealth in this agricultural
society.

This exciting conclusion was implicit in Greven's study of the founding
families of Andover, Massachusetts. He demonstrated that successive generations of these relatively privileged fathers had less land to distribute to their
heirs and that patterns of inheritance, property ownership, and migration
changed accordingly. It followed that fertility and mortality rates were as
influential as market forces in determining patterns of inequality. Lockridge
stated these relationships explicitly in his influential article "Land, Population, and the Evolution of New England Society, 1630–1780."[16] On the
basis of scattered empirical evidence, he posited an agricultural crisis in New
England by the third quarter of the eighteenth century: the sustained growth
of population through natural increase had overwhelmed the productive capacity of the available land; the result was a classic Malthusian subsistence
crisis.

Neither Lockridge's framework nor his conclusions were completely original. His interpretation was deeply influenced by the subsistence crisis discovered by Pierre Goubert in the Beauvais region of France in the 1690s and
by Charles S. Grant's *Democracy in the Connecticut Frontier Town of Kent*
(1961). Writing in the Turnerian tradition (but with Brown's thesis firmly in
mind), Grant had posited an evolutionary pattern of social development for
Kent. Founded in 1738, Kent's society was "predominately middle class in
1751, [but] included a growing class of propertyless men" by 1796. Grant
suggested that this change in the social structure was the result of "the
pressure of a population swollen by a fantastic birthrate against a limited

amount of land." Lockridge appropriated Grant's argument and applied it to
New England as a whole. Then in "Social Change and the Meaning of the
American Revolution" Lockridge speculated that these developments had
profound, if vaguely specified, political ramifications. "A shortage of land,
commercialization, and social differentiation. . . ," Lockridge maintained,
"must have activated and perhaps strained the political system," undermining the position of the "colonial elite" and perhaps prompting them to undertake a "purgative crusade" against British rule.[17]

Subsequent research has failed to demonstrate a strong causal relationship
between the "agricultural crisis" specified by Lockridge and the independence movement. In *The Minutemen and Their World* (1976), Robert A. Gross
confirms many of Grant's and Lockridge's findings in his empirical analysis
of the agricultural system of Concord, Massachusetts. Indeed, Gross argues
that mid-eighteenth century Concord farmers lived in "A World of Scarcity." Yet this microanalysis of this commercial farming town fails to detect a
dramatic relationship between a declining agricultural economy and the independence movement. The impetus to rebellion came from Boston and from
the British challenge to traditional colonial autonomy, Gross concludes, and
not from a shortage of prime agricultural land and increasing social stratification. At most, he concludes, "the continuing decay in their fortunes added a
special poignancy to their fears." Richard Bushman's astute analysis "Massachusetts Farmers and the Revolution" (1976) substantiates and extends this
interpretation. "It is not necessary to posit a social crisis to explain the
passionate reaction [of farmers] to parliamentary taxation," Bushman maintains, for their hostility stemmed primarily from a century-long tradition of
resistance to the creation of a burdensome political and religious establishment. These abiding fears were only accentuated by agricultural decline,
rising debts, and the specter of "slavish tenantry." "The transfer of fear from
debt to taxes was nearly automatic," Bushman concludes, "because taxes
were a form of debt, and were ultimately collected in the same way, by
forced land sales. . . ." Viewing these economic and political changes from a
transatlantic comparative perspective, Hermann Wellenreuther likewise located the resistance of the American freeholder population not in its progressive impoverishment but rather in the British challenge to its "share in the
political decision-making process." These studies posit an indirect relationship between a changing social structure and the revolutionary impulse. The
independence movement in the countryside was less the desperate revolt of a
recently impoverished agricultural population than the defense of a society of
small freeholders against the twin forces of agricultural stagnation and administrative reform.[18]

If the relationship between economic stagnation and political rebellion
remains problematic, these studies of families and their farms have revised
our understanding of the character of colonial society. In the first place, they
cast doubt on the Taylor-Main thesis of considerable per capita economic

growth and social mobility in the eighteenth century. Second, they provide an appropriate theoretical approach to the analysis of this agricultural society. As Bailyn argued in *Education and the Forming of American Society*, the family was the key institutional unit. It was the basic property-owning unit among the white population, and the family household was the prime productive unit, except on the larger plantations in the South. The dynamics of family existence thus form a crucial aspect of social process, whatever the extent of commercialization or geographic movement. Finally, this approach offers a structural framework for analysis. It suggests that the productive system did not change fundamentally between 1650 and 1750 and provides a set of conceptual categories to comprehend those changes that did occur.[19]

II

With this historiography in mind, let us turn to recent work in the field. My synthesis of this scholarship contains an argument: I will suggest that apart from one exception, changes in the American social structure over the course of the colonial period were primarily *extensive* in character. They involved the replication and modification of existing patterns rather than their transformation through a process of *intensive* development. This perspective disputes Taylor's interpretation of the growth of wealth during the colonial period; it modifies Main's discussion of changes in its distribution; and it challenges Lockridge's thesis of the "Europeanization" of the American social order. In the end, my emphasis will fall on the continuous creation and adaption of traditional modes of existence rather than their demise.

THE PRODUCTION OF WEALTH

The Taylor "thesis" lies in shreds. Not a single one of its hypotheses has survived detailed scholarly analysis. Critics directed their first attacks against Taylor's suggestion that the American economy stagnated, in terms of per capita GNP, between 1775 and 1840. While most analysts agreed that per capita *exports* and perhaps per capita *wealth* declined during the Revolutionary era, they maintained that substantial growth occurred between 1790 and 1840. Douglass North suggested an export-led process of development, beginning with the trade boom between 1792 and 1807. Conversely, Paul David emphasized internal factors: he argued that modest increases in farm productivity and a substantial expansion in the more efficient nonagricultural sector accounted for two surges, between 1790 and 1806 and between 1820 and 1835; these produced a per capita growth rate of 1.3 percent per annum in the half-century before 1840. Alice Hanson Jones also disputed the importance of the trade boom of the 1790s. Her data indicated a decline in real wealth per capita until 1805, after which wealth increased at an annual rate of

1.9 percent until 1850. Finally, Robert Gallman proposed an expansion rate for the early nineteenth century somewhat lower than those of David and Jones, but still above 1 percent per annum.[20] Whatever their differences with regard to timing and causation, these economic historians rendered a unanimous verdict with respect to the period as a whole. Gross national product per capita in the United States rose at least 50 percent between 1775 and 1840, with the entire increase coming after 1790.

These findings had significant implications. They indicated that over the short term the war for independence retarded American economic growth, and they supported the traditional interpretation of the 1780s as a "critical period." More important for our purposes, they showed that Taylor's estimate of per capita wealth of four hundred dollars for 1775 (in 1840 prices) was too high. This conclusion in turn undermined Taylor's hypothesis of a sustained high rate of growth during the eighteenth century.

A second series of studies yielded a similar result. Research on the seventeenth-century economy demonstrated major increases in productivity and wealth, especially between 1650 and 1680. European demand for Chesapeake tobacco rose until 1680, maintaining profits for producers despite falling commodity prices. More important, tobacco production per worker nearly doubled during the mid-century decades, thus increasing profit margins. Even thirty years of stagnating demand and level prices between 1680 and 1710 did not erode these sizable economic gains.[21] New England experienced a similar pattern of boom and stagnation. During the second generation of settlement farmers increased their productivity markedly and began to ship their surplus goods to the sugar islands of the West Indies. As a result, real wealth per capita rose at an annual rate of 1.6 percent between 1650 and 1680. Following this spurt, there was little or no growth for the subsequent three decades. Nevertheless, these mid-seventeenth-century bursts in productivity meant that colonial wealth levels were considerably higher in 1720 than Taylor had specified. Terry Anderson estimated that per capita income for New England was eleven pounds for the period 1700–1709, nearly double the five to six pounds proposed by Taylor.[22] Taken together, these findings were devastating: they indicated that Taylor had exaggerated the extent of colonial prosperity in 1775 and underestimated the level of wealth in 1720.

The implications are readily apparent. Per capita rates of growth during the eighteenth century were considerably below Taylor's proposed 1 percent per annum. Empirical data presented in various local and regional studies confirmed this deduction. The average wealth of decendents, as measured by probate records, in Hampshire County, Massachusetts, rose from an average of £208 in the first decade of the eighteenth century to £296 in the 1770s, yielding an annual growth rate of 0.54 percent. In Hartford, Connecticut, real wealth stagnated at pre-1675 levels until 1765, while in Guilford, Connecticut, mean ratable wealth per resident male taxpayer did not increase significantly during the first seven decades of the eighteenth century.[23] In sum, this research indicated a modest growth in per capita wealth in New England of 0.2 percent to 0.5 percent per year.

The Middle Colonies expanded output per capita at a much higher rate. The mean inventoried wealth of decedents in Chester County, Pennsylvania, leaped from £126 in 1714–31 to £200 in 1734–45. It then rose more slowly to £270 for those inventories filed in 1775–1790. The first spurt reflected the productivity gains accruing to the second generation of farmers and thus resembled the seventeenth-century experience of New England and the Chesapeake. It was the product of decades of patient labor. Fields had been cleared, houses and barns built, and roads constructed. The second rise stemmed from international price movements rather than hard-won increases in domestic farm productivity. In Pennsylvania output per farm worker expanded only at the rate of 0.2–0.3 percent per annum between 1730 and 1770.[24] Yet increases in export prices for wheat created an economic boom. Working from data on imports and exports (rather than probate records), Marc Egnal found a spectacular growth rate of 3–5 percent for the northern

Table 9.1
THE GROWTH OF WEALTH: SELECTED STATISTICS (IN POUNDS)

Hampshire County, Mass., Inventories		Guilford, Conn., Mean Ratable Wealth per Resident Male Taxpayer		Chester County, Pa., Mean Total Wealth Inventories		Prince George's County, Md., Inventories[a]		
1700–1709	209					1705	26.1	32.0
1710–19	269	1716	66.9	1714–31	126.5			
1720–29	301							
1730–39	391	1732	61.3	1734–45	200.6	1733	23.9	37.3
1740–49	258	1740	72.4					
		1749	62.7					
1750–59	381	1756	61.8	1750–70	240.6	1755	19.3	33.2
1760–69	344	1765	57.6					
1770–79	296			1775–90	270.8	1776	33.7	60.6
Average +0.54% per annum				Average +1.2% per annum				

Sources: Terry L. Anderson, "Economic Growth in Colonial New England: 'Statistical Renaissance,'" *Journal of Economic History* 39 (1979): 243–57; John J. Waters, Jr., "Patrimony, Succession, and Social Stability: Guilford, Connecticut in the Eighteenth Century," *Perspectives in American History* 10 (1976): 159; Duane E. Ball, "Dynamics of Population and Wealth in Eighteenth-Century Chester County, Pennsylvania," *Journal of Interdisciplinary History* 6 (1976), tables 5 and 6; Allan Kulikoff, "The Economic Growth of the Eighteenth-Century Chesapeake Colonies," *Journal of Economic History* 39 (1979): 275–88.

Note: All values have been deflated by an appropriate price index. Figures are not comparable, since not all were computed in pounds sterling.

[a]Measured in pounds per capita.

colonies as a whole between 1745 and 1760. In this propitious set of circumstances wealth grew at a rate of 1.2 percent per year in Chester County
between 1715 and 1790, although at a steadily declining rate. By 1774 the per
capita level of physical wealth in the Middle Colonies totaled £40.2 sterling,
as compared with £36.4 for New England.[25]

How should this economic performance be interpreted? Clearly, regional
differences were significant. A buoyant export market for grain quickly
raised living standards in the more recently settled Middle Colonies to a high
level. Yet the wealth of the New England colonies increased significantly as
well. And these gains came even as many towns quadrupled their population
and as the population of the older region increased by a factor of ten. Thus
the strongly negative relationship between wealth and population growth
posited by Lockridge no longer remained persuasive. The somewhat more
optimistic "Malthusian-Frontier Interpretation of United States Demographic History before c. 1815" proposed by Daniel Scott Smith was somewhat
more convincing. Like Lockridge, Smith began with population growth.
Because the northern colonies grew at a rate of 3 percent per annum, new
resources had to be brought into production continuously to keep per capita
wealth at a constant level. This task was so formidable that it absorbed most
of the productive energies of the society. Consequently, Smith argued, there
was *no* sustained increase in per capita output, and urban growth and commerce failed to keep pace with population. Export crops declined constantly
as a share of total agricultural output—from 20–30 percent in 1710 to 15–20
percent in 1770 to only 10–15 percent by 1790. The absence of intensive
development did not imply agricultural decline, a subsistence crisis, or an
increase in wealth inequality. Rather, the Malthusian rates of population
increase and the availability of an agricultural frontier resulted in an *extensive*
pattern of growth. Farms were hacked continually out of the wilderness for
an ever-growing population; the result was a static multiplication of productive units rather than a process of economic development and transformation.[26]

Smith's argument was astute but not completely persuasive. Growth was
primarily extensive, but the inhabitants of established regions slowly diversified their economies and accumulated greater wealth. Two examples will
suffice. In the early eighteenth century, inventoried wealth in Chester
County, Pennsylvania, consisted primarily of physical property; financial
assets amounted to only 11 percent of the total. By the 1770s, however, bills,
bonds, and debts accounted for nearly 50 percent of the inventoried wealth.
The composition of diet changed as well. The second generation of settlers in
Middlesex County, Massachusetts, shifted from a seasonal pattern of consumption of fresh and stored food to greater reliance on stored grains (corn
and rye, replacing wheat) and salt meats. Then, during the eighteenth century Middlesex residents increased the quantity and variety of their stored
provisions and substituted cider for beer. Finally, after 1750 the inhabitants

consumed a more varied diet. Potatoes and other vegetables appeared on their tables, and distinct dietary standards began to develop along class lines.[27] Diet thus became more assured, more sufficient, and more varied even as it reflected difficult agricultural adaptations in the face of population growth. Stored meats replaced fresh game; the planting of orchards allowed barley fields to be used for rye and corn; potatoes provided subsistence on shrinking farms. Interwoven with the pattern of extensive growth in the West was an equally important process of adaptation and modification in the East.

Southern development was also consistent, up to a point, with the Malthusian-frontier interpretation. The sudden introduction of tens of thousands of African slaves in the eighteenth century transformed the social structure, but it did not alter the productive capacity of the tobacco economy. In fact, the new slave regime initially cut agricultural productivity. In Prince George's County, Maryland, for example, per capita wealth declined slowly between 1700 and 1725; and despite the increase in tobacco prices, it decreased at a rate of 1 percent per year during the next quarter-century. This decline stemmed from three interrelated causes. First, the "dependency ratio" increased markedly. Because of an outmigration of white freedmen and a rising black birth rate, the number of dependents per worker inflated as the labor force changed in composition. African-born slaves were not as adept at tobacco cultivation as native-born blacks, servants, or freemen. Finally, the per capita wealth of the *white* population did increase over time: by 0.5 percent per year between 1705 and 1733 and by a roughly equal amount between 1733 and 1755 (if the value of slaves are included in the computation of assets). The capacity of the productive system remained stable, but its rewards were systematically expropriated by the slave-owning population.

The prosperity of whites increased even more dramatically in the subsequent two decades. The price of Chesapeake tobacco rose to 2–2.5 pence per pound (up from 1.25–1.75), and a largely native-born slave population brought higher productivity. In Prince George's County the export of grain generated additional revenue (10 percent of the total), while the ready availability of Scottish credit (£26 per household in 1776) encouraged economic expansion. These favorable developments drove up the price of slaves at a rate of 1.4 percent per annum between 1733 and 1776 and brought a massive increase in land prices—from 6.8 shillings per acre in 1733 to 8.4 shillings in 1755 to 27 shillings in 1776. By 1776 total household wealth for whites in the county averaged £357.[28] During the same years the dramatic growth of rice production brought even greater wealth to the white plantation owners of South Carolina.

A strong export economy and an exploited black labor force made white slaveowners the wealthiest group on the mainland. The average free wealthholder in the South had total physical resources of £395 in 1774, as compared with £161 for those in New England and £187 for the Middle Colonies.

Table 9.2

REGIONAL WEALTH COMPOSITION, 1774: AVERAGE PER FREE
WEALTHHOLDER, AND PER CAPITA (IN POUNDS STERLING)

	New England	Middle Colonies	South
Per free wealthholder:			
(1) Total physical wealth (2 + 3)	161.2	186.8	394.7
(2) Slaves and servants	0.7	7.2	132.6
(3) Total nonhuman wealth (4 + 5 + 6 + 7)	160.5	179.6	262.1
(4) Land (real estate)	115.1	115.5	181.1
(5) Livestock	12.3	21.3	34.9
(6) Other producers' goods	13.9	24.7	23.7
(7) Consumers' goods	19.2	18.0	22.4
Per capita:			
(8) Total nonhuman wealth (9 + 10 + 11 + 12)	36.4	40.2	36.4
(9) Land (real estate)	26.1	25.9	25.1
(10) Livestock	2.8	4.8	4.8
(11) Other producers' goods	3.1	5.5	3.3
(12) Consumers' goods	4.4	4.0	3.1

Source: Alice Hanson Jones, *Wealth of a Nation to Be: The American Colonies on the Eve of the Revolution* (New York, 1980), table 9.3.

These regional disparities persisted when slaves and servants were not count-ed as assets; the totals then became £161, for New England, £180 for the Middle Colonies, and £262 for the South. Yet the economy of the South was not more productive than the economies of other regions. For as line (8) of table 9.2 indicates, per capita wealth—land, livestock, producer and con-sumer goods—was almost exactly the same in 1774 in every region of the mainland.[29] White southerners had more wealth than white northerners only because black southerners had none.

Regional similarities in per capita wealth indicated that Smith's "Malthu-sian-Frontier" thesis of extensive growth applied to the South as well as to the North. Once again, however, it fails to capture important alterations in the economic social structure. First, as Aubrey Land and Edmund Morgan have demonstrated, thousands of whites bolstered their economic and social positions by becoming slaveowners. By 1745 all householders in Talbot County, Maryland, except tenants and small landowners owned slaves. In-deed, by 1774, 59 percent of all wealth holders in the South owned a slave (or servant).[30] Second, the economy of the Chesapeake gradually diversified. As Carville Earle and Paul Clemens have shown, during the first four decades of the eighteenth century wealthy planters became self-sufficient in food, clothing, and producer goods in order to weather cyclical fluctuations in the tobacco market. Subsequently they produced wheat and corn for export. By the 1760s at least two-thirds of gross agricultural income received by slaveowners in Talbot and Kent Counties, Maryland, came from wheat and corn; only tenant farmers and small landowners remained tied to the traditional tobacco economy. Finally, much of the increased wealth in the South (as in parts of Connecticut) resulted from a dramatic increase in land prices. In Talbot County, for example, the average price of land jumped from £0.46 per acre in the 1730s to £1.22 per acre in the 1760s. As a result, the number of landless laborers and tenants grew substantially. In All Hallow's Parish, Maryland, 33 percent of the adult white males did not own land in the 1710s, and nearly 50 percent were landless by the 1770s. Despite migration to the frontier, a substantial white underclass of tenant farmers appeared in most settled regions of the Chesapeake.[31]

Thus economic change in all mainland regions consisted of both the extensive growth of frontier regions and the intensive development of settled areas. Older settlements grew wealthier even as they diverted accumulated capital resources to open up new communities. The existence of an untapped agricultural frontier in turn relieved the strain on landed resources in eastern settlements while affording an adequate if hard-won livelihood for the migrant population. The net result was a modest increase in per capita wealth during the eighteenth century. This amounted to 0.5 percent per annum, roughly half of Taylor's optimistic estimate of 1 percent but considerably more than that allowed by Smith's hypothesis of a static economy. Growth was slow but sure.

THE DISTRIBUTION OF WEALTH

Initial studies of the distribution of wealth posited increasing concentrations over time and specified commercialization as the causal mechanism. Most analyses published during the following decade accepted this conceptualization. If the empirical data were not congruent with these hypotheses, the fit was close enough to discourage reformulation.[32] In 1976 three articles took issue with the evolutionary, mercantile framework propounded by Main and me. After a close analysis of assessment practices and other technical issues, G. B. Warden argued that the distribution of wealth in Boston did not change between 1687 and 1772. Main himself arrived at a similar conclusion with respect to Connecticut: he found cyclical fluctuations but no overall trend. Finally, Gloria Main's examination of probate records from Maryland and Massachusetts pointed towards a new interpretative framework: she argued that gross inequality became a permanent feature of southern life in the late seventeenth century and that a similar structural transformation occurred in the northern states in the early nineteenth century.[33]

This revisionist view was given coherent form by two economic historians, Peter Lindert and Jeffrey Williamson. Their analysis "Long Term Trends in American Wealth Inequality" revealed no significant changes in wealth distribution before 1800, followed by two major periods of transformation.

First, there was a "marked rise" in economic stratification during the first half of the nineteenth century. Then, in the second quarter of the twentieth century there was a "pronounced decline" in wealth concentrations, following "six decades of persistent and extensive inequality." These findings were significant, pinpointing the period between 1860 and 1930 as the most unequal in all of American history. Most important for our purposes, Lindert and Williamson argued that inequality in the nineteenth century was not the result of trends begun in the colonial period; rather, it was the sudden and unanticipated product of early industrialization. Empirical data provided graphic evidence for this interpretation. In 1774 the top 1 percent of the free wealthholders held 12.6 percent of total assets, and the wealthiest 10 percent owned about 50 percent. By 1860, however, the richest 1 percent held 29 percent, and the top 10 percent owned 73 percent.[34]

This revisionist perspective has considerable force, for it is stated with considerable care and complexity. Lindert and Williamson granted that wealth concentrations increased over time in settled areas and eventually in each frontier region. They pointed out, however, that new frontier communities (with low levels of per capita wealth and relatively low inequality) were "being added at a very rapid rate"; hence, "*in the aggregate* colonial inequality was stable at low levels." Along with other commentators, these authors also stressed the extent of age-related inequality. This took two forms. First, the major colonial cities attracted a larger proportion of young men and women in the late colonial period. This demographic phenomenon explains, at least in part, the apparent increase in urban inequality in the late colonial period—for few individuals have accumulated wealth in this phase of their life. Life-cycle analysis also accounted for a second pattern of inequality. Frontier agricultural communities became more stratified "naturally" as young parents aged and their propertyless sons appeared on the tax lists. As John Waters discovered in the long-settled town of Guilford, Connecticut, "age distribution was the most important factor in explaining both property distribution and officeholding." In Guilford (and also in the agricultural community of Wenham, Massachusetts, between 1731 and 1771) not a single father fell in the lowest 40 percent of wealth distribution; conversely, only a few young men ranked in the top 20 percent.[35] Lines of economic status existed in these communities, for some families had consistently more land and personal property over several generations, but inequality was often age-related. Taken together, the phenomena of age stratification and frontier migration provided considerable empirical support for an interpretation that emphasized the long-term stability of the distribution of colonial wealth.

Other scholars questioned the relationship between commercialization and inequality. The connections between the two turned out to be complex and ambiguous. The commercial tobacco economy of the Chesapeake certainly encouraged the early emergence of inequality. By 1700 the top 10 percent of the Virginia population owned one-half to two-thirds of the available acreage and 65 percent of the personal wealth. Most members of this elite owed their fortunes as much to mercantile activity as to tobacco cultivation.[36] Yet their economic success reflected the initial advantages resulting from their control of land and labor. These planters had imported indentured servants and received headright land allotments. Subsequently they sold or leased this land to new freemen, from whom they also extracted wealth by serving as storekeepers, tobacco merchants, and creditors.

Thus it was not "mere" commercialization or the cultivation of a staple crop that generated extreme inequality in the Chesapeake but rather the social context in which it occurred. Indeed, the market often worked to lessen inequality. Small planters prospered when the tobacco market was good, for that was their *only* form of cash income. Conversely, wealthy planters did relatively better in times of depression. Their control of labor permitted them to diversify agricultural and craft production, while their control of credit increased their leverage over small planters.[37] During the depressions in the tobacco trade of 1680–97 and 1727–33 the largest 10 percent of the plantations in All Hallow's Parish, Maryland, accounted for over 60 percent of the value of all plantations; during the boom of 1698–1704 this proportion fell to 32 percent.

Commercial expansion often produced greater equality in the northern colonies as well. In the heavily market-oriented colonies of New Jersey, Pennsylvania, and Delaware the top 10 percent of the free wealthholders owned 35 percent of the physical assets in 1774. By contrast, in subsistence-oriented New England the richest decile owned 47 percent of the wealth. Through an intensive analysis of the 1771 valuation list, Bettye Pruitt demonstrated that the same pattern appeared *within* Massachusetts. Many towns were both "poor" and unequal. The "poor" agricultural communities had low living standards and considerable inequality, with the wealthiest 10 percent owning 34 percent of the valued assets. Other towns had exactly the same distribution of wealth but a median level of individual wealth that was 50 percent higher. Moreover, in Sunderland, one of six "rich" agricultural communities in Massachusetts in 1771, the top decile owned only 24 percent of the total wealth.[38] In these farming regions market involvement did not automatically or inevitably produce greater inequality. Other factors were equally important: the quality of the soil; the structure of property ownership; the system of credit; and the fortuitous conjuncture of commodity-price rises with community or regional development.

Taken together, these findings forced major modifications in the evolutionary commercial model of wealth distribution suggested by Main in *The Social Structure of Revolutionary America*. Both in the countryside and in the cities the extent of inequality remained relatively stable. The share of wealth held by the top 30 percent of probated estates in Boston remained steady at 85 percent from 1700 to 1775; the percentage of wealth owned by the top 10 percent of taxpayers in New York stayed constant at 45 percent from 1695 to

1789; and there was a definite "ceiling" to wealth inequality in these preindustrial mercantile centers. Nowhere did the top 10 percent of the free
population own more than 60–65 percent of the assessed wealth; nowhere
did the Gini coefficient of inequality rise above 0.68. Yet by 1860 the Gini
coefficients for Boston, New York, and Philadelphia were 0.93, and the top 5
percent of the taxable population owned at least 70 percent of all urban
resources.[39] In the cities as in the larger society, early industrialization
brought a major structural transformation.

Class formation did take place during the colonial period, but it was different in degree and in kind from that of the early nineteenth century. Within
the colonial cities three important alterations took place. First, as Gary Nash
has demonstrated, a class of genuinely poor people numbering between 10
and 20 percent of the population appeared in Boston in the 1740s and in New
York and Philadelphia by the 1760s. Second, wealth became increasingly
concentrated at the very top of the social scale as a few merchants amassed
huge fortunes. By the end of the colonial period the top 5 percent of inventoried estates in Boston contained 46 percent of probated wealth, while in
Philadelphia the proportion soared to 55 percent. This incipient polarization
of the social order prompted institutional innovation. Wealthy merchants
established a variety of public asylums—almshouses, bettering houses, and
workhouses—to care for the poor and to supervise their economic lives.
These formal organizations both reflected and encouraged the formation of
class consciousness at each end of the social scale. Third, urban artisans
established craft lodges and mutual benefit societies and, during the independence crisis, articulated a distinct artisan ideology. Whatever the distribution
of urban wealth, class differences obviously were felt with greater intensity
and received more institutional expression as the eighteenth century advanced.

Yet these changes did not constitute a basic economic and social transformation. The augmented wealth of the merchant elite was derived from commercial enterprise, not industrial investments. Its new sense of cohesiveness
was striking, but mainly in relation to the previous lack of class identity. The
new artisan groups likewise merely resembled traditional craft organizations
in European preindustrial cities. Finally, many of the "poor" in the colonial
ports consisted, as in the past, of the old, the young, and the widowed. A
new and substantial group of propertyless wage-earning families appeared in
these urban areas, but its absolute size was small and its influence slight.[40]

In the predominant agricultural economy, there were two major structural
changes during the colonial period, one sudden, the other gradual. The
abrupt creation of a slave-based economy at the end of the seventeenth
century increased inequality and quickly changed the racial composition and
character of southern society. Beyond this, there was a slow but eventually
significant change in the scale of existence. The multiplication of farms, craft
shops, and merchant houses produced, especially in the northern colonies, a

more complex and diverse society. The greater density of population facilitated the formation of group identity and increased the prospect of organized political and social conflicts. If these changes in scale and density posed a threat to the dominance of established social and political elites, the cause was not "economic" in the narrow sense of the term, for the per capita wealth of the white population was growing and stratification was not dramatically increasing. Rather, these conflicts stemmed from greater ethnic, occupational, or religious cohesiveness among disadvantaged groups—frontier Scotch-Irish farmers, austere Virginia Baptists, and self-conscious urban artisans.

THE STRUCTURE OF SOCIETY

How, then, was the social history of colonial America to be conceptualized? Two models stressed the importance of European antecedents or influence. The first of these examined the English roots of seventeenth-century American society and the alterations induced by the conditions of life in the New World. Scholars treated this topic in three detailed studies. In his wide-ranging and important analysis *American Slavery-American Freedom*, Edmund Morgan underlined the exploitation of white indentured servants in the Chesapeake, thereby pointing to the English origins of the oppressive labor systems of the South. Seen from this perspective, racial slavery became less an anomalous American phenomenon than the logical culmination of upper-class behavior towards indentured servants and the poor in seventeenth-century England. David Grayson Allen posited an even more direct connection between the characters of the two cultures in *In English Ways: The Movement of Societies and the Transferal of English Local Law and Custom to Massachusetts Bay in the Seventeenth Century*. Allen's portrait of New England resembled a complex mosaic composed of a diverse assemblage of distinct regional and local social practices and institutions transplanted by cohesive groups of migrants. In his view, a common "New England" pattern of political leadership, wealth distribution, agricultural practice, and land allocation emerged only at the end of the seventeenth century.[41]

Morgan and Allen thus stressed the continuities as much as the differences between the European and the colonial American social orders. Their work, like that of many demographers and social historians, demonstrated that the claim for American "exceptionalism advanced by Louis Hartz, Daniel Boorstin, and other scholars during the 1950s rested on tenuous ground. Other scholars emphasized the complexity of the interaction between transplanted customs and new environmental conditions. Lois Green Carr and Lorena Walsh studied women's lives in relation to the demographic disasters that occurred in the seventeenth-century Chesapeake. High mortality, a skewed sex ratio, and low fertility prevented growth from natural increase. Early deaths disrupted most marriages; and few parents survived to see their children become adults. This fragmented family system undermined traditional patriarchal relationships with respect to the ownership and transmission of property. With no male kin on whom to rely, husbands bestowed greater legal authority on their wives by naming them to execute their wills. They also preferred their wives to their children in the distribution of property. Chesapeake widows commonly received more than their "dower rights" and a life interest in the estate that did not lapse upon remarriage. The appearance of more "normal" demographic patterns permitted the reintroduction of English inheritance customs. By the mid-eighteenth century most Chesapeake males wrote wills that named a male relative as their executor and as the guardian of their children; that restricted their wife's inheritances to the "widow's third" and limited its duration; and that systematically favored their male children at the expense of their marital partners.[42]

If these scholars suggested the slow or inconclusive "Americanization" of transplanted English customs and institutions, other historians proposed an increasing "Anglicization" of American provincial society during the eighteenth century. Jack P. Greene and Bernard Bailyn demonstrated the profound impact of English practices and ideology on the colonial political leadership with respect to both legislative prerogatives and constitutional thought.[43] Lockridge suggested that much of New England was "rapidly becoming more and more an old world society" characterized by small farms, an articulated social hierarchy, and substantial "poor" population. John Murrin and Rowland Berthoff likewise hypothesized a "feudal revival" in the Middle and Southern colonies in the late colonial period. They pointed out that between 1730 and 1745 the descendents of seventeenth-century proprietors successfully revived long-dormant claims to land and to quitrents. "By the 1760's," Murrin and Berthoff concluded, "the largest proprietors—and no one else in all of English America—were receiving colonial revenues comparable to the incomes of the greatest English noblemen and larger than those of the richest London merchants."[44]

Taken together, these formulations underlined the continuities and similarities between the metropolitan British experience and that of its American colonies. However, they related these histories to one another in two distinct ways. Some authors—Morgan, Allen, Bailyn, and Greene—demonstrated the direct impact of English values, ideas, and behavior patterns on American life. Others—Lockridge and Murrin and Berthoff—employed more problematic arguments by analogy. Just as Main's use of the modern concepts of social mobility and economic development failed to depict the character of preindustrial experience, so terms such as "Europeanization" or "feudal revival" distorted the dimensions of the American colonial existence. Unlike more detailed, more specific comparisons, they implied an unwarranted similarity between colonial and metropolitan life. Moreover, like all broad generalizations, these analogies reified the process of American social development and exaggerated the extent of our understanding of its logic.

In fact, two decades of research had not produced an accepted interpretation of the character of the colonial social structure. Tremendous—even outstanding—progress had been made. Historians could now specify, with considerable accuracy, the shape of the economic hierarchy in scores of towns and villages. Yet the surfeit of empirical data yielded confusion rather than certainty, for this material lacked a set of organizing principles. Commercialization and class stratification served to elucidate aspects of urban development but failed to depict the nature of social change in the dominant agricultural sector. The analysis of rural existence from the perspective of the family revealed the character of inheritance practices, farm life, and economic strategies but could not address important questions of change in the society as a whole. In these circumstances, a definitive synthesis is as impossible as it is unwise. A rapid survey of the literature on landholding and tenancy at the middle of the eighteenth century, however, can clarify the relationship between the production and the distribution of wealth on the one hand and the character of social structure and cultural values on the other.

Landlessness and tenant farming were everywhere on the increase in America in 1750, but nowhere did they approach English levels. In the mother country freeholders personally worked 30 percent of the land, and the nobility and gentry leased the remaining 70 percent to tenants. On the mainland of North America, by contrast, the proportions were reversed. Freeholding families controlled 70 percent of the land and except in the South represented a similar percentage of the total population. Marked differences in wealth holdings and lifestyles existed among freeholders, but poor farmers were not in a position of abject dependence.[45] Unlike wage laborers or slaves, they were not directly dependent on the wealthy for their subsistence. In addition, the numerical dominance of freeholders gave normative status to their social values and economic goals. Thus, in New England most tenants were either young men or families who needed (or wished) to augment their own holdings. Many owned their own tools or livestock; most would eventually acquire a small estate of their own by migration, savings, or inheritance. Tenancy assumed a more permanent form for many German and Dutch farmers in New York, for the manorial proprietors of the Hudson River Valley refused to subdivide their lands for sale. Yet the competition for agricultural labor remained keen until the end of the colonial period; as a result, most tenants received long leases and the right to sell their "improvements." Like their counterparts in New England, they "owned" productive property and shared many of the economic values of freehold farmers.[46] Even in the South tenancy varied widely. German tenants on the manor of Lord Baltimore in Frederick County, Maryland, had good land, long leases, and profitable wheat crops. Yet propertyless farmers in tobacco areas barely scraped by. In All Hallow's Parish in the 1740s the rental fee for one hundred acres was five hundred to eight hundred pounds of tobacco, while annual production of first-quality leaf (using household labor) was one thousand pounds. Given this narrow margin, few tenant families could live well or acquire property of their own. In the mid-1760s five out of six tenants on one of Baltimore's long-settled tobacco estates were either the original leaseholders or their direct descendents.[47]

If tenancy was ubiquitous, its causes were different and its effects were not equally onerous. As Richard Dunn has argued, patterns of propertylessness reflected regional systems of land use and agricultural production.[48] From the very beginning the Chesapeake colonies used the bound labor of indentured servants. Many rose to freeholder status before the collapse of the tobacco boom in 1670; thereafter most white freedmen clustered in the ranks of the propertyless, working as tenants, laborers, or overseers on the tobacco plantations of the wealthy. They constituted a permanent underclass of families divorced in condition and consciousness from the freeholding population. The legacy of indentured servitude in the Chesapeake was slavery for blacks and a grinding tenancy for many whites.

In the Middle Colonies tenancy took on an ethnic coloration as thousands of eighteenth-century German and Scotch-Irish immigrants worked on properties owned by their well-established countrymen or by Englishmen. Many of these indentured servants and redemptioners came with greater material resources than had their seventeenth-century counterparts and after a short period of service became tenants and then small landowners. They benefitted as well from the greater availability of freehold land, especially in Pennsylvania, and from the profitable transatlantic trade in grain. This fortunate combination of circumstances—their European background, liberal land policies, and international grain prices—made tenancy in the Middle Colonies less a treacherous dead-end path than a way station on the road to property ownership.

In long-settled regions of New England tenancy had unique causes and characteristics. For generations New England parents had routinely appropriated the youthful labor of their offspring. Throughout the seventeenth century the age at marriage for males was twenty-seven years in the small agricultural village of Wenham, in coastal Essex County, Massachusetts, and it remained high (26.2) until 1750 for nonmigrant males. These young men delayed marriage until they gained access to land, usually through inheritance. By this time Wenham and many other older towns had allocated all their land; generations of use had sapped the fertility of rich bottom land, and continued subdivision was economically unwise. The inability of parents to compensate their children with substantial inheritances slowly eroded the cultural pattern of "family" labor and prompted various creative "adaptions." In Guilford, Connecticut, many families adopted (or maintained) the "stem family" system of residence and inheritance. A married son or son-in-law lived in his parents' household and inherited the farm upon the death of the father; other siblings were given money, apprenticeship contracts, or encouragement to migrate to other communities. As a result, the town's population increased relatively slowly in the eighteenth century (1.4 percent per annum), and the level of assessed wealth per taxable resident remained stable.[49] In Wenham many males married early (age twenty-three) and migrated out of the community. Movement to interior hill towns or to the New Hampshire frontier, rather than family limitation or male celibacy, thus ensured social stability. As Darrett Rutman has shown, there was a direct relationship between the age of New Hampshire towns and their rate of growth; young towns expanded at more than 6 percent per annum, while older communities grew at the barely discernible rate of 0.03 percent.[50] The "safety valve" of the frontier limited the incidence of tenancy and growth of an agricultural proletariat.

In much of New England migration conflicted with a cultural preference for partible inheritance of land. In Chebacco (near Ipswich), Massachusetts, parents stretched limited resources to the limits of economic feasibility; 90 percent of all decedents with more than one son divided their land rather than bequeath the farm to a single heir. However unpromising at first sight, this strategy seems also to have allowed young families to preserve financial independence. Bettye Pruitt found that *communities* in Massachusetts remained viable productive units even as the size of individual farms decreased. An analysis of fourteen hundred farms on the 1771 valuation list indicated that only 47 percent had the exact number of the acres of pasture, tons of hay, and bushels of grain needed to feed their livestock; but 90 percent of all towns matched forage resources with livestock holdings. "Many farmers kept more cattle than their land could hold, and many kept fewer," Pruitt concludes, "and only in the town as a whole did it all balance out."[51] In dividing their land among their male offspring, Chebacco fathers were buying their sons "in" to an interdependent economic community.

This rapid survey of the contrasting patterns of landlessness and tenancy suggests the extent to which a common nomenclature obscures a diverse reality and underlines the significance of region in early America, a point made with some frequency in the essays in this volume. Finally, it suggests that wealth distribution and social structure are not autonomous subjects. Rather, they must be understood as part of a wider system of economic, social, and , ultimately, political relationships in a given community. In New England, for example, the exchange of economic goods—labor, land, and capital—took place according to three different types of cultural interactions. First, members of kinship groups cooperated with one another. Diaries document an elaborate exchange of female labor among kin-related households, especially with respect to textile production, and male exchange of tools and draft animals followed similar lines. In addition, there were "shucking bees" and other joint economic activities, based on kin or neighborhood connections and the principle of labor reciprocity. Money values figured more prominently in a second series of transactions. Hundreds of formal account books that survive for the period 1750–1820 detail an elaborate system of local exchange among farmers, artisans, and storekeepers. Fields were plowed in return for grazing rights or the repair of a tin pot; purchases of cloth and tools were repaid by labor or the delivery of produce. Each of these transactions received a monetary value, sometimes customary and sometimes reflecting current prices, but accounts were settled only after a year or two, usually with the transfer of a few pounds. The rest had canceled out. Finally, there were "commercial" transactions in the full sense of the term: the sale of surplus grain or livestock by farmers in return for cash or store goods.[52] Some of these patterns of exchange militated against wealth inequality, while others facilitated it; some tied the lives of the inhabitants together, while others accentuated religious and political divisions. Seen in this light, the prime task is not to analyze the production and distribution of wealth in quantitative terms but rather to comprehend the various sets of cultural interactions that constituted the social structure of the community. Thus, the autonomous treatment of the subjects of wealth and social structure inaugurated in the mid-1960s by Taylor and Main should cease. These topics should become important but subordinate parts of a wider social and political history based upon the dynamic interaction of individuals and social groups that had a distinct sense of their own identity.

The framework within which these actors operated is clear in outline if not in detail. Even at the end of the colonial period the economy of British North America remained agricultural. Unlike England, the mainland colonies boasted a strong class of freeholding farmers and were not burdened by a numerous group of underemployed farmer-artisans or landless laborers. Indeed, the "proto-industrial" cottage system of manufacturing, a longstanding and growing feature of English economic life, only began to develop in America during and after the war for independence.[53] This timing was not accidental. Freed from the competition posed by highly stratified and impoverished "proto-industrialized" areas of England, New England merchants found it profitable to organize the back-country production of shoes, cloth, and processed foods. Hence, the rise of cottage manufacturing in the United States occurred primarily after 1790, almost concurrently with the mechanization of production and the factory system. By the 1830s in New England twenty-thousand women and children labored full-time in textile factories, while some forty-thousand rural women and children worked part-time making four million palm hats each year. Four decades earlier, neither system of production had been in existence.[54]

The timing of American proto-industrialization addresses the major issues raised in this paper. First, it explains the relative stability of the per capita *production* of wealth in the colonial period: resources remained in the farming sector and were not diverted to more productive nonagricultural industries. Second, this chronology accounts for the comparative stability in the *distribu-*

tion of wealth in the northern colonies. The new social system of slavery brought an increase in inequality to the South after 1690, but a comparable shift occurred in the North only a century later as merchants and industrialists mobilized the rural labor force in a new productive system. Third, the discontinuity between the pre-1775 freeholder-dominated *social structure* of New England and other long-established northern regions and their rapid post-1790 development as proto-industrial areas raises important and as yet unanswered questions regarding the relationship between cultural values and economic development. The task before us is to explicate the distinct structures and patterns of existence in these pre-industrial societies and thus to comprehend the logic and dynamic of the lives of their inhabitants.

NOTES

1. The first detailed analysis of a "frontier" community came only in 1959: Merle Curti et al., *The Making of an American Community: A Case Study of Democracy in a Frontier County* (Stanford, 1959). See also Charles S. Grant, *Democracy in the Connecticut Frontier Town of Kent*, 1961; reprint, New York, 1972).

2. James Truslow Adams, *Provincial Society, 1690–1763* (New York, 1927), 85. See also Samuel Eliot Morison, *The Maritime History of Massachusetts, 1783–1860* (Boston, 1921).

3. Robert E. Brown, *Middle Class Democracy and the Revolution in Massachusetts, 1691–1780* (Ithaca, N.Y., 1955), 403; John Cary, "Statistical Method and the Brown Thesis on Colonial Democracy," *William and Mary Quarterly*, 3d ser., 20 (1963): 251–76; Richard Buel, Jr., "Democracy and the American Revolution: A Frame of Reference," ibid. 21 (1964): 165–90; J. R. Pole, "Historians and the Problem of Early American Democracy," *American Historical Review* 67 (1962): 626–46.

4. Robert Zemsky, *Merchants, Farmers, and River Gods: An Essay on Eighteenth-Century American Politics* (Boston, 1971), 31–38, 294–99. See also Jack P. Greene, "Foundations of Political Power in the Virginia House of Burgesses, 1720–1776," *William and Mary Quarterly*, 3d ser., 16 (1959): 485–506; and Jackson Turner Main, "Government by the People: The American Revolution and the Democratization of the Legislatures," ibid. 23 (1966): 391–407.

5. Robert E. Brown and B. Katherine Brown, *Virginia, 1705–1786: Democracy or Aristocracy?* (East Lansing, 1964). The lack of controversy engendered by the Virginia volume reflected its failure to convince rather than its success. Most scholars have preferred the "deferential," or "aristocratic," interpretation offered by Charles S. Sydnor, *Gentlemen Freeholders: Political Practices in Washington's Virginia* (Chapel Hill, 1952).

6. Jackson Turner Main, "The Distribution of Property in Post-Revolutionary Virginia," *Mississippi Valley Historical Review* 41 (1954): 241–58; idem, "The One Hundred," *William and Mary Quarterly*, 3d ser., 11 (1954): 354–84; idem, "Sections and Politics in Virginia, 1781–1787," ibid. 12 (1955): 96—112.

7. Bernard Bailyn, "Politics and Social Structure in Virginia" in *Seventeenth Century America*, ed. James M. Smith (Chapel Hill, 1960); idem, "Communications and Trade: The Atlantic in the Seventeenth Century," *Journal of Economic History* 12 (1953): 378–88; idem, *The New England Merchants in the Seventeenth Century* (New York 1955).

8. Main, *Social Structure of Revolutionary America*, vii.

9. W. W. Rostow, *The Stages of Economic Growth: A Non-Communist Manifesto* (Cambridge, 1960); by 1963 Rostow's book was in its ninth printing. Other works included Albert O.

Hirschman, *The Strategy of Economic Development* (New Haven, 1958); Bert F. Hoselitz, ed., *Theories of Economic Growth* (New York 1960); and Douglass C. North, *The Economic Growth of the United States, 1790–1860* (Englewood Cliffs, N.J., 1961).

10. James A. Henretta, "Economic Development and Social Structure in Colonial Boston," *William and Mary Quarterly,* 3d ser., 22 (1965): 75–92; Main, *Social Structure of Revolutionary America,* 276n and passim.

11. George Rogers Taylor, "American Economic Growth before 1840," *Journal of Economic History* 24 (1964): 427–44. See also Ralph Andreano, ed., *New Views of American Economic Development: A Selective Anthology of Recent Work* (Cambridge, Mass., 1965), 50–51; and Robert E. Gallman, "The Pace and Pattern of American Economic Growth," in *American Economic Growth: An Economist's History of the United States,* ed. Lance E. Davis et al. (New York, 1972), 17–25.

12. Clarence L. Ver Steeg, *The Formative Years, 1607–1763* (New York, 1964); Peter Laslett, *The World We Have Lost* (New York, 1965); Seymour Martin Lipset and Reinhold Bendix, *Social Mobility in Industrial Society* (Berkeley, 1963); Stephan Thernstrom, *Poverty and Progress: Social Mobility in a Nineteenth Century City* (Cambridge, Mass., 1964); Lawrence Stone, "Social Mobility in England, 1500–1700," *Past and Present,* no. 33 (1966): 16–55.

13. In Main, *Social Structure of Revolutionary America,* 287, 164, 286, 220.

14. It was not accidental that most of the previous work on wealth and social structure traced either the erosion of English status in the American environment or the social conflicts of the Revolutionary era, for these "problems" had been conceptualized by the Progressive historians. See, for example, Norman H. Dawes, "Titles as Symbols of Prestige in Seventeenth-Century New England," *William and Mary Quarterly* 3d ser., 6 (1949): 69–83; and William A. Reavis, "The Maryland Gentry and Social Mobility, 1637–1676," ibid. 14 (1957): 418–28.

15. John Demos, "Notes on Life in Plymouth Colony," *William and Mary Quarterly,* 3d ser., 22 (1965): 264–86; idem, *A Little Commonwealth: Family Life in Plymouth Colony* (New York, 1970); Philip J. Greven, Jr., "Family Structure in Seventeenth-Century Andover, Massachusetts," *William and Mary Quarterly,* 3d ser., 23 (1966): 234–56; idem, *Four Generations: Population, Land, and Family in Colonial Andover, Massachusetts* (Ithaca, N.Y., 1970); Kenneth A. Lockridge, "The Population of Dedham, Massachusetts, 1636–1736," *Economic History Review,* 2d ser., 19 (1966): 318–44; idem, *A New England Town: The First Hundred Years, Dedham, Massachusetts, 1636–1736* (New York, 1970).

16. Kenneth A. Lockridge, "Land, Population, and the Evolution of New England Society, 1630–1780," *Past and Present,* no. 39 (1968).

17. Quoted in Lockridge, "Evolution of New England Society," reprinted in *Colonial America: Essays in Politics and Social Development,* ed. Stanley N. Katz (Boston, 1971), 478; idem, "Social Change and the Meaning of the American Revolution," *Journal of Social History* 6 (1973): 403–39, as reprinted in Katz, *Colonial America,* 2d ed. (Boston, 1976), 501, 514.

18. Robert A. Gross, *The Minutemen and Their World* (New York, 1976), 107; Richard L. Bushman, "Massachusetts Farmers and the Revolution," in *Society, Freedom, and Conscience: The Coming of the Revolution in Virginia, Massachusetts, and New York,* ed. Richard M. Jellison (New York, 1976), 122,120; Hermann Wellenreuther, "A View of Socio-Economic Structures of England and the British Colonies on the Eve of the American Revolution," in *New Wine in Old Skins: A Comparative View of Socio-Political Structures and Values Affecting the American Revolution,* ed. Erich Angermann, Marie-Luise Frings, and Hermann Wellenreuther (Stuttgart, 1976), 14–40.

19. This argument is more fully developed in James A. Henretta, "Families and Farms: *Mentalité* in Pre-Industrial America," *William and Mary Quarterly,* 3d ser., 35 (1978): 3–32. Too often the analysis of the "early modern period" of European and American history has been undertaken with concepts and theories articulated originally to describe the industrializing society of the nineteenth century. Thus when Gary B. Nash compiled his useful anthology *Class and Society in Early America* (Englewood Cliffs, N.J., 1970), he used Bernard Barber's ahistorical survey "Social Stratification" (originally published in the *International Encyclopedia of Social Sciences,* ed. David L. Sills, 18 vols. [New York, 1968], 15:288–95) as his theoretical, or analytic, reading.

20. North, *Economic Growth of the United States;* Paul David, "The Growth of Real Product in the United States before 1840: New Evidence, Controlled Conjectures," *Journal of Economic History* 27 (1967): 151–97; Alice Hanson Jones, *Wealth of a Nation To Be: The American Colonies on the Eve of the Revolution* (New York, 1980), 305–7; Gallman, "Pace and Pattern." For an overview see John J. McCusker and Russell R. Menard, "The Economy of British America, 1607–1790: Needs and Opportunities for Study" (Draft for discussion, Conference on the Economy of British America, Williamsburg, Va., October 1980, mimeographed), chap. 15.

21. Russell R. Menard, "The Tobacco Industry in the Chesapeake Colonies, 1617–1730: An Interpretation," *Research in Economic History* 5 (1980): 109–77; Terry L. Anderson and Robert Paul Thomas, "Economic Growth in the Seventeenth-Century Chesapeake," *Explorations in Economic History* 15, no. 4 (1978): 368–87.

22. Terry L. Anderson, "Economic Growth in Colonial New England: 'Statistical Renaissance,' " *Journal of Economic History* 39 (1979): 243–58, and Anderson's other work cited therein.

23. Anderson, "Economic Growth," table 1; Jackson Turner Main, "The Distribution of Property in Colonial Connecticut," in *The Human Dimensions of Nation Making: Essays on Colonial and Revolutionary America,* ed. James Kirby Martin (Madison, Wis., 1976), tables 11, 13, and passim; John J. Waters, Jr., "Patrimony, Succession, and Social Stability: Guilford, Connecticut in the Eighteenth Century," *Perspectives in American History* 10 (1976): 159.

24. Duane E. Ball, "Dynamics of Population and Wealth in Eighteenth-Century Chester County, Pennsylvania," *Journal of Interdisciplinary History* 6 (1976), tables 5 and 6.

25. Marc Egnal, "The Economic Development of the Thirteen Continental Colonies, 1720 to 1775," *William and Mary Quarterly,* 3d ser., 32 (1975), table 2; Ball, "Dynamics of Population," table 6; Jones, *Wealth of a Nation To Be,* table 9.3. Studies such as Egnal's, which employed statistical data from exports and imports, tended to exaggerate the importance of overseas trade and the commercial economy. Works based on probate records did not measure the timing of economic change but rather gave a more accurate picture of economic performance.

26. Daniel Scott Smith, "A Malthusian-Frontier Interpretation of United States Demographic History before c. 1815," reprinted from *Urban History Review* in *Urbanization in the Americas: The Background in Comparative Perspective,* ed. Woodrow Borah, Jorge Hardoy, and Gilbert A. Stelter (Ottawa, 1980), 15–24.

27. Ball, "Economic Growth," 635; Sarah F. McMahon, "Providing a 'Comfortable Subsistence': The Composition of Diet in New England, 1630–1840," *William and Mary Quarterly,* forthcoming.

28. Allan Kulikoff, "The Economic Growth of the Eighteenth-Century Chesapeake Colonies," *Journal of Economic History* 39 (1979): 275–88. In All Hallow's Parish, Maryland, the adult-child ratio among slaves decreased from 3 to 1 in the 1680s, to 2.3 to 1 in the 1720s, to 1.04 to 1 in the 1760s (Carville V. Earle, *The Evolution of a Tidewater Settlement System: All Hallow's Parish, Maryland, 1650–1783* [Chicago, 1975], table 11).

29. Jones, *Wealth of a Nation To Be,* table 9.3; see table 9.2 in this chapter.

30. Edmund S. Morgan, *American Slavery—American Freedom: The Ordeal of Colonial Virginia* (New York, 1975), chap. 17; Aubrey C. Land, "Economic Base and Social Structure: The Northern Chesapeake in the Eighteenth Century," *Journal of Economic History* 25 (1965): 639–54; Jones, *Wealth of a Nation To Be,* table 7.9.

31. Paul G. E. Clemens, *The Atlantic Economy and Colonial Maryland's Eastern Shore: From Tobacco to Grain* (Ithaca, N.Y., 1980), 160–64; Earle, *Tidewater Settlement System,* 209.

32. See, for example, James T. Lemon and Gary B. Nash, "The Distribution of Wealth in Eighteenth-Century America: A Century of Change in Chester County, Pennsylvania, 1693–1802," *Journal of Social History* 2 (1968): 1–24. The authors found a "blurred, inconsistent, and often confusing picture" and suggested caution in generalizing about wealth distributions but in the end confirmed a "gradually increasing differentiation." In fact, Ball, "Population and Wealth," 636–38, supported the conclusion of increasing inequality, so the most recent evidence from Chester County remained consistent with the Main-Henretta model. Bruce C. Daniels, "Long Range Trends of Wealth Distribution in Eighteenth Century New England," *Explorations*

in Economic History 11, no. 2 (1973–74): 123–35, found considerable evidence of stability but used Main's evolutionary model to interpret the data. See also Donald W. Koch, "Income Distribution and Political Structure in Seventeenth-Century Salem, Massachusetts," *Essex Institute Historical Collections* 105 (1969).

33. G. B. Warden, "Inequality and Instability in Eighteenth-Century Boston: A Reappraisal," *Journal of Interdisciplinary History* 6 (1976): 49–84; Jackson Turner Main, "Property in Colonial Connecticut," 54–104; Gloria L. Main, "Inequality in Early America: The Evidence from Probate Records of Massachusetts and Maryland," *Journal of Interdisciplinary History* 7 (1977): 559–82.

34. Peter H. Lindert and Jeffrey Williamson, "Long Term Trends in American Wealth Inequality," in *Modeling the Distribution and Intergenerational Transmission of Wealth*, ed. James D. Smith (Chicago, 1980); see p. 10, table 1.3, and in general, 12–37.

35. Lindert and Williamson, "Long Term Trends," 14, 26–36; Waters, "Patrimony, Succession, and Social Stability." For Wenham see Douglas L. Jones, *Village and Seaport: Migration and Society in Eighteenth-Century Massachusetts* (Hanover, N.H., 1981), chap. 1, n. 14. Jones finds a pattern in the adjoining seaport of Beverly: there 25 percent of the fathers were in the lowest 40 percent of the wealth distribution. On the basis of seventeenth-century English probate records, Carole Shammas argued that occupation, age, and education taken together explain 32 percent of the variance in personal wealth and , further, that the decline in wealth after age sixty was most apparent among middling farmers and artisans but was not present among wealthy decedents and poor laborers ("The Determinants of Personal Wealth in Seventeenth-Century England and America," *Journal of Economic History* 37 [1977]: 675–89).

36. Main, "Inequality in Early America," 570–72. In her "Maryland and the Chesapeake Economy, 1670–1720," in *Law, Society, and Politics in Early Maryland*, ed. Aubrey C. Land, Lois Green Carr, and Edward C. Papenfuse (Baltimore, 1977), 134–52, Main confirmed Aubrey Land's "mercantile" interpretation of wealth accumulation in the Chesapeake. See Land, "Economic Behavior in a Planting Society: The Eighteenth-Century Chesapeake," *Journal of Southern History* 33 (1967): 469–85; but see also Morgan, *American Slavery—American Freedom*, chap. 10, which considered the impact of political profiteering, and Russell R. Menard, "From Servant to Freeholder: Status, Mobility and Property Accumulation in Seventeenth-Century Maryland," *William and Mary Quarterly*, 3d ser., 30 (1973): 37–64, which noted the decline in economic opportunity for former servants after 1660.

37. Earle, *Tidewater Settlement System*, 115, 128–32; Main, "Maryland and the Chesapeake Economy," 145–47.

38. Jones, *Wealth of a Nation to Be*, table 6.2; Bettye Hobbs Pruitt, "Agriculture and Society in the Towns of Massachusetts, 1771: A Statistical Analysis" (Ph.D. diss., Boston University, 1981), table 27 and pp. 172–79.

39. Daniels, "Trends of Wealth Distribution," 127; Gary B. Nash, "Urban Wealth and Poverty in Pre-Revolutionary America," *Journal of Interdisciplinary History* 6 (1976), table 1; Lindert and Williamson, "Long Term Trends," tables 1.A.3, 1.A.7, and 1.3.; Jones, *Wealth of a Nation to Be*, tables 8.6, 8.4, and 9.5. The only exception was the South and then only when all slaves were counted as potential wealthholders and given a wealth of zero; if slaves were counted only as property, the Gini coefficient for free wealthholders fell to 0.67 (ibid., table 9.4). By way of comparison, the Gini coefficient for Massachusetts rose from 0.55–0.62 in the late eighteenth century to 0.77 by 1830 and 0.825 in 1860. For all adult males in the South in 1870 the coefficient was 0.87. Clearly the industrialization of the North created a degree of wealth inequality comparable to that in the slave society of the South (See Main, "Inequality in Early America," 575).

40. Nash, "Urban Wealth and Poverty," tables 3, 4, 5, and 7. Nash provides a detailed treatment of the development of Boston, New York, and Philadelphia in *The Urban Crucible: Social Change, Political Consciousness, and the Origins of the American Revolution* (Cambridge, Mass., 1979).

41. Morgan, *American Slavery—American Freedom*, esp. 320–26; David Grayson Allen, *In English*

Ways: The Movement of Societies and the Transferal of English Local Law and Custom to Massachusetts Bay in the Seventeenth Century (Chapel Hill, 1981).

42. Lois Green Carr and Lorena S. Walsh, "The Planter's Wife: The Experience of White Women in Seventeenth-Century Maryland," *William and Mary Quarterly*, 3d ser., 34 (1977): 542–71; idem, "Women's Role in the Eighteenth-Century Chesapeake" (Paper presented at the Conference on Women in Early America, Williamsburg, Va., November 1981).

43. Jack P. Greene, *The Quest for Power: The Lower Houses of Assembly in the Southern Royal Colonies, 1689–1776* (Chapel Hill, 1963); Bernard Bailyn, *The Ideological Origins of the American Revolution* (Cambridge, Mass., 1967).

44. John M. Murrin and Rowland Berthoff, "Feudalism, Communalism, and the Yeoman Freeholder: The American Revolution Considered as a Social Accident," in *Essays on the American Revolution*, ed. Stephen G. Kurtz and James H. Hutson (Chapel Hill, 1973), 267; Lockridge, "Evolution of New England Society," passim.

45. Wellenreuther, "Socio-Economic Structures," 15–21.

46. See the concise argument in Patricia U. Bonomi, *A Factious People: Politics and Society in Colonial New York* (New York, 1971) or the more detailed but sometimes confusing analysis by Sung Bok Kim, *Landlord and Tenant in Colonial New York: Manorial Society, 1667–1775* (Chapel Hill, 1978).

47. Gregory A. Stiverson, "Landless Husbandmen: Proprietary Tenants in Maryland in the Late Colonial Period," in Land, Carr, and Papenfuse, *Law, Society, and Politics*, 197–211; Earle, *Tidewater Settlement System*, 207–13.

48. Richard S. Dunn, "Servants and Slaves: The Recruitment and Employment of Labor," in this volume.

49. Waters, "Patrimony, Succession, and Social Stability." See also Lutz K. Berkner, "The Stem Family and the Development Cycle of the Peasant Household: An Eighteenth-Century Austrian Example," *American Historical Review* 77 (1972).

50. Jones, *Village and Seaport*, chap. 5; Darrett B. Rutman, "The Social Web: A Prospectus for the Study of the Early American Community," in *Insights and Parallels: Problems and Issues of American Social History*, ed. William L. O'Neill (Minneapolis, 1973), 76n.

51. Christopher M. Jedrey, *The World of John Cleaveland: Family and Community in Eighteenth-Century New England* (New York, 1979), 80–83; Pruitt, "Agriculture and Society," 35.

52. For a fine theoretical statement see Michael Merrill, "Cash is Good to Eat: Self-Sufficiency and Exchange in the Rural Economy of the United States," *Radical History Review* 4 (1977): 42–69; see also Susan Geib, "'Changing Works': Agriculture and Society in Brookfield, Massachusetts, 1780–1835" (Ph.D. diss., Boston University, 1981).

53. See, for example, Hans Medick, "The Proto-Industrial Family Economy: The Structural Function of Household and Family during the Transition from Peasant Society to Industrial Capitalism," *Social History* 3 (1976): 291–316; Joan Thirsk, "Industries in the Countryside," in *Essays in the Economic and Social History of Tudor and Stuart England*, ed. F. J. Fisher (Cambridge, 1961), 70–88; and A. Soboul, "The French Rural Community in the Eighteenth and Nineteenth Centuries," *Past and Present*, no. 10 (1956): 78–95.

54. Thomas Dublin, "Women and the Dimensions of Outwork in Nineteenth-Century New England" (Paper presented at the Berkshire Conference on Women's History, June 1981), 10.

10

VALUE AND SOCIETY

JOYCE APPLEBY

n this essay I will discuss how historians during the past quarter-century have dealt with the subject of value and society. I will begin with the theoretical underpinnings for the proposition that values are the principal cohesive force in society. This concept of value has been particularly influential in recent writings on early America because of the widespread adoption of social science models that rely upon it. By using these models, colonial historians have become involved in two refractory issues: the relation between culture and behavior and the appropriateness of describing social change as the movement from traditional to modern mores. It is my intention here to look first at contemporary social theory and then at the application of social science models in colonial studies and then to assess the value of the "value and society" paradigm, or—to evoke the spirit of 1981—to consider whether the interest rates we are paying for having borrowed so heavily from the social sciences are too high.

In *The Theory of Social and Economic Organization*, Max Weber attributed to human beings "an inner necessity to comprehend the world as a meaningful cosmos and to know what attitude to take before it."[1] From this numinous need he extracted two propositions of fundamental importance to the study of society: (1) men and women carry inside them an imaginative reconstruction of reality; and (2) this model of the world affects their behavior. Karl Marx had set the problem for Weber with his assertion that world views were class artifacts produced by elites to be consumed by the masses. Assuming that human consciousness has a certain plasticity, Marx had attributed the transformation of belief systems to changes in economic organization. The relationship between ideas and class interests could be conveyed in an epigram: "At the date when, in England, people gave up the practice of burning witches, they began to hang the forgers of banknotes."[2] More interested in the psychological origins of believing, Weber could not find in class motives an adequate explanation for either the persuasiveness or the content of a society's world view. He therefore tested the implicit theory of behavior in Marx's writings on ideology and found it wanting.

Weber's celebrated case study *The Protestant Ethic and the Spirit of Capitalism* presented an alternative picture of the interaction of belief, behavior, and social change. Rather than attribute the modern Western mentality to the political program of a new class, as Marx had, he saw it as the adventitious outcome of the Protestant Reformation. Basic to Weber's argument was his skepticism about the presumed naturalness of economic endeavor. "A man does not by nature wish to earn more and more money," he wrote, "but simply to live as he is accustomed to live and to earn as much as is necessary for that purpose."[3] Nor did he find in the avarice and will of rising entrepreneurs the means, as distinct from the motives, for reorienting a society's values; instead, religious developments held the key for understanding how an ingrained way of life had given way in the early modern period to utterly new moral purposes. According to Weber's reformulation, the Calvinist injunction to glorify God through work invested mundane tasks with spiritual significance, while the Calvinists' anxieties about damnation promoted disciplined, rational, ceaseless economic activity. This dramatic reorganization of social sensibilities, Weber claimed, created modes of behavior powerful enough to overcome traditional restraints on private enterprise. A host of critics notwithstanding, Weber did not say that Calvinism caused capitalism; rather, he pointed to the way that certain religious commitments had created a spirit just as propitious for capitalism as developments in the material world.[4] Without minimizing the importance of class interests or economic influences, Weber insisted that ideology was an independent force capable of motivating as well as reflecting social action. In Weber's view, the most enduring legacy of the Protestant Reformation was rationalism. Once that expectation had penetrated the innermost temple of religious devotion, the venerable guidance of sentiment, tradition, and rule of thumb could be supplanted by explicit, abstract, calculable rules of procedure.[5] Rationalism, with its powers to demystify and instrumentalize social life, became for Weber the invisible force behind the modern transformation of Western society.

In his exploration of values Weber provided a model for the entire study of consciousness. He expanded and elaborated what others had contracted. His analysis of the connection between Calvinism and capitalism embraced the practical effect of rationalism, the psychological impact of predestination, and the social consequences of the celebration of work. In contrast to classical economic writers who had assumed that human beings were inherently geared to the strenuous pursuit of profit, Weber viewed this as novel behavior that had to be explained. By rejecting the universal economic impulse of liberal theories as well as Marx's dialectical materialism, Weber made social change a truly historical phenomenon to be understood on its own terms. His emphasis upon moral commitments and modes of thinking suggested also that change should not be reduced to the operation of mechanical causes. Society, with its ongoing processes, could be distinguished but not separated from culture, with its imaginative representations of those activities. Such a generous conception of historical reality and human complexity did much to neutralize the Marxist provenance of ideology for American scholars. Moreover, there was in Weber's work an explicit tension between purpose and contingency, materialism and morality, individual assent and social compulsion, which was particularly appealing to a generation of scholars whose intellectual inheritance had included the positivism of Comte, the determinism of Marx, and the relativism of Ruth Benedict.

Although Weber was widely read in the years following World War II, his great influence upon American colonial historiography came by way of two developing fields in the social sciences: the sociology of knowledge and structural functionalism. As was the case in so many other social inquiries, Marx had the original and stunning insight that detonated the liberal position. And he expressed it with typical succinctness: "It is not the consciousness of men that determines their being, but, on the contrary, their social being that determines their consciousness."[6] Since, for him, that social being was shaped by the class structure, which in turn reflected the mode of production, it followed that social consciousness was the creation of ruling classes using intellectual and artistic means to consolidate their power. Most scholars working after Marx abandoned the tendentious distinction between ideology as "ideas serving social interests" and false consciousness as "thought alienated from the real social being of the thinker."[7] It was not until the 1960s, however, that the logic of socially conditioned thought was pursued to the inexorable conclusion that cultural influences are manifest in all intellectual activity. Scientists may indeed subject their propositions to more rigorous testing, but like the man on the street, they begin with the "tacit knowledge" that makes all conceptualization possible. Of tremendous importance for the future of the study of ideology was the fact that those working in the sociology of knowledge were not overcome by that "vertigo of relativity" that had dampened the enthusiasm of their predecessors. Instead, following Weber's lead, they found a fascination in examining the human animal as a system-building and symbol-producing creature.[8]

The anthropologist Clifford Geertz and the sociologists Peter L. Berger and Thomas Luckmann have suggested what this new conception of belief could mean to historians' efforts to reconstruct the past. Writing as synthesizers, Berger and Luckmann explored both sides of the relationship between society as a socializing force and human beings, who act as the mediators of biological, psychological, and social influences. By accepting the essential ambiguity of the individual person's sense of self and sense of group membership, they attempted with some success to integrate the perspectives of Marx and Weber with those of Weber's distinguished contemporary Émile Durkheim. Starting with the premise that all reality is socially constructed, Berger and Luckmann worked out a theoretical base for the sociology of knowledge useful to both intellectual historians dealing with creative thinkers and social historians pursuing "the reality" in the minds of ordinary men and women. They also distinguished sharply between sociologists' questions and the epistemological concerns of philosophers. If men and women think that they possess free will, for instance, sociologists will not ask what this statement signifies but rather why people in some societies take free will for granted while others do not. Thus Berger and Luckmann have refurbished Marx's original formulation of ideology by making room for psychological and social imperatives that have weakened, without entirely displacing, class conflict as a causal force.[9]

The acknowledgment of the "inevitable historicity of human thought" made this new perspective particularly congenial to anthropologists working with nonliterate societies. Since abandoning nineteenth-century evolutionary theories these anthropologists had directed their attention to the actual operation of social systems, especially to the way that symbols and values interacted with routines and institutions. This functional approach also promoted a certain skepticism about Marx's position. Observing societies with limited economic resources, anthropologists became aware of the relation of culture to social survival. Just as Weber concluded that the content of the bourgeois world view could not be derived from purely economic influences, so anthropologists found it difficult to explain culture as the ideology of the elite. Not only did the evidence suggest that rulers were as immersed in the shared world view as other members of society but it also became apparent that culture was more profoundly rooted than the political purposes it presumably served. A society without classes could be imagined more readily than a society without culture.

More than any other anthropologist, Clifford Geertz has made explicit the implications of this conclusion for historians of the West. Affirming Weber's contention that values are subjectively experienced, Geertz has eloquently described man as "an animal suspended in webs of significance he himself has spun."[10] For him the sociology of knowledge has become the sociology of meaning, "for what is socially determined is not the nature of conception but the vehicles of conceptions." To know a society is to understand the means of expression open to its people—an assertion fairly bristling with opportunities for historians. In Geertz's writings the human mind figures as the repository for potentialities, dispositions, and capabilities, with a structural bias towards coherence. Weber's categories have thickened. Geertz has also added a historical dimension to the evolution of value systems. Whereas in small groups social action can be organized by ritual and custom, modern societies require more elaborate communication. "Ideology is ornate, vivid, deliberately suggestive," he has said. "By objectifying moral sentiment through the same devices that science shuns, it seeks to motivate action." And because ideas can motivate action, formal ideologies, Geertz has maintained, emerge and take hold at precisely the time when a society begins "to free itself from the immediate governance of received tradition."[11]

It needs to be noted that these hypotheses that hold out the possibility of treating the past as another culture are more suggestive than analytical. The extraordinary complexity of society makes it difficult to move from theory to empirical proof, and in the sociology of knowledge this step is further encumbered by the striking differences between nonliterate societies and the language-dominated societies historians study. A universal model for the interdependence of culture and society has been advanced, but the interaction between the two is far from clear. The sociologist Ernest Gellner has suggested that the more elaborate the structuring of a society—that is, the more exact the assignment of roles—the less the need for a culture carried by words. Modern societies, on the other hand, rely upon explanation and persuasion, often through the written word alone. "The burden of comprehension," Gellner explains, has shifted "from the context, to the communication itself."[12] Societies knit together by habit and ritual can dispense with words; this is not the case for modern societies: their no less urgent need for coherent social action actually heightens the importance of socially structured communication. Whereas Gellner talks about social identity, Geertz has focused upon the political significance of shared convictions. The "ornate, vivid, deliberately suggestive" language of ideology makes autonomous politics possible, he says, by providing the persuasive images crucial to the exercise of authority.[13]

Directing attention to the fact that the means of expression are important determinants of a society's intellectual life, these scholars have supplied historians with the theories necessary to examine belief in relation to behavior. In this enterprise they have also been greatly assisted by another historian, Thomas Kuhn. Working on the most recondite of all intellectual topics, the origins of scientific discovery, Kuhn asserted that all scientific inquiries are dependent upon established paradigms, which define the terms of discourse and organize the tasks of explanation. What has permitted historians to extrapolate from Kuhn's work on science is his insistence that scientific thinking is a social activity. Like the domain assumptions of an ideology, scientific truths require confirmation from the group, in this case the body of established practitioners.[14] Having, as David Hollinger commented, driven the Whig interpretation of history out of its best-defended enclave, Kuhn encouraged others to treat culture itself as a giant paradigm. His vivid description of established ways of scientific thinking under attack was easily seen as analogous to social revolutions, in which secure traditions were beset with novelty and confusion.[15] By revealing the unexamined assumptions underlying "normal science," Kuhn has made the most rarified intellectual labor congruent with the mundane thought of social existence: both rely upon consensus; both are exposed to contingent and subversive experiences. As J. G. A. Pocock enthusiastically wrote, Kuhn's work opened up the possibility of treating thought as both a linguistic and a political process.[16] Thus, refined, the sociology of knowledge held out the hope of joining belief with behavior. Ideas point people to their interests through a presentation of reality that makes connections and establishes priorities. Ideas also get some people to do what others want them to do. It becomes the business of historians to sort this all out for the past and, by clarifying the tacit understandings in a shared world view, to penetrate its logic. Historians' acceptance of this scholarly task is reflected in the use of *ideology* and *ideological* in contexts where *intellectual* would formerly have been used.[17]

Although Weber laid great stress upon the innovative, energizing quality of values, he did not deny that social norms become internalized through psychological mechanisms that act coercively. Indeed, in one of his most memorable passages he described his own society as an iron cage, "into which the individual is born and which presents itself . . . as an unalterable order of things in which he must live."[18] Where his convictions about the voluntary aspects of value formation become salient is in contrast to those of Durkheim. Both men accorded values the major role in creating solidarity, thus joining in bringing religion back from the periphery to the center of social study. Durkheim, however, subsumed values under the rubric "social facts."[19] People felt them as constraints; they were external in origin and repressive in effect. Yet, he regarded these elements of compulsion constructively: they established the boundaries that promoted the integration of potentially wayward individuals into prescriptively stable social systems. While he did not deny the human capacity of affirmation and dissension, Durkheim clearly feared the disruption of social equilibrium more than he feared the suppression of human freedom. Both men rejected the idea that history has an overarching rationale and hence did not share Marx's determinism, however indebted they were to him for his elucidation of social power. There was no destiny immanent in historical processes. Change was continuous but not necessarily progressive. The growth of rationality led only to an awareness, as George Lichtheim wrote, that it was not possible "to ground value judgments in a universally accepted doctrine of human nature."[20] It was indeed the problematic character of experience that rendered society and its study so central to all ameliorative efforts.

These particular features in the work of Weber and Durkheim bore fruit in the post–World War II period in the structural-functionalist theory of Talcott Parsons and his many collaborators. Like the cross-fertilization between the sociology of knowledge and intellectual history, Parsons's studies began immediately to exercise an influence upon social historians. As the principal translator of Weber's books, Parsons succeeded in bringing into mainstream American sociology the concept of culture as the hidden but shared matrix of attitudes, injunctions, and affirmations that guide social behavior.[21] Breaking out of the circularity of defining culture as the sum of the ways human beings behave and interpreting their behavior as the expression of their culture, he ambitiously set out to explicate what was implicit in Weber and Durkheim.[22] By pairing the systems he found operating in society with the social drives that produced them, he came up with a table of patterned variables. The resulting combination of complexity and precision gave social scientists a rather impressive set of categories for cataloging, if not actually interpreting, what they learned about societies, past and present. Under Parsons's relentless pressure, the definition of culture encompassing both material and spiritual expressions gave way to a purely psychological concept, a reworking that Parsons himself attributed to Weber and Durkheim's shared conviction that men (and presumably women) invest the acts and events in their world with "teleological meaning."[23]

Society became for Parsons a moral community in which rulers and ruled alike willingly participated because of their common need to legitimate behavior. The disposition of human beings to make moral distinctions and to defer biological gratification because of them offered a naturalistic theory of behavior that highlighted the spiritual and intellectual capacities of men and women. Especially appealing in this approach was the dethroning of the economic factors in Marxist and liberal theories. In the place of the economy Parsons put four functional exigencies: "goal attainment, adaptation, integration and pattern maintenance."[24] Despite the antiseptic social scientese of the formulation, the emphasis upon the specifically human qualities in social action impressed scholars cultivating more poetic insights. As Robert Berkhofer shrewdly noted, the new stress on man as a valuing animal enabled many humanists "to climb aboard the culture wagon."[25]

By giving equal time, as it were, to science, religion, politics, and the economy, Parsons provided theoretical support for studying such divergent topics as social status, kinship networks, adolescence, ethnicity, education, magic, inheritance patterns, and, of course, all religious movements. Whereas the classical liberal model had encouraged research on technology and economic institutions and Marxist analysis had promoted the study of class conflict, Parsons's theory put many arrows in the historians' quiver. All that any inquiry needed to do was relate the discrete social element to the overall structure. Thus the functionalists' absorption with how societies maintained their systems spawned a decade of "normal science." Lois Banner pointed the advantage out to social historians: subjects like women and the family could now be construed as elements in the dynamic process of social integration.[26] Differentiating the biological, psychological, and sociological aspects of human existence, with his new definition of culture as "a system of symbols by which man conveys significance upon his own experience" Parsons was able to indicate where and how they interacted.[27] Here was a conception of social life congenial to the humanist's view of men and women as purposeful creatures.

Where the Parsonian paradigm failed was in accounting for change. Originally more concerned with how social systems maintained themselves, the

Parsonians neglected the historical dimension. Contemporary events forced the issue: under the challenge to explain the great transformations of the modern era, sociologists returned to older writings on traditional and modern social forms, that is, to the gemeinschaft and gesellschaft of Ferdinand Tönnies. This rich literature in comparative studies offered a way to explicate social change without sacrificing grand theory to the crabbed particularities of national histories. Apparent variety, it was seen, masked real similarity. Change in the modern era in fact could be treated as a movement between two types of society, involving, as Dean Tipps has written, "a series of transitions from primitive, subsistence economies to technology-intensive, industrial economies; from subject to participant political cultures; from closed, ascriptive status systems to open, achievement-oriented systems; from extended to nuclear kinship units; from religious to secular ideologies."[28] Thus the new concept of modernization represented a joining of Parsons's patterned variables with the ideal types of Weber. What had begun as a means for analyzing social order ended by explaining in a single, embracive theory the momentous historical developments of the twentieth century. The rise of the West was not a cultural excrescence but the end towards which all other societies were inexorably moving through successive phases of differentiation, disruption, and reintegration.

Although originally conceived in the spirit of self-congratulation that American social scientists felt as they contemplated the Soviet bloc in the post–World War II period, modernization theory actually made it easier for historians to use both Parsonian and Marxist perspectives. The renewed emphasis upon purely material factors like capital and technology helped. When modernization theory was applied to contemporary Third World countries, the primacy of economic development was hard to deny, even among those who began with Weber's assumptions. Simultaneously, the discovery and reassessment of certain of Marx's writings revealed his view of ideas as autonomous forces in social life, more locked in a dialectic with material circumstances than passively following the realignments of classes.[29] With these two reinterpretations, Marx's old transition from feudalism to capitalism could be used, if not actually fused, with Parsons's conception of society as a system of interdependent and mutually reinforcing subsystems. Both offered a universal theory of the progression from traditional to modern social forms, and both saw change emanating from a disruption of the original relation between the material base and the superstructure. The residual differences about class power and social justice could be shelved while the new agenda for analyzing social processes got under way. Berger and Luckmann's theoretical union of Marx, Weber, and Durkheim was ready for historical application as a research strategy when the fading of cold-war stereotypes freed historians and their constituencies for more interesting tasks than that of defending American exceptionalism.

My purpose in expatiating upon the social scientists' models has been to show that they are firmly attached to specific explanations about change and to indicate what that means for colonial scholarship. The organizing themes of Weberian sociology carry with them unavoidable assumptions about the basic nature of human existence. Belief in the dominance of social reality has led to the abandonment of the old liberal story of individual endeavors, but like the Whig interpretation of old, the new models have structured the historians' imagination. The use of value as an organizing theme has shifted the attention of scholars from a progressive sequence of events to the patterned reception of those events in a multilayered society. Moreover, by defining society as a system of systems integrated through shared perceptions, the new approach has held out the hope of joining ideas and events in a single explanation.

Thirty years ago it would have been unthinkable—in the ideological sense of the word—to ask someone to summarize recent writings in early American intellectual history under the rubric "value and society." The "transit of civilization" perhaps, "the house of intellect," or even Samuel Eliot Morison's "pronaos," but not "value and society." When our conference organizers ranged such topics as "shifting intellectual orientations," "patterns of colonial and European thought," and "the contents of education" under this heading, they were implicitly recognizing the force of the social science influences that I have just discussed. Not that historians were indifferent to the formation of human values before Weber wrote and Parsons translated, but without an analytical mode for dealing with them, they had to make do with such notions as *Zeitgeist*, *Weltanschauung*, and climate of opinion or, more despairingly, repeat Herbert Butterfield's conclusion that men just put on new thinking caps. People in the past were presumed to have ideas and morals; the former one cataloged, the latter one hoped were proper while suppressing the cataloging impulse. The two have now been collapsed into value and linked to society by means of highly articulated models. We approach intellectual history mindful that a vast theoretical literature exists to explain why men and women believe—indeed, why they need to believe—and how this human predisposition manifests itself in elaborate codes, symbolic systems, and self-woven webs of significance. Just how these models have operated can be traced in recent scholarship on religion, political thought, and community life in colonial America.

As Henry May wrote in 1964, "The recovery of American religious history may well be the most important achievement of the last thirty years."[30] Since then social historians have worked in different but compatible ways to strengthen that development. Having attributed a metaphysical quality to human nature—what Berger and Luckmann have called "the craving for meaning"—Weber had created a way to break down the boundaries between religion and secularism. Not only could the profane contest for power go on in church affairs, as Perry Miller so brilliantly illuminated for Puritan New England, but what men and women believed about grace, worship, and congregational authority could no longer be confined under the heading of religion. Not waiting for Weber to be translated, Richard Niebuhr had demonstrated the fecundity of Weber's insights in his *Social Sources of Denominationalism*, a work that treated Anglo-American denominationalism as both a culture and a medium of class conflict.[31] The biting edge of the theologian's critique of the rebellion of the rich against the poor was blunted by the next generation of historians, who preferred to follow Paul Tillich in viewing religion as "the substance of culture and culture the form of religion."[32] The shift of emphasis is evident in Edward Gaustad's history of the Great Awakening. Insisting that the tumultuous eruption of evangelical fervor in the colonies cut across the lines of race, sex, and class, Gaustad opened the way for treating religious enthusiasm as an expression of both personal and social values.[33]

More compellingly, Perry Miller's delineation of how covenant theology structured Puritan experience offered a model for examining culture as the medium between the internal world of form and the external world of contingency and circumstance. Miller's theme of declension acted as a powerful corrosive on the facile assumption that American colonists anticipated the future greatness of the United States and hence accepted positively those developments leading to a mobile, prosperous, pluralistic society. Never had the essentially conservative role of values been more explicitly shown than in Miller's depiction of a set of social purposes guiding the institutional arrangements of Massachusetts Bay and conditioning all subsequent reflections upon change.[34] Although Miller has been criticized for exaggerating the influence of ideas in social life, the real power of his work lay not in reconstructing the New England mind but in making precise the connection between the Puritans' interpretation of reality and their response to it. Testing Miller's thesis of declension with indicators of popular behavior, Robert Pope uncovered evidence of traditional religious commitments. His findings made the clergy's support of the halfway covenant appear more political than doctrinal.[35] Similar investigations of the ebbs and flows in congregational membership have brought to light the importance of such factors as the age of prospective communicants, the character of their towns, the nature of parental authority, and the quality of clerical leadership.[36] These studies have strengthened the conviction that social context can illuminate the most recondite material.

Even more illustrative of the impact of the value-and-society paradigm on church history has been the outpouring of studies on the Great Awakening. Seen as the pivotal event before the Revolution, the Great Awakening has suggested to Alan Heimert a means for discriminating between two groups with fundamentally different orientations: the rationalists, who preached reason as a means to social order, and the evangelicals, who promoted disorderly holiness in the expectation of renewed brotherhood.[37] Heimert's thesis was not readily accepted, but his dichotomy between evangelical radicals and conservative rationalists has gained ground with Gary Nash, Rhys Isaac, and

Harry Stout. More than a religious movement, Nash has written, the Awakening must be seen as a profound cultural crisis involving the convergence of political, social, economic, and ideological forces; he goes on to point out the reckless thrust of the revivalists towards social leveling and antiauthoritarian acts.[38] This new work has made class conflict again a central theme in the interpretation of the Great Awakening, returning scholarship to Niebuhr's earlier insight that the churches of the disinherited served as emotional outlets for the poor.

Far more subtle and suggestive than the Progressive view which Gaustad upset, the new writings on evangelical radicalism have drawn upon the communications theory of Walter J. Ong. Writing with a *brio* rarely achieved in historical works, Isaac has presented the conflicts between simple Virginia Baptists and the arrogant Anglican gentry through dramaturgy. Isaac has shown, that, unlike the printed word, the spoken word is an event, taking its real significance from its *presentation*—the setting, the gestures, the expectations of the audience, the observance or lack of observance of conventions.[39] For Isaac and others, the baptismal gatherings at the river, the humble carriage of the converted, and their disdain for idle pleasures were challenges to the powers that were. But in this case the rebellion was directed towards the oppression of Durkheim's internalized values. More than doctrinal statements, the flow of words at revival meetings represented popular protest against a social world written, directed, and orchestrated by members of the elite. By exploring religious experience at its most basic level of expression, these historians have detached the subject from formal doctrine and reattached it to the practices of believers in particular places. By extending the range of evidence to include the symbolic action of deportment, rituals, and calculated ruptures of established mores, these same scholars have demonstrated the possibility of entering the minds of ordinary people. Thus, the concept of value as a determinant of behavior has pointed out areas of research that were closed when intellectual influences were defined in terms of formal ideas.

As indicated earlier, work done on the sociology of knowledge encouraged students of early American politics to employ the concept of ideology as an interpretive theme. Indeed, the assumption that shared and structured beliefs served as the integrating mechanism in societies indicated the importance of reconstructing the historically specific views that dominated particular public discources. Through the concept of ideology, ideas had acquired a motivational force; their analysis held out hope of understanding events in terms that were meaningful to the participants. Used in this way, ideology provided scholars with an alternative to historical explanations based on interest theory or a volitional model of belief. The kind of reworking this new approach suggested can be followed in the extended debate over Robert Brown's work in the 1950s and 1960s. Brown based his contention that colonial Massachusetts was both democratic and middle class on the fact that a high percentage of white adult males had held land and could vote.[40] Unconvinced that these statistical measures were sufficiently descriptive of the actual content of political beliefs, Roy Lokken, Richard Buel, and J. R. Pole examined colonial writings and uncovered a world of values unassimilable to twentieth-century norms.[41] By reconstructing contemporary thought on the function of political representation, Buel arrived at a more nuanced view of colonial perceptions of democracy, while Pole used the interpretive theme of deference to explain why ordinary men voted for their social superiors. Working in a different vein, Michael Zuckerman studied the operation of government in a cluster of eighteenth-century Massachusetts towns and found that what had appeared as participatory politics turned out to be the mechanisms for exercising social control.[42] Demonstrating how powerful an analytical tool the concept of culture could be, Zuckerman was able to extract from town records the purposes behind actual practices. His New Englanders pursued traditional community goals, suppressing those issues and individuals that might subvert them. Far from anticipating modern democracy, he concluded, the town meetings represented institutional devices for stifling free discussion.

By pushing to the fore the issue of present-mindedness, the controversy over Brown's thesis acted as a catalyst in the adoption of social science models that made values central to an understanding of political behavior. A new criterion for assessing the importance of ideas emerged from this "conceptual revolution": it was their capacity to elicit commitment and motivate action that made them historically significant. Formal discourse becomes powerful, Bernard Bailyn wrote, "when it mobilizes a general mood . . . when it crystallizes otherwise inchoate social and political discontent and thereby shapes . . . and directs it to attainable goals." But, Bailyn continued, the power of ideas is not autonomous; only moods, attitudes, and aspirations already present can be cast into ideologies.[43] In this view, between reality and its perception lies an intervening set of beliefs that serves both the inner need to render the world comprehensible and the social need for a shared perspective on experience. Understanding a society's political processes involves, therefore, a mastery of its beliefs. Only when that has been accomplished will the past be made intelligible to the present.

In their studies of prerevolutionary colonial politics, Bailyn and Jack Greene produced exemplars of the new approach. Although differing on the relative influence of seventeenth- and eighteenth-century English ideas, they treated them similarly, as determinants of behavior rather than disembodied propositions. Bailyn's opposition writings triggered men's emotions and aroused their fears. "This peculiar configuration of ideas," he wrote, "constituted in effect an intellectual switchboard wired so that certain combinations of events would activate a distinct set of signals." Greene found that the mimetic impulse of American leaders led them to take on the mantle of England's heroic parliamentarians, as well as the anxieties that accompanied "idealized English values." In both cases real circumstances fed into the adoption of the ideologies, but once in place, the ideologies became so deter-minative of the sensibilities of colonial politicians that they ran far "deeper than the surface of things." Greene's provincials took over the seventeenth-century system of thought *in toto*, "along with its patterns of perception and its cluster of imperatives, roles, and conventions."[44] Just six years earlier Edmund and Helen Morgan had presented the colonists' response to British measures as the principled defense of liberty.[45] With the protean concept of ideology this partisanship had been overcome. In its place Bailyn and Greene used a mode of analysis comprehending both English and American views, while rooting all belief in basic psychological and sociological drives. The rather straightforward "I believe" of intellectual history had become the infinitely more complicated "I feel, I want, I yearn for, I admire, I fear" of ideology. It was this stunning enlargement of the subject that raised Gordon Wood's hopes for joining the elusive, unmanageable, self-intensifying charac-ter of the colonists' ideas to the severe social strains of their provincial status.[46]

In addition to positing a different explanation for the way ideas operate in society, the ideological studies of the past two decades have led to a dramatic transformation of our understanding of the conceptual world of colonial America. By cracking the code, as it were, of political imagery, the new work has brought to light the colonists' attachment to an ornate interpretation of reality variously ascribed to the English commonwealthmen, Dissenters, Radical Whigs, and Country Opposition.[47] Most comprehensively explored by J. G. A. Pocock, the civic humanist tradition elaborated by the English Country party is now seen as having supplied the language of political dis-course on both sides of the Atlantic.[48] Derived from a Renaissance reading of classical texts and Anglicized during the English Civil War, this model of politics emphasized the essential vulnerability of civil order and the inherent corruptibility of men in power. Deeply imbued with a sense of history, Country thinkers became preoccupied with the cycles of degeneration dis-closed in the study of the past. For them, the supreme political achievement was to construct constitutions that would deliver society from the terrors of history. When this civic humanist mode of thought achieved a paradigmatic stature in the eighteenth century, it drew all observations into its interpretive matrix. Its prescriptions for stability determined attitudes towards com-merce; its characterization of the citizen's critical role made civic virtue the supreme value; its veneration of constitutional forms created a hostility to change. Subsequent studies on topics as diverse as colonial attitudes towards economic development and the emergence of a new conception of moral philosophy at Harvard have supplemented and enlarged upon the colonial preoccupation with virtue.[49] Scholars now see the colonists as deeply dis-turbed by the dissonance between their world of factional politics and indi-vidual striving and their civic humanist model of the good society. Gone is the assumption that they greeted the reordering of their world with the cool rationalism of Lockean philosophy. This emphasis upon the intellectual tensions present in colonial America has made these studies of political ideology particularly congruent with the research that was going on simultaneously on colonial families and towns.

The historians' accession of social science theory took place at a time when the scope of their inquiries was expanding greatly. New questions, innovative methods, and sophisticated models undergirt these inquiries. In 1970 communities studies burst upon the scholarly skyline like a meteor shower, leaving behind a trail of monographic meteorites. Reading through tables of cohort longevity and generational marriage patterns, it seemed hard to believe that just seven years earlier H. Stuart Hughes had addressed his colleagues as a body that knew not the social sciences. Hughes's essay, subsequently immortalized as a Bobbs-Merrill reprint, had urged historians to shed their fear of models and other schematic phobias. They should learn something about "mathematics, statistics and symbolic logic," he wrote, and carry on the speculative work of Max Weber.[50] Never was a gauntlet picked up so rapidly. In short order Andover, Dedham, and Plymouth yielded to the comprehensive questioning of Philip Greven, Kenneth Lockridge, and John Demos, while other scholars mined the continuous records of New England towns for quantifiable data on widowhood, income distribution, premarital pregnancy, social mobility, elite composition, and parental power.[51] Moving southward, historians examined Pennsylvania agriculture, Quaker marriage patterns, and mobility in the Chesapeake.[52] In some cases the dependence upon social science models was quite explicit: Lockridge's reliance upon anthropological work on peasant communities and Demos's use of Erik Erikson's developmental theory come to mind. But even in less theoretically self-conscious pieces the underlying assumptions revealed their origin: social history is the study of social process; human behavior is patterned; community life is structured. Of course, town studies had been done before. What set this scholarship apart was the emphasis placed upon the dynamics of population recovered through family reconstitutions and the prominence given to the methods themselves. Calling the new generation of colonial historians "sociodemographic model builders," John Waters rightly connected this identity with their eagerness to bring fresh conceptualizations to the task of rewriting history from the bottom up.[53]

It seems clear in retrospect that what the social sciences gave to historians was the courage to plough into the formless, massive accumulation of stuff in the public records, the detrita, as it were, of ordinary experience.[54] With their array of testable hypotheses, the social scientists pointed out theoretically significant relationships about society to study. If the story didn't move, at least the analysis could. Considering the dependence of conventional historians upon their readers' own sense of sequence, it is understandable that a substitute would have to be found for the "once upon a time" of narrative accounts. Writing as proponents for a different approach to the past, the new scholars in fact made their lists, tables, graphs, and statistics a part of what Carl Schorske has called the grammar of a work, that is, its apprehensible mental structure. David Landes and Charles Tilly summarized three characteristics of all social science history: the linkage of the recorded experience of large numbers of people to patterns of collective behavior, the explanation of collective behavior in terms of theoretical concepts, and the systematic comparison of past structures and systems.[55] More felicitously, Philip Greven singled out the shared conviction "that historians must seek to explore the basic structure and character of society through close, detailed examinations of the experience of individuals, families and groups in particular communities and localities."[56] With such an agenda, certain conclusions were inescapable. Patterns of collective behavior became reflections of an inherent coherence in society itself. Communities did not display random clusterings of qualities such as authoritarian political institutions and permissive childrearing. Rather, the component parts were seen as sustaining one another, as in Parsons's view of society as a system of systems. In deference to this premise, Harold Perkin commented that social history was not another aspect of the past but all of history from the social point of view. And for American colonial history the social point of view turned out to be dramatically different from all previous writing. Since it rests upon detailed examinations of family patterns, agricultural practices, population movements, town meetings, and church records, this depiction of early America will also have unusual staying power. For that reason alone, it is tremendously important to take stock of what has been learned and to discriminate between what we now know and what has been extrapolated from what we know.

Probably no historian ever completely subscribed to the old belief that America was born free, rich, and modern, but approximations of this view abound in texts.[57] These were the first and most likely the most permanent victims of "history from the social point of view." The reconstruction of ordinary life during the first three generations of American settlement has revealed a people immured in communities, preoccupied with kith and kin, and confined within the material limits of a largely subsistence economy. One by one the props under the notion of American exceptionalism have disappeared. Family reconstitutions have turned up an age of marriage conformable to Europe's; the geographic mobility of foot-loose Americans was, if anything, less than that in England; the nuclear family structure predominated on both sides of the Atlantic; the abandonment of primogeniture reflected American egalitarianism less than it reflected a new sentimentality coursing throughout the Western world; fathers in New England exercised a traditional patriarchal authority, which death denied many men in Europe; and the poor of Europe's cities found their counterparts in prosperous Philadelphia.[58] Even when the simple, first societies became more complex, they moved towards European norms rather than American ones. Thus historians have construed the social stratification accompanying commerical development as the Europeanization of northern society, while in the South they have seen English values inspire the planter class to establish itself as something brighter than a pale imitation of an English gentry.[59] John Murrin has argued persuasively that in the eighteenth century Massachusetts underwent an Anglicization that may have been going on elsewhere in the colonies.[60] With a provincial and emulative aristocracy presiding over the agrarian order in Virginia and the fathers of the towns in charge in New England, those who once seemed most typically American—Patricia Bonomi's factious New Yorkers, Lemon's liberal Pennsylvanians, and Stephanie Wolf's urban villagers—have become the exceptions.[61]

Three hundred years after John Clarke bemoaned the fact that "while Old England is becoming new, New England is become Old," historians have sustained his verdict and nailed down the specific mechanisms through which the transplanted English men and women perpetuated the Old World culture they had brought with them.[62] Addressing directly this question of purpose and value, Timothy Breen has shown us that the timing of the Puritan migration helps explain their less conspicuous institutional goals. Breen has interpreted the "persistent localism" they evinced as a reaction to the expansion of Charles I's authority. Thus, the alarming disruptions of England's century of revolution laid the groundwork for what Breen and Stephen Foster have heralded as "the Puritans' greatest achievement": their self-contained, cohesive, stable, nearly autonomous communities.[63] The American colonists were not only traditionalists: they were determined to be so and largely succeeded. This recovery of the long *durée* of the Euro-Americans' cultural memory has, of course, provided a very different starting point for the unfolding of our national history. The once familiar contrast between old regime Europe moving at glacial speed away from customary ways and newly minted America giving currency to every passing innovation has very nearly been reversed. What began as a new approach with theoretical underpinnings has concluded as a major revision with comprehensive implications.

Now that the original colonists, their children, and grandchildren look more and more at home in the Old World, it has been easy for social historians to switch allegiance from Adam Smith to Max Weber. The evident endurance of mores affecting the most personal aspects of human existence has strengthened belief in the reinforcing aspects of social systems. These theoretical propositions have come into play increasingly as historians have begun to interpret the long-term social development in the colonies. Traditional as they were, however, the American settlements did not stay as they were, and this phenomenon requires explanation. With the exception of Michael Zuckerman's sampling of rural towns in eighteenth-century Massachusetts, colonial studies have revealed considerable change over time.[64] Population growth, greater participation in the Atlantic trade, and the attenuation of religious commitments eventually transformed American communities. The "corporate utopianism" of Lockridge's Dedham, according to Edward M. Cook, changed drastically after 1725, when dissension, the open pursuit of self-interest, and the frequent election of new officeholders undermined the tightly meshed, undifferentiated institutions of yore.[65] With these developments, Dedham but held to the course that Richard Bushman had already marked out for colonial Connecticut. Although Bushman did not employ social science models in his beautiful evocation of the journey from Puritan to Yankee, his concentration upon social order made his account assimilable to the gemeinschaft-gesellschaft analysis.[66] Emphasizing the rhythms of ordinary lives paced by "annual, familial and ecological" time, James Henretta also found that the intrusion of commerce, the erosion of authority, and the divisiveness of conflict sped up the process of transformation in the colonies.[67] But as his title, *The Evolution of American Society*, suggests, Henretta believed that the patterns established in the seventeenth century provided the matrix into which the more fluid matter of political agitation flowed. Making explicit America's participation in the larger Western design of social change, Richard Brown has reinterpreted the whole pre–Civil War period as a particular example of the general phenomenon of modernization.[68]

Social science models have quite clearly added precision to our studies. The old words *larger, better, more, rarely, never*—approximations of size and intensity—have been flushed out of their evasive wetlands and into the shooting range of statistical analysis. The rigorous investigations of public records and explicit testing of hypotheses have heightened our expectations of verification. Ordinary people have been brought into our accounts by the most powerful vehicle possible: solid information about what they were doing. Many social processes have been tracked through colonial records to substantiate developments that eluded earlier researchers. The importance of the elite in the past has been greatly diminished simply because we now possess so much knowledge about their less showy contemporaries. Of the hundreds of scholars who have wrought this change in our histories we can say that never have so many done so much to the few. Going from measurements of behavior to explanations of the culture presumed to have produced that behavior, however, social historians have had to rely upon the normative functionalism of modern sociology.[69] Their acceptance of values as the principal cohesive force in society has predisposed them to see historical change as the transformation of social forms. In this view, values serve to sustain continuity; challenges to them represent disruptive forces. Distanced from the past by an approach that treats society as an integrated whole functioning to sustain itself, they have looked at evidence of change with attitudes akin to those of the Plains Indians watching the thin white line of Conestoga wagons. When they have descried signs of modernity on the horizon, their evaluation has been negative, an evaluation supported more by their models than by the testimony of contemporaries. It was this tendency that prompted me to suggest that we may be paying too high an interest rate on our debts to the social sciences.

The language of the social sciences has become particularly prominent in recent writings on early America. Intrinsically compatible with the scholarly enterprise of finding general laws, the social science lexicon conveys more than it says when applied to history. The most conspicuous offenders are such nouns as *process, pattern, system, organization,* and *structure.* These speak of permanence, uniformity, and continuity, yet the mere existence of a statistical distribution does not prove any of these qualities. When applied to percentages and rates, the words strongly suggest a form. Since most of the variables in marriage, migration, and income, for instance, show great variation from time to time and place to place, it can be misleading to use nouns that imply consistency. Generalizations are essential in all historical accounts, narrative as well as analytical, but the diction of the social sciences obscures diversity.

The conceptual vocabulary of the social sciences seems even more fraught with peril for historians. Nouns like *peasant, community,* and *network* appear to refer to something concrete but in fact are abstractions firmly attached to a theoretical literature. The discovery of traditional mores in the colonies has encouraged the use of *peasant* for farmers, which in turn has lent support to the notion that the anthropological literature of the Dinka of the Sudan or the Amahuaca of the Upper Amazon might illuminate the American experience.[70] If social forms are indeed more influential than the particularities of a society's own past, then information about one group of peasants would be helpful in explicating another. This assumption, however, needs to be made explicit and tested. In the case of *community,* the conceptual aspects are even more fugitive. Far more than a synonym for town or village, it is a word laden with connotative significance. Tied to the gemeinschaft-gesellschaft dichotomy, *community* refers more to shared sentiments than to shared space. The community's fragility is assumed by the fact that it is treated as an endangered species whenever the market intrudes. Rarely are the conditions for communal ties made explicit, however. And, in fact, some historians are beginning to argue that the community is an enduring form of social interaction.[71]

The belief that change can best be accounted for as the transformation of social forms—feudalism to capitalism, traditional to modern—is the one borrowing historians should return immediately. Although in its most egregious form of modernization theory it has gone into eclipse, it has by no means run its course in historical writing. This persistence is justified by the fact that Western societies did become modern. Perhaps more relevant, invoking the transition from one Weberian ideal type to another does get an otherwise immobile structural analysis to move. The need to get this particular story going, however, lies in the very theories that have created the problem. That is, it is the description of society as a system of systems established to achieve stability that has frozen the action in the first place. The sociologists' assumption that social change is an inexorable process has also encouraged historians to plug their own microscopic studies into the grander transitions that they presume to be going on.

Paul Boyer and Stephen Nissenbaum's fine study of the witchcraft craze in Salem provides an example. They place this unique event in a well-articulated analysis of the social structure of Salem and Salem Village. While the idiosyncracies of the main participants and the strange situation of Salem Village are by no means neglected, the goal of the book is clearly to join the structural analysis with a specific narrative to produce what James Henretta has called a *histoire problème*, a symbolic moment when persistent developments and extraordinary events collide.[72] Yet the uniting of the particular to the general in *Salem Possessed* depends upon a variant of modernization theory. We are told that Reverend Parris "was ultimately a representative man of his time, just as Salem Village was a representative community." Why? Because "all the elements of their respective histories were deeply rooted in the social realities of late seventeenth-century western culture—a culture in which a subsistence, peasant-based economy was being subverted by mercantile capitalism."[73] The typicality thus rests upon theory, and capitalism—another abstraction—has been called in to play *deus ex machina*.

Our acceptance of the sociologists' theoretical assumptions about the nature of society and social change has intruded itself upon our language in another way. This time it has to do with inferring meaning from behavior. Social historians have built up impressive data banks. At one time this accession of information suggested that literary evidence, with its impressionistic vagueness, might be left behind. But since the findings in themselves do not disclose how they were construed in the past, scholars have reached out for general explanations of social change in order to interpret their data. In the final analysis, they are no less dependent upon literary evidence, but in their case the literature comes from modern sociology rather than contemporary writings. As Lawrence Veysey has noted, "the slippery rubric of modernization" is summoned when social historians are forced to stitch their carefully researched detail onto a larger tapestry.[74] The normative quality given continuity and persistence then leads to an interpretation of change as the promoter of tensions, fear, anxiety, and guilt. Indeed, the whole range of pathological terms that figure in our histories comes from investing traditional society with a set of warm and wonderful features perpetually at risk. Twenty-three actions for the recovery of debt in a ten-year period, if twice that of an earlier decade, become poignant testimony to the disintegration of social solidarity or reflections of the unbearable tensions rending a once organic community. But, in fact, as Robert Berkhofer has pointed out, "we know far too little about the precise nature of the overall social system at any one time let alone its changing nature over time."[75] Theories designed to offer hypotheses for testing have ended up substituting for evidence.

The cumulative, substantive effect of recent research on colonial society has been to make more salient its conservative aspects. The recovery of a political tradition idealizing stability and civic virtue has led J. G. A. Pocock to suggest that the American Revolution be considered "the last great act of the Renaissance" instead of the beginning of a new revolutionary era.[76] In this scheme, the enlightened enthusiasms for science and social reform in the eighteenth century excited not admiration but fear among America's civic humanists. At the level of ordinary life, the persistence of the general structure of a preindustrial economy has made it plausible to think that the colonists were actually hostile to development. This case has been put forth most forcefully by James Henretta, who has argued that the farming families of the rural North resisted economic growth because they were enmeshed "in a web of social relationships and cultural expectations that inhibited the free play of market forces."[77] Yet evidence mounts that prerevolutionary America witnessed a steady commercialization of economic life: trades of all kinds increased; frontier communities quickly integrated themselves into market networks; large and small farmers changed crops in response to commercial incentives; new consuming tastes and borrowing practices proliferated.[78] If established leaders disdained the ordinary people's jostling for place and running into debt at the same time that the fathers of rural families repelled the materialistic mores spread by the market, we are left with an ill-defined group of entreprenuers initiating change. Deprived of cultural roots of their own, they flit in the background as the shadowy agents of a despised modernity. Yet if we attend to the value-creating capacity of human beings as carefully as we do their propensity to preserve values, we should be able to do more than dichotomize attitudes towards novelty. To interpret colonial society as either progressive or conservative is to despair of coming to terms with its variety, its fluidity, and its conflicting tendencies.

Social science models have given an intelligibility to what previously appeared as random and trivial details of everyday life, but the theory attached to the models overdetermines the interpretive outcomes. There is indeed a paradox in the fact that the theory points to the historicity of all social thought while simultaneously spreading belief in a pervasive human sentiment in favor of continuity. This implicit conclusion is particularly troubling when applied to the study of the seventeenth and eighteenth centuries, for then the first footings of modern society were laid. Clearly visible in England are the signs of that progressive economic development and participatory political style which give definition to Western institutions today. This raises the strong possibility that English culture itself carried values supportive of change, that indeed there is a dynamic towards diversity and movement traceable to "the peculiarities of the English." Now that we have acquired a sophisticated understanding of the forces working towards social stasis, it would be fruitful to examine those expectations and attributes that encouraged an openness to change. Within this range of definitions lies a measure of a society's receptivity to novelty. Assuming a different angle of vision on the operation of values in history might also reveal the way in which facts in the social realm influenced the imaginative construction of reality. For instance, did the relative weakness of legally defined status in England promote social theories like those of Thomas Hobbes and John Locke, which began with assertions about human equality? Highly critical of the application of sociological models to the English, Alan Macfarlane has traced family and landholding patterns back to the thirteenth century in order to demonstrate that "English peasant" is a contradiction in terms. Ordinary people in England, he has stressed, have always been "rampant individualists, highly mobile both geographically and socially, economically 'rational,' market-oriented and acquisitive, ego-centred in kinship and social life."[79] Although Macfarlane seems in danger of creating a timeless category known as Englishness, his challenge to conventional interpretations of medieval mores offers a new set of hypotheses to test among the transplanted English in the New World.

Approaching early American society by way of its culture has enabled historians to move beyond the liberal assumptions about a uniform human nature. We no longer appear as that "erudite reflection of the limited social perspectives of the average American" which Louis Hartz once described.[80] This should not stifle our curiosity about liberalism as a cultural artifact produced and disseminated by Anglo-Americans. Reacting to the universalism implicit in Western social science, Louis Dumont has urged us to stop using the qualities of our society as standards for a general theory about historical change. Describing Western culture as rooted in "a radically aberrant world view," he has suggested that we concentrate our efforts on finding out "how this unique development that we call modern occurred at all."[81] Is it possible that our prevailing distaste for contemporary developments has made us reluctant to explore as cultural those English peculiarities which promoted radical economic change. To read Macfarlane's list of characteristics is to foresee the march of "Big Mac" arches, toxic wastes, and multi-paycheck households. There is, moreover, as Louis Hacker pointed out long ago, an anticapitalist bias to most American historical writing. A popular college textbook gives definition to this bias: "Capitalism drained all mystery from the cosmos, dissolved the emotional network of social obligation and left a hollow, inexplicable void, at the core of society."[82] This resistance to viewing liberalism and its capitalistic underpinnings positively—that is, to recapturing the moral enthusiasm they once aroused—may also reflect the tensions engendered by them. R. N. Carew Hunt made this tension explicit when he drew attention to the fact that "for nearly two thousand years European civilization has rested upon a contradiction—between a philosophy and a religion which teach that all men are brothers, and an economic system which organises them as master and servant."[83] Liberalism sought to evade that contradiction by assuming that the moral order worked itself out in natural laws until, as Nietzsche said, that view was no longer tenable because it had conscience against it.[84] Turning to the past, we have found a more humane balance between moral affirmations and economic practices to celebrate. But if we no longer share Marx's faith in immanent solutions to historical problems, our invidious comparison between traditional and modern societies becomes nostalgic in the purest sense of the word, and history loses its capacity to prepare us to meet the future.

NOTES

1. From Max Weber, *Wirtschaft und Gesellschaft*, vol. 1 (Tübingen, 1947), as trans. and cited in Norman Birnbaum, "Conflicting Interpretation of the Rise of Capitalism: Marx and Weber," *British Journal of Sociology* 4 (1953): 123. In the discussion of Weber that follows I have relied upon the following works: Peter L. Berger and Thomas Luckmann, *The Social Construction of Reality: A Treatise in the Sociology of Knowledge* (New York, 1966); Clifford Geertz, *The Interpretation of Cultures: Selected Essays* (New York, 1973); Anthony Giddens, "Marx, Weber, and the Development of Capitalism," *Sociology* 4 (1970); Alvin Gouldner, *The Coming Crises of Western Sociology* (New York, 1970); George Lichtheim, "The Concept of Ideology," *History and Theory* 4 (1965); Ehud Sprinzak, "Weber's Thesis as an Historical Explanation," ibid. 11 (1972); David Little, *Religion, Order, and Law* (New York, 1969); Birnbaum, above; and idem, "The Sociological Study of Ideology," *Current Sociology* 9 (1960).

2. Karl Marx, *Capital*, 4th ed., trans. Eden Paul and Cedar Paul (London, 1928), 837, as cited in Birnbaum, "Conflicting Interpretations," 129.

3. Max Weber, *The Protestant Ethic and the Spirit of Capitalism*, trans. Talcott Parsons (New York, 1958), 60.

4. Weber's critics are legion. Most of them can be encountered in Robert W. Green, ed., *Protestantism, Capitalism, and Social Science: The Weber Thesis Controversy* (Lexington, Mass., 1959). On the relation between Weber and R. H. Tawney, *Religion and the Rise of Capitalism* (London, 1926), see Little, *Religion, Order, and Law*, 234–35. Only the shock of discussing religion and capitalism in the same analysis can explain readers' talking about a Weber-Tawney thesis. Where Weber emphasized the hold of Calvinism and its contribution to a new and powerful social order, Tawney blamed Calvinism for dissolving social ties, promoting individualism, and permitting Calvinists to use their new religion in instrumental ways.

5. Herbert Luethy, "Once Again: Calvinism and Capitalism," *Encounter* 22 (1964); Little, *Religion, Order and Law*, 9–13; Sprinzak, "Weber's Thesis as an Historical Explanation," 310.

6. Karl Marx, *A Contribution to the Critique of Political Economy* (1859), preface. See also Lawrence Krader, "Marxist Anthropology: Principles and Contradictions," *International Review of Social History* 20 (1975): 243–44.

7. Berger and Luckmann, *Social Construction of Reality*, 5–6; Geertz, "Ideology as a Cultural System" (1964) in *Interpretation of Cultures*, 232.

8. Berger and Luckmann, *Social Construction of Reality*, 5. For a similar point and Geertz's claim that *Patterns of Culture* was "probably the most popular book in anthropology ever published in this country" see Geertz, "The Impact of the Concept of Culture on the Concept of Man," in *Interpretation of Cultures*, 44. The role of symbols is discussed from a philosophical point of view in Suzanne Langer, *Philosophy in a New Key* (New York, 1942).

9. Berger and Luckmann, *Social Construction of Reality*, 187.

10. Geertz, "Thick Description: Toward an Interpretive Theory of Culture," in *Interpretation of Cultures*, 5.

11. Geertz, "Ideology as a Cultural System," 219.

12. Ernest Gellner, *Thought and Change* (London, 1964), 154–57. Gellner goes on to clinch the point: "The negative reason for the importance of culture has been indicated: the erosion of structure."

13. Geertz, "Ideology as a Cultural System," 231.

14. Thomas S. Kuhn, *The Structure of Scientific Revolutions* (Chicago, 1962). The only sociologist Kuhn cites is Bernard Barber. He does, however, credit Michael Polanyi and his concept of "tacit knowledge" as being a brilliant and similar theme (p. 44).

15. This idea has been well developed in David A. Hollinger, "T. S. Kuhn's Theory of Science and Its Implications for History," *American Historical Review* 78 (1973): 374–76.

16. J.G.A. Pocock, *Politics, Language, and Time: Essays on Political Thought and History* (New York, 1971), 14–15.

17. *Ideology* has come to refer to loosely associated propositions about reality that define social roles, distribute authority, and create values. It also suggests a level of belief more enduring and less accessible than that of opinions that change with experience. Little use has been made of the distinction made by Karl Mannheim, *Ideology and Utopia* (New York, 1936), between ideology as the justification of the status quo and utopia as an evocation of a reformed reality.

18. Weber, *Protestant Ethic and the Spirit of Capitalism*, 54.

19. Émile Durkheim, *The Rules of Sociological Method* (1895), trans. George E. G. Catlin (New York, 1964), 10.

20. Lichtheim, "The Concept of Ideology," 185. Marx and Hegel, Lichtheim goes on to say, had been saved from this relativistic conclusion by the belief that the nature of man and the logic of history could be grasped in an act of intellectual intuition.

21. See esp. Talcott Parsons, *The Structure of Social Action* (Glencoe, Ill., 1937); *The Social System* (New York, 1951); *Structure and Process in Modern Socieites* (Glencoe, 1960); with Neil Smelzer, *Economy and Society* (London, 1956); and with Edward Shils, eds., *Towards a General Theory of Action* (Cambridge, 1959). Just how much Max Weber needed to be rediscovered can be gauged by the fact that the only Max Weber listed in the 1955 edition of *Webster's Biographical Dictionary* was the American teacher of painting. Other Webers who made it were Theodor Weber, Wilhelm Eduard Weber, Ernst Heinrich Weber, Wilhelm Weber, George Weber, and Joseph Weber, of the American comedy team of Weber and Fields. Among the greats in the sociological tradition found in there are Comte, Tocqueville, Durkheim, and George Simmel. So much for editorial prescience.

22. Clifford Geertz, "After the Revolution: The Fate of Nationalism in the New States," in *Interpretation of Cultures*, 249–50.

23. Gouldner, *Coming Crises of Western Sociology*, 122.

24. James D. Stolzman, "Edward Shils on Consensus: An Appreciation," *British Journal of Sociology* 25 (1974): 4; see also Parsons, *Structure of Social Action*, 768.

25. Robert F. Berkhofer, Jr., "Clio and the Culture Concept: Some Impressions of a Changing Relationship in American Historiography," in *The Idea of Culture in the Social Sciences*, ed. Louis Schneider and Charles M. Bonjean, (Cambridge, 1973), 81.

26. Lois Banner, "On Writing History," *Journal of Interdisciplinary History* 2 (1971).

27. Geertz, "After the Revolution," 250.

28. Dean C. Tipps, "Modernization Theory and the Comparative Study of Societies: A Critical Perspective," *Comparative Studies in Society and History* 15 (1973): 204.

29. Alvin Gouldner, *For Sociology: Renewal and Critique in Sociology Today* (London, 1975), 418–23; Berger and Luckmann, *Social Construction of Reality*, 189; Anthony D. Smith, *The Concept of Social Change* (London, 1973), 17–19, 59.

30. Henry F. May, "The Recovery of American Religious History," *American Historical Review* 70 (1964): 79, 89. To be sure, other intellectual currents contributed to the rekindling of interest

in early American religion, particularly the neoorthodoxy in Protestant theology and existentialism, both secular and religious.

31. H. Richard Neibuhr, *The Social Sources of Denominationalism* (New York, 1929). Niebuhr quoted extensively from Weber's *Gesammelte Aufsatze sur Religionssoziologie*, but only from the first volume, which contained *The Protestant Ethic and the Spirit of Capitalism;* in fact, there are more index listings for Weber than for John Calvin and John and Charles Wesley put together.

32. As quoted approvingly by Sidney Mead, in "Prof. Sweet's Religion and Culture in America," *Church History* 22 (1953), who concluded that therefore "the center of the history of the West in general and of *all* aspects of American history in particular, is the history of Christianity."

33. Edward Gaustad, "Society and the Great Awakening in New England," *William and Mary Quarterly*, 3d ser., 11 (1954); idem, *The Great Awakening in New England* (New York, 1957).

34. Perry Miller, *The New England Mind: From Colony to Province* (Boston, 1953); idem, "Declension in a Bible Commonwealth," *Proceedings of the American Antiquarian Society* 51 (1941).

35. Robert G. Pope, *The Half-way Covenant: Church Membership in Puritan New England* (Princeton, 1969).

36. John Bumsted, "Religion, Finance, and Democracy in Massachusetts," *Journal of American History* 58 (1972); John W. Jeffries, "The Separation in the Canterbury Congregational Church: Religion, Family, and Politics in a Connecticut Town," *New England Quarterly* 52 (1979); Peter Onuf, "New Lights in New London: A Group Portrait of the Separatists," *William and Mary Quarterly*, 3d ser., 37 (1980); Harry Stout, "The Great Awakening in New England Reconsidered: The New England Clergy as a Case Study," *Journal of Social History* 8 (1974).

37. Alan Heimert, *Religion and the American Mind from the Great Awakening to the Revolution* (Cambridge, Mass., 1966).

38. Gary B. Nash, *The Urban Crucible: Social Change, Political Consiousness, and the Origins of the American Revolution* (Cambridge, Mass., 1979), 204, 211. Heimert's new following is discussed by Nathan O. Hatch in "New Lights and the Revolution in Rural New England," *Reviews in American History* 9 (1980), where he also draws attention to the very important consideration that the New Light churches were in decline by the time of the Revolution (p. 323).

39. Rhys Isaac, "Religion and Authority: Problems of the Anglican Establishment in Virginia in the Era of the Great Awakening and the Parsons' Cause," *William and Mary Quarterly*, 3d ser., 30 (1973); idem, "Evangelical Revolt: The Nature of the Baptists' Challenge to the Traditional Order in Virginia, 1765 to 1775," ibid. 31 (1974). See also Harry S. Stout, "Religion, Communications, and the Ideological Origins of the American Revolution," ibid. 34 (1977); and William McLoughlin, "Pietism and the American Character," *American Quarterly* 17 (1965). Also responsive to Heimert's thesis of two conflicting ideologies is Philip J. Greven, Jr., who has written that "Heimert's work provides the indispensable link between the seventeenth and the nineteenth century" (*The Protestant Temperament* [New York, 1977], 11).

40. Robert E. Brown, "Democracy in Colonial Massachusetts," *New England Quarterly* 25 (1952); idem, *Middle Class Democracy and the Revolution in Massachusetts, 1691–1780* (Ithaca, N.Y., 1955).

41. Roy Lokken, "The Concept of Democracy in Colonial Political Thought," *William and Mary Quarterly*, 3d ser., 16 (1959); John Cary, "Statistical Method and the Brown Thesis on Colonial Democracy," ibid. 20 (1963); J. R. Pole, "Historians and the Problem of Early American Democracy," *American Historical Review* 67 (1962); Richard Buel, Jr., "Democracy and the American Revolution: A Frame of Reference," *William and Mary Quarterly*, 3d ser., 21 (1964).

42. Michael Zuckerman, "The Social Context of Democracy in Massachusetts," *William and Mary Quarterly*, 3d ser., 25 (1968); idem, *Peaceable Kingdoms: New England Towns in the Eighteenth Century* (New York, 1970).

43. Bernard Bailyn, "The Central Themes of the American Revolution: An Interpretation," in *Essays on the American Revolution*, ed. Stephen G. Kurtz and James H. Hutson (Chapel Hill, 1973), 11.

44. Bernard Bailyn, *The Ideological Origins of the American Revolution* (Cambridge, Mass., 1967), 22; idem. *The Origins of American Politics* (New York, 1968); Jack P. Greene, "Political Mimesis: A Consideration of the Historical and Cultural Roots of Legislative Behavior in the British Colonies in the Eighteenth Century," *American Historical Review* 75 (1969): 344, 348. Interestingly, Bailyn supplied psychological and sociological roots for Greene's "mimetic impulse" in "Politics and Social Structure in Virginia," in *Seventeenth Century America*, ed. James M. Smith (Chapel Hill, 1960), 112–15.

45. Edmund S. Morgan and Helen M. Morgan, *The Stamp Act Congress: Prologue to Revolution* (Chapel Hill, 1953).

46. Gordon S. Wood, "Rhetoric and Reality in the American Revolution," *William and Mary Quarterly*, 3d ser., 23 (1966): 22, 26–32.

47. For a recapitulation of this scholarship see Robert E. Shalhope, "Toward a Republican Synthesis: The Emergence of an Understanding of Republicanism in American Historiography," ibid. 29 (1972).

48. J.G.A. Pocock, *The Machiavellian Moment: Florentine Political Thought and the Atlantic Republican Tradition* (Princeton, 1975).

49. J. E. Crowley, *This Sheba, Self: The Conceptualization of Economic Life in Eighteenth-Century America* (Baltimore, 1974); Norman Fiering, *Moral Philosophy at Seventeenth-Century Harvard: A discipline in Transition* (Chapel Hill, 1981).

50. H. Stuart Hughes, "The Historian and the Social Scientist," in *Generalizations in Historical Writing*, ed., Alexander V. Riasanowky and Barnes Riznik (Philadelphia, 1963), 26–29, 42, 58–59.

51. Philip J. Greven, Jr., *Four Generations: Population, Land, and Family in Colonial Andover, Massachusetts* (Ithaca, N.Y., 1970); Kenneth A. Lockridge, *A New England Town: The First Hundred Years, Dedham, Massachusetts, 1636–1736* (New York, 1970); John Demos, *A Little Commonwealth: Family Life in Plymouth Colony* (New York, 1970). The shorter studies are Alexander Keyssar, "Widowhood in Eighteenth-Century Massachusetts: A Problem in the History of the Family," *Perspectives in American History* 8 (1974); Donald W. Koch, "Income Distribution and Political Structure in Seventeenth-Century Salem, Massachusetts," *Essex Institute Historical Collections* 105 (1969); Daniel Scott Smith and Michael S. Hindus, "Premarital Pregnancy in America, 1640–1971: An Overview and Interpretation," *Journal of Interdisciplinary History* 5 (1975); Linda A. Bissel, "From One Generation to Another: Mobility in Seventeenth-Century Windsor, Connecticut," *William and Mary Quarterly*, 3d ser., 31 (1974); P.M.G. Harris, "The Social Origins of American Leaders: The Demographic Foundations," *Perspectives in American History* 3 (1969); and Daniel Scott Smith, "Parental Power and Marriage Patterns: An Analysis of Historical Trends in Hingham, Massachusetts," *Journal of Marriage and the Family* 35, no. 3 (1973).

52. James T. Lemon, *The Best Poor Man's Country: A Geographical Study of Early Southeastern Pennsylvania* (Baltimore, 1972); Robert V. Wells, "Quaker Marriage Patterns in a Colonial Perspective," *William and Mary Quarterly*, 3d ser., 29 (1972); Darrett B. Rutman and Anita H. Rutman, "Of Agues and Fevers: Malaria in the Early Chesapeake," ibid. 33 (1976).

53. John J. Waters, Jr., "From Democracy to Demography: Recent Historiography of the New England Town," in *Perspectives of Early American History: Essays in Honor of Richard B. Morris*, ed. Alden T. Vaughan and George Athan Billias (New York, 1973), 240.

54. Charles Wilson and Geoffrey Parker estimate that it takes twenty thousand working hours, or eight years, of a single researcher's time to produce a century-long study of a town with eighty thousand persons (*An Introduction to the Sources of European Economic History, 1500–1800* [Ithaca, N.Y., 1977], preface), and the Cambridge Group for the Study of Population and Social Structure consider a year of full-time research necessary to reconstitute the families of a twelve-hundred-person parish over a three-hundred-year period.

55. David Landes and Charles Tilly, *History as Social Science* (Englewood Cliffs, N.J., 1971), 71–73.

56. Greven, *Four Generations*, vii–viii.

57. See, for example, Carl Degler, *Out of Our Past* (New York, 1959), 1–8; and Joyce O. Appleby, ed., *Materialism and Morality in the American Past* (Reading, Mass., 1974), 1–5.

58. Greven, *Four Generations*, 33; Peter Laslett and John Harrison, "Clayworth and Cogenhoe," in *Historical Essays*, ed. H. E. Bell and R. L. Ollard (London, 1963); Peter Laslett, ed., *Household and Family in Past Time* (Cambridge, 1972); Philippe Aries, *Centuries of Childhood*, trans. Robert Baldick (New York, 1962); Gary B. Nash, "Urban Wealth and Poverty in Pre-Revolutionary America," *Journal of Interdisciplinary History* 6 (1976); idem, "Up from the Bottom of Franklin's Philadelphia," *Past and Present*, no. 77 (1977).

59. Lockridge, *New England Town*, 177; Bailyn, "Politics and Social Structure in Virginia." See also Rowland Berthoff and John M. Murrin, "Feudalism, Communalism, and the Yeoman Freeholder: The American Revolution Considered as a Social Accident," in Kurtz and Hutson, *Essays on the American Revolution*.

60. John M. Murrin, "Anglicizing an American Colony: The Transformation of Provincial Massachusetts" (Ph.D. diss., Yale University, 1966).

61. Patricia U. Bonomi, *A Factious People: Politics and Society in Colonial New York* (New York, 1971); Lemon, *Best Poor Man's Country*; Stephanie Graumann Wolf, *Urban Village: Population, Community, and Family Structure in Germantown, Pennsylvania, 1683–1800* (Princeton, 1976).

62. John Clarke, *Ill Newes from New England or a Narrative of New England's Persecution*, as cited in Sidney Mead, *The Lively Experiment: The Shaping of Christianity in America* (New York, 1963), 25–26.

63. T. H. Breen, "Persistent Localism: English Social Change and the Shaping of New England Institutions," *William and Mary Quarterly*, 3d ser., 32 (1975); T. H. Breen and Stephen Foster, "The Puritans' Greatest Achievement: A Study of Social Cohesion in Seventeenth-Century Massachusetts," *Journal of American History* 60 (1973).

64. Zuckerman, *Peaceable Kingdoms*.

65. Edward M. Cook, "Social Behavior and Changing Values in Dedham, Massachusetts, 1700 to 1775," *William and Mary Quarterly*, 3d ser., 27 (1970).

66. Richard L. Bushman, *From Puritan to Yankee: Character and the Social Order in Connecticut, 1690–1765* (Cambridge, Mass., 1967).

67. James A. Henretta, *The Evolution of American Society, 1700–1815: An Interdisciplinary Analysis* (Lexington, Mass., 1973), 206–14.

68. Richard Brown, *Modernization: The Transformation of American Life, 1600–1865* (New York, 1976).

69. On this point see Smith, *Concept of Social Change*, 3–4.

70. See, for instance, Lockridge, *New England Town*; John J. Waters, Jr., "The Traditional World of the New England Peasants: A View from Seventeenth-Century Barnstable," *New England Historical and Genealogical Register* 129 (1976); and Michael Zuckerman, "The Fabrication of Identity in Early America," *William and Mary Quarterly*, 3d ser., 34 (1977).

71. Thomas Bender, *Community and Social Change in America* (New Brunswick, N.J., 1978); Richard R. Beeman, "The New Social History and the Search for 'Community' in Colonial America," *American Quarterly* 29 (1977); and Douglas Greenberg, "Of Courts and Communities," *Reviews in American History* 9 (1980).

72. Paul Boyer and Stephen Nissenbaum, *Salem Possessed: The Social Origins of Witchcraft* (Cambridge, Mass., 1974); James A. Henretta, "Social History as Lived and Written," *American Historical Review* 84 (1979): 1319–21.

73. Boyer and Nissenbaum, *Salem Possessed*, 178.

74. Lawrence Veysey, "The 'New' Social History in the Context of American Historical Writing," *Reviews in American History* 7 (1979): 5.

75. Robert F. Berkhofer, Jr., "Comment on 'Social History as Lived and Written,'" *American Historical Review* 84 (1979): 1328.

76. J.G.A. Pocock, "Virtue and Commerce in the Eighteenth Century," *Journal of Interdisciplinary History* 3 (1972): 120.

77. James A. Henretta, "Families and Farms: *Mentalité* in Pre-Industrial America," *William and Mary Quarterly*, 3d ser., 35 (1978): 19.

78. Marc Egnal, "The Economic Development of the Thirteen Continental Colonies, 1720 to 1775," ibid. 32 (1975); Carville V. Earle and Ronald Hoffman, "Staple Crops and Urban Development in the Eighteenth-Century South," *Perspectives in American History* 10 (1976); Paul G. E. Clemens, *The Atlantic Economy and Colonial Maryland's Eastern Shore: From Tobacco to Grain* (Ithaca, N.Y., 1980); Winifred B. Rothenberg, "The Market and Massachusetts Farmers, 1750–1855," *Journal of Economic History* 61 (1981).

79. Alan Macfarlane, *The Origins of English Individualism: The Family, Property and Social Transition* (Oxford, 1978), 163.

80. Louis Hartz, *The Liberal Tradition in America: An Interpretation of American Political Thought since the Revolution* (New York, 1955), 29.

81. Louis Dumont, *From Mandeville to Marx: The Genesis and Triumph of Economic Ideology* (Chicago, 1977), 7.

82. As cited in Edwin Burrows, "The Transition Question," *Radical History Review* 8 (1978).

83. R. N. Carew Hunt, *The Theory and Practice of Communism* (New York, 1951), 3.

84. As quoted in Karl Lowith, *Meaning in History* (Chicago, 1949), vii.

11

RELIGION AND SOCIETY:
PROBLEMS AND
RECONSIDERATIONS

DAVID D. HALL

he meaning of religion to the peoples of colonial America is not easy to recapture.[1] The stories that we tell of them evoke a wide spectrum of experience. Roger Williams and Mary Dyer listen to the voice of private conscience and are cruelly punished for it by the "theocrats" of Massachusetts. James Logan, of newly founded Pennsylvania, adjusts his Quaker principles to suit political realities. Venturing into the backwoods of North Carolina, William Byrd encounters squatters who have never heard a sermon. Out in Stockbridge, on the edge of the New England frontier, Jonathan Edwards fashions an intricate defense of high Calvinism. Nathan Cole hastens to hear George Whitefield preach, and in mid-eighteenth-century Virginia evangelical preaching brings a new rhythm into the lives of ordinary people.

Out of such images and actions grow several of the major themes and issues in the history of religion in colonial America. The oldest of these issues surely must be the controversial relationship between church and state in Puritan New England. Soon after settlement began critics were denouncing the policy of the colonists, and historians unsympathetic to the Puritans would continue to misstate the nature of the system well into the 1930s. Not until agendas shifted in that decade did the issue seem to lapse.[2] With that shifting of agendas came what Henry May has called the "rediscovery of religion" in American history.[3] One thrust of this new movement lay in emphasizing the coherence and vitality of ideas. Another lay in realizing that immigrant religions had all passed through a process of adaptation to American circumstances. These achievements were substantial: Jonathan Edwards and the Puritans were rescued from centuries of detraction, and church history broke free of its denominational isolation.

The significance of these achievements diminished in the 1960s as social historians began to question whether ideas had really mattered. Behavior and belief seemed discrepant. Already in 1640s Boston most people could not fit into the meetinghouse. In the North and the South colonists seemed more concerned with land and family than with God. The impotence of Sudbury's Reverend Edmund Brown in a dispute over land was widely construed to mean the isolation of the ministry. As a learned elite, the ministry was suspect from another point of view. Historians were increasingly eager to describe the lives of ordinary people. Together with a sympathy for the dispossessed and the inarticulate, this eagerness would lead away from verbal and explicit statements to other languages—the movements of a crowd, the gestures of a preacher. Meanwhile, the emphasis on Americanization was being challenged as the continuities between Europe and America became more visible. Institutions like the family now seemed astonishingly "traditional," a discovery that seemed to lessen the significance of any ideology concerned with how the family should be organized.[4] Altogether, the trends in recent social history worked against the "rediscovery" of religion.

Beyond either of these positions, the one so resolutely behavioral, the other cheerfully open to ideas, lies the mediating ground this essay will explore. Backwoods squatters and Jonathan Edwards, Roger Williams and James Logan—these references suggest the range of possibilities for a history of religion in colonial America. Among these many possibilities, four themes seem most important. Americanization continues to demand attention, if only because the problem of American exceptionalism will not disappear. Nor will ideas evaporate; the history of religion in colonial America remains in part the history of doctrinal systems. From the "new" social history comes a third important theme, the "radical religion" of the dispossessed and discontented. Social patterns in colonial America fall somewhere in between the ideal types of "modern" and "traditional." The fourth theme turns these categories into a question: How did religion and emerging capitalism interact?

I

When James Logan bent his principles to the winds of political reality, his gesture was in keeping with a larger process. The Quaker faith, born in England amid the circumstances of the English Revolution and transported in full vigor to America, would gradually come to terms with its new environment. English Quakers, used to being excluded, were suddenly in command of a pluralistic colony. The Puritans in charge of Massachusetts faced similar adjustments. Purists wanted to maintain the ideal of a gathered church; others, more accommodating, preferred the compromising halfway covenant.

This transformation of European institutions into patterns that were recognizably American was an overriding theme for many of the historians who wrote on religion in colonial America in the years after World War II. As in Quaker Pennsylvania and Puritan New England, so everywhere the story was of *American* religion, not of religion *in* America. Immigrants all, the colonists had passed through a subtle process of acculturation that had stripped them of their European ways.

Sidney Mead was the preeminent church historian of these postwar years. The subtle dialectics of his essays seemed both to capture and to explain the process by which Europeans became Americans. In the opening pages of "The American People: Their Space, Time and Religion," Crèvecoeur appears to testify that the American is a "new man," a European transformed by a veritable "revolution" into something "unique." In terms of church history, the nature of this uniqueness lay in a freedom without parallel in Europe, a freedom to which the immigrant religious groups responded by acknowledging the legitimacy of their competition. Toleration on such a scale was unprecedented. In moving from state church to pluralism, the colonists had to "begin anew, unfettered by" the "ancient restraints" of "habit, custom and tradition." Old attitudes and institutions were useless in the vast expanses of America. Like Turner and W. W. Sweet, though perhaps with more complexity, Mead invoked the "frontier" to explain this transformation.[5]

Turning to the structure of the church and the ministry, Mead argued in his famous essay "The Rise of the Evangelical Conception of the Ministry: 1607–1850" that a European, "sacerdotal" form of ministry could not be sustained in the New World. The structure of a sacerdotal ministry was hierarchical. Much of its authority came from its being closely linked with a stable, centralized state. Americanization shattered both these patterns. A new kind of ministry emerged, "evangelical" in relying on informal means of persuasion and wholly separate from the state. In other essays Mead argued that the free conditions of American life transformed European models of the church into a new form, the denomination. The real emergence of denominationalism occurred in the aftermath of the Revolution. But the tendencies that would culminate in the institution were present from the outset–for example, the "voluntary principle," by which the "several religious groups became voluntary associations, equal before, but independent of the civil power and of each other." The denomination and the evangelical ministry were forms that coincided with the fluidity and openness of American society.[6]

In support of this interpretation, other historians described the process of Americanization in specific contexts. Leonard Trinterud wrote of conflict in colonial Presbyterianism between a native-born and an immigrant clergy.

Scottish immigrants supported the authority of synods while insisting that candidates for the ministry return to Scotland for their university degrees. This "clericalism" was opposed by native-born ministers, who were moving towards a freer understanding of their office. The immigrants disliked the new revival movements which the native-born were leading.[7] The theme of revivalism as peculiarly American would reappear in Perry Miller's essays on church history. As early as *The New England Mind: The Seventeenth Century* (1939), Miller was differentiating the intellectual life of the colonists from its European sources. New England Puritans were unique, he argued, in combining Ramist logic, covenant theology, and Congregationalism. In later work, as in his interpretation of Solomon Stoddard, Miller invoked the "wilderness" as the reason for new movements and ideas.[8]

The argument for an "American" style of Protestantism was taken up by historians who argued that a general process of accommodation was at work in the colonial period. For an influential version of this point of view, we may turn to Oscar Handlin's essay of 1959, "The Significance of the Seventeenth Century." Handlin argued that the expectations of the colonists were badly matched to the realities of their new environment. A series of disrupting experiences separated the immigrants from accustomed ways of doing things: the transatlantic crossing itself, the high rates of mortality among children and adults. The fundamental abnormality was the shift from order to disorder: "Old habits did not apply to new circumstances; and it was hard for individuals to fulfill the personal, family, religious, or communal roles they were expected to play. . . . The lack of stability or orderliness even in the home was particularly troublesome. . . . The lack of permanence, the constant mobility that shifted individuals and families . . . exacerbated all these tensions." Tensions arising from insecurity and disorder, said Handlin, explain the crises that mark the colonial period. Conflict occurred as people tried to adapt old beliefs to new realities or sought vainly to preserve familiar roles.

What Handlin said of religion was in keeping with his basic categories of order and disorder. He regarded Congregationalism in New England as an improvised, ad hoc development; as in the vestry system of Virginia, churches in America "developed a de facto congregational form, despite the fact that their communicants theoretically held to a belief in centralized authority." In Europe power had been concentrated in a bureaucratic state and a hierarchical, established church. In America power flowed outward into local units like the vestry and the town. This trend enhanced a general "looseness of social structure."[9]

Other historians picked up on the themes of instability and strain and used them to interpret such events as the antinomian controversy of 1636–38 and the Keithian schism of the 1690s among Pennsylvania Quakers. As one historian explained the schism, Pennsylvania society was swept with conflict because no institutional structures could achieve stability. Chronic factionalism had its origins in the very openness of a new society, where traditional restraints and deferential patterns were never reproduced. As people moved off into the wilderness, "a sense of corporateness" yielded to an "atomizing" tendency. In their new environment, moreover, the Quakers lacked the pressures for agreement that came from being persecuted in their mother country. Altogether, these factors "put insupportable burdens on institutions which were inherently frail, and fragile institutions encouraged resistance to authority."[10]

It would not do to underestimate the virtues of this point of view. The historians who argued for Americanization were adept at suggesting connections between the history of religion and the history of society. In drawing those connections, they lifted church history out of sectarian or denominational categories that had kept it isolated from the mainstream of interpretation. The special grace of the Americanist perspective lay in moving back and forth between religion and society, and in exploiting the ambiguities of that relationship. That some of these historians, in their assumption that America was uniquely "free," also shared the liberal ideology of the postwar years is something we can see in retrospect. And in arguing that America was fundamentally different from Europe several were conscious or unconscious spokesmen for an ancient fable, namely, that this country began anew.

The fable lingers, but with diminished power. Beginning in the 1960s a strong reaction against American exceptionalism became evident as colonial historians rediscovered the continuities and connections between the Old World and the New World. "One thing is certain," Joyce Appleby has recently declared in summing up this tendency. "The old story of individualism and free enterprise coming with the first boatloads of English colonists no longer is credible." The most striking of these continuities concerned the family. When demographers discovered the capacity of the New England family to preserve and even to enhance its structure, they demolished a key instance of Americanization, the disintegration of traditional roles in a fluid, destabilizing society.[11] Another major step was a new awareness of the many variations in European social patterns. Increasingly it seemed possible to explain the colonial period in terms of how the colonists chose among these variations. Conflict in Quaker Pennsylvania may have been the consequence of contradictions strictly within Quakerism as it evolved from its primitive millennial commitment—in England as in Pennsylvania—into a structured, intergenerational community.[12] In New England the colonists brought with them a highly ambivalent understanding of the ministry, responsive to both "evangelical" and "sacerdotal" ideals.[13] Eighteenth-century Presbyterianism was a hybrid of Scottish, Irish, and native-born factions; coming out of different social and political circumstances than the Scots, the Irish brought with them to America many of the attitudes that Trinterud had regarded as "American."[14] In a systematic response to Trinterud and Mead, Jon Butler has argued that the origins of New World denominationalism lay in England, where strong clerical leadership had become an intellectual assumption, or fact of life, among the groups that later settled in the Delaware Valley. All groups but the Anglicans were able to maintain this clerical authority once they reached the colonies.[15] In intellectual history, too, the continuities have begun to loom as more significant than change. We know that Solomon Stoddard borrowed his ideas from English Presbyterians of the mid-seventeenth century and that Edwards borrowed some of his from a well-developed tradition of moral philosophy.[16]

Enough has been accomplished, then, to demonstrate the limitations and inadequacies of Americanization or exceptionalism as an overriding theme. Continuity deserves an equal if not greater emphasis. It may well be, however, that this emphasis on continuity is now in need of criticism. In turning against exceptionalism, some historians have gone to the extreme of insisting that colonial society was more "traditional" in its nature than European society of the same period.[17] This inversion of perspective ignores the processes of adaptation and selection that *did* occur. With an overblown exceptionalism no longer in the way, it may again be possible to take account of differences in the social and religious histories of Europe and America. We know that in most respects the material conditions of life in colonial America were better than in Europe; the colonists ate more, lived longer, and had access to more land. Race relations were distinctive in the New World. So too were certain aspects of religion. In most denominations a contractual relationship prevailed between the clergy and their parishes, a situation that was echoed in the general absence of any legal power to enforce church punishments or moral standards. Only one of Europe's several different theological traditions was successfully transplanted. The dominance of this type—Calvinism, to call it by its most convenient name—would have far-reaching consequences.

II

The lonely Edwards in his study is an image that evokes the history of religion as a system of ideas. Even in his rural outpost, Edwards was not isolated from the great traditions of Western Christianity. At the Yale that he attended, the books and course of study put him in touch with most of the intellectual apparatus on which Christianity had depended since the Middle Ages. This intellectual apparatus—the classics that were rediscovered in the Renaissance, the arts of logic and rhetoric, the sciences of physics, mathematics, and astronomy, the philosophical and theological principles that joined in scholasticism—was, with the one exception of the inquiry into natural science, the sum and substance of *learning* in colonial America.[18]

When Edwards drew upon this learning, it was on behalf of Christianity in the form of Calvinism. To say that Edwards was a Calvinist is again to remove him from isolation, for Calvinism was the common faith of people in America before the Revolution. It was the theology of the Puritans in seventeenth-century New England. But it was also the theology of the Baptists who arose out of the Great Awakening and of the Presbyterians who flooded into the middle colonies in the early eighteenth century. Princeton graduates carried this religious system to the furthest reaches of colonial settlement and even to the West Indies.[19] Baptists followed close behind in their missionary outreach. Some Anglicans had started down the road to "rational" religion, as had some eighteenth-century Congregationalists. But in the main the Anglican and Congregational communities were still bound up with Calvinism.[20] Taken as a whole, the language of religious discourse in colonial America was surprisingly uniform.

This is not a language that twentieth-century historians, many of them secular or liberal in their thinking, instinctively comprehend. Some indication of their distance from this system lies in the adjectives that recur so often in descriptions of Calvinism: *rigid, deterministic, arbitrary, logical.* Or there may be statements that suggest how out of date this system was. Even so distinguished a historian as Carl Van Doren, comparing Benjamin Franklin with Jonathan Edwards, fell into this way of speaking: "the defeated Edwards, who all his life upheld a cause which even in his youth was lost, had he but known it, and who seems on most of his pages to speak of forgotten issues in a forgotten dialect."[21]

The word that rounds out and sums up this point of view is *orthodoxy,* which in this context means a system set apart from real life by a logical structure that allows no ambiguity. The uses and abuses of this word form a story that, however fascinating, belongs elsewhere. Important here are two consequences of orthodoxy's long association with Calvinism. One of these consequences is revealed in the statement by Van Doren. It is what may be termed the "one-horse shay" phenomenon: orthodoxy *cannot* be a living, vital system, which is why it necessarily died out. The other consequence is to construe the evolving discourse of a theological tradition as a history of declension from a fixed and perfect standard; orthodoxy becomes an arbitrary yardstick, and all change is deviation.

Little more than a decade after Van Doren offered his characterization of Edwards, a youthful Richard Niebuhr moved to reconsider the "defeated Edwards." The issue, declared Niebuhr, was not the stultifying effects of Calvinism but the losses *we* had suffered in giving up its understanding of God and man. The Edwards of the famous "hellfire" sermons was no more out of date than ever. "Placed in their proper context [of divine sovereignty, these sermons] represent Edwards' intense awareness of the precariousness of life's poise, of the utter insecurity of men and of mankind which are at every moment as ready to plunge into the abyss of disintegration, barbarism, crime and the war of all against all, as to advance toward harmony and integration."[22] In reclaiming Edwards, Niebuhr reclaimed the whole of Calvinism

from the blight of orthodoxy. On the heels of his decisive gesture, Perry
Miller could declare in 1938 that the Puritans had much to offer modern man:
"The optimism and cheerfulness to which the revolters against Puritanism
turned now threatened to become rather a snare and a delusion than a liberation. . . . We are terribly aware once more . . . that men are not perfect or
essentially good. The Puritan description of them, we have been reluctantly
compelled to admit, is closer to what we have witnessed than the description
given in Jeffersonian democracy or transcendentalism."[23] This perspective
would culminate in Miller's tour-de-force insistence, in his intellectual biography *Jonathan Edwards* (1949), that Edwards was "one of America's five or
six major artists."

Miller reclaimed the Puritans as vigorous and important intellectuals. Yet
the great irony of his revisionism is that he continued to think of orthodoxy in
ways akin to that of Van Doren. The Calvin who appears in the pages of *The
New England Mind: The Seventeenth Century* is "rigid," "arbitrary," and fiercely "logical." Miller's Calvin preaches a God who is absolutely sovereign, a
God who demands of man that he surrender all initiative and freedom. This
conception of Calvin and his God becomes, for Miller, a fixed point from
which to measure the adherence (or lack of it) by Puritans to Calvinism.
Miller thought of orthodoxy as valuable, but he also thought of it as something static, a given, laid out in perfect logic once and for all. When he came
to describe the covenant theology and its evolution in New England, he told
a story of declension from the starting point of Calvinism.[24]

Miller regarded the covenant theology as a compromise between Calvin's
insistence on man's helplessness and a more liberal approach to human initiative. Comparing Puritan formulations with a wholly artificial orthodoxy, he
was startled to discover that the God of the Puritans seemed willing to
accommodate himself to man. Putting the pieces together, Miller concluded
that the covenant theology harnessed in uneasy alliance a sovereign God
(Calvinism) and a language of conditionality. When he came to interpret the
antinomian controversy, he saw it as a struggle between orthodoxy in the
person of John Cotton and emerging liberalism in the person of the "legal"
preachers.[25]

Miller's distinction between orthodoxy and the covenant theology has become a truism in the historical literature, a truism invoked by countless
others who have followed his authority. Here is a fairly direct translation: "If
God were to respond to man in a purely Calvinistic manner, then nothing
could be known of the Divine Will ahead of its appointed fulfillment. But the
Federal or Covenant Puritans were not Pure Calvinists, and Mather embraced the Congregational principle by which man's deeds could influence
God's response."[26] As in this analysis of Increase Mather, so in many other
biographies or histories much effort went into uncovering deviations.[27] The
failing was widespread, and perhaps not really Miller's doing. We may look

past his example to the general problem of understanding orthodoxy, a problem that seems to inhere in the very word itself.

The alternative to a static conception of Calvinism is to recognize that Calvinism remained ambivalent in important ways and accordingly could change or grow. Referring to another intellectual tradition in which orthodoxy has often been an issue, Raymond Williams has protested against the misuses of the concept:

> But now that I knew more of the history of Marxism, and of the variety of selective and alternative traditions within it, I could at last get free of the model which had been such an obstacle, whether in certainty or in doubt: the model of fixed or known Marxist positions, which in general had only to be applied, and the corresponding dismissal of all other kinds of thinking as non-Marxist, revisionist, neo-Hegelian, or bourgeois. Once the central body of thinking was itself seen as active, developing, unfinished and persistently contentious, many of the questions were open again.[28]

The crucial shift, as Williams indicates, is from a rigid to an open-ended understanding of orthodoxy or tradition.

To take this step is only the beginning. The change to an "active" understanding of orthodoxy would in turn reopen many of the questions that are raised about the development of Calvinism. Where this reconsideration has occurred is in the work of a group of historians I wish to call the Yale school.[29] The Yale school and its allies dissent from much of Miller's argument about the course of New England theology. He saw it as a compromise with Calvinism, and one that steadily deteriorated through internal decay as the seventeenth century wore on. In place of compromise the Yale historians see ambivalence; in place of change they put continuity.

In keeping with the recovery of ambivalence, William Stoever has shown that a language of conditionality coexisted in Reformed dogmatics with a language of absolute grace. For Stoever, therefore, the covenant theology was a natural outgrowth and expansion of an orthodoxy rich in possibilities.[30] Similarly, Norman Pettit has demonstrated that the Scripture itself offered diverse messages about "preparation for salvation." Preachers in New England were faithful to both the Scripture and tradition in urging it upon the colonists.[31] Brooks Holifield is even more emphatic concerning the possibilities for compromise and change within the Calvinist tradition. Describing the doctrines of baptism and the Lord's Supper in Reformed and Puritan theology, he has argued that both doctrines could accommodate widely varying interpretations of the Lord's Supper, from Calvin's assertion of a real presence to Zwingli's "memorialist" position. Few Reformed or Puritan ministers settled for a fixed, inflexible position. Close analysis of New England texts concerned with baptism led Holifield to discover that "the Puritans were ambidextrous theologians: what the right hand took away, the left hand

could retrieve. For almost every negation in their baptismal doctrine there
was a qualifying affirmation. Baptism did not convey saving grace, yet it was
a means of grace. The sacrament could not save an infant, but it could
facilitate the process of salvation." As Holifield goes on to demonstrate, this
persisting ambivalence was the framework within which every seventeenth-
and early eighteenth-century minister taught the meaning of the sacraments.[32]

The consequences of this flexible, more open-ended understanding of
orthodoxy were several. Stoever could show that the "legal" party in the
antinomian controversy stood on firm ground; they were not, as Miller had
suggested, introducing changes into Calvinism. From Pettit's point of view,
the debate concerning preparation for salvation was rooted in sixteenth-
century (and for that matter Scriptural) tendencies. Holifield questioned the
emphasis on differences among the New England clergy and found new
origins for Stoddardeanism among seventeenth-century English Presbyterians. In each instance, the Yale school was exploiting the interpretative
possibilities of an orthodoxy that lacked rigid boundaries. The same approach also opened up fresh ways of understanding Congregationalism. De-
bating the nature of the ministry in the 1630s and 1640s, the colonists vacil-
lated between conceptions of it as a special order and conceptions of it as
subordinated to lay governance. Both concepts left their mark upon the
Cambridge Platform of 1648; and both had long been part of the Reformed
tradition.[33]

The Yale school and its allies turned also to rethinking the century between the Cambridge Platform and the Great Awakening. From Perry Miller's point of view, the compromises of the covenant theology had become
increasingly explicit in the course of the seventeenth century and reached
their nadir in Cotton Mather. Mather, Miller argued, was far along the road
to rational religion. Only with Jonathan Edwards and the Great Awakening
was the process of "declension" halted, and Edwards had to break with the
past in order to refashion Calvinism.[34] This way of reading the years between the Platform and the Awakening was sharply disputed, first perhaps
by David Levin and soon afterwards by Robert Middlekauff. Levin and
Middlekauff were persuasive in reattaching Cotton Mather to the Puritan
mainstream.[35] This step made "declension" seem less probable. Holifield's
discovery of a "sacramental renaissance" among the preachers of the later
seventeenth century went further in the same direction: renewal now seemed
just as likely as decline.[36] As early as the 1690s Mather himself was giving
emphasis to themes that figure in the rise of pietism. In and through his
efforts, New England Calvinism may have passed intact into the eighteenth
century.[37]

It is true, of course, that by the early eighteenth century the themes of
liberal religion were being voiced in the colonies. Important intellectuals—
Benjamin Franklin, John Adams, and young Jefferson—broke away entirely.

But the rise of liberalism was not equivalent to the collapse of traditional beliefs. The Calvinist system was resiliant, possibly because right from its outset it struck a fundamental compromise between the workings of the Holy Spirit and a legalistic insistence on man's own actions. This compromise enabled different persons to find in Calvinism what they wanted, whether it was John Cotton's emphasis upon the witness of the Spirit or the legalism of a Richard Baxter. Neither was more "orthodox."[38] Ambivalence provoked sharp argument whenever certain groups or persons tried to force the system into tighter definition. But usually the compromise emerged anew. Edwardseans and Old Lights found that they could work together; John Cotton ended up accepting Thomas Shepard. The long development and reign of Calvinism is evidence that systems can renew themselves.

Whenever ministers preached this system, they clothed its doctrinal bones in a language that made religion something to be lived and daily reexperienced. Calvinism survived and flourished because it was a way of life, a veritable culture. This culture proved remarkably persistent and deeprooted. In 1765 as in 1700, the primers used in countless schools and households continued to include the Westminister Confession or a catechism of the seventeenth century. The psalms and hymns of Isaac Watts became so widely known as to achieve the status of folk poetry. For people who grew up within this culture, its meaning reached a special focus in conversion. Conversion was no abstract process: many ordinary persons, like a Nathan Cole, could write or speak about it in literal, direct prose.[39] Dozens of such testimonies made their way into print, and circulated for decades as a leading type of popular literature. In these books lies further proof of Calvinism's transformation into popular belief.[40] Not the Calvinism of doctrinal systems but the Calvinism that was heard and understood as the great evangelical question, Are you saved? As wave after wave of revivals beat upon the colonists, this question came close to being dominant in eighteenth-century America.

III

When Nathan Cole and Mary Dyer set out on journeys of dissent from orthodoxy, neither could foresee the outcome. For Mary Dyer, the end was Quakerism—and the hangman's noose on Boston Common. The end for Nathan Cole lay in the Baptist movement. These two paths are illustrations of a process that was extraordinarily significant in colonial America, a process of dissent becoming radical.

The possibilities for radical religion all had their roots in the Protestant Reformation. The Reformation was scarcely under way before a leftwing tendency developed. The major issue that divided "radical" from "magisterial" Protestants was restitution versus reformation. Leftwing Protestants were eager to destroy "root and branch" the corrupted, worldly church in order to restore it to its primitive condition, as a gathered fellowship of true believers. This gesture was inevitably sectarian: in separating from the world, the radicals repudiated any notion of the church as a means of grace to all. Some of these sectarians carried the doctrine of the priesthood of all believers to its logical end, eliminating any formal ministry. Others asserted a spiritualism that legitimated direct communion with the Holy Spirit.[41]

The left wing of the Reformation went down to defeat a century before the founding of the English colonies in North America. Even so, its influence transcended space and time to have an impact in America. Quaker Pennsylvania became a haven for groups that had survived the great repression of the left. By the time they reached America, these sectarians had turned inward and become passive in their social outlook. The other point of contact between the left wing of the Reformation and colonial America was the Puritan movement. Puritanism was not directly indebted to continental radicalism, yet some connections can be drawn, for in the Puritan program the ambition to restore the primitive church broke out anew. Congregationalists in New England and Quakers in Pennsylvania would represent this ambition in the colonies.[42]

In both Pennsylvania and New England, radical religion became a powerful factor in the making of social and political institutions. The "congregational way" was genuinely democratic in its empowering of the laity. The role of freemen in the civil government was also large. The church in New England had none of the powers of the state church in England—no power to tax, no courts, no civil penalties for excommunication, no bishops sitting in the House of Lords. These changes were in keeping with a broader animosity against the structures of feudalism, an animosity that made early New England something of a utopia in terms of law courts, town government, and land ownership. Compromise was inevitable as the colonies became more pluralistic and as the crown began to intervene. But the utopian impulse lingered on, to reappear in times of crisis, like the Great Awakening, when laymen once again demanded an effective role in church government.

The antinomian controversy of the 1630s brought into play another strand of Puritan radicalism, a spirit mysticism that continued to find advocates throughout the early period. Repudiating Calvin, these mystics argued that the Old and New testaments stood for separate and distinct covenants. Repudiating the Old Testament as legalistic, they insisted that the New Testament taught the doctrine of "free grace." Spirit mystics eliminated the traditional structure of the means of grace, the sacraments and ministry. Challenging the validity of any church not founded on the continuity of revelation, they based their own authority on the immediate witness of the Holy Spirit. These were motifs of the antinomian party in 1630s Massachusetts, and of the Rogerenes of New London in the early eighteenth century.[43]

This spirit mysticism appears in Quakerism, as does the impulse to restore the church of Christ. The early history of Pennsylvania, like the early history of New England, was marked by a conscious utopianism. Here too, the situation changed to one of compromise. Penn himself grew concerned more with what his rights were as proprietor than with his vision of a peaceful kingdom. The millennial fervor of the Quaker movement faded as Quaker grandees rose to power and as merchants made accommodations with the world. Yet here as in New England, the founders' vision never vanished altogether. Sedate, mature Quakerism remained in tension with its origins.[44]

Thus far in this discussion of radicalism, our reference point has been the left wing of the Reformation. But this is not the only source, or even the most influential, from which the concept has been taken. When historians of the English Revolution speak of "radical" religion, they mean the criticism of social class that groups such as the Levellers were expressing. In the ferment of the Revolution the "common people" rose up against "their betters" to question, and if possible to overturn, the institutions and ideas of the gentry and the merchants. It is the potential for disrupting the class structure that makes certain religious ideas seem "radical" or "popular." Radical religion enables ordinary people to take control of their lives, or at least to give themselves more freedom.[45]

Historians from Eduard Bernstein to Christopher Hill have regarded the Levellers and their kin as the great exemplars of this process. But the search for radical or popular belief has passed beyond the boundaries of the English Revolution. Hill has widely influenced many historians of early modern Europe and colonial America who find in other groups and movements— Huguenot printers, say, or New Light evangelicals—the same fusion of social and religious discontent.[46] Some historians also assume—and here the influence comes from French interpretations of popular culture—that "elite" and "popular" cultures were intrinsically distinct. Carried over into religious history, these categories are understood as meaning that only the elite was Christian in belief. The peasants, the illiterate, the "lower orders" had another mental world, a melange of magic, superstition, and elements of Christianity.[47]

By these routes, and in keeping with a broader sympathy for social conflict, radicalism has broken free of the Reformation to become a pervasive theme in the history of religion. Because it lends itself to different uses the category can become confusing, and because it means so much it can also end up meaning very little. Let me start upon the task of discrimination by observing that radicalism in colonial America was highly situational in ways that may preclude consistent definition. The Quaker challenge to social hierarchy subsided as the group matured. Once in power, New Lights in Connecticut behaved like Old Lights in manipulating church and state to their advantage. John Cotton acknowledged the message of the "legal" preachers; George Keith became an Anglican.

Nor does it seem possible for historians to fix the social meaning of specific doctrines. Are we to assume, as T. Wilson Hayes has argued, that the doctrine of original sin served the interests of an "ecclesiastical tyranny by diminishing the control and self-confidence of ordinary people"? Or is William McLoughlin correct in declaring that the Baptists in seventeenth-century New England were radical because they repudiated the compromises of the covenant theology in favor of a more rigorous Calvinism?[48] And there is always room for the observation, in this case referring to Virginia Baptists of the eighteenth century, that evangelicals who seem defiantly individualistic in belief were not really out to change the world.[49] Richard Niebuhr once noted that "the liberty in which [eighteenth-century evangelicals] were interested was not the liberty defined in the Declaration of Independence."[50] For every example of religious ideas that do explode into social protest, there is another example where the relationship is confusing or ambiguous, even among the "lower orders."

A case in point is millenarianism. To assert that earthly hierarchies will vanish once Christ returns to earth seems intrinsically a radical idea. From the millenarian perspective, the social order of this world remains provisional and corrupted. In the world to come, the saints, the persecuted, and the lowly will finally be empowered. Not surprisingly, therefore, historians have frequently assumed that millenarianism was the religion of the dispossessed and an instrument of social change. This assumption lingers despite the fact that every effort to link millenarianism with the dispossessed runs up against the problem of exceptions. The evidence is contradictory. There are out-groups that remain indifferent to millenarianism, as well as groups professing or enjoying stability whose world view is apocalyptic.[51] Again the English Revolution tantalizes, with its examples of millenarianism at high pitch evolving into social radicalism. Even if we leave aside the equivocal evidence on social class in some of these examples, they do not prove that millenarianism always moved in this direction. The American evidence is equivocal: millenarian ideas were so common as to be almost domesticated, retaining only fitfully a connection with "enthusiasm."

Sometimes this domesticated millenarianism had radical consequences. Expectations of the coming kingdom moved John Cotton and his fellow ministers to sharpen the requirements for church membership, a move resisted by conservatives in England and New England who feared the democratic consequences of the gathered-church ideal.[52] The Mathers' vivid hopes for the second coming may have strengthened their commitment to lay privileges at a time when many other ministers were turning "presbyterian." The Great Awakening infused expectations of the coming kingdom with a new energy and perhaps with a new political significance. Alan Heimert's argument to this effect has won a certain sympathy. The Edwardsean–New Light party, Heimert argues, emerged out of the Awakening with a socially progressive, optimistic eschatology. This eschatology warranted vigorous action to hasten on the kingdom. As Heimert construes them, Edwards's concepts of "union" and "true virtue" were democratic alternatives to the status-minded, proto-capitalistic voluntarism of the liberals.[53]

Edwards was not unusual in his fascination with Scripture prophecy and the history of redemption. For nearly two centuries the Anglo-American Protestant community had put enormous effort into deciphering the meaning of the prophecies. This intellectual tradition was neither radical nor conservative in its social implications. When ministers spoke of the coming kingdom, as they did without cease throughout the colonial period, they associated it with the experience of conversion and communal cycles of affliction, repentance, and assurance. Eschatological language was bound up with the evangelical imagery of man's pilgrimage from sin to grace. Living "in but not of" the world, the people who had been converted were confident of overcoming all their lapses into sin or their persecution by the devil in the knowledge that these moments figured in the history of redemption. Eschatology was continuous, therefore, with fundamental themes of evangelical Protestantism: conversion and the never-ending cycle of sin and repentance; persecution and God's providence. None of these themes was in the least bit political, as James Davidson argues convincingly in *The Logic of Millennial Thought*. New Light preaching of the mid-eighteenth century may have emphasized the motif of the coming kingdom, but always within a traditional context. To regard New Light eschatology as "optimistic" is an error, and it is another error to say that Edward's social ethics were progressive. He had much to say about love as a quality of the regenerate, "but he was content to leave the external trappings of the social order as they stood. . . . [His] millennial world was a society notably traditional in its social ethics."[54]

At best, therefore, millenarian thinking was ambiguously radical in the colonial period. The same can be said of anticlericalism, which touched immense numbers of persons in both centuries. In and of itself, anticlericalism had no fixed meaning. Congregationalists would attack Anglican sacerdotalism, and Quakers would assail Congregationalists for their "hireling ministry." Puritans and deists alike would decry "priestcraft," though for utterly different reasons. Anticlericalism was a constantly shifting and evolving language. Nonetheless, it was a powerful factor in numerous situations. It shows up in the behavior of the deputies in the Massachusetts Bay Colony General Court and especially in the massive anger about the introduction of the halfway covenant. The authority of the minister was an issue in early eighteenth-century Connecticut and again in the Great Awakening, when Separatist Congregationalists reaffirmed the validity of lay prophesying and lay ordinations.[55] The relationship between lay vestries and Anglican missionaries in the southern colonies was colored by anticlericalism; and Rhys Isaac has shown how the issue looms behind the rise of evangelical groups.[56] An essentially evangelical form of anticlericalism was complemented in the eighteenth century by a second kind that stemmed from deistic and Whig assumptions about liberty. Its development and expression extends into

Jeffersonianism and the labor radicalism of the early nineteenth century. In brief, anticlericalism was a means by which ordinary people—and many of the lay elite—expressed their resentment of special privilege and their fear of consolidated power. We badly need a history of this important theme.

There is one other strain of radicalism to consider: the evangelicalism of the Virginia New Lights, whom Rhys Isaac has studied. The methodological significance of Isaac's work lies in its analysis of evangelicalism as a cultural style or code, a style that is related to modes of communication and in turn to literacy. Via these associations, evangelicalism becomes popular religion, a religion of "the people": popular because it is oral and therefore easily accessible, because it plays off the cultural style of the gentry, and because it validates an unspecialized, spontaneous form of religion. Harry S. Stout has extended parts of this interpretation to the whole of the New Light movement. He argues that revivalists who adopted a rhetorical strategy of extemporaneous speech were challenging a different rhetoric, the print-oriented modes of the conservatives. The one style was egalitarian, the other hierarchical, since print itself, Stout reasons, embodied symbols of a deferential social order. Evangelical rhetoric thus involved "a shift in authority."[57]

The strength of this argument lies in directing our attention to matters of style and cultural communication and in demonstrating that religious themes can carry or imply other kinds of messages. Isaac and Stout succeed in demonstrating that religious commitments spill over into social history by complex and subtle routes. Yet the argument for style as socially significant fails to reckon with the fact that "spontaneous" rhetoric quickly becomes formalized; in this regard, language itself is more patterned and ambiguous than either Stout or Isaac recognizes.[58] But perhaps the most interesting ambiguity in the concept of evangelical radicalism concerns its relationship to social class. Are the "people" of whom Isaac speaks the dispossessed, the "lower orders" of colonial society?

Gary Nash moves in this direction in *The Urban Crucible*. As the Great Awakening unfolds in Boston (its trajectory was different in Philadelphia and New York), it becomes a "class-specific movement," dividing common people from the middle and upper classes. The appeal of evangelical preachers was partly a matter of style; Whitefield's "frenetic body movements and magnificent voice control replaced dry, logical, rigidly structured theological lectures. . . ." Whitefield also "challenged traditional sources of authority . . . and implicitly attacked the prevailing upper-class notion that the uneducated mass of people had no minds of their own." Tennent and Davenport went further, denouncing wealth, capitalistic individualism, and the clergy. The rise of lay exhorting

> gave a new importance to the oral culture of common people, whose spontaneous outpourings contrasted sharply with the literary culture of the gentry, established among them the notion that their destinies and their souls were in

their own hands instead of the hands of the elite clergy, and turned the world upside down in allowing those who had traditionally been consigned to the bottom of society to assume roles customarily reserved for educated, adult men.

This is language that echoes Isaac, Heimert, E. P. Thompson, and Natalie Davis and in doing so reflects the great enrichment of American social history in the 1970s. But by itself this language does not answer the important questions Nash is asking: Was enthusiastic religion a response to deprivation in mid-eighteenth-century New England? Did the sermons of the clergy embody a hierarchical class code?[59] Until we are more confident about the social situation of the people who responded to revivalism, most historians may prefer Rhys Isaac's answer to the first of these questions. He believes that evangelicalism drew converts from all parts of society; his is a nonclass phenomenon. And his Baptists are alternately individualistic and communal in their social ethos.[60]

The heightening of interest in radical or popular religion owes much to historians of early modern Europe—Christopher Hill, Thompson, Davis, Keith Thomas, Jean Delumeau. As the themes and categories of such work are carried over increasingly into interpretations of religion in colonial America, this process must be one that reckons with certain differences between Europe and the colonies. It is not obvious, for example, that the world of "magic" and occult belief Keith Thomas has so magisterially described ever had the same hold on Americans.[61] In early modern Europe, Christianity may have clashed with pre-Christian beliefs that survived among the peasantry. The situation on this side of the Atlantic seems less clear-cut. If certain folk beliefs were clearly present, the culture of the middle and northern colonies was nonetheless predominantly Christian, the outcome of a long tradition of local clergy, an abundance of religious books written in the vernacular, and a relatively high rate of literacy.[62] Puritanism itself may be regarded as a religion of the people. Among some of the immigrant groups in the middle colonies, and on the frontier that William Byrd visited, organized religion was scarcely evident in the early stages of settlement. But the situation changed with the arrival of missionaries. The "dark corners" of eighteenth-century America may not deserve comparison with those in early modern Europe.[63]

Words like *popular* and *radical* summon up a society that is sharply divided. There are reasons to be skeptical about these implications. For one, historians may have failed to allow for the ideological origins of a category such as popular. Eighteenth-century rationalists attached the label "superstition" to beliefs that did not fit their mental world. Historians cannot use the same distinction as if these superstitions constitute a true religion of the people. For another, historians must recognize the constant interchange between elite and popular versions of religion. Elite culture was not so dominant, nor popular culture so dominated, that each could not at once both influence the other and be accommodating. As many European historians have begun to recognize, popular and radical are categories that have no fixed, inherent meaning.[64]

Aside from New Light evangelicalism, the religious expression of women in colonial America seems most open to analysis in terms of dominant and subordinate relationships. Far more women than men joined the gathered churches of colonial New England.[65] No women members could vote in church affairs or hold church office. Most of the persons accused and convicted of witchcraft were women, as were many of the dissidents from Puritanism. The most famous woman "rebel" of the seventeenth century, Anne Hutchinson, was angrily denounced by the magistrates and ministers for breaching the proper boundaries of her gender.[66] How all these situations fit together is not clear. Lyle Koehler argues that women in seventeenth-century New England responded to "oppression" by becoming deviants—antinomians, Quakers, Gortonists, or witches. His interpretation makes no allowance for the logic of Puritan spirituality, which could easily sweep men *and* women into radical religion. It is likely that women found more freedom of expression in sectarian religions such as Quakerism, but this is not to say that those who joined the sects were consciously rebellious. As for the church membership of women, two cultural factors seem entangled with their high rate of joining: they wanted the children they would bear to receive the sacrament of baptism, and they found in Christianity a language that exalted them as spiritual teachers, "transforming weakness into gentleness, obscurity into humility, changing worldly handicaps into spiritual strengths." Is it fair to conclude, therefore, that dominating and dominated fit some aspects of women's experience but not others? In any case, no one would argue that women were without recourse or initiative in their relationship to Christianity.[67]

IV

The last of my themes is religion and emerging capitalism. No less than *orthodoxy* and *radicalism*, these words have implications that reverberate throughout the historiography. *Capitalism* denotes one great mode of society and economy, a mode for which we recently have been using synonyms like *modern* and *industrial*. Perhaps the most important question facing students of colonial America is to specify the bearing of these categories on the century and a half before the Revolution. Had society and economy advanced into the modern phase or, as most of us are inclined to argue, did they remain suspended between it and its opposite, the "traditional" and the "preindustrial"? Community and family structures, the rural and the craft economy, urban life and politics—all seem to bear some marks of the preindustrial and others of the coming age of capitalism.[68]

Ideally, historians of religion could help resolve this question. A classic argument, the one associated with Max Weber, is that Protestantism functioned as a solvent of traditional restraints. Ascetic Calvinism, with its logic of new order and its ethic of unrelenting work, broke sharply with the values of traditional society. The Calvinist saint, disciplined, confident, and entrepreneurial, became an agent of change. And of conflict also: inevitably the zeal to transform and reorder became explosive, for groups less touched by rationalizing tendencies or empowered by the status quo vigorously resisted the demands for change. Like other sociologists of his day, Weber viewed modernization as a source of social strain and conflict.[69]

Oddly enough, this rich framework of interpretation has never been adopted by historians of colonial America. Instead, they have argued that emerging mercantile capitalism clashed with disciplined, ascetic religious cultures. According to Bernard Bailyn's influential *The New England Merchants in the Seventeenth Century*, merchants resented the communal norms of the Puritan ministry, preferring in their place the greater freedom of the marketplace.[70] A variation on this argument is to suggest that religion looked both backwards to communal values and forward to more freedom. In Richard Bushman's *From Puritan to Yankee*, written in the days before historians began to look in rural communities for signs of their resistance to emerging capitalism, a new form of social character—a kind of individualism—came into being in eighteenth-century Connecticut aided and accompanied by revivalism. But revivalism was also a vehicle for resisting change; or better yet, for releasing tensions that accumulated as behavior varied from official norms. In Bushman's scheme, the evangelicals seem both entrepreneurial and unhappy. Virginia Baptists have it both ways as well. Their social program was implicitly individualistic and contractual, in keeping with an underlying shift in material and economic systems; yet in moments of collective ecstasy, as in their "strict evangelical code," the Baptists were engaged in "a comforting sacred return to a communal sharing."[71]

A similar ambivalence turns up in Paul Boyer and Stephen Nissenbaum's Salem villagers. *Salem Possessed* is based on a comparison of two mentalities, the one rationalizing and capitalistic, the other rural, communal, and traditional. The villagers face in both directions. Sometimes they are precapitalistic, and their outburst against suspect witches is a means of striking back at change. Or else they are baffled and confused by the very mixture of feelings in themselves; they have tried being entrepreneurs, but without success, even as they also are responsive to older values. Either way, Puritanism is linked with an older communalism, as it is in *The New England Merchants in the Seventeenth Century*.[72]

The ways of linking society, economy, and religion in *Salem Possessed* extend beyond the contrast between old community and new capitalism. Boyer and Nissenbaum owed their interpretation of witchcraft in part to Michael Walzer's *Revolution of the Saints*, in which Puritanism is construed as a response to the crumbling of traditional social order. Walzer's Puritans strive to restore order and authority, but in ways that make them innovators. Boyer and Nissenbaum also drew into their eclectic synthesis the argument, which we may call the deprivation thesis, that a Malthusian process was at work in Salem Village as the average size of landholdings decreased sharply. All of these assumptions deserve reconsideration.[73] The imperative task is to detach religion from a backward-looking communalism and, simultaneously, to rethink the connection between witchcraft or revivalism and encroaching deprivation. Certainly, modes of belief could change in keeping with the development of urbanized, commercial society; eighteenth-century "Arminianism" in New England was overwhelmingly a phenomenon of coastal towns, as the maps in Conrad Wright's *Beginnings of Unitarianism* vividly reveal.[74] It seems true that Protestantism, and perhaps especially the Reformed tradition, helped dissolve or create certain structures and mentalities. But we should not say that emerging capitalism determined the path of religious development. Though it was conditioned by social change and social forces, religion retained important powers of autonomy; religion was a mediating force, able to select among and rearrange the elements of capitalism.[75] Historians who have emphasized ambivalence among the colonists have been trying, perhaps, to make this very point, though their doing so has been hampered by their oversimple contrast between "community" and "individualism." The fairest statement may be that in trying to connect religion and society, historians of colonial America possess a stock of half-truths each of which tends to be reductive of a complex, interactive process. Religious movements do not really seem dependent on patterns of wealth distribution or changes in the economy.

The lesson to be learned from these unsuccessful efforts is that we need a framework more responsive to religion as a culture. One modest way of proceeding in this direction is to reflect upon the ritual process. Ritual represents and acts out a myth of collective identity. It is a process that reaffirms the social bond. Yet it also may become expressive of contradictions and alternatives. We have the beginnings of a history of ritual in Rhys Isaac's studies of Virginia; and there is much in the work of historians like Davis and Le Roy Ladurie to stimulate comparisons with early modern Europe.

Let me start upon a larger history by describing Calvinism as a symbolic order. The central myth in New England Calvinism concerned the separation of the saints from evil-doers and their progress towards the coming kingdom. In effect, the transition from "world" to "church" was a ritual process of inversion whereby one set of values or realities—the greed and conflict that ran rampant in the world—was transposed in favor of the values of the outcast: peace, charity, consensus. To be a pilgrim, to live "in but not of" the world, to be as though a martyr—such were commonplace motifs of this inversion. The world is satanic and dark, a realm of bondage and tyranny; the kingdom to come is filled with light and offers freedom. Symbol and myth converge on three occasions: the Sabbath, which as sacred time becomes a liminal moment, a time for entering momentarily the freedom of the kingdom; the covenanted church, where again the passage into freedom is experienced; and conversion, the basic rite of passage from darkness to light.[76]

(This transposition from the language of doctrine to the language of symbol and myth may serve as another reminder that religion was no abstract matter for the colonists. Richard Baxter's father was called a Puritan because of his habit of "reading Scripture when the rest were dancing on the Lord's Day . . . and for talking sometimes a few words of Scripture and the Life to come." For most of the colonists, as for this man, life was bounded by highly charged symbolic structures. Here as elsewhere, the symbols were not esoteric, as we sometimes take formal creeds to be; they were as simple as the image of the Pope as Antichrist or "set" prayer as humane invention. In colonial New England the accouterments of everyday life were saturated with such symbols—the almanac, for example, cleansed of red-letter days, lacking any table of kings, invoking gunpowder plots but not the martyrdom of Charles I, and referring to months and days by number. Accordingly, the almanac becomes evidence of a religion that is truly popular and authentically Puritan, even if some persons attended church infrequently, were anticlerical, or never came forward to receive the sacraments.)[77]

Ritual structures in colonial New England grew out of the obligation to repurify the kingdom. Foremost among the *public* rituals was the fast day. People stopped work to spend their time in prayer and fasting. They lamented all their actions that indicated that worldliness had crept into the kingdom—their covetousness, their quarreling over power, their breaches of the Sabbath. Fast days were moments for restoring boundaries.[78] Foremost among the *private* rituals was the "way of death." Here the reconciliation lay between the dying person and his Savior. But in publicizing this experience, the colonists turned death into something larger: a ritual structure that reimpressed on everyone the boundary between good and bad behavior.[79]

As social change impinged upon these rituals, their structures shifted. Fast days fell out of favor when people disagreed as to which problems should be mentioned in official proclamations. A process meant to heal became enmeshed in conflict.[80] Renewal of covenant was a temporary alternative, but not until the Great Awakening did another, lasting structure, the revival, come about. Revivals played upon deep feelings for cohesion; and the people in New London who burned their jewelry and fine clothes were acting out a cleansing process that many others also yearned for and experienced. The code and structure of this process remained rooted in the zealous sectarianism of the founders of New England. In this regard, revivalism was not new at all. Indeed, it could be argued that Calvinism led directly to a sense of crisis whenever people felt themselves becoming "worldly." The very culture of the colonists—that is, the basic symbols through which they understood reality—dictated that they live according to the rhythm of alternations between purity and corruption. These cycles tended to be mediating, relieving tensions and allowing ordinary business to resume when liminal conditions no longer existed. If revivals also drew on social discontent, as Gary Nash has argued, the process may have reenacted not cohesion but reversal, "a world turned upside down." Guy Fawkes Day was another ritualized event whose meaning may have changed as social discontent increased.[81] It seems possible that the wealthy and more educated withdrew from certain ceremonies and created new ones more in keeping with gentility.[82] The "way of death" would clearly change by 1800. Old symbols vanished, as did the broadside elegies that publicized the "King of Terrors." Death became more private, perhaps in sympathy with greater individualism.[83]

All this is quite preliminary. Of each ritual, and especially of the fast day and revival, we need more careful studies. In their absence, may I emphasize the continuities in ritual structure? The moral economy of the jeremiad, with its invocations of a purified society, played a key role in the Revolution and may have lasted well into the nineteenth century. Here was a ritual offering both purity and progress, as though the two were reconcilable.[84] Perhaps that reconciliation betokened some fundamental compromise between the moral order and emerging capitalism, a compromise that may sum up the paradoxical melange of old and new in the making of colonial America.

From the vantage point of ritual process, the themes and issues I began with all find some common ground. To say that Calvinism was a set of ritual structures is to emphasize anew that religion is not merely the history of ideas or of the ministry. It was the formal task of the clergy to administer these rituals and also to control their meaning. Yet never were the clergy really strong enough to do so. A history of the ministry is not, therefore, the same as a history of religion in colonial America. To say that Calvinism was a set of rituals is also to recognize that New World Protestantism remained latently radical, retaining alternatives like lay prophesying or withdrawal from the "world" beneath the surface until some crisis brought them into play. And it is to recognize that colonial Americans enjoyed a distinctive repertory of symbol, myth, and ritual, a repertory that, while deeply linked with European culture, was also very much their own.

NOTES

1. In this essay I limit myself to the peoples who came from Europe to settle in America. The Christianity of these immigrants is my concern. A history of religion in triracial America would have to encompass the beliefs of native Americans and of the Africans who came as slaves.

2. William McLoughlin, *New England Dissent, 1630–1833: The Baptists and the Separation of Church and State* (Cambridge, Mass., 1971), exemplifies a "relative or historically contextual" approach to church and state which has replaced the older story of freedom and oppression.

3. Henry F. May, "The Recovery of American Religious History," *American Historical Review* 70 (1964): 79–92.

4. Darrett B. Rutman, *Winthrop's Boston: Portrait of a Puritan Town, 1630–1649* (Chapel Hill, 1965), chap. 4; Sumner C. Powell, *Puritan Village: The Formation of a New England Town* (Middletown, Conn., 1963), chap. 8. Cf. Peter Laslett's remark that the only false note in Edmund S. Morgan's *The Puritan Family* (1944) was the word *Puritan* in the title. (Laslett, ed., *Household and Family in Past Time* [Cambridge, 1972], 23). The assumption that many people went unchurched in colonial America is effectively challenged by Patricia U. Bonomi and Peter R. Eisenstadt, "Church Adherence in the Eighteenth-Century British American Colonies," *William and Mary Quarterly*, 3d ser., 39 (1982): 245–86.

5. Sidney Mead, *The Lively Experiment: The Shaping of Christianity in America* (New York, 1963), 1–15.

6. Mead, "The Rise of the Evangelical Conception of the Ministry in America: 1607–1850," in *The Ministry in Historical Perspectives*, ed. H. Richard Niebuhr and Daniel D. Williams (New York, 1956); Mead, *The Lively Experiment*, chap. 7.

7. Leonard J. Trinterud, *The Forming of an American Tradition: A Re-Examination of Colonial Presbyterianism* (Philadelphia, 1949), passim and esp. 92, 118, 122.

8. Perry Miller, "From the Covenant to the Revival," *Nature's Nation* (Cambridge, Mass., 1967); idem, *The New England Mind: The Seventeenth Century* (Cambridge, Mass., 1954), 374; idem, *The New England Mind: From Colony to Province* (Cambridge, Mass., 1953), 228–37.

9. Oscar Handlin, "The Significance of the Seventeenth Century," in *Seventeenth-Century America*, ed. James M. Smith (Chapel Hill, 1959), 3–12. The overall logic of this position is beautifully—if in its essence as history incorrectly—expressed in the following passage from Stanley Elkins's *Slavery* (Chicago, 1959), 28:

> The shadow of an Anglican church, disestablished in the wake of the Revolution and its doom forever sealed by the yearly anarchy of the camp meeting, was all that remained in the South of vested ecclesiastical authority; and in New England the Congregational church, which had once functioned as a powerful state establishment, was deprived of its last secular supports early in the century. . . . As a source both of organized social power and internal discipline the church had undergone a relentless process of fragmentation.

It is a minor irony that Elkins transposes to the nineteenth century the developments that Handlin locates in the seventeenth. But this language of breakdown was irresistible!

10. Bernard Bailyn, *The New England Merchants in the Seventeenth Century* (Cambridge, Mass., 1956), 39–40; Gary B. Nash, *Quakers and Politics: Pennsylvania, 1681–1726* (Princeton, 1968), 161–79.

11. Joyce O. Appleby, "The Radical Double-Entendre in the Right to Self-Government," in *The Origins of Anglo-American Radicalism*, ed. Margaret C. Jacob and James R. Jacob (London, 1983); Philip J. Greven, Jr., *Four Generations: Population, Land, and Family in Colonial Andover, Massachusetts* (Ithaca, N.Y., 1970). The demography of the seventeenth-century Chesapeake was quite different, though this fact was not known to the historians of the 1950s.

12. Joel Meyerson, "A Quaker Commonwealth: Society and the Public Order in Pennsylvania, 1681–1765" (Ph.D. diss., Harvard University, 1971).

13. David D. Hall, *The Faithful Shepherd: A History of the New England Ministry in the Seventeenth Century* (Chapel Hill, 1972).

14. Elizabeth Nybakken, "New Light on the Old Side: Irish Influences on Colonial Presbyterianism," *Journal of American History* 68 (1982): 813–32.

15. Jon Butler, "Power, Authority, and the Origins of American Denominational Order: The English Churches in the Delaware Valley, 1680–1730," *Transactions of the American Philosophical Society* 68, pt. 2 (1978). In a paper for the Philadelphia Center for Early American Studies Seminar (1981), "Sect, Church, and Secularization: Religion in Colonial Pennsylvania," J. William Frost argues convincingly that "pluralism" did not necessarily result in greater or more

rapid secularization in eighteenth-century Pennsylvania; nor in other respects did it lead to weakened commitment, as some Americanists have implied. The opposite could be true, and often was, among the sects that coexisted in Pennsylvania.

16. Norman Fiering, "The First American Enlightenment: Tillotson, Leverett, and Philosophical Anglicanism," *New England Quarterly* 54 (1981): 318; E. Brooks Holifield, *The Covenant Sealed* (New Haven, 1974), 192–93; Norman Fiering, *Jonathan Edwards's Moral Thought and Its British Context* (Chapel Hill, 1981).

17. As Kenneth A. Lockridge risks doing in *A New England Town: The First Hundred Years, Dedham, Massachusetts, 1636–1736* (New York, 1970) and especially in *Literacy in Colonial New England* (New York, 1974).

18. This apparatus is described in Samuel Eliot Morison, *Harvard College in the Seventeenth Century* (Cambridge, Mass., 1936), and in Richard Warch, *School of the Prophets: Yale College, 1701–1740* (New Haven, 1973).

19. James McLachlan, *Princetonians* (Princeton, 1976), passim.

20. Babette Levy, *Early Puritanism in the Southern and Island Colonies* (Worcester, Mass., 1960); Richard Beale Davis, *Intellectual Life in the Colonial South*, vol. 2 (Knoxville, 1978), chap. 4, and cf. 580–84; Joseph Ellis, *The New England Mind in Transition: Samuel Johnson of Connecticut* (New Haven, 1973); Gerald J. Goodwin, "The Myth of 'Arminian-Calvinism' in Eighteenth-Century New England," *New England Quarterly* 41 (1968): 213–37. It should be noted that Dutch and German Reformed communities were broadly Calvinistic; and the Quakers, though openly hostile to certain doctrines, were sympathetic to others.

21. Carl Van Doren, ed., *Benjamin Franklin and Jonathan Edwards: Selections from Their Writings* (New York, 1920), ix.

22. H. Richard Niebuhr, *The Kingdom of God in America* (1937; reprint, New York, 1959), 137–38. Another reappraisal was Joseph Haroutunian, *Piety versus Moralism* (New York, 1932).

23. Perry Miller and Thomas H. Johnson, eds., *The Puritans* (New York, 1938), 63.

24. For an earlier argument to this effect, together with citations to *The New England Mind: The Seventeenth Century*, see David D. Hall, "Understanding the Puritans," in *The State of American History*, ed. Herbert Bass (Chicago, 1970), 330–49. My brief note, "A Reader's Guide to *The New England Mind: The Seventeenth Century*," *American Quarterly* 34 (1982): 31–36, is also relevant.

25. Perry Miller, "The Marrow of Puritan Divinity," in *Errand into the Wilderness* (Cambridge, Mass., 1956), 50–53; idem, "'Preparation for Salvation' in Seventeenth-Century New England," in Miller, *Nature's Nation*. Miller romanticized the tough-mindedness of orthodoxy. A recent comment by Donald Davie is relevant: "More certainly, there is an unpleasantness about extolling the heroically uncompromising consistency of the old Puritans when they maintained their doctrines in all their primitive ferocity, and then going on to speak sneeringly of temporizers and compromisers. . . . This is how Leslie Stephen—himself safely outside the Christian fold, and watching from the sidelines—treats of the Baxterian compromise" (*A Gathered Church: The Literature of the English Dissenting Interest, 1700–1930* [New York, 1978], 10).

26. Mason Lowance, *Increase Mather* (New York, 1974), 62. Miller had used the phrase "pure Calvinism" in "The Marrow of Puritan Divinity," p. 53.

27. B. Richard Burg, *Richard Mather of Dorchester* (Lexington, Ky., 1976), chap. 4.

28. Raymond Williams, *Marxism and Literature* (Oxford, 1977), 3–4.

29. The term is something of a misnomer; the historians to whom I refer did not consciously act as a school, or even think of themselves as being in agreement. For example, Holifield and Stoever are critical of Pettit's emphasis on "preparation." Nonetheless, a common point of view pervades a number of books originating as theses in New Haven or written by persons who received their degrees there. One aspect of this point of view is a confidence in intellectual history.

30. William Stoever, *'A Faire and Easie Way to Heaven'* (Middletown, Conn., 1978), 14, 41, 97, 109–10; see also Norman Fiering, "Will and Intellect in the New England Mind," *William and Mary Quarterly*, 3d ser., 29 (1973): 516.

31. Norman Pettit, *The Heart Prepared* (New Haven, 1966).

32. Holifield, *The Covenant Sealed*, 27–28, 57, 104, 107, 155, 227.

33. Hall, *The Faithful Shepherd*, chap. 6.

34. Miller, *The New England Mind: From Colony to Province*, passim and esp. chap. 24.

35. David Levin, "Introduction," in Cotton Mather, *Bonifacius* (1710; reprint, Cambridge, Mass., 1966); Robert Middlekauff, *The Mathers* (New York, 1971).

36. Holifield, *The Covenant Sealed*, chap. 7; Robert Pope, *The Half-Way Covenant: Church Membership in Puritan New England* (Princeton, 1969).

37. Richard F. Lovelace, *The American Pietism of Cotton Mather: Origins of American Evangelicalism* (Grand Rapids, Mich., 1979).

38. Geoffrey Nuttall, *Richard Baxter and Philip Doddridge: A Study in a Tradition* (London, 1951); Melvin B. Endy, Jr., *William Penn and Early Quakerism* (Princeton, 1973), chap. 1.

39. Michael J. Crawford, "The Spiritual Travels of Nathan Cole," *William and Mary Quarterly*, 3d ser., 33 (1976): 89–126.

40. These statements are based on a work I have in progress on popular religion in colonial America.

41. George Williams, *The Radical Reformation* (Philadelphia, 1962).

42. The discussion in Endy, *William Penn and Early Quakerism*, of the relationships between Puritanism and Quakerism, and between these two and the "radical reformation," is authoritative. The relevant secondary literature is surveyed in his bibliography.

43. James F. Maclear, "'The Heart of New England Rent': The Mystical Element in Early Puritan History," *Mississippi Valley Historical Review* 42 (1956): 621–52; Stoever, '*A Faire and Easie Way to Heaven*,' chaps. 8–9; Geoffrey Nuttall, *The Holy Spirit in Puritan Faith and Experience* (Oxford, 1946), chap. 5. The longer tradition is sketched in Ronald A. Knox, *Enthusiasm: A Chapter in the History of Religion* (1950; reprint, New York, 1961).

44. Endy, *William Penn and Early Quakerism;* Frederick B. Tolles, *Meetinghouse and Countinghouse: The Quaker Merchants of Colonial Philadelphia, 1682–1763* (Chapel Hill, 1948).

45. Christopher Hill, *The World Turned Upside Down* (New York, 1972).

46. Natalie Davis, "Printing and the People," in *Society and Culture in Early Modern France* (Stanford, 1975).

47. Keith Thomas, *Religion and the Decline of Magic* (New York, 1971); Robert Muchembled, *Culture populaire et culture des elites dans la France moderne* (Paris, 1978); James Obelkevitch, *Religion and Society: South Lindsay, 1825–1875* (Oxford, 1976).

48. T. Wilson Hayes, "John Everard and the Familist Tradition," in Jacob and Jacob, *The Origins of Anglo-American Radicalism;* McLoughlin, *New England Dissent*, vol. 1, 28. Cf. Hill, *The World Turned Upside Down*, chap. 7. It is impossible to reconcile these two positions. The one grows out of the Marxist point of view that considers religion, and especially Calvinism, an ideology that protects the interests of the dominant classes. The other reflects the sympathy for Calvinism that American cultural historians would begin to feel in the 1930s. For these historians, the essential conflict was not between social classes but between a shallow optimism and a tragic sense of man's limitations.

49. Rhys Isaac, "Radicalized Religion and Changing Lifestyles: Virginia in the Period of the American Revolution," in Jacob and Jacob, *The Origins of Anglo-American Radicalism.*

50. Niebuhr, *The Kingdom of God in America*, 123.

51. Sylvia Thrupp, ed., *Millennial Dreams in Action: Essays in Comparative Study* (The Hague, 1962); Norman Cohn, *The Pursuit of the Millennium*, rev. ed. (New York, 1970). Cohn pursued a functional interpretation of "millenarianism," tying it to the dispossessed and to revolution, an approach that was also taken in E. J. Hobsbawm, *Primitive Rebels: Studies in Archaic Forms of Social Movement in the 19th and 20th Centuries* (Manchester, 1959). Bernard McGinn has indicated the shortcomings of this interpretation in his introduction to *Visions of the End: Apocalyptic Traditions in the Middle Ages* (New York, 1979), a book which should be required reading for anyone who writes on this theme, not least because of the distinction McGinn draws between apocalypticism and millenarianism. Also useful is Bernard Capp, "*Godly Rule* and English Millenarianism," *Past and Present*, no. 52 (1971), 106–17. Luther was once asked what he would do if he knew the

world would end tomorrow. His answer: plant an apple tree. Apocalypticism can proceed hand-in-hand with institution building and social stability, a point I have been reminded of by Steven Ozment.

52. Geoffrey Nuttall, *Visible Saints: The Congregational Way* (Oxford, 1957); Joy B. Gilsdorf, "The Puritan Apocalypse: New England Eschatology in the Seventeenth Century" (Ph.D. diss., Yale University, 1964); James F. Maclear, "New England and the Fifth Monarchy: The Quest for the Millennium in Early American Puritanism," *William and Mary Quarterly*, 3d ser., 32 (1975): 223–60. The relevant literature, especially on English Puritanism, is enormous; the key issues tend to turn up in the pages of *Past and Present*.

53. Alan Heimert, *Religion and the American Mind from the Great Awakening to the Revolution* (Cambridge, Mass., 1966).

54. James Davidson, *The Logic of Millennial Thought: Eighteenth-Century New England* (New Haven, 1977), passim and esp. 216–19.

55. Paul R. Lucas, *Valley of Discord: Church and Society along the Connecticut River, 1636–1725* (Hanover, N.H., 1976), chap. 9; C. C. Goen, *Revivalism and Separatism in New England, 1740–1800* (New Haven, 1962).

56. Rhys Isaac, "Religion and Authority: Problems of the Anglican Establishment in Virginia in the Era of the Great Awakening and the Parsons' Cause," *William and Mary Quarterly*, 3d ser., 30 (1973): 3–36. In general, cf. James F. Maclear, "The Making of the Lay Tradition," *Journal of Religion* 33 (1953): 113–36; Christopher Hill, *Economic Problems of the Church* (Oxford, 1956), chaps. 5–6; and Margaret James, "The Political Importance of the Tithes Controversy in the English Revolution, 1640–1660," *History* 26 (1941): 1–18.

57. Rhys Isaac, "Evangelical Revolt: The Nature of the Baptists' Challenge to the Traditional Order in Virginia, 1765–1775," *William and Mary Quarterly*, 3d ser., 31 (1974): 345–68; Harry S. Stout, "Religion, Communications, and the Ideological Origins of the American Revolution," ibid. 34 (1977): 519–41.

58. I question whether a description of modes of language is also a description of audience or social groupings; after all, the new style of the evangelists was practiced by ordained clergy within the Anglican Church. The evangelicals were not hostile to print. The very rhetoric that Stout describes as formal originated as the "plain style" in opposition to high-style, courtly literary structures in the seventeenth century. Literary historians are increasingly skeptical about these categories. See Stanley Fish, *Self-Consuming Artifacts: The Experience of Seventeenth-Century Literature* (Berkeley, 1972). On the larger issue of the Bible as a model for prose style see Erich Auerbach, *Mimesis* (1946; reprint, Princeton, 1968), chap. 1.

59. Gary Nash, *The Urban Crucible: Social Change, Political Consciousness, and the Origins of the American Revolution* (Cambridge, Mass., 1979), chap. 8 and esp. 204–12; E. P. Thompson, "The Moral Economy of the English Crowd in the Eighteenth Century," *Past and Present*, no. 50 (1971): 76–136; Davis, "The Rites of Violence," in *Society and Culture in Early Modern France*. In an unpublished study of the Great Awakening in Connecticut, Peter Onuf argues that revivalism in the major towns became more "enthusiastic" because only a small percentage of the townspeople in such places were church members and used to accepting the authority of the incumbent minister. In smaller towns these conditions were reversed, and the progress of the revival was far less agitated. Patricia Tracy's study of the relationship between deprivation and revivalism in Northampton is not persuasive (*Jonathan Edwards, Pastor: Religion and Society in Eighteenth-Century Northampton* [New York, 1979]).

60. Isaac, "Radicalized Religion and Changing Lifestyles."

61. Jon Butler, "Magic, Astrology, and the Early American Religious Heritage," *American Historical Review* 84 (1979): 317–46; Herbert Leventhal, *In the Shadow of the Enlightenment* (New York, 1976). The larger issues are two, and both of them, in my opinion, are mishandled by Butler. They arise out of the practice of dividing belief into the "rational" and the "irrational," the "religious" (or Christian) and the "magical." On the one hand these categories, by assigning certain beliefs to the margins of the cultural system or to specific social groups, can easily become ideological. On the other, they read conflict into a situation that, in early modern

Europe and America, was actually one of comfortable accommodation. There was no warfare between astrology and Christianity in early modern Europe; and many "superstitions" were as prevalent among the educated and the clergy as among the uneducated. Important arguments that point beyond the opposition of religion and magic include: Natalie Zemon Davis, "Some Tasks and Themes in the Study of Popular Religion," in *The Pursuit of Holiness in Late Medieval and Renaissance Religion*, ed. Charles Trinkaus with Heiko A. Oberman (Leiden, 1974), 307–36; R. W. Scribner, *For the Sake of Simple Folk: Popular Propaganda for the German Reformation* (Cambridge, 1981); and Michael MacDonald, *Mystical Bedlam: Madness, Anxiety, and Healing in Seventeenth-Century England* (Cambridge, 1981).

62. David D. Hall, "The World of Print and Collective Mentality in Seventeenth-Century New England," in *New Directions in American Intellectual History*, ed. John Higham and Paul Conkin (Baltimore, 1979), 166–80.

63. John B. Frantz, "The Awakening of Religion among the German Settlers in the Middle Colonies," *William and Mary Quarterly*, 3d ser., 33 (1976): 266–88.

64. Roger Chartier, "La 'culture populaire': un decoupage questioné" (Paper delivered at the Conference on Popular Culture in Europe and America, Ithaca, N.Y., April 22–24, 1982).

65. Richard D. Shiels, "The Feminization of American Congregationalism, 1730–1835," *American Quarterly* 33 (1981): 46–62.

66. David D. Hall, ed., *The Antinomian Controversy, 1636–38: A Documentary History* (Middletown, Conn., 1968), 267–69.

67. Lyle Koehler, *A Search for Power: The 'Weaker Sex' in Seventeenth-Century New England* (Urbana, 1980); Laurel Thatcher Ulrich, *Good Wives: Image and Reality in the Lives of Women in Northern New England, 1650–1750* (New York, 1982), 216; Mary Maples Dunn, "Saints and Sisters: Congregational and Quaker Women in the Early Colonial Period," in *Women in American Religion*, ed. Janet Wilson James (Philadelphia, 1978), 27–46; Keith Thomas, "Women and the Civil War Sects," *Past and Present*, no. 13 (1958): 42–62.

68. James A. Henretta, "Families and Farms: *Mentalité* in Pre-Industrial America," *William and Mary Quarterly*, 3d ser., 35 (1978): 3–32.

69. Max Weber, *The Protestant Ethic and the Spirit of Capitalism*, trans. Talcott Parsons (reprint, New York, 1958).

70. Bailyn, *New England Merchants*, chaps. 2–3.

71. Richard L. Bushman, *From Puritan to Yankee: Character and the Social Order in Connecticut, 1690–1765* (Cambridge, Mass., 1967); Isaac, "Radicalized Religion and Changing Lifestyles."

72. Paul Boyer and Stephen Nissenbaum, *Salem Possessed: The Social Origins of Witchcraft* (Cambridge, Mass., 1974), 88, 99, 101–2, 104–7; see esp. the portrait of Samuel Parris in chap. 7.

73. Michael Walzer, *The Revolution of the Saints: A Study in the Origins of Radical Politics* (1965; reprint, New York, 1968); Boyer and Nissenbaum, *Salem Possessed*, chap. 4. Important corrections in, if not a downright refutation of, the deprivation thesis appear in Christopher M. Jedrey, *The World of John Cleaveland: Family and Community in Eighteenth-Century New England* (New York, 1979), chap. 3. The relationship between religion and society is thoroughly reappraised in Christine Heyrman, *Commerce and Culture: The Maritime Communities of Colonial Massachusetts, 1690–1750* (New York, 1983), in ways that depart from all of Boyer and Nissenbaum's assumptions. Heyrman relocates the actual witchcraft accusations in a context of responses to *religious* deviance. The argument in favor of village feuding, pure and simple, continues to deserve respect (see Abbie Peterson Towne and Marietta Clark, "Topsfield in the Witchcraft Delusion," *Topsfield Historical Society Collections* 13 [1908]:23–38). A masterful review of New England witchcraft that lifts it out of older categories is Carol Karlsen, "The Devil in the Shape of a Woman" (Ph.D. diss., Yale University, 1981).

74. Conrad Wright, *The Beginnings of Unitarianism in America* (Boston, 1955); Daniel W. Howe, "The Decline of Calvinism: An Approach to Its Study," *Comparative Studies in Society and History* 14 (1972): 306–27.

75. Joyce O. Appleby, "Modernization Theory and the Formation of Modern Social Theories

in England and America," *Comparative Studies in Society and History* 20 (1978): 259–85; John Bossy, *The English Catholic Community* (London, 1975), 144–46.

76. This description draws on several of the essays in *The American Puritan Imagination*, ed. Sacvan Bercovitch (New York, 1974), and on·Charles Hambrick-Stowe, *The Practice of Piety* (Chapel Hill, 1982).

77. Quoted from *Reliquiae Baxterianae* in Hall, *The Faithful Shepherd*, 22.

78. W. DeLoss Love, Jr., *The Fast and Thanksgiving Days of New England* (Boston, 1895), provides a superb basis for studying the fast day. Cf. Bossy, *English Catholic Community*, 110.

79. David Stannard, *The Puritan Way of Death: A Study in Religion, Culture, and Social Change* (New York, 1977); Allan Ludwig, *Graven Images: New England Stonecarving and Its Symbols, 1650–1815* (Middletown, Conn., 1966); Ola Winslow, *American Broadside Verse* (New Haven, 1930).

80. Hall, *The Faithful Shepherd*, chap. 10.

81. As Alfred Young has argued in an unpublished essay on "Pope's Day." An exemplary essay on ritual change is Charles Pythian-Adams, "Ceremony and the Citizens: The Communal Year at Coventry, 1450–1550," in *Crisis and Order in English Towns, 1500–1700*, ed. Peter Clark and Paul Slack (London, 1972).

82. Rodris Roth, "Tea Drinking in Eighteenth-Century America: Its Etiquette and Equipage," *Contributions from the Museum of History and Technology* (Washington, D.C., 1969), 61–91.

83. Philippe Ariès, *The Hour of Our Death*, trans. Helen Weaver (New York, 1981); Winslow, *American Broadside Verse*, xxv; James Deetz and Edwin S. Dethlefsen, "Death's Head Cherub Urn and Willow," *Natural History* 76 (1967): 28–37.

84. Sacvan Bercovitch, *The American Jeremiad* (Madison, Wis., 1978); Edmund S. Morgan, "The Puritan Ethic and the American Revolution," *William and Mary Quarterly*, 3d ser., 24 (1967): 3–43. Cf. Roland A. Delattre, "The Rituals of Humanity and the Rhythms of Reality," *Prospects* 5 (1980): 35–49.

12

AMERICAN HIGH-STYLE AND
VERNACULAR CULTURES

RICHARD L. BUSHMAN

o we now have the materials for an integrated cultural history of the American colonies? Or to pose a more difficult question, can we realistically expect to compose an ordered history from the thousands of existing studies of chairs, folk songs, farm tools, poems, flags, election rituals, games, diet, costume, festivals, gravestones, pottery, and so on? Restricting the definition of culture to the older idea of the arts and manners of the cultivated classes does not ease the task appreciably. The scholarly work on high style seems hopelessly diverse and unconnected. The academy divides the study of high culture among departments of art history, literature, music, history, and others, each with its own canons of evidence and significance, and they are only part of the story. Art and antique dealers and museum curators further confuse the picture with their catalogs and descriptions. The aesthetic and monetary value of cultural objects generates an intense, demanding scholarship with only secondary interest in integration. If we add to this work the materials encompassed by an anthropological definition of culture, the prospect of an integrated cultural history grows dim indeed.[1] And yet our language betrays a conviction that it can be done. Use of the word *culture* implies a belief that chairs, pageants, and costumes can be related systematically, as wheat, pipe staves, and shipping relate systematically to the economy. It should be possible, our vocabulary says, to write cultural history as coherently as economic history. High-style culture especially appears to invite integrative studies, with labels like *baroque*, *rococo*, and *neoclassical* applied generally to painting, architecture, and furniture. Those labels imply integrative forces working through diverse channels the analysis of which should form the substance of cultural history. Despite the notorious weakness of the cultural sections in survey texts and our reluctance in recent years to attempt comprehensive

345

histories of American colonial culture, the logic of our convictions compels us to ask how to proceed.[2]

Thirty and forty years ago a generation of historians showed less reticence than scholars do now in tackling cultural history. Within the fifteen-year period from 1942 to 1957, Carl and Jessica Bridenbaugh, Louis B. Wright, Michael Kraus, and Thomas J. Wertenbaker attempted summaries with titles like *The Atlantic Civilization: Eighteenth-Century Origins* or *The Golden Age of Colonial Culture*. The survey text *Art and Life in America*, though written by an art historian, Oliver Larkin, attempted a similar integrated study of American society and American arts. Chapter titles like "Books, Libraries, and Learning," "Drama, Music, and Other Diversions," and "Architecture and the Decorative Arts" reveal that these scholars uncritically assumed that culture meant the culture of the cultivated classes, but they nonetheless attempted broad studies comprehending a substantial part of the whole.[3]

Our own efforts to return to broadly conceived cultural history may logically begin with the work of this generation, perhaps properly with the most thoughtful and original among them, Carl and Jessica Bridenbaugh. Carl Bridenbaugh entered the armed services before the completion of *Rebels and Gentlemen: Philadelphia in the Age of Franklin*, and an aura of wartime patriotism shines faintly from the pages. Students reading too rapidly may mistake the book for a catalog lauding Philadelphia's high culture. But the Bridenbaughs' inclination to vaunt American achievements would have pleased many intellectuals for other reasons. Constance Rourke died in 1941, and *The Roots of American Culture* appeared in 1942, the same year as *Rebels and Gentlemen*. Rourke had led the drive in the 1930s to confute 1920s critics of American culture who wrote of the desiccated, materialistic American cultural landscape as an uninhabitable environment for artists and writers. Lewis Mumford and Van Wyck Brooks made the migration of Benjamin West and John Singleton Copley back to Europe in the eighteenth century signify the hostility of the American provinces to talent. What art did appear here, they said, was imitative and retarded. Rourke and others such as John Kouwenhoven were attempting to recover a past from which twentieth-century artists could draw nourishment. The Bridenbaughs' pride in eighteenth-century Philadelphia, more than mere chauvinism, may be read as an effort to join forces with Rourke in the creation of a usable cultural past.[4]

Part of the difficulty under which this group of American apologists labored was the prevailing idea that high culture and civilization were synonymous, that is, that societies could be ranked on a scale of civilization, measured by the quality of their art, literature, and manners. A society lacking high culture was that much closer to barbarism. America's deficiencies lowered it on the scale of human life. Rourke argued in her *Roots of American Culture* for a broader definition of culture that would include humor, or, as Kouwenhoven later argued, vernacular tools. A culture strong in vernacular house forms or native wit could nourish its people, including its artists, and claim standing among cultures more richly endowed with painters and poets. The task of historians was not to measure America by European standards but to discover the roots of the truly American culture, including in the search native craftsmen and spinners of yarns. The idea, though simple, was liberating: the search for the emergent American in American culture, for the qualities distinguishing American from European, became the governing question of the American studies movement.[5]

The Bridenbaughs' contribution was to distinguish rebels from gentlemen, that is, authentic Americans from Europeans. Gentlemen imitated English culture in a slavish effort to ape the gentry of the mother country; rebels were true to American circumstances. The gentlemen felt that "colonial artistic output should be as nearly as possible an echo of that of contemporary London." Others "whom instinct and experience told that America was already developing its own way of life" thought America was "capable of distilling its own forms of artistic expression." These more prescient Americans were drawn from "the great middle class" which brought forth craftsmen, artists, and scientists with an inclination "to re-form European culture in an American mold." American art was realistic, robust, practical, emphasizing "simple beauty of line," in contrast to formal, artificial, sophisticated European works with their "elaborate elegance." The American "leaven worked beneath the surface" until the early 1770s, when the "actuality of the chasm separating the two cultures and two ways of life" forced itself to the attention of Americans and emboldened them to revolt.[6]

The Bridenbaughs took it upon themselves to judge the degree of commitment to American standards of each artistic medium, even of individual works. An aura of disloyalty hung over those still dependent on Europe. The theater "owed little to colonial Philadelphia," they observed, and became "ultimately the butt of attack from emergent patriotism." To their discredit, American "cabinetmakers largely failed to develop a style of their own." Architecture did better, but the prize art was painting, "the art to attain most complete naturalization." By conforming to "already established native traditions and local taste," with "little reference to British conventions or European theories," painting succeeded best in realizing its American potential. The glaring exception was Benjamin West, who left Philadelphia at an early age to become the historical painter to George III. West "may be regarded," the Bridenbaughs said, "as an unfortunate accident" in the history of American art "from which it required more than a century to recover." West's defection "led directly to the artistic tragedy of Copley, a somber drama that was often to be repeated in the national period." Copley's magnificent achievements as a provincial painter were thrown in jeopardy by West's insistent invitations. "Copley, a lukewarm Tory, fled to Italy and artistic ruin when he cut himself off from his native land." This treatment of the

West-Copley migrations became the trademark of the generation committed to establishing the merit of America's independent cultural resources.[7]

After forty years, *Rebels and Gentlemen* has gone out of print, and the story of Constance Rourke's battles with Mumford and Brooks has been long forgotten by her spiritual grandchildren. From today's perspective, the particular division that the Bridenbaughs drew between patrons and producers of the arts no longer seems real. These gentlemen patrons, "in their admiration of current standards of English taste, often crystallized to the point of decadence," supposedly carried American culture one way, while the painters who did their portraits and the architects who constructed their houses marched in the opposite direction. *Rebels and Gentlemen* separates patrons from artists and craftsmen, as if the two could function independently of one another. In actuality the craftsmen were as attuned to London fashions as anyone. When Swan's *British Architect* was published in Philadelphia in 1775, 172 of 186 subscribers were carpenters. To gain customers, craftsmen had no better way to advertise themselves than to announce their recent arrival from London. Painter after painter followed West to England for instruction in his studio. The artists and craftsmen appear to have followed European fashions as avidly as their patrons. The search for a distinctive colonial democratic culture is illusory, William Pierson observes. "For the most part colonial architecture was imitative from beginning to end." How could it be otherwise, when the patrons of the arts wanted and paid for the best in English taste?[8]

Today the necessity of discovering the roots of an indigenous American culture no longer presses upon us. We have no need to isolate a native strain or to prove that the colonies were capable of bearing civilization. Considering the changed circumstances, is anything to be learned from the Bridenbaughs and their generation? Perhaps the most trustworthy foothold for a cultural history is an assumption common to both them and their antagonists, the assumption summed up in the word *imitation*. Mumford and Brooks pitied American imitation, and the Bridenbaughs scorned it, but neither side denied its reality. In a less impassioned time, we can accept imitation as simply signifying American participation in an Anglo-American cultural system. Rather than hunt for the roots of a uniquely American culture, we can begin with the fact that the American colonies were cultural provinces of London, as were Ireland, Scotland, and the west country. Philadelphia was one among a dozen comparable provincial British cities, each with its peculiarities. Before we attempt to identify distinctive American qualities, as the Bridenbaughs tried to do, the colonies must be securely located in this larger system. The true meaning of imitation and American exceptionalism, the traditional issues in American cultural studies, must emerge from an understanding of Anglo-American provinciality as a whole. The sketch that follows seeks to explicate England's cultural networks as they influenced high culture and vernacular.[9]

The Great Houses

The Bridenbaughs' gentry culture did not flower anywhere along the American seaboard until the eighteenth century. There was wealth in the seventeenth century, as well as display and attempts at fashion, but cultural life entered a new era after 1700. The houses themselves tell of the change, and nowhere more clearly than in Virginia. The most ambitious seventeenth-century Virginia houses, extant or on record, were basically enlarged farmhouses. Greenspring, the house of Governor William Berkeley and the largest of the seventeenth-century houses (with the possible exception of Fairfield, built in 1692), had four rooms, arranged according to a traditional farmhouse plan that was a common vernacular form. Bacon's Castle of 1665 went further than any houses before it in assuming the exterior dress of a fashionable house, but its interior followed a familiar two-room plan.[10]

The Governor's Palace in Williamsburg marked the beginning of a new era in Virginia. Conceived by Governor Francis Nicholson and erected between 1706 and 1714 largely under the eye of Alexander Spotswood, the palace was in conception and purpose a departure in Virginia architecture. For years it was debated whether its design was by Sir Christopher Wren. It now seems beyond question that it was designed in London, possibly in His Majesty's Office of Works, of which Wren was the surveyor, but it seems unlikely that Wren himself had a hand in the design. The question has been worthy of discussion because the palace was built in a style current in England. It resembled the innumerable small houses of the middle class going up all over England, many of them scaled-down versions of Wren's great buildings. The palace had four rooms on the first floor and a grand staircase to the chambers on the second, which were also usable for purposes of state. In plan and style the palace was a mansion.[11]

The completion of the Governor's Palace signaled the beginning of a building boom in great houses that was to last for the remainder of the colonial period. Already in 1722, in a new passage in his *History*, Robert Beverley noted that the houses in Virginia "of late . . . have made their stories much higher than formerly, and their windows larger, and sashed with crystal glass, adorning their apartments with rich furniture." Two score known buildings of great magnitude and cost went up before the Revolution, a dozen in the 1720s and 1730s, in the first wave, and more than two dozen in a second wave between 1750 and 1776. In the first wave William Byrd II built Westover. In 1704 Byrd inherited from the first William Byrd twenty-six thousand acres, along with a position on the provincial council and a place at the pinnacle of Virginia society. Yet the second Byrd was content with his father's simple frame house until 1730, when he began the construction of Westover, within a few years of the time when John Fitzhugh, Thomas Lee, Charles Chiswell, Mann Page, John Randolph, Thomas Nelson, Benjamin Harrison, and various branches of the Robert King Carter family put up

their fashionable mansions. Other planters, like the Washingtons, transformed older houses into large and stylish residences. The Washingtons
remained content with a simple, single-story frame farmhouse until the period after 1740, when in two stages a story was added and rooms were constructed at both ends and to the back to make the Mount Vernon home we
know today. It was in the 1720s and 1730s that the great house, usually with
four large rooms on the first floor, elegantly fitted with paneling, marble
fireplaces, pedimented doorways, and elaborate cornices in the main rooms
and grand staircases, became inextricably interwoven into the Virginia planter's way of life. If not built in the architectural style of the exact moment,
the houses clearly drew on fashionable English models and compared favorably to construction in other provincial regions.[12]

New England house building passed through a similar transition about the
same time. After the first few years of settlement in the seventeenth-century,
house construction converged on a remarkably similar pattern over the entire
region: the classic two-room hall-and-parlor plan with a huge chimney pile at
the center, chambers above, and often a lean-to addition for kitchen and
storage in the rear. Although the salt-box can be traced to English precedents, it became the dominant form in New England folk architecture of the
early period. In the houses of the wealthy, decoration was added and the
rooms grew larger, but the basic outline remained the same.[13]

The first heralds of a new house type, the 1679 central-passage house of
Peter Sargeant and the precocious Palladian, three-story structure put up by
the merchant John Foster in Boston in 1688, foreshadowed developments of
the coming century. The eighteenth-century great houses were usually built
for merchants in port towns like Newport, Portsmouth, Marblehead, and
Salem and, unlike the country houses in Virginia, followed an English town-
house pattern. A number of these, such as the Isaac Royall House in Med-
ford, which was a two-stage expansion of an older house (1733–37 and
1747–50), and the Jeremiah Lee mansion in Marblehead, were three-story
structures with blank end walls. Although they stood alone, they assumed
the possibility of another house close by, as along a city street. These merchant town houses and a few remaining rural equivalents, such as the Old
Manse in Deerfield (1768), show unmistakable signs of provincial awkward-
ness in proportion and decoration, but they broke cleanly with the traditional
New England house and, with their quoins, pedimented doorframes, and
classical pilasters, represented an obvious effort to copy English fashions.[14]

As in New England, so in Pennsylvania it was merchants and successful
urban artisans who built the great houses. Because Philadephia was not
founded until 1682, no sharp break divides a seventeenth-century folk house
from the stylish town houses of the eighteenth century. The Letitia Street
house of the merchant Thomas Chalkeley, built in 1713–15, though small,
was designed with blank end walls for a densely packed urban street and
stylistically could serve as a starting point for the enlargement of Philadelphia

town houses towards the elegant three-story houses of Samuel Powel and John Cadwalader built in the 1760s and remodeled in the 1770s. Insurance records and a number of extant houses offer proof that fashionable great houses lined Philadelphia streets well before the Revolution. The occupants added another touch of English gentility with the construction of country houses along the Schuylkill River and in nearby Germantown. The Philadelphians' country houses, mostly within ten miles of the city, an easy morning's ride, allowed their owners to follow the city-country rhythms that delighted their English counterparts.[15]

A closer look at one Philadelphia town house, that of Samuel Powel III, on Third Street, offers a hint as to the meaning of these expensive residences springing up along the Atlantic seaboard in the eighteenth century. Born in 1738, Powel attended school at the Academy of Philadelphia and entered the College of Philadelphia at eighteen, graduating in 1759. As prospective heir to two fortunes, he was reared as a gentleman to no trade, although he maintained membership in the Carpenters' Company. For seven years after 1760 he traveled in Scotland, Italy, and France, where he was well received in fashionable circles, had his portrait painted by Angelica Kaufman, and traded Quaker for Anglican beliefs. In 1769 Samuel, then thirty-one, married Elizabeth Willing, whose mother's Shippen family, as well as her father Charles Willing, gave young Samuel connections with two of Philadelphia's most eminent mercantile families.[16]

Powel purchased his Third Street house five days before his marriage and proceeded at once to remodel. The house as eventually completed suggests how a Philadelphia gentleman conceived of his life and his society. The three-bay house had just two rooms on each floor and a generous stair hall to one side. None of the practical areas of housekeeping—kitchen, washing rooms, or servants' quarters—were in this main block; they were all housed in a two-story wing, four rooms long, extending from the back. The two parlors on the first floor and the two rooms on the second apparently were used primarily for entertainment. The largest and most prodigiously decorated space was the ballroom, on the second floor to the front. All four rooms on the first two floors were public rooms. They had pedimented interior doorways, marble fireplace surrounds, classical chimney pieces, wainscoted or paneled walls, and in the drawing room fluted pilasters and marvelous plasterwork on the ceiling. By contrast, the two chambers on the third floor, apparently family bedrooms, had a simple chair rail and baseboard, no mantel, and, like bedrooms in other great Philadelphia houses, little other decoration.[17]

Although both of Powel's children, two sons, were to die in infancy before 1775, he did not know that he was to be denied a family when the remodeling was done. And yet the family spaces of the house were given a secondary position. They were pushed to the top and back, where absence of decoration gives an indication of their role. The expensive ornament, the largest spaces, and central location were devoted to the rooms for public entertainment. Under the date of September 8, 1774, John Adams made note of dinner at the Powels with five gentlemen and "many others." "A most sinfull Feast again! Every Thing which could delight the Eye, or allure the Taste, Curds and Creams, Jellies, Sweet meats of various sorts, 20 sorts of Tarts, fools, Trifles, floating Islands, whipped Sillabubs etc., etc.—Parmesan Cheese, Punch, Wine, Porter, Beer." The splendor of the repast matched the splendor of the decor, suggesting the significance of such events to the Powels. A glance at the floor plans of virtually all the great houses in Virginia and New England reveals entertainment rooms of similar size, prominence, and grandeur. It is not surprising that the second quarter of the eighteenth century saw the appearance of formal cupboards to display the expanding array of ceramics and dinnerware. In the same vein, householders purchased more chairs to accommodate guests. In seventeenth-century Newbury the number of chairs per household was less than five; by 1735–40 the average number of chairs was over eleven. Probably for the same reason, eighteenth-century dinnerware and silverware began to come more commonly in sets, and the card table became a common form.[18]

The appearance of the great house in the eighteenth century seems to have marked the emergence of formal entertainment by the American upper middle class. Thinking broadly for a moment, we can envision late medieval entertainments as encompassing the whole village or all the dependents of a lord. In the nineteenth century the nuclear family takes a central place in the house. The eighteenth-century houses gave precedence to a middle group, a select company, not a collection of the entire society nor a close-knit family group, but men and women of similar social class and breeding. In those marvelously adorned public rooms we can picture them displaying their clothing, their wit and worldly knowledge, their fine manners and physical grace—all within a beautiful space suitable for a civil and refined society. Underlying the high culture of eighteenth-century provincial Americans was an urge to enjoy the pleasures of fine company in a fine environment.[19]

THE IDEAL OF CULTIVATION

The word *imitation* does an injustice to the occupants of the great houses. The dinners, the fine wines, the silver and glass, the carriages, the costumes, the country houses surely meant more than simple emulation of a distant society that many of them had never known. They must have been striving for some good whose force they experienced directly in their drawing rooms and gardens. The knowledge that England's most exalted families sought the same good and embodied it in their manners and houses doubtless intensified the strivings of the American gentry, but the ideal had power of its own apart from the repetition of English behavior.

Personal cultivation and the presentation of self in a select company was a protean ideal with undefined boundaries, no real center, and far-reaching effects, but it is the key to understanding life in the great houses. Its meaning in the eighteenth century can perhaps best be recovered now through extreme statements, such as the famous letters of Philip Dormer Stanhope, the fourth earl of Chesterfield, to his son. Trying to capture the elusive but potent image of human refinement, Chesterfield urged upon young Stanhope the example of the late duke of Argyle, who combined "a most genteel figure, a graceful, noble air, an harmonious voice, an elegance of style." Chesterfield's main themes were the aesthetics of appearance and bearing and the achievement of grace in every act and word. He was impatient for a drawing of the boy, he noted at one point. "I want to see your countenance, your air, and even your dress." In a summary list of necessary accomplishments he urged, among other things, "a genteel carriage and graceful motions, with the air of a man of fashion: a good dancing-master, with some care on your part, and some imitation of those who excel, will soon bring this about." Stanhope was to be "extremely clean" in his person "and perfectly well dressed, according to the fashion." Presumably in his own life Chesterfield extended his aesthetic sense to all of his surroundings. He gave his personal attention to the house and gardens in South Audley, Mayfair, assembling a substantial collection of paintings to adorn the rooms.[20]

Chesterfield emphasized especially the aesthetics of speech. He foresaw a diplomatic career for young Stanhope, wherein eloquence was an everyday necessity. To persuade public assemblies, Chesterfield told his son, "a certain degree of good sense and knowledge is requisite." "But beyond that, the purity of diction, the elegance of style, the harmony of periods, a pleasing elocution, and a graceful action, are the things which a public speaker should attend to the most." Effectiveness depended on the presentation of self. Returning to the duke of Argyle, Chesterfield remembered that "he forcibly ravished the audience; not by his matter certainly, but by his manner of delivering it." There was social power in the form of address, and Stanhope was ever to attend to it. "Consider your style, even in the freest conversation and most familiar letters."[21]

The desired presence and manner of which Chesterfield wrote is preserved for us in English portraiture from Van Dyck through Sir Joshua Reynolds and Thomas Gainsborough. Portraits were painted, the contemporary art critic Jonathan Richardson freely admitted, in order that the viewer may "conceive a better opinion of the beauty, good sense, breeding, and other good qualities of the person than from seeing themselves." After viewing Van Dyck's picture of Queen Henrietta Maria, Sophia of Bavaria marveled when she saw the actual person, dumfounded that one "who looked so fine in painting, was a small woman raised up on her chair, with long skinny arms and teeth like defense works projecting from her mouth."[22]

And to what end the constant attention to countenance, bearing, speech—

all that went into making a figure? Chesterfield must have had in view power over the common people on those stages where as justices and magnates the aristocracy were called to play their parts. Stanhope likewise was to seek influence in the Parliament and with dignitaries. Still, the promise of practical success loomed less large in the letters than the prospect of "pleasing and shining as a man of the world." Stanhope was assured of a seat in the Commons, and Chesterfield told him that he "must first make a figure there, if you would make a figure, or a fortune, in your country," as if politics were an avenue to some greater success. He pressed upon his son the necessity of frequenting the best company, for the purpose of discipline and instruction. He was to seek out "veteran women of condition, who having lived always in the grande monde . . . form a young fellow better than all the rules that can be given him." Though ever practical, Chesterfield brought the point around less often to the preparation for diplomacy or to the exercise of power than to becoming like the models. The ultimate end was "to shine as an agreeable, well-bred man" and to take one's place as a polished member of the best company.[23]

Chesterfield wrote as no armchair theorist or frustrated recluse. He was himself a former member of Parliament, ambassador to The Hague, and later in life leader of the opposition in the House of Lords. After Walpole fell in 1742, Chesterfield was brought into the ministry as Lord Lieutenant of Ireland, where, in contrast to his image as a hopeless snob, he was noted for sensitivity to the plight of the Irish peasantry and hostility to the landlords. From 1746 to 1748 he was secretary of state for the northern department. And yet through the years of his most active political career, from the time his son was five, in 1743, until young Stanhope's premature death in 1768, Chesterfield wrote the letters, usually two or three a week, each one nearly a finished essay. After his own son reached maturity, Chesterfield started another series to his godson, a distant cousin also named Philip Stanhope. The task of teaching a young person to shine in the world held endless fascination. He remarked to his son, "I wish to God that you had as much pleasure in following my advice, as I have in giving it to you."[24]

The fascination was not singular to Chesterfield. A year after his death in 1773, his daughter-in-law, Mrs. Eugenia Stanhope, disappointed by his neglect, sold the letters to the publisher Dodsley for fifteen hundred pounds, more than double the amount paid to Fielding for *Tom Jones*. Although Chesterfield's survivors tried to stop publication, the letters went through five editions within the year. By 1776 they were translated into French and German. James Humphreys published a four-volume edition in Philadelphia in 1774, and a reprint appeared in Newburyport and Boston in 1779. Within a decade Chesterfield's name had become a byword in the household of literate families. Seventeen-year-old Nabby Adams's first reaction to Royall Tyler when he began to pay suit to her in Braintree in 1782 was to object that

Tyler was "practicing upon Chesterfield's plan, that is the essence and quintessence of artfulness."[25]

Five years later, after Nabby had thrown him over, Tyler wrote *The Contrast* in condemnation of Billy Van Dumpling, a "ruddy youth" from New York who, having traveled in Europe, became Billy Dimple and was "metamorphosed into a flippant, pallid, polite beau, who devotes the morning to his toilet, reads a few pages of Chesterfield's letters, and then minces out, to put the infamous principles in practice upon every woman he meets." Tyler's criticism of Chesterfield echoed the reaction of Samuel Johnson after the publication of the *Letters:* "They teach the morals of a whore and the manners of a dancing-master." The condemnation juxtaposed to the *Letters'* popularity reflects the deep ambivalence in which gentility was ensnared. The ideal of cultivation both inspired admiration and evoked disgust.[26]

Courtesy literature, the tradition of writings on personal conduct, in which Chesterfield's *Letters* stood, was a blend of two partly incompatible streams. One descended from medieval Christian exhortations to monarchs on their duties as vice-regents of God. The other originated in the Renaissance, with Baldassare Castiglione's *Book of the Courtier* as an outstanding example and model for numerous imitations. The first emphasized sturdy virtues and the responsibilities of rulers, as in Thomas Eliot's *The Book Named the Governor* or in Benjamin Franklin's list of thirteen virtues. The second, though written to instruct servants of the prince, enlarged on personal grace and accomplishments and the importance of beauty. The two crossed and intermingled. Although Chesterfield, whose letters stood in the tradition of Castiglione, earned the wrath of Samuel Johnson, that gentleman thought *The Book of the Courtier* the best ever written on the subject of personal conduct. In denouncing Chesterfield, his eighteenth-century critics did not mean to repudiate gentility. It was artificiality and falseness they disliked, the apparent emphasis on appearances and manners to the exclusion of solid virtues and real substance. Addison depicted a member of Sir Roger de Coverley's family as elegant in manner but idle, wasteful, and careless. The spendthrift, mendacious, artful rake, "the flippant, pallid, polite beau," repelled the moralists, who at the same time admired the gracious, generous, accomplished gentlemen.[27]

As early as 1703 Solomon Stoddard, in a critique of Harvard, complained that "tis not worth the while for persons to be sent to the College to learn to compliment men and court women." Puritanism was not congenial to Renaissance civility, nor was republicanism. John Adams, who warned Royall Tyler away, wishing his daughter to have nothing to do with "any, even reformed Rake," associated polite society with monarchy and informed Mercy Warren that to enjoy republican "Hardiness, Activity, Courage, Fortitude and Enterprise, the many noble and Sublime Qualities in human Nature," they must forgo the other. "A Monarchy would probably, somehow or other make me rich, but it would produce so much Taste and Politeness, so much Elegance in Dress, Furniture, Equipage, so much Musick and Dancing, so much Fencing and Skaiting, so much Cards and Backgammon; so much Horse Racing and Cockfighting, so many Balls and Assemblies, so many Plays and Concerts that the very Imagination of them makes me feel vain, light, frivolous and insignificant." The ideal of cultivation had to make its way against a general English suspicion of the fop and the rake, against Puritanism, and late in the century against republicanism.[28]

On its side, true gentility had many allies, among them Joseph Addison and Richard Steele, whose *Tatler* and *Spectator* strove to make the polite religious and the religious polite, that is, to reconcile the Renaissance and the Christian strains in the courtesy literature. Genteel ideals did not squarely contradict Christian principles. Gentility needed only to be purged of its excesses, and the moralist literature, including the novels of both Richardson and Fielding, were dedicated to that purpose. With the work of purgation and reconcilation going forward on every hand, the remaining ambiguities did not prevent the ideal of cultivation from inspiring the American gentry.[29]

The desire for refinement, as we would expect, seems to have preceded the construction of the great houses in the 1720s. In 1702 Robert King Carter expressed a hope for the training of "a set of better polished patriots," and actually the work of polishing the American planter had begun much earlier among the wealthiest. William Byrd sent William II to England for his education in 1681, at the age of seven. When Governor Spotswood gave a dinner and a ball for the provincial council in 1711, Byrd was well aware of who danced well and regretted that "the president [of the council] had the worst clothes of anybody there." Spotswood, the finisher of the Governor's Palace, had an eye for such things and received credit from Hugh Jones in 1724 in *The Present State of Virginia:* "The country may be said to be altered and improved in wealth and polite living within these few years since the beginning of Colonel Spotswood's government, more than in all the scores of years before that, from its first discovery."[30]

Young George Washington grew up in the 1730s and 1740s without the benefit of a great house. Mount Vernon was still at best a generous farmhouse, and his father intended it for Lawrence, not George. But George was drawn into the circle of the Fairfax family. Their Belvoir, though merely a "tolerable cottage" by Fairfax standards, was, with its two elaborately furnished sitting rooms, a mansion to George. Faced with the usual youthful problems of personal conduct and yearning for acceptance at Belvoir, at age thirteen he laboriously copied maxims from "Youth's Behavior or Decency in Conversation Amongst Men," a seventeenth-century courtesy book which schooled him in genteel manners.

> 13th. Kill no Vermins as Fleas, lice ticks etc in the Sight of Others, if you See any filth or thick Spittle put your foot Dexteriously upon it if it be upon the

Cloths of your Companions, Put it off privately, and if it be upon your own Cloths return Thanks to him who puts it off.

29th. When you meet with one of Greater Quality than yourself, Stop, and retire especially if it be at a Door or any Straight place to give way for him to Pass.

66th. Be not forward but friendly and Courteous; the first to Salute hear and answer and be not Pensive when it's a time to converse.

Driven by his ambitions to rigorous self-discipline, in time George Washington became a model of true gentility to which all Americans could aspire.[31]

Gentility also encircled the lives of young women. The proper education of planters' and merchants' daughters became a minor industry in colonial cities. More than fifty fashionable boarding schools advertised their existence in Charleston in the fifty years preceding the Revolution. Rebecca Woodin promised to teach "the different branches of Polite Education." Her advertisement told the standard curriculum: "Reading, English and French, Writing, Arithmetic, Needlework: and Music and Dancing by Proper Masters." Ornamental needlework as a genteel craft became a high-fashion activity. A 1772 Virginia advertisement offered needlework instruction "after the newest taste."[32]

The emphasis on dancing, needlework, and music notwithstanding, the education of genteel ladies was not frivolous. The polishing of young women who were to host grand entertainments in the great houses required attention and self-discipline. At boarding school or under private tutelage, girls were expected to submit to a demanding regimen. The schedule Jefferson prepared for his daughter Martha at age eleven was not exceptional:

from 8. to 10 o'clock practise music
from 10. to 1. dance one day and draw another
from 1. to 2. draw on the day you dance, and write a letter the next day
from 3. to 4. read French
from 4. to 5. exercise yourself in music
from 5. till bedtime read English, write, etc.

It required no small effort to win the compliment of William Eddis just before the Revolution: "There are throughout these colonies, very lovely women, who have never passed the bounds of their respective provinces, and yet, I am persuaded, might appear to great advantage in the most brilliant circles of gaiety and fashion."[33]

By the mid-eighteenth century the ideal of cultivation infused the great houses wherever they stood along the seaboard, blending with other cultural currents originating in Christianity, politics, and the economy. Thomas Jefferson had the opportunity to observe at close hand Governor Francis Fauquier in Williamsburg, whose popularity with the Virginia gentry was

partly due to their perception of him as a "compleat gentleman." Jefferson
practiced the violin three hours a day so as to perform with the governor and
John Randolph in weekly concerts at the palace. Boston had not escaped the
influence of gentility. A visitor in 1740 noted that "the ladies here visit, drink
tea and indulge every little piece of gentility to the height of the mode and
neglect the affairs of their families with as good grace as the finest ladies in
London." Benjamin Franklin had a copy of the *Spectator* not long after it
appeared in London, as did Jonathan Edwards, Cotton Mather, and William
Byrd. By 1721 Harvard students had a periodical of their own named the
Telltale, modeled after the *Spectator*. In 1726 a group of more serious literati—
Mather Byles, Thomas Prince, and others—began the *New England Weekly
Journal*, assigning the editor the nom de plume "Proteus Echo," again in
imitation of the *Spectator*. Although reprehensible to Samuel Sewall, there
were balls at the governor's house, races in Cambridge, and rumors of plays
performed in the provincial council chambers. During the eighteenth century at least seven Boston boarding schools offered to teach the young ladies
of New England music, art, dancing, and needlework. Indeed, in 1744 Alexander Hamilton judged that Boston excelled Philadelphia and New York
"both for politeness and urbanity tho only a town."[34]

The ideal of cultivation as experienced by the American gentry, though
diffuse as it was powerful, combined three interrelated aspects. The first was
personal refinement, meaning grace of bearing and manner, along with fitting accomplishments: dancing above all but also music, drawing, riding,
letterwriting, needlework (for women), and knowledge of science, languages,
and history. The second was the assemblage of cultivated persons into select
companies for entertainment in the houses or for balls and assemblies in more
public spaces. Here refined persons met to display their wit, grace, beauty,
and gentle manners for the benefit of one another and to enjoy the pleasure of
shining in the best company. The third aspect was the preparation of environments fitting for such assemblies, appropriately adorned in the best
taste with proper accouterments for dinners, dancing, and card-playing.
The great house was the primary stage for such assemblies, but gardens and
later assembly halls and baths joined the group of favored places. In time
cities planned for promenades, public gardens, and vistas where ladies and
gentlemen could stroll, talk, and observe one another. A series of words tied
together the three interrelated aspects of genteel living and signaled to listeners and readers that the entire ideal was being invoked. Among them at
least were *polite, polished, well-bred, genteel, refined, gay, urbane, civil*, and also
taste, fashion, beau monde, and *grace*.[35]

So powerful was the ideal that it became inextricably associated with
human progress itself. The degree to which a person, a people, or a place had
achieved gentility and urbanity was a measure of progress from barbarism to
civilization. A common theme of histories of the colonies and of travelers'
accounts was the manners of the people, their learning, the size and taste of

their buildings. Alexander Hamilton, the Edinburgh-educated Annapolis physician who rode to Maine and back in 1744, constantly judged the vulgarity or refinement of the persons he encountered. "The landlord's name I cannot remember, but he seemed to be a man of tollerable parts for one in his station," typified his observations. The ferry at the Susquehanna was "kept by a little old man whom I found att vittles with his wife and family upon a homely dish of fish without any kind of sauce." Invited to eat with them, Hamilton declined. "They had no cloth upon the table, and their mess was in a dirty, deep, wooden dish which they evacuated with their hands, cramming down skins, scales, and all. They used neither knife, fork, spoon, plate, or napkin because, I suppose, they had none to use." The scene fascinated Hamilton. Every detail of the family's manners, their possessions, and their diet spoke to his finely calibrated sense of human progress. "I looked upon this as a picture of that primitive simplicity practiced by our forefathers long before the mechanic arts had supplyed them with instruments for the luxury and elegance of life." The ferryman's meal brought to Hamilton's mind the course of history from the primitive to the civilized, including, as indicated by the words *elegance* and *luxury*, a fashionable tinge of regret for lost simplicity. Hamilton summed up his findings on the American colonies in the concluding sentence of the itinerarium: "As to politeness and humanity, they are much alike except in the great towns where the inhabitants are more civilized, especially att Boston."[36]

The spread of gentility created in America a conscious class of gentlemen united by common standards across colony lines. Before leaving Annapolis in 1744, Hamilton obtained letters of introduction to prominent gentlemen in each town. He recognized urbanity wherever he went, from Maryland to Maine, and in his turn was welcomed by men of civility. Despite regional variations, houses were similar, learning was comparable, and manners and dress universally conspicuous. A common culture facilitated regional marriages. William Byrd III married the sister of Samuel Powel's wife and moved in next-door. Later in the century, as the imperial crisis came to a head, gentility was both a resource and a problem for politicians. It was a resource in that leaders of distant colonies who had never seen one another could judge their new colleagues by dress, manner, and speech. The outward signs of gentility were assurance of common assumptions and predictable behavior, of a commitment to reason, tolerance, and respect. Governor Gooch's observation in 1727 soon after his arrival in Williamsburg that "the gentlemen and ladies are perfectly well-bred, not an ill dancer in my government" was not entirely silly. Dancing, personal grace, and manners signified engagement to a code of conduct that enabled gentlemen to deal with one another.[37]

The prevalence of gentility was a problem to those who did not subscribe to, or who consciously flaunted, its standards, like Patrick Henry or Samuel Adams. Adams's deficiencies of dress worried his friends as the patriot was preparing for the journey to the Continental Congress in 1774. One by one, so the story goes, they arranged for a new suit of clothes, additional linen, a new wig and hat, silk hose, and six pairs of shoes. Adams and the other delegates, including cousin John, set out from Boston in "a coach and four, preceded by two white servants who were mounted and arm'd, with four blacks behind in livery, two on horseback and two footmen." Connecticut rang bells and set off cannon as the entourage passed through. In New York merchants threw an elegant dinner at the Exchange Tavern, where the foresight of Adams's friends was vindicated. The speaker Philip Livingston alarmed the Bostonians with remarks about "Goths and Vandals" accompanied by uneasy glances in their direction. The ability of John Adams to enter easily into the company at Samuel Powel's and to enjoy the conversation as well as the whipped sillabub was not entirely unimportant to the success of the Massachusetts delegation in Philadelphia.[38]

THE DIFFUSION OF GENTEEL CULTURE

The diffusion of genteel culture in eighteenth-century America has been attributed to growing wealth alone. It has been assumed that when the hardships of settlement began to recede, and slave labor and trade provided leisure and prosperity, the great planters and merchants turned their eyes to England for cues to fine and stylish living. This assumption should be modified. We do not need to deny the significance of wealth in order to recognize that broader cultural developments, in England as well as America, sustained the spread of gentility. We must not forget that England itself was changing. We are inclined to think of the colonies as primitive and coarse and the mother country as refined and advanced from the beginning. But this was not so. England was a cultural province of France, Italy, and particularly the Netherlands through the sixteenth and much of the seventeenth century. Even England's most aristocratic nobles had not always been committed to taste and fashion. Taste was a creation of the Italian Renaissance; like all ideas, it had to spread and be adopted. It spread to the upper reaches of the class structure in England in the sixteenth century and seeped downward into the middle classes after the Restoration. The construction of stylish houses for the English middle class commenced not many years before the appearance of the great houses in America. The flowering of high culture in the colonies was not due to their increasing prosperity alone but to the quickening pace of cultural activity in England as well.

Castiglione's *The Book of the Courtier*, perhaps more than any other single carrier, brought the Renaissance idea of civility to England. Baldassare Castiglione (1478–1529) began his service to Duke Guidobaldo da Montefeltro at the court of Urbino in 1503 and continued in his service and that of his heir Francesca della Rovere until 1524, when Pope Clement VI sent Castiglione to Spain as papal nuncio to the Emperor Charles V. Castiglione began work on *The Courtier* in 1508 and published it in Venice in 1528, one year before his death. Sir Thomas Hoby translated *The Book of the Courtier* in 1561 for a receptive English audience. Sir Philip Sidney carried it with him whenever he went abroad. Ben Johnson praised it, as in later generations did Richard Steele and Samuel Johnson.[39]

The acceptance of *The Courtier* signified more than a British interest in things Italian. Castiglione's popularity, it can be seen in light of Lawrence Stone's analysis, was related to a crisis among the English aristocracy in the sixteenth century. *The Courtier* helped with the difficult transition from medieval knight to client of the king, as the aristocracy's base of power shifted from the armies they could raise to their position at court. Obtaining the favor of the crown and the management of court politics called for new manners, a new ethic, and a new set of accomplishments. The feudal warrior lacked the necessary polish of the new man of honor. Castiglione and his many imitators provided an appropriate social character for the new role. Gentility had its origins in the powerful needs of this first generation of courtiers.[40]

Fundamentally, the aristocracy needed to justify their right to office. They pursued education above all as a key to control of office in competition with clerics, whose learning and skills had long given them advantage. But from there the nobility went on to many forms of display to manifest their largesse, cultivation, and grandeur. The extravagant prodigy houses of the Elizabethan and early Stuart eras were only the most blatant attempts to attract royal favor and exhibit prowess. The huge country seats, erected at immense cost, were designed with the single aim of entertaining Elizabeth or James in the course of the royal progress. A wide, long stairway rose through the house to a great room where the queen could be greeted and seated to preside over the entertainment of the court. The houses were the scene of prodigal feasts and pageants put on at an expense few could lightly bear.[41]

Despite the excesses, the aristocracy must be credited for training themselves to excel at court. Lord Burghley, who as chancellor of Cambridge and master of the court of wards directed the education of fatherless young noblemen, was merciless in his demands. The twelve-year-old earl of Oxford in 1562 had a program of study laid down for him that went from morning to night.

A.M.	7–7:30	Dancing
	7:30–8	Breakfast
	8–9	French
	9–10	Latin
	10–10:30	Writing and Drawing
	10:30	Prayers and Dinner
P.M.	1–2	Cosmography
	2–3	Latin

3–4	French
4–4:30	Writing
4:30	Prayers and Supper

In the training stages, gentility was a discipline more than an indulgence. The Continental tours for purposes of learning dancing, riding, languages, history, fencing, and music were not extended vacations. After emphasis shifted from scholarship to art with the transition from James I to Charles I, the aristocracy studied painting, sculpture, and architecture as well. Only by careful cultivation of the self could one achieve the easy grace and confidence that was the mark of the perfect cavalier. The end result of their efforts was the deep implantation of the ideal of cultivation which inspired English society for three centuries or more.[42]

Interwoven with the aesthetic side of gentility was the principle of taste, an innovation in English cultural life in the sixteenth century. Taste incorporated the idea of a center of glory where the best was known and practiced, as well the hope of borrowing glory by adopting similar manners or appearance. The power of taste influenced all who recognized the center's glory and were willing to follow the lead of the occupants of the most honored places. As gentility gained sway, taste preempted the position of tradition in determining costume, housing, and diet and marked a reorientation away from the local to the metropolitan and the foreign.[43]

Next to costume, houses were the foremost statement of taste. Until the mid-sixteenth century noblemen were housed much as in the late Middle Ages. In the prodigy houses and other buildings of the late Tudor era an aesthetic of symmetry made its first impression on the facades, indicating a yearning for the classical and Italian and a responsiveness to the influence of foreign fashions. Attention to architectural fashion arrived later in the city, according to John Summerson. "Taste in architecture reached London about 1615: Taste, that is, in the exclusive, snobbish sense of the recognition of certain fixed values by certain people. Taste was a luxury import from abroad, received and cherished by a small group of noblemen and artists whose setting was the unspectacular palaces of James I." In architecture as in furniture, taste at first meant the adoption of Italianate forms in place of English traditional forms. Inigo Jones's return from Italy marked the beginning of high-style taste in architecture. About the same time, furniture makers spread discontent with native English styles by offering Italianate designs from Flemish and German copybooks. So engulfing were Italian styles that they provoked a backlash in Shakespeare's contemptuous observation on polished youths:

Reports of fashions in proud Italy
Whose manners still our tardy apish nation
Limps after in base imitation.[44]

Harold Perkin has observed that fashions moved in half-century cycles in the sixteenth and seventeenth centuries, gradually speeding up until in the eighteenth century fashion changed by the decade. The pattern holds for furniture and architecture. Jacobean style in furniture persisted through the first part of the seventeenth century, until more rapid changes were introduced after 1660. But fashions in costume changed with breathtaking speed from the sixteenth century on. Tailors on the lookout for new cuts are said to have spied on the gallants from behind the pillars of St. Paul's. An anonymous poet around 1635 could not have been the only one to find the dizzying pace ridiculous and immoral.

> He that will have the world to his minde,
> Must search well his wits new fashions to finde,
> And study new fangles to pleasure fond fooles,
> For wantons are willing to follow bad rules.

But moralists could not stop the tide. It became increasingly true that the pursuit of cultivation entailed a commitment to fashion.[45]

The high cost of gentility at first sharply divided the nobility and wealthiest merchants from the squirearchy and the more modest middle class. The middle class could not afford to be fashionable. The polish and refinement available through education and travel, the great houses with their glittering furnishings, and incessant alterations in costume were possible only for those with large fortunes. Not until after the Restoration did increasing prosperity, combined with a scaling down of fashionable life to suit people of more modest circumstances, permit a large segment of the English population to aspire to taste and personal refinement. The middle class in England began its great period of growth around 1660, accelerating as the eighteenth century approached, with profound effects on the economy as well as on culture.[46]

This expansion created a large new market for fashionable goods and activities which eventually touched many artists and tradesmen. The contrasting studio practices of Anthony Van Dyck and Peter Lely exemplify the change. Van Dyck (1599–1641), the Flemish court painter to Charles I, succeeded through his marvelous ability to portray the aristocracy as the polished courtiers they aimed to be. Successful as Van Dyck was, in his decade in England he produced only a fraction as many paintings as Lely (1618–80), court painter to Charles II, who turned out four or five hundred pictures. Lely began sittings as early as seven in the morning and was booked up days in advance. To increase productivity, he hired specialist journeymen painters to do postures, backgrounds, ornaments, and draperies. Lely's busy practice at the pinnacle of society echoed through the provincial towns, where in the late seventeenth century portrait painters in substantial numbers opened studios to meet the needs of an expanding market.[47]

The same pattern holds true for architecture. Inigo Jones (1573–1651) and Christopher Wren (1632–1723) affected the architectural environment quite differently as the social environment changed through the century. As surveyor of the royal works for James I and Charles I, Jones had the supervision of palace construction. He and his contemporary Roger Pratt (1620–84) pioneered Italian Palladian architecture in England, but they built only great houses in the grandest manner. The masons and carpenters who put up lesser English buildings, even those employed in the Office of Works, failed to follow Jones's lead. Wren, appointed surveyor in 1669, received similar commissions—royal palaces, churches, and university buildings. But Wren inspired, although he did not build, structures on a scale that merchants and master artisans could afford. In Wren's time carpenters and masons reacted to high-style taste. Townhouses in the Wren style went up on the streets and squares of every provincial city. The Governor's Palace in Williamsburg was one manifestation of a broad architectural movement.[48]

The growing middle-class desire for fashionable goods and activities touched one sphere after another. Cane chairs, in imitation of high styles, were turned out in cheaper models by methods approaching mass production. They were sold in sets of six, eight, or twelve to achieve the proper effect in the new spaces designed for entertainment. J. H. Plumb has surveyed the vast enlargement of fashionable leisure activities after the Restoration and especially after 1690: fishing, yachting, racing, theater, gardening, pets, baths. In the cities, middle-class aspirations made themselves visible not only in stylish houses on fashionable squares and terraces but in assembly halls, gardens, and promenades.[49]

The taste for the appearance if not always the substance of gentility reached so far down in society and so far out to the provincial corners of the land that by 1763 the *British Magazine* complained that "the present vogue for imitating the manners of high life hath spread itself so far among the gentle folks of lower life that in a few years we shall probably have no common people at all." By the early eighteenth century country gentlemen, who earlier had despised the royalist extravagance of Inigo Jones's buildings, were in danger of ridicule on the London stage or in the *Tatler* as booby squires if they failed to follow fashion. John Summerson attributed the great wave of London building in the first decade of the eighteenth century to country magnates setting up town houses, where they could enter better into urbane society. In the opening lines of *She Stoops to Conquer*, Mrs. Hardcastle scolds her old-fashioned squire husband: "Is there a creature in the whole country, but ourselves, that does not take a trip to town now and then, to rub off the rust a little?"[50]

Learning, absorbing, and manifesting civility required a host of tradesmen: among many others, barbers, gardeners, musicians, and dancing masters in the service lines; jewelers, clockmakers, booksellers, tailors, upholsterers, and cabinetmakers in the crafts. The growing market for luxury goods drew into apprenticeships many who found reason to believe they could succeed in one of the expanding lines. The flow of these craftsmen into the apprenticeships and out into shops of their own followed a course that for a century shaped the structure of provincial culture, as shown, for example, in the development of clockmaking. In the early 1600s foreign craftsmen dominated English clockmaking, turning out costly and beautiful clocks for nobility and the wealthiest gentry. A few English-born makers constructed less expensive iron lantern clocks for a limited custom. In 1656 there were just fifty clockmakers in the Clockmakers Company. The simplest clock cost £2.10, and a typical mantel clock, £40. In 1658 Christopher Huygens's invention of a clock pendulum combined with an anchor escapement resulted in a small clock that actually kept time. The new clocks, plus the increased demand, tripled the membership of the Clockmakers Company by 1662, as more young men arrived from the provinces to take up the trade.[51]

Although benefiting from the generally enlarging market, the demand for clocks and the supply of clockmakers could never be perfectly synchronized. When supply exceeded demand, London-trained clockmakers flowed back to the provincial towns, where new tastes were also creating a market. By 1700 there were a dozen important provincial clockmaking centers; apprentices trained in these centers in turn left for villages and hamlets when the supply-and-demand cycle repeated itself in the provinces. The first clockmakers in America, William Davis and David Johnson, arrived in Boston in 1683 and 1687, respectively, to import and repair clocks. The first actual manufacture of clocks occurred in Philadelphia after Samuel Bispham immigrated in 1696, followed by Abel Cottey in 1700 and Peter Stretch in 1702.[52]

We can envision culture being carried from the metropolis to the provinces in the late seventeenth century in the minds and hands of English craftsmen moved by the currents of supply and demand. The construction of the great Virginia houses may have been delayed until competent carpenters, joiners, and plasterers were available to handle large structures and finished interiors. There were never enough skilled masons to erect Palladian buildings in stone, as fashion required, and no one in eighteenth-century America could lay up a vault. American builders simulated stone by mixing sand into paint to achieve a Palladian effect. The deficiencies of American styles, where they existed, may be attributed as much to delays and imperfections in the transfer of craftsmen as to rusticity in taste.[53]

The diffusion of fashion-oriented craftsmen into the provinces and the middle-class desire for the "genteelest taste" in time created a market for another polite commodity, the fashion book. The arrival of craftsmen who advertised themselves as newly from London continually challenged established tradesmen. Because their customers' preferences followed London fashions, craftsmen with knowledge of recent trends had the advantage. From around 1700 to the Revolution eighty-seven different architectural books are referred to in American libraries or book lists. Familiarity with such books became almost as advantageous as English experiences in winning customers. John Arris, a native Virginian who studied architecture in England, advertised in the *Maryland Gazette* in 1751 his ability to design "either in the Ancient or Modern Order of Gibbs' Architect."[54]

Cabinetmakers and other artisans borrowed designs and patterns from the architectural books, one general book serving several crafts. But Thomas Chippendale's success with *The Gentleman's and Cabinetmaker's Director*, published in 1754, indicated that the demand for recent information throughout the English provinces also warranted more specialized books. By the mid-eighteenth century guide books to virtually every phase of genteel living were available. Edmund Hoyle's *Short Treatise on the Game of Whist* went through fifteen editions between its first appearance in 1742 and Hoyle's death in 1769. There were cookbooks on high-style cuisine, gardening books, music books, travel books. In 1762 John Dunlap reprinted in Philadelphia a collection of jests, bon mots, and humorous tales entitled *The Wits of Westminster*, a book to enliven provincial conversation.[55]

From the late seventeenth century onward, waves of craftsmen flowed outward from London to the provinces and eventually to the colonies, followed by shipments of books carrying the means of acquiring genteel culture. Earlier a similar wave had reached American shores from the Netherlands. The Low Countries were a century ahead of England in many aspects of cultural development, particularly in painting. The names of eight thousand painters are known for the seventeenth-century Netherlands, compared with a few score in England. This source supplied the English court from Van Dyck through Lely and did the same for the Dutch colonies. The low-country surplus spilled over into the provinces in the seventeenth century, just as clockmakers later spilled out of London. The number of Dutch painters practicing in New Netherlands and New York belies the belief that culture waited entirely on wealth and the passing of frontier conditions. Dutch painters found patrons when New Amsterdam and Albany were still tiny outposts. The arrival of English painters like John Smibert and John Wollaston in the eighteenth century probably reflected less colonial economic maturity than the accumulation for the first time of a surplus of English painters in the home country, some of whom chose to seek customers in America.[56]

Colonial cultural development was linked to England far more intricately than is implied in the word *imitation*. Cultural evolution in England and America was a single integrated process. American planters and merchants could not build fashionable houses until their English counterparts resolved to create a polite society for themselves and learned to modify aristocratic housing tastes. Until middle-class Englishmen adapted the architecture of Inigo Jones and Christopher Wren for their town houses and small country seats, there could be no Governor's Palace. American manifestations of gentility, taste, and urbanity awaited their appearance in English provincial centers and the subsequent dispersal of producers and purveyors to the colonies.[57]

The colonies were not much slower to respond to the new stimuli than provinces in England. Boston imported cane chairs in large numbers in the 1680s, just as English chairmakers geared up to produce them. Soon after early Georgian forms appeared in England, cabinetmakers able to produce them arrived in the colonies. In Newbury, a Massachusetts outpost, a cabinetmaker with skills equal to the new styles took over local customers from a traditional joiner by the 1720s. William Fussell in Philadelphia produced a rococo chair at least four years before Chippendale's *Director* popularized the style. Dancing masters, theater companies, and wigmakers showed up in Williamsburg and Philadelphia about the same time as they did in Bristol and Lincoln. In 1745 Charles Willson Peale's father was teaching fencing and dancing in Chestertown, Maryland, a cultural center two or three levels below the top. By the time of the Revolution many fashions reached American style centers in a matter of months. America was a cultural province of London, as most of England itself was, linked by nerves and arteries to the source of cultural ideas.[58]

London and the Colonies

Besides receiving cultural information from London, the colonies dispatched painters and writers back to England for training and fulfillment. London was an irresistible lure. The concentration of aristocratic society around the government at Westminster gave the city immense power over the nation's cultural life, and provincial artists yearned to partake of it. Ultimately the success of a fashion, of an individual artist, or of a craftsman depended on the endorsement of the aristocracy. The assembling of the most distinguished people of the realm during the London season created a testing ground where reputations, ideas, and taste were made and destroyed. Only in that fiery furnace could true refinement and the highest success be achieved.[59]

London threw its spell over colonial America's two greatest artistic talents, Benjamin West (1738–1820) and John Singleton Copley (1738–1815). West left Philadelphia in 1759 to study in Italy for three years before settling in London, where he quickly rose to become historical painter to George III. Copley submitted *The Boy with the Squirrel* to the exhibition of London's Society of Artists in 1766 and received back a thrilling letter from Sir Joshua Reynolds: "If you are capable of producing such a piece by the mere efforts of your own genius, with the advantages of example and instruction you would have in Europe you would be a valuable acquistion to the art and one of the first painters in the world." That was a promise to be made and fulfilled only in London, and it put Copley in a dilemma. The flow of painters was from London to the provinces, where a better living could be made than amidst the competition of the metropolis. "I should be glad to go to Europe," Copley wrote West in 1768, "but cannot think of it without a very good prospect of doing as well there as I can here. You are sensable that three hundred Guineas a Year, which is my present income, is a pretty living in America, and I cannot think You will advise me to give it up without a good prospect of something at least equel to it." Copley delayed for six more years before uprooting himself in 1774. He left America with the intention of an instructional tour, but in the event made London his permanent home.[60]

Unlike Copley, other Americans returned home after a time in Europe. David Hume deplored Franklin's departure from urbane Edinburgh for Philadelphia, believing so promising a philosopher must surely perish in the wilderness. Franklin's suave reply spoke a basic truth: "You have here at present . . . such a plenty of wisdom. Your people are, therefore, not to be censured for desireing no more among them than they have; and if I have any, I should certainly carry it where, from its scarcity, it may probably come to a better market." The American market stood over against the hope of fame in England, opposing poles pulling on talent. The Bridenbaughs held Benjamin West responsible for the migration of American artists to Europe in the ensuing century and for the continuing oscillation of others between metropolis and province, but West was not responsible. Polarity and oscillation were inherent in the structure of Anglo-American culture.[61]

All of the provinces yielded up their poets and painters to London for a time, some few to rise to fame, others to return instructed and frustrated, but in one respect the American provinces differed from the rest: America partook of London culture but not of London society. The society that assembled for the London season and then moved off to watering places for more theater, balls, and conversation returned at last to their country seats scattered across the face of the land. With them they brought London culture. The aristocracy hired London craftsmen to build and furnish their country houses. Thomas Chippendale traveled to country seats all over England to take notes, returned to London to design and construct, and then shipped out the furniture, along with assistants to install it. The best collections of fine paintings, silver, porcelains, hangings, glassware, and furniture were not concentrated in the metropolis alone but were dispersed throughout the realm. And the people who bought the upholstered chairs, dined from Wedgwood's plates, and sponsored the balls and assemblies dispersed with the objects, bringing a rich, full portion of London culture to the provinces—the wit, the manner, the costume, the taste.[62]

America enjoyed bits and pieces of London. William Byrd ordered wrought-iron gates for Westover from Thomas Robinson, the most prominent smith in London. In 1735 Thomas Hancock furnished his Beacon Hill house with forms imported from London. The gorgeous paneling in Carter's Grove was done by Richard Bayliss, an English carpenter brought to Virginia for that purpose. By the same token, John Cadwalader of Philadelphia or Peter Manigault of Charleston, after years of experience in European society, returned to the provinces as polished, urbane gentlemen. But none of the American gentry mingled yearly with the court, heard the latest gossip, caught the nuances of politics, savored the wit of the best raconteurs, saw firsthand the costumes, the jewelry, and the dinnerware of England's highest society.[63]

Whatever the efforts to attain civility, a shade of rusticity tinged American life. In the eyes of Europe, the wilderness overhung the most advanced American cities. When Wedgwood began large-scale exports, he sent the cheapest wares to America, as if he doubted Americans' capacity to value his best. Five years after his arrival in America, Dr. Alexander Hamilton's thought as he started his trip to Maine in 1744 was to measure American civility, and he was often disappointed. Reflecting on Philadelphia after seeing it coming and going, he wrote, "I could not apprehend this city to be so very elegant or pritty as it is commonly represented. In its present situation it is much like one of our country market towns in England. When you are in it the majority of the buildings appear low and mean, the streets unpaved and therefor full of rubbish and mire. It makes but an indifferent appearance att a distance, there being no turrets or steeples to set it off to advantage."[64]

The lingering fear of backwardness moved some eighteenth-century Americans to a renewed boosterism. In his 1720 account of Virginia Hugh Jones claimed of Williamsburg:

> Here dwell several very good families, and more reside here in their own houses at public times. They live in the same neat manner, dress after the same modes, and behave themselves exactly as the gentry in London, most families of any note have a coach, chariot, berlin or chaise. The habits, life, customs, computations, etc., of the Virginians are much the same as about London, which they esteem their home.

Other, more sophisticated Americans adopted England's view of American life and made the best of it. William Byrd admitted his rusticity and tried to gain moral advantage from the fact. He wrote to an English correspondent in 1729 of the absence of plays, operas, and masquerades. "We that are banished from these polite pleasures are forced to take up with rural entertainments. A library, a garden, a grove, and a purling stream are the innocent scenes that divert our leisure." Virginia was purer if duller than London. Franklin did his best to import English ideas of urbanity to Philadelphia, working to pave the streets, light them, and establish a library soon after the library rage struck London. Yet at the end he acceded to the European view and concealed his deep civility under a beaver cap. Embarrassed through the colonial period by their country's crudity, many colonials recognized the virtues in their own rusticity only after revolutionary republicanism ennobled simplicity. Then, as John Adams wrote to Mercy Warren, polite society made him feel "vain, light, frivolous, and insignificant," and Americans could take pride in their hardiness, activity, and courage.[65]

Vernacular Culture

The culture of the less pretentious colonial population also had its origins in a homeland, primarily Britain, Germany, or Africa, but it was structured much differently from high culture. Vernacular culture had no London. Its base, as the term *vernacular* implies, was the province, a particular locale, with only tenuous connections to the metropolis. While high culture was cosmopolitan and fashion-conscious, vernacular was placebound and enduring. Much of it was carried down within what E. P. Thompson has called the "circular space" of locality, where practices and norms were "reproduced down the generations within the slowly differentiating ambience of 'custom.' "[66]

Because of the structural differences, Henry Glassie has observed that

> in general, folk material exhibits major variations over space and minor variation through time, while the products of popular or academic culture exhibit minor variations over space and major variation through time. The natural divisions of folk material are, then, spatial, where the natural divisions of popular material are temporal; that is, a search for patterns in folk material yields regions, where a search for patterns in popular material yields periods.

As applied to the eighteenth century, this principle means that high, or academic, culture, emanating from the metropolitan center, imparted a common appearance to the cultivated classes across all Anglo-American regions. Style changes through time in furniture, clothing, painting, and architecture are the usual modes of analysis. Vernacular culture, slower to change through time, varied from region to region. Space is the key. The analysis of colonial American vernacular must begin with an understanding of how culture moved from places on one side of the Atlantic to places on the other, how various local cultures intermixed when they arrived in one place, and how out of this process American regional cultures came into being.[67]

Recent work has been making more of the connections between English and American regions. David Grayson Allen has shown how practices from specific English shires and towns shaped farming, government, and leadership in five New England towns linked to England by migrating families. Robert Blair St. George has attributed the furniture traditions of southeastern New England to certain regional patterns in England. The many variations in New England house types in the first generation of settlement suggest regional influences in floor plans and construction methods. Common sense compels us to expect the discovery of more such connections, given scholars with the persistence to pursue them in the narrow passages of Anglo-American local archives.[68]

But fascination with the local should not obscure the remarkably rapid dissolution of imported variations, leaving as a residue a broad regional culture. There may have been many house types in the first round of construction in New England, but in less than a generation a single major type predominated. The extant houses from the seventeenth century, as William Pierson has observed, show both a "common plan and common structural methods," so that "a coherent image of the seventeenth-century New England house emerges." A similar phenomenon repeated itself among Pennsylvania German immigrants. The innumerable variations in material culture brought from homes along the Rhine melted within a generation into a common Pennsylvania German culture, which within two generations began to blend with other ethnic patterns in Pennsylvania to create an interwoven if not homogeneous Middle Atlantic regional culture. The traces of English regionalism in New England town government and agriculture also washed out by the end of the seventeenth century.[69]

The rapid appearance of a dominant New England house type is a reminder that culture expresses group membership. Adoption of a certain vernacular style represented a commitment to one's neighbors and to the norms that the local community valued. Without a community to sustain them, cultural forms were drained of their power. The first immigrants could hold a remote English or German community in their imaginations and honor that group with house styles and decorative carvings, but in time the force of the present community irresistibly made itself felt. The current need to form a new community, to link person to person for purposes of marriage, trade, and decency in intercourse, pressed hard on the forms of cultural expression. The mixture of migrants from various regions within a single town intensified the need for a common culture to overarch English or German regional and religious peculiarities. The movement within New England during the first generation, while the large initial wave of migrants sought comfortable locations, made the formation of a broad regional culture a functional necessity.[70]

Along with this homogenization of English, German, and African local cultures went a diminution. The examples of vernacular culture in Robert Malcolmson's *Popular Recreations in English Society, 1700–1850* or Peter Burke's *Popular Culture in Early Modern Europe* remind us how much was lost in transit. Where were the morris dancers, the wassailing, the annual wakes, the craft holidays, the maypoles? Was Saint Monday observed anywhere in the colonies in the seventeenth century? One of the reasons for the loss is connected with the local base of custom. While harvest festivals and wakes were celebrated widely throughout European peasant culture, the details of how and when to proceed were strictly local. In Fallow, a hamlet of the parish of Sparsholt in Berkshire, the feast was held on "the Sunday following the feast of St. James" and doubtless in a certain place with an established distribution of duties, all fixed by custom. When a family moved from one old place to another old place, merging customs from two locations, there was never a question of which customs were to prevail in public events. Authority lay with the locale. In a vacant new place entirely empty of customs how were migrants from many places to mediate their differences? Place exercised no authority. In the confusion old customs disappeared.[71]

The absence of so much else from Old World society contributed to the attrition. In England the gentry structured and enlivened large segments of vernacular culture. The largesse of manor lords and large farmers provided feasts for the crew of laborers brought on to the land for harvest. The gentry provided prizes for horse races and cockfights, bred the cocks and horses, and sponsored pugilists. They paid for morris dancers and wassailers. Their gambling lent zest to the races. Gentry sponsored celebrations at coronation time or royal birthdays and treated the voters on election day. What was to become of all these with no great landlords in the seventeenth-century colonies to superintend and sustain public festivities?[72]

And what of the vocational culture of shoemakers, weavers, woodcutters, masons, herdsmen, shepherds, miners, beggars, and thieves? The great bulk of the early migrants dissolved into the farm population, and where there were craftsmen they were dispersed. One or two shoemakers in a town could scarcely do justice to Saint Crispin's feast. And the great scenes of popular recreation, the markets and fairs, were not soon to appear in any strength amid the thinly scattered American population.[73]

The public culture of the common people was to a large extent cut off from its source in the customs of a place and became more heavily dependent on government and the literate culture of clergy and print. In New England particularly the people came together at the meetinghouse, where the authority and knowledge of the minister prevailed. Sermons, the sacraments, and church meetings to admit converts substituted for harvest feasts and annual wakes. The immense devotional literature flooding English villages and hamlets was all the more potent in New England for a lack of competition. When a tradition did begin to form, such as the thanksgiving and fast days carried over from European Calvinist practice, custom was insufficient to determine the proper times; the colony government proclaimed the days.[74]

Seventeenth-century colonial vernacular culture—I have New England in mind primarily—was weak on the side of local, customary, folk forms of expression and overbalanced on the side of literate, ecclesiastical, and civil culture. That weighting was not to last. Places rebuilt their customary authority, and people generated culture of their own, adaptations of European vernacular but bearing an American mark. By the end of the century there were many evidences of it. A reference to a cornhusking as early as 1687 sounds as if this mixture of entertainment and work at the end of the harvest season was a familiar event. The harvest feast provided by the manor lord had been replaced by an egalitarian gathering to deal with a uniquely American crop. The same for apple-parings, maple sugar–makings, timber-rollings, and sheep shearings. An English visitor in 1699 noted that elections, militia training days, and the Harvard commencement were the principal holidays in New England, replacing, it might be added, Christmas, the annual wake, harvest feasts, and annual fairs. After 1730 President Wadsworth moved commencement to Friday to allow "less remaining time in the week to be spent in frolicking." The emergent gentry began to assume their traditional roles on these holidays. At the marksmanship contests on training days Samuel Sewall offered a silver cup as prize, and on another occasion a silver-headed pike. From election days came in time " 'lection cake," "a sort of rusk rich with fruit and wine," and elsewhere " 'lection beer." In the south horse races and reaping frolics carried society directly back to English customs. By the 1740s evidence is found of an original, indigenous folk song, "Yankee Doodle," with innumerable verses and variations.[75]

VERNACULAR AND GENTEEL

Evidence accumulates of a full-bodied vernacular culture emerging as the eighteenth-century began, weighted with local customs and folk expressions to balance the input of ministry, print, and government. This deepening of vernacular culture occurred in about the same period that the great house sprang up, filling itself with genteel company. In America patrician and plebian, as E. P. Thompson has termed the two cultures, grew in strength simultaneously, raising the question of how the two were related.[76]

Vernacular culture cannot be thought of as self-contained, walled in, and defensive like a medieval town. Quite to the contrary: it was porous and absorptive, each segment borrowing from neighboring vernacular groups and from polite society. Henry Glassie has noted how the symmetrical Georgian house, with its center-passage entry hall and rooms on each side, changed vernacular forms in all the regional cultures—the salt-box in New England and the I-form in the South (two stories, one room deep, two or more rooms wide). The Wren house, so useful to the middle class, was adapted for other levels of society. In the same manner, gravestone carving accepted neoclassical design. After a century and a half of slow evolution from death's head to cherub, abruptly around 1800 classical patterns and symbols appeared on gravestones in remote country villages and within twenty years had taken over the field from the traditional. Not long after, Greek Revival architecture, begun in the most auspicious public buildings, penetrated every corner of the land, to "blossom into one of the most remarkable flowerings of folk art in Western history." Nathaniel Ames's almanacs from their first appearance in 1725 brought to their huge readership the best English poetry.[77]

Vernacular craftsmen seemed willing to borrow from the high culture, especially when they wished to exalt an object such as a gravestone, but to call that borrowing imitation again distorts the meaning. Vernacular artists used genteel designs, as they borrowed from Africans or Indians, to elaborate or enrich the culture of their own communities. Once assimilated, the new patterns tended to endure; Greek Revival lasted in American villages long after it was obsolete among high-style architects. Builders and craftsmen maintained old forms, heedless of metropolitan taste, when the old served better to strengthen the tradition of the group. Nineteenth-century chair factories in New Jersey produced Dutch and German chairs virtually unchanged from their seventeenth-century forms. Eighteenth-century Philadelphia chairmakers turned out as many slat-back chairs as they did fashionable bannister-back chairs, even though they could be produced for roughly the same price, because some group in the city, oblivious to the demands of fashion, preferred the traditional.[78]

Exchange and assimilation went on constantly, but the porousness of the boundaries does not mean that no boundaries existed. In the minds of the people a sharp line divided plain and genteel culture, just as they distinguished in their minds a class of people called gentlemen. "Polite," "fashionable," "gentlemen" were the categories of a widespread vernacular sociology. Gentlemen travelers like Alexander Hamilton, dependent for their own social well-being on the capacity to discriminate genteel and vulgar, certainly gauged speech and appearance by their degree of civility. Franklin's famous china bowl is evidence that people from below made similar distinctions.

> My breakfast was for a long time bread and milk, (no tea), and I ate it out of a two penny earthen porringer with a pewter spoon. But mark how luxury will enter families and make a progress in spite of principle. Being called one morning to breakfast I found it in a china bowl, with a spoon of silver. They had been bought without my knowledge by my wife, and had cost her the enormous sum of twenty-three shillings, for which she had no other excuse or apology to make but that she thought *her* husband deserved a silver spoon and china bowl as well as any of his neighbors. This was the first appearance of plate and china in our house which afterwards in a course of years, as our wealth increased, augmented gradually to several hundred pounds in value.

Franklin, his wife, and the neighbors knew the social value of china and silver. Moreover, Franklin knew he was crossing a line when they appeared on his table. He recognized it as a dangerous crossing but also as the beginning of the ascent that carried him upwards to gentility and the amenities of a polite life. The earthenware and the china bowls stood for a sharp social distinction.[79]

Were relationships antagonistic along the line between patrician and plebian? E. P. Thompson has argued that they were. The gentry paraded their wealth and their manners in the courts, at races, and in other theaters of display, Thompson says, to remind the people of the gentleman's superiority and the majestic justice of the law. The people in riots and acts of near violence displayed the strength of their numbers to remind the gentry of the limits on power. Thompson's analysis jibes with the accounts of Boston's 1748 impressment riot and of the mob's destruction of Thomas Hutchinson's house in 1765. Given provocation, the people of the street could compel the people of the great houses to withdraw.[80]

But direct political antagonism was but a small part of life along the boundary between civility and vulgarity. One of Alexander Hamilton's encounters gives an idea of the crosscurrents beating on those who approached that line. At New Castle, Delaware, on his way to Philadelphia, Hamilton joined three travelers, one of whom, a William Morison, had been inquiring about a land title in the Annapolis land office. Hamilton found Morison "a very rough spun, forward, clownish blade, much addicted to swearing, att the same time desirous to pass for a gentleman." Morison's natural boorishness betrayed him, as he himself knew, and he repeatedly apologized for his excesses as "right down plain dealing." To his chagrin, the landlady at the inn, observing his "greasy jacket and breeches and a dirty worsted cap," took him for a ploughman and gave him cold veal scraps for breakfast. Enraged, Morison threatened to throw out the scraps and "break her table all to pieces should it cost him 100 pounds for damages." He ripped off his worsted nightcap, pulled a linen one out of his pocket, and clapped it on his head. " 'Now,' says he, 'I'm upon the borders of Pennsylvania and must look like a gentleman.'" "He told us that tho he seemed to be but a plain, homely fellow, yet he would have us know that he was able to afford better than many that went finer: he had good linnen in his bags, a pair of silver buckles, silver clasps, and good sleeve buttons, two Holland shirts, and some neat night caps; and that his little woman att home drank tea twice a day."[81]

The story tells many things about fashion and gentility: how clothes and appearance registered one's class at a glance and elicited scraps instead of good meat from landladies; how the fashionable held the unfashionable in humorous scorn; how the plain people thought linen, silver buckles, and tea twice a day were the signs of gentility, while their manners and speech forever betrayed lack of breeding; how those just below the line hated and at the same time envied those above it—and possibly, if Morison had told the story, how Hamilton would have appeared the butt of the joke. So complex and powerful were the forces in play that innumerable subtleties, inversions, and ambiguities characterized the relationship.

No single word can sum up the meanings of *vernacular* and *genteel*. Rather than hunt for one metaphor to describe the meeting of the two cultures, we should think of them as two great forces that in combination could be drawn on for many purposes. From the time of Royall Tyler's *The Contrast* on, the appeal and pitfalls of fashion became a theme of American drama. The broad but good-hearted country boy and the refined city girl became stock characters. The reconciliation of politeness and simplicity, with their contrasting virtues, defects, and dangers, was a theme of unfailing appeal. In real life the two cultures entered into judgments of city and country, Europe and America, rich and poor, and in politics the worthy and the licentious. The course of individual aspiration and the development of industry were partially laid down according to the norms of fashion and the ideals of civility. Many of the great themes of nineteenth-century social and cultural life had their origins in the encounter of vernacular and genteel. The task of analysis is not to fix a single definition but to explicate the variations on the general theme and to discover the many ways that these cultural strains played themselves out first in colonial and then in national life.[82]

NOTES

1. For bibliographies of high culture consult Wendy Cooper, *In Praise of America: American Decorative Arts, 1650–1830* (New York, 1980); Wendell D. Garrett and Jane Garrett, comps., and Walter Muir Whitehill, *The Arts in Early American History: Needs and Opportunities for Study* (Chapel Hill, 1965); Charles F. Montgomery, comp., *A List of Books and Articles for the Study of the Arts in Early America* (Winterthur, Del., 1970); and Louis B. Wright et al., *The Arts in America: The Colonial Period* (New York, 1966). For bibliographies of the material aspects of vernacular culture see Kenneth L. Ames, *"Beyond Necessity": Art in The Folk Tradition: An Exhibition from the Collections of the Winterthur Museum at the Brandywine River Museum* (Winterthur, Del., 1977); Henry H. Glassie, *Folk Housing in Middle Virginia: A Structural Analysis of Historic Artifacts* (Knoxville, 1975); and idem, *Pattern in the Material Folk Culture of the Eastern United States* (Philadelphia, 1968). Charles Haywood, *A Bibliography of North American Folklore and Folksong* (New York, 1951), offers 1,292 pages of source materials arranged regionally, ethnically, and occupationally.

2. The anthropological conception of culture is discussed in Clyde Kluckhohn, "The Concept of Culture," in *The Science of Man in the World Crisis*, ed. Ralph Linton (New York, 1945), 78–106; Melville J. Herskovits, *Cultural Anthropology* (New York, 1963); and Leslie A. White, *The Science of Culture* (New York, 1969). I was persuaded not to attempt an explanation of style as the basis of cultural history by George Kubler, *The Shape of Time: Remarks on the History of Things* (New Haven, 1962); Donald Greene, "What Indeed Was Neo-Classicism?" *Journal of British Studies* 10 (1970): 69–79; and Robert Rosenblum, *Transformations in Late Eighteenth-Century Art* (Princeton, 1967). Jules David Prown makes the case for historical study of style in "Style As Evidence," *Winterthur Portfolio: A Journal of Material Culture* 15 (1980): 197–210.

3. Carl Bridenbaugh and Jessica Bridenbaugh, *Rebels and Gentlemen: Philadelphia in the Age of Franklin* (1942; reprint, London, 1968); Thomas Jefferson Wertenbaker, *The Golden Age of Colonial Culture* (1949; reprint, Ithaca, N.Y., 1975); Oliver Larkin, *Art and Life in America* (New York, 1949); Louis B. Wright, *The Cultural Life of the American Colonies, 1607–1763* (New York, 1957).

4. The story of Constance Rourke is brilliantly illuminated in Joan Shelley Rubin, *Constance Rourke and American Culture* (Chapel Hill, 1980). John Kouwenhoven's classic work was published as *Made in America* (New York, 1948) and republished as *The Arts in Modern American Civilization* (New York, 1967).

5. Carl Bridenbaugh argued for a broader definition of culture while revealing his own ambivalence about high culture in *Myths and Realities: Societies of the Colonial South* (Baton Rouge, 1952). Clyde Kluckhohn published his influential discussion of the anthropological definition of culture "The Concept of Culture," in 1945, just as the new views were affecting American studies.

6. Bridenbaugh and Bridenbaugh, *Rebels and Gentlemen*, 176, 365, 197, 203–4.

7. Ibid., 175–77, 205. For a repeat of the Copley story see Larkin, *Art and Life*, 64–66.

8. Bridenbaugh and Bridenbaugh, *Rebels and Gentlemen*, 223; Margaret B. Tinkcom, "Cliveden: The Building of a Philadelphia Country Seat, 1763–1767," *Pennsylvania Magazine of History and*

Biography 88 (1964): 15–16; William H. Pierson, Jr., *American Buildings and Their Architects: The Colonial and Neo-Classical Styles* (1970; reprint, Garden City, N.Y., 1976), 155–56, 60.

9. The concept of the American colonies as one among many English provinces is discussed in John Clive and Bernard Bailyn, "England's Cultural Provinces: Scotland and America," *William and Mary Quarterly*, 3d ser., 11 (1954): 200–213. See also Margaret B. Tinkcom, "Urban Reflections in a Trans-Atlantic Mirror," *Pennsylvania Magazine of History and Biography* 100 (1976): 287–313.

10. On Virginia high-style houses see Thomas Tileston Waterman, *The Mansions of Virginia, 1706–1776* (Chapel Hill, 1946). The most recent information on seventeenth-century vernacular housing is reported in Cary Carson et al., "Impermanent Architecture in the Southern American Colonies," *Winterthur Portfolio: A Journal of Material Culture* 16 (1981): 135–96.

11. The argument for Wren as architect of the Governor's Palace is made in Waterman, *Mansions*, 30–38. A more recent view is in Pierson, *American Buildings*, 61–73.

12. Robert Beverley, *The History and Present State of Virginia*, ed. Louis B. Wright (Chapel Hill, 1947), 289. For a summary of construction dates of extant and recorded Virginia houses see Waterman, *Mansions*, 413–24. On the growth of Mount Vernon see Thomas Flexner, *Washington: The Indispensable Man* (Boston, 1974), 45.

13. The basic work on New England houses is now Abbott Lowell Cummings, *The Framed Houses of Massachusetts Bay, 1625–1725* (Cambridge, Mass., 1979), but see also Richard M. Candee, "A Documentary History of Plymouth Colony Architecture, 1620–1700," *Old-Time New England* 59 (1969): 59–71, 105–11; 60 (1969): 37–53. Older works include J. F. Kelly, *The Early Domestic Architecture of Connecticut* (New Haven, 1924); and M. S. Briggs, *The Homes of the Pilgrim Fathers in England and America, 1620–1685* (London, 1932).

14. Pierson, *American Buildings*, 89–93; S. Fiske Kimball, *Domestic Architecture of the American Colonies and of the Early Republic* (1922; reprint, New York, 1966), 17–93. Cary Carson connects Bacon's Castle, the Peter Sargeant and Foster-Hutchinson houses, and a number of other American structures with the mannerist houses that English merchants built in the ports, in market towns, and in the home counties in the 1630s and 1640s. Meant to display wealth and gain attention, they were not imitations of courtly styles, Carson argues, but the expressions of an emergent class of commercial figures who felt at home with neither courtly nor traditional culture (Paper delivered at Winterthur Summer Institute, July 21, 1981). In my estimation, they were also the advance wave of the much broader middle-class adaptation of high style that occurred at the end of the seventeenth century.

15. George B. Tatum, *Philadelphia Georgian: The City House of Samuel Powel and Some of Its Eighteenth-Century Neighbors* (Middletown, Conn., 1976); Nicholas B. Wainwright, *Colonial Grandeur in Philadelphia* (Philadelphia, 1964); Richard Webster, *Philadelphia Preserved: Catalog of the Historic American Buildings Survey* (Philadelphia, 1976); Thompson Westcott, *The Historic Mansions and Buildings of Philadelphia*, rev. ed. (Philadelphia, 1895); Anthony N. B. Garvan et al., *The Architectural Surveys, 1784–1794* (Philadelphia, 1976).

16. Tatum, *Philadelphia Georgian*, 6–25.

17. Ibid., 103, 106.

18. John Adams, *Diary and Autobiography of John Adams*, ed. L. H. Butterfield, 2 vols. (Cambridge, Mass., 1961), 1:127; Susan Mackiewicz, "Woodworking Traditions in Newbury, Massachusetts, 1635–1745" (Master's thesis, University of Delaware, 1981), 28; Helen Comstock, *American Furniture: Seventeenth, Eighteenth, and Nineteenth Century Styles* (New York, 1962), 74, 189. On social life in a Rhode Island great house see Wendy Cooper, "The Furniture and Furnishings of John Brown, Merchant of Providence, 1736–1803" (Master's thesis, University of Delaware, 1971).

19. Irene Brown, of the University of Connecticut, is developing the idea of select company as a characteristic eighteenth-century social group in European society. For family relationships in the Chesapeake see Daniel Blake Smith, *Inside the Great House: Planter Family Life in Eighteenth-Century Chesapeake Society* (Ithaca, N.Y., 1980).

20. The edition of Chesterfield's letters used for this study was *Letters to His Son by the Earl of*

Chesterfield: On the Fine Art of Becoming a Man of the World and a Gentleman, ed. Oliver H. Leigh (New York, 1937). Chesterfield's life is conveniently summarized in *Dictionary of National Biography*, "Stanhope, Philip Dormer." s.v. On the origins of the ideal of cultivation see Norbert Elias, *The Civilizing Process*, trans. Edmund Jephcott (New York, 1978).

21. Chesterfield, *Letters*, 253–55. On letter writing as a genteel art see Louis B. Wright, *Middle-Class Culture in Elizabethan England* (Chapel Hill, 1935), 139–46; and Howard Anderson, Philip B. Daghlian, and Irvin Ehrenpreis, eds., *The Familiar Letter in the Eighteenth Century* (Lawrence, Kans., 1966).

22. The quotations are from Ellis Waterhouse, *Painting in Britain, 1530 to 1790*, 4th ed. (Harmondsworth, 1978), 74.

23. Chesterfield, *Letters*, 283–86, 255. On manner as a source of political power see E. P. Thompson, "Patrician Society, Plebeian Culture," *Journal of Social History* 7 (1974): 382–405. On shining in society see John Edward Mason, *Gentlefolk in the Making: Studies in the History of English Courtesy Literature from 1531 to 1774* (Philadelphia, 1935), 286.

24. *DNB*, s.v. "Stanhope, Philip Dormer"; Chesterfield *Letters*, 292.

25. For publication information see *DNB*, s.v. "Stanhope, Philip Dormer"; and Bridenbaugh and Bridenbaugh, *Rebels and Gentlemen*, 80. For Nabby Adams's reaction see Ada Lou Carson and Herbert L. Carson, *Royall Tyler* (Boston, 1979), 17–18.

26. *The Contrast* is conveniently reprinted in Edwin Harrison Cady, ed., *Literature of the Early Republic* (New York, 1950); the quote is found on pp. 396–97. The famous Johnson quote is in *DNB*, s.v. "Stanhope, Philip Dormer."

27. On the traditions of the courtesy literature see Mason, *Gentlefolk in the Making*, 34, 106, 187; Virgil B. Heltzel, *Chesterfield and the Tradition of the Ideal Gentleman* (Chicago, 1925, microfilm); Gertrude E. Noyes, *Bibliography of Courtesy and Conduct Books in Seventeenth-Century England* (New Haven, 1937); Virgil B. Heltzel, comp., *A Checklist of Courtesy Books in the Newberry Library* (Chicago, 1942).

28. Thomas Goddard Wright, *Literary Culture in Early New England, 1620–1730* (1920; reprint, New York, 1966), 119; Carson and Carson, *Royall Tyler*, 18; John Adams to Mercy Warren, Braintree, January 8, 1776, in *Warren-Adams Letters*, [ed. Worthington C. Ford], 2 vols. (Boston, 1917–25), 1:201–2.

29. Ian Watt, *The Rise of the Novel: Studies in Defoe, Richardson, and Fielding* (Berkeley, 1957), 51. On the task of reconciliation see Mason, *Gentlefolk in the Making*, chap. 9.

30. Pierre Marambaud, *William Byrd of Westover, 1674–1744* (Charlottesville, 1971), 191; Hugh Jones, *The Present State of Virginia*, ed. Richard L. Morton (Chapel Hill, 1956), 87. On southern and Caribbean gentility see Louis B. Wright, *The First Gentlemen of Virginia: Intellectual Qualities of the Early Colonial Ruling Class* (San Marino, Calif., 1940); Julia Cherry Spruill, *Women's Life and Work in the Southern Colonies* (Chapel Hill, 1938); George C. Rogers, *Charleston in the Age of the Pinckneys* (Columbia, S.C., 1969); Harold E. Davis, *The Fledgling Province: Social and Cultural Life in Colonial Georgia, 1733–1776* (Chapel Hill, 1976); Edward Brathwaite, *The Development of Creole Society in Jamaica, 1770–1820* (Oxford, 1971).

31. Douglass Southall Freeman, *George Washington: A Biography*, vol. 1, *Young Washington* (New York, 1948), 75–76, 200; J. M. Toner, ed., *Washington's Rules of Civility and Decent Behavior in Company and Conversation* (Washington, D.C., 1888), 14, 18, 26. For a discussion of the rules see Edwin Harrison Cady, *The Gentleman in America: A Literary Study in American Culture* (Syracuse, 1949), 8–9; and Moncure D. Conway, *George Washington's Rules of Civility Traced to Their Sources and Restored* (New York, 1890).

32. Spruill, *Women's Life*, 197–98, 200.

33. Ibid., 195–96; Thomas Jefferson to Martha Jefferson, Annapolis, November 28, 1783, in *The Portable Thomas Jefferson*, ed. Merrill D. Peterson (New York, 1975), 366–67. William Eddis is quoted in Spruill, *Women's Life*, 93.

34. Dumas Malone, *Jefferson the Virginian*, vol. 1, *Jefferson and His Time* (Boston, 1948), 77–79; John Marshall Phillips, *American Silver* (New York, 1949), 76; Wright, *Literary Culture*, 214, 213, 201–2, 104–5; Carl Bridenbaugh, ed., *Gentleman's Progress: The Itinerarium of Dr. Alexander*

Hamilton, 1744 (Chapel Hill, 1948), 193. For other aspects of civility and enlightenment in the colonies see Norman Fiering, "The Transatlantic Republic of Letters: A Note on the Circulation of Learned Periodicals to Early Eighteenth-Century America," *William and Mary Quarterly*, 3d ser., 33 (1976): 642–60; and Carl Bridenbaugh, *Early Americans* (New York, 1981).

35. On gentility in America see Cady, *Gentleman in America*; Gerald Carson, *The Polite Americans: A Wide-Angle View of Our More or Less Good Manners over 300 Years* (1966; reprint, Westport, Conn., 1980); Howard Mumford Jones, *O Strange New World: American Culture: The Formative Years* (New York, 1967), 114–21, 241–55; Stow Persons, *The Decline of American Gentility* (New York, 1973); and Arthur M. Schlesinger, *Learning How to Behave: A Historical Study of American Etiquette Books* (1946; reprint, New York, 1947).

36. Bridenbaugh, *Gentleman's Progress*, 10, 8, 199. See also Bridenbaugh's introduction, ibid., xxvi; and Bridenbaugh and Bridenbaugh, *Rebels and Gentlemen*, 135.

37. Tatum, *Philadelphia Georgian*, 14, 145 n. 16; Richard L. Morton, *Colonial Virginia*, vol. 2 (Chapel Hill, 1960), 502. For gentility among English provincial merchants see R. G. Wilson, *Gentlemen Merchants: The Merchant Community in Leeds, 1700–1830* (Manchester, Eng., 1971), chaps. 9, 10.

38. John C. Miller, *Sam Adams: Pioneer in Propaganda* (1936; reprint, Stanford, 1974), 214–15. On the larger movement towards civility see Elias, *The Civilizing Process;* and Edwin S. Ramage, *Urbanitas: Ancient Sophistication and Refinement* (Norman, Okla., 1973). I am indebted to George Basalla and Kenneth Ames for these references.

39. The original English translation of Castiglione is available in modern edition: Baldassare Castiglione, *The Book of the Courtier*, trans. Thomas Hoby (London, 1959). On its popularity in England see Mason, *Gentlefolk in the Making*, 34.

40. Lawrence Stone, *The Crisis of the Aristocracy, 1558–1641*, abr. ed. (London, 1967), esp. chaps. 10, 12; Peter Burke, *Popular Culture in Early Modern Europe* (New York, 1978), 276.

41. Stone, *Crisis*, 303–4; Mark Girouard, *Life in the English Country House: A Social and Architectural History* (New Haven, 1978), chap. 4. On pageantry see G. P. V. Akrigg, *Jacobean Pageantry, or the Court of King James I* (London, 1962); and Lewis Einstein, *Tudor Ideals* (New York, 1921).

42. Stone, *Crisis*, 307, 309–14, 318–24.

43. On diffusion of culture see Lord Raglan, "The Origins of Vernacular Architecture," in *Culture and Environment: Essays in Honor of Sir Cyril Fox*, ed. L. I. Foster and L. Alcock (London, 1963); and George Duby, "The Diffusion of Cultural Patterns in Feudal Society," *Past and Present*, no. 39 (1968): 3–10.

44. John Summerson, *Georgian London*, 3d ed. (Cambridge, Mass., 1978), 27; idem, *Architecture in Britain: 1530 to 1830*, 4th ed., rev. (Baltimore, 1969), chaps. 4, 5. The Shakespearean passage is from *Richard II*, act 1, sc. 1; The charge was inappropriate for the time of Richard II but squarely on target for the era of James I.

45. Poem quoted in John Gloag, *The Englishman's Chair: Origins, Design, and Social History of Seat Furniture in England* (London, 1964), 84. On style changes see H. J. Perkin, *The Origins of Modern English Society, 1780–1880* (London, 1969), 94; Ralph Fastnedge, *English Furniture Styles from 1500–1830* (Harmondsworth, 1955); Helen Comstock, *American Furniture;* and Stone, *Crisis of the Aristocracy*, 257.

46. Stone, *Crisis of the Aristocracy*, 328–29. On the emergence of the middle class see Alan Everitt, *Change in the Provinces: The Seventeenth Century*, Department of English Local History Occasional Papers, 2d ser. 1 (Leicester, 1969); Peter N. Borsay, "The English Urban Renaissance: The Development of Provincial Urban Culture, c 1680–c 1760," *Social History* 5 (1977): 581–604; John Brewer, J. H. Plumb, and Neil McKendrick, *The Birth of the Consumer Society: Commercialization in Eighteenth-Century Britain* (London, 1979); J. H. Plumb, *The Commercialization of Leisure in Eighteenth-Century England* (Reading, 1973); and Wright, *Middle-Class Culture in Elizabethan England*. The last is a mine of information on genteel culture but in some instances confuses middle-class and aristocratic culture.

47. Waterhouse, *Painting in Britain*, 70–77, 92, 114.

48. Pierson, *American Buildings*, 61–73. Recent work by Daniel D. Reiff shows that middle-class

adaptations of high-style houses preceded Wren by at least a decade (Reiff, "Small Georgian Houses in England and Virginia: Origins and Development through the 1750s" [forthcoming]).

49. Gloag, *Englishman's Chair*, 77, 78, 84; Plumb, *Commercialization of Leisure*; Borsay, "English Urban Renaissance;" C. W. Chalkin, *The Provincial Towns of Georgian England: A Study of the Building Process, 1740–1820* (Montreal, 1974).

50. Perkin, *Origins of Modern English Society*, 93; Penelope Corfield, "A Provincial Capital in the Late Seventeenth Century: The Case of Norwich," in *Crisis and Order in English Towns, 1500–1700: Essays in Urban History*, ed. Peter Clark and Paul Slack (Toronto, 1972), 306n; John C. Loftis, *Comedy and Society from Congreve to Fielding* (Stanford, 1959), 68–76; Summerson, *Georgian London*, 24; Oliver Goldsmith, *Poems and Plays*, ed. Tom Davis (London, 1975), 69.

51. Stone, *Crisis of the Aristocracy*, 267; Richard Thomson, *Antique American Clocks and Watches* (Princeton, 1968), chap. 2; Brian Loomes, *Country Clocks and Their London Origins* (Devon, 1976), 16, 26–28, 40–43, 55–57; Eric Bruton, *The Longcase Clock* (London, 1964), 30–38.

52. Loomes, *Country Clocks*, chap. 3; Arthur Hagger and Leonard F. Miller, *Suffolk Clocks and Clockmakers* (Ramsgate, Eng., 1974), 37–159; H. Miles Brown, *Cornish Clocks and Clockmakers* (Devon, 1961), 63–94; Chris H. Bailey, *Two Hundred Years of American Clocks and Watches* (Englewood Cliffs, N.J., 1975), 15–16, 31–32. Gordon Sands supplied the references and the ideas in the paragraphs on clocks.

53. Pierson, *American Buildings*, 213, 83, 90.

54. Helen Park, "A List of Architectural Books Available in America before the Revolution," *Journal of the Society of Architectural Historians* 20 (1961): 115–30. The quotation is in Pierson, *American Buildings*, 115. Among the guides to notices and advertisements of tradesmen are George Francis Dow, *The Arts and Crafts in New England, 1704–1775* (Topsfield, Mass., 1927); James H. Craig, *The Arts and Crafts in North Carolina, 1699–1840* (Winston-Salem, N.C., 1965); and Alfred Coxe Prime, comp., *The Arts and Crafts in Philadelphia, Maryland, and South Carolina, 1721–1785* (New York, 1969). There are many biographical dictionaries of tradesmen and artists, among them George C. Groce and David H. Wallace, *The New York Historical Society's Dictionary of Artists in America, 1564–1860* (New Haven, 1957).

55. Charles F. Hummel, "The Influence of English Design Books upon the Philadelphia Cabinetmakers, 1760–1780" (Master's thesis, University of Delaware, 1955); Watt, *Rise of the Novel*, 51, 42; Plumb, *Commercialization of Leisure*, 56; Bridenbaugh and Bridenbaugh, *Rebels and Gentlemen*, 93. On Hoyle see Ronald Paulson, *Popular and Polite Art in the Age of Hogarth and Fielding* (Notre Dame, Ind., 1979), chap. 7.

56. Edgar P. Richardson, *Painting in America: From 1502 to the Present* (New York, 1956), 26. On colonial American painting see, in addition to Richardson, James T. Flexner, *First Flowers of Our Wilderness: American Painting* (1947; reprint, New York, 1969); Virgil Barker, *American Painting: History and Interpretation* (New York, 1950); and Ian M. G. Quimby, ed., *American Painting to 1776: A Reappraisal* (Charlottesville, 1971).

57. Neil Harris, "The Making of an American Culture: 1750–1800," in *American Arts, 1750–1800: Towards Independence*, ed. Charles F. Montgomery and Patricia Kane (Boston, 1976), 22–31; J. H. Plumb, "America and England: 1720–1820, The Fusions of Cultures," in ibid., 14–21; Perkin, *Origins of Modern English Society*, 91–96.

58. Susan Mackiewicz, "Woodworking Traditions in Newbury," chaps. 2, 3; Benno M. Forman, "Delaware Valley 'Crookt Foot' and Slat-Back Chairs: The Fussell-Savery Connection," *Winterthur Portfolio: A Journal of Material Culture* 15 (1980): 41–64; Comstock, *American Furniture*, 18, 17; Benno M. Forman, "Urban Aspects of Massachusetts Furniture in the Late Seventeenth Century," in *Country Cabinetwork and Simple City Furniture*, ed. John D. Morse (Charlottesville, 1970), 22, 24, 26; Robert F. Trent, ed., *Pilgrim Century Furniture: An Historical Survey* (New York, n.d.), 139; Marambaud, *William Byrd*, 194; Bridenbaugh and Bridenbaugh, *Rebels and Gentlemen*, 143; Wright, *Cultural Life*, 110. The basic cultural pattern was described in Dixon Ryan Fox, *Ideas in Motion* (New York, 1935), 6.

59. For a brilliant analysis of Josiah Wedgwood's calculated manipulation of the London aristocracy see Neil McKendrick, "Josiah Wedgwood: An Eighteenth-Century Entrepreneur in Sales-

manship and Marketing Techniques," *Economic History Review*, 2d ser., 12 (1960): 408–33. On London's culture and social power see F. J. Fisher, "The Development of London as a Centre of Conspicuous Consumption in the Sixteenth and Seventeenth Centuries," *Transactions of the Royal Historical Society*, 4th ser., 30 (1948): 37–50; E. A. Wrigley, "A Simple Model of London's Importance in Changing English Society and Economy, 1650–1750," *Past and Present*, no. 37 (1967): 44–70.

60. Richardson, *Painting in America*, 59–60; Jules David Prown, *John Singleton Copley*, 2 vols. (Cambridge, Mass., 1966), 1:45–51.

61. Benjamin Franklin, cited in Bridenbaugh, *Gentleman's Progress*, xii.

62. For the interplay of a London craftsman and the owners of great country houses see Christopher Gilbert, *The Life and Work of Thomas Chippendale* (London, 1978).

63. Waterman, *Mansions*, 146; Wright, *Cultural Life*, 40; Pierson, *American Buildings*, 119.

64. McKendrick, "Josiah Wedgwood," 431; Bridenbaugh, *Gentleman's Progress*, 192–93.

65. Jones, *Present State*, 71, 80; William Byrd, quoted in Marambaud, *William Byrd*, 147; John Adams to Mercy Warren, Braintree, January 8, 1776, *Warren-Adams Letters*, 1:202. The ambivalence about simplicity and elegance continued after the Revolution: see Robert Ralph Davis, Jr., "Diplomatic Plumage: American Court Dress in the Early National Period," *American Quarterly* 20 (1968): 164–79.

66. E. P. Thompson, "Eighteenth-Century English Society: Class Struggle Without Class," *Social History* 3 (1978): 152–53.

67. Glassie, *Pattern in the Material Folk Culture*, 33.

68. David Grayson Allen, *In English Ways: The Movement of Societies and the Transferal of English Local Law and Custom to Massachusetts Bay in the Seventeenth Century* (Chapel Hill, 1981); Robert Blair St. George, "Style and Structure in the Joinery of Dedham and Medfield, Massachusetts, 1635–1685," in *Winterthur Portfolio*, ed. Ian M. G. Quimby, vol. 13 (Chicago, 1979), 1–46; James Deetz, "Plymouth Colony Architecture: Archaeological Evidence from the Seventeenth Century," *Architecture in Colonial Massachusetts* (Boston, 1979), 43–59; Candee, "A Documentary History of Plymouth Colony Architecture;" Cecil A. Hewett, "Some East Anglican Prototypes for Early Timber Houses in America," *Post Medieval Archaeology* 3 (1970): 100–121; James Deetz, *In Small Things Forgotten: The Archaeology of Early American Life* (Garden City, N.Y., 1977), 95–99. On agriculture see James T. Lemon, "The Agricultural Practices of National Groups in Eighteenth-Century Southeastern Pennsylvania," *Geographical Review* 56 (1966): 467–96. On costume see Don Yoder, "Sectarian Costume Research in the United States," in *Forms upon the Frontier: Folklife and Folk Arts of the United States*, ed. Austin Fife, Alta Fife, and Henry H. Glassie (Logan, Utah, 1969), 41–75. For an overall analysis applicable to early New England see John J. Waters, Jr., "The Traditional World of the New England Peasants: A View from Seventeenth-Century Barnstable," *New England Historical and Genealogical Register* 130 (1976): 3–21. On English regional culture see Christopher Gilbert, "Regional Traditions in English Vernacular Furniture," in *Arts of the Anglo-American Community in the Seventeenth Century*, ed. Ian M. G. Quimby (Charlottesville, 1975), 43–77; and J. T. Smith, "The Concept of Diffusion in Its Application to Vernacular Building," in *Studies in Folk Life*, ed. Geraint Jenkins (London, 1969), 59–78.

69. Pierson, *American Buildings*, 47–49; Abbott Lowell Cummings, "Summary Abstracts of the Structural History of a Significant Sample of First Period Houses at Massachusetts Bay," in Deetz, *Architecture in Colonial Massachusetts*, 125–92; idem, *Framed Houses*, 22–44; Glassie, *Pattern in the Material Folk Culture*, 36; Forman, "Delaware Valley 'Crookt Foot' and Slat-Back Chairs," 52–54. On later regionalism see Charles F. Montgomery, "Regional Preferences and Characteristics in American Decorative Arts: 1750–1800," in Montgomery and Kane, *American Arts*, 50–65.

70. Jack Michel presents an illuminating picture of rural Pennsylvania material culture before 1735 in "'In a Manner and Fashion Suitable to Their Degree': A Preliminary Investigation of the Material Culture of Early Rural Pennsylvania," *Working Papers from the Regional Economic History Research Center* 5 (1981): 1–83. The interplay of African and local American materials in the

formation of Afro-American culture has been the subject of a debate whose outlines can be discerned in Daniel J. Crowley, ed., *African Folklore in the New World* (Austin, Tex., 1977). See also John Michael Vlach, *The Afro-American Tradition in Decorative Arts* (Cleveland, 1978). For provocative general statements on the interpretation of folk culture see Ames, *Beyond Necessity;* Raglan, "The Origins of Vernacular Architecture"; and Smith, "The Concept of Diffusion."
71. Robert W. Malcolmson, *Popular Recreations in English Society, 1700–1850* (Cambridge, 1973); Burke, *Popular Culture in Early Modern Europe;* Thompson, "Patrician Society, Plebeian Culture," 392. For evidence that traditional folk culture was waning in England by the time of American settlement see Charles Phythian-Adams, "Ceremony and the Citizen: The Communal Year at Coventry, 1450–1550," in Clark and Slack, *Crisis and Order in English Towns,* 57–85; and E. K. Chambers, *The English Folk-Play* (New York, 1964). For summaries of seventeenth-century American folklore, particularly in New England, see Richard M. Dorson, *American Folklore* (Chicago, 1959), 17–38; and idem, *American Folklore and the Historian* (Chicago, 1971), 29–32.
72. Malcolmson, *Popular Recreations,* 56–66.
73. Burke, *Popular Culture in Early Modern Europe,* 29–47; Thompson, "Patrician Society, Plebeian Culture," 392, 396.
74. David D. Hall, "The World of Print and Collective Mentality in Seventeenth-Century New England," in *New Directions in American Intellectual History,* ed. John Higham and Paul Conkin (Baltimore, 1979), 166–80; W. DeLoss Love, Jr., *The Fast and Thanksgiving Days of New England* (Boston, 1895); George Francis Dow, *Everyday Life in the Massachusetts Bay Colony* (Boston, 1935); Margaret Spufford, "First Steps in Literacy: The Reading and Writing Experiences of the Humblest Seventeenth-Century Spiritual Autobiographers," *Social History* 4 (1979): 407–36.
75. J. A. Leo Lemay, "The American Origins of 'Yankee Doodle,'" *William and Mary Quarterly,* 3d ser., 33 (1976): 435–64; Alice Morse Earle, *Customs and Fashions in Old New England* (1893; reprint, Rutland, Vt., 1973), chap. 9; Bridenbaugh, *Myths and Realities,* 24, 26; T. H. Breen, "Horses and Gentlemen: The Cultural Significance of Gambling among the Gentry of Virginia," *William and Mary Quarterly,* 3d ser., 34 (1977): 239–57. On funeral customs see David E. Stannard, *The Puritan Way of Death: A Study in Religion, Culture, and Social Change* (New York, 1977). Evidence of folk painting and folk song is meager (although some songs were very popular) until after the Revolution: Jean Lipman and Alice Winchester, *Primitive Painters in America, 1750–1950: An Anthology* (New York, 1950); Mary Black and Jean Lipman, *American Folk Painting* (New York, 1966); Nina Fletcher Little, *American Decorative Wall Painting, 1700–1851* (New York, 1972); David Ewen, *American Popular Songs from the Revolutionary War to the Present* (New York, 1966). Witchcraft acitvity may also have diminished in America in the early part of the century as compared with that in England, and then grown in strength at the end of the century. See John Demos, *Entertaining Satan: Witchcraft and the Culture of Early New England* (New York, 1982); and George Lyman Kittredge, *Witchcraft in Old and New England* (Cambridge, Mass., 1929). See also Alan Macfarlane, *Witchcraft in Tudor and Stuart England* (New York, 1970); and Keith Thomas, *Religion and the Decline of Magic* (New York, 1971).
76. Thompson, "Patrician Society, Plebeian Culture"; idem, "Eighteenth-Century English Society." On three aspects of eighteenth-century vernacular culture see George Lyman Kittredge, *The Old Farmer and His Almanack* (Cambridge, Mass., 1904); Tristram Potter Coffin, *Uncertain Glory: Folklore and the American Revolution* (Detroit, 1971); and Dean A. Fales, Jr., *American Painted Furniture, 1660–1880* (New York, 1972).
77. Henry Glassie, "The Impact of the Georgian Form on American Folk Housing," in Fife, Fife, and Glassie, *Forms upon the Frontier,* 23–25; idem, *Pattern in the Material Folk Culture,* 49; Pierson, *American Buildings,* 214, 451–52; Wright, *Literary Culture,* 214. Amidst the voluminous literature of gravestones the following are basic: Allan Ludwig, *Graven Images: New England Stonecarving and Its Symbols, 1650–1815* (Middletown, Conn., 1966); Dickran Tashjian and Ann Tashjian, *Memorials for the Children of Change* (Middletown, Conn., 1974); Peter Benes, *The Masks of Orthodoxy* (Amherst, 1977); idem, ed., *Puritan Gravestone Art, Annual Proceedings of the Dublin Seminar for New England Folk Life* 1 (1976); and idem, ed., *Puritan Gravestone Art II,* ibid. 3 (1978). I am indebted to Paul Bourcier for insights into gravestone sculpture. For the assimilation of

Dutch barn-building techniques see Peter O. Wacker, "Dutch Barns and Barracks in New Jersey," in Fife, Fife, and Glassie, *Forms upon the Frontier*, 27.

78. Robert F. Trent, *Hearts and Crowns: Folk Chairs of the Connecticut Coast, 1720–1840* (New Haven, 1977); idem, *Pilgrim Century Furniture*, 139; Forman, "Delaware Valley 'Crookt Foot' and Slat-Back Chairs"; Morse, *Country Cabinetwork*, 281–83. On the general point of continuity in vernacular culture see Pierson, *American Buildings*, 15–16; Burke, *Popular Culture in Early Modern Europe*, 280–88; and Thompson, "Eighteenth-Century English Society," 153.

79. Benjamin Franklin, *The Autobiography and Selections from His Other Writings*, ed. Hervert W. Schneider (Indianapolis, 1952), 78–79. Franklin voiced his attitudes towards the accouterments of gentility in his Anthony Afterwit essay in *Pennsylvania Gazette*, July 10, 1732.

80. Thompson, "Patrician Society, Plebeian Culture"; Edmund S. Morgan and Helen M. Morgan, *The Stamp Act Crisis: Prologue to Revolution*, rev. ed. (New York, 1962), chaps. 8, 9; John Lax and William Pencack, "The Knowles Riot and the Crisis of the 1740's in Massachusetts," *Perspectives in American History* 10 (1976): 163–214; Peter Shaw, *American Patriots and the Rituals of Revolution* (Cambridge, Mass., 1981); Dirk Hoerder, *Crowd Action in Revolutionary Massachusetts, 1765–1780* (New York, 1977). On similar tensions in the Chesapeake see Rhys Isaac, *The Transformation of Virginia, 1740–1790: Community, Religion, and Authority* (Chapel Hill, 1982).

81. Bridenbaugh, *Gentleman's Progress*, 13–14.

82. Gordon S. Wood, *The Creation of the American Republic, 1776–1787* (Chapel Hill, 1969), chap. 12.

13

THE INTERNATIONAL AND
IMPERIAL CONTEXT

W. A. SPECK

Historians addressing themselves to the relationship between the mother country and the colonies from the imperial point of view have rung changes on four main questions. First, did the imperial authorities pursue a coherent set of policies towards their American and West Indian possessions? Second, were the attitudes of successive English and British governments consistent, or can distinct periods be discerned between 1607 and 1763? In particular, did the year 1763 mark a major turning point? Third, did political developments in Britain play a role in determining the attitudes of successive ministries towards colonial problems? Fourth, what effects did developments in America have on the relationship? While these remain the principal lines of inquiry, recent answers to them differ significantly from traditional solutions.

One traditional approach to the first can be summed up in the word *mercantilism*. Like other isms that have been identified as historical agents, such as feudalism and capitalism, mercantilism is an elastic concept that can mean different things to different scholars. To give a brief resumé of a phenomenon to which whole books have been devoted is to risk misrepresentation. Nevertheless, the risk must be run, for a synopsis of the concept is required before recent criticisms of it can be evaluated.

Those who found the concept useful claimed that colonial policy could be fitted into a framework of mercantilist theory. Mercantilists were held to believe that a country's wealth was represented by its stock of silver and gold bullion. Consequently they advocated a favorable balance of trade, whereby a nation's exports were more valuable than its imports, the difference being made up in shipments of precious metals from its trading partners. To establish a favorable balance the state should encourage the importation of raw materials and the exportation of manufactured articles and discourage the importation of manufactured articles and the exportation of raw materials. These goals could be achieved by a complete ban on the movement of certain commodities, such as the prohibition of raw wool exports, or by financial penalties and inducements. Tariffs on foreign manufactures, for example, or bounties on the export of certain English products were advocated as a means whereby the government could regulate trade to produce a favorable balance.

The colonies fitted these assumptions admirably, since they could be made to supply the mother country with primary produce available only outside the British Isles and at the same time they could be prevented from developing industries that would compete with rather than complement English manufactures. As Adam Smith put it, "When those establishments were effectuated, and had become so considerable as to attract the attention of the mother country, the first regulations which she made with regard to them had always in view to secure to herself the monopoly of their commerce."[1]

The arrangements made to regulate the Chesapeake tobacco trade, it was said, illustrated the implementation of mercantilism. The first regulation that the English government made to secure the monopoly of colonial trade was an order in council of 1621 directing "that all tobacco of the growth of any English plantations whatsoever be brought into this kingdom." Thus Virginia's cash crop could only be exported to the mother country. Although this regulation prevented Virginia tobacco growers from sending their produce to the most profitable market overseas, they were to some extent protected by the same order, which forbade the importation into England of any tobacco not grown in English colonies and even prohibited the cultivation of the weed in England itself. Nevertheless, the Privy Council definitely held colonial tobacco to be more of an asset to England than it was to Virginia.

Mercantilism was also seen as a system of economic nationalism. The state was expected to intervene in international trade to protect and enlarge its own country's share. Moreover, since it was assumed that the volume of world trade was more or less static, this could be achieved only by restricting the share of their trading rivals by economic regulations, and, ultimately, by war. In the mid-seventeenth century England's main commercial rival was the Dutch Republic, which virtually monopolized the carrying trade of Europe. In order to relax the Dutch strangle hold on English trade, therefore, the Rump Parliament of the Commonwealth passed its Navigation Ordinance in 1651.

As far as the colonies were concerned, the most important measures adopted were restrictions on their trade. No colonial produce could be exported to England other than in English or colonial vessels. No European produce could be imported into the colonies except in English ships or those of the country where the goods were produced, "or most usually are first shipped for transportation." Because the ordinance had been passed by the Rump without the consent of the House of Lords, which it had abolished, or of the king, whom it had executed, it was held to be null and void when

Charles II was restored in 1660. However, the convention that assumed the role of a parliament at his restoration passed a similar measure, the Navigation Act. It also enumerated certain colonial products that could only be shipped directly to England—including sugar, tobacco, cotton, indigo, ginger, and fustic and other dyeing woods—which paid a duty upon arrival in English ports. What was not foreseen at the time was a loophole in this act whereby the enumerated commodities could be shipped from one colony to another and then exported to Europe without payment of a duty. This loophole was blocked in 1673 with the Plantation Duties Act, whereby duties were levied in the colonies themselves on commodities not destined to be shipped to England. The navigation acts allowed European produce to be conveyed directly from Europe to the colonies, provided it was shipped in English vessels or those of the country where it originated. The Staple Act of 1663, however, laid down that it had first to be brought to England before being conveyed to the colonies. The only exceptions were servants, horses, and victuals from Scotland and Ireland, salt meant for the fishing industries of New England and Newfoundland, and wine from Madeira or the Azores.

Although further acts were passed to regulate colonial trade, the basic legislation was enacted between 1650 and 1673. One of the fundamental problems in trying to appreciate the English government's attitude towards its colonies, therefore, is to explain why both the republic and the restored monarchy, two very different regimes, passed similar laws to control their commerce.

Ever since Adam Smith attacked these restrictions upon free trade it has been commonplace to criticize them on the grounds that they favored the distributors rather than the consumers of goods. Smith attributed the policy behind them to the political influence of merchants, who had made their interests paramount in the passing of the necessary legislation. Modern studies of economic theory and parliamentary practice, however, have raised serious objections to Smith's view. A recent penetrating study of works by seventeenth-century precursors of Smith has denied that those who wrote with a view to furthering mercantile interests generally did so by advocating restrictions upon commerce. Studies of the personnel of Stuart and Hanoverian governments and of the social composition of parliaments in the colonial period suggest that Smith exaggerated the political clout of the business community in the formulation of policy.

In *Economic Thought and Ideology in Seventeenth-Century England* Joyce Appleby analyzes an extensive range of economic tracts and treatises and concludes that until the end of the century at least, they do not document a system of mercantilism. On the contrary, many contemporaries speculating upon the operations of the economy came to conclusions quite distinct from those allegedly common to mercantilists. They were not all bullionists, for example, nor did they agree on prohibiting the importation of foreign manufactures. Indeed, some influential economic thinkers justified the export of bullion to India in order to pay for cotton textiles. This was almost the reverse of the balance-of-trade theory said to be the principal contribution of economists to policy making in the seventeenth century. The classical economists who attacked their predecessors for advocating "mercantilism" were attributing to the seventeenth century policies that only came to be implemented after the Revolution of 1688. According to Appleby, it was John Locke who persuaded the post-Revolutionary regime to adopt bullionism and the balance of trade; this became the conventional wisdom until Adam Smith attacked them in the 1770s.

Appleby sees a close relationship between the theories and policies devised by economists, and trends in the English economy. In general, she argues that writers were reacting to the rise of a market economy from the subsistence economy of the late Middle Ages. In her view, the breakdown of face-to-face economic relationships and the emergence of impersonal market forces freed economics from metaphysical explanations of reality and allowed its development as a separate science of human behavior. Economists could observe developments in the economy with detachment and recommend "scientific" responses to them. In particular, she regards Thomas Mun's *England's Treasure by Foreign Trade*, for example, as a reaction to the commercial recession of the 1620s, and John Locke's recommendations of bullionism and a favorable trading balance as a response to the crisis caused by the deplorable state of the silver coinage and the depression that brought an end to a period of rapid economic expansion under Charles II.[2]

Although this attempt to place seventeenth-century economic thought into the actual development of a market economy is open to challenge, the conclusion that it does not document a system of mercantilism appears to be unexceptionable. It follows therefore that the navigation acts were not the statutory embodiment of such a system. The Commonwealth and Restoration regimes were not imposing a theoretical blueprint upon the colonies. Instead, as D. C. Coleman observes, the legislation emerged as a result of a "bargaining process, as, so to speak, a series of games involving Crown, parliament and sets of interest groups. The varying strengths of the contending parties determined the outcome." In his view, the central executive "rarely possessed anything remotely describable as 'economic policy', but it always had financial problems for the solution of which it had to parley with both the creators of wealth and the payers of taxes."[3]

One of the problems in explaining the undoubted preoccupation of imperial authorities with commercial affairs is that relatively few businessmen stalked the corridors of power. Perhaps the Rump, which passed the Navigation Ordinance of 1651, had a larger proportion of merchants in it than any other parliament of the period, yet even there they "were heavily outnumbered in the House by rural landlords."[4] It has been argued that they were able, nevertheless, to exert an influence disproportionate to their numbers, while colonial merchants were particularly influential in the Rump's deliberations. Many of the men engaged in trade with the colonies have been identified as the younger sons of country gentlemen rather than as being associated with the established city oligarchy. Unlike the oligarchs, who incorporated themselves into chartered companies, colonial merchants preferred to trade individually. The civil war toppled the companies from their paramount position in trading circles and brought to the fore those engaged in colonial trade, who asserted their own priorities.[5] Among them were Maurice Thompson and his associates, who were influential if not instrumental in the framing of the Navigation Ordinance.[6]

After the Restoration, however, Parliament was flooded with country gentlemen, and mercantile representation was reduced to its norm for the period, no more than 10 percent of the House of Commons. Moreover, the return of the king also restored the House of Lords and the court. In both, the presence of landowners rather than of businessmen was paramount. Of course their interests were never mutually exclusive. Peers and country gentlemen, for example, invested in trading activities, whether in joint-stock companies or individual ventures. There is even evidence that they were particularly interested in colonial commerce, for landowners featured prominently in subscriptions to the Virginia and Providence island companies.[7] However, the degree of overlap of landed and mercantile interests fostered by such investment can be exaggerated. Merchants formed a substantial majority of investors in any venture, while the bulk of the landed gentry did not invest in trade, either because they lacked surplus capital to do so or through choice.

The question therefore remains, Why were regimes dependent overwhelmingly on landed aristocrats and country gentlemen persuaded to adopt measures that apparently benefitted primarily the mercantile community? The problem does not admit of a single or a simple explanation, but one answer to it lies in a consideration of some of the functions of government in early modern England. As Blair Worden observed regarding the passing of the Navigation Ordinance by the Rump:

> Whoever inspired the navigation act, the important question is why the Rump agreed to it. If one reads the memoranda, the pamphlets, and the record of discussions bearing on the formulation of the government's commercial policies, one is reminded time and again of a pervasive and time-honoured concept of the proper relationship between trade and the public interest. The precarious economic circumstances of the Commonwealth period dictated firm economic priorities, clearly reflected in the instructions given to the Council of Trade. The fear of poverty, the need to spread wealth equally through the land, the concern for fiscal stability, the emphasis on strengthening shipping and improving inland communications—these were age-old matters of national economic survival, to which private interests had invariably to be subordinated. The Rump worked closely with merchants who were prepared to assist it, but negotiations were conducted strictly on the government's terms.[8]

No function of government, whether that of the Republic or of the Restored monarchy, was more important than defending national security. It was a truism to contemporaries that they lived on a seagirt island and that any attack, from the Spanish Armada to the invasion of the Prince of Orange exactly a century later, could only come by sea. The Royal Navy alone was not adequate for the task of defending the country and in an emergency drew on the merchant marine for both ships and manpower. Any scheme that developed the merchant navy or proved to be a "nursery for seamen" was therefore bound to appeal to governments in this period. The navigation acts of 1651 and 1660 both had as a prime aim, stated in their preambles, "the increase of shipping and encouragement of the navigation of this nation." This aim "under the good providence and protection of God," was conducive to the welfare of the Commonwealth according to the Rump's ordinance, and to the wealth and strength of the kingdom according to the Restoration statute; but each stressed its importance for the "safety" of the nation.

The degree to which the mother country's relations with the colonies were caught up in preparations for and involvement in war was of concern primarily to strategic historians until recently. Those historians who stress the commercial nature of the relationship tend to emphasize also that the colonies developed largely without governmental interference. Many of course did, and, as Edmund Burke expressed it in 1757, "the settlement of our colonies was never pursued upon any regular plan; but they were formed, grew, and flourished, as accidents, the nature of the climate, or the dispositions of private men happened to operate."9 But some, such as Jamaica, New York, New Jersey, and Nova Scotia, were acquired by conquest. Those on the American mainland had to be protected from French, Spanish, and Indian attack. These military aspects of the colonial enterprise have been emphasized by Stephen Webb in *The Governors-General: The English Army and the Definition of the Empire, 1659–1681*. The very title chosen for the chief executives in the colonies, he claims, was military. Colonial governors practiced what he calls "garrison government," a term he illustrates with extensive case studies of Jamaica and Virginia. Between 1660 and 1730, 110 out of 180 governors were army officers. "The governmental institutions of England's colonies," he asserts, "whether in Ireland, the West Indies or North America, thus were shaped by military men, intent on establishing security and imposing social order within their jurisdictions and determined to spread crusading Christianity and English authority over conquered territories and 'native' peoples. Here were elements of empire."

Indeed, Webb maintains that "the structure of the imperial constitution was completed on January 27, 1682." This was when Lord Culpeper's commission as governor of Virginia was redrafted to systematize a form of garrison government that he had introduced into the Old Dominion in the aftermath of Bacon's Rebellion. "It was then imposed on colony after colony, for a century to come, as the organic law of the English empire." The model was one of "limited local legislative authority, provincial taxes for imperial use, and unfettered military prerogative." "Thus," he concludes, "Anglo-American relations were not primarily shaped by a commercial system, in which the strongest element was 'colonial self-government.' Rather, they were predominantly directed by a military system, in which the strongest political element was Anglo-American imperial government."[10]

The Governors-General is in fact the first installment of the theme of garrison government. A sequel dealing with the first duke of Marlborough and the military aspects of empire is apparently imminent. Meanwhile, Professor Webb has indicated the broad themes of his study as they will be subsequently substantiated. It appears that two concepts of empire, the commercial and the military, coexisted in the century or so before America's War of Independence. Between 1676 and 1722 the concept of garrison government was in the ascendant. Under Walpole, however, the commercial concern became dominant. Then the wars of 1739–48 and 1754–63 brought the militarist view of empire to the fore again.

Webb's work is a salutary reminder that the interests of the governing classes in England were not necessarily the same as those of the business community. One sector of the English political elite clearly did conceive of the colonies as being involved in the military function of government. How far this added up to an imperial view of the colonial system, however, is disputable. Indeed, the alleged distinction between imperial and mercantilist attitudes is open to question. While the assertion that authorities in London did conceive of the colonies as forming an empire is a convincing refutation of assertions that such a concept is anachronistic for the period, it does not necessarily follow that this conception was advocated as an alternative to commercial considerations. Both objectives could be pursued simultaneously, as indeed they were under James II. Philip Haffenden observes of his colonial activities that "the objective . . . was the reduction of the remaining independent governments overseas, and their regrouping, with the royal provinces, to form viceroyalties comparable in size to the Spanish territories to the South and greater in military strength than the French power to the North."[11] Yet at the same time the navigation acts were strictly enforced, the number of ports of entry in New England, for example, being reduced to five for more efficient supervision of colonial trade.

While the dominion of New England fits Professor Webb's concept of an empire based on garrison government, his claim that James II's brother had sought similar objectives is not confirmed by John Childs's investigation, *The Army of Charles II*. On the contrary, Childs's conclusion from the experience of the expedition sent out to mop up the aftermath of Bacon's Rebellion is very different: by 1681 it was in considerable arrears in pay and seemed likely itself to become disaffected. In 1682 it was disbanded.[12]

Webb himself admits that "there are questions about the efficacy of English soldiers as the physical base of garrison government in America. The garrisons were diseased, dispersed, and undisciplined, and their numbers were small. In the seventeenth century there were seldom more than one thousand regular soldiers on the North American continent. Often there were no more than three hundred." This scarcely constitutes a military presence strong enough to justify the assertion that the military function was a paramount consideration of the government in England. Nor is the ingenious attempt to show that "in proportion to populations, the garrisons often were larger than the armies commanded by the present-day authoritarian regimes" convincing.[13] There is a point where the absolute size of the armed forces is more important than their relative size. Three hundred soldiers were manifestly not enough to sustain a system of government. Between 1692 and 1769 it was considered necessary to maintain twelve thousand troops in Ireland alone. When John Trenchard and Thomas Gordon distinguished two sorts of colonies, "one to keep conquered countries in subjection" and "the other . . . for trade and intended to encrease the wealth and power of the native kingdom," they put Ireland in the first category and the American and West Indian colonies in the second.[14]

Moreover, the fact that many colonial governors were military men holding commissions analogous with those of garrison commanders in Britain might not be as significant as it at first appears. British garrisons were a very insignificant part of the military machine. They were generally used as easy postings for men who had come to the end of their active career in the army, being commanded for the most part by superannuated officers and often garrisoned by invalids. Except in emergencies like the Jacobite risings of 1715, they played a completely negligible role in civil government, and even in those crises their powers were minimal. Although several towns maintained them, in no way could one talk about "garrison government" in Carlisle or Chester, for example. Rather they offered rest homes for old soldiers and semiretirement for officers who had been put out to pasture. The commands of these dilapidated fortresses were little more than perquisites for their holders, many of whom were nonresident. In this way they formed a small part of the elaborate patronage system of Hanoverian politics. One suspects that colonial governorships, even when given to commissioned officers, were regarded in much the same light.

Certainly the duke of Newcastle included them in the colonial patronage he had at his disposal as secretary of state, appointing George Burrington to the governorship of North Carolina in 1731, the first of several gubernatorial appointments during his secretaryship. Other colonial posts were bestowed on his supporters at home in order to consolidate his interests, an electoral agent in Sussex, for example, obtaining the secretaryship of New Jersey in 1733. As James Henretta observes, "For a brief time in the 1740s and 1750s the American colonies had become less a national than a Sussex preserve, operated by Newcastle for the political benefit of his family."[15]

Although patronage was one function of government that could make the

British ruling elite as interested in the colonies as commercial opportunities made the merchants, it is not in itself a completely satisfactory explanation. All commentators observe that the actual amount of patronage available to the British government in colonial America was very limited. The secretary of state for the South, for instance, had only forty-six places at his disposal in 1724, and while this rose to eighty-five by 1748, it was still of little significance.

As far as the government was concerned, indeed, the small advantage to be gained from bestowing posts in the colonial establishment upon its supporters had to be offset by the administrative costs that many of them entailed. It was estimated in 1763, for example, that the revenue arising from customs duties in America and the West Indies was not "sufficient to defray a fourth part of the expence necessary for collecting it."[16] The Plantation Duties Act of 1673, on which the customs were based, was originally passed, not to bring in money, but to divert the flow of colonial commerce across the Atlantic. As the Lord Treasurer put it at the time, the intention was "to turn the course of a trade rather than to raise any considerable revenue to his Majesty."[17] When colonial produce was landed in England, however, it did raise a considerable revenue. Something like half of Charles II's total regular income came from the customs, amongst which duties on imports from the colonies loomed large, those on tobacco and sugar alone amounting to nearly 20 percent of the duties levied.[18] Yields from customs alone explain the acute interest in the regulation of colonial trade on the part of governments anxious to exploit every source of income. This was particularly true of the insolvent reign of Charles II, who sought every means available to raise his revenues to the level of his extravagant expenditure. As the Plantation Duties Act itself explained, the evasion of the intentions of the Navigation Act by colonial merchants had been a "great hurt and diminution of your Majesty's customs." Controls on colonial commerce above all made Charles II less dependent upon parliamentary supplies, and the boom in Atlantic trade towards the end of his reign finally made him altogether independent of those politically troublesome sources.

In this connection it is interesting that several customs officials were associated with the legislation of the years 1660 to 1673 which formed the pattern of the Restoration government's relations with the colonies. John Shaw and George Downing, both involved in the passage of these laws through Parliament, were also employed in the customs service. Another indication of the regime's financial interest in the navigation acts is that the commissioners of the customs were charged with the duty of enforcing them in the colonies. The Plantation Duties Act stipulated that "for the better collection of the several rates and duties . . . this whole business shall be ordered and managed and the several duties hereby imposed shall be caused to be levied by the commissioners of the customs in England." In November 1673 the first officials were appointed for the colonies, a collector and a surveyor being assigned to Maryland, Virginia, and the Carolinas. By 1677 they had been introduced into all colonies south of New England. In 1678 Edward Randolph was sent out as collector, surveyor, and searcher of the customs in New England, thus completing the system. Randolph had no doubt about the purpose of his mission, for he claimed that evasions of the navigation acts in Massachusetts alone were costing the English revenue over one hundred thousand pounds a year.[19]

Randolph's experiences showed that the difficulties facing the English government in its dealings with the colonies were not simply administrative problems resulting from their being three thousand miles across the Atlantic but also political. As Lawrence Harper put it, "Seventeenth-century administrators like present day radio technicians, found that their problems of remote control arose not so much from the mere physical distance to be covered as from the interference likely to be encountered."[20] There was resistance to the navigation acts in several colonial quarters, particularly in the virtually autonomous colonies of New England and in those directly under proprietors rather than the crown. Both Charles II and James II therefore tried to increase the crown's power over the colonies. These attempts were felt more immediately by New England, though there are signs of a policy aimed at bringing colonial proprietors to heel as well.

Randolph claimed that the only way to force Massachusetts to obey the navigation laws was to make it a crown colony. Although his proposal encountered stiff resistance in New England and less than full backing at home, he stuck doggedly to it until he eventually obtained a quo warranto against the colony "for usurping to be a body politick," and the charter was annulled in October 1684. This development coincided with a review of several colonial charters, including those of Connecticut, Rhode Island, and Maryland. Some historians have seen in this a coherent policy of extending royal authority in North America by reducing all the colonies to the status of crown colonies. They have had difficulties, however, in squaring this with the grant of Pennsylvania to William Penn in 1681, the largest proprietorial donation ever conceded by the crown. Of course it could be that, as in other spheres of activity, the left hand of Charles II's government did not know what the right hand was doing.[21] Yet if we see his aim as being to maximize his revenues from the colonies rather than to extend his power over them, then we can perceive an overall consistency. Penn's powers were more circumscribed than those of the proprietors of Maryland and the Carolinas precisely in the prescription of his colony's financial obligations to the mother country. The charter stressed, for instance, that Pennsylvania should conform to the navigation acts. All the colony's produce shipped abroad was to be sent to England. Although it could then be reexported, this was "provided always that they pay such customs and impositions, subsidies and duties for the same to us, our heirs and successors, as the rest of our subjects of our kingdom of England, for the time being, shall be bound to pay."

Even with the advent of parliamentary monarchy after the Revolution of 1688, kings and their ministers were as interested in the financial advantages of colonies as they were in the stimulation of trade, if not more so. As P. W. J. Riley noted in his observations upon the making of the treaty of union with Scotland, "When officers of state talked about encouraging trade, as from time to time they did, they usually had in mind not a sleek and contented mercantile community but an increase in customs yield. . . . This was true of them all."[22]

Unlike James II, however, they had to pay attention to the interests of those social groups that were represented in Parliament. Where these groups desired to be left alone to conduct their own local affairs, they did not advocate similar noninterference with colonial matters. On the contrary, they took as keen an interest in the development of the colonies to the advantage of the mother country as any Stuart king had done. To be sure, this interest was not primarily with an eye to the financial advantage of the crown. As Klaus E. Knorr concluded from a survey of literature on the relationship between Britain and the colonies, "The proposition that colonisation would lead to enlarged revenues from export and import duties was of distinctly subordinate if not negligible significance. Indeed it was maintained only vaguely if at all and, on the whole, served merely to increase the number of arguments that could be cited in support of colonisation."[23]

There were several arguments in favor of colonies and colonial trade that might have appealed indirectly to the country gentlemen who sat on the benches of the House of Commons in this period. The strategic and naval arguments were of concern to many of them, especially those who argued that the sea was England's natural element and that any active foreign policy should be maritime rather than military. This "blue water policy" was attractive not only to their patriotism but also to their pockets. Involvement in land wars on the Continent was far more expensive, and they bore the brunt of direct taxation. The land tax, levied largely on their rents, was raised to its maximum rate of four shillings in the pound during periods of warfare in Europe.

Similar prudential considerations also led them to look favorably upon the protection and encouragement of colonial trade. The "mercantilist" argument for engineering a favorable balance of trade by government regulation was not merely advanced by bullionists, who saw in it a means of increasing the "wealth" of the nation as expressed in its holdings of precious metals. It was also proposed as a method of protecting English manufactures from foreign competition and thereby of employing the laboring poor in productive occupations. Those not thus employed were forced back onto parochial relief. The poor rate was levied to a large extent on the same basis as the land tax, that is, on an assessment of rental values of the estates of country gentlemen. There are signs of an increasing concern about the weight of this burden, especially after the Revolution of 1688, when landlords were faced with the additional demand of four shillings in the pound to finance nearly twenty years of war with Louis XIV. At no time before the twentieth century were landlords in England taxed as heavily as in the years 1689 to 1713. Any scheme to reduce the incidence of direct taxation was listened to sympathetically, while any policy that threatened to increase it yet further was stubbornly resisted.

Trade played a vital role in this context. A proposal to remove the tariff barriers against France, put forward by the Tory ministry in 1713, was defeated after a rebellion by Tory backbenchers. Among the reasons that persuaded them to oppose the measure was that French goods would compete with English manufactures, putting manufacturers out of business and creating unemployment amongst artisans and laborers, which in turn would lead to an increase in the poor rate for parochial relief. When the Board of Trade was set up in 1696, it had among its avowed aims, besides "inspecting and improving our plantations in America," "proper methods for setting on work and employing the poor, thereby easing our subjects of that burden."

The answer to the first question—whether the mother country had a coherent colonial policy—therefore would seem to be that imperial authorities did not proceed from theoretical concepts when formulating their views of colonial questions, but reacted in a pragmatic way to the problems and opportunities presented to them by the colonies. Above all, they were not implementing a body of doctrines that can be called mercantilism. Indeed, the notion that such a concept existed can no longer be seriously maintained. Rather, they were responding to needs and circumstances as they arose. Although the enactment of navigation acts by both the Commonwealth and Restoration regimes appears to indicate that economic theory rather than political contingency dictated policy, each was in fact concerned to meet the challenge of Dutch mercantile supremacy. The one unquestionable continuity from 1650 to 1675 is that three Anglo-Dutch wars were fought. While the extent to which the navigation acts caused these conflicts is disputable, the fierce rivalry between the two nations undoubtedly brought the legislation into being. Other considerations behind it and similar measures were such problems as the need to maximize revenues, to encourage navigation, and to keep down the poor rate.

The problem of periodization admits of various solutions. Perhaps the first date to determine is when imperial authorities began to try to get a grip on the colonies. Initially the colonists had been allowed to develop more or less independently of the mother country. Although when Virginia became a crown colony the king proclaimed that he intended to provide "one uniform course of government" for all the English plantations, this policy was not implemented. Four years later the Massachusetts Bay Company obtained its charter, and three years after that Lord Baltimore was granted a charter to establish the first proprietary colony on the mainland. Thereafter the English Civil War disrupted the Anglo-American world and postponed the possibility of imposing any uniform design upon it until the 1650s. As we have seen, in the period 1650–75 a framework of legislation for developing colonial commerce was fashioned. It was not until around 1675, however, that the crown seriously tried to assert its authority over its American and West Indian possessions. From the mid-1670s until the Glorious Revolution there were attempts to make the colonies more of an asset to the crown than they had been.

Even after the Revolution the aim of subordinating the colonies to the mother country remained an imperial objective. The chief means of realizing this end, the Board of Trade, was established in 1696. There had been other bodies to supervise relations with the colonies, but these had been relatively short-lived. The board established in 1696 was to last until 1782 and was to play a major role in the administration of the colonies, at least until the creation of a separate colonial secretariat in 1768. The Board of Trade was charged with advising the Privy Council on such personnel of colonial government as governors, deputy governors, councillors, and secretaries. It was also authorized to see that colonial legislation was compatible with the interests of the crown, particularly to ensure that it did not contravene the navigation laws.

Because it was an advisory body, the Board of Trade could not always exercise a decisive influence over governmental policies towards the colonies. One problem was that at least until the eve of the War of Independence there was no central agency with overall responsibility for the colonies. Instead there were several authorities whose jurisdiction overlapped. First and perhaps foremost before the establishment of a secretariat for the colonies was the secretaryship of state. Two secretaries were responsible for Britain's foreign relations, one for the north, who dealt with northern Europe, and one for the south, who dealt with southern Europe and, in theory, British colonial dependencies. Under the Hanoverians, however, the secretary of state for the north became the senior partner and often supervised colonial business. Then there was the Board of Customs, which, though technically a subdepartment of the Treasury, as we have seen regulated colonial commerce. The Treasury actually forebade the Board of Trade to correspond directly with the commissioners of the customs. Indeed the Treasury itself exerted an important and increasing influence over colonial affairs during the eighteenth century. The Admiralty played a part too, since the navy policed American waters to apprehend violators of the navigation laws.

The Board of Trade was thus one of several bodies with an interest in colonial affairs, and it complained in 1721 to the king that "no one office is thro'ly informed of all matters relating to the Plantations."[24] How far it could make its influence felt depended upon two considerations: the determination of its members to assert its authority; and the willingness of other interested parties to allow it. Historians have detected three phases in the board's activities in the period 1696–1768. The first, which lasted until 1720, was characterized by the board's taking the lead in shaping the government's approach to colonial problems. During the second, which extended until 1748, the board became subordinate to the secretaries of state. In the third period, from 1748 to 1768, the board again played a dynamic if not decisive role in relations between Britain and her colonies.

The first period began with a vigorous approach to the regulation of colonial commerce. The year 1696 was marked not only by the establishment of the Board of Trade but also by the passage of an act "for preventing frauds and regulating abuses in the Plantation Trade." This navigation act tightened up previous measures, insisting, for instance, that vessels trading with the colonies should be built in England, Wales, Ireland, or America and should not be owned merely by men residing there. This stipulation was aimed not at the Dutch so much as at Scots, who had been interloping in colonial trade. The enforcement of navigation laws was enjoined on colonial governors, who were obliged "to take a solemn oath to do their utmost that all the clauses matters and things contained in the . . . acts of parliament heretofore passed, and now in force, relating to the said colonies and plantations, and all and every the clauses contained in the present act, be punctually and bona fide observed." Failure of governors to uphold the laws would result in their removal and a fine of one thousand pounds, a warning that their previous connivance with breaches of the regulations would not be tolerated in future. The Act of Frauds of 1662 was now extended to the colonies. This act empowered customs officials to search ships and confiscate their cargoes and even to enter houses or warehouses in search of contraband. In the exercise of these duties, they could issue general search warrants, or writs of assistance. All forfeitures arising from successful prosecutions were recoverable in any of the law courts at Westminster or in Ireland or "in the court of Admiralty held in his Majesty's plantations." This act also sanctioned the use of vice-admiralty courts in the colonies to enforce the navigation laws, the first being introduced in 1697.

The Navigation Act of 1696 thus systematically subordinated colonial commerce to control by the mother country. As Thomas C. Barrow observes, "In no instance did the machinery of enforcement evolved depend on colonial participation." The principal officers to enforce the system were appointed by the commissioners of the customs. Prosecutions for breaches of the laws could be undertaken at Westminster or in the court of Admiralty, both jurisdictions outside colonial control. To quote Barrow again, "In all its varied aspects the Act of 1696 centered authority on London."[25] In the same year, too, the American customs service was made wholly independent of colonial control by putting it on the payroll of the English Exchequer.

Like Randolph in Charles II's reign, the Board of Trade regarded the corporate and proprietary colonies as the chief culprits in the evasion of the navigation laws. It therefore reported in 1698 that "if the proprietors and charter governments do not speedily comply with what is required of them, we see no means to prevent a continuance of this mischief without calling in the further assistance of parliament." The suspect colonies in fact did not do what was required of them, and in 1701 the board concluded that their charters should be resumed "and all of them put into the same state of dependency as those of your Majesty's other plantations." A bill for "reunion with the Crown" was actually introduced in the House of Lords. One of the reasons adduced to justify the measure was that corporate and proprietary colonies were prejudicial to the royal revenue because of the encouragement they gave to illicit trade. The Lords, however, dropped it from their proceedings, and although it was again introduced into Parliament in 1702, the death of William III put an end to discussion of it. The only concrete achievement of such moves at this time, therefore, was the resumption of New Jersey by the crown.

Between 1702 and 1720 the Board of Trade gradually lost authority. The departure in 1707 of William Blathwayt, who in addition to being a commissioner was also surveyor and auditor general of colonial revenues, was one sign of its diminishing importance. Increasing complaints from the board that it was impotent to bring recalcitrant colonies to heel were another. These provoked a series of reports urging the crown to assume more direct power over its transatlantic dependencies. Until 1748, however, such reports were shelved. Despite the board's decline, it nevertheless continued to function as a "clearing house" for colonial interests, processing petitions from the colonies to the Privy Council.[26] These normal day-to-day activities went on regardless of the periods that historians have detected in the Board of Trade's history.

The second such period, from 1720 to 1748, is generally regarded as being characterized by "salutary neglect." Although it has become customary to distinguish it thus ever since Burke first used the expression, some historians have questioned its appropriateness. James Henretta, for instance, has suggested that the British government continued to take an active interest in colonial affairs until the mid-1730s. Indeed, he even detects a period of dynamic intervention between the mid-1720s and the mid-1730s. That decade saw the resumption of the Carolinas by the crown, the establishment of Georgia, and the passage of the Hat and Molasses acts. It was only when the duke of Newcastle managed to achieve almost complete control of colonial affairs that the government began to neglect them. Even then, in Henretta's view, the neglect was scarcely salutary. On the contrary, he concludes that "as Southern Secretary for a quarter of a century Newcastle failed to make a single positive contribution to the functioning of the colonial system. Not one administrative measure, not a solitary piece of legislation was connected with his name. His was an era devoid of achievement and vision, a period of culpable mismanagement and negligence which led directly to many of the intractable problems of the next generation."[27]

This sad state of affairs only came to an end, in the view of Newcastle's critics, when Lord Halifax became president of the Board of Trade in 1748. Halifax's new initiative at the Board of Trade is widely seen as foreshadowing the functions of the secretaryship for the colonies (established in 1768) and even as anticipating the policies that were to necessitate its establishment. For example, he issued instructions to governors commanding them to curb the pretensions of the colonial assemblies. As far as the intentions of the British government were concerned, it is consequently claimed, the year 1748 marks the real turning point in the relationship between the mother country and the colonies. Only the outbreak of hostilities in 1754 prevented them from being realized, postponing their implementation until 1763.

This contrast between the allegedly incompetent Newcastle and the efficient Halifax has been overdrawn, however, for two reasons. First, it exaggerates the duke's ineptitude in colonial matters and inflates the earl's abilities. Second, and more important, they did not have different views on how to approach colonial problems. Whatever initial misgivings Newcastle might have had about Halifax's appointment to the Board of Trade, they were soon working together. Indeed, it was Newcastle who obtained the king's agreement in 1752 for Halifax to attend meetings of the cabinet when the colonies were under discussion. During the critical period before the outbreak of war between the British and the French, according to Roy Clayton, "reports of French encroachments in North America were passed from the Board of Trade to the Duke of Newcastle by the Earl of Halifax. That intelligence only further confirmed Newcastle in the opinion that he had expressed on many occasions after 1749 that the French intended to provoke a resumption of war when they had insinuated themselves into a position stronger than their situation at the end of the War on the Austrian Succession in 1748."[28]

It was realization that the treaty of Aix-la-Chapelle marked a truce rather than a peace in North America, and not the accession of Lord Halifax to the presidency of the Board of Trade, which really made 1748 a turning point in imperial policies. As P. J. Marshall observes, "The end of the war in 1748 brought no real reduction in British military involvement overseas. Louisburg was returned to France at the peace, but a garrison of 4,000 men costing an average of about £95,000 a year, a figure totally out of proportion with all previous spending, was established in Nova Scotia; and Halifax was built up as a base and made the home of the Royal Naval squadron maintained in North America after 1745."[29]

The government's attitude towards the American colonies varied with the rhythm of international, and especially Anglo-French, relations. Between 1689 and 1713, when England was at war with France for all but four years of uneasy peace, military activity in America took priority over commercial considerations. During King William's War the government tried to persuade the reluctant colonies to cooperate against the French threat. In the interval of peace following the treaty of Ryswick the newly formed Board of Trade presented a report on colonial union, proposing to unite New England

and New York under one governor for military purposes. Despite colonial objections, the scheme went ahead, and the earl of Bellomont was appointed to the new governorship. The board also empowered him to draw on the Treasury for up to two thousand pounds to repair forts, which he found to be in a critically weak condition. Although the experiment was dropped on Bellomont's death in 1701, attempts to get the colonies to cooperate against the French were resumed during Queen Anne's War. In 1709 the board even approved plans for an attack on Quebec by twenty-five hundred troops from the middle and northern colonies in conjunction with two battalions of regulars and six warships from England, though it proved abortive when the English contribution was called off. Despite colonial resentment of this development, another joint attack was planned against Port Royal; this time the attack was executed, resulting in the acquisition of Nova Scotia. A subsequent attempt on Canada in 1711, however, was a dismal failure. Nevertheless, the British war effort did culminate with French recognition of Britain's claim to Hudson Bay, Newfoundland, and Nova Scotia in North America and Nevis and St. Kitts in the West Indies. The 1713 treaty of Utrecht thus ended a period of military involvement and territorial aggrandizement in the colonies.

Between 1713 and 1744 Britain and France remained technically at peace and, apart from clashes along the Canadian borders, were not involved in hostilities in North America. More serious friction indeed occurred with Spain in the Caribbean and on the borders with the Carolinas, especially during the short-lived Anglo-Spanish war of 1727. It was partly to provide a bulwark against the Spanish settlements in Florida that Georgia was established in 1732. Until the war of Jenkins' Ear broke out in 1739, however, defense was not a major concern of the British government in its dealing with the colonies. Hence the relative neglect of them, whether it was salutary or not.

The period 1739–63, by contrast, witnessed almost constant military activity on the American side of the Atlantic. Even in the years of peace between 1748 and 1754, as we have seen, there were active preparations for renewed conflict on both sides. Throughout this period imperial defense again superseded economic relations in the thinking of the authorities in Whitehall.

The war years, therefore, mark a significant shift in the importance that British ministers ascribed to the colonies, as well as in the attention that they consequently gave to North America. They feared that unless priority were given to colonial defense, the French might well sweep the board there. Instead, of course, the British swept the French from the continent in the Seven Years' War. The process of doing so, however, drastically altered the imperial and international context of the colonies.

One crude measure of this alteration is the amount Britain spent on its North American empire. Between 1740 and 1748 the annual average was

£148,000. During the interval between the wars it actually rose to £268,000. From 1756 until the end of the Seven Years' War it reached £998,000. These averages conceal the real trend. As Julian Gwyn has pointed out, "The change of British policy in America, if the serious spending of money by parliament is a reasonable guide, can be said to date not from 1756–63, as is traditionally recorded, but from 1745–6 with the Louisbourg expedition and the planned invasion of Canada."[30] Yet Louisbourg was returned to France when peace terms were eventually agreed upon in 1748. It was not until the Seven Years' War that a determined effort was made to conquer Canada. The conquests of Quebec and Montreal led to insistence on the acquisition of all French possessions in North America at the peace of Paris in 1763. By this treaty the territorial context of the empire was vastly extended, which altered the scale of administrative problems from the point of view of Whitehall. The proclamation of 1763, defining the westward limits of colonial expansion, might have been a stopgap measure, but it brought the crown into the arena of North American sectional, racial, and economic controversy more directly than ever before. The Grenville ministry also made the fateful decision to recoup some of the costs of colonial defense from the colonists themselves, initiating a sequence of events which culminated in the American Revolution.

Yet if many of those who resisted the British in that struggle were to look back at the year 1763 as the start of all the trouble, in truth the relationship between the colonies and the mother country had deteriorated before that, during the mid-century wars. Imperial authorities criticized the colonists for not pulling their weight in the war effort. For their part, the colonists felt that they had fully cooperated and were resentful that their contribution was unappreciated in Britain.[31] They also had for the first time a taste of real military government, which fed their inherited fear of the threat that a standing army posed to freedom.[32] Things were never again to be quite the same as they had been before 1739.

Many historians have sought to link these changing imperial attitudes to political developments in England between 1607 and 1763. Indeed, almost every shift in colonial policy from the taking over of Virginia by the crown to the so-called Grenville program has been attributed to tensions in English politics. Thus the dissolution of the Virginia Company was at one time held to have represented the triumph of absolutist forces at the court of James I over the advocates of limited monarchy and parliamentary representation, while the Grenville program was seen as evidence of a conspiracy to undermine liberty on both sides of the Atlantic by the men who came to power after the accession of George III. These simple equations have long been at a discount, along with similar simplistic notions such as the alleged favoring of Puritan New England by the Roundheads and the Whigs and the inclination towards "Cavalier" Virginia attributed to Royalists and Tories.

Despite the difficulties of establishing connections, however, historians still continue to be intrigued by the problem. Of late, the coincidence that the years 1675–1720 witnessed both the first serious attempt by the imperial authorities to tighten their hold on the colonies and the rise of the first political parties in England has led to speculation about possible relationships between the two. Stephen Webb develops his distinction between imperial and mercantilist attitudes by ascribing the first to a militaristic court Tory ethos and the second to a commercial republican Whig outlook.[33] David Lovejoy has forged links between those in England and in America who resisted the crown in the Glorious Revolution.[34] Alison Olson places the Board of Trade's attempt to put the crown again in control of the colonies— and its failure—in the context of the party struggle during the reigns of William and Anne, claiming that the policy appealed to Whigs, while the proprietors found support among the Tories.[35]

Although there is something to be said in favor of these views, the exact nature of the interrelationship still remains elusive. The main problem concerns the development of parties on the English side of the Atlantic, which some colonial historians apparently regard as the rise of a two-party system. This view exaggerates the extent to which the political nation was polarized even in what has been called "the first Age of Party." While there were two parties, the Tories and the Whigs, they did not necessarily result in a two-party system, in which each party in turn monopolized authority as it came to power. On the contrary, apart from very short intervals, neither the Tories nor the Whigs completely controlled the distribution of posts in the administration before the accession of George I. What offset the rise of such a system was the influence of the crown, which "trimmed" between the parties under Charles II, William III, and Anne and even, to some extent, under James II. Political life in England cannot therefore be discussed exclusively in terms of the division into two parties. Certainly politicians in Charles II's reign were not divided along the lines of court Tory or republican Whig, as Professor Webb seems to be suggesting. Indeed, his notion that the first Whigs held republican views in itself accepts at face value the propaganda of their opponents. Their own political theories were a great deal more subtle than that. Those who took part in the Glorious Revolution in America had to come to terms with the new rulers in England as well as with the political parties, as Leisler learned. An examination of the personnel of the Board of Trade also reveals difficulties in ascribing to it a party political role. At no time between 1696 and 1714 did either party monopolize its membership. Moreover, for much of that period there was relatively little turnover of members, despite several changes of ministry. Between 1697 and 1707, indeed, there was a nucleus of four men who did much of its work: William Blathwayt, Sir Philip Meadowes, John Pollexfen, and George Stepney. These were not party zealots, for although they can all be given partisan labels, Blathwayt and Meadowes being Tories and Pollexfen and Stepney Whigs, they were such moderate politicians that they are best labeled court supporters. They were in fact a new breed of administrator who appealed more to the court "managers" than to the party leaders.

The "managers," such as the earl of Sunderland in William's reign and Lord Godolphin and Robert Harley in Anne's, played a vital role in post-Revolutionary politics. They tried to prevent the crown from becoming too dependent upon either the Tories or the Whigs by building up a party of court supporters from moderate men on both sides. One way of doing this was to keep some areas of the administration free from the party spoils system, reserving them for such moderates. The Board of Trade fell into this category, and its members were more like nonpolitical civil servants than party hacks. Although the party leaders tried to encroach on this preserve by getting their own supporters appointed to the board—Tories from 1702 to 1704 and again from 1712 to 1714 and Whigs from 1708 to 1710—they never succeeded in wresting control from the "managers" completely. Prime ministers Godolphin and Harley, both Lord Treasurers, protected the board from the takeover bids of such partisan secretaries of state as the earls of Nottingham and Sunderland and Henry St. John Viscount Bolingbroke. Under their administrations it was used as an active instrument of royal policy and played a major role in colonial relations.

After Anne's death nobody took over the role of "manager" for the crown. Instead, Whig party leaders triumphed and engrossed all patronage. They not only stripped Tory zealots of their posts but even invaded those areas of the administration that Godolphin and Harley had tried to preserve from the spoils system. By 1720 the Board of Trade had succumbed, being staffed by Whig placemen rather than by moderates. The result was that until Lord Halifax became its president the board remained subordinate to the wishes of the Whig ministers.

The triumph of the Whigs meant that the colonists could no longer exploit party political differences to their own advantages. Where before 1714 colonial agents attached themselves to rival English politicians, since there was a rapid turnover of ministries and therefore a party in opposition could expect a spell in office, under George I it became increasingly clear that only Whigs associated with Walpole could be of service to the colonies. Most agents therefore lobbied Whig politicians associated with the prime minister. Those who looked to the opposition for support were left out on a limb when the excise scheme of 1733 pitted Walpole's opponents against colonial interest groups. As Alison Olson observes; "It is not too much to suggest that the Excise scheme and the dilemma into which it put the English opposition was a turning-point in Anglo-American history, for two reasons. First, it seems to have completely changed the approach of the opposition leaders towards the colonies for the next thirty years. . . . Secondly, it destroyed the promising transatlantic connections of Queen Anne's reign."[36] It was to some extent possible for colonial agents to play off one group of ministers against another, for example, the disgruntled commissioners of trade against the secretary of state in the 1730s, or the duke of Bedford's connection against the Newcastle Whigs in the 1740s.[37] But there was far less room for maneuver than there had been. The result was that the links between English and American politics were fewer and frailer by 1763 than they had ever been, just when they were about to be subjected to the greatest strain.

How far the strain was exerted by developments in America as well as by initiatives from Britain has always interested historians concerned with the international and imperial context of the colonial era. Were the American colonies growing along lines which made a break with the mother country inevitable, so that political events were merely contingent to the timing of it? Did an American society exist before an American nation? Did the Revolutionary rhetoric mask material ambitions to throw off the alleged restraints of empire? Although these have been perennial problems, our appreciation of changes in colonial society has expanded so greatly in recent years, as the other contributions to this volume testify, that they can now be approached from fresh perspectives. Indeed, the most interesting lines of inquiry into the relationship between Britain and her American possessions seem likely to take the form of detailed comparative studies of the two societies based on our expanded knowledge of them.

So far, there have been relatively few close studies of their interaction, in comparison with analyses of the truly Revolutionary years, which are beyond the scope of this essay. There is a cluster of works on New England's relations with old England under the later Stuarts which show how a knowledge of realities on both sides of the Atlantic can deepen our perception of the imperial connection.[38] These demonstrate that the colonies were not just passive entities, reacting only to stimuli from the mother country, but developed their own dynamics, to which England had to respond.

The rhythm of response in Whitehall to events in America might have dictated the phases in colonial policy as much as did changes in the attitudes of successive British regimes. As has already been observed, Lord Halifax's fresh approach to colonial affairs after 1748 was partly inspired by the seriousness with which the government regarded the French threat to the mainland colonies. It has also been suggested that the ministers were aware of the enormous growth in population and the expansion of the economy in the colonies. This made them acutely conscious of the increasing importance of trade with them for the economic well-being of Britain and apprehensive that the colonists were flexing their recently developed muscles to assert themselves against the prerogatives of their governors and ultimately of the crown.[39]

One of the major changes in attitude towards the colonies in the century between the Restoration of Charles II and the accession of George III was a shift in the order of priorities from the Caribbean to the mainland. Under the later Stuarts Barbados and Jamaica were regarded as the jewels in the imperial crown. In this respect, Webb is absolutely right to place the emphasis on the West Indies rather than on the somewhat overworked New England colonies under the restored monarchy. The sugar islands were the key to imperial policy until well into the Hanoverian era. At what stage the North American colonies became more significant, until Canada was held to be preferable to Guadeloupe, and why are questions that can be satisfactorily answered only by a close examination of the interaction over decades of several interests on both sides of the Atlantic: the power of the West Indian lobby as a pressure group in British politics and the leverage of other colonial agencies; the impact on imperial thinking of social and economic trends in North America and the Caribbean; changes in strategic and logistic considerations.

Clearly a comparative approach to the imperial context of colonial history will pay dividends as our knowledge of the societies involved is enhanced. At the same time, those who attempt to synthesize current research into a new transatlantic framework must be careful to distinguish between those colonial trends discerned by modern historians and those perceived by contemporaries. This obvious point can be stressed by the hoary old problem of whether or not the navigation acts laid a heavy burden on colonial trade. Recent quantitative analyses have concluded that on the whole they did not.[40] Yet some American colonists clearly thought that they did, and their subjective consciousness was important in shaping their attitudes towards Britain. Students of the colonial relationship from the imperial viewpoint should try to ascertain how developments three thousand miles away were seen by British observers. Even the best-informed politicians in Whitehall could be only dimly aware of some trends now a commonplace of colonial history, while they would be totally ignorant of others. The reader of this book will be better briefed on the colonies than the Board of Trade was at the time.

NOTES

1. Adam Smith, *The Wealth of Nations*, vol. 2 (London, 1950), 103.

2. Joyce O. Appleby, *Economic Thought and Ideology in Seventeenth-Century England* (Princeton, 1978), 37–41, 250–51, passim.

3. D. C. Coleman, "Mercantilism Revisited," *Historical Journal* 23, (1980): 790.

4. B. Worden, *The Rump Parliament* (Cambridge, 1974), 32.

5. Robert Brenner, "The Social Basis of English Commercial Expansion, 1550–1650," *Journal of Economic History* 32 (1972): 361–84.

6. J. E. Farnell, "The Navigation Act of 1651, the First Dutch War and the London Merchant Community," *Economic History Review*, 2d ser., 16 (1964): 439–54.

7. Lawrence Stone, *The Crisis of the Aristocracy, 1558–1641* (Oxford, 1965), 368–75; T. K. Rabb, *Enterprise and Empire: Merchants and Gentry Investment in the Expansion of England, 1575–1630* (Cambridge, Mass., 1967), 39–44.

8. Worden, *Rump Parliament*, 157–58.

9. Quoted in Jack P. Greene, ed., *Great Britain and the American Colonies, 1606–1763* (New York, 1970), xi.

10. Stephen S. Webb, *The Governors-General: The English Army and the Definition of Empire, 1569–1681* (Chapel Hill, 1979), 447.

11. Philip Haffenden, "The Crown and the Colonial Charters, 1675–1688," *William and Mary Quarterly*, 3d ser., 15 (1958): 297–311, 452–66.

12. J. Childs, *The Army of Charles II* (London, 1976), 160.

13. Webb, *Governors-General*, 454.

14. *Cato's Letters*, no. 106: "Of plantations and colonies," in *Cato's Letters*, by T. Gordon and J. Trenchard, 4 vols. (1755), 4:1–12.

15. James A. Henretta, *"Salutary Neglect": Colonial Administration under the Duke of Newcastle* (Princeton, 1972), 238–39.

16. Order in Council, October 4, 1763, printed in Jack P. Greene, ed., *Colonies to Nation, 1763–1789* (New York, 1967), 14.

17. Quoted in Charles McLean Andrews, *The Colonial Period of American History*, vol. 4 (New Haven, 1938), 121.

18. D. Chandaman, *The English Public Revenue, 1660–1688* (Oxford, 1975), 9–36.

19. M. G. Hall, *Edward Randolph and the American Colonies, 1676–1703* (Chapel Hill, 1960), 35, where it is noted that Randolph probably exaggerated.

20. Lawrence H. Harper, *The Navigation Laws* (New York, 1964), 151.

21. Cf. Jack M. Sosin, *English America and the Restoration Monarchy of Charles II: Transatlantic Politics, Commerce, and Kinship* (Lincoln, Nebr., 1980), 181: "The government of Charles II had no overall plan; it reacted to disparate events as they occurred in the individual American colonies."

22. P. W. J. Riley, *The Union of England and Scotland: A Study in Anglo-Scottish Politics of the Eighteenth Century* (Manchester, Eng., 1978), 205.

23. Klaus E. Knorr, *British Colonial Theories, 1570–1850* (London, 1963), 59.

24. T. Barrow, *Trade and Empire: The British Customs Service in Colonial America, 1660–1775* (Cambridge, Mass., 1967), 108.

25. Ibid., 59.

26. Alison G. Olson, "The Board of Trade and London-American Interest Groups in the Eighteenth Century," in *The British Atlantic Empire before the American Revolution*, ed. P. J. Marshall and G. Williams (London, 1980), 33–50.

27. Henretta, 'Salutary Neglect,' 270–71.

28. T. Roy Clayton, "The Duke of Newcastle, the Earl of Halifax and the American Origins of the Seven Years' War," *Historical Journal* (1981): 571–603.

29. P. J. Marshall, "The British Empire in the Age of the American Revolution: Problems of Interpretation," in *The American Revolution: Changing Perspectives*, ed. W. M. Fowler and W. Coyle (Boston, 1979), 200.

30. J. Gwyn, "British Government Spending and the North American Colonies, 1740–1775," in Marshall and Williams, *The British Atlantic Empire*, 77.

31. Jack P. Greene, "The Seven Years' War and the American Revolution: the Causal Relationship Reconsidered," ibid. 85–105.

32. Alan Rogers, *Empire and Liberty: American Resistance to British Authority, 1755–1763* (Berkeley, 1974).

33. Webb, *Governors-General*, 446–47, 461, where Whig supporters are even described as "levelling"!

34. David S. Lovejoy, *The Glorious Revolution in America* (New York, 1972).

35. Alison G. Olson, *Anglo-American Politics, 1660–1775: The Relationship between Parties in England and Colonial America* (Oxford, 1973), 104; Cf. Ian K. Steele, *Politics and Colonial Policy: The Board of Trade in Colonial Administration, 1696–1720* (Oxford, 1968), 60–61.

36. Olson, *Anglo-American Politics*, 118.

37. Ibid., 128–35, 149–53.

38. Sosin, *English America and the Restoration Monarchy*; Philip Haffenden, *New England in the English Nation, 1689–1713* (Oxford, 1974); Richard C. Simmons, "The Massachusetts Charter of

1691," in *Contrast and Connection: Bicentennial Essays in Anglo-American History*, ed. H. C. Allen and R. Thompson (Athens, Ohio, 1976); Richard R. Johnson, *Adjustment to Empire: The New England Colonies, 1675–1715* (New Brunswick, N.J., 1981).

39. Jack P. Greene, "'A Posture of Hostility:' A Reconsideration of Some Aspects of the Origins of the American Revolution," *Preachers and Politicians: Two Essays on the Origins of the American Revolution* (Worcester, Mass., 1977).

40. For a recent review of the debate and current conclusions see the contributions by F. J. A. Broeze, P. D. McClelland, Gary M. Walton, and D. J. Loschky to the *Economic History Review*, 2d ser., 26 (1973): 668–91.

14

POLITICAL DEVELOPMENT

JOHN M. MURRIN

e now have a rather clear idea of what the nature of early American politics was not," observed Jack P. Greene in his 1966 survey of the relevant historiography, "but we are still not very sure about what exactly it was." Greene described the dominance of the Progressive school in the first half of the twentieth century and emphasized its rapid disintegration after 1950 until it had become "little more than a series of clichés" which are "either totally inapplicable or seriously distorting at every point for which there has been a detailed study." But because numerous monographs in a field of vigorous activity had also left the impression "that the politics of every colony was completely idiosyncratic, that there were as many species of political life as there were political environments," he called for attempts at synthesis and ventured one of his own, based primarily upon a typology of factionalism.[1]

Since 1965 studies have continued to appear, but the pace has slackened in recent years as political history rather suddenly yielded priority to social history in the early 1970s. Nonetheless, enough research now exists to enable us to detect major lines of development in the large colonies of Massachusetts, New York, Pennsylvania, Virginia, North Carolina, South Carolina, and Jamaica, with eighteenth-century Connecticut well covered and work in progress on Rhode Island, New Jersey, and Maryland.[2] Despite the dampening of interest in politics, attempts at a general synthesis have proliferated as never before. Most of the participants for the period before 1763 share Greene's conviction that the Progressives were wrong, but they remain far from agreed among themselves as to just who or what is right. Despite numerous obituaries over Progressive history, it has never quite died and in the wake of Vietnam has shown renewed vitality which is just beginning to appear in the field of colonial politics. In fact, if such a specialty can provide a decent test, the gap between Progressive and Consensus historians may be less relevant now than at any time since 1950.

Some participants at an international conference might be forgiven for wondering why they should care how power was acquired, distributed, and used on the farthest fringe of the Atlantic world two and three centuries ago. In fact, colonial politics have long occupied a strategic position in the larger historiography of the American nation. It may be worth a little trouble to see why.

I

Greene's survey of the historiography to 1965 remains comprehensive and authoritative, thorough enough that any attempt to retrace the same ground may seem about as exciting as a guided tour of one's own backyard. That risk hardly seems worth taking, but a few points do deserve emphasis. First, Greene adopted broad chronological boundaries for colonial politics, ranging even beyond the Revolution and into the Confederation era. Because the present volume investigates what we know about the *colonial* period and has no essay specifically devoted to the Revolution, in this essay I shall try without belaboring the point to remove colonial political development out of the shadow of that later upheaval. Such an effort can produce surprising results. When one asks, for example, what Progressives had to say about strictly *colonial* politics, the answer is almost nothing beyond a systematic contention for a limited electorate.[3] Charles H. Lincoln, Carl Becker, Orin G. Libby, Charles Beard, Arthur M. Schlesinger, Sr., and nearly all of their followers through Merrill Jensen and his Wisconsin doctoral students concentrated their energies so intensely on the Revolution that few of them ventured back before the 1750s, much less as far as the seventeenth century, except in a few textbooks or surveys.[4] These general works assumed that numerous adult males were disfranchised and pointed out that immigration and westward expansion created conflicts of interest between the seaboard and the back country (Frederick Jackson Turner) and that the growth of wealth in the eighteenth century generated tensions between those who had it and those who did not (Beard). But when they tried to explain what was happening in actual politics, Progressives simply borrowed what others made available to them.

Overwhelmingly, these others belonged to the Imperial school, which believed that true history must study major institutions and public law, not vague social forces. Because the source of legitimacy lay in Whitehall and Westminster, these historians insisted on studying early American history from an imperial perspective broad enough to include, for most of them, the West Indies and Nova Scotia. Nearly all the hard data about colonial politics amassed before 1950 derived from the weighty publications of Herbert L. Osgood, George Louis Beer, Charles M. Andrews, and a long generation of graduate students at Columbia and Yale. The Anglophile sentiments of the

northeastern elite explain much of this emphasis, but not all. Beer, of German Jewish ancestry, closed his life trying to undo the Revolution by reunit-
ing Britain and America. Osgood, despite his Yankee Congregational background, quietly sympathized with Germany in World War I, while
Andrews, a Connecticut Episcopalian, hardly idealized the governing elite of
Hanoverian Britain. It "can hardly be said that in 1776 the Englishmen of the
ruling classes," he proclaimed in the last sentence of a famous essay, "were
governed by any ideals that were destined to be of service to the future of the
human race."[5] Yet he shared Osgood's conviction that American patriots
fought under a "false philosophy" whose inevitable triumph it became part of
the school's melancholy duty to chronicle.[6]

Admiration for England juxtaposed with American loyalties, and regional
pride set against a strong distaste for Puritanism, were only two of the
tensions that beset the Imperial approach at its very core. Disgusted with the
rhetorical bombast of George Bancroft's providential nationalism as an organizing principle for American history, Osgood and Andrews banished
providence but kept the nationalism, which they dislodged from the seventeenth century only to provide it with more genial quarters in the eighteenth.
"The seventeenth century shows us an English world in America, with but
little in it that can strictly be called American," Andrews explained; "the
eighteenth everywhere presents to the view an Anglo-American conflict."[7]
At root, early American political history became a process whereby New
England principles of resistance to the English court spread to the other
mainland colonies in some way never described and finally became institutionalized in the triumph of the assembly after 1689. The decline of royal
government, which sometimes seemed well advanced before it had any
chance to rise, became a major theme of Imperial scholarship, closely linked
to the primacy of New England in American national identity.[8]

This formulation had little attraction for loyal Virginians such as Alexander Brown and Thomas Jefferson Wertenbaker, who knew instinctively
that when American political development becomes properly understood,
the Old Dominion will have to dominate the story. Confronted with all those
monographs and with Virginia's embarrassing contentment under royal government during the fifty years after 1720, they had no other way to assert the
colony's priority but to return to the seventeenth century. Two events provided immense consolation: the creation of the Virginia assembly (*before* the
Pilgrims landed) amidst the struggles between the London Company and the
Stuart court, and Bacon's Rebellion in 1676. Both firmly linked Virginians to
the triumph of liberty in England at a time when Massachusetts labored
under a repressive "Puritan oligarchy" that showed more interest in hanging
witches than in defending freedom. Especially for Wertenbaker, a liberty-
loving yeomanry was the natural condition in early Virginia. Outside
forces—specifically, the crown and the London merchant community, in-

cluding the navigation acts—had to intervene to corrupt a nascent democracy into a slaveowning planter aristocracy.[9]

This Virginia alternative to both Imperial and Progressive history had a rather short life, terminated through the efforts of a southerner with a strong distaste for regional apologetics, Wesley Frank Craven. Before 1950 Craven undermined both aspects of what Wertenbaker still actively defended. The struggle over the London Company, Craven showed in 1932, had virtually nothing to do with any emerging contest in England between prerogative and privilege, court and Parliament. And whatever else may have caused it, Bacon's Rebellion was primarily about Indians and had only the most ambiguous overtones of political liberty.[10]

Apart from the Virginians, actual writing about colonial politics fell overwhelmingly to Osgood, Andrews, and their students. Progressives borrowed what they found useful in this array of scholarship to explain the conditions necessary, in their mind, to generate a revolution after 1750 or 1763. Their search for general causes prompted them to reject the extreme Imperial emphasis on public law and formal institutions that compelled Andrews, for instance, to discuss Maryland with Barbados as a proprietary colony rather than with neighboring Virginia as a tobacco society. Progressives liked to detect underlying realities transcending artificial colonial boundaries. Their officeholding coastal elites were closely tied to transatlantic commerce and patronage by the 1750s and ready to resist demands for change from below or from the interior. Wealthy opponents with weaker patronage claims resented this domination and often favored moderate commercial and political reforms, but they too feared popular tumult. Having demonstrated that any successful revolution would have to decide who ruled at home along with home rule, Progressives turned quickly to their main story.

Partly because they never seriously addressed colonial history proper, Progressives also never adequately confronted the central ambiguity implicit in their own work. If Turner's free land really did differentiate America from Europe, did it not also render difficult the emergence of the class tensions essential to Beard? Turner and Beard were aware of their differences; most of their admirers were not. Uninterested in any theory of land and labor that might make slavery part of the answer to this question,[11] Progressives subsumed class and sectionalism under the general heading "economic conflict." Nearly all Progressive historians were westerners who believed their region had had to fight a continuing battle against exploitation by a northeastern elite. The resulting equation seemed almost too obvious to state explicitly: Sectionalism plus Class = Real America. Fittingly, the most resounding response came from another westerner trained in the Progressive bastion of Wisconsin and almost incapable of thinking in any but Progressive terms. Robert E. Brown finally exposed the latent vulnerability of his mentors. He conscripted Turner to demolish Beard. For him, Land minus Class = Democratic America. The Revolution, he insisted, was fought to preserve, not change, the social order. He thus extended to all of colonial America what Wertenbaker had once set apart as the peculiar glory of early Virginia. By demonstrating that most adult white males could vote if they chose, he turned the mainland provinces into "middle-class democracies," and he explained away any contrary tendencies as encroachments by malign outside forces, usually based in the British crown and aristocracy. Brown and his wife Katherine dominated the study of early American politics for several years by forcing numerous counts and recounts of eligible and actual voters, until J. R. Pole suggested a plausible alternative when he lent Americans the English notion of deference in 1962. This concept helped explain why even a broad electorate routinely chose gentlemen for office, and it also shifted attention to broader patterns of Anglo-American political development, a theme that Pole would later extend well beyond the Revolution.[12]

Something larger than Brown separated the Progressives from the younger historians who would soon be called a new Consensus school. That event was World War II, which seemed to demonstrate one overpowering fact: America was a success story. The nation worked—better than Britain, better than all of Europe, better than any other society at any other era in history. Much as the assumed agenda of the Progressives had been to trace evolving patterns of exploitation and the popular response they elicited at each stage of the past, Consensus scholars set about answering the question most of them were too polite to phrase directly, Why had the United States become the greatest and freest nation in the world? Their responses shared an often strident rejection of Progressivism (especially Beard) and usually reflected renewed interest in colonial politics as the seedbed of what flourished later. But taken as a body, their efforts proved even more contradictory and irreconcilable than Turner and Beard.

For the Browns, democracy remained a simple fact of economic, social, and political life in colonial America. Even when settlers praised aristocracy and damned democracy, Katherine insisted, they really meant to idealize the kind of broadly based representative institutions that Massachusetts Bay possessed by 1634 and that the United States has always had.[13] Louis Hartz, Daniel Boorstin, and Bernard Bailyn all found this problem more perplexing than the Browns and ventured different solutions to it.

Of the three, Hartz's position remains the most complex, and with an unwitting assist from his elliptical prose, he has been misunderstood more often than not. Ideologically, he does not belong with any Consensus school dedicated to celebrating American success. Rather, American history became in his hands a potential tragedy, the story of a people imprisoned by ideas that they cannot recognize or examine critically. In brief, the United States has been disabled by its own past from understanding the modern revolutionary world in which it must learn to survive. Hartz explained this process in terms of an American "liberal tradition," quintessentially Lockean and consensual, accepted so completely by the settlers that they did not even know that their emerging "American way of life" represented one distinct hue in Europe's ideological spectrum. Or, as Hartz later rephrased his argument, the United States was a "liberal fragment" of Europe, cut off from dialectical exchange with feudalism, and therefore incapable of evolving into socialism. Obviously the colonial political experience had to play a central role in this larger story, but like the Progressives, Hartz saw no need to investigate it in detail. He too hurried to get on with the real story—that American consensus *is* the tragedy. He merely summarized what he assumed everyone already knew about colonial politics.[14]

Boorstin did celebrate "the American way of life," with a zest that almost illustrated Hartz's main contention. For him America represented the failure and finally the conscious rejection of all European ideologies. New World experiences shaped a pragmatic people whose political spokesmen avoided ideological commitment and specialized in compromise.[15]

As late as 1961 Bailyn's formulation seemed to mediate between Hartz and Boorstin in novel ways. Where earlier historians (such as Perry Miller) had seen an ideologically charged seventeenth century yield to social complexity in the eighteenth, Bailyn reversed the formula. He emphasized seventeenth-century social change and eighteenth-century ideas. Despite their different origins, he argued, New England, New York, and Virginia had all reached a similar stage of social development by about 1700. In each colony a new elite of recent immigrants with excellent transatlantic contacts reshaped the political system in the late seventeenth century while absorbing the salient lessons taught by the New World. Access to fresh lands, for example, undercut primogeniture, entail, and the whole social logic that stressed transmission to the next generation of a consolidated, paternal estate. When Enlightenment ideas reached mid-eighteenth-century America, they were embraced and studied seriously, not because they inspired a radical reshaping of the social landscape, but because they legitimated (often for the first time) a broad set of social and political changes that had already occurred. An initial Boorstinian pragmatism thus led by 1960 to a generation of ideologues more self-conscious about their ruminations than either Boorstin or Hartz could admit. Yet this change was possible only because the social cost of ideology remained uniquely light in America.[16]

Bailyn extended and in some fundamental ways altered his position over the next six years. A sweeping category such as "Enlightenment ideas" no longer seemed very helpful in describing the intellectual armament of the settlers after 1750. Detailed study of their pamphlets, newspapers, and sermons revealed a world view characterized, not by celebration of the status quo, but by persistent fears and tensions. While not specifically anti-Lockean, these attitudes owed little to Locke, deriving instead mostly from second-echelon English opposition writers already studied by Caroline Robbins and still under intensive investigation by J.G.A. Pocock and Isaac Kramnick.[17] By

1967 Bailyn was ready to offer the most thoroughly revisionist interpretation of colonial politics yet undertaken, one that left little room for a simple importation of Enlightenment categories to legitimate and extol the unadorned realities of American public life. More systematically than any earlier attempt, Bailyn's revision derived from a careful comparison of Britain and the colonies, with particular attention to the structure of politics and the role of ideology in each. In brief, he introduced the concept of "political culture" to early Americanists. Its impact has been tremendous. Even Bailyn's critics have had to adopt much of his language.

Bailyn distinguished between the "formal" and "informal" constitutions in Britain and North America. In the home islands, formal prerogatives such as the royal veto and the power to dissolve Parliament fell into disuse in the generation after the Glorious Revolution, but the crown's informal powers, particularly its use of patronage to control Parliament, achieved unprecedented effectiveness. Opposition spokesmen, whether Real Whigs like John Trenchard and Thomas Gordon or Tories like Lord Bolingbroke, drew upon a sophisticated tradition of civic humanism to warn that "corruption" threatened to undermine the delicate balance of Britain's mixed government by king, Lords, and Commons. Within the active political nation, however, these views remained a minority position incapable of undermining the kind of political stability finally achieved under Sir Robert Walpole and the Court Whigs.

The colonies, Bailyn insists, greatly admired Britain's balanced constitution and readily drew analogies between it and their own regimes under governor, council, and assembly. But in America formal prerogatives (veto, dissolution, judicial tenure at royal pleasure, and so on) remained anachronistically powerful, while informal weapons of persuasion and influence continued to be quite weak. Governors could not dominate their assemblies, much less manipulate elections, in the way that Walpole managed Britain. This vacuum between bloated pretensions and diminished reality became filled by a "milling factionalism" that often reduced public life "to an almost unchartable chaos of competing groups" whose leaders everywhere imported British opposition rhetoric to legitimate their resistance to royal demands. What remained a minority position in Britain became a habit of mind in America. As early as the 1730s, Bailyn now insisted, colonial politics had become "latently revolutionary." When the home government tightened its pressures after 1760 and tugged at political wires that were not tied to social realities, these "latent tendencies of American politics moved swiftly to their ultimate fulfillment." Almost imperceptibly, a dread of improbable corruption perilously close to paranoia had thus replaced the legitimation of benign social change as his central theme for late colonial politics.[18]

At the broadest level, anti-Progressives tried to reintrepret the significance of colonial politics for American history at large, but their efforts did not form a coherent whole and at several key points were utterly incompatible by the mid-1960s. Hartz's instinctive Lockeans, whose commitment to liberty and property ran too deep for systematic articulation, could not inhabit a polity built by Boorstin's fiercely anti-ideological pragmatists, content to improvise from their novel experiences in the wilderness. Neither fit well with Bailyn's fearful settlers, who first created a disturbingly unfamiliar social order and then, more than a century after the initial settlements, imported in a body a complex ideology that exaggerated their anxieties while purporting to rationalize their social and political institutions. Bailyn evoked a civilization inhabited by a more intensely ideological people than existed anywhere else in the world at that time, a vision acceptable to neither Hartz nor Boorstin. And almost any reader of *The Origins of American Politics* had to wonder whether Bailyn had provided the prehistory for Richard Hofstadter's "paranoid style" in American politics. Hofstadter investigated a recurring phenomenon on the fringes of American public life. Bailyn had taken the fringe and almost turned it into the center.[19]

II

Each grand synthesis of the American past seems to require an outsized role for colonial politics. How have the specialists met this challenge? Most content themselves with medium-range generalizations about a single colony or historical generation and hesitate to speculate magnificently about its deeper meaning for all of the American past. The cumulative effect has been rather curious. Implicit Hartzian assumptions now seem to thrive only in colonial New England, where apparently the Puritans could not avoid liberty, despite some rather heroic efforts. Covenant did evolve into reverence for contract, deeply affecting even militia organization.[20] Boorstin's world finds support in the Middle Colonies, particularly New York. In that province ethnic pluralism and the pursuit of economic gain produced a politics of interest groups who invoked fashionable ideologies only for momentary convenience while they set about their real task, the creation of the pragmatic political culture of the nineteenth century. Before the 1760s, Bailyn's country ideology now seems characteristic of eighteenth-century Virginia and South Carolina and of particular opposition groups elsewhere. As modified by Greene and Robert M. Weir, it does not function quite the way he posited in any of these societies. The political culture of the seventeenth-century southern colonies has, meanwhile, slipped quietly away from all of these formulations. Finally, colonial Pennsylvania may be emerging as the best example of what Progressives were trying to describe but never demonstrated adequately. Its political history has been studied more thoroughly than that of any other colony, and it does seem to lead to a genuine crisis over who shall rule at home. For that matter, so does New York's.

Perhaps the best way to get at these developments is to proceed chronologically. Implicit in any such attempt is, of course, a meaningful scheme of periodization. This essay suggests a division into three periods, each with flexible boundaries to permit precocious evolution in one colony or lagging change in another. The idea is not to be dogmatic about precise transitions but to organize an enormous quantity of information in a way that helps us to understand it and to recognize some important, basic shifts.

The first period, extending to about 1675 (later in the Quaker colonies), brought forth an astonishing array of political experiments, ranging from Puritan and Quaker utopianism at one extreme through proprietary feudalism and absolutism at the other. In the second era, which ran from 1675 to the 1720s, the British Empire assumed the institutional shape it would hold until the American Revolution, with important ramifications for every participating colony. Simultaneously, Britain's political culture also achieved a high degree of definition within the framework of Whig stability. This development in turn strongly influenced the various patterns of stabilization that began to appear in the colonies between the 1720s and roughly 1760, the decades that constitute the last of our three periods.

Broad generalizations about the significance of colonial politics for the nation's history can draw primarily from any of the three eras. Long ago the first heavily predominated. Scholarly leaps from Virginia's first assembly or the Mayflower Compact to Jefferson's Declaration seemed natural and inevitable. No longer. If anything, the period before 1675 is becoming increasingly depoliticized, or at least set apart from later events. Of major recent synthesizers, only Kenneth Lockridge has placed heavy weight on the politics of the founding years. He posits a continuing tension over legitimacy between transatlantic norms and local communitarianism. This dilemma, he argues, emerged very early, affected each geographical region of the continent, and remained unresolved until after Independence. His emphasis explains a lot about the beginning and end of his story, but it ignores too much in between, particularly during the half-century after 1690, when questions of legitimacy visibly receded even while the gulf between cosmopolitans and localists remained and probably intensified.[21]

No other recent interpretation of colonial politics draws principally on the years of settlement. The second period has fared better. Jack M. Sosin and Stephen Saunders Webb both have begun multivolume works, Alison G. Olson has produced a short synthesis, and Richard R. Johnson a massive study of a single region, all of which see the decades of imperial consolidation as absolutely critical to what would come later. But most attempts at synthesis draw heavily upon the third period or use it for a launching platform into the Revolution. Bailyn, Pole, Greene, Lawrence H. Leder, George Dargo, and Marc Egnal all have published efforts of this kind since 1965. Because the evidence relevant to the Pole and Egnal interpretations lies chiefly in the Revolution itself, their studies fall mostly beyond the scope of this paper.[22] The others will be discussed under the period that seems proper to each.

III

One way to catch a glimpse of the astounding variety of colonial experiments is to glance around the colonial world as of 1675, just before imperial reforms significantly altered the political scene. The chartered corporation resident in England had provided the major impetus for settlement into the 1620s, but half a century later only one example survived, and its days in Bermuda were numbered.[23] One corporation, the Massachusetts Bay Company, had actually crossed the ocean and turned itself into a colony. From the Bay other Puritans with either less or more rigid views of a godly society had created numerous settlements outside the company's patent. This centrifugal tendency had continued into the 1640s, threatening for a time to create a cartographic mosaic almost as perplexing as the map of the Holy Roman Empire. Dissenters from Massachusetts founded four towns around Narragansett Bay that seemed almost as suspicious of one another as they were of the orthodox magistrates from whom they had fled. Only with great difficulty did they finally coalesce into the colony of Rhode Island, whose very survival would remain precarious for the rest of the century.[24] By the 1650s the situation in New England had simplified somewhat. The English towns on both shores of Long Island Sound offered allegiance to Hartford, New Haven, or New Amsterdam, while further inland Springfield and its offshoots accepted rule from Boston after a brief flirtation with Connecticut. Massachusetts also extended its government over the sprawling settlements of northern New England when direct supervision from England collapsed during the interregnum.

As of 1660 only one of New England's five remaining colonies possessed a government whose legitimacy had been sanctioned by royal charter, and the crown was just beginning the long duel with Massachusetts that would lead to the revocation of that patent a generation later. Until then, the structure of English commercial corporations provided the most obvious model for governmental institutions throughout New England, but into these common forms the settlers proved capable of breathing different types of community life. Massachusetts and New Haven confined voting privileges in colony elections to visible saints; the other three did not. Only Massachusetts had a bicameral General Court, except on judicial questions, when the two houses voted together. Throughout the region the General Court retained broad judicial powers, preeminently in Plymouth, where that body probably devoted more time to resolving law suits and routine criminal cases than to passing legislation.[25] By the mid-1660s both Rhode Island and Connecticut had obtained a royal charter, and by the terms of the latter document, New Haven Colony ceased to exist; it was absorbed under Hartford's jurisdiction.

The London Company's venture on Chesapeake Bay had collapsed in bankruptcy after the Opechancanough massacre of 1622, producing by default the royal colony of Virginia. As late as 1675 it remained the only royal province on the mainland under a governor who was only loosely supervised from England and a legislature that became bicameral in the 1640s.[26] Already Virginia had acquired important siblings in the West Indies, where Barbados, the Leeward Islands, and Jamaica had all gone royal after the Restoration.

Beginning in the 1630s, proprietary forms characterized nearly all attempts to plant new colonies from England. By 1675 only Maryland survived intact from the pre-1640 batch, but in roughly the decade before 1675 it was joined by the Bahamas, Carolina, New York, and New Jersey. Bahama would long remain a lonely outpost inhabited mostly by buccaneers. It would not even acquire a permanent assembly until 1729. Carolina and New Jersey, like Maryland, were evolving governments by proprietor, council, and assembly, an arrangement that was strictly bicameral only in Maryland. Since 1670 Carolina had been toying with what was potentially a tricameral legislature, one aspect of the Harringtonian idealism that the proprietors tried to inflict upon unwilling settlers. In the Hudson Valley the duke of York had recently launched a different kind of proprietary regime since the conquest of New Netherland in 1664. For nearly twenty years his governors ruled autocratically, as had the Dutch to 1664. Every one of these proprietary experiments, we should note, loudly proclaimed its religious tolerance, and for a time they all tried to keep their promise.

Ranging from autonomy to autocracy, these colonies represented a sweeping devolution of power in a century noted in Europe for the consolidation of authority. Even though this trend had already started to reverse in the islands and would soon do so on the mainland, after 1675, aspiring settlers had still not exhausted their fondness for novelty. Between 1674 and 1681 the Quakers would invade the Delaware Valley with still another bracing experiment, and for a while in the 1680s they seemed likely to engulf nearly the entire Middle Atlantic region.

In roughly three generations the New World had become a place for practical men to try unsuccessfully to replicate England's basic institutions while making their personal fortunes, for solitary visionaries who wished to resurrect a purified medieval past, for Puritans and Quakers who sought a gateway to the millennium in the forests of America, for a royal heir who could experiment in America with a kind of absolutism that would have been extremely dangerous in England, for Harringtonians armed with the newly discovered laws of history which they intended to convert into a new secular utopia, and even for ordinary seamen and other social outcasts who resented their lowly place in the world and devised buccaneering communities with rules that suggest an intriguing level of discontent with the social order of Europe.[27]

Political activity of such bewildering diversity ought to be a fascinating subject for comparative study, but it has attracted little interest in recent years, perhaps because the weighty volumes of Osgood and Andrews are both daunting and dull. Numerous questions demand analysis that has not been forthcoming. For example, every colonialist knows that something like a general crisis overtook most colonies between 1675 and 1692, but no one has yet pointed out that the 1640s may have been equally critical. New England had to restructure its economy after immigration ceased, consolidate its political and ecclesiastical systems under severe internal pressures, and build a viable system of regional defense amidst the continual Indian alarms that the settlers generated. New Netherland almost disintegrated in the long Indian conflict that followed the Pavonia massacre of 1643. Maryland collapsed politically in the 1640s and may have been reduced to a few hundred settlers at the peak of these troubles. Virginia, largely cut off from English aid, reeled under the second Opechancanough war of 1644–46. Politics remained stormy in the Carribbean, where the legitimacy of every regime was precarious and the sugar revolution was transforming both the economy and the social structure. What common denominators, if any, characterized these separate situations? We shall not know until we ask.[28]

Another question equally transcends colonial boundaries and historiographical categories. Turner—along with most American historians since him, including Hartz, Boorstin, and Bailyn—assumed that America was "born modern," that it never had an old regime to reject. Some recent findings indicate that the settlers conceptualized their world in more complex ways than we care to recognize. In England part of the transition from medieval to modern was the crown's assault on bastard feudalism, which meant disarming most of the population in the interests of public order. The colonies moved in the opposite direction, compelling all freemen to arm. Fear of Indian attack powerfully stimulated this reversal of English norms, but as the Quaker rejection of this alternative suggests, the desire to terrorize Indians into compliant submission may have been just as weighty.[29] Similarly, the crown had created an efficient legal system in England through itinerant justices, who rode circuit throughout the kingdom and brought uniformity to the law. The colonies reverted to stationary local courts of gentlemen amateurs (some of them not very genteel) and occasionally legislated *against* anyone overly trained in the law. In England, Parliament became a modern legislature partly by breaking the medieval ties between MPs and their local constituencies and also by stressing its lawmaking function over its judicial role. But in most colonies, representation reverted to the medieval concept of attorneyship, often enforced by strict residency requirements. And most colonial assemblies highly valued their judicial activities throughout the seventeenth century. To a degree, the settlers merely carried with them the English localist resistance to the emerging demands of a centralizing state. Yet much of the liberation that colonists sought was really an emancipation from some of the most modern aspects of English life. Maybe Lord Baltimore was foolish to imagine a wilderness society built upon the loyalty between lord and man, but he differed from many other colonizers only in the content, not in the fact, of his nostalgia.

Turnerian logic also posits a close correlation between liberty and a favorable ratio of land to labor. That ratio has never been higher than in the seventeenth century, and yet liberty struggled to survive, while in large parts of the New World the settlers laid a foundation for a kind of slavery that did not even exist in England. Before 1675 trial by jury, except for capital offenses, nearly disappeared south of New England. In the land of the saints it thrived in civil cases but was hardly ever used for crime, except when life was at stake.[30]

Nearly every colony did much better in establishing some form of representative government, usually within a decade of the first permanent settlements; but what Michael Kammen pointed out in 1969 remains true today: we understand little of how the colonists conceptualized these activities—what they thought they were doing and why. In most colonies for most of the century, assemblies ratified or sanctioned measures initiated by the council or the executive, but when Carolina and Pennsylvania invoked Harrington to convert this custom into a rigid requirement, the proprietors quickly ran into trouble. The widespread fascination of many colonies for formal legal codes along with other judicial activities may indicate that assemblymen shared a rather static concept of law, one that did not leave much room for continuing legislative initiative. Finally, although nearly every assembly antedated the establishment of royal government in its colony and had acquired a formidable body of customary privileges before the crown took control, these claims often rested on a precarious social base.[31] In Massachusetts and New Haven the requirement that freemen be church members steadily reduced the percentage of adult males eligible to vote.[32] New York's first assembly in 1683 derived from pressures among the English settlers (a minority), and it adopted a sufficiently aggressive policy of Anglicization to leave the Dutch majority more antagonized by this change than reconciled to it.[33] Probably no New World assembly exceeded early Maryland's deliberate imitation of the House of Commons, inspired by the proprietary family's awesome array of prerogatives. Yet complaints appeared rather often against frequent meetings of the assembly and the tax burden they placed on the people. The Calverts, much like contemporary royal governors in Virginia, achieved some success after 1675 by reducing the size of the lower house. On the whole, relations between governor and assembly were fairly cordial in Maryland and Virginia between 1660 and 1675, but particularly in Virginia this harmony at the top masked ugly resentments farther down the social ladder. Consensus in politics does not necessarily reflect harmony in society.

These antagonisms, rather than political narrative as such, have inspired some of the best history written about early America. Historiographers often describe Edmund S. Morgan as a "neo-Whig" or "Consensus" man. He has always rejected the latter label, and there is nothing consensual about his *American Slavery—American Freedom: The Ordeal of Colonial Virginia*. He departs sharply from previous ways of understanding that province's development, all of which were at root political. He tells a depressing story of a turbulent, violent, death-ridden society organized primarily around the need to exploit labor. Freedom enters his narrative as a vision of Elizabethan promoters and a substantial attribute of eighteenth-century planters, but it almost disappears as a discernible element of the seventeenth-century tale. The combination of exploitative landholders with landless ex-servants created a menace to social stability and nearly tore the colony apart in Bacon's Rebellion. In the next generation, great planters met this dilemma by replacing servants with slaves and by showing much greater respect to small planters. Only then could the white population indulge a fondness for freedom that would culminate in Jefferson. Many historians had recounted the rise of slavery as an unfortunate exception to a heritage that is otherwise libertarian. Morgan is the first to ground liberty in slavery, to make bondage a necessary precondition for the rise of a free white Virginia in the eighteenth century.[34]

Until the 1970s, ironically, colonial Maryland, judged by strictly political standards, had always appeared to be more anachronistic, tumultuous, and ungovernable than Virginia. This account still seems fair enough for the period before 1660, when the province barely managed to survive. However, students of Restoration Maryland now find little of the tension between established planters and exploited freedmen that energizes Morgan's Virginia. Indeed, the research of Lois Carr, Russell Menard, and others now seems poised to suggest that in virtually every way that mattered, Maryland had somehow become a more stable polity than Virginia. Reasons for this contrast remain obscure, but the details are hard to refute. Factional rivalries did create bitter antagonisms among the planting elite and threatened to start rebellions in 1676 and 1681. Yet these discontents never did mobilize the freedmen, much less servants, and thus no public disturbance after 1660 approached the destructiveness of Bacon's Rebellion in Virginia. On the other hand, recent studies of the seventeenth-century Caribbean resemble or even magnify Morgan's paradigm for Virginia. They treat sugar, slavery, and exploitation as the really significant elements of the story. Political life has become epiphenomenal.[35]

Thus partly by default, most political history since 1965 of the era of experimentation has concentrated upon New England, particularly Massachusetts. (Connecticut and New Haven, for whatever reason, remain sadly ignored, although one can learn much about their politics from monographs on other subjects.)[36] Timothy H. Breen, in tracing how political thought evolved from godliness to property rights, has produced the only serious study of political theory in seventeenth-century America. Breen has also stressed the relevance of English political issues for decisions taken in Massachusetts during the first generation, and he has demonstrated the pervasiveness of the covenant idea in virtually all new forms of social relations.

He and Stephen Foster have argued that New Englanders created the most stable polities anywhere in the English world of the seventeenth century, and they give Puritanism much of the credit.[37]

This judgment is almost certainly correct. One reason beyond those they cite may well be that only New Englanders satisfactorily resolved the Lockridge problem, which was inherent in the colonial relationship everywhere else. Power, legitimacy, and even basic community aspirations had to meet demands from both sides of the Atlantic. Every proprietary colony experienced acute discord at times because of this situation. Even in Virginia the ruling elite had to satisfy first the London Company and later the crown and London merchants while preserving the loyalty of its settlers. Governor Sir John Harvey could not negotiate this barrier and was thrust from the colony in 1635. When Governor Sir William Berkeley heeded crown desires and built expensive and useless forts to deter Dutch attacks that succeeded anyway, he lost much of his credibility. A similar tension can also be found in the early years of Plymouth Colony until the settlers could pay off their English investors. Massachusetts, Connecticut, and eventually Plymouth vastly simplified their political problems by evading most of these pressures. But autonomy alone cannot explain the region's stability; it also rested upon ethnic homogeneity, intense lay religiosity, and a family pattern of settlement.[38]

Though stable and autonomous, the New England colonies did not escape persistent tensions peculiar to themselves. These have now been well studied for Massachusetts. Much of the solidity of the Bay Colony grew from its ability to institutionalize in satisfactory ways those difficulties that would not disappear. At least three major tensions can be traced as far back as the 1640s, and into the 1680s they usually pitted a majority of magistrates and ministers against a majority of deputies. These issues were relations with England, toleration of religious dissent (primarily Baptists and Quakers), and what became by 1662 the halfway covenant. Magistrates and ministers usually preferred some kind of accommodation to English demands, if only symbolic, while deputies favored resistance. Assistants and clerics advocated persecution in defense of orthodoxy, but deputies showed a real reluctance to harass tender consciences. Magistrates and preachers supported the halfway covenant, which deputies accepted only grudgingly and then refused to implement in their churches.[39]

We still remain ignorant about several aspects of these struggles. First, because of the peculiar nature of Massachusetts politics, the debates that have been investigated all involve divisions among the saints. Both the Robert Child affair and the visit of the royal commission in 1664 provided a rare opportunity for those among the growing band of nonsaints to register their discontent. Most did not, but the documents associated with these incidents deserve more careful study than they have received. Second, we do not know whether the divisions among the saints constituted competing world views.

If forced to choose, did most magistrates and ministers regard nonseparation as a primary value, long after the restored Church of England had banished dissenters into outer darkness? Did their universe threaten to crumble unless it contained a thoroughly orthodox New England capable of perpetuating itself across the generations until on some glorious day it would again be poised to regenerate old England? On the other hand, had ordinary saints opted for de facto separatism, rooted in personal godliness and integrity? Whether anyone in England approved of their actions apparently mattered less to them than the protection of their regenerate churches from corruption by the crown or other manifest sinners, including their own children. They preferred to make allowances to overheated saints, such as Quakers and Baptists, rather than compromise with the world. On a topic of this kind, political, religious, intellectual, and social history could all converge fruitfully with a study of popular culture to produce a striking analysis.

New England's atypical success in the seventeenth century raises a final issue about colonial historiography, for it rested more on the Puritanism that the settlers brought with them than on what they found in the New World. Apparently only religious commitment could forge bonds strong enough to overcome the conflicts of interest present in every society and often out of control in early America. One large exception to this generalization merits brief attention. The biggest asset that North America offered the Puritans was accidental and unexpected: an extraordinarily healthy environment that allowed them to multiply out of all proportion to their original numbers among émigrés from England. Chesapeake settlers probably exceeded Yankees by six or seven to one in the seventeenth century. By 1700 the two regions had roughly equal populations. A demographic lottery played quite unconsciously three centuries ago has had a gigantic impact on all subsequent American history.

How, then, should we summarize this age of experimentation? Boorstin displays no doubts on this subject. "America began as a sobering experience," he proclaimed in 1958. "The colonies were a disproving ground for utopias. . . . A new civilization was being born less out of plans and purposes than out of the unsettlement which the New World brought to the ways of the Old." America meant liberation from the dogmatic systems and antisystems of Europe. In some mysterious way that Boorstin never analyzed rigorously, the American "wilderness"—Turner's frontier in thin disguise—undermined Europe's utopian dreams.[40]

Beyond any question, this process did occur. The utopian elements in early Maryland and Carolina quickly disintegrated. Puritan New England survived by becoming less Puritan and by reinterpreting its past to make the different eighteenth-century reality more acceptable. Pennsylvania's pacifists lost control in the twenty years after 1755, when the province faced first war and then revolution. Very likely the organized benevolence project that became Georgia was always as hopeless as Boorstin claims.

Yet what should we make of these failures? What matters most—the ultimate collapse or the duration of the attempt? For over half a century the
American wilderness allowed some Englishmen to try out in practice those
ideals of religious and social organization that could not take firm root in
England. All of these efforts had political implications, and their great variation in longevity suggests that America served less as an active dissolvent
than as a neutral ground on which they could explore their inherent social
logic, perhaps even their true merit. Nowhere else in the world could pacifists have retained control of an important polity for almost a century. Puritanism disintegrated in America, but it endured much longer than in England.
The real significance of utopias in America is not that they failed, for that
would have happened anywhere, but that they could be tried at all.

IV

West Jersey's radical Concessions and Agreements of 1677 (which may
have been Leveller-inspired)[41] and Pennsylvania's four "frames of government" to 1701 showed that the age of experimentation had not yet exhausted
itself, but from about 1675 (even earlier in the Caribbean) a pattern of imperial consolidation had begun which would overwhelmingly characterize the
next forty or fifty years. Simply put, all colonies had to adjust to the centralizing demands of the emerging English state. At least since Leonard
Labaree, historians have known that the West Indies, not Virginia or any
other part of the mainland, provided the laboratory for royal government in
which commissions and instructions were drafted, modified, standardized,
and rendered capable of application to other colonies as the entire system
expanded.[42] By 1720, after a provincial revolt overturned the Carolina proprietors, royal government had become the manifest norm for English colonies, with the few surviving proprietary and corporate settlements serving as
increasingly odd exceptions.

Much like the American Revolution, the late seventeenth century has its
plausible Whig interpretation. The 1680s have always possessed the great
virtue of bringing events on both sides of the ocean into common focus upon
the classic theme of liberty. Even though much of the scholarship of the past
twenty years has run in the other direction, the Whig approach still has able
defenders. Philip Haffenden, for example, has placed the assault on colonial
charters within the context of the Stuart reaction that followed the Exclusion
crisis. David Lovejoy has explained the Glorious Revolution in America as
an affirmation by the settlers that they would insist upon equal liberty with
subjects of the realm. According to this view, Stuart absolutism at home
found its colonial counterpart in a sustained assault upon colonial assemblies
in the 1680s. The Revolution of 1688–89 resolved the impasse in both England and America.[43]

Both Richard S. Dunn and Wesley Frank Craven have expressed doubts that Charles II ever developed a comprehensive colonial policy. Pennsylvania, for instance, launched its Quaker experiment in 1681–83 under a proprietary charter from Charles, and New York received its first assembly from James, just when the court was entering the final phase of its struggle against the Massachusetts patent. At first the dominion was actually rather popular among some of the bored descendants of the Puritan founding fathers, as Dunn has shown in his fascinating account of the Winthrop dynasty.[44] On one point everyone who studies this era now seems agreed. Following Bailyn's lead, they all emphasize the critical significance of the informal social links that tied together merchants, planters, officeholders, and even clergymen across the Atlantic barrier. These shifting personal alignments affected public life profoundly.

Alison G. Olson and Stephen S. Webb believe that the pattern of Anglo-American interaction created around 1675 not only defined the nature of the first British Empire but also created the preconditions of the American Revolution. They do not agree, however, on what those patterns were or on how to evaluate them. In Olson's estimation, as the expanding English state collided with entrenched colonial autonomy, royal officials suddenly discovered that they could obtain leverage for their policies by stimulating and working through dissident factions in the settlements. In brief, factionalism in America became almost a condition of royal success. But once a particular "party" in a province had identified itself as a court faction, its opponents quickly recognized the advantage of appealing to opposition connections in England. As Whigs and Tories shifted in and out of power between the Exclusion crisis and the Hanoverian succession, competing members of the separate colonial patriciates attached themselves to the interests of particular English politicians and similarly found themselves in and out of favor at Whitehall and Westminster. Because of these relationships, both sides of any major dispute in a colony could obtain a lengthy hearing in London and had a real chance of winning. The emphasis on patience and adroitness reduced the sense of urgency in America, discouraged violence, and in general helped to channel public life in the colonies into a calmer direction after the Glorious Revolution.

Olson makes no effort to connect electoral behavior in the two environments, and she posits a colonial factionalism more systematic than others believe it to be. We now know that voters' impact on English politics in the Augustan Age was greater than at any earlier time and greater than it would be again until the nineteenth century. Whether this dynamic behavior affected the colonists remains all but unstudied. Olson does not even discuss the colonial electorate until the mid-eighteenth century, but she is convinced of one central point: as the Whig triumph of 1714–15 evolved into the long Walpole-Pelham ascendancy, these complex transatlantic connections disintegrated. Opposition groups in Parliament, instead of cultivating colonial leaders, found that they could embarrass the ministry by demanding repressive measures towards America. Discontented settlers turned for support to their constituents, not to England. A naked confrontation between the British state and its overseas possessions had become a real possibility even before 1760. Recently Olson had expressed some second thoughts about the chronology of disintegration. In a fascinating study of the Board of Trade, she argues that it functioned quite usefully as a clearing house for competing interest groups until the early 1760s. With the collapse of this role, no effective buffer remained between imperial and provincial demands.[45]

Webb, in the first of a projected three-volume study, so far has carried the story only to 1681, but he has offered a few glimpses of what shall follow. His chronology of empire strikingly resembles Olson's but with far greater emphasis upon the Caribbean. After a period of royal experimentation in the West Indies, he posits a takeoff for imperial demands following the fall of Lord Shaftesbury in 1674. Colonial (specifically Jamaica's) resistance to royal pressures achieved a compromise in 1681 from which emerged nothing less than the colonial constitution as it would exist until the American Revolution. In greater detail than Olson, Webb recounts the elaborate maneuvers that drew colonial factions into the cauldron of English politics during the Exclusion crisis until his compromise somehow bubbled to the top. The Lords of Trade, he points out, rapidly and successfully imposed the Jamaica settlement upon Virginia. Under aggressive soldier governors, Webb's empire also reached its zenith under Queen Anne, only to fall victim to Walpolean sloth. By attempting to revive the original vision of empire after 1760, George III's ministers would produce the Revolution instead.

This similarity in chronology masks a huge difference in the underlying dynamic at work for Olson and Webb. What preserved the empire for Olson undermined it for Webb. In fact, Webb's book is the most provocatively revisionist interpretation of the British Empire to appear in this century, so sweeping that if it is finally accepted, even the history of the realm will have to be restructured to give greater weight to the army and much less to the county community. Although Webb is very much in the Imperial school's tradition of colonial history (London is the proper vantage point, the West Indies deserve equal treatment with the mainland, formal institutions really do matter), he strongly challenges Andrews's conception of the fundamental nature of the empire. Andrews always stressed the commercial basis of English colonization and imperial government. He even argued that a dramatic shift from commercial gain to the military conquest of territory changed the empire's central character in the 1750s and triggered the American Revolution. Webb, by contrast, describes an empire that was from the start essentially military, even militaristic, along with the English state that it served. From the conquest of Jamaica under Oliver Cromwell until the death of Anne, England's prophets of empire, her true imperial visionaries, spokesmen, architects, and nearly all her colonial governors were soldiers.

They were determined to rule by force when necessary and were quite willing to subordinate English commerce to their central goal. New York's governors, for example, routinely encouraged trade with Amsterdam. Webb associates the idea of a commercial, voluntaristic, and localist empire with Shaftesbury and the emerging colonial patriciates, all of whom had to be subdued to achieve the institutional structure that finally emerged in the 1680s. Like Olson, he emphasizes the importance of transatlantic factional alignments, but he insists that real victory went to the men in arms and that the future of the empire depended upon their continuing success. Maybe at some level colonial planters and merchants do belong in the same camp with Shaftesbury, the drafters of the navigation acts, and the English merchants who specialized in the plantation trade. But at least through the 1680s the most articulate resistance to the navigation acts came precisely from colonial leaders who, in Webb's account, ought to have recognized a commercial empire as the one viable alternative to the military model that threatened their autonomy. Barbados planters, North Carolina settlers, Virginia's Governor Berkeley, Maryland's proprietary leaders (who actually murdered one customs official), New York's wealthy merchants, and the Massachusetts General Court all registered an overwhelming preference for freer trade than Parliament cared to permit.

We badly need for the mainland what Richard Sheridan has given us for the islands, that is, a study of when, how, and why the colonies accepted English commercial regulation as a legitimate demand to be challenged only in detail, not in substance. Perhaps only then can we recognize precisely how trade and politics affected one another in the era of imperial consolidation. Nevertheless, Webb has superbly documented the wide variety of ways in which prior military experience shaped the political expectations of *most* governors before 1720. How far he can push this phenomenon remains to be seen. At the very least, he has already transformed existing concepts of the origins of royal government.[46]

Jack M. Sosin has also published the first book in a multivolume history of the politics of the old empire. Although carefully researched and ably developed, his argument is mostly a composite of points that others have made before. He rejects Webb's emphasis on the central role of the army in English politics and imperial expansion. Like Bailyn, he finds a social basis for empire in the numerous commercial and religious ties that spanned the Atlantic, but he does little to integrate this theme with his broader narrative. Entering an old argument, he denies that the navigation acts embodied a coherent vision of a self-contained, mercantilistic empire. Following Craven and Dunn, he doubts that the later Stuarts ever had a systematic colonial policy, but he does insist that support for religious toleration in England and the colonies provided one of their points of consistency. He has nothing favorable to say about proprietary governments, which he considers chaotic and inefficient, and he regards the imposition of crown rule as a positive step. Yet the only royal alternatives that he discusses, Virginia through Bacon's Rebellion and its aftermath and New Hampshire under Edward Cranfield in the 1680s, both led to fiascos rather more spectacular than any proprietary debacle of the period. Strangely, he ignores the West Indies, the one region that might demonstrate his point for the Restoration era. His most original suggestion involves Massachusetts: Had the "commonwealth party" there been willing to make the most minimal concessions to royal demands around 1664, its fate would have been no more horrifying than the Connecticut charter of 1662, or something quite like it. But English regimes had changed with such bewildering rapidity since 1640 that Bay leaders expected, or prayed, that the Restoration would prove equally transitory. Instead the colony's resistance brought the Dominion of New England upon itself. For Sosin, as for Craven and Dunn, the particular autocratic form that the dominion assumed reflected only a series of ad hoc political decisions, not a grim determination to impose absolutism everywhere in English America.[47]

New York ought to be a critical piece in the puzzle of empire, if only because James II while duke of York had been lord proprietor of that colony from 1664 to 1685. In a fine book, Robert C. Ritchie has dissected the political life of Restoration New York. He notes the lack of firm provincial loyalties among a highly disparate population (Dutch, Yankee, English immigrant), the predatory habits of the colony's military governors after Richard Nicolls (1664–68), whom alone he admires, and the contempt of the ruling clique for the navigation acts. Like all previous New York historians, he believes that the assembly of 1683 provided a real opportunity to solve the colony's difficulties, until James abolished it after his accession to the throne. On dubious grounds, he even credits the assembly with reviving a faltering economy.

For our purposes, New York's significance lies in its intercolonial context. Webb correctly stresses the centrality of Jamaica, and then Virginia, in forcing a colonial policy upon Charles II. But most of James's experience with colonial rule came through New York. Beyond all reasonable doubt, that colony provided a working (or poorly working) model for the Dominion of New England, a point Massachusetts historians have missed because they seldom bother to study New York. Even though the duke's experiment in proprietary absolutism fell apart in the New York City tax revolt of 1681 and its aftermath, James and his one-time governor of New York Sir Edmund Andros did not forget what they had tried there. Every major component of the dominion had been regular policy in New York: reliance on a military garrison, government without an assembly, restriction of the power of town meetings, reorganization of the land system to emphasize quitrents, religious toleration, and even the insistence that the major church in the capital share its physical facilities with intruding Anglicans. If Ritchie and Webb are correct, Andros took the navigation acts more seriously in Boston than he ever had in New York, but if Sosin proves right on this point, the two situations are again fully comparable. Interestingly, James extended the dominion to include almost exactly the same area covered by his first venture into colonial activity—the royal commission of 1664 that had conquered New Netherland before trying without success to reform New England.[48]

In other words, no *fixed* colonial constitution had yet emerged by the 1680s, despite royal decisions on Jamaica and Virginia. James probably did have distinct ideas about the proper organization of colonial government, notions that he put into practice whenever he had a free hand. Whether he seriously intended to extend the dominion beyond the northern colonies remains dubious and probably unknowable. But the possibility was there. Had the dominion survived, it would have given the Lords of Trade two model constitutions to choose between: Jamaica's and New York's. It failed, not because of colonial initiative, but because William of Orange drove James from the throne. Only with the collapse of the dominion was the crown reduced to the Jamaica example as its one viable option for royal government. The dominion's fall also illustrated something else as its component societies reasserted themselves amidst the wreckage. England, not the settlers, had tried to unite America, or at least northern America. By 1690 the settlers had demonstrated their strong preference for autonomy—that is, division.

The Glorious Revolution gave English liberty a legitimacy in America it had never had before. Under the old charter, Massachusetts had shown more concern for the protection of the saints than for the rights of Englishmen. In its continuing bid for popular support, the intercharter government expanded freemanship but had to turn to London for legitimacy. The charter of 1691 shattered the old link between church membership and suffrage and also imposed toleration for Protestants upon the colony. The final compromise, for whatever reason, closely resembled the demands of the royal commission of 1664. It gave Massachusetts a royal governor and permitted both the royal disallowance and judicial appeals to the Privy Council. The governor appointed militia officers and, with the council's consent, all justices. On the other hand, town government remained intact, annual assemblies were guaranteed, the council again became elective (by the legislature, not the freemen), and the General Court retained control over the disposal of land—a crown prerogative in other royal colonies. In effect, William III accepted as given, or hopelessly irremediable, much of the previous history of the region.

No one has done a more impressive job of analyzing the accompanying changes in New England political culture than Richard R. Johnson, whose marvelously nuanced insights illuminate every stage of the region's painful adjustment to empire between King Philip's War and the Treaty of Utrecht. By comparing royal and nonroyal colonies in the area, he can isolate the impact of crown control upon the expanding concern for English liberty. He uses military campaigns to trace New England's emergence from self-imposed isolation into a symbiotic relationship with the English state, despite persisting suspicions and uneasiness on both sides. He charts the progress of a "tory" faction in building effective barriers to prerogative in Massachusetts when it encountered a governor it could not control. Above all, he stresses the permanency and importance of the revolution settlement once "Rome's procurator ruled in Israel." As in England, "the improvised and, in part, wholly fortuitous arrangements patched together in the years immediately following William's succession ultimately attained authority and even sanctity less out of any widespread conviction that they deserved to be definitive than by virtue of their capacity to survive all attempts at alteration." And survival meant an expansion of function. Paradoxically, he claims, the effort "to circumscribe government was also to stimulate its institutional growth through codification and definition. Limiting the business of government became part of the business of government." Johnson realizes that authority became hesitant and uncertain throughout New England in the 1690s only to revive in the next decade, but he may underrate the extent of the collapse. A massive generational shift in leadership challenged the old order more than he concedes, even though he does point out that only three assembly leaders out of more than sixty in the quarter-century after 1692 had served as deputies under the first charter. Stephen Innes carries the argument further. In a compelling local study of the Springfield area, he shows that internal pressures and discontents very nearly disintegrated the western Massachusetts militia in the 1690s, however urgent the wartime need for defense. John Pynchon sustained his once unchallenged ascendancy only through frequent, exasperated appeals to Boston.[49]

Jacob Leisler's overwhelmingly Dutch revolt against the dominion overturned a New York elite that had brought English liberties to the colony in 1683 and then retained office after James II revoked these gains. When the dislodged patriciate angrily returned to the province in 1691 and reenacted their Charter of Liberties of 1683 at almost the exact moment that they sanctioned the execution of Leisler and Jacob Milborne, English rights seemed destined to remain polarized against the common interests and aspirations of the Dutch majority. Instead, working first through The Hague, the Leislerians established effective contacts with English Whigs, secured the backing of one royal governor at the end of the decade, and began to learn how to use English liberty as a weapon against its anti-Leislerian advocates. After a brief return to power, they lost in a series of ferocious electoral and administrative struggles. Yet in all probability, these contests gave the structure of the regime and the territorial boundaries of the province a legitimacy neither had possessed before, even if the hold of any one group upon high office remained tenuous. New York politics would be highly volatile for a quarter-century after 1689. Perhaps the biggest winner was the royal governor, who, by pitting one faction against another, converted his position into what was probably the most lucrative office in British North America. Even this trend could not become clear until Robert Hunter managed to overcome the discredit that the greedy and inept Lord Cornbury had inflicted upon the governorship.[50]

Maryland emerged from its upheaval of 1680 with its basic social and political institutions intact, Catholics barred from office, the Church of England established by law—all of this achieved with a minimum of violence. Whatever tensions may have existed between servants or freedmen and established planters, none of them reached the political surface in 1689. The colony experienced nothing like the turmoil of Bacon's Rebellion, and it became a royal province until the next generation of Calverts converted to Canterbury and got their colony back as a reward in 1716.[51]

Virginia narrowly escaped revolt in 1689 when its Catholic governor conveniently departed, permitting the orderly proclamation of William and Mary. Beset by memories of 1676, the plundering by Berkeley's men in the years that followed, the tobacco-cutting riots of 1682, and the Burgesses' capitulation to royal governors in the 1680s, the colony's planter elite was beginning to acquire a new appreciation for the protective value of English liberties. They also learned that their own political position would remain precarious unless a firmer basis for confidence between small and large planters could be created. This took time, of course, and slavery provided part of the answer. Meanwhile the continuing struggle between governor and council underscored the urgency of the need, especially when Sir Francis Nicholson displayed an alarming capacity to rally small planters and ordinary clergymen against their social superiors. When the council acquired executive control in 1706, it ruled without an assembly for five years. Virginia's political contests would continue for another decade before the colony discovered its ideal balanced constitution in materials already at hand.[52]

Ironically, the articulation of liberty in late-seventeenth-century America owed less to the inherent convictions of the settlers before 1689 than to the continuing dialectical exchange between crown and colony, forcing each into proven patterns of institutional legitimacy. Without the permanent presence of royal or proprietary authority, few settlers would have discovered that they had always been destined to be free. This achievement took hold, not when land was most abundant, but during a generation of almost constant war with the French and the Indians. This weary struggle compressed the frontiers, frustrated attempts at expansion, and jeopardized existing trading patterns, but it also compelled London and the colonies to find satisfactory ways of accommodating one another. American liberty acquired firm roots only when the settlements were old enough to project a newly awakened sense of their Anglo-colonial past into viable institutional patterns for the future.

If the Glorious Revolution overturned the dominion and the Maryland proprietary and offered new opportunities for the institutional elaboration of traditional liberties, war with France created the eighteenth-century English state (army, patronage, national debt, Bank of England), the neo-Harringtonian political culture that went with it, and new imperial needs. Interestingly, the Navigation Act of 1696 did not significantly modify the commercial goals of its predecessors, and the new Board of Trade at its most ambitious thought of nothing more alarming than extending the Jamaica model of royal government to all corporate and proprietary colonies. Transatlantic politics proved too much for the board, and after only five or six years of reformist activity it settled into the comfortable administration of routine chores.[53]

Within a few years on either side of 1700 virtually every institutional feature that we associate with the eighteenth-century British Empire had taken shape. How particular colonies would behave within this system remains to be seen.

V

Recent students of the eighteenth-century empire have found little flattering to say about imperial administration after 1715 or 1720. For different reasons, Webb and Olson detect patterns of disastrous decay in these decades, undermining for Webb the soldierly basis of royal power and for Olson the informal transatlantic network that had forced restraint upon crown and Parliament. On somewhat different grounds, James Henretta strongly concurs. He stresses the petty-mindedness, ineptitude, and sheer incompetence of the duke of Newcastle's long colonial administration. So bleak a picture do these scholars draw that we almost wonder why revolution was averted until after 1763.[54]

Yet if we examine the situation from a North American perspective, a curious irony emerges. By almost any measurable standard we try to impose, imperial rule was more effective by mid-century than ever before. Compliance with the basic navigation acts had been minimal in the seventeenth century, but by the eighteenth century colonial trade sailed on British vessels, colonial staples went to England or Scotland, and most European and Asian imports reached America through England. Similarly, if one cared to trace the pattern of intercolonial cooperation in each war from the Anglo-Dutch conflict of 1652 to the fall of Canada in 1760, the pattern would undoubtedly show a marked increase over time in colonial response to imperial war needs, culminating in mass mobilization in most colonies by the late 1750s. Finally, a comparable catalog of strong or successful royal governors, colony by colony, would find them concentrated quite disproportionately in this period—Henry Grenville and Charles Pinfold in Barbados, Edward Trelawny in Jamaica, Henry Ellis in Georgia, James Glen and William Henry Lyttelton in South Carolina, William Tryon in North Carolina, Sir William Gooch and Francis Fauquier in Virginia, Sir Francis Bernard and William Franklin in New Jersey, William Shirley and Thomas Pownall in

Massachusetts, and Benning Wentworth in New Hampshire. Of the mainland governors, only New York's Robert Hunter (1710–19) and, for much of his administration, Virginia's Alexander Spotswood (1710–22) seem to provide huge exceptions to this chronological pattern. Pre-1720 governors may have had the advantage of a lucid military vision, and colonial politicians did possess better contacts in London before 1720 than after. Maybe that was the problem: the second asset tended to check the first.

If Queen Anne's reign really did herald the zenith of the old empire, a lot of governors could not detect this trend amidst the political turmoil in which they found themselves mired. Joseph Dudley quarreled fiercely with the Massachusetts assembly from 1701 to 1704 and from 1707 to 1708, and he let New Hampshire affairs mostly drift before he settled into a more effective pattern. Cornbury alienated New York and New Jersey so completely that Hunter could not put the pieces together again before 1715. Virginia councillors drove Nicholson back to England in 1705 and ruled the colony for five years with neither governor nor assembly. Antigua planters brutally assassinated the irascible Daniel Parke, a hero of Blenheim, in 1710.[55] Between the Glorious Revolution and the Stamp Act no other period saw so many governors simultaneously in political trouble except possibly the years 1748–54, when contemporaneous struggles in New Hampshire, New York, New Jersey, Virginia, North Carolina, Bermuda, and Jamaica alarmed the Board of Trade and started it on the reformist path that would lead finally to the Grenville program, despite strong recovery almost everywhere in the later 1750s.[56] More typical of the era from 1720 to 1760 was intermittent conflict, intense somewhere at almost any given time but never coalescing into an intercolonial pattern. Massachusetts and South Carolina exploded in the 1720s but quieted down before the John Peter Zenger affair disrupted New York in the mid-1730s. New York calmed again before the land bank embroiled Massachusetts in 1740–41, and Massachusetts relaxed once more before the governors of New York and North Carolina lost control of their provinces later in the decade.[57]

The most important new variables were the political transformations occurring within Britain and the colonies after about 1720. Quite suddenly under Walpole, J. H. Plumb has argued, England achieved political stability, which Plumb defines as "the acceptance by society of its political institutions, and of the classes of men or officials who control them."[58] To restate the matter in a slightly different way, the English state that had arisen in response to war learned under Walpole how to perpetuate its techniques of political control in peacetime. Plumb underscores two elements of the system: ministerial use of patronage to dominate the Commons; and neutralization of the electorate through the Septennial Act, gentlemanly understandings to prevent contests whenever possible, and the invocation of legal technicalities to reduce the number of voters when disputes did occur. Yet, as others have shown, stability fell far short of political omnipotence. Fear of

the voters imposed real restraints upon government. Walpole could not reform the customs service in 1733 in the face of a public uproar against his
excise, nor could he avoid a popular Spanish war that he personally opposed
in 1739 nor avert his own downfall in its wake. Henry Pelham could not even
naturalize Jews, and George Grenville's cider tax produced a fiasco. Here the
need for balanced analysis seems obvious. Stability was quite real if only
because the Walpolean system endured without fundamental change for over
a century, and under it Britain reached her peak in global power despite the
loss of America. But that stability always had limits. A prudent scholar
ought to discover what they were. For example, the government rarely won
active support in large, open constituencies.[59]

Plumb confines his stability to England and perhaps the Lowlands of
Scotland, specifically excluding the Highlands, Ireland, and the American
colonies. Although Bailyn had already formed his own views when Plumb's
book appeared, he obviously accepts the same contrast. To the extent that
America could not replicate England, it remained unstable. "The similarities
in government were superficial; the differences in politics profound." Had
colonial governors possessed something like Walpole's patronage, they could
have disciplined opposition groups and secured their own power. Lacking
these advantages, colonial politics became the playground for "milling factionalism" and country ideology.[60]

Bailyn was only one of several historians searching for common denominators in colonial politics during the late 1960s and early 1970s. Writing at
almost the same time as Bailyn and thus uninfluenced by him or Plumb,
Lawrence H. Leder found the structure of the empire (rather than particular
colonies) flawed and brittle, the settlers varied and often inconsistent in their
perception of their rights, and most colonists rather vague about all liberties
except trial by jury and no taxation without representation. Concentrating on
the decades from 1720 to 1760, he emphasizes the growing importance of the
press (which some other scholars have found dull, conventional, and even
rather cautious about intruding into politics), the emancipation of political
debate from religious preconceptions that had inhibited discussion of the
origins and nature of power, and the de facto legitimation of religious pluralism. Leder's world does not contradict Bailyn's, but it is more varied, less
certain about its convictions, and far less inevitable in its momentum or
direction of movement. A few years later George Dargo accepted much of
Bailyn's description, but, a bit perversely, he has managed to convert it into a
kind of proto-modern form of stability. Already, he argues, the colonies had
anticipated much—perhaps most—of the political and constitutional stability
of the United States in the nineteenth century.[61]

The most thorough challenge to Bailyn has come from Jack P. Greene and
his students. Denying that country ideology had anything like a uniform
impact on the colonies before the 1760s, Greene in 1969 extended a theme he
had developed before, the tendency of colonial assemblies to imitate the

House of Commons. In that process, he believes, the colonists absorbed an older language of English political expression. It was essentially legalistic, pitting royal prerogative against parliamentary privilege, with elaborate emphasis upon precedent. Country ideology, by contrast, dichotomized power and liberty within a balanced constitution, isolated corruption as the dynamic threat to that balance, and projected this struggle throughout recorded history in a way that left the British world a solitary and therefore terribly vulnerable oasis of freedom. Bailyn simply assumes that his country tracts and essays spoke for a majority of the assembly and thus help to measure a governor's weakness. Greene contends that when assembly majorities did resist governors, they used their strongest weapon, which was precedent, not country ideology. Conversely, manifestations of country ideology as an opposition weapon (it could assume other forms, as we shall see) occurred when a faction could not win the assembly to its side. In other words, these explosions reflected a governor's strength rather than his weakness and to that degree cannot provide a useful way of distinguishing Britain from colonial America. One caveat applies equally to Bailyn and Greene: neither formulation helps us much to understand developments in Connecticut and Rhode Island, where elective governors with limited patronage undermined the local relevance of both forms of expression. The two colonies managed to join the Revolution anyway.[62]

As we have seen, Greene had already argued that colonial factionalism was not "chaos," that it was far from universal, and that it could be typed. Over the past decade he has elaborated this analysis into a claim that most colonies by the middle decades of the eighteenth century had achieved maturity, or a real form of political stability. His own account of Virginia stresses the disappearance of both factionalism and confrontation between governor and Burgesses after the pivotal administration of Alexander Spotswood (1710–22). Taking their place was a highly ritualized politics of harmony in which governor and assembly showed extraordinary respect for one another and learned to cooperate willingly to obtain necessary legislation. Robert M. Weir, a Greene student, has found a similar pattern taking hold in South Carolina during the 1730s, and he observes that country ideology, far from reflecting unresolvable political tensions, became a common denominator of public life, a way of *describing* the new stability. Georgia fell into the same mold almost from the moment that royal government was established there in the mid-1750s.[63] No one has yet extended this model to North Carolina or Maryland, and probably no one should try. Factionalism and executive-legislative discord occurred too frequently in both. In fact, North Carolina carried down to Independence much the same constellation of problems that had baffled Virginians in the previous century—an immigrant elite without strong affective ties to the rest of the community; a huge and continuous influx of new settlers without deep loyalties to local or provincial institutions; and a remarkably underdeveloped sense of the public good among leading politicians.[64] A new element, severe sectional antagonisms among tobacco, rice, and back-country areas, vastly complicated public life.

While the system described by Greene and Weir did characterize most of the southern mainland provinces, it apparently did not extend to the West Indies, if Jamaica is an adequate guide. Conflicts between governor and assembly remained frequent and often ill-tempered, factional alignments arose around the competing claims of Spanish Town and Kingston, and even when a group (the Jamaica Association) emerged that advocated something quite like the politics of harmony, it failed. Throughout the Caribbean, assemblies scored striking gains at the expense of governors, only to fall before Parliament in the next century. If a moral is needed, the West Indian experience may suggest not only that the rise of the assembly cannot be an adequate explanation for the Revolution but that without a revolution to confirm it, even that rise could become an eventual victim to the demands of the centralizing state.[65]

Where the system did take hold, the politics of harmony involved government by persuasion, not through placemen and patronage, and it worked. Its spokesmen believed that their colonies really had achieved the ideals enunciated by English opposition writers, that their constitutions were stable, and that their political practices were fully compatible with loyalty to crown and empire. Indeed one might carry this argument another step. Contrary to Bailyn's expectations, Walpolean tactics were actually dysfunctional in this environment, as Spotswood learned in Virginia when the voters massacred his placemen in the election of 1715. John Seymour had met the same fate in Maryland in the previous decade, but the restored Calverts rejected the lesson and retained a high level of political tension through their ceaseless but unsuccessful efforts to dominate the assembly through patronage.[66]

Quite a different kind of stability emerged in New Hampshire and Massachusetts in the 1740s and 1750s after seemingly unpromising beginnings. As in Augustan England, the most important catalyst was war. Defense needs armed governors with unusual moral authority and also provided the kind of patronage with which to build an effective court party in the assembly. Especially in Massachusetts, occasional outbursts of country rhetoric reflected the frustration of opposition groups unable to dismantle Governor William Shirley's legislative coalition. Boston's James Allen (a mentor of Samuel Adams) fought specie resumption in 1748 and was expelled from the House of Representatives for his pains. Nor could a barrage of country tracts (all emanating from Boston, much as English country expression centered in London) prevent enactment of an unpopular excise in 1754.[67]

As in the case of Britain, however, we cannot posit a stability in America without investigating its limits. Interestingly, the southern country constitutions appeared in decades of peace and were best adapted to this environment. To be sure, South Carolina and Virginia both passed through the Seven Years' War without great political turmoil. Virginia mobilized more effectively than at any time since 1644–46, and South Carolina assumed a heavy tax burden, but neither had to sustain an effort proportional to that of the northern colonies. South Carolina failed dismally at raising men rather than money and survived the Cherokee War of the early 1760s as well as it did only with massive British support. By contrast, the New England colonies fought virtually the whole of the Seven Years' War outside the boundaries of their region. They sent aid to beleaguered neighbors in Nova Scotia, New York, and the Caribbean. They thus became, certainly in their own conception and to a considerable degree in hard reality as well, junior partners in empire, not utterly dependent provinces in desperate need of defensive assistance.[68]

Could a stability that arose in war make the difficult transition to peace? Massachusetts had experienced this problem once before, in the decade after the Treaty of Utrecht, when, as William Pencak shows, Dudley's effective wartime rule had collapsed into ferocious factionalism by the 1720s. We know that after 1760 royal government would again break down in Massachusetts. Whether wiser British policies might have perpetuated Shirley's system remains one of those intriguing and important counterfactual questions that can never be resolved with certainty. Two points are worth making, however. First, much of the apparatus of Shirley's success had already appeared by the mid-1730s under Jonathan Belcher, permitting Shirley to achieve some spectacular political reforms (peaceful liquidation of the land bank, reduction of the currency supply, protection for the king's woods, jury reform) *before* the outbreak of war with France. Shirley's coalition also held together against vehement opposition from 1748 to 1754 and even abolished paper money, a hugely unpopular measure carried out at a time when other royal regimes faced something close to political paralysis. Thus royal domination did possess an independent base in Massachusetts society, despite articulate opposition to Shirley's goals. Second, Walpole had survived the Bubble and Excise crises far better than royal government weathered the 1760s in Massachusetts. The regime did have a significant social base, but it was much more vulnerable than Walpole's to electoral pressures, which it could continue to ignore only at the price of its own legitimacy. In this sense, it was also less stable, or its stability was always conditional, dependent upon an identity of interest between crown and colony that fell apart after 1765.[69]

New York and Pennsylvania offer fascinating variations on these themes. Specialists in New York politics emphasize the colony's endemic factionalism, the importance of powerful English connections for both governor and opposition, and the shallowness of ideological commitment before the 1760s. Lewis Morris, for example, could emerge as a court manipulator after 1710, introduce country ideology to the province during his opposition phase of the 1730s, and revert to an extreme prerogative type after he became royal governor of New Jersey in 1738, scorning with majestic disdain many of the reform demands he had recently insisted upon in New York. The larger province did its best to remain neutral during Queen Anne's War, against the wishes of its governors. When Governor George Clinton tried to force a recalcitrant New York assembly to support aggressive imperial expansion in the 1740s, he utterly lost control—along with many of his prerogatives—while enduring one humiliation after another. Until 1754, it seems, war destabilized New York politics mostly because it threatened the profitable Albany-Montreal trade. Peacetime governors, even some incredibly greedy ones, usually did retain ascendancy over the assembly. Only in the 1750s, when opposition leader James Delancey happened to become acting governor, did New York's executive prove capable of leading the province in an effective war effort. Any system that behaved this fitfully cannot be called stable without showing undue contempt for the lamentations of royal officials who did have to govern, however clumsy and corrupt some of their efforts may have been.[70]

Recently Alan Tully, backed by Greene, has advanced an argument of elegant clarity for political stability in mid-eighteenth-century Pennsylvania. Conceding that early Pennsylvania politics were as factional, uproarious, and antiauthoritarian as Gary Nash has brilliantly portrayed them, Tully insists that the situation had changed by the late 1720s. Quakers finally wearied of their internal quarrels and pulled together to form a coherent "party" that would dominate the assembly until Independence. A proprietary "faction" did exist, but it had no significant electoral support and oscillated between cooperation with the Quakers and impotent antagonism towards them. Thus the Quaker party controlled public life, provided the kind of government that nearly all settlers desired, and proved highly responsive to the demands of constituents. Just over half of the legislation passed by the assembly responded directly to petitions from voters. Unfortunately, Tully leaves off his account on the eve of the Seven Years' War, just as his generalizations encountered their most critical test prior to the Revolution itself.[71]

Tully's Pennsylvania does not meet Plumb's definition of stability, the acceptance by society of its existing political institutions and rulers. Only if we omit the entire executive branch of government from this equation can we apply it successfully to Pennsylvania, whose political institutions were surely bizarre by any other than Quaker standards. The most anticlerical group to come to the colonies, the Quakers denied that they had a ministry and thus felt free in the early years to fill high offices with "public friends," their unordained preachers. Even when this custom ceased, the Yearly Meeting routinely chose the Quaker party's annual slate of candidates for the assembly, and by mid-century these men usually were elected without opposition. Only in Pennsylvania could the separation of church and state become virtually indistinguishable from the union of sect and state. Similarly, the Charter of Privileges of 1701 seemingly abolished bicameralism but also inaugurated a decade of paralyzing political stalemate. Then in 1710 the wealthy merchants of the governor's advisory council finally broke the deadlock by running for assembly seats and winning. In this remarkable contest every single incumbent was replaced. Only in Pennsylvania could an abolished upper house reappear *within* the lower. The colony was also a pacifist bastion, lacking any legally sanctioned militia until the 1750s. When French invasion seemed possible in 1747, Benjamin Franklin organized a "volunteer" militia, thereby giving the colony an armed force potentially under private rather than public control. Only in Pennsylvania did opposition to war threaten to revive a kind of feudal anarchy, as worried proprietary spokesmen specifically pointed out. This danger never materialized, but Franklin did use his volunteers to intimidate a governor on at least one occasion early in the next war. Finally, the Pennsylvania assembly claimed and exercised greater privileges than any other legislative body in the empire—so great that it avoided comparisons with the House of Commons because any such exercise would *reduce* its powers. When country ideology made a conspicuous appearance in Pennsylvania, Provost William Smith used it to defend the executive (and balanced government) *against* the assembly, whose extreme claims had, he insisted, corrupted a mixed constitution.

Yet when we ask how the assembly used its extraordinary array of powers, we are somewhat startled to learn that it seldom did anything with them. The Quaker legislature was the least active in America. For half a century after 1701 it passed no statutes whatever in about one year out of three. England's Addled Parliament of 1614, ridiculed for its failure to enact any laws or taxes, almost threatened to become a standard for emulation in Pennsylvania. During Tully's generation of stability (1726–54) the province averaged under four laws per year—slightly fewer than tiny and disorganized Delaware in the same period, not many as small New Hampshire and New Jersey produced even in times of turmoil, perhaps a third of South Carolina's average, a fifth of New York's or Virginia's, and a sixth of Massachusetts's. Tully's claim for exceptional responsiveness to constituents translates into not quite two acts per year, which was exceeded several times over in other colonies where the phenomenon has been studied. A more plausible reading of these data is that compared with the case in other colonies, Pennsylvania constituents expected less from their legislature and got it. Robert S. Hohwald has described this paradoxical behavior as "passive sovereignty." The assembly showed far less interest in governing Pennsylvania than in preventing anyone else from organizing the colony in a manner inimical to pacifists.[72]

If such a system represented stability, it marked a peculiarly brittle variety. Beginning in 1754–55 Pennsylvania confronted a series of simultaneous crises severe enough, not just to test its political system, but to threaten the colony's very survival. Lord Baltimore still claimed a northern boundary that, if allowed, would include Philadelphia. Virginia dispatched George Washington (and a year later Edward Braddock's regulars) to secure her own title to the forks of the Ohio (modern Pittsburgh). Connecticut used the

Albany Congress of 1754 to purchase the Susquehanna Valley in north-eastern Pennsylvania, and finally in 1755 the Delaware Indians brought war to Pennsylvania's settled frontier for the first time in the colony's history. Government by the old rules threatened nothing less than disintegration of the province by 1755.

Pennsylvania had to change or die. It is a tribute to much of Tully's analysis to note that the province changed as little as possible while meeting unavoidable emergencies. Despite bitter antagonism towards the proprietary, Benjamin Franklin took command of a reorganized and somewhat secularized Quaker party willing to wage defensive wars. The assembly sponsored heavy military expenditures that also involved another novelty, a hefty tax burden. Not incidently, these actions also secured the colony's claims to its prewar borders. Nonetheless, the Quaker paradigm had great staying power and reasserted itself to a surprising degree after Pontiac's War. The militia expired, per capita taxes eventually fell, and while the legislature never quite returned to its earlier torpor, the volume of its business lagged well behind that of other large colonies. After 1770 the Quaker party even began to cooperate openly with its proprietary rivals as both faced new political enemies within the province. It took a genuine revolution to sweep aside Quaker rule. That event lies beyond the scope of this essay, but it is worth observing that Richard Ryerson, a Greene student, has gone a long way towards resurrecting Progressive categories in his fascinating effort to explain how that happened.[73]

The concept of political stability has acquired considerable explanatory power for Anglo-America, but we should not exaggerate what it can accomplish. It enables us to distinguish many of the dynamic elements of political change in diverse societies and to compare their impact in a variety of situations, but it does not—and probably cannot—account for an event as massive as the American Revolution, which often became a direct challenge to that stability. That upheaval swept across the effective "court" constitutions of New Hampshire and Massachusetts, through their less successful cousins in New York and New Jersey, into the troubled polities of Pennsylvania and Maryland, over the flourishing "country" regimes of Virginia, South Carolina, and Georgia, and into their failed imitator in North Carolina. Adding Rhode Island, Connecticut, and Delaware to the list, one finds that by 1760 colonial governments spanned nearly the whole spectrum of political possibilities for the English-speaking world of that age. Yet all thirteen provinces overcame their differences long enough to embrace a common revolution. "Stability" can tell us important things about colonial politics, but as an encompassing explanation for revolution, it evaporates into a metaphor without power. Like "social maturity," it begs precisely the questions it ought to resolve and fails to sort out what must be differentiated.

Nor has "political stability" yet told us much about the relationship between those who participated actively in government and the rest of society, although here it has greater potential. What expectations did ordinary settlers have about public life? What did they ask from government, and what did they get? Whom did they blame when things went badly? What happened when fissures opened between the few and the many, or within the few, or among the many?

VI

So far the analysis in this essay has proceeded very much at a macro-level. To get beneath the surface of public events in all of these colonies between 1607 and 1760 is hardly possible in an essay of this scope, but a few generalizations do seem to emerge from the literature.

Although seventeenth-century government was on the whole more authoritarian than eighteenth-century rule, it was also weaker. Outside New England, regimes toppled easily if their legitimacy fell into doubt, as Maryland and East Jersey learned several times and even Massachusetts eventually discovered. Peter Stuyvesant may have been an autocrat, but he could not persuade the residents of New Amsterdam to resist English attack in 1664, nor did an English governor fare any better when the Dutch returned in 1673. Colonists, on the other hand, observed interesting boundaries to their animosities. Bacon's Rebellion was a major upheaval, but for all the posturing with muskets at "sieges" and "battles," fewer than half a dozen settlers were killed—far below the expected toll (even during Bacon's Rebellion) when colonists turned their rage against Indians, for example, or when buccaneers assailed the Spanish. No deaths complicated Boston's overthrow of Andros or John Coode's demolition of Maryland's proprietary regime. Leisler's New York revolt produced fatalities only as his enemies retook the province in 1691. Judicial reprisals could be much more severe, but Bacon's Rebellion seems quite a singular episode in this regard. While government claimed broad powers, its real authority was always more limited than it could afford to admit, and so were the forms that resistance assumed.

As regimes stabilized on both sides of the Atlantic after 1689, legitimacy greatly diminished as a problem, and political life became more patterned and predictable. Governments made fewer exalted claims but in most colonies probably wielded greater effective power, especially in time of war. More young men found that civic responsibility might include extensive military service. Courts dispatched an expanding volume of cases per capita. Government created and regulated paper money, collected more taxes, and sometimes established public loan offices. In the process, the state made economic decisions that benefitted some groups and injured others. Against small-planter opposition, for example, Virginia imposed tobacco regulation in 1730, a device that Maryland resisted until 1747. After 1714, as printing presses became an accepted adjunct of public life in northern cities, extended pamphlet (and eventually newspaper) debate of political and economic issues frequently occurred. When the policy-making few divided over public versus private land banks in Massachusetts, over imposts versus land taxes in New York, or over paper money in Philadelphia, antagonists increasingly appealed to the public and hoped for a response. Members of the elite politicized the people against the bad guys only to find that the same weapons could threaten themselves. Special interests jostled one another more openly than before and struggled to find a language that could legitimate their aspirations within the framework of the common good. In the process, still more city dwellers could be mobilized in a way that had seldom happened in the seventeenth century.[74]

Amongst those who still felt cut off from the political process and angered by government, rioting and violent resistance again became common in the generation after 1745. As in the previous century, rioters seldom killed anyone except Indians, but government had grown more effective in its retaliation. None of these disturbances, unlike their seventeenth-century progenitors, overturned a colonial regime before 1775. Government had indeed become more powerful. Its collapse in 1775 required an onslaught gigantic enough to change decisively the values and norms of public life.[75]

That government became bigger hardly explains how it worked. For twenty years now deference has been the most widely used concept to explain how these structures functioned in the eighteenth century. With few full-time civil servants, government remained in the hands of gentlemen amateurs who used their offices to work with (or against) the governor. The officeholder asked the voters to embrace his political choices much as they recognized and accepted his social superiority. We now know enough about eighteenth-century politics to modify this picture somewhat.[76]

Officeholding did become measurably more elitist. In no mainland colony, for example, did the size of the assembly keep pace with population growth. Representatives tended to serve longer terms in bodies that sat for a greater portion of the year to transact a much higher volume of business. Pure deference, in which the many willingly yield to the superior judgment of the few, probably does characterize some of these regimes. South Carolina by mid-century had few contested elections, and not many voters were likely to show up. The absence of competing factions argues for a lack of planter discontent in rice and indigo areas (as against the back country by the 1760s). In Virginia contested elections were the norm, but because these struggles had no factional base in society after 1720, they assumed a carnival air. As Morgan explains the process, the few ostentatiously treated the many, expressing public respect for their integrity and gratitude for their support. The many, for a day or two, behaved as though vox populi really was vox dei before surrendering real power to the gentry for another seven years. Ritually, the world was turned upside down in contests without issues, only to right itself with the result—affirmation of the social order through election of a great planter, who nearly always happened also to be a local magistrate. Deference in these colonies ratified and confirmed the status quo.[77]

Joy and Robert Gilsdorf are uncovering a rather different system in eighteenth-century Connecticut, one that might be called "achieved deference." In studying the colony's elective council, they find that socioeconomic indicators—family, wealth, education—contribute little to explaining who got promoted. Connecticut voters, unlike their Virginia counterparts, had to choose men they most likely had not even met because the elections were colonywide. Successful candidates had to demonstrate their superiority through outstanding service in the assembly, with news of their exceptional merit reaching the voters through local deputies. Once elected, a member of the council could normally expect to serve for life, but he got that far only by hard work and proven ability, at least until the Great Awakening began to complicate loyalties. In Connecticut the voters may have been applauding the virtues of their government more than they affirmed any particular hierarchical vision of their society.[78]

Massachusetts hovered somewhat precariously between deference and outright "influence," a system in which a superior can command support because of the benefits he can extract from above and bestow on those below. From the 1730s on, voters increasingly elected officeholders (especially justices of the peace, who were patronage men in Massachusetts in a way that they were not in Virginia) to the House of Representatives, with the total surpassing 70 percent by 1763. As the demands of government escalated, presumably it helped to have a man with strong connections mediate between the town and the authorities in Boston. But these men also owed their appointive offices to the governor and could often be persuaded to support unpopular measures. In every domestic crisis from 1735 to 1765 the percentage of justices in the House fell markedly in the next election, only to climb again in subsequent years. Voters, in short, punished representatives who valued their offices above the perceived good of the town. Perhaps such a system can be described as "suspicious deference" or "deference-influence." More than before, representatives were part of a recognizable elite, the county court of sessions. But voters did not automatically defer to their superior judgment on public issues.[79]

Finally, in the belt of colonies from New York to Maryland deference did not work very well. Election struggles were generally ferocious and bitter into the 1720s. Patterns diverged in separate colonies over the next generation, but by mid-century Maryland, New Jersey and New York were publishing roll-call votes by the hundreds, presumably to permit voters to evaluate performance. The normal stance of the electorate was antiadministration. Government men learned to fear elections.

While population expanded rapidly in the Middle Atlantic region, the assemblies grew very slowly and for long stretches not at all. Maryland voters consistently elected "country party" majorities against the proprietary regime. Pennsylvania electors endorsed the Quaker party (in most years without opposition), which in turn battled the Penn family. Until mid-century, New Jersey voters behaved in much the same way. In a tradition culminating in the stormy administration of Lewis Morris (1738–46) they usually returned antiadministration men, sometimes even against a governor who sponsored such populist causes as broader suffrage. When governor and assembly learned to cooperate effectively around mid-century, contested elections also became rarer, which might indicate voter satisfaction. On the other hand, the number of single-term assemblymen rose sharply, doubling after 1749 until it accounted for nearly two-thirds of the men chosen. Nearly all representatives continued to come from deeply entrenched elite families in their counties. One wonders whether the gentry deflected voter wrath in an age of land riots, war, and heavy taxation by swapping assembly terms among themselves, thereby diffusing responsibility.[80]

Perhaps the most striking such pattern developed in New York, where the elite were nearly always divided. Those out of favor appealed to the voters, particularly in the city. Those in power tried to avoid elections. To be sure, deference continued to function in certain safe constituencies for each side— if deference it was. The widespread landlord-tenant relationship does raise the specter of coercion, in which inferiors *unwillingly* yield to the judgment of superiors. But in a small assembly New York City's four seats could often tip the balance, and the city was much too large to manipulate through defer-ence. Accordingly, when the Lewis Morris faction gained a comfortable majority in 1716, it put off a general election for ten years, meanwhile losing *every* by-election along the way. The triumphant Adolph Philipse faction likewise avoided an election between 1728 and 1737. Hence the Zenger crisis of 1733–34, in which the Morrisites began to scramble back through by-elections. Anyone "who dares publickly cry out agt a Governour and tells the people they are oppressed and Sets up for a patriot and defender of the Liberties and priviledges [of the] Country," observed James Alexander, "will soon thereby make an Interest here and when he desists that he as soon Loses it." Passage of a septennial act in 1743 only institutionalized the process. From 1754 to the last contest in December 1775, the governing faction was almost routinely defeated in general elections in New York.[81]

In other words, we shall understand deference better and sharpen its use as an analytical tool once we have established the *boundaries* of what it can explain. That process may bring us back towards unfashionable ideas, such as the growth of oligarchy. Everybody concedes its importance for Britain, but not since the Progressives has the concept been widely applied to the colonies. The planter elites of South Carolina and Virginia were decidedly oligarchic. They offered scant opportunity for a small planter to cross the watershed that separated ordinary mortals from gentlemen. True, Virginia enjoyed a participatory oligarchy in which *most* voters could expect to hold minor offices, perhaps rising as high as the grand jury. Lacking severe clashes of interest, the system was quite stable and, if we can ignore the slaves, not repressive. Possibly slavery even made pure deference feasible by reducing the need for chains of overt dependency and influence within the white community.[82]

New England never lacked families with similar pretensions to dominance, but in their efforts to sustain their claims they always confronted major obstacles, even when the Massachusetts electorate became increasingly pro-government from 1735 to 1760. The Middle Atlantic settlements display the clearest examples of oligarchy both affirmed and resisted. Of the five assemblies from New York to Maryland, not one formally repudiated the empire in 1775–76. Oligarchy had risen far enough to become unresponsive to social inferiors, despite the noisy rhetoric of elections, which the voters may have believed more readily than the purveyors. There alone, so far as I am aware, did numerous assemblymen join appointive officeholders as loyalists against the wishes of their constituents, while some others defied loyalist constituents and subordinates to become patriots. There alone, as Gary Nash has shown in a powerful revival of Progressive thinking, did urban radicals grope their way to a frank evocation of class consciousness. (In Boston, where economic conditions had long been more severe but Puritan communalism remained a living force, opposition writers continued to distingush between good and bad gentlemen.) Up to a point, the tendency towards oligarchy encouraged the emergence of men sufficiently educated and experienced to set forth the rights and claims of their communities with far greater clarity than earlier generations had shown. Beyond that point (and we should not expect to find it at the same location in different societies), the same men could become insensitive to similar demands upon themselves.[83]

Colonial behavior was not latently revolutionary in 1730 or even 1760. If anything, it seemed to be moving in the opposite direction, towards greater imperial integration. Ironically, the region with the most suspicious electorate by 1760 was also the least rebellious part of America in 1775 and would not have left the empire on its own initiative. By contrast, the most loyal colonies in the previous generation led the movement for Independence. Even in the 1750s, as Greene has contended, allegiance was conditional. But, then, so is all allegiance. Limits always exist. The historian's job is to find them and discover how and why they change over time.[84]

VII

The study of colonial politics must seem rather disappointing to anyone whose expectations have derived from the high historiography of the past thirty years. Consensus history demanded a consensual revolution, one whose work had mostly been done before the event itself. Brown, Hartz, Boorstin, and Bailyn all sensed the need but produced incompatible answers.

Inevitably, colonial politics became an arena for auditioning a series of daring new actors, each trying to play the American Character convincingly. Like the Progressives before them, they failed to sustain the role. The Progressives had oversimplified and overgeneralized, sometimes from naive assumptions, but they did know that the Revolution was a violent and messy affair with decisive results. No Revolution, no America. On that fundamental point, they saw more clearly than their successors.

I hope that this long excursion into the recent literature of colonial politics has not been only destructive. Slowly a more modest version of the subject has been emerging, and while the parts have not yet been put together satisfactorily, a surprising number of them seem to spell a foul, three-letter word: *war*.

England's empire, and the colonial politics that lagged behind it, evolved in stages that reflected cycles of international war. While free from most of these constraints, the colonies could experiment with an amazing assortment of political institutions. By 1675 that phase had ended except among Quakers, whose bold logic prompted them to pursue a dream of peace surrounded by a world at war. Already Anglo-Dutch commercial competition had produced the first navigation act, which triggered a cycle of three Anglo-Dutch wars from 1652 to 1674, which in turn stimulated England's earliest serious experiments in overseas conquest, royal government, and autocracy, with Jamaica (taken from Spain) and New York (from the Dutch) as the laboratories. Deficiencies and humiliations revealed by these efforts inspired a broader colonial reorganization after 1675 in which both the Jamaica and New York models encroached on earlier forms. This period also inaugurated a pattern of elaborate transatlantic politics among those out of power as well as those in. The Glorious Revolution destroyed the New York (dominion) option and ended the first cycle.

In the second wave of Anglo-French wars, from the Glorious Revolution to the Treaty of Utrecht, the eighteenth-century British state achieved its developed form, and so did British political culture and the institutional apparatus of empire. Once again the colonial response lagged behind the British stimulus. By about 1720 every mainland colony except Georgia (founded in 1732), North Carolina, and Nova Scotia had acquired the formal political system it would hold until Independence, and in the generation after 1720 the settlers vitalized these forms with derivative political cultures that borrowed selectively from the parent. What they appropriated served different functions in different colonies. Country ideology became an indispensable component of the new stability of Virginia and South Carolina, but in Massachusetts and New York it replicated its English function as a rhetorical outlet for a powerless minority. It remained quite idiosyncratic to political life in Pennsylvania.

The third cycle, which includes Britain's wars against France and Spain from 1739 to 1763, produced the most paradoxical results. It brought British arms greater success abroad than they had ever known before and witnessed a higher degree of cooperation between metropolis and colonies than had ever yet occurred, even if colonial efforts often failed to overcome the exasperation of British officers trying to win the war. Much of the initiative for this support arose in America. Most colonists were proud of their contribution, especially in provinces that made extraordinary efforts. Yet London read the experience quite differently, enough so to begin a serious rethinking of imperial policy. Alarmed by a series of political crises in several colonies after 1748 and by initial difficulties in winning colonial cooperation from 1754 to 1757, imperial authorities assumed a "posture of hostility" towards America. Instead of embracing the voluntarist lessons of a great common victory, London seemed to blame even ardently anti-French New England for not having done more. The home government tried to implement reforms that would make recurrence of these difficulties impossible. In that intriguing sense, Whitehall's policy was *literally* reactionary, an effort to avert an earlier crisis. Britain sought an empire efficient enough to thrive without colonial consent. She lost the consent—and the empire with it.[85]

No sizable colonial group actively approved of Britain's postwar policies—not the Hutchinson bloc in Massachusetts, the Delanceys in New York, or the Quaker party in Pennsylvania, all of whom eventually rejected the Revolution anyway. Only once before had the home government attempted something that unpopular. The Dominion of New England had endured less than three years, and once resistance began, the regime collapsed in a matter of hours or days, depending on the colony. By contrast, the imperial system erected in the eighteenth century survived for a decade after 1765 under immense pressures. This contrast demonstrates how dramatically imperial power had grown in the intervening generations. The long-term trend in America had not been towards revolution but towards closer integration with Britain.

The third cycle of imperial wars thus coincided with the fullest development of colonial politics in their third (or stabilization) phase. It also provided the essential conditions for a fourth cycle of war and a fourth stage of American politics. The two became indistinguishable. They were the Revolution.

The Revolution had to become truly revolutionary because it had to reverse the dominant integrative trend of the century. It had to shatter loyalties and patterns of behavior that were becoming quite venerable. The stabilization phase of colonial politics has always made better sense in Imperial or Consensus categories than in Progressive terms. But to succeed against Britain's awesome might, the Revolution did open social fissures and resentments that were just becoming visible before 1750 and indeed may have been more characteristic of seventeenth-century than of early eighteenth-century colonies. If we are ever to draw together the history of colonial politics, the empire and the Revolution, we shall have to absorb the best that all of these schools can offer us.[86]

NOTES

1. Jack P. Greene, "Changing Interpretations of Early American Politics," in *The Reinterpretation of Early American History: Essays in Honor of John Edwin Pomfret*, ed. Ray Allen Billington (San Marino, Calif., 1966), esp. 151, 156, 170–71, 152, 176–77.

2. Relevant items will be cited in context below. The work in progress is by Edward M. Cook, on Rhode Island, Thomas L. Purvis, on New Jersey; and Edward C. Papenfuse, who is supervising a three-volume history of Maryland politics through the Confederation period.

3. The outstanding exception to this generalization, although never published, is Beverly McAnear, "Politics in Provincial New York, 1689–1761" (Ph.D. diss., Stanford University, 1935); James Truslow Adams, *Revolutionary New England, 1691–1776* (Boston, 1923), also devoted slightly more than half its space to events before 1763. See also Albert E. McKinley, *The Suffrage Franchise in the Thirteen English Colonies in America* (Philadelphia, 1905), esp. 473–88.

4. Carl L. Becker, *Beginnings of the American People* (Boston, 1915); Charles A. Beard and Mary Beard, *The Rise of American Civilization*, 2 vols. (New York, 1927); Marcus Wilson Jernegan, *The American Colonies, 1492–1750* (New York, 1929); and Curtis P. Nettels, *The Roots of American Civilization: A History of American Colonial Life* (New York, 1938). Nevertheless, Greene is quite correct to stress the pervasiveness of Progressive themes until after World War II. One good index is the massive textbook by Samuel Eliot Morison and Henry Steele Commager, *The Growth of the American Republic*. The second and third editions (New York, 1942, 1950) incorporated every major Progressive theme and even introduced the Federal Constitution under the heading "Thermidor." This emphasis disappeared in the fifth edition (1960).

5. Biographical information derived from Dixon Ryan Fox, *Herbert Levi Osgood, American Scholar* (New York, 1924); Charles McLean Andrews et al., *George Louis Beer, A Tribute to His Life and Work in the Making of History and the Moulding of Public Opinion* (New York, 1924); and A. S. Eisenstadt, *Charles McLean Andrews* (New York, 1956). The quotation is from Andrews, "The American Revolution: An Interpretation," *American Historical Review* 31 (1925–26): 232.

6. Compare Herbert Levi Osgood, "England and the Colonies," *Political Science Quarterly* 2 (1887): 440–69, esp. 463–65, with Charles McLean Andrews, *The Colonial Period*, Home University Library (London, 1912), esp. 252.

7. Charles McLean Andrews, *The Colonial Period of American History*, vol. 1 (New Haven, 1934), xiii.

8. This link is made explicitly in Andrews, *Colonial Period* (1912), 60, 66–67, 105. It is strongly implicit in Osgood's "England and the Colonies" and in Claude H. Van Tyne, *The Causes of the War of Independence* (Boston, 1922), chap. 2.

9. Alexander Brown, whose early writings defended James I and attacked Captain John Smith, reversed himself in *English Politics in Early Virginia History* (Boston, 1901). Thomas Jefferson Wertenbaker's main argument about Virginia can be found intact in *Virginia under the Stuarts* (Princeton, 1914) and *The Planters of Colonial Virginia* (Princeton, 1922), although he elaborated on these points in several later publications. For his New England contrast see esp. *The Puritan Oligarchy: The Founding of American Civilization* (New York, 1947).

10. Wesley Frank Craven, *Dissolution of the Virginia Company: The Failure of a Colonial Experiment* (1932; reprint, Gloucester, Mass., 1964); idem, *The Southern Colonies in the Seventeenth Century, 1607–1689* (Baton Rouge, 1949), chap. 10.

11. Turner derived many of his ideas about democracy and free land from the Italian economist Achille Loria, but he ignored that part of Loria's argument which made slavery equally an offshoot of free land (Lee Benson, *Turner and Beard: American Historical Writing Reconsidered* [New York, 1960], 1–40 and passim). For a modern revival of this theme see Evsey D. Domar, "The Causes of Slavery or Serfdom: A Hypothesis," *Journal of Economic History* 30 (1970): 18–32.

12. Robert E. Brown, *Middle-Class Democracy and the Revolution in Massachusetts, 1691–1780* (Ithaca, N.Y., 1955); Robert E. Brown and B. Katherine Brown, *Virginia, 1705–1786: Democracy or Aristocracy?* (East Lansing, 1964). On deference see J. R. Pole, "Historians and the

Problem of Early American Democracy," *American Historical Review* 67 (1961–62): 626–46; and idem, *Political Representation in England and the Origins of the American Republic* (London, 1966), pts. 1 and 2.

13. B. Katherine Brown, "A Note on the Puritan Concept of Aristocracy," *Mississippi Valley Historical Review* 41 (1954–55): 105–12.

14. Louis B. Hartz, *The Liberal Tradition in America: An Interpretation of American Political Thought since the Revolution* (New York, 1955), and his "A Theory of the Development of New Societies," and "United States History in a New Perspective," in *The Founding of New Societies: Studies in the History of the United States, Latin America, South Africa, Canada, and Australia*, ed. Hartz (New York, 1964), 1–122.

15. Daniel Boorstin, *The Americans: The Colonial Experience* (New York, 1958); idem, "The Myth of an American Enlightenment," in *America and the Image of Europe: Reflections on American Thought* (New York, 1960); and idem, *The Genius of American Politics* (Chicago, 1953).

16. Bernard Bailyn, *The New England Merchants in the Seventeenth Century* (Cambridge, Mass., 1955); idem, "Politics and Social Structure in Virginia," in *Seventeenth-Century America: Essays in Colonial History*, ed. James M. Smith (Chapel Hill, 1959), 90–115; idem, "Communications and Trade: The Atlantic in the Seventeenth Century," *Journal of Economic History* 13 (1953): 378–87; idem, "The Beekmans of New York: Trade, Politics, and Families: A Review Article," *William and Mary Quarterly*, 3d ser., 14 (1957): 598–608; idem, "Political Experience and Enlightenment Ideas in Eighteenth-Century America," *American Historical Review* 67 (1961–62): 339–51.

17. Bernard Bailyn, *The Ideological Origins of the American Revolution* (Cambridge, Mass., 1967), a somewhat shorter version of which had already appeared as an introductory essay to *Pamphlets of the American Revolution, 1750–1776*, vol. 1 (Cambridge, Mass., 1965); Caroline Robbins, *The Eighteenth-Century Commonwealthman: Studies in the Transmission, Development and Circumstance of English Liberal Thought from the Restoration of Charles II until the War with the Thirteen Colonies* (Cambridge, Mass., 1959); J. G. A. Pocock, "Machiavelli, Harrington, and English Political Ideologies in the Eighteenth Century," *William and Mary Quarterly*, 3d ser., 22 (1965): 549–83; idem, *The Machiavellian Moment: Florentine Political Thought and the Atlantic Republican Tradition* (Princeton, 1975); Isaac Kramnick, *Bolingbroke and His Circle: The Politics of Nostalgia in the Age of Walpole* (Cambridge, Mass., 1968); John Dunn, "The Politics of Locke in England and America in the Eighteenth Century," in *John Locke, Problems and Perspectives: A Collection of New Essays*, ed. John W. Yolton (Cambridge, 1969), 45–80.

18. Bernard Bailyn, *The Origins of American Politics* (New York, 1968), esp. 64, 160, 161; this study first appeared in *Perspectives in American History* 1 (1967).

19. Richard Hofstadter, *The Paranoid Style in American Politics and Other Essays* (New York, 1965), 3–40.

20. Compare T. H. Breen, *Puritans and Adventurers: Change and Persistence in Early America* (New York, 1980), 24–45, with F. W. Anderson, "Why Did Colonial New Englanders Make Bad Soldiers? Contractual Principles and Military Conduct during the Seven Years' War," *William and Mary Quarterly*, 3d ser., 38 (1981): 395–417.

21. Kenneth A. Lockridge, *Settlement and Unsettlement in Early America: The Crisis of Political Legitimacy before the Revolution* (Cambridge, Mass., 1981).

22. Marc Egnal, "The Pattern of Factional Development in Pennsylvania, New York, and Massachusetts, 1682–1776," in *Party and Political Opposition in Revolutionary America*, ed. Patricia U. Bonomi (Tarrytown, N.Y., 1980), 43–60; idem, "The Origins of the Revolution in Virginia: A Reinterpretation," *William and Mary Quarterly*, 3d ser., 37 (1980): 401–28. That portion of Pole's contribution that deals with deference will be discussed below in section VI.

23. Richard S. Dunn, "The Downfall of the Bermuda Company: A Restoration Farce," *William and Mary Quarterly*, 3d ser., 20 (1963): 487–512.

24. Sydney V. James, *Colonial Rhode Island: A History* (New York, 1975).

25. Mary Patterson Clarke, *Parliamentary Privilege in the American Colonies* (New Haven, 1943), 24–25.

26. On this question, Jon Kukla's "Robert Beverley Assailed: Appellate Jurisdiction and the Problem of Bicarmeralism in Seventeenth-Century Virginia," *Virginia Magazine of History and Biography* 88 (1980): 415–29, supersedes Wesley Frank Craven's "'. . . And so the Form of Government Became Perfect,'" ibid. 77 (1969): 131–45, which postponed bicameralism until the 1680s.

27. Marcus Rediker, "'Under the Banner of King Death': The Social World of Anglo-American Pirates, 1716 to 1726," *William and Mary Quarterly*, 3d ser., 38 (1981): 203–27, deals with a later period, but an earlier classic shows that much of the same ethos was already present half a century before: see A. O. Exquemelin, *The Buccaneers of America* (1678), trans. from the Dutch by Alexis Brown (Baltimore, 1969).

28. In addition to material that will be cited in context below, see Allen W. Trelease, *Indian Affairs in Colonial New York: The Seventeenth Century* (Ithaca, N.Y.), 1960, chap. 3; Russell R. Menard, "Maryland's 'Time of Troubles': Sources of Political Disorder in Early St. Mary's," *Maryland Historical Magazine* 76 (1981): 124–40; Richard L. Morton, *Colonial Virginia*, 2 vols. (Chapel Hill, 1960), 1: 153–56; and Harry J. Bennett, "The English Caribbees in the Period of the Civil War, 1642–1646," *William and Mary Quarterly*, 3d ser., 24 (1967): 359–77.

29. See esp. Francis Jennings, *The Invasion of America: Indians, Colonialism, and the Cant of Conquest* (Chapel Hill, 1975); and Richard Slotkin, *Regeneration through Violence: The Mythology of the American Frontier, 1600–1860* (Middletown, Conn., 1973). For England see Lawrence Stone, *The Crisis of the Aristocracy, 1558–1641* (Oxford, 1965), pt. 5; and Lindsay Boynton, *The Elizabethan Militia, 1558–1638* (London, 1967).

30. John M. Murrin, "Magistrates, Sinners, and a Precarious Liberty: Trial by Jury in Seventeenth-Century New England," in *Saints and Revolutionaries: Essays in Early American History,* ed. David D. Hall, John M. Murrin, and Thad W. Tate (New York, 1983).

31. Michael Kammen, *Deputyes & Libertyes: The Origins of Representative Government in Colonial America* (New York, 1969); J. R. Pole, *The Seventeenth Century: The Sources of Legislative Power* (Charlottesville, 1969). For an imaginative effort to rethink the meaning of representation in England prior to 1640 see Derek Hirst, *The Representative of the People? Voters and Voting in England under the Early Stuarts* (Cambridge, 1975). So far Hirst's efforts have had no impact upon the way colonialists discuss their seventeenth-century provinces.

32. Of a voluminous literature see esp. Richard C. Simmons, "Godliness, Property, and the Franchise in Puritan Massachusetts: An Interpretation," *Journal of American History* 55 (1968–69): 495–511; and Robert E. Wall, Jr., "The Decline of the Massachusetts Franchise, 1647–1666," ibid. 59 (1972–73): 303–10.

33. John M. Murrin, "English Rights as Ethnic Aggression: The English Conquest, the Charter of Liberties of 1683, and Leisler's Rebellion in New York" (Paper delivered at the annual convention of the American Historical Association, San Francisco, Calif., December 1973). For a different view see David S. Lovejoy, "Equality and Empire: The New York Charter of Libertyes, 1683," *William and Mary Quarterly*, 3d ser., 21 (1964): 493–515.

34. Edmund S. Morgan, *American Slavery—American Freedom: The Ordeal of Colonial Virginia* (New York, 1975).

35. Russell R. Menard, "Economy and Society in Early Colonial Maryland" (Ph.D. diss., University of Iowa, 1975), contains a fresh discussion of very early Maryland politics but thereafter sticks to social history. For a published narrative of the Restoration era one must still use such older works as Andrews, *Colonial Period of American History*, vol. 2, chap. 9; but see also Susan R. Falb, "Advice and Ascent: The Development of the Maryland Assembly, 1635–1689" (Ph.D. diss., Georgetown University, 1976), chaps. 9–10. For the islands see Carl Bridenbaugh and Roberta Bridenbaugh, *No Peace beyond the Line: The English in the Caribbean, 1624–1690* (New York, 1972); and Richard S. Dunn, *Sugar and Slaves: The Rise of the Planter Class in the English West Indies, 1624–1713* (Chapel Hill, 1972).

36. Mary J. A. Jones, *Congregational Commonwealth: Connecticut, 1636–1662* (Middletown, Conn., 1968), is thin and disappointing; Paul R. Lucas, *Valley of Discord: Church and Society along the Connecticut River, 1636–1725* (Hanover, N.H., 1976), although not specifically about politics, is much more stimulating. The best studies of the New England periphery are David E. Van

Deventer, *The Emergence of Provincial New Hampshire, 1623–1741* (Baltimore, 1976); and Charles E. Clark, *The Eastern Frontier: The Settlement of Northern New England, 1610–1763* (New York, 1970).

37. T. H. Breen, *The Character of the Good Ruler: A Study of Puritan Political Ideas in New England, 1630–1730* (New Haven, 1970); T. H. Breen and Stephen Foster, "The Puritans' Greatest Achievement: A Study of Social Cohesion in Seventeenth-Century Massachusetts," *Journal of American History* 60 (1973–74): 5–22; Breen, *Puritans and Adventurers*, 3–45.

38. J. Mills Thornton III, "The Thrusting Out of Governor Harvey: A Seventeenth-Century Rebellion," *Virginia Magazine of History and Biography* 76 (1968): 11–26; Morgan, *American Slavery—American Freedom*, on Berkeley. For the demographic contrast between New England and the Chesapeake compare Philip J. Greven, Jr., *Four Generations: Population, Land, and Family in Colonial Andover, Massachusetts* (Ithaca, N.Y., 1970), and Kenneth A. Lockridge, *A New England Town: The First Hundred Years, Dedham, Massachusetts, 1636–1736* (New York, 1970), with the essays in *The Chesapeake in the Seventeenth Century: Essays on Anglo-American Society*, ed. Thad W. Tate and David L. Ammerman (Chapel Hill, 1979).

39. Robert E. Wall, Jr., *Massachusetts Bay: The Crucial Decade, 1640–1650* (New Haven, 1972); Timothy J. Sehr, "Colony and Commonwealth: Massachusetts Bay, 1649–1660" (Ph.D. diss., Indiana University, 1977); Paul R. Lucas, "Colony or Commonwealth: Massachusetts Bay, 1661–1666," *William and Mary Quarterly*, 3d ser., 24 (1967): 88–107; E. Brooks Holifield, "On Toleration in Massachusetts," *Church History* 38 (1969): 188–200; Richard C. Simmons, "The Founding of the Third Church in Boston," *William and Mary Quarterly*, 3d ser., 26 (1969): 241–52; Robert G. Pope, *The Half-Way Covenant: Church Membership in Puritan New England* (Princeton, 1969); and David D. Hall, *The Faithful Shepherd: A History of the New England Ministry in the Seventeenth Century* (Chapel Hill, 1972).

40. Boorstin, *The Americans: The Colonial Experience*, esp. 1, 149–50.

41. Caroline Robbins, "Laws and Governments Proposed for West New Jersey and Pennsylvania, 1676–1683," *Pennsylvania Magazine of History and Biography* 105 (1981): 373–92.

42. Leonard W. Labaree, *Royal Government in America: A Study of the British Colonial System before 1783* (New Haven, 1930); A. P. Thornton, *West India Policy under the Restoration* (Oxford, 1956).

43. Philip Haffenden, "The Crown and the Colonial Charters, 1675–1688," *William and Mary Quarterly*, 3d ser., 15 (1958): 297–311, 452–66; David S. Lovejoy, *The Glorious Revolution in America* (New York, 1972).

44. Richard S. Dunn, *Puritans and Yankees: The Winthrop Dynasty in New England, 1630–1717* (Princeton, 1962), chap. 11; Wesley Frank Craven, *The Colonies in Transition, 1660–1713* (New York, 1968).

45. Alison G. Olson, *Anglo-American Politics, 1660–1775: The Relationship between Parties in England and Colonial America* (Oxford, 1973); idem, "The Board of Trade and London-American Interest Groups in the Eighteenth Century," *Journal of Imperial and Commonwealth History* 8 (1979–80): 33–50. On parties and elections in England see J. H. Plumb, "The Growth of the Electorate in England from 1600 to 1715," *Past and Present*, no. 45 (1969): 90–116; W. A. Speck, *Tory and Whig: The Struggle in the Constituencies* (London, 1970); Geoffrey Holmes, *The Electorate and the National Will in the First Age of Party* (London, 1976); and idem, *British Politics in the Age of Anne* (London, 1967).

46. Stephen S. Webb, *The Governors-General: The English Army and the Definition of Empire, 1569–1681* (Chapel Hill, 1979); idem, "Army and Empire: English Garrison Government in Britain and America, 1569 to 1763," *William and Mary Quarterly*, 3d ser., 34 (1977): 1–31. See also E. E. Rich, "The First Earl of Shaftesbury's Colonial Policy," *Transactions of the Royal Historical Society*, 5th ser., 7 (1957): 47–70, for the localist-voluntary model that Webb projects far beyond Shaftesbury; and Richard B. Sheridan, *Sugar and Slavery: An Economic History of the British West Indies, 1623–1775* (Baltimore, 1974), 1–74, for acceptance of the navigation acts in the islands.

47. Jack M. Sosin, *English America and the Restoration Monarchy of Charles II: Transatlantic Politics, Commerce, and Kinship* (Lincoln, Nebr., 1980).

48. Robert C. Ritchie, *The Duke's Province: A Study of New York Politics and Society, 1664–1691*

(Chapel Hill, 1977). See John M. Murrin, "Pluralism and Predatory Power: Early New York as a Social Failure," *Reviews in American History* 6 (1978): 473–79, for amplification of some of these points.

49. Richard R. Johnson, *Adjustment to Empire: The New England Colonies, 1675–1715* (New Brunswick, N.J., 1981); Stephen Innes, *To Labor in a New Land: Dependency, Exchange, and Community in Seventeenth-Century Springfield* (Princeton, 1983). See also Richard R. Johnson, "The Search for a Usable Indian: An Aspect of the Defense of Colonial New England," *Journal of American History* 64 (1977): 623–51; Breen, *Puritans and Adventurers,* chap. 5, on the emergence of new "brokers" between town and province under the pressure of war; and Philip Haffenden, *New England in the English Nation, 1689–1713* (Oxford, 1974), which anticipated a number of themes developed by Johnson and does more with actual warfare after the early 1690s.

50. Thomas J. Archdeacon, *New York City, 1664–1710: Conquest and Change* (Ithaca, N.Y., 1976); Beverly McAnear, *The Income of the Colonial Governors of British North America* (New York, 1967), chap. 2.

51. Lois Green Carr and David W. Jordan, *Maryland's Revolution of Government, 1689–1692* (Ithaca, N.Y., 1974).

52. In addition to Morgan's *American Slavery—American Freedom,* see John C. Rainbolt, "A New Look at Stuart 'Tyranny': The Crown's Attack on the Virginia Assembly, 1676–1689," *Virginia Magazine of History and Biography* 75 (1967): 387–406; and idem, "The Alteration in the Relationship between Leadership and Constituents in Virginia, 1660 to 1720," *William and Mary Quarterly,* 3d ser., 27 (1970): 411–34.

53. J. R. Jones, *The Revolution of 1688 in England* (New York, 1972); J. R. Western, *Monarchy and Revolution: The English State in the 1680s* (London, 1972); J. P. Kenyon, *Revolution Principles: The Politics of Party, 1689–1720* (Cambridge, 1977); P. G. M. Dickson, *The Financial Revolution in England: A Study in the Development of National Credit* (London, 1967); Pocock, *Machiavellian Moment;* H. T. Dickinson, *Liberty and Property: Political Ideology in Eighteenth-Century Britain* (London, 1977); Joyce O. Appleby, *Economic Thought and Ideology in Seventeenth-Century England* (Princeton, 1978), which sees a proto-liberal subculture emerging along with Pocock's country ideology; and Ian K. Steele, *Politics of Colonial Policy: The Board of Trade in Colonial Administration, 1696–1720* (Oxford, 1968).

54. James A. Henretta, *"Salutary Neglect": Colonial Administration under the Duke of Newcastle* (Princeton, 1972).

55. Recent studies include Patricia U. Bonomi, *A Factious People: Politics and Society in Colonial New York* (New York, 1971); David Alan Williams, "Anglo-Virginia Politics, 1690–1735," in *Anglo-American Political Relations, 1675–1775,* ed. Alison G. Olson and Richard M. Brown (New Brunswick, N.J., 1970), 76–91; and for Antigua, Dunn, *Sugar and Slaves,* 143–46.

56. Jack P. Greene, "'A Posture of Hostility': A Reconsideration of Some Aspects of the Origins of the American Revolution," *Proceedings of the American Antiquarian Society* 87 (1977): 27–68.

57. For recent accounts see Robert M. Zemsky, *Merchants, Farmers, and River Gods: An Essay on Eighteenth-Century American Politics* (Boston, 1971); M. Eugene Sirmans, *Colonial South Carolina: A Political History, 1663–1763* (Chapel Hill, 1966); and Stanley N. Katz, *Newcastle's New York: Anglo-American Politics, 1732–1753* (Cambridge, Mass., 1968).

58. J. H. Plumb, *The Origins of Political Stability: England, 1675–1725* (Boston, 1967), esp. xvi–xviii.

59. Paul Langford, *The Excise Crisis: Society and Politics in the Age of Walpole* (Oxford, 1975); G. A. Cranfield, "The 'London Evening Post' and the Jew Bill of 1753," *Historical Journal* 8 (1965): 16–30. Lawrence Henry Gipson, *The British Empire before the American Revolution,* 15 vols. (New York, 1936–70), vol. 10 (1961), chap. 9 (on the cider tax). No adequate published study exists of Walpole's final years in office, but Brian Hill, *The Growth of Parliamentary Parties, 1689–1742* (London, 1976), is helpful. For antagonism between the administration and the larger political nation see J. H. Plumb, "Political Man," in *Man versus Society in Eighteenth-Century Britain: Six Points of View,* ed. James L. Clifford (Cambridge, 1968), 1–21; and Linda Colley, *In Defiance of*

Oligarcy: The Tory Party, 1714–60 (Cambridge, 1982). That Walpolean rule was socially repressive is powerfully argued in E. P. Thompson, *Whigs and Hunters: The Origins of the Black Act* (New York, 1975).

60. Plumb, *Origins of Political Stability*, xviii n. 1; Bailyn, *Origins of American Politics*, 66.

61. Lawrence H. Leder, *Liberty and Authority: Early American Political Ideology, 1689–1763* (Chicago, 1968); George Dargo, *Roots of the Republic: A New Perspective on Early American Constitutionalism* (New York, 1974); Stephen Botein, "'Meer Mechanics' and an Open Press: The Business and Political Strategies of Colonial American Printers," *Perspectives in American History* 9 (1975): 127–225.

62. Jack P. Greene, "Political Mimesis: A Consideration of the Historical and Cultural Roots of Legislative Behavior in the British Colonies in the Eighteenth Century," with a reply by Bailyn and a rejoinder by Greene, *American Historical Review* 75 (1969–70): 337–67. For Connecticut see Richard L. Bushman's brilliant study of the slow erosion of a seventeenth-century polity, *From Puritan to Yankee: Character and the Social Order in Connecticut, 1690–1765* (Cambridge, Mass., 1967). For a striking anticipation of nineteenth-century liberal politics see Sydney V. James, "Colonial Rhode Island and the Beginnings of the Liberal Rationalized State," in *Essays in Theory and History: An Approach to the Social Sciences*, ed. Melvin Richter (Cambridge, Mass., 1970), 165–85. The Massachusetts excise controversy of 1754 provides an instructive example of the difference between the Bailyn and Greene assumptions when applied to a concrete issue. Bailyn read the large volume of tracts denouncing the measure and simply took it for granted that the excise was defeated. In fact, it passed despite an outpouring of hostile instructions from the towns. Compare Bailyn, *Origins of American Politics*, 145–46, with Paul Boyer, "Borrowed Rhetoric: The Massachusetts Excise Controversy of 1754," *William and Mary Quarterly*, 3d ser., 21 (1964): 328–51.

63. Jack P. Greene, "The Growth of Political Stability: An Interpretation of Political Development in the Anglo-American Colonies, 1660–1760," in *The American Revolution: A Heritage of Change*, ed. John Parker and Carol Urness (Minneapolis, 1975), 26–52; idem, "'Virtus et Libertas': Political Culture, Social Change, and the Origins of the American Revolution in Virginia, 1763–1766," in *The Southern Experience in the American Revolution*, ed. Jeffrey J. Crow and Larry E. Tise (Chapel Hill, 1978), 55–108; Robert M. Weir, "'The Harmony We Were Famous For': An Interpretation of Pre-Revolutionary South Carolina Politics," *William and Mary Quarterly*, 3d ser., 26 (1969): 473–501; W. W. Abbot, *The Royal Governors of Georgia, 1754–1775* (Chapel Hill, 1959). A. G. Roeber explores tensions emerging within the Virginia gentry after mid-century, and Rhys Isaac examines the growing hostility between gentry culture and an expanding Baptist and Methodist counterculture. Both subjects belong more properly to a discussion of the Revolutionary era than to the main theme of this paper (Roeber, *Faithful Magistrates and Republican Lawyers: Creators of Virginia Legal Culture, 1680–1810* [Chapel Hill, 1981]; Isaac, *The Transformation of Virginia, 1740–1790* [Chapel Hill, 1982]).

64. A. Roger Ekirch, *"Poor Carolina": Politics and Society in Colonial North Carolina, 1729–1776* (Chapel Hill, 1981).

65. George Metcalf, *Royal Government and Political Conflict in Jamaica, 1729–1783* (London, 1965); Frederick G. Spurdle, *Early West Indian Government, Showing the Progress of Government in Barbados, Jamaica and the Leeward Islands, 1660–1783* (Palmerston North, N.Z., n.d.).

66. The best discussions of these Virginia and Maryland elections are in David Alan Williams, "Political Alignments in Colonial Virginia Politics, 1698–1750" (Ph.D. diss., Northwestern University, 1959); and David W. Jordan, "The Royal Period of Colonial Maryland, 1689–1715" (Ph.D. diss., Princeton University, 1966).

67. Jere R. Daniell, "Politics in New Hampshire under Governor Benning Wentworth, 1741–1767," *William and Mary Quarterly*, 3d ser., 23 (1966): 76–105; Zemsky, *Merchants, Farmers, and River Gods*; John A. Schutz, *William Shirley, King's Governor of Massachusetts* (Chapel Hill, 1961).

68. Sirmans, *Colonial South Carolina*, 348–51; Jack P. Greene, "The Seven Years' War and the American Revolution: The Causal Pattern Reconsidered," *Journal of Imperial and Commonwealth*

History 8 (1979–80): 85–105; John M. Murrin," "Anglicizing an American Colony: The Transformation of Provincial Massachusetts" (Ph.D. diss., Yale University, 1966), chap. 3.

69. William Pencak, *War, Politics, & Revolution in Provincial Massachusetts* (Boston, 1981).

70. In addition to material already cited, see Stanley N. Katz, "Between Scylla and Charybdis: James DeLancey and Anglo-American Politics in Early Eighteenth-Century New York," in Olson and Brown, *Anglo-American Political Relations*, 92–108; Eugene R. Sheridan, *Lewis Morris, 1671–1746: A Study in Early American Politics* (Syracuse, 1981); and John Strassburger, "The Origins and Establishment of the Morris Family in the Society and Politics of New York and New Jersey, 1630–1746" (Ph.D. diss., Princeton University, 1976).

71. Alan Tully, *William Penn's Legacy: Politics and Social Structure in Provincial Pennsylvania, 1726–1755* (Baltimore, 1977).

72. Gary B. Nash, *Quakers and Politics: Pennsylvania, 1681–1726* (Princeton, 1968); Jon Butler, "Gospel Order Improved': The Keithian Schism and the Exercise of Quaker Ministerial Authority in Pennsylvania," *William and Mary Quarterly*, 3d ser., 31 (1974): 431–52; Thomas Wendel, "The Keith-Lloyd Alliance: Factional and Coalition Politics in Colonial Pennsylvania," *Pennsylvania Magazine of History and Biography* 92 (1968): 289–305; Robert S. Hohwald, "The Structure of Pennsylvania Politics, 1739–1776" (Ph.D. diss., Princeton University, 1978). The data on legislative behavior are my own compilations from published statute collections for all of the thirteen colonies except Georgia, Maryland, Connecticut, and Rhode Island. On petitioning cf. Raymond C. Bailey, *Popular Influences upon Public Policy: Petitioning in Eighteenth-Century Virginia* (Westport, Conn., 1979); William Pencak, "Warfare and Political Change in Mid-Eighteenth-Century Massachusetts," *Journal of Imperial and Commonwealth History* 8 (1979–80): 51–73, esp. 53; and Thomas L. Purvis, "The New Jersey Assembly, 1722–1776" (Ph.D. diss., The Johns Hopkins University, 1979), chap. 5.

73. James H. Hutson, *Pennsylvania Politics, 1746–1770: The Movement for Royal Government and Its Consequences* (Princeton, 1972); Richard A. Ryerson, *The Revolution Is Now Begun: The Radical Committees of Philadelphia, 1765–1776* (Philadelphia, 1978). Much more can still be done on Pennsylvania's participation in the Seven Years' War.

74. See esp. John C. Rainbolt, ed., "The Case of the Poor Planters in Virginia under the Law for Inspecting and Burning Tobacco," *Virginia Magazine of History and Biography* 79 (1971): 314–21; and Gary B. Nash, "The Transformation of Urban Politics, 1700–1765," *Journal of American History* 60 (1973–74): 605–32.

75. Of the extensive literature on popular disturbances see esp. Edward Countryman, "The Problem of the Early American Crowd," *Journal of American Studies* 7 (1973): 77–90; idem, " 'Out of the Bounds of the Law': Northern Land Rioters in the Eighteenth Century," in *The American Revolution: Explorations in the History of American Radicalism*, ed. Alfred F. Young (De Kalb, Ill., 1976), 37–69; Thomas L. Purvis, "Origins and Patterns of Agrarian Unrest in New Jersey, 1735 to 1754," *William and Mary Quarterly*, 3d ser., 39 (1982): 600–27; Pauline Maier, "Popular Uprisings and Civil Authority in Eighteenth-Century America," ibid. 27 (1970): 3–35; Richard Maxwell Brown, "Back Country Rebellions and the Homestead Ethic in America, 1740–1799," in *Tradition, Conflict, and Modernization: Perspectives on the American Revolution*, ed. Richard Maxwell Brown and Don E. Fehrenbacher (New York, 1977), 73–99; and John Lax and William Pencak, "The Knowles Riot and the Crisis of the 1740's in Massachusetts," *Perspectives in American History* 10 (1976): 163–214.

76. J. G. A. Pocock, "The Classical Theory of Deference," *American Historical Review* 81 (1976): 516–23, provides conceptualization for this problem. For the colonies see Pole, "Historians and the Problem of Early American Democracy."

77. Jack P. Greene, "Legislative Turnover in British America, 1696 to 1775: A Quantitative Analysis," *William and Mary Quarterly*, 3d ser., 38 (1981): 442–63; Robert J. Dinkin, *Voting in Provincial America: A Study of Elections in the Thirteen Colonies, 1689–1776* (Westport, Conn., 1977); Edmund S. Morgan, "The People's Choice: The Electoral Carnival in Eighteenth-Century England and America" (Paper delivered at the Lionel Trilling Seminar, Columbia University, April 6, 1982); Charles S. Sydnor, *Gentlemen Freeholders: Political Practices in Washington's*

Virginia (Chapel Hill, 1952); Lucille Griffith, *The Virginia House of Burgesses, 1750–1774*, rev. ed. (University, Ala., 1970).

78. Joy B. Gilsdorf and Robert R. Gilsdorf, "Elites and Electorates: Some Plain Truths for Historians of Colonial America," in Hall, Murrin, and Tate, *Saints and Revolutionaries*.

79. John M. Murrin, "Review Essay," *History and Theory* 11 (1972): 257–70. For the concept of "brokers" and intermediaries see Breen, *Puritans and Adventurers*, chap. 5. For elections and the structure of officeholding in the towns see Michael Zuckerman, "The Social Context of Democracy in Massachusetts," *William and Mary Quarterly*, 3d ser., 25 (1968): 523–44; and Edward M. Cook, Jr., *The Fathers of the Towns: Leadership and Community Structure in Eighteenth-Century New England* (Baltimore, 1976).

80. Robert J. Dinkin, "Elections in Proprietary Maryland," *Maryland Historical Magazine* 73 (1978): 129–36; Thornton Anderson, "Eighteenth-Century Suffrage: The Case of Maryland," ibid. 76 (1981): 141–58; David W. Jordan, "Elections and Voting in Early Colonial Maryland," ibid. 77 (1982): 238–65; Richard A. Ryerson, "Portrait of a Colonial Oligarchy: The Quaker Elite in the Pennsylvania Assembly, 1729–1776" (Paper delivered at the Philadelphia Center for Early American Studies, 1981); Thomas L. Purvis, "'High-Born, Long-Recorded Families': Social Origins of New Jersey Assemblymen, 1703 to 1776," *William and Mary Quarterly*, 3d ser., 37 (1980): 592–615; Richard P. McCormick, *Voting in New Jersey: A Study of the Development of Election Machinery, 1664–1911* (New Brunswick, N.J., 1953), chap. 2. No serious study of Delaware politics exists, but the best general history suggests a period of high factional discord into the 1720s, yielding to a quieter era of cooperation with the Penn proprietors. This pattern eventually produced a high ratio of loyalists (John A. Munroe, *Colonial Delaware: A History* [Millwood, N.Y., 1978]).

81. Much of my thinking about voter behavior in the Middle Atlantic colonies has been stimulated by John Strassburger, "'To My Fellow Citizens': Elites and Politics in Early New York," (Paper, 1980). The Alexander quotation is from Sheridan, *Lewis Morris*, 125. Other major contributions not yet cited include Edward Countryman, *A People in Revolution: The American Revolution and Political Society in New York, 1760–1790* (Baltimore, 1981), chaps. 1, 3; and Roger Champagne, "Family Politics versus Constitutional Principles: The New York Assembly Elections of 1768 and 1769," *William and Mary Quarterly*, 3d ser., 20 (1963): 57–73.

82. Martin H. Quitt, "Virginia House of Burgesses, 1660–1706: The Social, Educational, and Economic Bases of Political Power" (Ph.D. diss., Washington University, 1970); Aubrey C. Land, *The Dulanys of Colonial Maryland: A Biographical Study of Daniel Dulany, the Elder (1685–1753) and Daniel Dulany, the Younger (1722–1797)* (Baltimore, 1955); Emory G. Evans, *Thomas Nelson of Yorktown, Revolutionary Virginian* (Williamsburg, 1975); David Alan Williams, "The Small Farmer in Eighteenth-Century Virginia Politics," *Agricultural History* 43 (1969): 91–101. For a strikingly different pattern of elite officeholding in South Carolina see Richard Waterhouse, "South Carolina's Colonial Elite: A Study in the Social Structure of a Southern Colony, 1670–1760" (Ph.D. diss., The Johns Hopkins University, 1973), chaps. 4–5.

83. Gary B. Nash, *The Urban Crucible: Social Change, Political Consciousness, and the Origins of the American Revolution* (Cambridge, Mass., 1979).

84. Jack P. Greene, "An Uneasy Connection: An Analysis of the Preconditions of the American Revolution," in *Essays on the American Revolution*, ed. Stephen G. Kurtz and James H. Hutson (Chapel Hill, 1973), 32–80, esp. 52 (on conditional loyalty). The fullest argument for extreme disaffection in North America during the 1750s is put forth by Alan Rogers in *Empire and Liberty: American Resistance to British Authority, 1755–1763* (Berkeley, 1974), who never notices that little of his evidence extends past 1757 or 1758, when Britain began to win the war.

85. Greene, "The Seven Years' War and the American Revolution"; John M. Murrin, "The French and Indian War, the American Revolution, and the Counterfactual Hypothesis: Reflections on Lawrence Henry Gipson and John Shy," *Reviews in American History* 1 (1973): 307–18. See also T. Roy Clayton's revisionist interpretation of the origins of the war in his "The Duke of Newcastle, the Earl of Halifax, and the American Origins of the Seven Years' War," *Historical Journal* 24 (1981): 571–603; and Jack P. Greene, "Social Context and the Causal Pattern of the

American Revolution: A Preliminary Consideration of New York, Virginia and Massachusetts," in *La Révolution Américaine et l'Europe*, Colloques internationaux du Centre National de la Recherche Scientifique, no. 577 (1979): 25–63.

86. For a fuller discussion see John M. Murrin, "The Great Inversion, or Court versus Country: A Comparison of the Revolution Settlements in England (1688–1721) and America (1776–1816)," in *Three British Revolutions: 1641, 1688, 1776*, ed. J. G. A. Pocock (Princeton, 1980), 368–453.

15

THE PROBLEM OF A COLONIAL
LEGAL HISTORY

STANLEY N. KATZ

I

egal history remains something of a poor relation within the family of American colonial history. Why this should be so is not entirely clear, although some of the reasons that would have been given twenty-five years ago for the improverishment of legal history are probably still pertinent. The field requires technical expertise, but so, obviously, do demographic and economic history. It suffers from an unevenness of source materials, almost all of which are in manuscript form, but this applies to much of colonial history. Reading legal records is frequently dull, and many individual items seem intellectually trivial, but this is hardly news to the practitioners of the new social history.

The sad truth appears to be that although the past ten years have seen the emergence of American legal history as a recognizable and independent field of study, colonial legal history has not flourished in the same way as the legal history of the nineteenth century. Before reviewing the status of the colonial period, therefore, it will be useful to survey briefly the history of American legal history over the past generation or so.

There have been four major scholarly traditions in American legal-constitutional history.[1] The first of these is really not in American history at all but rather is the settled tradition of English legal and constitutional history, which flows from the work of William Stubbs and Frederic William Maitland.[2] By the standards of English history this is not, of course, a very ancient tradition, being barely a hundred years old, but it continues to exercise a profound impact on American historians of English legal history and historians of American legal history. The tradition really leads in quite opposite directions: towards the macrohistorical study of the larger constitutional forms and trends and towards the microhistorical study of ideas, institutions, and documents.

Another profound influence of the British tradition has been its emphasis on medieval studies. For Maitland and his followers, the "modern" era began with Henry VII and history ended with the English Civil War. The method not only focused on earlier periods of modern history, but in the hands of its lesser practitioners it tended to be teleological and Whiggish, two attributes that were accepted rather uncritically by American practitioners of the art. The result was particularly disastrous, and it is still with us—the tradition of discovering the "origins" of everything, especially the Constitution of 1787 and the American Bill of Rights.

Still, the contributions of the English school have been enormous. At the micro-level they have led to an understanding of the origins of common-law rules, procedures, and court systems and an appreciation of classic texts; they have also contributed to the tradition of documentary editing which is so important to research in legal history. The macro-level contributions also are not to be despised, leading as they have to speculation on the origins of legislation, the nature of constitutionalism, and other conceptual problems of substantial significance.

Obviously, the English historical tradition is still exceedingly strong in the United States. From the point of view of colonial legal history, perhaps its most significant early scholars were Charles H. McIlwain and Robert Livingston Schuyler, who were later joined by George E. Woodbine, Samuel E. Thorne, William H. Dunham, Julius Goebel, and others.[3] The mantle is now worn by such scholars as Thomas G. Barnes, Donald Sutherland, Morris Arnold, Richard Helmholz, Thomas Green, and John Beckerman.[4] The most recent striking example of the sophistication of this group is the Festschrift for Thorne edited by Arnold, Green, Sally Scully, and Stephen White.[5] It seems to me that the English tradition is in most ways even more central for the legal historian than for other historians of colonial America. Not only must the legal historian know the seventeenth- and eighteenth-century context of the legal system but he must have a sound appreciation of medieval legal history as well. Surely this is the ideal for all colonialists, but it is certainly a prerequisite for the legal historian.

The second major tradition in the writing of legal history has been what might be termed the law school tradition. This was the earliest teaching tradition in American legal history, and it was also probably the origin of modern scholarship in the field. It flows out of the microhistorical strain of English legal history. There have been two major sources of influence here. The first, and oldest, is the Columbia Law School tradition begun by Julius Goebel, Jr., and Joseph H. Smith, Goebel's successor as the George Welwood Murray Professor of Legal History.[6] Goebel and Smith taught American legal history to Columbia law students for nearly fifty years while at the same time producing massive sets of teaching materials for that purpose. Their emphasis was on English medieval and colonial American history— even the last edition of Smith's materials devotes only a few pages to the period after the American Revolution.[7] Smith and Goebel focused on fairly narrow legal issues, and brought to them an incredible expertise in the history of English law for their explication. The results have been devastating to the interest of all but the most stalwart students in law school, but they have been enlightening for most scholarly students of the field. They also devoted much of their scholarly effort to documentary editions, the most significant of which are their *The Law Practice of Alexander Hamilton* and Smith's *Court Records of Prince George's County, Maryland, 1696–1699* and *Colonial Justice in Western Massachusetts, 1639–1702: The Pynchon Court Record*.[8]

The second institutional source of the law school tradition has been Harvard, where Mark DeWolfe Howe and John P. Dawson, later joined by Samuel E. Thorne, taught courses from the early 1950s. (In a sense, of course, the scholarly tradition at Harvard began with Zechariah Chafee and Roscoe Pound just after the turn of the century.) Dawson's interests have always been largely in English history, and, like Goebel and Smith, he has emphasized the colonial period and its English antecedents.[9] Howe, while writing originally in the colonial period, later turned to the Oliver Wendell Holmes biography and to legal history courses, which carried him into the twentieth century. More than any other single man, Howe is the link between the older law school tradition and the more modern traditions pioneered by Willard Hurst.[10]

By and large, however, the law school tradition has had an Anglo-American colonial orientation, according to which the point of the exercise is to trace the transit of legal ideas and institutions from the old country to the new. My suspicion is that the focus on the colonial period is in part due to the constraints of time in teaching a one-semester course on American legal history—if one begins with the Conquest, it is very difficult to get past the Revolution in twelve weeks! Indeed, most of the older law school courses focused on the seventeenth-century American experience as a way of distinguishing American ideas and institutions from those of our English forebears. The principal subjects treated in these courses were the capacity of Americans for rude adaptation of older institutions to frontier conditions in the seventeenth century, the reception of the common law in the eighteenth century, and the separateness of the legal systems in the several colonies. The courses tended to be characterized by the technical rigor of legal analysis, the commitment to research in sources, a tendency to be tough, dry, and unpopular with law students, and, at the same time, an ironic present-mindedness. This last attribute is probably the most important, for in an effort to justify the very existence of their courses to law school deans the early teachers were forced to argue (although it certainly seems to have been their own firm belief) the contemporary relevance of the historical material they were studying. This drove them in the direction of demonstrating the rootedness of current legal ideas in ancient ideas and practices. They could demonstrate very nicely that contemporary lawyers and law students did not understand the origins of equity, although it was somewhat more difficult to show that this deficiency made any real difference in the practice of law.

The lawyer-historians were strongly associated with the documentary editing tradition begun in England, and they developed institutional financial support for their efforts, especially in the Littleton-Griswold Fund of the American Historical Association (publisher of the nine volumes of the American Legal Records Series), the William Nelson Cromwell Foundation (publisher of Smith's *Pynchon Court Record*, Goebel and Smith's *Law Practice of Alexander Hamilton*, and Wroth and Zobel's *Legal Papers of John Adams*),[11] and the Harvard Law School's Ames Foundation (publisher of medieval legal texts). These materials are, of course, almost entirely on the colonial period, and they have contributed importantly to the development of scholarship in the field, as have more recent projects such as Herbert A. Johnson, Charles Cullen, and Charles Hobson's *The Papers of John Marshall* and William E. Nelson and David T. Konig's *Plymouth Court Records*.[12] The law school teaching tradition remains strong among a younger generation, probably best exemplified by the work of John P. Reid and William E. Nelson at New York University Law School, Thomas A. Green at the University of Michigan Law School, and John H. Langbein at the University of Chicago Law School.[13] Smith and Spencer Kimball, then at the University of Michigan Law School, have published their teaching materials, and until 1980 these were the only published materials in the field.[14]

I do not mean to suggest that the scholarship of the law school teachers is to be ignored. Far from it: it has provided a solid base for the study of colonial legal history. Among those historians already mentioned, special attention should be given to Goebel and Naughton's *Law Enforcement in Colonial New York*, Smith's *Appeals to the Privy Council from the American Plantations*, and Howe's *The Garden and the Wilderness*,[15] as well as the other works by these scholars. Although so far as I know, he has never taught a general course on the subject, special attention ought also to be paid to the University of Pennsylvania Law School lawyer-historian George L. Haskins, whose *Law and Authority in Early Massachusetts* had a major effect on the field and whose long series of articles have also been very influential.[16] The character of the work done by these men is probably best epitomized in the collection of essays put together by David H. Flaherty, *Essays in the Early History of American Law*.[17]

The third significant tradition in American legal history is what might be called the arts and sciences school, which has ancient and honorable origins. It is possible to identify at least five aspects of the tradition, and I will do so at the risk of being rather arbitrary in my taxonomy.

1. The oldest of these graduate school traditions is, of course, in British constitutional history, which has had a number of eminent practitioners in the United States. Even today British constitutional history remains an important field of study at both the graduate and undergraduate levels in the

United States (increasingly more so at the undergraduate level), but it is also a derivative field, parasitic on models and traditions developed in Great Britain. We are all indebted to the work of such scholars as Charles H. McIlwain, Helen Maud Cam (of course an Englishwoman, but my own teacher at Harvard), William H. Dunham, Robert Livingston Schuyler, and many others who taught the field even though they did not do scholarship in it—such as my Princeton colleague Joseph R. Strayer. From the point of view of colonial history, this school probably reached its high point of significance almost exactly fifty years ago, in the debate between McIlwain and Schuyler on the constitutional origins of the American Revolution, a subject only recently taken up again by Barbara Black.[18]

2. Another strong but short-lived strain of colonial legal history developed in the earlier part of this century out of the English imperial school founded by Charles McLean Andrews at Yale. Viola F. Barnes, Mary P. Clarke, Dora Mae Clark, and Leonard Labaree all did work of considerable significance for colonial legal history, although surely none of them would have considered herself or himself a "legal" historian. It is clear, however, that Andrews's combination of training in British history, interest in the formal structure of empire, and perception of the centrality of legal forms for understanding local institutions led to research on basic questions of legal history. The most dramatic result of this interest is surely Labaree's *Royal Instructions to the Colonial Governors*, but an excellent example of technical legal history is Viola Barnes's article on land tenure in seventeenth-century New England in the Andrews Festschrift.[19] This "school" did not replicate itself, since Labaree's interests moved in other directions and most of the other students who did this sort of work were relegated to teaching in colleges that did not train graduate students. Viola Barnes seems precisely the sort of historian who might have made important contributions to colonial legal history had not the sexism of American higher education quarantined her in an undergraduate institution without satisfactory library resources. In any case, the legal structure of the empire is a subject that has gone almost totally unexamined since the early 1930s save in the important work of Joseph H. Smith.[20]

3. A third and also short-lived strain of the graduate school tradition in American legal history is represented by the work of Richard T. Ely and John R. Commons. The most significant contributions are Commons's *Legal Foundations of Capitalism* and his magisterial collections: *Documentary History of American Industrial Society* and *History of Labour in the United States*.[21] Ely and Commons were the first Americans to explore the significance of law as a fundamental element in the structure of modern capitalism and thus to assert openly the proposition that is now likely to be taken as self-evident, namely, that the Anglo-American common law is not a value-free system. This insight, which obviously owes much to the work of Marx, Weber, and the continental sociological tradition, was of course followed up more systematically in the context of European history than in that of Anglo-American

history. Still, this first "Wisconsin school" disappeared from sight until it was resurrected under the leadership of Willard Hurst.

4. One of the most obvious sources for the contemporary concern with colonial legal and constitutional history is clearly the longstanding graduate school tradition in the study of constitutional law by political scientists. Two institutions stand out as the twin homes of work in the field, for clearly most of the major scholars have been trained at Princeton and Columbia. The Princeton tradition arguably goes back to Woodrow Wilson and to the brief tenure of Charles McIlwain, but, especially to Edward Corwin and Alpheus Thomas Mason (and now Walter Murphy).[22] At Chicago the tradition was begun by Hermann Von Holst and continued by Andrew C. McLaughlin and W. T. Hutchinson in the history department, William Winslow Crosskey in the law school, and C. Herman Pritchett and Herbert Storing in the political science department.[23] With the exception of Crosskey, all of these men were outstandingly successful trainers of graduate students in history and political science, but even the political scientists were trained in a tradition that is essentially one of constitutional history.

The constitutional history tradition obviously still continues a strong, although subordinate element in American political science, but its difficulties are demonstrated by the general decline of historical scholarship and sensitivity within the field of political science and also by the reluctance or inability of major departments (for instance, the Government Department at Harvard) to attract or retain historically oriented professors of public law.

The constitutional history tradition has also continued within history departments, its leading practitioners having been such notable scholars as Henry Steele Commager of Columbia, Arthur E. Bestor of Washington University, Leonard Levy of the Claremont Graduate School, Harold Hyman of Rice, Paul Murphy of Minnesota, and Stanley I. Kutler of Wisconsin.[24] Until fairly recently, if "legal" history was taught at all in history departments, it was probably taught as constitutional history. Over the past ten years, however, where departments have had a choice, they have tended to hire scholars trained in legal rather than constitutional history.

It will be apparent that the constitutional history tradition flows naturally out of certain broad historiographical trends, and in that sense Bancroft was probably the first of the great modern constitutional historians. Recently, however, historians of law have tended to downplay constitutional history as a lesser field—technically less demanding, less likely to reveal original insights, and epiphenomenal to basic socioeconomic change. As much as anything else, the transition to legal from constitutional history probably reflects the disdain of leading law teachers for constitutional law as a field. What is prized in the law schools is hard legal analysis, and constitutional analysis is deprecated as "mere" policy preference. In this respect Morton Horwitz's strictures are typical:

. . . another, more crucial distortion has been introduced by the excessive equation of constitutional law with "law." Because of the peculiar intellectual and institutional background of judicial review, the study of constitutional law focuses historians on the nay-saying function of law and, more specifically, on the rather special circumstances of judicial intervention into statutory control. Yet judicial promulgation and enforcement of common law rules constituted an infinitely more typical pattern of the use of law throughout most of the nineteenth century. By thus focusing on private law we can study the more regular instances in which law, economy, and society interacted.[25]

Constitutional history is certainly not dead, but it is not flourishing and its significance for colonial history is not altogether obvious.

5. The fifth and perhaps most important traditional source of legal history has been what might be called the Columbia Graduate School approach. In part, this is obviously the product of Henry Commager's scholarship and his influence on a number of outstanding students, of whom Leonard Levy, Harold Hyman, and William Leuchtenburg are probably preeminent. Levy and especially Hyman have been active in training graduate students in legal history, and it well may be that no teacher has been quite so prolific as Hyman. They all began rather solidly in the constitutional history tradition, but all three have displayed an increasing interest in the legal side of the field.

There is no doubt, however, that Richard B. Morris has been the dominant figure, both as scholar and as trainer of graduate students. Morris's *Studies in the History of American Law: with Special Reference to the Seventeenth and Eighteenth Centuries*, based on his dissertation, and his *Government and Labor in Early America* marked outstanding efforts by a historian to work squarely within the parameters of what might properly be called "legal" history.[26] Morris was content to study the manuscript records of civil courts of all kinds, and he is really the first historian to make a frontal attack on the problem of the relationship of ordinary legal doctrine to social process. His first book was fraught with minor errors and methodological difficulties, and Morris was attacked savagely in the law reviews for his presumption in treading upon the supposed terrain of the lawyers. There is little doubt that he was at least somewhat frightened off the field because of this response, but he nevertheless continued to explore legal sources and to encourage his students to work with them. Milton M. Klein and Herbert A. Johnson are only two of the outstanding examples of Morris's impact as a trainer of legal historians,[27] and until recently he was virtually the only colonial historian to take seriously the challenge of stimulating work in legal history. The truth of the matter is that although legal historians have appeared from time to time, prior to 1970 there was virtually no systematic attempt to train in the field, nor was there, so far as I am aware, an endowed history department chair in American legal history prior to the creation of the Class of 1921 Bicentennial Professorship at Princeton in the mid-1970s.

Returning to my list of the major traditions in American legal history, the fourth, and clearly the most important, is that begun after World War II by James Willard Hurst at the University of Wisconsin Law School. The Hurstian tradition has proved far and away most persuasive with a younger generation of historians, and it is the tradition that has provided what is currently the most persuasive methodology for work in the field. Hurst has surely been the most prolific of American legal historians since the war, but his influence among younger practitioners has been the result not so much of the content of his work as of his methods, which have suggested entirely new ways to *do* legal history.

Hurst has focused on the economy as the central element in American legal history, somewhat after the fashion of his Wisconsin school predecessors. He has emphasized state and local history as being the level at which the actual machinery of social process can best be determined. He has extended the list of those institutions that must be considered "legal," and he has stressed institutions rather than ideas—with the result that the traditional focus of legal history on legal doctrine, or at least case law, has been diminished. Correspondingly, Hurst has struggled to shift the focus of legal historians from courts, especially appellate courts, to legislatures and regulatory agencies. He has insisted upon the primacy of the study of the nineteenth and twentieth centuries for understanding the origins of our contemporary legal system, and he has displayed a marked sympathy for the social sciences as handmaidens of historians, although his own work is not particularly suffused with modern social-science methodology.

None of this will sound particularly dramatic or exciting to an audience of colonial historians. Nevertheless, it seems to have come as news to a good many traditional legal historians working at the time Hurst began to propagate his message, and his influence has been enhanced by his continuing interest in writing about historical methodology and by his attempts at system building. Hurst began these efforts in 1950 with his taxonomic treatise *The Growth of American Law: The Law Makers*, which he followed up ten years later with his Cooley lectures at the University of Michigan Law School, published under the title *Law and Social Process in United States History*. He has continued the tradition with his Carl Becker lectures at Cornell in 1976, entitled *Law and Social Order in the United States*, but doubtless his outstanding contribution to the understanding of the general role of law in American history was his 1955 Julius Rosenthal lectures at Northwestern University School of Law, entitled *Law and the Conditions of Freedom in the Nineteenth Century United States*.[28] Hurst's influence has been most profound and immediate upon his own colleagues at Wisconsin, Lawrence Friedman (now at Stanford Law School), Stanley I. Kutler, and Robert W. Gordon (and, doubtless, upon myself), but by the mid-1960s it became clear that his writings had become persuasive for a great many younger historians attracted to legal history as a primary field of study. This attraction was doubtless hastened by the intelligently adulatory articles written about Hurst by David Flaherty and Harry Scheiber.[29]

The catholicity of Hurst's appeal is evident from the beginning of his Becker lectures.

> At first sight, the study of the legal history of the United States is a specialized inquiry, dealing with only one dimension of complex events. Yet it is an unusual speciality, for the events of which the law was a part range over most of the country's experience. One can more readily separate out from the other aspects of the society the history of the family, or the church, or the school than he can the history of law. That this was a law-minded, law-using people, whose affairs were touched by legal processes at many points, is a basic fact that quickly enforces itself on one who examines legal elements in the life of the United States. Legal history is a way of studying the general history of the country's character and development.[30]

Hurst continues to make a characteristic argument about the immediacy of legal history:

> Basic also is the way that people generally have used law in a narrowly practical way. Typically they were concerned with law more as an instrument for desired immediate results than as a statement of carefully legitimated, long-range values. . . the values that people wrote into law and more or less implemented through law did not add up to a neatly balanced, conceptually complete pattern of human interest. . . .
>
> That uses of law reach broadly through the life of the country without also embodying a comparably broad philosophy of these uses creates problems for telling the history of law. What went on is such a mixture of calculation as to defy neat relation. There can be no single point of view from which all United States legal history falls into a coherent sequence. Rather, the subject must be turned this way and that, to catch different but relevant aspects of a complex reality.[31]

In other words, what Hurst has captured is Americans' pervasive sense that their society is uniquely lawbound. Most of us share the more or less unexamined feeling that law is central to the American experience in ways that we cannot very precisely specify; Hurst has tried to indicate to a new generation of historians the ways in which we can avoid descending into Tocquevillian generalities in dealing with the problem of law in American society. That he has implicitly argued for the democratic and liberal tendencies of American law has been seldom noticed and little criticized; what is perhaps most relevant for his impact on the study of the colonial period is that he has strenuously argued against it.

I remember quite well the moment in 1965 when, upon arriving in Madison, I had my first interview with Hurst. I described to him my project for investigating the history of chancery courts and equity law in the eighteenth century in the hope of understanding the persistent political struggle in colonial America over the legitimacy of chancery courts. First a look of puzzlement passed across the face of this, the world's kindest man, and then he gently remarked that the subject was of no contemporary significance. He suggested to me, very quietly, that if I were truly interested in understanding the origins of the American legal system, I would address myself to the period after 1870, when the industrial corporation had transformed American life to such an extent that American history before 1870 was essentially discontinuous with what followed. It was a shattering experience for a fledgling colonial historian, especially one who was even less confident of his ability as a legal historian. The fact of the matter is, however, that the thrust of Hurst's ideology has been both Whiggish and present-minded and that it has captured the imagination of many of the best young legal historians, with the result that they have tended to abandon the colonial period as irrelevant to their professional concerns. And that, essentially, is the point of this historiographical excursus.[32]

A brief foray into the sociology of legal history will be helpful at this point. What needs to be stressed is that as a field, American legal history is only about ten years old, if we define "field" as an area of study with the sense of its own intellectual integrity and with an organized institutional structure to promote it. Although the American Society for Legal History has just celebrated its twenty-fifth birthday and the *American Journal of Legal History* is likewise a quarter of a century old, the organization and the journal were originally dominated by a small group of law professors and practitioners whose interests were more antiquarian than scholarly. It was only in the late 1960s, when George Haskins reorganized the society and began to recruit history-trained members, that the society began to play an intellectual role in the development of the field. At about this time the journal was also reorganized under the editorship of William E. Nelson (a lawyer and history Ph.D. student of Bernard Bailyn), and for the first time a legal history monographic series was established at the Harvard University Press, under my editorship.[33]

The Harvard Law School played a central role in the new developments. I have already remarked that members of the Harvard faculty have been teaching and writing in American legal history since the time of Roscoe Pound, but in the late 1950s the first-year program was reorganized, and both Mark Howe and Jack Dawson began to offer elective courses in legal history on a regular basis. At about this time the school received a grant from the Carnegie Corporation to establish fellowships in law and humanities, intended to bring humanists to the school for a year in order to give them sufficient legal training to bring legal perspectives to bear on their humanistic work. This program and others like it which sprang up elsewhere (particularly at Yale) have provided a large number of historians (including myself) with the technical training necessary to pursue the field seriously. Upon the death of Professor Howe in 1967, unable to lure Hurst from his post at Wisconsin, the school (at the urging of Jerome A. Cohen) began to devote the income from Howe's Charles Warren Professorship of the History of American Law to train young lawyers, notably Morton J. Horwitz and William E. Nelson, as legal historians. The school also undertook to place young legal historians in law school teaching posts and in 1969 hired Horwitz as an assistant professor. By 1971 products of the Harvard program occupied permanent positions in legal history at the Harvard, University of Pennsylvania, and University of Chicago law schools, and it quickly became apparent that for law schools legal history had become an "in" field. This occurred at the moment that the employment market for history Ph.D.'s began to decline, and thus the field of legal history suddenly seemed quite attractive, since if it had no other allure, it could pay its way.

Ten years ago, then, the field of American legal history was terribly exciting and seemed to promise great scholarly progress in a relatively short period of time. In some ways that promise has been fulfilled. The monographic series at Harvard reached nine volumes, at least a few of them truly distinguished; now transplanted to North Carolina, the series has almost doubled in size. One of the volumes in the original series, Horwitz's *The Transformation of American Law*, won the Bancroft Prize and has attracted considerable attention, while one of the most recent publications in the new series, David Allen's *In English Ways*,[34] was awarded the Jamestown Prize for Early American History. The quality of writing in the *American Journal of Legal History* has improved dramatically, and courses in American legal history are now offered much more regularly in law schools and history departments. The law schools, at least, have come to see the field as a necessary component of a sophisticated curriculum, and history departments have sensed the marketability of legal history, if not necessarily its intellectual significance. Joint appointments between law schools and history departments have become more common, existing now at such institutions as Chicago, Michigan, Case Western Reserve, Virginia, and Florida, to name only those institutions that come immediately to mind. Superficially, all is well.

II

For a colonial historian the retrospect is distressing. We have simply not made the progress anticipated ten years ago, and it seems to me that there is very little reason to believe that the situation will improve in the foreseeable future. So far as I know, there are few courses specifically in the field; indeed, I am not sure whether since I ceased teaching my own course in American colonial legal history at Wisconsin, in 1971, anyone regularly teaches such a course. Much more important, we have not been producing significant numbers of young Ph.D.'s in the field. To be sure, there have been some bright lights on the horizon, younger scholars who have done significant work in colonial legal history, but the truth is that very few of them would consider themselves to be primarily legal historians, and a good many of them are not very likely to do further work in the field. Several have left history departments, or even the teaching profession, and even fewer are in a position to train graduate students in the field. Most of the members of this distinguished list are historians who have used legal sources, but for most of them, law is not the necessary or central focus of their work. It has provided the source materials for work in social, intellectual, or political history without being the central focus of scholarly effort. Legal history, even colonial legal history, is at the moment increasingly the preserve of law schools and law teachers, and this raises significant problems for the future development of scholarship.

I have already mentioned some of the apparent reasons why the legal history of colonial America has not developed satisfactorily; now I would like to return to them. The first, and most obvious, is the fact that virtually all of the sources for colonial legal history are in manuscript, and even these are scattered, incomplete, and difficult to use. They can be distinguished from the sorts of manuscript sources most of us have used in writing more traditional forms of colonial history by the fact that no single or discrete body of records is likely to yield very much information. Legal history generally requires the examination of great quantities of material, for it is ordinarily quite low-yield ore. A second difficulty is the technical obscurity of much of colonial law. Few colonial historians know enough legal doctrine or procedure to deal satisfactorily with hard legal questions, and in fact it is very difficult to acquire the necessary expertise, since the law schools themselves do not attend to the problems of such old law. Third, and very significant, is the fact that current scholarship in English legal history tends to stop short in the late Middle Ages or at best in the mid-seventeenth century. Thus, the Americanist cannot readily discover the antecedents of or analogies to colonial problems in the mother country, since his English counterparts have not taken the trouble to investigate the modern history of their own law. Finally, it is probably necessary to admit that much research in legal history is difficult, tedious, and intellectually unchallenging. The nature of the materials and the questions that need to be answered before we can rise to a higher level of historical questioning have not proved attractive to younger scholars, and this is not surprising. We do not yet understand the basic procedures of seventeenth-century or even early eighteenth-century American law; it is probably necessary, for instance, to learn much more about the nature of systematic efforts to record deeds before we can make sensible generalizations about patterns of property inheritance.[35]

Faced with these problems, most young historians have turned either to other problems within colonial history or, if they were sufficiently committed to legal history, to the study of postcolonial history. Alas, one of the most significant problems for the colonial field is that the intellectual argument for disregarding the period as irrelevant to the national history of American law has been resurrected over the past several years, and it is to this problem that I shall turn briefly.

The historical profession is now methodologically sophisticated enough to realize that periodization is a substantive rather than a procedural issue. For legal history, periodization has been an absolutely central issue, one that has negatively affected colonial scholarship. The difficulty first surfaced in the 1936 Livingston lectures, delivered by Roscoe Pound at Tulane University in 1936 and published in 1938 as *The Formative Era of American Law*.[36] Pound was commemorating the one hundredth anniversary of the death of Edward Livingston, the great codifier, and he marked the occasion by describing the era "extending from independence to the time of the Civil War" as the "formative era of American law."[37] Pound described the colonial era as "the age of Coke," not the "age of Mansfield."

> It was heavily burdened with the formalism of the strict law. Its ideals were those of the relationally organized society of the Middle Ages and so quite out of line with the needs and ideas of men who are opening up the wilderness. It spoke from an era of organization while the colonists represented an oncoming era of individualism. But there was little need for law until the economic development of the colonies and the rise of trade and commerce in the eighteenth century. Then there began to be trained lawyers practicing in the courts and courts manned by trained lawyers, so that the reception of the common law and reshaping it into a law for America were well begun at the time of the Revolution. The Revolution, however, and its results in the years immediately following, set back this development for a time and led to a critical period in the history of our law. The conservatism characteristic of lawyers led many of the strongest men at the bar to take the royalist side and decimated the profession. . . . Moreover, political conditions gave rise to a general distrust of English law.[38]

"Social and geographical conditions contributed also to make the work of receiving and reshaping the common law exceptionally difficult," Pound contended.

> The idea of a profession was repugnant to the Jeffersonian era. The feeling was strong that all callings should be on the same footing. . . . Geographical conditions completed the process of decentralizing the law and deprofessionalizing the lawyers. In a country of long distances at a time of slow and expensive travel, the common law system of central courts and a centralized bar imposed an intolerable burden upon litigants. For a time there was a veritable cult of local law.[39]

As opposed to this picture of stasis and even decay, Pound imagined a creative "formative era" whose task it was, "in the face of these difficulties, to work out from our inherited legal materials a general body of law for what was to be a politically and economically unified land." He concluded, rather startlingly, that "whether they thought to make over or to build anew, the lawyers and judges and teachers of the formative era found their creating and organizing idea in the theory of natural law."[40] Pound's three lectures work out this notion of the use of natural law in the formulation of modern American law with elegance and in a way that was immediately attractive to his intended audience, members of the legal profession of the 1930s. His approach was also intended to glorify the task of the legal scholar and the law teacher. Arguing that the founders of the American legal tradition had little to go on save their own intuition and appreciation of the values of natural law, Pound acknowledged the tremendous outpouring of judicial creativity during the nineteenth century and the consequent immensity of law, litigation, and technical detail that confronted twentieth-century judges. "If they are to do their work well, there must be a thorough working over of the law which has come down to us as only jurists and law writers can do it. And no one who has followed the history of American law can doubt that the jurists and law writers who are to do this will be law teachers."[41]

Pound's interpretation, for all of its difficulties, was immensely influential with legal scholars, and I now recall with some amusement that my first historiographical effort in legal history was an attempt to argue the case for a fundamental continuity between eighteenth-century and post-Revolutionary American law.[42] Fifteen years ago my feeling was that given the sophistication with which colonial history was being written and the distinction of the colonial historians within the field of American history, the integral place of colonial law in American legal history would become increasingly obvious. In fact, so far as I can tell, mine was a voice crying in the wilderness, and recent scholarship in legal history has tended to reinforce Pound's periodization, although for reasons that would have horrified the Harvard dean.

A few examples will suffice to make my point clear. I have already referred to Willard Hurst's modernism, but it is worth noting his very brief reference to colonial legal history in his most influential work, *Law and the Conditions of Freedom*. Hurst sees individualism as the most profound value in American culture, and he acknowledges that nineteenth-century law "drew on values rooted in our colonial past."

> But there was a difference and tension between social-economic and legal growth in the colonial years. Social and economic development tended to create a way of life and a pattern of human relations which generated an individual's habits of independence and expectations of mobility in social status or influence. But through a good part of the colonial years the dominant tone in the law was defensive rather than expansive, furthering stability rather than change and emphasizing the security or strength of the colony more than the freedom of the individual. So far as we use law to meet the challenge of environment, colonial statute books imply that we sought primarily to enlarge the range of options of the community as a social entity.[43]

Hurst argues that "security was a natural emphasis in colonial law," especially as expressed in loyalty legislation. He acknowledges the pervasiveness of morality in law but argues that "in the background was the consciousness of lonely communities on trial before God and the hard facts. There was all too little strength to meet the challenge of our situation; we must hold closely together, save and not waste, and prevent internal dissentions born of envy and unseemly striving."[44] Colonial law, that is, was communal, conservative, and moralistic, whereas truly American law (the law of the nineteenth century) was creative, expansive, and pragmatic. For Hurst, not much can be learned from the colonial experience to explain the emergence of a national law.

Perry Miller, ironically, lent credence to this periodization, if not to its rationale. In *The Life of the Mind in America from the Revolution to the Civil War*,[45] Miller honors the idea of "the legal mentality" by ignoring the colonial period altogether. Without going far into his fascinating account, it would appear that he equates the emergence of American law with the rise of a profession of lawyers, which he saw as occurring in the new republic. The story of law was forced into the mold of a conflict between Heart and Head, a morality play in which the democratizing instincts of the codifiers lost out to the aristocratic instincts of the pseudoscientific Common Lawyers. The substance of Miller's critique is not at issue in this paper, but it is obviously significant that one of the leading historians of colonial intellectual life should choose to ignore entirely the significance of law prior to the Revolution.

More recently, the traditional periodization was elegantly (if unconvincingly) restated in Grant Gilmore's *The Ages of American Law*. Gilmore argues that the notion of "a generalized theory of the common law" dates from the late eighteenth century.

> Blackstone had no predecessors. By the end of the century, lawyers had put aside their plumbers' image and become philosophers—an upgrading of status which the legal mind naturally found irresistible. . . .
>
> The eighteenth century invented not only law or jurisprudence but also history, economics and sociology—that is, the whole range of what came to be called the social sciences.[46]

Gilmore understands Blackstone's achievement as profoundly conservative—an attempt to defend traditional legal values against the incredible change which the industrial revolution was wreaking upon English society. In his view, the pace of legal change increased exponentially in the late eighteenth century because of the self-conscious attempt by the judges to bring the law into conformity with what they perceived as the new social requirements of the era.

> We might say, making use of the famous eighteenth-century formulation, that in its own time the Blackstonian thesis (which represented what the conservative establishment wanted the law to be) was confronted with its Mansfieldian antithesis (which represented what the courts were actually doing with the law during a period of extraordinary change). The resultant nineteenth-century

synthesis . . . came out muddy and blurred . . . but with the Blackstonian
element on the whole in the ascendant.[47]

This same tension was the source of what Gilmore describes as the "beginnings" of American law, which he dates from "1800 or thereabouts." He
acknowledges that this periodization "seems to pass over, with cavalier dis-
regard, the nearly two hundred years of our colonial history," but he dis-
misses the colonial era with the assertion that "the development of legal
institutions during those two centuries, which makes a fascinating story, is,
for a variety of reasons, irrelevant to our discussion." He believes that "the
law of the primitive agricultural settlements which were painfully hacked
from the wilderness in the seventeenth century . . . had no more relevance
to the law of our own industrial society than the law of the Sioux or the
Cheyennes."[48] He recognizes that a legal profession emerged in the eighteenth century but says that since there were no published law reports and
since there was not a centralized court system, "it is pointless to speak of an
'American law' before the 1880s."[49] Indeed, for Gilmore, the distinctive
feature of American law is that it was created out of whole cloth in the
nineteenth century, that it did not emerge organically in the way that English
law had. "Our system was, from the beginning, consciously designed as a
sort of formal garden instead of being allowed to come up as it might from the
compost heap of the centuries. Our English cousins have been the romantics
of the law. We have been—at least we have tried to be—the classicists."[50]
The colonial historian hardly knows where to begin in dealing with such
nonsense.

But the real damage has doubtless been done by two of the finest historians
to emerge in the last decade, William E. Nelson and Morton J. Horwitz.
Starting from radically different premises, Nelson and Horwitz both reject
the significance of colonial law. The titles of their two books—Nelson's
Americanization of the Common Law, 1760–1830 and Horwitz's *The Transformation of American Law, 1780–1860*—make the point sufficiently clear.

Nelson views the Revolutionary War as the motivating force in the "Americanization" of law: "The War of Independence ushered in the beginning of a
new legal and social order of Massachusetts. Although little legal change
occurred during the war itself, the attempts of the revolutionary generation
to explain and justify the war and its political results set loose new intellectual and social currents which ultimately transformed the legal and social
structure of the new state."[51] He views the prerevolutionary eighteenth
century through idealizing lenses and images Massachusetts society as characterized by ethical unity, communitarianism, and stability, all of which
were undermined by the socioeconomic effects of the Revolution.

> Whether it was made by the courts or legislatures, law in nineteenth-century
> America had ceased to be a mechanism for the preservation of local power and
> the building of local consensus or to be a mirror of stable and widely shared

ethical values. In part it had become a mechanism for giving individuals liberty to choose their own ethical values and for enforcing choices they made. More often, however, the function of the law was to resolve disputes among individuals seeking control over a particular economic resource. In resolving those distributional disputes, the law came to be a tool by which those interest groups that had emerged victorious in the competition for control of lawmaking institutions could seize most of the society's wealth for themselves and enforce their seizure upon the losers.[52]

Horwitz's account is in an even more precarious position—on a tightrope stretched between Marx and Hurst.

In his tremendously influential *Transformation of American Law*, Horwitz begins by agreeing with the traditional acknowledgment of the formative impact of the early nineteenth century upon American law. He contends that before the nineteenth century American judges "almost never self-consciously employed the common law as a creative instrument for directing men's energies toward social change." "What dramatically distinguished nineteenth century law from its eighteenth century counterpart," he says, "was the extent to which common law judges came to play a central role in directing the course of social change."[53]

He views eighteenth-century law as based on the common law, "a body of essentially fixed doctrine to be applied in order to achieve a fair result between private litigants in individual cases."[54] For Horwitz, however, it is not the Revolution that accounts for the "transforming surge of postrevolutionary legal activity" but rather an "alliance between intellect and power"[55]— that is, an alliance between judges and the commercial classes of early nineteenth-century America, which deliberately overturned the stable legal system of the eighteenth century.

> By 1820 the legal landscape in American bore only the faintest resemblance to what existed forty years earlier. While the words were often the same, the structure of thought had dramatically changed and with it the theory of law. Law was no longer conceived of as an eternal set of principles expressed in custom and derived from natural law. Nor was it primarily regarded as a body of rules designed to achieve justice only in the individual case. Instead, judges came to think of the common law as equally responsible with legislation for governing society and promoting socially desirable conduct. The emphasis on law as an instrument of policy encouraged innovation and allowed judges to formulate legal doctrine with the self-conscious goal of bringing about social change. And from this changed perspective, American law stood on the verge of what Daniel Boorstin has correctly called one of the great "creative outbursts of modern legal history."[56]

Thus Nelson and Horwitz, like Pound, believe that colonial law is to be either ignored or caricatured as stable, unchanging, and in the end uninteresting.

I have labored my argument about the "formative era" deliberately. The best of the new work that accepts the old chronological parameters does so for sound, substantive reasons. Nelson and Horwitz have coherent views of the nature and functioning of modern American law which lead them to focus on certain aspects of early national law in order to explain the sources of persistent problems in American law. They cannot be challenged, then, simply by rejecting their periodization.

It might be noticed at this point, however, that even if I am wrong in my rejection of the argument for the discontinuity of colonial and national law, it would still be appropriate to stress the importance of the early period. We should know more than we currently do about "stable, preindustrial communities" in order to comprehend the distinctiveness of "modern" legal systems; that is, we must know what modern law is *not*. Also, the study of colonial, preindustrial law would help us to identify the ways in which industrial society requires particular legal regimes. It would be especially helpful to understand the cultural changes that transform the American understanding of such concepts as authority and property.[57]

III

I believe that a coherent and compelling interpretation of the colonial period which makes the colonial era relevant to a national history of law and is the unfulfilled challenge to the current generation of colonial legal historians can be put forward. A fair amount of effort, especially by younger historians, has been spent in working through the materials of colonial legal history. Thus, at the very least, we know more than we ever did about the context and nature of colonial legal behavior. What remains quite unclear, however, is the relationship of the colonial legal experience to the larger fabric of colonial history and, equally, to the contours of American national history. I will devote the remainder of this paper to an impressionistic account of these problems.

As long ago as 1945, Zechariah Chafee, Jr., addressed the Massachusetts Historical Society on the nature of colonial law and the various strategies that had been propounded for analyzing it.[58] The problem for Chafee was to understand what the colonists meant by "the common law," and he suggested three possible scholarly answers to the question. The first was that the common law of England was substantially in force in the colonies from the time of their settlement.[59] Only Joseph Story and Lemuel Shaw could be cited in support of this view, although it is arguable that Jefferson himself supported the position in *Notes on Virginia*. Chafee concluded that there was really no evidence for this position.

The second hypothesis was that "the colonists had in large measure their own kind of law for a long time after their settlement in America." This position was first put forward by Paul S. Reinsch as early as 1899, and it was also supported by the work of Charles J. Hilkey.[60] The general hypothesis of Reinsch and Hilkey can be stated in two propositions: "First, the original law of the colonies was for the most part very different from English law and had a rude, popular nature. Secondly, eventually a reception of most of the rules of the English common law took place. This was a process somewhat resembling the well-known Reception of Roman Law into Germany and Holland during the Renaissance."[61] Chafee rejected this proposition, since it was apparent, even in 1945, that systematic study of seventeenth-century American legal records refuted the notion that American law was entirely or even predominantly a crude response to frontier conditions. The records revealed a quite sophisticated, if not necessarily systematic, use of formal legal concepts and procedures in the early colonies. Likewise, Chafee could not ascertain any particular break in colonial legal history that would correspond to a dramatic "reception" of the common law.

The third hypothesis suggested in the literature reviewed by Chafee was "that colonial law was English local law."[62] This, of course, was largely the argument put forward in Julius Goebel's brilliant 1931 essay, "King's Law and Local Custom in Seventeenth-Century New England."[63] Chafee quoted Goebel's famous statement that "so accustomed are we to focus our attention upon the expansion of the King's law that we have closed our eyes to the fact that at the outset of the seventeenth century local custom and local courts were still an immensely important part of the law administration in England."[64] Goebel, of course, stressed that this proposition did not place him in agreement with Reinsch that seventeenth-century American law was primitive. On the contrary, he contended that the earliest colonists were drawing upon quite sophisticated notions of local and customary law in organizing their legal behavior.

Chafee concluded, not very surprisingly, that something of all three theories might account for the actual fact; he termed this "the synthetic-rubber hypothesis because it endeavors to combine several elements with an elastic common law"!

> It may turn out that Winthrop and Penn and the rest brought over the common law as a body of principles, and not as the mass of case-law which Story knew; that it was always binding on the settlers, but required to be supplemented from other sources of unwritten law in order to meet their increasingly complex needs, with which local legislation could not possibly keep pace. Reinsch and Goebel and other critics of Story have supplied valuable information about these auxiliary sources of colonial law, but have perhaps exaggerated their importance and underestimated that of the common law. According to this surmise, there was no "reception" of the common law in the colonies. It was there from the start in some form, yet not the same form. I think of it as an outline map which was gradually filled in as the growth of law libraries and serious legal students brought more and more case-law and detailed doctrines from England. Law was a function of law-books.

Such a developing common law would naturally play an increasing part in the administration of justice outside the scope of colonial statutes and it would tend to displace whatever existed of homemade law or English local law. The long process can be considered at an end when the records show judges and lawyers in an American court reasoning and using precedents like their contemporaries in an English court. Yet something may still remain of the factors stressed by Reinsch and Goebel, especially in petty litigation and in situations where English rules of action are plainly unsuited to American conditions.[65]

I have quoted from Chafee at considerable length because, although he was writing almost forty years ago, his "synthetic-rubber" hypothesis is probably about as sophisticated as any currently in use. And that is precisely the problem.

Legal historians and, I suspect, general historians have been operating on the basis of very crude assumptions about the general character of the colonial legal system. Exaggerating for effect, let me describe what I take the model to be. The earliest colonists brought with them primitive notions of English royal as well as local law but adapted it fairly freely as local circumstance and a lack of legal expertise permitted. They had the rudiments of what they imagined to be the English common-law system in mind and in fact attempted to implement it insofar as they were able. As the economy and social structure of the colonies matured in the last thirty years of the seventeenth century, however, the colonists were driven to employ lawyers and therefore to imitate English reality much more closely than they had previously.[66] This was an organic process which proceeded largely under the spur of the commercialization of the early eighteenth century (in a process we might as well call Anglicization) and, with the emergence of an increasingly numerous class of lawyers and the increasing importance of English law books, resulted by 1750 in a colonial legal system substantially like that of the mother country. The similarity of the colonial legal system to the common law, when placed in the context of British constitutionalism in the seventeenth century, resulted in colonial dissatisfaction with British authoritarianism both in 1689 and, more important, in the Revolutionary era. The Americans of the late eighteenth century were thus confronted with the apparent contradiction of a commitment to common-law values and procedures and a rejection of things British, which they resolved by anti-British rhetoric and common-law reality. It is, in fact, not a bad model, but it needs to be articulated more carefully than hitherto has been done.

From the point of view of general history, some such overview will probably suffice to locate the proximate role of law in cultural development. But it cannot do more, and it may prove to be seriously misleading when more scholarly returns are in. Such a hypothesis is still modeled upon the old "sources" of our legal-tradition approach. The question that Reinsch, Hilkey, Goebel, and Chafee were putting was essentially one of cultural patterning, although it is clear that Chafee was trying to break out of this tradition. It was assumed that the colonists must have had preformed notions of appropriate legal behavior and that in order to understand their behavior, it was the primary task of the legal historian to understand the *original* pattern. There are anthropological difficulties with such assumptions, but even more significant, they tend to shift the attention of historians from the legal behavior of the colonists and their own articulated assumptions to the search for precolonial origins. The "sources" analysis is the seventeenth-century analogy to the "origins" approach to the constitutional history of the early republic, which has focused so devastatingly on the intentions of the framers and the late eighteenth-century governmental experience. My objection is that it is essentially a diversionary approach, distracting us from concentration upon the primary phenomena which we ought to be studying.

IV

Despite my lamentations at the outset of this paper, it is clear that a great deal of progress has been made in studying the operational character of colonial law and legal institutions. No one who has read the work of David Konig and David Grayson Allen, not to mention that of George L. Haskins, on the seventeenth century or the writings of Douglas Greenberg and A. G. Roeber, not to mention those of John Murrin, on the eighteenth century could fail to understand a great deal more about the functioning of law in colonial American society.[67] Some of these historians are themselves adept in technical legal analysis, and they are all sensitive to the various ways in which law actually worked as a social artifact. To summon up a single example, if one compares the present-day sophisticated approach to the Salem witch trials of 1692–93 with the previously existing interpretations, one cannot fail to be impressed by a new subtlety and sensitivity to a multiplicity of social processes.[68]

Thus, at least two important steps forward have been taken in the past decade. First, the pool of historically trained investigators competent to understand the internal operation of legal process has increased; second, the notion that the history of law is inextricably entwined in the fabric of general social behavior has been accepted, so that the history of law must be attended to by any historian with serious pretentions to understanding social change. My one real satisfaction with the progress of the field is that the use of legal materials has been made more possible by the gradual demystification of law and by their increasing use by historians who would not consider themselves "legal" historians. I suppose an excellent example of this phenomenon would be the remarkable use that John Demos has made of Essex County legal materials in research for his witchcraft study.[69] Even in this area progress can still be made, but so long as an increasing number of legal historians are present in history departments to guide students by instruction and example, it is likely that increasing use will be made of previously neglected legal sources. But this will not necessarily augment the sophistication of the legal history of the colonial era.

Just as one difficulty—the "mystery" of law—has been diminished, another problem has emerged. It arises out of the professional bifurcation of the field, that is, between historians and law teachers. Fifty years ago, such lawyer-historians as Julius Goebel dismissed the scholarship of historically trained scholars as technically incompetent and trivial—one needs only to remember the immediate response to Richard Morris's dissertation.[70] The historians, to be sure, responded in kind, denying that the lawyers knew enough of the historical context to write useful history and, more serious, arguing that the lawyers espoused a view of legal history that was "internalist" and thus irrelevant to the study of general history. Such controversy is now rare, and it would certainly be misplaced. Historians may or may not agree with Morton Horwitz, but the Bancroft selectors were surely correct in labeling him non-dismissible.

What the historically trained legal historian now encounters, however, is the intellectual dilemma of the law teacher: is law a scholarly discipline? Without going into this vexing problem, it is sufficient to say that an increasing uncertainty as to the intellectual integrity of law taken as a discipline by itself has led some of the brightest members of the new generation of law teachers to search outside of the legal system for intellectual legitimacy. The most creative efforts in this direction have taken diametrically opposed political orientations: on the one hand, the conservative law and economics movement; on the other hand, the new "Critical" legal studies movement. The Critical Studies scholars have been especially committed to the study of history. Their commitment and example have forced legal historians, especially in law schools, to contend with an ideological debate of tremendous pertinence to their intellectual orientation. To locate one's self ideologically, then, has become a central problem in a way that it has not been for the general historian since the early 1950s. The new orientations bring with them exciting possibilities for historical interpretation, but they also bring the usual dangers of ideological history, and they tend to be diversions from the main task of understanding the past.[71]

The Critical scholars have been particularly forceful in challenging the validity of the now traditional categories of liberal political thought (such as the distinctions between state and civil society, law and economy, public and private). They emphasize the inherent contradiction in liberal social organization:

> Most participants in American legal culture believe that the goal of individual freedom is at the same time dependent on and incompatible with the communal coercive action that is necessary to achieve it. Others (family, friends, bureaucrats, cultural figures, the state) are necessary if we are to become persons at all—they provide us the stuff of our selves and protect us in crucial ways

against destruction. . . . But at the same time that it forms and protects us, the universe of others . . . threatens us with annihilation and urges upon us forms of fusion that are plainly bad rather than good . . . [but] the abolition of these illegitimate structures, the fashioning of an unalienated collective existence, appears to imply such a massive increase of collective control over our lives that it would defeat its purpose.[72]

The insight is psychological as well as historical, for "the very structures against which we rebel are necessarily within us as well as outside us."[73] The political task of the Critical legal historian, therefore, is to identify liberal categories that provide false justification for the present legal systems of domination and individual unfreedom and to provide the intellectual means of individual self-liberation. This is heavy stuff. It makes the enterprise of legal history much more than an intellectual exercise; so far the Critical scholars have not had much impact on legal historians trained in history.[74]

One problem of historical interpretation that the pressure of ideological debate has thrust to center stage is the concept of the "autonomy" of law. Put too simply, the difficulty is to ascertain the degree to which law is a truly independent institution, existing and changing according to rules generated from within the system, and developing without any necessary synchronization with general social change. It is a problem that has been a commonplace of Marxist scholarship for nearly a century and a half, but it has taken on new urgency in the current intellectual climate. A wide variety of specific theories have been put forward to account for the interdependence of law and society, ranging from a liberal interpretation of Willard Hurst (and followers such as Lawrence Friedman) to the Gramscian views of Eugene Genovese.[75]

Genovese's sophisticated view of the role of law in southern slave society typifies the nature of this concern. He criticizes "the fashionable relegation of law to the rank of a superstructural and derivative phenomenon" as obscuring "the degree of autonomy" that law creates for itself. He regards law as serving the "hegemonic function" of facilitating class domination. "Ruling classes differ, and each must rule differently. But all modern ruling classes have much in common in their attitude toward the law, for each must confront the problem of coercion in such a way as to minimize the necessity for its use, and each must disguise the extent to which state power does not so much rest on force as represent its actuality." Law serves such a purpose for the ruling class.

> The juridicial system may become, then not merely an expression of class interest, nor even merely an expression of the willingness of the rulers to mediate with the ruled; it may become an instrument by which the advanced section of the ruling class imposes its viewpoint upon the class as a whole and the wider society. The law must discipline the ruling class and guide and educate the masses. To accomplish these tasks it must manifest a degree of even-handedness sufficient to compel social conformity; it must, that is, validate itself ethically in the eyes of the several classes, not just the ruling class.

The argument is, then, that the law serves an integrative purpose by assuring members of the society "that their particular consciences can be subordinated—indeed morally must be subordinated—to the collective judgment of society."[76]

It seems likely that in time a theory of the superstructural character of law will emerge out of the work of the historical anthropologists, such as Isaac, Roeber, Innes, and Breen, acting under the influence of the cultural anthropology of Clifford Geertz and Victor Turner.[77] Our attention has turned, then, from the "sources" of law to the functional relationship of law to general social process. This is doubtless a step forward in sophistication, but it also launches the historian into an arena of methodological speculation, at which he is not ordinarily very adept. Thus, the dangers are as great as the opportunities.

One striking advantage of the concentration on legal autonomy has been the manner in which it has exposed the insufficiency of traditional models for understanding the colonial legal system. We have already considered one discarded set of models—the tension between imitation of earlier English institutions and the model of pragmatism (of the Reinsch-Boorstin variety). Another pervasive model that, so far as I know, has never been criticized directly has probably (and certainly correctly) been discarded by most historians working in the field. This is what might be termed the "human development" model, according to which the legal system was analogized to the human life cycle, proceeding from infancy to maturity over the course of the two centuries of colonial experience. The language of the life cycle has been used with maddening frequency and with a total inattention to the intellectual and historical significance of such a conceptualization. One could probably state it this way: the period to 1660 represents the infancy of the colonial legal systems, struggling to find their way in an unfamiliar social environment; the era from the Restoration to about 1715 represents adolescence, with legal systems discovering their own personalities and adapting themselves to the requirements of the larger society; the last fifty years of the colonial era therefore represent the maturity of the system, embracing total conformity with the external society and symbolizing that sophistication by the reception of the common law. It seems to me that I hardly have to comment on the intellectual problems of such a model, and yet I would contend that it has been the unconscious model for most legal historians over the past fifty years. We would do better to turn to anthropology and political economy rather than to such crude psychodynamics.

By viewing the colonial legal system from the perspective of social theory, the totality of the American legal experience, and, still more important, an internationally comparative perspective, we are beginning to drive fresh insight into the operation of colonial legal systems. Perhaps the best example of such intellectual progress is David Konig's recent book, *Law and Society in Puritan Massachusetts: Essex County, 1629–1692*. The central intellectual problem for Konig is to understand the social significance of the incredible amount of litigation in late-seventeenth-century Essex County. Earlier historians, such as George Haskins, and even sociologists, such as Kai Erikson,[78] have treated litigiousness as a sign of social dysfunction. Konig, however, takes a diametrically opposed view: he perceives the same failure to achieve communitarianism that historians since Darrett Rutman have perceived,[79] but his argument is that the emergence of formal court systems and regularized legal conflict was in fact a measure of functionality in the context of Massachusetts society. "Litigation," he notes, "not only removes disputes from the emotionally charged arena of the town meeting; confrontation in the court room also serves to facilitate a social process that had taken place years earlier in parts of England: placing people 'far enough apart, so to speak, to be able to hate each other without repercussions on a mystical plane.'"

> Litigation as an agent of orderly social change in economic growth—not just as a final barrier against chaos—had proved vital to Essex society. In a rapidly evolving culture it was essential that people be able to meet and synthesize new ground rules for interaction—in neighborhoods, congregations and business ventures. The crowded colonial courtroom served more than the litigants, however. Anyone appearing there formally or merely to watch and listen— learned something about standards of behavior. He gained invaluable social information from listening to a drawn-out law suit, and from the court's decision he learned what society approved. . . . The formulas asserted in court were brought back to a community where they were, in turn, communicated to people. People in Essex would not shun litigation, nor would their leaders try to discourage them from going to court to obtain a satisfactory solution.
>
> Through that medium the residents of Essex were able to remain a contentious and well-ordered people, and even many who once distrusted the courts came to recognize that the legal system could be a source of their own protection.[80]

I am not altogether persuaded by Konig's argument, but he has raised the problem to a higher intellectual plane than have previous historians, and he has at least identified one of the central problems that the legal historian must confront. Unfortunately, such insights have been few and far between in colonial legal history, although they have been much more common in modern American legal history.

V

Reviewing the field as a whole, to me it seems apparent that a number of areas cry out for new investigation. One is the problem of legislation in the colonial period. The Hurstians have long reminded us that legal history should not concentrate exclusively on courts, though that surely has been the want of colonial legal historians. The rules created by legislatures are obviously of significance in understanding social change, but the actual rule-making function of colonial legislatures has never been studied with the same intensity as have other political, legal, or social phenomena. In part, this is because we have more or less unconsciously accepted the model of Parliament as satisfactory for understanding the nature and function of colonial legislatures, and we all know that the scope of parliamentary legislation until the mid-eighteenth century is remarkably narrow. Several years ago Bernard Bailyn offhandedly suggested that rules made by eighteenth-century American legislatures in fact affected a much wider range of activities than did those made by Parliament (citing only, I think, a seminar paper written by a graduate student).[81] The point is clearly worth examining more systematically. Those who, like David Allen and David Konig, have attended to the impact of legislative rules on the mundane aspects of village life have begun to sensitize us to the importance of social ordering conducted in legislatures (and, for that matter, on the administrative side of county courts). Fencing laws, to name only one example, were obviously of critical socioeconomic importance in colonial communities.

More important to the legal historian, however, is the fact that we have never clearly worked out the process by which legislation and adjudication became distinguishable activities in the colonial period. McIlwain's work on England prior to the settlement of America should have alerted colonial historians to the fact that colonial legislatures in the seventeenth century were in some sense throwbacks to a Tudor past in which little distinction was made between legislating and judging.[82] An offhand impression would be that, in fact, this functional bifurcation did not generally take place until after the Glorious Revolution and that this is a process which needs careful examination. Indeed, it seems to me arguable that the separation of adjudication from legislation marks a critically important point in the political development of several colonies, especially in Massachusetts Bay. This, I would guess, is part of a crisis of the 1690s that requires much more careful examination than it has hitherto been given.

Similarly, what might be called "the problem of the seventeenth century" needs to be addressed. Although Konig and Allen have recently added dramatically to our knowledge of the legal history of the period, since the early 1960s no one has seriously attempted to conceptualize the period as a whole,[83] and we are left hanging somewhere between the views of Julius Goebel and those of Paul Reinsch in our quest for a general interpretation. This becomes particularly important if we are to escape the "life cycle" model. Allen has surely put us on the right track by returning to Powell's systematic attempt to relate colonial development to metropolitan development, but the effort is still in a primitive stage from the point of view of both theory and empirical investigation.

Another example of an area in need of study is the history of the legal profession in colonial America, an area in which some progress has been made. Here there has been a good deal of work, in both dissertation and published form, yet save for Stephen Botein's recent essay and Greg Roeber's recent book, there has been relatively little effort to sum up this work and assess its significance.[84] Historians as diverse as Zechariah Chafee and Greg Roeber have stressed the relationship between book learning, the professionalization of lawyers, and the sophistication of legal systems; and yet my feeling is that we still do not adequately understand either this process or its larger social significance. Here, however, the signs are very hopeful since social historians have proved so sensitive to this problem.

Finally, it is important to note that the development of new subfields within colonial history can have an invigorating impact upon legal history. The best example is women's history. The recent production of admirable books and articles on women makes it clear that we have understood little about woman's role.[85] Women's history alerts us to a series of questionable assumptions that characterize traditional legal history. Perhaps the best example arises out of work on the law of marriage, in which we have assumed that the classic Blackstonian account of the legal unity of husband and wife was the bench mark against which American developments might be measured. The authoritative account has been Richard Morris's argument that in comparison with the English legal subjection of husband to wife, colonial practice permitted substantial freedom (if not equality) to the colonial married woman. Morris based his argument upon apparently extensive manuscript research, which seemed to be supported by the contemporary writing of Mary Beard, and his optimistic picture of colonial wives has been accepted even by recent feminist historians.[86]

The ongoing research of Marylynn Salmon challenges every element of Morris's account. Salmon denies that Blackstone's report of English law was accurate (things were better for married women than he admits), and she documents widespread evidence that the legal lot of colonial women was not one of near equality. She insists that we must learn more about the state of seventeenth- and eighteenth-century English law before we can make adequate comparisons between it and that in the colonies, and she shows that we cannot assume uniformity of colonial legal behavior with respect to women's rights. "Perhaps we will discover," she concludes, "that questions concerning legal improvements or losses in relationship to England are not the best questions to investigate." Salmon believes that "intercolonial variations, or changes over time in single colonies may reveal more significant information about female status.[87]

While I think that scholars might be more charitable to Morris, whose work in this area was done over half a century ago, the perspective of women's history clearly enables us to gain a new purchase on old problems. By questioning traditional assumptions about the acceptability of the subordination of women, Salmon and others have opened up an avenue to exploring the coercive (or at least socially confirming) role of law in colonial society.

This is precisely the way in which progress in general history and improvement in legal history should march hand and hand.

When I wrote a similar essay in 1966, I began by noting, cautiously, "a modest revival of interest in the early history of American law." I was correct in both my general diagnosis and my caution, but it is certainly true that our knowledge of colonial legal history and of the relevance of law to general colonial history has increased over the past fifteen years. In 1966 I was particularly concerned with demonstrating the interconnectedness of colonial and national legal history, and I still see that as an important concept for the understanding of American national legal history. From the point of view of the colonial period, however, it seems to me that we are well along with my original concern, which was the study of "ordinary" legal process in colonial society. We have been made much more aware of the existence and usefulness of legal source materials, and at an intellectual level there has been a general appreciation of the significance of law for the understanding of colonial culture.

So far, so good. Colonial legal historians have made some progress, but not nearly enough. What seems to me most critical at the present moment of scholarly development is theory. We must, I believe, have a more systematic understanding of how law relates to society, and we must employ such theory to identify those areas that most urgently require investigation. We need an intellectual agenda, now that we have a method, if we are to make ourselves heard amongst the important voices in the colonial field.

NOTES

I would like to thank the members of the Oxford Conference for their helpful comments, and I would especially like to acknowledge the aid of Robert W. Gordon, of Stanford University Law School, whose criticisms were central to the revision of this essay for publication.

1. I acknowledge the crude construction of these categories. They reify a complex reality and slip awkwardly from the analytic to the institutional. Nevertheless, I think they may be useful in guiding the newcomer's first steps upon the unfamiliar terrain of legal history. The two most helpful bibliographical essays on colonial legal history are Herbert A. Johnson, "American Colonial Legal History: A Historiographical Interpretation," in *Perspectives on Early American History: Essays in Honor of Richard B. Morris*, ed. Alden T. Vaughan and George Athan Billias (New York, 1973), 250–81; and Robert W. Gordon, "J. Willard Hurst and the Common Law Tradition in American Legal Historiography," *Law and Society Review* 10 (1976): 9–56.

2. William Stubbs, *The Constitutional History of England, in Its Origin and Development* (London, 1880); Frederic William Maitland, *The Constitutional History of England* (Cambridge, 1908); Frederick Pollock and Frederic William Maitland, *The History of English Law*, 2 vols. (1895; reprint, with a new introduction by S. F. C. Milson, London, 1968).

3. Charles H. McIlwain, *Constitutionalism, Ancient and Modern* (Ithaca, N.Y., 1940); Robert Livingston Schuyler, *The Constitution of the United States: An Historical Survey of Its Formation* (New York, 1923); Henry Bracton, *De Legibus et Consuetudinibus Angliae*, ed. George E. Wood-

bine, 4 vols. (New Haven, 1915–42); Samuel E. Thorne, *Sir Edward Coke, 1552–1952* (London, 1957); William H. Dunham, *Lord Hastings' Indentured Retainers, 1461–1483: The Lawfulness of Livery and Retaining under the Yorkists and Tudors* (Hamden, Conn., 1955); Julius Goebel, Jr., *Felony and Misdemeanor: A Study in the History of English Criminal Procedure* (New York, 1937).

4. Thomas Garden Barnes, *The Clerk of the Peace in Caroline Somerset* (Leicester, 1961); Donald W. Sutherland, *The Assize of Novel Disseisin* (London, 1973); idem, *Quo Warranto Proceedings in the Reign of Edward I, 1278–1294* (London, 1963); Morris Arnold, ed., *Yearbook of Richard II* (Cambridge, Mass., 1975); Richard Helmholz, *Marriage Litigation in Medieval England* (Cambridge, 1974); Thomas A. Green, "The Jury and the English Law of Homicide, 1200–1600," *Michigan Law Review* 74 (January 1976): 414–99.

5. Morris Arnold et al., eds., *On the Laws and Customs of England* (Chapel Hill, 1981).

6. Julius Goebel, Jr., and T. Raymond Naughton, *Law Enforcement in Colonial New York* (New York, 1944); Julius Goebel, Jr., and Joseph H. Smith, *The Law Practice of Alexander Hamilton*, 4 vols. (New York, 1964–80); Joseph H. Smith, *Appeals to the Privy Council from the American Plantations* (New York, 1950); idem, *Colonial Justice in Western Massachusetts, 1639–1702: The Pynchon Court Record* (Cambridge, Mass., 1961).

7. Joseph H. Smith, *Cases and Materials on the Development of Legal Institutions* (St. Paul, 1965). See also n. 10 below.

8. Goebel and Smith, *Law Practice of Alexander Hamilton;* Joseph H. Smith and Philip A. Crowl, *Court Records of Prince George's County, Maryland, 1696–1699* (Washington, D.C., 1964); Smith, *Colonial Justice.*

9. John P. Dawson, *Gifts and Promises: Continental and American Law Compared* (New Haven, 1980); idem, *The Oracles of the Law* (Ann Arbor, 1968); idem, *A History of Lay Judges* (Cambridge, Mass., 1960).

10. Mark De Wolfe Howe, *The Garden and the Wilderness: Religion and Government in American Constitutional History* (Chicago, 1965). For a new view in the law school casebook field see Stephen B. Presser and Jamil S. Zainaldin, eds., *Law and American History: Cases and Materials* (St. Paul, 1980). Presser and Zainaldin devote one chapter to "The English Background" and one chapter to "Legal and Constitutional Perspectives on The American Revolution;" altogether only 139 of 846 pages are devoted to the period before 1787. In Joseph H. Smith's casebook (*Cases and Materials on the Development of Legal Institutions*) 414 of 744 pages are devoted to English medieval law, and fewer than 200 pages are devoted to select questions in national law. Spencer L. Kimball (*Historical Introduction to the Legal System* [St. Paul, 1966]) devotes 262 of his 598 pages to English law and a substantial proportion of 200 pages to problems in modern legal history. For a different perspective see Stephen Botein, *Early American Law and Society: Essay and Materials in Law and American History* (New York, 1983).

11. L. Kinvin Wroth and Hiller B. Zobel, *Legal Papers of John Adams*, 3 vols. (Cambridge, Mass., 1965).

12. Herbert A. Johnson, Charles Cullen, and Charles Hobson, eds., *The Papers of John Marshall*, 3 vols. to date (Williamsburg, 1974–); William E. Nelson and David T. Konig, eds., *Plymouth Court Records*, 3 vols. to date (Wilmington, Del., 1978–).

13. John Phillip Reid, *In a Defiant Stance* (University Park, Pa., 1977); idem, *In a Rebellious Spirit* (University Park, Pa., 1979); idem, *In Defiance of the Law* (Chapel Hill, 1981); William E. Nelson, *Americanization of the Common Law: The Impact of Legal Change on Massachusetts Society, 1760–1830* (Cambridge, Mass., 1975); idem, *Dispute and Conflict Resolution in Plymouth County, Massachusetts, 1725–1825* (Chapel Hill, 1981); Thomas A. Green, "The Jury and the English Law of Homicide, 1200–1600," *Michigan Law Review* 74: 415–99; John H. Langbein, *Prosecuting Crime in the Renaissance: England, France and Germany* (Cambridge, Mass., 1974).

14. Kimball, *Historical Introduction to the Legal System;* see also n. 10 above.

15. Goebel and Naughton, *Law Enforcement in Colonial New York;* Smith, *Appeals to the Privy Council;* Howe, *The Garden and the Wilderness.*

16. George L. Haskins, *Law and Authority in Early Massachusetts: A Study in Tradition and Design* (New York, 1960).

17. David H. Flaherty, *Essays in the Early History of American Law* (Chapel Hill, 1969).

18. Barbara Black, "The Constitution of Empire: The Case for the Colonists," *University of Pennsylvania Law Review* 124 (May 1976): 1157–1211; Charles H. McIlwain, *The American Revolution: A Constitutional Interpretation* (New York, 1923); Robert Livingston Schuyler, *Parliament and the British Empire: Some Constitutional Controversies Concerning Imperial Legislative Jurisdiction* (New York, 1929).

19. *Essays in Colonial History Presented to Charles McLean Andrews by His Students* (New Haven, 1931); Leonard W. Labaree, *Royal Instructions to British Colonial Governors, 1670–1776* (New York, 1935).

20. Notably Smith, *Appeals to the Privy Council;* and idem, "Administrative Control of the Courts of the American Plantations," *Columbia Law Review* 51 (1961), reprinted in Flaherty, *Essays,* 281–335.

21. John R. Commons, *Legal Foundations of Capitalism* (1923; reprint, Madison, Wis., 1957); idem, *Documentary History of American Industrial Society,* 10 vols. (Cleveland, 1910–11); idem, *History of Labour in the United States,* 4 vols. (New York, 1918–35).

22. Woodrow Wilson, *Constitutional Government in the United States* (New York, 1908); Edward Corwin, *The Constitution and What It Means Today* (Princeton, 1920); Alpheus Thomas Mason and William M. Beaney, *American Constitutional Law: Introductory Essays and Selected Cases* (Englewood Cliffs, N.J., 1954); Alpheus Thomas Mason, *Brandeis: Lawyer and Judge in the Modern State* (Princeton, 1933); idem, *Harlan Fiske Stone: A Pillar of the Law* (New York, 1956); Walter Murphy and Joseph Tanenhaus, *Comparative Constitutional Law: Cases and Commentaries* (New York, 1977).

23. Andrew C. McLaughlin, *The Foundations of American Constitutionalism* (New York, 1932); William T. Hutchinson and William M. E. Rachal, eds., *Papers of James Madison,* 10 vols. to date (Chicago, 1962–); William Winslow Crosskey, *Politics and the Constitution in the History of the United States,* 3 vols. (Chicago, 1953–80); C. Herman Pritchett, *The American Constitution* (New York, 1959); Herbert Storing, *The Complete Antifederalist,* 7 vols. (Chicago, 1981), esp. vol. 1, *What the Anti-Federalists Were For.*

24. Henry Steele Commager, *Majority Rule and Minority Rights* (New York, 1943); Harold Hyman and Leonard W. Levy, eds., *Freedom and Reform: Essays in Honor of Henry Steele Commager* (New York, 1967); Arthur E. Bestor, Jr., "State Sovereignty and Slavery," *Illinois State Historical Society Journal* 54 (1961): 148–74; idem, "The Civil War as a Constitutional Crisis," *American Historical Review* 69 (1964): 327; Leonard W. Levy, *Judgments: Essays on American Constitutional History* (Chicago, 1972); Harold Hyman, *A More Perfect Union: The Impact of the Civil War and Reconstruction on the Constitution* (New York, 1973); Paul Murphy, *The Constitution in Crisis Times, 1918–1969* (New York, 1972); Stanley I. Kutler, *Privilege and Creative Destruction* (New York, 1971).

25. Morton Horwitz, *The Transformation of American Law* (Cambridge, Mass., 1977), xii. See also Harry N. Scheiber, "American Constitutional History and the New Legal History: Complementary Themes in Two Modes," *Journal of American History* 68 (1981): 337–50.

26. Richard B. Morris, *Studies in the History of American Law: With Special Reference to the Seventeenth and Eighteenth Centuries* (1930; reprint, New York, 1964); idem, *Government and Labor in Early America* (1946; reprint, New York, 1965).

27. Milton M. Klein, "New York Lawyers and the Coming of the American Revolution," *New York History* 55 (1974); idem, "The Rise of the New York Bar: The Legal Career of William Livingston," *William and Mary Quarterly,* 3d ser., 15 (1958); Herbert A. Johnson, *Imported Eighteenth-Century Law Treatises in American Libraries, 1700–1799* (Knoxville, 1978); idem, *The Law Merchant and Negotiable Instruments in Colonial New York, 1664–1730* (Chicago, 1963).

28. James Willard Hurst, *The Growth of American Law: The Law Makers* (Boston, 1950); idem, *Law and Social Process in United States History* (Ann Arbor, 1960); idem, *Law and Social Order in the United States* (Ithaca, N.Y., 1977); idem, *Law and the Conditions of Freedom in the Nineteenth-Century United States* (Evanston, 1956; reprint, Madison, Wis., 1964).

29. David H. Flaherty, "An Approach to American History: Willard Hurst as a Legal Histo-

rian," *American Journal of Legal History* 14 (1970): 222; Harry N. Scheiber, "At the Borderland of Law and Economic History: The Contributions of Willard Hurst," *American Historical Review* 75 (1970): 744–56.

30. Hurst, *Law and Social Order*, 23.

31. Ibid., 23–25.

32. I am told that the current three-year research and fellowship program in American legal history at the University of Wisconsin, sponsored by the National Endowment for the Humanities, is rigidly limited to projects in the period *after 1870*—at the insistence of Willard Hurst. Ironically, however, the first Willard Hurst Prize in American legal history (Law and Society Association) was awarded in Madison in June 1981 to Julius Goebel, Jr. (posthumously), and Joseph H. Smith for their edition of the legal papers of Alexander Hamilton. I confess to having been a member of the Hurst Prize selection committee. Unfortunately for the profession, Smith died very suddenly in December 1981.

33. The series of both the Harvard University Press and the University of North Carolina Press are called Studies in Legal History. The editors at North Carolina have been Morris Arnold (University of Pennsylvania Law School) and, currently, G. Edward White, of the University of Virginia Law School.

34. David Grayson Allen, *In English Ways: The Movement of Societies and the Transferal of English Local Law and Custom to Massachusetts Bay in the Seventeenth Century* (Chapel Hill, 1981).

35. John J. Waters, Jr., "Patrimony, Succession, and Social Stability: Guilford, Connecticut in the Eighteenth Century," *Perspectives in American History* 10 (1976): 131–60.

36. Roscoe Pound, *The Formative Era of American Law* (Boston, 1938).

37. Ibid., 3.

38. Ibid., 6–7.

39. Ibid., 7–8.

40. Ibid., 8, 12.

41. Ibid., 165.

42. Stanley N. Katz, "Looking Backward: The Early History of American Law," *University of Chicago Law Review* 32 (1966): 867–84.

43. Hurst, *Law and the Conditions of Freedom*, 37.

44. Ibid., 37–38.

45. Perry Miller, *The Life of the Mind in America from the Revolution to the Civil War* (New York, 1965). See Katz, "Looking Backward," 877–82, for my criticism of *Life of the Mind*.

46. Grant Gilmore, *The Ages of American Law* (New Haven, 1977), 3.

47. Ibid., 7–8.

48. Ibid., 8.

49. Ibid., 9.

50. Ibid., 11.

51. Nelson, *Americanization of the Common Law*, 5.

52. Ibid., 173–74.

53. Horwitz, *Transformation of American Law*, 1.

54. Ibid.

55. Ibid., 266.

56. Ibid., 30.

57. I owe this point to a discussion with Robert W. Gordon.

58. Zechariah Chafee, Jr., "Colonial Courts and the Common Law," *Massachusetts Historical Society Proceedings* 68 (1952): 132–59; reprinted in Flaherty, *Essays*, 53–82. Further references are to the Flaherty reprint.

59. Ibid., 61–64.

60. Paul S. Reinsch, "The English Common Law in the Early American Colonies," in *Select Essays in Anglo-American Legal History*, vol. 1 (Boston, 1907–), 367–415; Charles J. Hilkey, "Legal Developments in Colonial Massachusetts, 1630–1686," *Columbia Studies in History, Economics and Public Law* 37 (1910).

61. Chafee, "Colonial Courts and the Common Law," 66.

62. Ibid., 76–78.

63. Julius Goebel, Jr., "King's Law and Local Custom in Seventeenth-Century New England," *Columbia Law Review* 31 (1931): 416.

64. Chafee, "Colonial Courts and the Common Law," 76–77.

65. Ibid., 79.

66. Allen, *In English Ways*, is a more modern and sophisticated example of this tendency.

67. David T. Konig, *Law and Society in Puritan Massachusetts: Essex County, 1629–1692* (Chapel Hill, 1979); Allen, *In English Ways*; Haskins, *Law and Authority in Early Massachusetts;* Douglas Greenberg, *Crime and Law Enforcement in the Colony of New York, 1691–1776* (Ithaca, N.Y., 1976); A. G. Roeber, *Faithful Magistrates and Republican Lawyers: Creators of Virginia Legal Culture, 1680–1810* (Chapel Hill, 1981); John M. Murrin, "The Legal Transformation: The Bench and Bar of Eighteenth-Century Massachusetts," in *Colonial America: Essays in Politics and Social Development,* ed. Stanley N. Katz (Boston, 1971), 415–49; Michael Hindus, *Prison and Plantation* (Chapel Hill, 1980).

Kermit Hall, professor of law and history at the University of Florida, has recently published a bibliography of over seventeen thousand entries on the subject of American legal and constitutional history: *A Comprehensive Bibliography of American Constitutional and Legal History, 1896–1979* (Millwood, N.Y., 1983); these entries will be kept up to date by periodic supplements. It should also be noted that Morris Cohen, the Yale Law School librarian, has for years been preparing a massive, multivolume list of American legal imprints prior to 1860.

68. Konig, *Law and Society in Puritan Massachusetts*, chap. 7; Paul Boyer and Steven Nissenbaum, *Salem Possessed: The Social Origins of Witchcraft* (Cambridge, Mass., 1974).

69. John Demos, "John Godfrey and His Neighbors: Witchcraft and the Social Web in Colonial Massachusetts," *William and Mary Quarterly*, 3d ser., 33 (1976): 242–65; idem, *Entertaining Satan: Witchcraft and the Culture of Early New England* (New York, 1982).

70. See reviews of Morris's book by Theodore F. T. Plucknett, *New England Quarterly* 3 (1930): 574–77; and Karl N. Llewellyn, *Columbia Law Review* 31 (1931): 729–33. Llewellyn summarized his thoughts about the book in the first sentence of the review: "This is a book depressing and grotesque."

71. See Duncan Kennedy, "Form and Substance in Private Law Adjudication," *Harvard Law Review* 89 (1976): 1685; idem, "The Structure of Blackstone's Commentaries," *Buffalo Law Review* 28 (1979): 205–382; Mark Tushnet, "A Marxist Analysis of American Law," *Marxist Perspectives* (1978); Isaac Balbus, "Commodity Form and Legal Form: An Essay on the 'Relative Autonomy' of the Law," *Law and Society Review* 11 (1977): 571; Roberto Unger, *Law in Modern Society* (New York, 1976). Another influence, one that will surely make itself felt in the near future, is the recent work of the Thompson school: Douglas Hay et al., eds., *Albion's Fatal Tree: Crime and Society in Eighteenth-Century England* (New York, 1975); E. P. Thompson, *Whigs and Hunters: The Origins of the Black Act* (London, 1975); Robert W. Gordon, "New Developments in Legal Theory," in *The Politics of Law*, ed. David Kairys (New York, 1982), 281–93.

72. Kennedy, "The Structure of Blackstone's Commentaries," 211–12.

73. Ibid., 212.

74. My discussion of the Critical school has been informed by the analysis of Robert W. Gordon. The "institutional" expression of the Critical school is a very loose organization that has held annual meetings for the past few years, the Conference on Critical Legal Studies.

75. Lawrence M. Friedman, *A History of American Law* (New York, 1973); Eugene D. Genovese, *Roll, Jordan, Roll* (New York, 1974).

76. Genovese, *Roll, Jordan, Roll*, 25–27.

77. T. H. Breen and Stephen Innes, *"Myne Owne Ground": Race and Freedom on Virginia's Eastern Shore, 1640–1676* (New York, 1980); Rhys Isaac, "Preachers and Patriots: Popular Culture and the Revolution in Virginia," in *The American Revolution: Explorations in the History of American Radicalism*, ed. Alfred F. Young (De Kalb, Ill., 1976), 125–56; Clifford Geertz, *The Interpretation of Cultures: Selected Essays* (New York, 1973); Victor W. Turner, *Dramas, Fields, and Metaphors*

(Ithaca, N.Y., 1974). See also Mircea Eliade, *Images and Symbols* (New York, 1961); Wendell C. Beane and William G. Doty, eds., *Myths, Rights, Symbols*, 2 vols. (New York, 1966); Peter L. Berger and Thomas Luckmann, *The Social Construction of Reality: A Treatise in the Sociology of Knowledge* (New York, 1966); P. Bohannon, *Justice and Judgment among the Tiv* (London, 1975); L. Fallers, *Law Without Precedent* (Chicago, 1969); M. Gluckman, *The Judicial Process among the Barotse* (Manchester, Eng., 1955); K. Llewelyn and E. A. Hoebel, *The Cheyenne Way* (Tulsa, 1941); and S. Schlegel, *Tiruray Justice* (Berkeley, 1970).

78. Kai Erikson, *Wayward Puritans: A Study in the Sociology of Deviance* (New York, 1966).

79. Darrett B. Rutman, *Winthrop's Boston: Portrait of a Puritan Town, 1630–1649* (Chapel Hill, 1965).

80. Konig, *Law and Society in Puritan Massachusetts*, 188–89.

81. Bernard Bailyn, *The Origins of American Politics* (New York, 1968), 101–4. But see the discussion of legislation in Rhys Isaac, *The Transformation of Virginia, 1740–1790: Community, Religion, and Authority* (Chapel Hill, 1982).

82. Charles H. McIlwain, *The High Court of Parliament* (New Haven, 1934).

83. George Athan Billias, *Law and Authority in Colonial America* (Barre, Mass., 1965).

84. Roeber, *Faithful Magistrates and Republican Lawyers;* Stephen Botein, "The Legal Profession in Colonial North America," in *Lawyers in Early Modern Europe and America*, ed. Wilfred Prest (New York, 1981); Dennis R. Nolan, *Readings in the History of the American Legal Profession* (Indianapolis, 1980).

85. Mary Beth Norton, *Liberty's Daughters: The Revolutionary Experience of American Women, 1750–1800* (Boston, 1980); Linda K. Kerber, *Women of the Republic: Intellect and Ideology in Revolutionary America* (Chapel Hill, 1980); Lyle Koehler, *A Search for Power: The 'Weaker Sex' in Seventeenth-Century New England* (Urbana, 1980); Carol Ruth Berkin and Mary Beth Norton, eds., *Women of America: A History* (Boston, 1979).

86. Morris, *Studies in the History of American Law*, chap. 3; Mary R. Beard, *Woman as a Force in History: A Study in Traditions and Realities* (New York, 1946); Gerda Lerner, "The Lady and the Mill Girl: Changes in the Status of Women in the Age of Jackson, 1800–1840," *Midcontinent American Studies Journal* 10 (1969): 5–14; revised and reprinted in *A Heritage of Her Own: Toward a New Social History of American Women*, ed. Nancy F. Cott and Elizabeth H. Pleck (New York, 1979), 182–96; Joan Hoff Wilson, "The Illusion of Change: Women and the American Revolution;" in Young, *The American Revolution;* Ann D. Gordon and Mari Jo Buhle, "Sex and Class in Colonial and Nineteenth-Century America," in *Liberating Women's History*, ed. Berenice Carroll (Urbana, 1976), 278–300.

87. Marylynn Salmon, "The Legal Status of Women in Colonial America: A Reappraisal" (Paper presented at the Conference on Women in Early America, Williamsburg, Va., November 1981), p. 23; the paper is a sustained attack on the scholarship of Morris's book, with suggestions for new scholarly research. See also Salmon, "The Property Rights of Women in Early America: A Comparative Study" (Ph.D. diss., Bryn Mawr College, 1980).

NOTES ON THE CONTRIBUTORS

JOYCE APPLEBY (b. 1929) is professor of history at the University of California at Los Angeles.

T. H. BREEN (b. 1942) is professor of history and American culture at Northwestern University.

RICHARD L. BUSHMAN (b. 1931) is professor of history at the University of Delaware.

RICHARD S. DUNN (b. 1928) is professor of history at the University of Pennsylvania.

JACK P. GREENE (b. 1931) is Andrew W. Mellon Professor of the Humanities at The Johns Hopkins University.

DAVID D. HALL (b. 1936) is professor of history at Boston University.

JAMES A. HENRETTA (b. 1940) is professor of history and director, Program in American and New England Studies, at Boston University.

STANLEY N. KATZ (b. 1934) is Bicentennial Professor of the History of American Law and Liberty at Princeton University.

JAMES T. LEMON (b. 1929) is professor of geography at the University of Toronto.

JOHN M. MURRIN (b. 1935) is professor of history at Princeton University.

GARY B. NASH (b. 1933) is professor of history at the University of California at Los Angeles.

J. R. POLE (b. 1922) is Rhodes Professor of American History and Institutions at Oxford University.

JIM POTTER (b. 1922) is reader in economic history with special reference to the United States at The London School of Economics and Political Science.

JACOB M. PRICE (b. 1925) is professor of history and chairman, Department of History, at the University of Michigan.

RICHARD B. SHERIDAN (b. 1918) is professor of economics at the University of Kansas at Lawrence.

W. A. SPECK (b. 1938) is G. F. Grant Professor of History at the University of Hull.

491

INDEX

Abbot, John, 185, 186; family of, 185–86
Absenteeism, among Caribbean sugar elite, 49, 52
Academy of Philadelphia, 351
Adam, Nabby, 354, 355
Adams, James Truslow, 263
Adams, John, 326, 352, 355, 360, 368
Adams, Samuel, 359, 360, 436
Addison, Joseph, 355, 356
Africa: cultural and ethnic diversity of immigrants from, 200; rice growing areas supply slaves to South Carolina, 53
Africans. *See* Afro-Americans
Afro-Americans: distribution of, 137–39, 149–50; formation of culture of, 211, 217–18, 224–25, 256; patterns of demographic growth of, 136–39, 149–50; perception of whites of, 202; ratio of, to whites, 210–12; regional variations in societies and cultures of, 255–56; relations of, with Indians, 225–26; relations of, with whites, 218–19; social adaptation of, 255–56; social development of, 254–56; white attitudes toward, 166–67
Age structure: character of, 149; of United States population in 1800, 145–46
Agriculture: diversification of, in Chesapeake colonies, 46; dominance of, in American economic and social development, 284–85; and production in colonies, 43–55, 57, 60–62; and self-sufficiency of Chesapeake plantations, 47
Alden, John R., 2
Alexander, James, 444

Allen, David Grayson, 93–94, 201, 207, 279, 280, 370, 467, 477, 482
Allen, James, 436
American exceptionalism: and demographic development, 128–32; and interpretation of colonial period, 3–4, 10, 279, 305–6; reaction to concept of, 321–22
Americanization: of colonial religion, 318–22; process of, in colonies, 3, 279–80, 346–48
American Journal of Legal History, 466
American Revolution, and interpretations of colonial period, 2–3
American Society for Legal History, 466
American studies movement, and interpretations of colonial period, 3
Ames, Nathaniel, 373
Ames Foundation, 460
Anderson, Terry L., 58, 270
Andrews, Charles M., 2, 20, 33, 195, 409, 410, 411, 461
Andros, Sir Edmund, 428
Anglicization, process of, in colonies, 15, 87–88, 221–23, 279–80, 304–6, 347–73
Animal raising, in Caribbean colonies, 51
Annales school: criticisms of, 10; influence of, upon colonial historians, 6–7, 8, 124, 234
Anticlericalism, in colonies, 331–32
Antigua. *See* Caribbean colonies
Appleby, Joyce, 8, 9, 11, 321, 386–87
Archdeacon, Thomas J., 62
Argyle, Duke of, 353

493